IRISH HOTELS FEDERATION

13 Northbrook Road, Dublin 6, Ireland
Telephone +353 1 497 6459   Fax: +353 1 497 4613

Web Site: www.irelandhotels.com

Be Our Guest

2001

**Featuring over 1,000 Hotels & Guesthouses
as well as details on
Golfing
Angling
Conference Facilities
and
Touring Maps**

The Irish Hotels Federation does not accept any responsibility for errors, omissions or any information whatsoever in the Guide and members and users of the Guide are requested to consult page 19 hereof for further information.

If dialling Northern Ireland directly from the Republic of Ireland replace the prefix code 028 with the code 048.

*Printed & Published by The Wood Printcraft Group, Greencastle Parade, Clonshaugh, Dublin 17.
Tel: +353 1 847 0011. Fax: +353 1 847 5570.
Design & Origination by Printcraft Imaging, Unit 95 Newtown Industrial Estate, Clonshaugh, Dublin 17.*

*Telephone and fax numbers may change in some areas during 2001,
please consult directory enquiries in case of difficulty.*

CONTENTS

FACILITIES

🛏	Total number of rooms	🎱	Games room
🛏	Number of rooms with bath/shower and toilet	🏃	Squash court
☎	Direct dial facilities	♘	Horse riding/pony trekking on site or nearby
▯	TV in all bedrooms	▶9	9-hole golf course on site
⬍	Elevator/Lift	▶18	18-hole golf course on site
T	Can be booked through travel agent / tourist office and commission paid	↗	Angling on site or nearby
⚖	Childrens playground	♫	Evening Entertainment
🐴	Childrens playroom	P	Car parking
C	Price reduction for children	🐾	Facilities for pets
🍼	Babysitter service	S	Price reduction for senior citizens excl. July/August and subject to availability
CM	Childrens meals	⚲	Wine Licence only
CS	Creche	🍾	Dispense Bar Service Only
✿	Garden for visitors use	⚱	Licensed to sell all alcoholic drink
⛲	Indoor swimming pool	alc	À la carte meals provided
⛲	Outdoor swimming pool	☕	Tea/coffee making facilities in bedroom
🔲	Sauna	♿	Facilities and services are accessible to disabled persons
🏋	Gym only	👤	Suitable for disabled persons, with the assistance of one helper
⌂	Leisure Complex (including sauna / swimming pool / gym)	Inet	Modem access in room
		FAX	Fax machine in room
♞	Tennis court - hard / grass	☺	Special Offer

 Denotes that premises are members of the Irish Hotels Federation as at 18 September 2000.

 Denotes that premises are members of the Northern Ireland Hotels Federation as at 18 September 2000.

ACTIVITY SECTIONS

Green symbols Illustrated below denote that the hotel or guesthouse is included in a particular activity section. Further details of the facilities available and the arrangements made on behalf of guests for participation in these activities are shown on pages 398 to 442.

 Golf   Angling   Ⲧ Conference

MARKETING GROUPS

Many of the hotels and guesthouses in the guide are members of Marketing Groups. Those properties which are members of the Marketing Groups will have the name of the group displayed within their entry. Some of these groups operate a central reservation system and can make reservations for you.

SELECTING YOUR HOTEL AND GUESTHOUSE

REGIONS

Begin by selecting the region(s) you wish to visit. This guide divides into eight separate Regions – North West, North, East Coast, Midlands / Lakelands, South East, South West, Shannon and West – and they are represented in that order.

COUNTIES

Within each region, counties are presented alphabetically.

LOCATIONS – CITIES, TOWNS, VILLAGES

Within counties, locations are also presented alphabetically, see Index Pages 4 & 6.

PREMISES

Hotels and guesthouses are also presented in alphabetical order, see Index Pages 468 to 480.

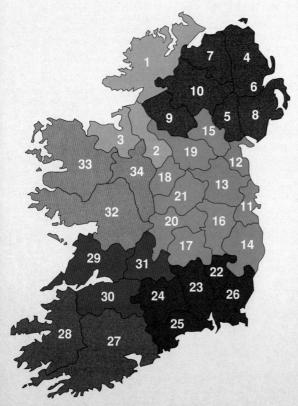

	COUNTIES	REGION	PAGES
1	DONEGAL	North West	Page 26 to 38
2	LEITRIM	North West	Page 38 to 40
3	SLIGO	North West	Page 40 to 45
4	ANTRIM	North	Page 47 to 51
5	ARMAGH	North	Page 52 to 52
6	BELFAST CITY	North	Page 53 to 56
7	DERRY	North	Page 56 to 58
8	DOWN	North	Page 58 to 62
9	FERMANAGH	North	Page 62 to 64
10	TYRONE	North	Page 65 to 65
11	DUBLIN	East Coast	Page 67 to 129
12	LOUTH	East Coast	Page 129 to 133
13	MEATH	East Coast	Page 133 to 138
14	WICKLOW	East Coast	Page 138 to 149
15	CAVAN	Midlands & Lakelands	Page 151 to 153
16	KILDARE	Midlands & Lakelands	Page 153 to 159
17	LAOIS	Midlands & Lakelands	Page 159 to 161
18	LONGFORD	Midlands & Lakelands	Page 161 to 161
19	MONAGHAN	Midlands & Lakelands	Page 162 to 163
20	OFFALY	Midlands & Lakelands	Page 163 to 166
21	WESTMEATH	Midlands & Lakelands	Page 167 to 170
22	CARLOW	South East	Page 172 to 174
23	KILKENNY	South East	Page 174 to 182
24	TIPPERARY SOUTH	South East	Page 183 to 189
25	WATERFORD	South East	Page 190 to 202
26	WEXFORD	South East	Page 202 to 215
27	CORK	South West	Page 217 to 258
28	KERRY	South West	Page 258 to 303
29	CLARE	Shannon	Page 305 to 328
30	LIMERICK	Shannon	Page 329 to 338
31	TIPPERARY NORTH	Shannon	Page 339 to 340
32	GALWAY	West	Page 342 to 380
33	MAYO	West	Page 381 to 393
34	ROSCOMMON	West	Page 393 to 395

INDEX TO LOCATIONS

GUINNESS.

4

AVOCA
HANDWEAVERS

Welcome to the colourful world of Avoca, where our seven magical shops are crammed
with beautiful things, most of which are made exclusively by Avoca. Savour our restaurants
where our delicious lunches are legendary. Visit any one of our shops and be
sure of a warm welcome and an experience with a difference.

Tel: 01 286 7466
Fax: 01 286 2367
Open 7 Days

Kilmacanogue	Avoca Village	Powerscourt House Shop	Molls Gap	Bunratty	Letterfrack	Suffolk St.
Bray, Co. Wicklow	Avoca Co. Wicklow	Enniskerry Co. Wicklow	Killarney, Co. Kerry	Co. Clare	Co. Galway	Dublin 2.

INDEX TO LOCATIONS

GUINNESS.

6

live
life
to
the
power
of

Mary Fitzgerald
President, Irish Hotels Federation

Hotels and Guesthouses in Ireland are very special. The majority are family owned with the proprietor and members of the family there to welcome guests and to extend to them renowned Irish hospitality. Even when they are owned by a company, or are part of a group, they still retain the character and ambience of a family premises - a place where you will be truly welcome.

The Irish hotel is unique, in that more often than not, it acts as a social centre for the community. Hotels offer a lot more than just a bed and a meal - they are fully fledged social, leisure, business and community centres with every imaginable facility and amenity, providing food, accommodation, sports, leisure facilities, entertainment and other attractions.

If you are moving around the country, you'll find that "Be Our Guest" is an invaluable help in choosing your next location.

Ireland's hoteliers and guesthouse owners want to welcome you and want to play their part in ensuring that your stay in Ireland is a happy one. We hope that you will stay with us and that you will use this guide to select the hotel or guesthouse of your choice, so that we can personally invite you to -

Be Our Guest

Ní haon ní coitianta é an Óstlann nó an Teach Lóistín in Éirinn. Is i seilbh teaghlaigh iad a bhformhór acu agus bíonn an t-úinéir agus baill den teaghlach romhat chun fáilte Uí Cheallaigh a chur romhat. Fiú nuair is le comhlacht iad, nó is cuid de ghrúpa iad, baineann meon agus atmaisféar áitreabh teaghlaigh leo – áiteanna ina gcuirfí fíorchaoin fáilte romhat.

Rud ar leith is ea an óstlann in Éirinn agus is dócha ná a mhalairt go bhfeidhmíonn sí mar lárionad sóisialta don phobal. Cuireann an óstlann i bhfad níos mó ná leaba agus béile ar fáil - is lárionad sóisialta,a siamsaíochta, gnó agus pobail ar fheabhas í chomh maith agus gach aon áis faoin spéir aici, a chuireann bia, lóistín, imeachtaí spóirt, áiseanna siamsíochta agus só agus tarraingtí nach iad ar fáil.

Agus tú ag taisteal timpeall na tíre gheobhaidh tú amach go mbeidh "Bí i d'Aoi Againn" an-áisiúil agus an chéad suíomh eile á roghnú agat.

Is mian le hóstlannaithe agus le lucht tithe lóistín na hÉireann fáilte a chur romhat agus a bheith in ann a dheimhniú go mbainfidh tú sult as do sheal in Éirinn. Tá súil againn go bhfanfaidh tú linn agus go mbainfidh tú leas as an treoir seo chun do rogha óstlann nó teach lóistin a aimsiú, i dtreo is go mbeimid in ann a rá leat go pearsanta -

Be Our Guest

Les hôtels et les pensions en Irlande sont d'un caractère particulier.

Ils sont très souvent gérés par le propriétaire et des membres de sa famille, présents pour accueillir les visiteurs et leur faire découvrir la célèbre hospitalité irlandaise. Même s'ils appartiennent à une entreprise ou font partie d'un groupe de sociétés, ils possèdent toujours ce caractère et cette ambiance des lieux familiaux - un endroit où vous serez sincèrement bien accueillis.

L'hôtel irlandais est unique en ce qu'il joue très souvent le rôle de centre social pour la communauté. Les hôtels offrent beaucoup plus qu'un lit et un repas - ce sont, pour la communauté, de véritables centres sociaux, de loisirs et d'affaires, équipés de toutes les infrastructures et installations imaginables.
Ils vous proposent le gîte et le couvert, mais aussi activités sportives et de loisir, divertissements et autres attractions.

Si vous voyagez dans le pays, vous trouverez que le guide "Be Our Guest" est d'une aide précieuse pour vous aider à choisir votre prochaine destination.

Les hôteliers et les propriétaires de pensions irlandais veulent vous accueillir et être là pour vous assurer un séjour agréable en Irlande. Nous espérons que vous resterez avec nous et que vous utiliserez ce guide pour sélectionner l'hôtel ou la pension de votre choix, afin que nous ayons le plaisir de vous compter parmi nos visiteurs.

Be Our Guest

Die Hotels und Pensionen in Irland sind von ganz besonderer Art.

Zum größten Teil handelt es sich dabei um private Familienbetriebe, in denen der Besitzer und die Familienmitglieder ihre Gäste mit der vielgerühmten irischen Gastfreundschaft willkommen heißen. Aber auch wenn sich diese Häuser in Unternehmensbesitz befinden oder einer Kette angehören, strahlen sie dennoch den Charakter und die Atmosphäre von Familienbetrieben aus - ein Ort, an dem Sie immer herzlich willkommen sind.

Hotels in Irland sind einzig in ihrer Art und dienen oftmals als Mittelpunkt geselliger Treffen. Hotels haben viel mehr zu bieten als nur ein Bett und eine Mahlzeit - sie sind Gesellschafts-, Freizeit-, Geschäfts- und öffentlicher Treffpunkt mit allen nur erdenklichen Einrichtungen und Annehmlichkeiten, angefangen bei Essen, Unterkunft, Sport und Freizeitmöglichkeiten bis zur Unterhaltung und anderen Anziehungspunkten.

Auf Ihren Reisen im Land werden Sie feststellen, daß Ihnen der "Be Our Guest"-Führer eine wertvolle Hilfe bei der Suche nach der nächstgelegenen Unterkunft leistet.

Irlands Hotel- und Pensionsbesitzer heißen Sie gerne willkommen und möchten ihren Anteil dazu beitragen, daß Ihnen Ihr Aufenthalt in Irland in angenehmer Erinnerung bleibt. Wir hoffen, daß Sie uns besuchen werden und diesen Führer bei der Auswahl Ihres Hotels oder Ihrer Pension zu Rate ziehen, so daß wir Sie persönlich willkommen heißen können.

Be Our Guest

+800 36 98 74 12

resireland

www.ireland.travel.ie

QUALITY   QUALITY

HOTEL   GUESTHOUSE

I R I S H
HOTELS
F E D E R A T I O N

Why not visit our Website at

www.irelandhotels.com

to view any one of more than 1,000 Hotels and Guesthouses featured in the Be Our Guest guide.

With on-line bookings from

Spring 2001

it has never been easier to "Be Our Guest".

IRISH
HOTELS
FEDERATION

Magical Blarney

TOURIST BOARD OFFICES

GUINNESS.

IRISH TOURIST BOARD OFFICES
www.ireland.travel.ie

IRELAND

Dublin
Bord Fáilte - Irish Tourist Board,
Baggot Street Bridge, Dublin 2.
Tel: 1850 23 03 30
Fax: 01 - 602 4100

NORTHERN IRELAND

Belfast
Bord Fáilte - Irish Tourist Board,
53 Castle Street, Belfast BT1 1GH.
Tel: 028 - 9032 7888
Fax: 028 - 9024 0201

Derry
Bord Fáilte - Irish Tourist Board,
44 Foyle Street, Derry BT48 6AT.
Tel: 028 - 7136 9501
Fax: 028 - 7136 9501

EUROPE

Great Britain
Bord Fáilte - Irish Tourist Board,
150 New Bond Street,
London W1S 2AQ.
Tel: 020 - 7493 3201
Fax: 020 - 7493 9065

All Ireland Information,
Britain Visitor Centre, 1 Regent Street,
London SW1Y 4XT.

France
Office National du Tourisme Irlandais,
33, rue de Miromesnil, 75008 Paris.
Tel: 01 - 70 20 00 20
Fax: 01 - 47 42 01 64

Italy
Ente Nazionale del Turismo Irlandese,
Via S. Maria Segreta, 6, 20123 Milano.
Tel: 02 - 482 96 060
Fax: 02 - 869 03 96

Germany
Irische Fremdenverkehrszentrale,
Untermainanlage 7,
D-60329 Frankfurt am Main.
Tel: 069 - 66 80 09 50
Fax: 069 - 92 31 85 88

Netherlands
Iers Nationaal Bureau voor Toerisme,
Spuistraat 104, 1012VA Amsterdam.
Tel: 020 - 504 06 89
Fax: 020 - 620 80 89

Belgium
Irish Tourist Board,
Avenue Louise 327 Louizalaan
1050 Brussels.
Tel: 02 - 275 01 71
Fax: 02 - 642 98 51

Spain
Oficina de Turismo de Irlanda,
Paseo de la Castellana 46, 3™ Planta,
28046 Madrid.
Tel: 91 - 745 64 20
Fax: 91 - 577 69 34

Sweden
Irlandska Turistbyran,
Sibyllegatan 49,
PO Box 5292, 10246 Stockholm
Tel: 08 - 662 85 10
Fax: 08 - 661 75 95

Denmark
Det Irske Turistkontor, Klostergaarden,
Amagertorv 29B, 3,
DK 1160 Kobenhavn K.
Tel: 33 - 15 80 45
Fax: 33 - 93 63 90

Finland
Irlannin Matkailutoimisto,
Embassy of Ireland,
Erottajankatu 7A,
PL33 00130 Helsinki.
Tel: 09 - 608 966/961
Fax: 09 - 646 022

USA & CANADA

New York
Irish Tourist Board,
345 Park Avenue,
New York NY 10154.
Tel: 1800 22 36 470
Fax: 212 - 371 9052

JAPAN

Tokyo
Irish Tourist Board,
Ireland House 4th floor,
2-10-7 Kojimachi,
Chiyoda-ku, Tokyo 102 - 0083
Tel: 03 - 5275 1611
Fax: 03 - 5275 1623

SOUTH AFRICA

Braamfontein
Irish Tourist Board
c/o Development Promotions
Everite House, 7th floor,
20, De Korte Street,
Braamfontein 2001, Johannesburg
Tel: 011 - 339 4865
Fax: 011 - 339 2474

AUSTRALIA

Sydney
Irish Tourist Board,
5th Level, 36 Carrington Street,
Sydney, NSW 2000.
Tel: 02 - 9299 6177
Fax: 02 - 9299 6323

NORTHERN IRELAND TOURIST BOARD

Belfast
Northern Ireland Tourist Board,
59 North Street,
Belfast BT1 1NB.
Tel: 028 - 9023 1221
Fax: 028 - 9024 0960

Dublin
Northern Ireland Tourist Board,
16 Nassau Street,
Dublin 2.
Tel: 01 - 679 1977
Fax: 01 - 679 1863

Glasgow
Northern Ireland Tourist Board,
98 West George Street,
7th Floor, Glasgow G2 1PJ.
Tel: 0141 - 572 4030
Fax: 0141 - 572 4033

London
Northern Ireland Tourist Board,
24 Haymarket,
London SW1Y 4DG.
Tel: 020 - 7766 9920
Fax: 020 - 7766 9929

France
Northern Ireland Tourist Board,
Centre PO 166,
23 rue Lecourbe,
75015 Paris
Tel: 01- 49 39 05 77

Germany
Northern Ireland Tourist Board,
Westendstr. 16-22
D-60325, Frankfurt
Tel: 0049 69 - 234504
Fax: 0049 69 - 233480

United States
Northern Ireland Tourist Board,
551 Fifth Avenue, Suite 701,
New York, NY 10176.
Tel: 212 - 922 0101
Fax: 212 - 922 0099

Canada
Northern Ireland Tourist Board,
2 Bloor Street West, Suite 1501,
Toronto, ON M4W 3E2.
Tel: 416 - 925 6368
Fax: 416 - 925 6033

LOCAL TOURIST INFORMATION OFFICES

The offices below operate throughout the year; approximately one hundred others are open during the summer months.

Aran Islands
Kilronan
Tel: 099 - 61263

Armagh
40 English Street
Tel: 028 - 3752 1800
Fax: 028 - 3752 8329

Athlone
Tel: 0902 - 94630

Belfast (From March 2001)
35 Donegall Place
Tel: 028 - 9024 6609
Fax: 028 - 9031 2424
www.discovernorthernireland.com

Blarney
Tel: 021 - 438 1624

Newgrange
Bru na Boinne Visitor Centre
Donore, Co. Meath
Tel: 041 - 988 0305

Carlow
Town Centre
Tel: 0503 - 31554

Clonmel
Town Centre
Tel: 052 - 22960

Cork City
Tourist House,
Grand Parade
Tel: 021 - 427 3251
Fax: 021 - 427 3504

Derry
44 Foyle Street
Tel: 028 - 7126 7284
Fax: 028 - 7137 7992

Dublin
Dublin Tourism Centre,
Suffolk Street, Dublin 2
Ferry Terminal,
Dun Laoghaire Harbour
Arrivals Hall, Dublin Airport
Baggot St. Bridge, Dublin 2
The Square Town Centre,
Tallaght
O'Connell Street, Dublin 1
E-mail:
reservations@dublintourism.ie
Internet: www.visitdublin.com

For reservations in Dublin
contact Ireland Reservations
Freephone
Tel: +800 668 668 66

Dundalk
Jocelyn Street
Tel: 042 - 933 5484
Fax: 042 - 933 8070

Dungarvan
Town Centre
Tel: 058 - 41741

Ennis
Arthur's Row
Tel: 065 - 682 8366

Enniskillen
Wellington Road
Tel: 028 - 6632 3110
Fax: 028 - 6632 5511

Galway
The Fairgreen,
Forster Street
Tel: 091 - 563081
Fax: 091 - 565201

Giant's Causeway
Bushmills
Tel: 028 - 2073 1855

Gorey
Town Centre
Tel: 055 - 21248

Kilkenny
Rose Inn Street
Tel: 056 - 51500
Fax: 056 - 63955

Killarney
Beech Road
Tel: 064 - 31633
Fax: 064 - 34506

Killymaddy
Dungannon (off A4)
Tel: 028 - 8776 7259

Letterkenny
Derry Road
Tel: 074 - 21160
Fax: 074 - 25180

Limerick City
Arthur's Quay
Tel: 061 - 317522
Fax: 061 - 317939

Mullingar
Market House
Tel: 044 - 48650
Fax: 044 - 40413

Newcastle (Co. Down)
10-14 Central Promenade
Tel: 028 - 4372 2222
Fax: 028 - 4372 2400

Omagh
1 Market Street
Tel: 028 - 8224 7831
Fax: 028 - 8224 0774

Rosslare, Kilrane
Tel: 053 - 33622 /33232
Fax: 053 - 33421

Shannon Airport
Tel: 061 - 471664

Skibbereen
North Street
Tel: 028 - 21766
Fax: 028 - 21353

Sligo
Temple Street
Tel: 071 - 61201
Fax: 071 - 60360

Tralee
Ashe Hall
Tel: 066 - 7121288

Tullamore
Tullamore Dew
Heritage Centre
Bury Quay
Tel: 0506 - 52617

Waterford
The Granary
Tel: 051 - 875823
Fax: 051 - 876720
Waterford Crystal
Tel: 051 - 358397

Westport
James Street
Tel: 098 - 25711
Fax: 098 - 26709

Wexford
Crescent Quay
Tel: 053 - 23111
Fax: 053 - 41743

Wicklow
Fitzwilliam Square
Tel: 0404 - 69117
Fax: 0404 - 69118

Be Our Guest

2001
HOTEL AND GUESTHOUSE RESERVATIONS FREEPHONE

To book any of the premises in this Guide ring toll free on

* +800 36 98 74 12

Be Our Guest

or visit our web site at

www.irelandhotels.com

On-line Reservations from Spring 2001

* + denotes international access code in country where call is made
e.g. from UK   access code 00
          USA   access code 011

Powered by: 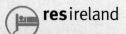 **res**ireland

Ireland's Tourist Information Network

Tourist Information

WELCOME TO IRELAND and to the services provided by our Tourist Information Network. In addition to tourist information and room reservation, many of our offices provide a wide range of services, all designed to aid you in your holiday planning and help you to enjoy to the full, all that Ireland has to offer.

OUR SERVICES AT A GLANCE

- Accommodation Booking Service
- Bureau de Change Facilities
- Computer speeded Gulliver reservation service
- Guide Books for sale
- Itinerary and route planning
- Local and national Information

- Local Craft Display
- Map Sales
- Multi-lingual facilities
- Souvenirs
- Stamps and postcards
- What's on in the area and nationally

* Some tourist information offices may not provide all of the service or facilities listed here.

Follow the Shamrock

LOOK FOR THE SHAMROCK SIGN on accommodation. It is your guarantee that premises on which it is displayed provide accommodation which is inspected and whose standards are approved and regulated by agencies supervised by Bord Fáilte, the Irish Tourist Board.

Of course all accommodation booked on your behalf through Tourist Information Offices is fully approved and regulated in this manner.

Ask for our free guide to the locations of all 123 Tourist Information Offices throughout the country - your guide to better service and a happier holiday.

INTRODUCTION

It is essential that when booking your accommodation you request the "Be Our Guest 2001" Rate

Our Guide features a broad selection of Irish Hotels, including stately Country Houses, luxurious Castles, old-world Inns and homely Guesthouses. The majority of these hotels and guesthouses are members of the Irish Hotels Federation or the Northern Ireland Hotels Federation and we hope that the illustrations and descriptions of these premises and the amenities they offer will help you to choose the most suitable premises for your holiday.

All of the hotels and guesthouses registered at the time of going to print (10th Oct 2000) and the facilities and services they provide have been inspected by Bord Failte / Irish Tourist Board or by the Northern Ireland Tourist Board, in accordance with the Statutory Registration Regulations which they administer. (*See also Activity Sections pages 398-442*)

RATES

The only rates featured in this publication relate to Per Person Sharing or a Room Rate.

<u>Per Person Sharing:</u> relates to the cost of Bed & Full Breakfast per person per night, on the basis of two persons occupying a double/twin bedded room, most having private bath/shower.

<u>Room Rate:</u> relates to the cost of a room per night. There may be a restriction on the number of persons allowed to share the room. It is advisable to check this when making your reservation.

The rates range from minimum to maximum and are those generally in operation throughout the year, but may not apply during special occasions such as Public Holiday Weekends, Christmas and New Year, International Events, Major Festivals and Sporting Fixtures, or on such other occasions as individual premises may decide.

The rates are guideline rates, please ensure that you contact the premises to vertify the rates applicable to your reservation.

Rates are inclusive of Value Added Taxes at current (2000) rates and Services Charges (if any).

<u>Supplements</u> may be payable for suites or superior / de luxe rooms. Also, where single or double / twin bedded rooms are occupied by one person, a supplement may be payable. Correspondingly, if more than two persons share a family room, special reduced rates may be arranged.

In the case of hotels and guesthouses in the Republic of Ireland, rates are quoted in IR£, whereas in Northern Ireland they are quoted in STG£.

Rates are also quoted in Euros except in the case of Northern Ireland. 1 € = IR£ 0.787564

STANDARD SPECIAL OFFERS (Per Person Sharing) ☺

Many of the hotels / guesthouses in the Guide feature special offers :

- **Weekend Specials** include 2 nights' accommodation, 2 Breakfasts and 1 Dinner.
- **Midweek Specials** include 3 nights' accommodation and 3 breakfasts.
- **Weekly Partial Board** includes 7 nights' accommodation, 7 breakfasts and 7 dinners.

Alternative Special Offers may be featured

HOTEL CLASSIFICATION

FIVE STAR ★★★★★

These include Ireland's most luxurious hotels, all of which are of high international standard. They range from elegant, stately castles to prestigious country clubs and top class city hotels catering for both the business and tourist visitor. All guest accommodation is luxurious and spacious suites are also available.

These fine hotels boast of some of the country's best restaurants and offer table d'hôte and / or à la carte lunch and dinner menus. Exceptional service and a personalised welcome are the norm in these hotels.

FOUR STAR ★★★★

These include contemporary hotels of excellent quality and charming period houses renovated to very high standards complete with all modern comforts. All guest accommodation is luxurious with suites and half suites available in most cases. Restaurant facilities provide

follow in a giant's footsteps.
start with his breakfast.

Next time you fancy a holiday break, try Northern Ireland for size. The massive, mysterious Giant's Causeway (built by giant Finn MacCool, some say, to reach his lady love in Scotland) will take your breath away. And just wait till you see the size of the breakfasts we serve here. One on its own is enough to keep you going for a whole holiday!

We're big on welcomes, too. Nobody's a stranger for long in Northern Ireland - because making new friends is one of our favourite hobbies. Just you try *not* joining in with the music, the singing and the chat when you spend an evening in one of our pubs!

It's ever so easy to get here - and there's so much to see and do you'll never, ever find yourself at a loose end.

Enjoy a wander along one of our beautiful, uncrowded beaches. Take a picnic to your very own secret, hideaway glen (there are nine in County Antrim alone!) or head for our magnificent rolling hills and blow a few cobwebs away.

Come and live it up in our superb restaurants, famous theatres and night clubs. Stroll our first class shopping avenues. Feed your mind in our heritage

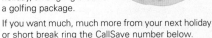

parks, galleries and museums. Come pony trekking, mountain biking or hang gliding. Or relax on a boating holiday, an angling break or a golfing package.

If you want much, much more from your next holiday or short break ring the CallSave number below.

It's easy to find out more. CallSave

1850 230 230

(Mon - Fri, 9.15am - 5.30pm. Sat, 10am - 5pm.)

16 Nassau Street, Dublin 2.
(www.discovernorthernireland.com)

Ireland. It's a different holiday altogether.

GUINNESS.

excellent cuisine and service for the discerning diner. Table d'hôte and / or à la carte lunch and dinner menus are available.

THREE STAR

These range from small, family operated premises to larger, modern hotels. Guest rooms are well decorated with the emphasis on comfort and all have a private bathroom with a bath and/or shower. Some hotels may also have colour TV, direct dial phones, hairdryers, tea/coffee facilities and room service. Many hotels also have leisure facilities, car parking, safety deposit boxes.

Restaurants offer high standards of cuisine in relaxed and hospitable surroundings. Table d'hôte and / or à la carte dinner menus are available.

GUESTHOUSE CLASSIFICATION

FOUR STAR ★★★★

This is the top classification for guesthouses in Ireland. Guest accommodation includes half suites and all guest rooms have private bathroom with bath and / or shower, direct dial telephone, colour TV and radio. Room service offers full breakfast. Many premises provide dinner, with table d'hôte and / or à la carte menus. Guesthouse facilities include car parking, safety deposit boxes, fax.

THREE STAR

All guest rooms have private bathroom with bath and / or shower and direct dial telephone. Guesthouse facilities include a TV lounge, travellers cheques are exchanged and major credit cards are accepted. Restaurant facilities are available in some guesthouses.

TWO STAR ★★

Half or more of the guest rooms have private bathroom with bath and / or shower. Guesthouse facilities include a reading / writing room or lounge area for residents' use. Restaurant facilities are available in some guesthouses.

ONE STAR ★

These premises meet all the mandatory requirements for guesthouses and offer simple accommodation, facilities and services to a satisfactory standard. Restaurant facilities are available in some guesthouses.

TWO STAR ★★

These are more likely to be family operated premises, selected for their charm and their comfortable facilities.

All guest rooms have a telephone and most have a private bathroom with a bath and / or shower. Full dining facilities are available, representing excellent value and good wholesome food.

ONE STAR ★

Here you can enjoy the comforts of a pleasantly simple hotel where a warm welcome prevails. These premises offer all the mandatory services and facilities to a satisfactory standard, necessary for a most enjoyable and relaxed visit. Some guest rooms have a private bathroom with a bath or a shower.

OPENING DATES

Some of the premises featured in the guide were not open at the guide print date (10 October 2000). The planned date of opening as supplied by these premises is displayed.

Hotels and Guesthouses may have the symbols, U, N, R, P, CR for the following reasons:

U Under the terms of the classification scheme a premises may opt to remain unclassified and will be shown U in this guide. Of course these premises meet all the mandatory requirements for hotel/guesthouse registration.

N These are premises that have recently registered with Bord Fáilte / Northern Irish Tourist Board but, at the time of going to print, have not been long enough in operation for their standards to be fully assessed.

R These premises were undergoing major refurbishment at the time of printing this guide. Their classification will be assessed when the work is completed.

P Applied to Bord Fáilte/Northern Ireland Tourist Board for registration at time of going to print.

CR Classification Rescinded - At the time of going to print (10 October 2000) the classification of these properties had been rescinded and the registration was under review by Bord Fáilte.

RESERVATIONS

Courtesy Onward Reservations

If you are moving around the country, the premises in which you are staying will be delighted to help you select and make your next accommodation reservation from the Be Our Guest Guide.

The following are other ways in which a booking can be made :

1. Advance enquiries and reservations may be made directly to the premises by phone, fax, e-mail or letter and details of the reservation should be confirmed by both parties. A deposit should be forwarded if requested.

2. Some of the hotels and guesthouses in the Guide participate in a Central Reservations system which may be indicated in their entry.

3. Travel Agent - your travel agent will normally make a booking on your behalf without extra charge where the premises pays travel agents' commission (this is indicated by the symbol T in the Guide). In other cases, agents will usually charge a small fee to cover the cost of telephone calls and administration.

4. Book your accommodation online (from Spring 2001) at:

www.irelandhotels.com

Which features all premises listed in the Be Our Guest guide.

5. Some Irish Tourist Board offices listed in this guide (see pages 12 & 13) operate an enquiry and booking service and will make an accommodation reservation on your behalf.

6. "resireland" - Ireland's tourism information and reservations system. This system enables visitors to make reservations with ease. To book any premises in the guide ring toll free on + 800 36 98 74 12.

COMPLAINTS

Should there be cause for complaint, the matter should be brought to the notice of the Management of the premises in the first instance. **Failing satisfaction, the matter should be referred to the Tourist Information Office concerned (see list on pages 12 & 13) or The Irish Tourist Board, Baggot Street Bridge, Dublin 2.** In the case of Northern Ireland premises, complaints should be addressed to the Customer Relations Section, **Northern Ireland Tourist Board, 59 North Street, Belfast BT1 1NB.**

ERRORS AND OMISSIONS

The information contained in the accommodation section has been supplied by individual premises. While reasonable care has been taken in compiling the information supplied and ensuring its accuracy and compliance with consumer protection laws, the Irish Hotels Federation cannot accept any responsibility for any errors, omissions or misinformation regarding accommodation, facilities, prices, services, classification or any other information whatsover in the Guide and shall have no liability whatsoever and howsoever arising to any person for any loss, whether direct, indirect, economic or consequential, or damages, actions, proceedings, costs, claims, expenses or demands arising therefrom.

The listing of any premises in this guide is not and should not be taken as a recommendation from the IHF or a representation that the premises will be suitable for your purposes.

THINK ABOUT INSURANCE

We strongly advise you to take out an insurance policy against accidents, cancellations, delays, loss of property and medical expenses. Such travel and holiday insurance policies are available quite cheaply and are worth every penny for peace of mind alone.

CANCELLATIONS

Should it be necessary to amend or cancel your reservation, please advise the premises immediately, as there may be a cancellation penalty. Please establish, when making a reservation, what cancellation policy applies.

GUINNESS

SAMPLE ENTRY

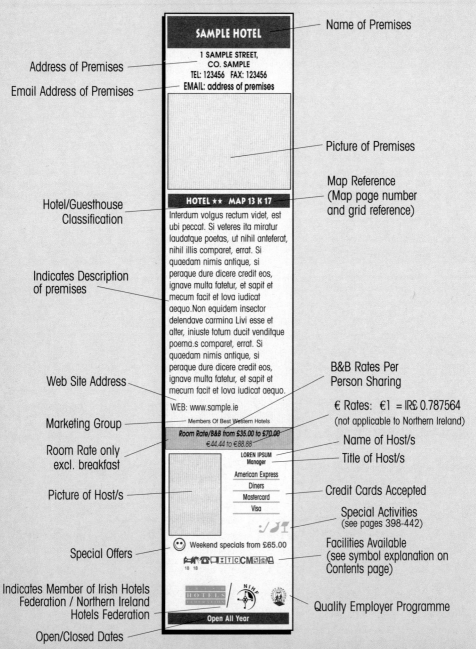

Name of Premises

Address of Premises

Email Address of Premises

SAMPLE HOTEL

1 SAMPLE STREET,
CO. SAMPLE
TEL: 123456 FAX: 123456
EMAIL: address of premises

Picture of Premises

Map Reference
(Map page number
and grid reference)

Hotel/Guesthouse
Classification

HOTEL ★★ MAP 13 K 17

Interdum volgus rectum videt, est
ubi peccat. Si veteres ita miratur
laudatque poetas, ut nihil anteferat,
nihil illis comparet, errat. Si
quaedam nimis antique, si
peraque dure dicere credit eos,
ignave multa fatetur, et sapit et
mecum facit et Iova iudicat
aequo.Non equidem insector
delendave carmina Livi esse et
alter, iniuste totum ducit venditque
poema.s comparet, errat. Si
quaedam nimis antique, si
peraque dure dicere credit eos,
ignave multa fatetur, et sapit et
mecum facit et Iova iudicat aequo.

Indicates Description
of premises

Web Site Address

WEB: www.sample.ie

Members Of Best Western Hotels

B&B Rates Per
Person Sharing

€ Rates: €1 = IR£ 0.787564
(not applicable to Northern Ireland)

Marketing Group

Room Rate/B&B from £35.00 to £70.00
€44.44 to €88.88

Room Rate only
excl. breakfast

LOREN IPSUM
Manager

Name of Host/s

Title of Host/s

American Express
Diners
Mastercard
Visa

Credit Cards Accepted

Picture of Host/s

Special Activities
(see pages 398-442)

Weekend specials from £65.00

Special Offers

Facilities Available
(see symbol explanation on
Contents page)

18 18

IRISH
HOTELS
FEDERATION

NIHF

Indicates Member of Irish Hotels
Federation / Northern Ireland
Hotels Federation

Quality Employer Programme

Open All Year

Open/Closed Dates

GUIDELINE EXCHANGE RATES

Rates in the Guide are quoted in IR£ and euros, except in the Northern Ireland section where they are quoted in Stg£. Listed below are some guideline exchange rates applicable at the time of going to press (10th October, 2000). Visitors to Ireland are advised to check current exchange rates before travelling.

IR£1 =	Currency =	€uro 1
IR£1 =	0.7527 UK Sterling =	0.5928
IR£1 =	1.0885 US Dollar =	0.8573
IR£1 =	118.1237 Japanese Yen =	93.030
IR£1 =	9.4519 Danish Krone =	7.444
IR£1 =	10.7810 Swedish Krona =	8.4908
IR£1 =	431.3681 Greek Drachma =	339.7300
IR£1 =	1.9359 Swiss Franc =	1.5247
IR£1 =	10.0278 Norwegian Krone =	7.8975
IR£1 =	1.6606 Canadian Dollar =	1.3078
IR£1 =	2.0825 Australian Dollar =	1.6401
IR£1 =	5.0048 Polish Zloty =	3.9416
IR£1 =	334.3030 Hungarian Forint =	263.2850
IR£1 =	8.4871 Hong Kong Dollar =	6.6842
IR£1 =	1.8919 Singapore Dollar =	1.4900

Note: €1 = IR£0.787564

QUALITY EMPLOYER PROGRAMME SYMBOL
AN ASSURANCE TO GUESTS OF THE HIGHEST
STANDARDS OF EMPLOYMENT

Readers will notice our Quality Employer Programme (QEP) logo in the right hand corner of a large number of hotel and guesthouse entries throughout this guide. It is an assurance to you, as a guest, that the property you choose offers excellence in all standards of employment and treatment of staff. This ultimately benefits all guests, as the staff in these premises enjoy high job satisfaction, which in turn leads to an enhanced quality of service for you to experience.

The QEP is a defined code of practice with standards set in all areas of employment including; training, personnel relations, rostering and the arrangement of work hours. It also makes recommendations on meals, uniforms and pensions. Once a property has fulfilled all elements of the programme, it faces an annual review to ensure that standards are achieved and maintained. The QEP development by the Irish Hotels Federation is, in effect, a guarantee to you that the accredited properties have reached an important standard in relation to all their employment practices in these areas. It also means that staff are trained to carry out their job to set criteria and receive ongoing training to update their skills. All in all, this means a better service for guests.

The QEP status enjoyed by the properties in this guide also means that they attract the highest calibre of staff. Highly skilled staff in the hospitality sector want to work in the best of hotels and guesthouses, so that they can experience the best conditions of employment and career progression.

So you when you choose a QEP hotel or guesthouse, you can be assured you will experience Irish hospitality and friendliness at its best.

Ireland's North West spans a huge variety of landscape, from the rolling drumlins and tranquil lakes of counties Cavan and Monaghan in the east, to the lovely valleys of Leitrim and Sligo and the dramatic wild landscape of Co. Donegal in the west. Three of the counties, Donegal, Leitrim and Sligo bathe their feet in the restless Atlantic and the Shannon Erne Waterway connects the other great water courses in the region, the Shannon and the Erne Rivers.

FESTIVALS AND EVENTS

The North West offers many unexplored peaceful beauty spots, but lively action too. Festivals and events abound, from the Letterkenny and Ballyshannon Folk Festivals, Sligo International Choral Festival, the Mary from Dungloe International Festival, to the Yeats International Summer School and the North Leitrim Walking Festival and the Monaghan Jazz Festival.

MAJOR ATTRACTIONS

Two major attractions are Bundoran's Waterworld and the Visitor Centre at Carrowmore near Sligo, the largest and most important megalithic site in Europe. Also not to

Lough Muckno Park, Co. Monaghan

be missed in Co. Donegal are the Lakeside Museum at Dunlewy, Glencolumbkille Folk Museum, Glenveagh National Park, Donegal Castle and the Vintage Car Museum in Buncrana. Parke's Castle on the shore of Lough Gill on the Sligo/Leitrim border is located in the heart of Yeats' country.
Visit Cavan Crystal, Parian China and Celtic Weave in Ballyshannon, Swan Island Open Farm in Co. Leitrim, the Patrick Kavanagh Centre in Inniskeen and the award winning Monaghan County Museum, or follow the sculpture trail through Hazelwood, near Sligo Town.

Tra Na Rosann Bay, Co. Donegal

ENTERTAINMENT

In Sligo, experience the Yeats' Candle-Lit Supper - a 3 course evening meal with entertainment, dramatising the loves and frailties of the Nobel poet, William Butler Yeats. Alternatively, discover our culture in the lively traditional music sessions that are held in pubs throughout the region
For further information and assistance in planning your holiday and making accommodation reservations please contact:–

The North West Tourism Authority,
Temple Street, Sligo.
Tel: 071 61201. Fax: 071 60360
OR
Tourist Information Office,
Derry Road, Letterkenny, Co. Donegal.
Tel: 074 21160. Fax: 074 25180.

Guinness Mary from Dungloe International Festival, Co. Donegal.
July / August

Yeats International Summer School, Co. Sligo.
July / August

Event details correct at time of going to press

ABBEY HOTEL

THE DIAMOND, DONEGAL
TEL: 073-21014 FAX: 073-23660
EMAIL: whitegrp@iol.ie

HOTEL ★★★ MAP 13 | 18

A comfortable 3*** hotel. All bedrooms are en suite equipped with modern facilities, some rooms with delightful views of Donegal Bay. Situated in the centre of Donegal Town it is an ideal base for touring the scenic County of Donegal. Available locally: sandy beaches, golf, fishing, boating, pitch & putt, all water sports, horse riding, hill walking. In our Abbey Restaurant we serve a full à la carte menu, a dinner menu daily and lunches, hot meals/snacks in our Eas Dun Bar.

WEB: www.whites-hotelsireland.com

Member of White's and Associated Hotels

B&B from £45.00 to £55.00
€57.14 to €69.84

JIM WHITE
Proprietor

American Express
Diners
Mastercard
Visa

2 Nights B&B & 1 Dinner from £90.00

Closed 25 - 27 December

CENTRAL HOTEL, CONFERENCE & LEISURE CENTRE

THE DIAMOND, DONEGAL
TEL: 073-21027 FAX: 073-22295
EMAIL: centralhotel@eircom.net

HOTEL ★★★ MAP 13 | 18

The Central Hotel, Conference & Leisure Centre is a 3*** hotel based in the centre of Donegal Town, with views of Donegal Bay. It is an ideal base for discovering our beautiful countryside and unspoilt beaches. There is also horse riding, golfing and angling near by. Our leisure centre has a fully equipped gym, indoor swimming pool, steam room, jacuzzi and solarium. An experience you won't forget.

Member of White's and Associated Hotels

B&B from £45.00 to £60.00
€57.14 to €76.18

MICHAEL NAUGHTON
General Manager

American Express
Diners
Mastercard
Visa

Weekend specials from £100.00

Open All Year

HARVEY'S POINT COUNTRY HOTEL

LOUGH ESKE, DONEGAL TOWN, CO. DONEGAL
TEL: 073-22208 FAX: 073-22352
EMAIL: harveyspoint@eircom.net

HOTEL ★★★ MAP 13 | 18

If you enjoy fine food cooked with flair and attention to detail, coupled with a warm Irish welcome, then Harvey's Point is your destination. Hidden in the hills of Donegal, this exclusive, 20 bedroomed hotel is situated on the shores of Lough Eske, 6km from Donegal Town. Michelin Guide listed, AA 3 Rosette award 1992-2000, RAC Blue Ribbon award 2000.

B&B from £49.00 to £75.00
€62.22 to €95.23

DEIRDRE MCGLONE & MARK GYSLING Proprietors

American Express
Diners
Mastercard
Visa

Closed 01 November - 31 March

B&B rates are IR£ per person sharing per night incl. Breakfast

MILL PARK HOTEL, CONFERENCE CENTRE & LEISURE CLUB

THE MULLINS, KILLYBEGS ROAD, DONEGAL TOWN, CO. DONEGAL
TEL: 073-22880 FAX: 073-22640
EMAIL: millparkhotel@eircom.net

HOTEL P MAP 13 I 18

The Mill Park Hotel is set in its own grounds just a few minutes' walk from the centre of Donegal Town. With pebble drives, mill pond and spacious gardens this new hotel opened in 2000 has 37 bedrooms, 2 Suites and 4 Conference Suites. A luxurious leisure centre with swimming pool, gym solarium and jacuzzi. All bedrooms are extra large and luxuriously furnished. The Granary which is our main Bar Restaurant Reception Lounge has high open beamed ceilings, old stone fireplaces.

WEB: www.millparkhotel.com

Member of Village Inn Hotels

B&B from £32.50 to £79.50
€41.27 to €100.94

TONY MCDERMOTT

American Express
Diners
Mastercard
Visa

🙂 Weekend specials from £85.00

39 39

PS 🔲 alc

Closed 24 - 26 December

ST ERNAN'S HOUSE HOTEL

DONEGAL TOWN, CO. DONEGAL
TEL: 073-21065 FAX: 073-22098
EMAIL: info@sainternans.com

HOTEL ★★★★ MAP 13 I 18

St Ernan's House Hotel is situated on its own wooded island and joined to the mainland by a causeway. This graceful house offers a homely atmosphere where good food and tranquillity is a way of life. Golfing, swimming and angling are close by. The surrounding countryside offers beautiful scenic tours of mountains, sea and lakes. St Ernan's is the perfect respite from the hectic pace of life. Children under 6 not catered for. Member of Irish Country Houses and Restaurants Association.

WEB: www.sainternans.com

Member of I.C.H.R.A.

B&B from £78.00 to £85.00
€99.04 to €107.93

BRIAN O'DOWD
Proprietor

Mastercard
Visa

11 11

Closed 29 October - 20 April

NESBITT ARMS HOTEL

MAIN STREET, ARDARA, CO. DONEGAL.
TEL: 075-41103 FAX: 075-41895
EMAIL: nesbitta@indigo.ie

HOTEL U MAP 13 H 18

Built in 1838 and named after the last Whaling family in Ireland, The Nesbitt Arms lies at the hub of the heritage town of Ardara, famed for its handwoven tweeds and handknits. Unspoilt sandy beaches and scenery, Maghera Caves, Glencolmcille, Slieve League and Glenveigh National Park. Choice of dining in Weavers à la carte Restaurant or in our Bar Bistro. Seafood specialities. Traditional Music and Lively Bar.

Member of Village Inn Hotels

B&B from £29.00 to £36.00
€36.82 to €45.71

MICHAEL MOLLOY M.D.
NESSA MOLLOY Manageress

Diners
Mastercard
Visa

🙂 Weekend specials from £69.00

19 19

Open All Year

WOODHILL HOUSE

ARDARA,
CO. DONEGAL
TEL: 075-41112 FAX: 075-41516
EMAIL: yates@iol.ie

GUESTHOUSE ★★★ MAP 13 H 18

An historic country house, the site dates back to the 17th century. The house is set in its own grounds, overlooking the Donegal Highlands. There is a quality restaurant, with fully licensed bar and occasional music. The area, famous for its Donegal tweeds and woollen goods, also offers salmon and trout fishing, shooting, pony trekking, golf, boating, cycling, bathing beaches, many archaeological sites, Sheskinmore Wildlife Reserve and some of the most unspoiled scenery in Europe.

WEB: www.woodhillhouse.com

B&B from £35.00 to £45.00
€44.44 to €57.14

NANCY & JOHN YATES
Owners

American Express
Diners
Mastercard
Visa

Closed 24 - 27 December

JACKSON'S HOTEL

BALLYBOFEY,
CO. DONEGAL
TEL: 074-31021 FAX: 074-31096
EMAIL: bjackson@iol.ie

HOTEL ★★★ MAP 13 J 19

Jackson's award winning family run hotel is situated in its own gardens with all 88 bedrooms en suite with mod cons. Relax at the log fire at reception or enjoy breathtaking views of the River Finn and Drumboe Woods. Close to Glenveagh National Park and ideal for golf, fishing, hill walking and horse riding. Indulge in fine cuisine in the Bally Buffet Bistro or Garden Restaurant. Leisure club with swimming pool, jacuzzi, sauna, sun beds, massage and gym.

B&B from £41.50 to £65.00
€52.69 to €82.53

MARGARET & BARRY JACKSON
Proprietors

American Express
Diners
Mastercard
Visa

Open All Year

KEE'S HOTEL

STRANORLAR, BALLYBOFEY,
CO. DONEGAL
TEL: 074-31018 FAX: 074-31917
EMAIL: info@keehotel.ie

HOTEL ★★★ MAP 13 J 19

This charming historic family run hotel in its pleasant village situation overlooking the Blue Stack Mountains has that special atmosphere, a combination of excellent facilities, caring staff and management, which draws guests back time and again. The elegant Looking Glass Restaurant awarded 2 AA Rosettes of Excellence. The Old Gallery Restaurant for more casual dining. Delightful en suite rooms with TV, tea/coffee facilities, hairdryer, trouser press. Comprehensive leisure club.

WEB: www.keeshotel.ie

B&B from £45.00 to £53.00
€57.14 to €67.30

RICHARD & VICKY KEE
FRED SOUTY

American Express
Diners
Mastercard
Visa

Weekend specials from £93.00

Open All Year

B&B rates are IR£ per person sharing per night incl. Breakfast

DORRIANS IMPERIAL HOTEL

MAIN STREET, BALLYSHANNON, CO. DONEGAL
TEL: 072-51147 FAX: 072-51001

HOTEL R MAP 13 I 17

Town centre family run hotel (built 1781). All rooms en suite with TV, phone and tea/coffee making facilities. Small leisure centre - gym, jacuzzi and steamroom. Private car park. Hotel recently renovated embracing old and new decor, elevator. Ideally suitable for touring North West Donegal, Fermanagh, Sligo and Derry. Ideally located for golfing, fishing and a base for discovering the North of Ireland, Sligo 45km, Belfast 202km, Dublin 216km.

Member of Logis of Ireland

B&B from £35.00 to £49.50
€44.44 to €62.85

BEN & MARY DORRIAN
Proprietors

Mastercard

Visa

Weekend specials from £85.00

47 47

Closed 23 - 31 December

FORGE

ROSSNOWLAGH ROAD, BALLYSHANNON, CO. DONEGAL
TEL: 072-22070 FAX: 072-22075

GUESTHOUSE P MAP 13 I 17

Crafted with care, easy on the eye, this unique Irish country guesthouse and restaurant is definitely worth a visit. Ideally located about 3 miles from Ballyshannon and the same from Rossnowlagh Beach. With 10 superb en suite bedrooms you can relax in comfort. We have combined traditional charm, modern design and gracious hospitality. Dedicated to the highest standard the Forge Restaurant features contemporary creative cuisine that will excite your palate.

B&B from £29.50 to £32.50
€37.46 to €41.27

COLM & FIONA ROPER

American Express

Mastercard

Visa

Weekend specials from £75.00

10 10

Closed 23 - 26 December

OSTAN GWEEDORE HOTEL & LEISURE COMPLEX

BUNBEG, CO. DONEGAL
TEL: 075-31177 FAX: 075-31726
EMAIL: boylec@iol.ie

HOTEL ★★★ MAP 13 I 20

Luxury hotel, all major guides approved, with 36 bedrooms & 3 executive suites, leisure centre with 19m swimming pool, children's pool, sauna, steam room & jacuzzi. Our award winning restaurant, overlooking the Atlantic, specialises in salmon & lobster fresh from the ocean. The Library Bar is the ideal place to relax with a quiet drink and a good book. 9-hole golf course & fishing available locally.

WEB: www.ostangweedore.com

B&B from £50.00 to £75.00
€63.49 to €95.23

CHARLES BOYLE
Managing Director

American Express

Mastercard

Visa

Weekend specials from £110.00

39 39

Closed 01 December - 31 January

Room rates are IR£ per room per night

OSTAN RADHARC NA MARA

SEA VIEW HOTEL, BUNBEG, CO. DONEGAL
TEL: 075-31159   FAX: 075-32238
EMAIL: ostanradharcnamara@eircom.net

HOTEL ★★   MAP 13 I 20

In an area where nature remains untouched, the air is rich and pure, ensuring a heavy appetite. In the Seaview Hotel, guests are treated to wonderful food. The à la carte menu always includes a seasonal selection of fresh, local seafood dishes, with salmon, trout, lobster and oysters a speciality.

B&B from £30.00 to £35.00
€38.09 to €44.44

JAMES BOYLE
General Manager

Mastercard

Visa

39 39

Open All Year

INISHOWEN GATEWAY HOTEL

RAILWAY ROAD, BUNCRANA, INISHOWEN, CO. DONEGAL
TEL: 077-61144   FAX: 077-62278
EMAIL: inigatho@iol.ie

HOTEL ★★★   MAP 14 K 20

Luxurious hotel, 63 bedrooms, Peninsula Restaurant, exciting barfood menu, conference & banqueting, disabled facilities, Keycard security, free carparking, Gateway health and fitness club. 20m deck level swimming pool, sauna, steam room, jacuzzi, fitness suite and aerobics studio. Coastal location, white sandy beaches, coastal walks, fresh sea breeze, breathtaking views, free golf, inexpensive rates.

Member of Irish Family Hotels

B&B from £36.00 to £49.00
€45.71 to €62.22

SEAN O'KANE
General Manager

American Express

Mastercard

Visa

63 63

Open All Year

LAKE OF SHADOWS HOTEL

GRIANAN PARK, BUNCRANA, CO. DONEGAL
TEL: 077-61902   FAX: 077-62131

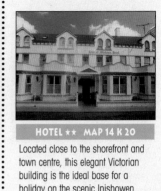

HOTEL ★★   MAP 14 K 20

Located close to the shorefront and town centre, this elegant Victorian building is the ideal base for a holiday on the scenic Inishowen Peninsula. All bedrooms have bathroom en suite, satellite TV, video, direct dial phone, hairdryer and hospitality tray. White sandy beaches, championship golf links, game/sea angling, watersports, horseriding, coastal walks available locally. Weekly live entertainment, excellent hospitality and a genuine warm welcome awaits you here.

Member of Logis of Ireland

B&B from £26.00 to £30.00
€33.01 to €38.09

PATRICK DOHERTY
Proprietor

American Express

Mastercard

Visa

23 23

Closed 24 - 26 December

B&B rates are IR£ per person sharing per night incl. Breakfast

ALLINGHAM ARMS HOTEL

MAIN STREET, BUNDORAN,
CO. DONEGAL
TEL: 072-41075 FAX: 072-41171
EMAIL: allinghamarmshotel1@eircom.net

HOTEL ★★★ MAP 13 I 17

Hospitality is a Donegal tradition and nowhere is the tradition more honoured than at the Allingham Arms Hotel. The Allingham's comfortable rooms, good food and considerate personal attention contribute to the stress-free atmosphere which many clients feel is a holiday in itself. Entertainment at weekends and nightly during the summer season.

B&B from £30.00 to £45.00
€38.09 to €57.14

PETER MCINTYRE
Manager

American Express
Diners
Mastercard
Visa

88 88

Closed 22 - 27 December

GRAND CENTRAL HOTEL

MAIN STREET, BUNDORAN,
CO. DONEGAL
TEL: 072-42722 FAX: 072-42656

HOTEL ★★★ MAP 13 I 17

Situated in Bundoran, Co. Donegal we provide the perfect base for touring Donegal, Sligo, Leitrim and Northern Ireland. The hotel consists of 62 bedrooms, all tastefully decorated with the emphasis on luxury and relaxation. Large family rooms and rooms with facilities for the disabled are also available. Our restaurant and bar is known locally for its varied and interesting dishes and boasts a reputation for excellence in both cuisine and service. Multi purpose gym available with steam room and games room.

B&B from £35.00 to £45.00
€44.44 to €57.14

GEORGINA WHITTLE
Manager

American Express
Diners
Mastercard
Visa

62 62

Open All Year

GREAT NORTHERN HOTEL

BUNDORAN,
CO. DONEGAL
TEL: 072-41204 FAX: 072-41114
EMAIL: reservations@greatnorthernhotel.com

HOTEL U MAP 13 I 17

The Great Northern Hotel and Leisure Centre, Bundoran is situated in the middle of its own 18 hole championship golf course overlooking Donegal Bay. This hotel has all en suite bedrooms, a restaurant, grill room, lounge, ballroom and syndicate rooms. Leisure centre with swimming pool, gymnasium, private jacuzzi, sauna, steam room, plunge pool, beauty salon and hairdressing salon. We now offer a new state of the art conference centre.

WEB: www.greatnorthernhotel.com

Member of Brian McEniff Hotels

B&B from £70.00 to £75.00
€88.88 to €95.23

PHILIP MCGLYNN
General Manager

American Express
Mastercard
Visa

😊 Weekend specials from £125.00

96 96

Open All Year

Room rates are IR£ per room per night

CO. DONEGAL
CULDAFF / DOWNINGS

MCGRORYS OF CULDAFF

CULDAFF, INISHOWEN,
CO. DONEGAL
TEL: 077-79104 FAX: 077-79235
EMAIL: mcgr@eircom.net

GUESTHOUSE ★★★ MAP 14 L 21

Modern family run guesthouse, bar and restaurant, incorporating Mac's Backroom Bar (famous live music venue). Specialising in music, all tastes are catered for from traditional sessions to Rock and Jazz. The restaurant at McGrorys offers great food in a stylish setting and includes locally sourced seafood. Situated on the scenic Inishowen Peninsula, McGrorys is an ideal base for golfing, angling and leisure breaks.

WEB: www.mcgrorys.ie

B&B from £30.00 to £45.00
€38.09 to €57.14

JOHN & NEIL MCGRORY/
ANNE DOHERTY

American Express
Mastercard
Visa

Weekend specials from £75.00

10 10

Closed 23 - 27 December

OSTAN NA TRA (BEACH HOTEL)

DOWNINGS, LETTERKENNY,
CO. DONEGAL
TEL: 074-55303 FAX: 074-55907

HOTEL ★ MAP 13 J 21

The Beach Hotel is family run, situated on the breath taking Atlantic Drive, having safe Downings Beach at the back door. In the heart of Rosguill golf enthusiasts can avail of both Carrigart and Rosapenna 18 hole championship course. Ideally placed for angling, diving and walking, within easy driving distance of Glenveagh National Park, Glebe Gallery, Horn Head and Letterkenny. Sea trips to Tory Island, and diving for wrecks and shark fishing easily arranged.

B&B from £28.00 to £30.00
€35.55 to €38.09

CHARLIE & MAIREAD
McCLAFFERTY

20 14

Closed 31 October - 01 April

ROSAPENNA HOTEL

DOWNINGS,
CO. DONEGAL
TEL: 074-55301 FAX: 074-55128
EMAIL: rosapenna@eircom.net

HOTEL ★★★★ MAP 13 J 21

Rosapenna is a 4**** hotel situated in North West Donegal beside the fishing village of Downings. Set in 700 acres between Sheephaven and Mulroy Bays, the hotel has its own 18 hole course designed by Old Tom Morris of St. Andrews in 1893. New private pool, whirlpool, steam room, spacious lounges and a magnificent dining room overlooking the bay all contribute to a relaxing atmosphere. Fresh seafood, locally caught, served daily. Rosapenna, a place to remember and return to.

WEB: www.rosapenna.ie

B&B from £52.50 to £57.50
€66.66 to €73.01

HILARY & FRANK CASEY
Owners

American Express
Diners
Mastercard
Visa

Special Offer: 3 Dinners, B&B and 3 Green Fees from £202.50

53 53

Closed 29 October - 16 March

32 **NORTH WEST**   B&B rates are IR£ per person sharing per night incl. Breakfast

ARNOLDS HOTEL

DUNFANAGHY,
CO. DONEGAL
TEL: 074-36208 FAX: 074-36352
EMAIL: arnoldshotel@eircom.net

HOTEL ★★★ MAP 13 J 21

Situated at the entrance to the village and overlooking Sheephaven Bay and Horn Head, the hotel has been in the Arnold Family for three generations. Good food, the friendly relaxed atmosphere and our helpful staff are just some of the compliments we receive from our guests who return each year. We are an ideal base for touring North West Donegal, Glenveagh National Park and Gardens. GDS Access Code UI Toll Free 1-800-44-UTELL.

Member of Coast and Country Hotels

B&B from £42.00 to £52.50
€53.33 to €66.66

ARNOLD FAMILY
Proprietors

American Express
Diners
Mastercard
Visa

Mid Week Sun-Fri 5 nights
Dinner, B&B from £295.00

30 30

Closed 05 November - 16 March

ATLANTIC HOUSE

MAIN STREET, DUNGLOE,
CO. DONEGAL
TEL: 075-21061 FAX: 075-21061

GUESTHOUSE ★★ MAP 13 I 19

The Atlantic House is family run. It is within easy access of the airport, golf courses, pitch 'n putt course, shopping and lots of beaches to choose from. There is also lake fishing, sea angling and hill walking close by. We have one of the most beautiful coastlines in Ireland as well as some of the most beautiful scenery to offer the tourist who just wants a quiet, peaceful holiday.

B&B from £18.00 to £25.00
€22.86 to €31.74

JAMES & MARY CANNON
Owners

Mastercard
Visa

10 10

Closed 20 - 30 December

OSTAN NA ROSANN

MILL ROAD, DUNGLOE,
CO. DONEGAL
TEL: 075-22444 FAX: 075-22400
EMAIL: ostannarosann@iol.ie

HOTEL ★★★ MAP 13 I 19

The hotel is situated in the rugged area of the Rosses amidst some of the finest scenery in Ireland and is an ideal location for golf, fishing, riding, walking and sailing. All 48 bedrooms are en suite and come fully equipped with TV, tea/coffee making facilities, hairdryer and direct dial phone. The hotel features a leisure centre with a splendid heated indoor swimming pool. The function room can cater for up to 330 people. Fresh local produce is used in all our menus.

WEB: www.ostannarosann.com

B&B from £40.00 to £52.00
€50.79 to €66.03

LEWIS CONNON
General Manager

American Express
Mastercard
Visa

48 48

Open All Year

Room rates are IR£ per room per night

BAY VIEW HOTEL & LEISURE CENTRE

MAIN STREET, KILLYBEGS,
CO. DONEGAL
TEL: 073-31950 FAX: 073-31856
EMAIL: bvhotel@iol.ie

HOTEL ★★★   MAP 13 H 18

One of Donegal's newest hotels, overlooking the splendour of Donegal Bay. We offer 40 en suite bedrooms with satellite TV, hair dryer, trouser press, tea/coffee makers, D.D., wheelchair rooms, lift. Theme bar and carvery, seafood restaurant. Fully equipped leisure centre, indoor swimming pool. Deep sea angling, fresh water fishing, golf, hill walking. Guided tours of the Veronica, when in harbour, the queen of the Irish fishing fleet. An ideal touring base.

WEB: www.bayviewhotel.ie

B&B from £45.00 to £58.00
€57.14 to €73.64

NOEL O'MAHONY
Managing Director

American Express
Mastercard
Visa

Weekend specials from £76.00

40 40

Closed 25 - 27 December

MOORLAND GUESTHOUSE

LAGHEY, DONEGAL TOWN,
CO. DONEGAL
TEL: 073-34319 FAX: 073-34319

GUESTHOUSE ★★★   MAP 13 I 18

Have a break from the hustle and bustle. A guesthouse with family character, situated in a wild, high moor/hill landscape. We offer good cuisine. Available on the premises:- cosmetic treatment, reflexology, massage, lymphatic drainage, chiropody and sauna. The ideal starting point for unlimited walks, angling, bicycle tours, riding and touring. Excellent golf links and sandy bathing beaches nearby. Very quiet and remote. German spoken.

B&B from £19.00 to £25.00
€24.12 to €31.74

ROSEMARIE & WALTER
SCHAFFNER Proprietors

Mastercard
Visa

Weekend specials from £60.00

8 8

Open All Year

CASTLE GROVE COUNTRY HOUSE HOTEL

BALLYMALEEL, LETTERKENNY,
CO. DONEGAL
TEL: 074-51118 FAX: 074-51384

HOTEL ★★★★   MAP 13 J 19

Castle Grove is a 17th Century country house set on its own rolling estate overlooking Lough Swilly. Its bedrooms are spacious and with all modern facilities. Downstairs in both drawing room and library you find a perfect blend of old and new. The dining room offers excellent cuisine, much of its produce from the Walled Garden. To the discerning guest Castle Grove has to be visited to be appreciated. While here you can fish, golf, or simply enjoy the locality.

B&B from £40.00 to £65.00
B&B €50.78 to €82.53

RAYMOND & MARY T. SWEENEY
Owners

American Express
Diners
Mastercard
Visa

14 14

Closed 23 - 28 December

B&B rates are IR£ per person sharing per night incl. Breakfast

GALLAGHERS HOTEL

100 MAIN STREET, LETTERKENNY,
CO. DONEGAL
TEL: 074-22066 FAX: 074-21016

HOTEL ★★ MAP 13 J 19

Gallaghers Hotel situated in the centre of Letterkenny in the heart of Donegal. The hotel offers the ultimate in comfort and personal attention with its home-like atmosphere and friendly staff. Each bedroom complete with private bath/shower, colour satellite T.V. and direct dial telephone, personal hair dryers, tea/coffee making facilities. Enjoy delicious food served in our restaurant and bar daily. 18-hole golf course nearby and leisure complex - 5 mins walk, convenient to all shops, bars, nite clubs.

B&B from £25.00 to £30.00
€31.74 to €38.09

AIDAN COMISKEY
Owner

American Express
Diners
Mastercard
Visa

☺ Weekend specials from £75.00

27 27

Open All Year

LETTERKENNY COURT QUALITY HOTEL

MAIN STREET, LETTERKENNY,
CO. DONEGAL
TEL: 074-22977 FAX: 074-22928
EMAIL: stay@irishcourthotels.com

HOTEL N MAP 13 J 19

The Letterkenny Court Quality Hotel, opened in Nov '99. 84 luxurious bedrooms, 30 of which are apartment-style luxury suites. All rooms have direct dial phone, hair dryer, tea/coffee making facilities, cable TV. Dillons Bar serves food all day. Private car parking.

WEB: www.irishcourthotels.com

Member of Irish Court Hotel Group

B&B from £35.00 to £85.00
€44.44 to €107.93

SEAN LYNE
Proprietor

American Express
Diners
Mastercard
Visa

84 84

Closed 25 December

MOUNT ERRIGAL HOTEL & LEISURE CENTRE

BALLYRAINE, LETTERKENNY,
CO. DONEGAL
TEL: 074-22700 FAX: 074-25085
EMAIL: info@mounterrigal.com

HOTEL ★★★ MAP 13 J 19

The hotel is situated approximately 1km from Letterkenny on main entry road from Galway, Dublin and Derry. The hotel has 82 bedrooms, all en suite with all facilities. The hotel has an indoor leisure centre which has a swimming pool, sauna, gym, steam room, jacuzzi, sun beds and massage available. Entertainment at weekends and nightly during the summer season.

WEB: www.mounterrigal.com

B&B from £40.00 to £54.00
€50.79 to €68.57

TERRY MCENIFF
General Manager

American Express
Diners
Mastercard
Visa

☺ Weekend specials from £92.00

82 82

Closed 23 - 27 December

Room rates are IR£ per room per night

SILVER TASSIE HOTEL

RAMELTON ROAD, LETTERKENNY, CO. DONEGAL
TEL: 074-25619   FAX: 074-24473
EMAIL: silvertassie@eircom.net

HOTEL ★★★   MAP 13 J 19

Nestled in the beautiful hills of Donegal overlooking Lough Swilly. The Silver Tassie Hotel combines old world charm with modern comfort and elegance. Our spacious and plush bedrooms offer unrivalled comfort and luxury with an old country house feel. Our restaurant has a reputation for the best food around. Friendly service in relaxed surroundings with open fires. Ideal touring base with local golf courses, fishing and hill walking.

WEB: www.silvertassiehotel.com

B&B from £30.00 to £35.00
€38.09 to €44.44

CIARAN & ROSE BLANEY

Mastercard
Visa

Weekend specials from £69.00

11 11

Closed 24 - 25 December

MALIN HOTEL

MALIN, INISHOWEN, CO. DONEGAL
TEL: 077-70645   FAX: 077-70770
EMAIL: malinhotel@eircom.net

HOTEL ★★   MAP 14 L 21

Situated on the scenic Inishowen Peninsula the newly-refurbished old world style family-run hotel offers a large variety of good homecooked food and locally caught seafood in pleasant surroundings. Ideal area for walking, cycling, etc. Golf locally (10 minutes drive). All rooms en suite, direct dial phone, colour TV, tea / coffee making facilities and hair dryer.

WEB: www.inishowen.com

B&B from £30.00 to £35.00
€38.09 to €44.44

MARTIN & BRIDIE MCLAUGHLIN
Proprietors

Mastercard
Visa

Weekend specials from £60.00

10 10

Open All Year

SHANDON HOTEL & LEISURE CENTRE

MARBLE HILL STRAND, PORT-NA-BLAGH, CO. DONEGAL
TEL: 074-36137   FAX: 074-36430
EMAIL: shandonhotel@eircom.net

HOTEL ★★★   MAP 13 J 21

Nestled into the lee of a hill, in its own grounds that slope down to Marble Hill Strand. All our rooms command panoramic views of Sheephaven Bay (a sheltered inlet, warmed by the Gulf Stream, where dolphins can be seen). 18 superior bedrooms, air conditioned dining room, conservatory and sun terrace. A purpose-built children's play centre. Our leisure centre has a 17.5m swimming pool, children's pool, whirl-pool spa, sauna and steam room. The Blue Flag 2000 beach is ideal for swimming, boating and windsurfing. Beautiful walks and drives.

WEB: www.shandonhotel.com

B&B from £50.00 to £75.00
€63.49 to €95.25

CATHERINE & DERMOT MCGLADE
Proprietor/Manager

American Express
Mastercard
Visa

2 Nights B&B and 1 Dinner from £120.00

70 70

Closed 04 November - 17 March

B&B rates are IR£ per person sharing per night incl. Breakfast

FORT ROYAL HOTEL

RATHMULLAN, LETTERKENNY,
CO. DONEGAL
TEL: 074-58100   FAX: 074-58103
EMAIL: fortroyal@eircom.net

HOTEL ★★★   MAP 14 K 20

One of the most beautifully situated hotels in Ireland with 7 hectares of lovely grounds and gardens beside Lough Swilly include a sandy beach, hard tennis court, par 3 golf course. Especially friendly welcome accounts for the large number of regular visitors from all parts of the world to this peaceful unspoilt part of Donegal. Awarded two rosettes for food by AA. Member of Manor House Hotels, Irish Tourist Board and AA ***. GDS Access Code: UI Toll Free 1-800-44-UTELL

WEB: www.fortroyalhotel.com

Member of Manor House Hotels

B&B from £50.00 to £65.00
€63.49 to €82.53

ANN & ROBIN FLETCHER
Owners

American Express
Diners
Mastercard
Visa

😊   Special offers on request

15 15

Closed 01 November - 31 March

RATHMULLAN HOUSE

LOUGH SWILLY, RATHMULLAN,
CO. DONEGAL
TEL: 074-58188   FAX: 074-58200
EMAIL: rathhse@iol.ie

HOTEL ★★★★   MAP 14 K 20

A country house with a glorious seaside setting on Lough Swilly amid award winning gardens which stretch down to a sandy beach. Inside, elegant sitting-rooms are in period style. Bedrooms vary in size and cost, from family rooms to luxurious suites. Renowned for good food. Indoor heated pool, steamroom and tennis. 4 golf courses nearby. Special weekend and half board rates on request. Member of Blue Book. RAC*** (Comfort Award). Dublin - 3.5 hours, Belfast - 2 hours.

WEB: www.rathmullanhouse.com

Member of Ireland's Blue Book

B&B from £55.00 to £60.50
€69.84 to €76.82

ROBIN & BOB WHEELER
Hosts

American Express
Diners
Mastercard
Visa

😊   Weekend specials from £143.00

24 24

Closed 02 January - 09 February

REDCASTLE HOTEL

REDCASTLE, MOVILLE,
CO. DONEGAL
TEL: 077-82073   FAX: 077-82214

HOTEL ★★★   MAP 14 L 21

Redcastle Hotel is ideally situated along the banks of Lough Foyle in the beautiful Inishowen Peninsula. The hotel's challenging 9 hole golf course and indoor leisure centre provides the perfect form of relaxation. Cochranes Restaurant offers a wide choice of dishes with warm and friendly service guaranteed. The welcoming staff look forward to greeting old and new customers.

B&B from £35.00 to £55.00
€44.44 to €69.84

MARGARET PATTERSON
General Manager

American Express
Diners
Mastercard
Visa

😊   Weekend specials from £95.00

31 31

Open All Year

Room rates are IR£ per room per night

COS. DONEGAL - LEITRIM
ROSSNOWLAGH - BALLINAMORE

SAND HOUSE HOTEL

ROSSNOWLAGH,
CO. DONEGAL
TEL: 072-51777 FAX: 072-52100
EMAIL: info@sandhouse-hotel.ie

HOTEL ★★★★ MAP 13 I 17

A delightful seaside setting overlooking the Atlantic Ocean on Donegal Bay. This small 4* luxury hotel, a transformed mid 19th century fishing lodge, is an oasis of comfort and relaxation on a 2ml golden sandy beach. It combines elegant accommodation, open log fires and an award winning restaurant. A splendid location to explore the spectacular Donegal landscapes. Nearby 3 Ch'ship golf links courses. Described as one of Ireland's west coast treasures. Dublin 3 1/2hrs, Shannon 4hrs.

WEB: www.sandhouse-hotel.ie

Member of Manor House Hotels

B&B from £50.00 to £77.50
€63.49 to €98.40

PAUL DIVER
Manager

American Express
Diners
Mastercard
Visa

45 45

Closed 30 October - 01 April

GLENVIEW GUESTHOUSE

AUGHOO, BALLINAMORE,
CO. LEITRIM
TEL: 078-44157 FAX: 078-44814
EMAIL: glenvhse@iol.ie

GUESTHOUSE ★★ MAP 11 J 15

Glenview House, 2 miles south of Ballinamore is a holiday haven, 500m from the Shannon-Erne Waterway with its boating, canoeing, fishing and tranquil walks. Exclusive restaurant, private tennis court, games room, museum and play area. Enjoy golf, boat trips, cycling and hill walking locally. Self catering houses within grounds.

B&B from £25.00 to £28.00
€31.74 to €35.55

TERESA KENNEDY

Mastercard
Visa

6 6

Open All Year

RIVERSDALE FARM GUESTHOUSE

BALLINAMORE,
CO. LEITRIM
TEL: 078-44122 FAX: 078-44813

GUESTHOUSE ★★★ MAP 11 J 15

Riversdale is an impressive residence beautifully situated in parkland overlooking the Shannon-Erne Waterway. Spacious rooms and lounges mean a comfortable and peaceful ambience. We have our own heated indoor pool, squash court, sauna, fitness suite and games room for when the weather is unkind - or hot! Local golf, horse riding, walking, riverbus, boat trips and scenic drives. Wide choice of interesting day trips. Brochure available - special family suites.

B&B from £28.00 to £32.00
€35.55 to €40.63

THE THOMAS FAMILY
Owners

Mastercard
Visa

☺ Midweek specials from £69.00

10 10

Closed 16 - 31 December

B&B rates are IR£ per person sharing per night incl. Breakfast

AISLEIGH GUEST HOUSE

DUBLIN ROAD, CARRICK-ON-SHANNON, CO. LEITRIM
TEL: 078-20313   FAX: 078-20313
EMAIL: aisleigh@eircom.net

GUESTHOUSE ★★★   MAP 10 I 14

A warm welcome awaits you at our family run guest house situated 1km from the centre of the picturesque town of Carrick on Shannon, Ireland's best kept secret. Facilities include en suite bedrooms with TV, direct dial telephones (fax also available) games room, and sauna. Local genealogy a speciality. Nearby there is golfing, swimming, tennis, squash, cruising, fishing (tackle & bait supplies) horse riding, walking, cycling, etc.

WEB: homepage.eircom.net/~aisleigh

B&B from £19.00 to £19.00
€24.13 to €24.13

SEAN & CHARLOTTE FEARON
Owners

American Express

Mastercard

Visa

😊 Weekend specials from £50.00

10 10

Open All Year

BUSH HOTEL

CARRICK-ON-SHANNON, CO. LEITRIM
TEL: 078-20014   FAX: 078-21180
EMAIL: bushhotel@eircom.net

HOTEL ★★★   MAP 10 I 14

An hotel of ambience, style and comfort, the Bush Hotel (one of Ireland's oldest) has recently undergone major refurbishment whilst retaining its olde world character and charm. Centrally located in the village, the hotel backs onto courtyard, gardens and N4 by-pass with private access and parking. 28 en suite bedrooms, theme bars, coffee shop, restaurant overlooking courtyard. Amenities: National Parks, period houses, River Shannon.

WEB: www.bushhotel.com

Member of Logis of Ireland

B&B from £32.00 to £37.00
€40.63 to €46.98

JOSEPH DOLAN
Managing Director

American Express

Mastercard

Visa

28 28

Closed 24 - 26 December

LANDMARK HOTEL

CARRICK-ON-SHANNON, CO. LEITRIM
TEL: 078-22222   FAX: 078-22233
EMAIL: landmarkhotel@eircom.net

HOTEL N   MAP 10 I 14

Overlooking the majestic River Shannon and its picturesque marinas. This beautifully appointed property is just a stroll from the town centre. Luxurious accommodation, Boardwalk Café & Bar, Ferrari's Restaurant and La Gondola continental/Italian cuisine. Extensive leisure centre - 20 metre deck level pool, sauna, steamroom, jacuzzi & fully equipped gym. Health & Beauty Studio. Activities available in this beautiful unspoilt location include cruising, golf, hill walking, equestrian and watersports.

WEB: www.thelandmarkhotel.com

B&B from £50.00 to £80.00
€63.49 to €101.58

SIOBHAN SMYTH
Operations Manager

Mastercard

Visa

😊 Midweek specials from £137.50

51 51

Closed 24 - 26 December

Room rates are IR£ per room per night

COS. LEITRIM - SLIGO
MOHILL - SLIGO TOWN

GLEBE HOUSE

BALLINAMORE ROAD, MOHILL,
CO. LEITRIM
TEL: 078-31086 FAX: 078-31886
EMAIL: glebe@iol.ie

GUESTHOUSE ★★★ MAP 11 J 14

Dating back to 1823 this lovely Georgian former rectory set in fifty acres of woods and farmland has been completely restored by the Maloney Family. Enjoy the tranquillity of this peaceful part of Ireland. Plenty to see and do. Visit the stately homes and gardens, sample golf, horse riding, pony trekking, fishing and cruising. Or take to the country roads by bike or on foot. Assistance given with genealogy. 10% discount on bookings if more than one night. Special discount for seniors.

WEB: www.glebehouse.com

B&B from £26.50 to £32.00
€33.65 to €40.63

JOHN & MARION MALONEY
Proprietors
American Express
Mastercard
Visa

Open All Year

CLARENCE HOTEL

WINE STREET,
SLIGO
TEL: 071-42211 FAX: 071-45823
EMAIL: clarencehotel@eircom.net

HOTEL U MAP 10 H 16

Listed for its striking architectural design, the hotel is situated in the centre of Sligo. Its location makes it the perfect base to explore one of Ireland's most beautiful counties. You will find all of Sligo's business, shopping and historic centres just steps away with a modern new entertainment complex adjoining the hotel. Our restaurant, a gourmet delight, atmospheric throughout brings an exciting dimension to wining and dining in Sligo. All rooms en suite with all amenities.

B&B from £30.00 to £47.00
€38.09 to €59.68

CARMEL FOLEY
Managing Director
American Express
Diners
Mastercard
Visa

Open All Year

HOTEL SILVER SWAN

HYDE BRIDGE,
SLIGO
TEL: 071-43231 FAX: 071-42232
EMAIL: hotelsilverswan@eircom.net

HOTEL U MAP 10 H 16

Uniquely situated on the banks of the Garavogue River and close to shops, art gallery and theatre. All rooms recently refurbished and our de-luxe rooms have aero-spa baths. Relax and watch the swans glide by as you dine in the Cygnet Restaurant renowned for excellent French cuisine with a special emphasis on fresh oysters, lobster and game in season. Traditional Irish music Wednesday nights. A member of Logis of Ireland.

Member of Logis of Ireland
B&B from £28.00 to £40.00
€35.55 to €50.79

MICHAEL HIGGINS
Manager
American Express
Diners
Mastercard
Visa

Weekend specials from £75.00

Closed 25 - 28 December

B&B rates are IR£ per person sharing per night incl. Breakfast

INNISFREE HOTEL

**HIGH STREET,
SLIGO
TEL: 071-42014 FAX: 071-45745**

HOTEL ★★ MAP 10 H 16

Located in the heart of Sligo Town, this comfortable hotel has a special, friendly atmosphere. All rooms are en suite with TV, direct dial phone and tea making facilities. Excellent food served all day or visit the lively Ark Bar with its seafaring theme. Convenient to theatre and shops. Explore W.B. Yeats' breathtaking countryside, the Lake Isle of Innisfree, Glencar, Lisadell, renowned for its golf courses and seaside resorts. Specialising in commercial traveller rates and golf holidays.

B&B from £30.00 to £40.00
€38.09 to €50.79

GERRY & CATHERINE GURN
Owners

Mastercard

Visa

☺ Midweek specials from £100.00

19 19

Closed 24 - 26 December

LISADORN

**DONEGAL ROAD,
SLIGO
TEL: 071-43417   FAX: 071-46418
EMAIL: cjo'connor@eircom.net**

GUESTHOUSE ★★★ MAP 10 H 16

Sligo Town's 1st and only 3* guesthouse situated on the N15 within 5 minutes of town centre. Ideal base for North bound traffic. All rooms en suite, remote control colour TVs, direct dial telephones, fax, hairdryers and hospitality tray. Beside pitch & putt and 10 minutes to Rosses Point. Beside Sligo's Tennis & Squash Club. In the heart of Yeats' Country. It's the ultimate in luxury accommodation. A friendly welcome and service is guaranteed.

B&B from £19.50 to £22.50
€24.76 to €28.57

CYRIL O'CONNOR
Proprietor

Mastercard

Visa

7 7

Open All Year

RIVERSIDE HOTEL

**MILLBROOK,
SLIGO
TEL: 071-48080 FAX: 071-48060
EMAIL: stay@irishcourthotels.com**

HOTEL P MAP 10 H 16

Opened in October '99, this 66 bed-roomed hotel is situated in the centre of Sligo Town overlooking the River Garavogue. All rooms are en suite with cable TV, direct dial telephone, hair dryer. Indoor swimming pool, gym, jacuzzi, sauna & steam room. The Mill Bar serves food all day or you can dine in the Mill Restaurant offering excellent cuisine. Ideal base for touring the north west region.

WEB:www.irishcourthotels.com

Member of Irish Country Houses & Restaurants

B&B from £35.00 to £85.00
€44.44 to €107.93

TADHG LYNE
Proprietor

American Express

Diners

Mastercard

Visa

66 66

Closed 25 - 25 December

Room rates are IR£ per room per night

SLIGO PARK HOTEL

PEARSE ROAD,
SLIGO
TEL: 071-60291 FAX: 071-69556
EMAIL: sligopk@leehotels.ie

HOTEL ★★★ MAP 10 H 16

Situated one mile south of Sligo on the Dublin Road, the Sligo Park Hotel is set on seven acres of gardens. A 3*** hotel with 110 bedrooms, the hotel has one of the finest leisure centres in the country. In the heart of the Yeats country, the Sligo Park is surrounded by some of the most scenic countryside in Ireland ranging from the majestic Benbulben to the gentle waters of Lough Gill. For that special break, the Sligo Park has all the facilities for your enjoyment.

WEB: www.leehotels.ie

Member of Lee Hotels

B&B from £42.00 to £55.00
€53.33 to €69.84

MICHELE HAUGH
General Manager

American Express
Diners
Mastercard
Visa

Weekend specials from £85.00

110 110

SLIGO'S SOUTHERN HOTEL & LEISURE CENTRE

STRANDHILL ROAD,
SLIGO
TEL: 071-62101 FAX: 071-60328
EMAIL: reservations@sligosouthernhotel.com

HOTEL ★★★ MAP 10 H 16

The Sligo Southern Hotel is situated in the heart of Sligo Town, adjacent to the railway and bus stations. The Sligo Southern Hotel blends old world intimacy with every modern convenience. All 99 rooms are en suite, cable TV, phone, hairdryers, tea/coffee making facilities. Indoor swimming pool, gym, jacuzzi, sauna and steam room. Indoor bowls and bridge tables available. Entertainment most nights in high season. Reservations 1 850 520052 or Free phone NI & UK 0800 783 9024.

WEB: www.sligosouthernhotel.com

Member of Brian McEniff Hotels

B&B from £36.00 to £75.00
€45.71 to €95.23

KEVIN MCGLYNN
Manager

American Express
Diners
Mastercard
Visa

Weekend Specials from £79.00

99 99

TOWER HOTEL

QUAY STREET,
SLIGO
TEL: 071-44000 FAX: 071-46888
EMAIL: towersl@iol.ie

HOTEL ★★★ MAP 10 H 16

A Tower Group Hotel - located in the heart of Sligo Town, the hotel has immediate access to Sligo's shopping facilities and has a host of lively bars on its doorstep. It also makes an ideal base from which to play the great links courses of the North West. With 60 bedrooms it is small enough to offer a truly personal service but provides an impressive range of guest facilities.

WEB: www.towerhotelgroup.ie

Member of Tower Hotel Group

B&B from £35.00 to £50.00
€44.44 to €63.49

IAN HYLAND
General Manager

American Express
Diners
Mastercard
Visa

Midweek specials from £99.00

60 60

B&B rates are IR£ per person sharing per night incl. Breakfast

CROMLEACH LODGE

**CASTLEBALDWIN, VIA BOYLE,
CO. SLIGO
TEL: 071-65155   FAX: 071-65455
EMAIL: info@cromleach.com**

HOTEL ★★★★   MAP 10 H 16

Good Hotel Guide - Hotel of the Year 1999. Cromleach Lodge is set in the quiet hills above Lough Arrow - a spectular vista of unspoiled mountain, lake & woodlands. The superior minisuites are appointed to a very high standard & each enjoys the breathtaking panorama. The atmosphere is warm & relaxed with complimentary liqueurs, fruit, newspapers & the scent of fresh flowers everywhere. But Cromleach's *pièce de résistance* is its Restaurant, where the creations of Moira & her team are a gastronomic delight.

WEB: www.cromleach.com

Member of Ireland's Blue Book

B&B from £65.00 to £95.00
€82.53 to €120.63

MOIRA & CHRISTY TIGHE
Proprietors

American Express
Diners
Mastercard
Visa

10 10

alc

Closed 01 November - 01 February

MARKREE CASTLE

**COLLOONEY,
CO. SLIGO
TEL: 071-67800   FAX: 071-67840
EMAIL: markree@iol.ie**

HOTEL ★★★   MAP 10 H 15

Charles and Mary Cooper have restored Sligo's oldest inhabited house and made it a spectacular family hotel. Home of the Cooper family since 1640 and set in the middle of a large estate, Markree boasts spectacular plasterwork, a fine Irish oak staircase yet all the comforts of a 3* hotel. Good food, peace, quiet, lots of space and warm family welcome. Riding is also available on the estate.

WEB: www.markreecastle.ie

B&B from £58.00 to £65.00
€73.64 to €82.53

CHARLES & MARY COOPER
Owners

American Express
Diners
Mastercard
Visa

30 30

Closed 24 - 27 December

CASTLE ARMS HOTEL

**ENNISCRONE,
CO. SLIGO
TEL: 096-36156   FAX: 096-36156**

HOTEL ★★   MAP 10 F 15

The Castle Arms Hotel is a 2** family run hotel and upholds the tradition of offering a warm and friendly welcome with excellent home cooking and 27 rooms. It is adjacent to a three mile long sandy beach, an 18 hole championship golf links, aqua leisure centre, sea-weed and steam health baths, tennis courts and many other amenities. For other information contact a member of the Grimes family at 096 36156.

WEB: www.castlearms.hotel.com

B&B from £27.50 to £30.00
€34.92 to €38.09

LIAM & SHANE GRIMES

Mastercard
Visa

☺ Weekend specials from £72.50

27 27

Open All Year

CO. SLIGO
MULLAGHMORE / ROSSES POINT

BEACH HOTEL AND LEISURE CLUB

THE HARBOUR, MULLAGHMORE, CO. SLIGO
TEL: 071-66103 FAX: 071-66448
EMAIL: beachhot@iol.ie

HOTEL ★★ MAP 13 H 17

Set in the centre of the picturesque seaside village of Mullaghmore, overlooking the Atlantic Ocean. All rooms en suite (bath & shower), direct dial phone, TV & tea/coffee facilities. The hotel boasts an excellent leisure club; heated indoor swimming pool, jacuzzi, sauna, steam room & gymnasium. Discount at 5 golf courses, sea, game & coarse angling, horse riding, watersports & boat trips locally. Free Kiddies Club, Murder Mystery & activity weekends. Fall under the spell of the hotel.

B&B from £25.00 to £40.00
€31.74 to €50.79

COLM HERRON & AUDRI MCARDLE
Proprietor/Gen Manager

American Express
Mastercard
Visa

Open All Year

PIER HEAD HOTEL

MULLAGHMORE, CO. SLIGO
TEL: 071-66171 FAX: 071-66473
EMAIL: pierhead@eircom.net

HOTEL N MAP 13 H 17

With its unique setting in the picturesque seaside/fishing resort of Mullaghmore this family run hotel offers superb bay & harbour views. All rooms en suite, cafe style bar, restaurant, function rooms and conference facilities. Regular entertainment by top Irish and international artistes. Next door is the renowned Olde Quay Bar & upstairs Seafood Restaurant with its attractive stone facade and old world nautical charm, making it a popular haunt for locals and tourists alike.

B&B from £30.00 to £45.00
€38.09 to €57.14

JOHN MCHUGH

American Express
Diners
Mastercard
Visa

Week partial board from £270.00

Open All Year

YEATS COUNTRY HOTEL AND LEISURE CLUB

ROSSES POINT, SLIGO, CO. SLIGO
TEL: 071-77211 FAX: 071-77203
EMAIL: yeatscountry@eircom.net

HOTEL ★★★ MAP 10 H 16

A family run, 3*** hotel. All rooms en suite, cable TV, direct dial phone, tea/coffee facilities, hairdryer. 3km of sandy beaches and Sligo's 18 hole ch'ship golf courses at concession rates locally. Amenities include de-luxe leisure club with 18m swimming pool, sauna, jacuzzi, steam room and hi-tech gymnasium. Also available tennis, basketball, indoor bowling. Supervised creche and indoor play areas on bank holiday weekends/July/August. Local activities: golf, yachting, fishing, scenic drives.

WEB: www.cisl.ie/sligoaccommodation/yeats

Member of Brian McEniff Hotels

B&B from £30.00 to £80.00
€38.09 to €101.58

FIONA MCENIFF
Managing Dierctor

American Express
Diners
Mastercard
Visa

Weekend specials from £79.00

Closed 02 January - 02 February

B&B rates are IR£ per person sharing per night incl. Breakfast

OCEAN VIEW HOTEL

STRANDHILL, CO. SLIGO
TEL: 071-68115 FAX: 071-68009
EMAIL: oceanviewhotel@eircom.net

HOTEL ★★★   MAP 10 H 16

Ocean View Hotel, nestling at the foot of Knocknarea Mountain, overlooking the Atlantic, is a long established family hotel which offers a unique blend of all modern comforts with old-fashioned courtesy and charm. Its Rollers Restaurant is renowned for its home oak-smoked salmon and fresh local produce. Bar food also available. This picturesque area invites you to stroll its sandy beaches, pony trek, golf, explore the hidden glens, visit the oldest megalithic tombs in Europe.

Member of Village Inn Hotels

B&B from £35.00 to £47.50
€44.44 to €60.31

SHAY BURKE/JEAN BURKE
Proprietors

American Express
Diners
Mastercard
Visa

IRISH HOTELS FEDERATION

Closed 24 December - 01 March

CAWLEY'S

EMMET STREET, TUBBERCURRY, CO. SLIGO
TEL: 071-85025 FAX: 071-85963

GUESTHOUSE ★★   MAP 10 G 15

Cawley's, a large 3 storey family run guesthouse. We offer high standards in accommodation with tastefully decorated rooms. Our home cooking and personal service makes this premises your home for the duration of your stay. Private parking, landscaped gardens, easily accessed by air, rail and bus. Local amenities include fishing, 9 hole golf, horse riding. Seaside resorts close by. Major credit cards accepted.

B&B from £25.00 to £35.00
€31.74 to €44.44

JEAN CAWLEY
Proprietor

Mastercard
Visa

IRISH HOTELS FEDERATION

Closed 25 - 26 December

WATCH FOR THE SYMBOL OF QUALITY

THIS SYMBOL OF QUALITY GUARANTEES YOU, THE VISITOR, A HIGH STANDARD OF ACCOMMODATION AND SERVICE WHICH IS EXPECTED OF IRISH HOTELS & GUESTHOUSES.

QUALITY

BORD FÁILTE - IRISH TOURIST BOARD

★ ★ ★

HOTEL

Room rates are IR£ per room per night

follow in a giant's footsteps.
start with his breakfast.

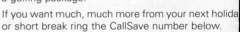

Next time you fancy a holiday break, try Northern Ireland for size. The massive, mysterious Giant's Causeway (built by giant Finn MacCool, some say, to reach his lady love in Scotland) will take your breath away. And just wait till you see the size of the breakfasts we serve here. One on its own is enough to keep you going for a whole holiday!

We're big on welcomes, too. Nobody's a stranger for long in Northern Ireland - because making new friends is one of our favourite hobbies. Just you try not joining in with the music, the singing and the chat when you spend an evening in one of our pubs!

It's ever so easy to get here - and there's so much to see and do you'll never, ever find yourself at a loose end.

Enjoy a wander along one of our beautiful, uncrowded beaches. Take a picnic to your very own secret, hideaway glen (there are nine in County Antrim alone!) or head for our magnificent rolling hills and blow a few cobwebs away.

Come and live it up in our superb restaurants, famous theatres and night clubs. Stroll our first class shopping avenues. Feed your mind in our heritage parks, galleries and museums. Come pony trekking, mountain biking or hang gliding. Or relax on a boating holiday, an angling break or a golfing package.

If you want much, much more from your next holiday or short break ring the CallSave number below.

It's easy to find out more. CallSave

1850 230 230

(Mon - Fri, 9.15am - 5.30pm. Sat, 10am - 5pm

Ireland

Northern Ireland Tourist Board

16 Nassau Street, Dublin

(www.discovernorthernireland.com

Ireland. It's a different holiday altogether.

ADAIR ARMS HOTEL

BALLYMONEY ROAD, BALLYMENA,
CO. ANTRIM BT43 5BS
TEL: 028-2565 3674   FAX: 028-2564 0436
EMAIL: reservations@adairarms.com

HOTEL ★★★   MAP 15 O 19

A warm welcome awaits you at the
Adair Arms Hotel, which is owned
and run by the McLarnon Family.
The hotel was built in 1846 by Sir
Robert Adair, and designed by the
famous architect Charles Lanyon.
Situated in the heart of Ballymena,
ideally located for touring the
romantic Glens of Antrim, Slemish
Mountain and North Antrim Coast.
The hotel has recently been
refurbished and has the added
attraction of a new 18 hole golf
course within one mile, courtesy
transport provided for guests.

WEB: www.adairarms.com

B&B from £35.00 to £42.50

G MCLARNON
Manager/Proprietor

American Express
Diners
Mastercard
Visa

Weekend specials from £75.00

44 44

Closed 25 - 26 December

TULLYGLASS HOUSE HOTEL

178 GALGORM ROAD,
BALLYMENA, CO. ANTRIM BT42 1HJ
TEL: 028-2565 2639   FAX: 028-2564 6938
EMAIL: guest@tullyglass.com

HOTEL ★★★   MAP 15 O 19

Situated in its own private grounds
close to the North Antrim Coast and
Glens of Antrim, Tullyglass House
Hotel has something for everyone
with 27 beautifully decorative en
suite bedrooms, all with tea/coffee
making facilities, trouser press,
hairdryer, direct dial telephone, 3
bars, a superb restaurant and daily
carvery. Regular entertainment and a
choice of conference and wedding
facilities. Activities close by include
fishing, horseriding and golf.

WEB: www.tullyglass.com

B&B from £34.00 to £40.00

MR & MRS C MCCONVILLE

American Express
Mastercard
Visa

Weekend specials from £75.00

27 27

Closed 25 - 26 December

BUSHMILLS INN

9 DUNLUCE ROAD, BUSHMILLS,
CO. ANTRIM BT57 8QG
TEL: 028-2073 2339   FAX: 028-2073 2048
EMAIL: mail@bushmillsinn.com

HOTEL ★★★   MAP 14 N 21

It's one of those places where you
hope it rains all day so you have an
excuse to snuggle indoors. At the
home of the world's oldest distillery
between the Giant's Causeway and
Royal Portrush Golf Club this award
winning hotel and restaurant, with its
open peat fires, pitched pine and
gas lights, has been outstandingly
successful in re-creating its origins
as an old coaching inn and mill
house.

WEB: www.bushmillsinn.com

Member of Best Loved Hotels of The World

B&B from £44.00 to £64.00

ALAN DUNLOP & STELLA
MINOGUE Managers

American Express
Mastercard
Visa

32 32

Open All Year

Room rates are Stg£ per room per night

CAUSEWAY HOTEL

**40 CAUSEWAY ROAD, BUSHMILLS,
CO. ANTRIM BT57 8SU
TEL: 028-2073 1226 FAX: 028-2073 2552**

HOTEL ★★ MAP 14 N 21

Situated on the North Antrim Coast at the entrance to the world famous Giant's Causeway and the new visitors' centre, this old family hotel established in 1836 has been tastefully renovated and restored to provide modern facilities while retaining its old grandeur and charm. The thirty centrally heated bedrooms have TV, telephone, tea/coffee making facilities and bathrooms en suite.

WEB: www.giants-causeway-hotel.com

B&B from £32.50 to £35.00

STANLEY ARMSTRONG
Proprietor

Mastercard

Visa

🖙🏠☎🅿©🖙CM✱♪🄿🄰a/c☕
28 28

Open All Year

LONDONDERRY ARMS HOTEL

**20 HARBOUR ROAD, CARNLOUGH,
CO. ANTRIM BT44 0EU
TEL: 028-2888 5255 FAX: 028-2888 5263
EMAIL: info@comforthotelportrush.com**

HOTEL ★★★ MAP 15 P 20

This beautiful Georgian hotel was built in 1847. Once owned by Sir Winston Churchill, it is now owned and managed by Mr Frank O'Neill. With its open log fires, private lounges and award-winning restaurant this premier hotel in the Glens of Antrim is the perfect place to stay and discover the north eastern part of Ireland.

WEB: www.comforthotelportrush.com

Member of Northern Ireland Best Kept Secrets

B&B from £40.00 to £50.00

FRANK O'NEILL
Proprietor

American Express

Diners

Mastercard

Visa

😊 Weekend specials from £85.00

🖙🏠☎🄳🄱🅃©🖙CM✱♪🄿🄿
🅂🄰a/c☕

Open All Year

QUALITY HOTEL

**75 BELFAST ROAD, CARRICKFERGUS,
CO. ANTRIM BT38 8PH
TEL: 028-9336 4556 FAX: 028-9335 1620
EMAIL: info@qualitycarrick.co.uk**

HOTEL ★★★ MAP 15 P 18

3*** Mediterranean style hotel situated just 15 minutes from Belfast City Centre, en route to the beautiful Antrim Coast. With two bars and the Boardwalk Restaurant the hotel offers a variety of menus to suit all tastes. Each of the deluxe 68 en suite bedrooms offers a hospitality tray, trouser press, kingsize bed, hairdryer, direct dial phone and colour TV with satellite channels.

WEB: www.qualityinn.com

Member of Choice Hotels International

Room Rate from £60.00 to £85.00

FRANK BARBER
General Manager

American Express

Diners

Mastercard

Visa

😊 Weekend specials from £69.00

🖙🏠☎🄳🄱🅃©🖙CMʊ♪🄿🄵
a/c☕

Closed 24 - 26 December

B&B rates are Stg£ per person sharing per night incl. Breakfast

KEEF HALLA COUNTRY HOUSE

20 TULLY ROAD, NUTTS CORNER,
CRUMLIN, CO. ANTRIM BT29 4SW
TEL: 028-9082 5491 FAX: 028-9082 5940
EMAIL: info@keefhalla.com

GUESTHOUSE ★★★★ MAP 15 P 18

Keef Halla Country House is the nearest 4**** guesthouse to Belfast International Airport. All 7 bedrooms are elegantly decorated and include, STV, direct dial phone, trouser press, tea/coffee and refreshments. It is ideal for business people and holiday travellers requiring a central base for visiting Northern Ireland. We are conviently located to Antrim, Belfast, Crumlin, Dunadry, Lisburn and Templepatrick. Excellent value for money.

WEB: www.keefhalla.com

B&B from £22.50 to £25.00

CHARLES & SIOBHAN KELLY
Owners

American Express
Mastercard
Visa

7 7

Open All Year

ALEXANDRA

11 LANSDOWNE CRESCENT,
PORTRUSH, CO. ANTRIM
TEL: 028-7082 2284 FAX: 028-7082 2284
EMAIL: mcalistermary@hotmail.com

GUESTHOUSE U MAP 14 N 21

The Alexandra, a charming period townhouse, traditionally furnished but with modern day facilities offers the discerning visitor an ideal base to explore the surrounding countryside. Your choice of room will range from cosy and charming to spacious and gracious. Located in a tranquil crescent with uninterrupted sea views and ample car parking.

B&B from £22.50 to £30.00

MARY MCALISTER

Mastercard
Visa

9 5

Open All Year

CAUSEWAY COAST HOTEL & CONFERENCE CENTRE

36 BALLYREAGH ROAD, PORTRUSH,
CO. ANTRIM BT56 8LR
TEL: 028-7082 2435 FAX: 028-7082 4495
EMAIL: info@causewaycoast.com

HOTEL ★★★ MAP 14 N 21

Located one mile from Royal Portrush Golf Course on the coast road between Portrush and Portstewart, overlooking the Atlantic Ocean and within easy reach of the Giant's Causeway, Carrick-a-Rede Rope Bridge, Dunluce Castle. Ideal base to relax and play golf at Royal Portrush, Portstewart, Castlerock, Ballycastle, Bushfoot, Gracehill and Galgorm Castle Golf Courses. Private car park. Comfort Hotel, Portrush opening February 2001, Sister Hotel (50 Bedrooms).

WEB: www.causewaycoast.com

Member of Kennedy Hotel Group

B&B from £35.00 to £50.00

MARY O'NEILL
Group Marketing Manager

American Express
Mastercard
Visa

21 21

Open All Year

Room rates are Stg£ per room per night

CLARMONT

**10 LANSDOWNE CRESCENT,
PORTRUSH, CO. ANTRIM
TEL: 028-7082 2397   FAX: 028-7082 2397
EMAIL: clarmont@talk21.com**

GUESTHOUSE ★★ MAP 14 N 21

Clarmont, a spacious period townhouse, situated on Lansdowne Crescent, an award winning Victorian stucco-style resort terrace, designed to take maximum advantage of its seafront position on the famous Causeway Coast. With the renowned Royal Portrush Golf Club on its doorstep, the Clarmont enjoys an international golfing clientele. Also an ideal base for enjoying the many splendours & attractions of Ireland's North Coast. Convenient to pubs & restaurants. Ample parking.

WEB: www.clarmont.com

B&B from £22.50 to £27.50
€28.57 to €34.92

JOHN & FRANCES DUGGAN
Owners

Mastercard

Visa

🖐️🚗🅿️T🅲❄️♨️🕺🛎️
10 10

Closed 20 - 30 December

COMFORT HOTEL PORTRUSH

**71 MAIN STREET, PORTRUSH,
CO. ANTRIM BT56 8BN
TEL: 028-7082 6100   FAX: 028-7082 6160
EMAIL: info@comforthotelportrush.com**

UNDER CONSTRUCTION OPENING FEB 2001

HOTEL P MAP 14 N 21

Comfort Hotel opening February 2001, sister hotel of the Causeway Coast Hotel. 50 en suite bedrooms with interlinking and ambulant disabled rooms. Lift, private car park. Overlooking the Atlantic Ocean situated in the centre of Portrush. Ideal for golfing, walking, cycling, angling, sightseeing, families, tour parties, conference, golf at Royal Portrush, Portstewart, Castlerock, Ballycastle, etc. Rooms will accommodate 2 adults/2 children with TV, phone, hospitality tray, trouser press and internet access from bedroom telephone.

WEB: www.comforthotelportrush.com

Member of Choice Hotels Europe

Room Rate from £49.95 to £59.95

MARY O'NEILL
Group Marketing Manager

American Express

Diners

Mastercard

Visa

✓ 🍴

🖐️🚗☎️🅿️T🅲C🅼♨️🎵🅿️🆂🛎️
50 50

📶 Inet

Open All Year

MAGHERABUOY HOUSE HOTEL

**41 MAGHERABOY ROAD,
PORTRUSH, CO. ANTRIM
TEL: 028-708 23507   FAX: 028-708 24687
EMAIL: admin@magherabuoy.co.uk**

HOTEL ★★★ MAP 14 N 21

Overnight in the centre of the Causeway Coast's golfers dream. The Magherabuoy is only a short driving time to Royal Portrush, Portstewart and Castlerock Golf Clubs. Quality location with views over Portrush Town. Members of A Taste of Ulster boasting best of Ulster produce. Unique to the Magherabuoy is on site aromatherapy/reflexology and our own specialist cook shop. NITB Welcome Host Gold Award winners 1999 and 2000.

WEB: www.magherabuoy.co.uk

B&B from £30.00 to £50.00

T. CLARKE
General Manager

American Express

Diners

Mastercard

Visa

✓ 🍴

😊 Midweek specials from £70.00

🖐️🚗☎️T🅲C🅼♨️🍴♨️🕺🎵🅿️
38 38

🆂🛏️🅰d

Closed 24 - 26 December

B&B rates are Stg£ per person sharing per night incl. Breakfast

BALLYMAC

7A ROCK ROAD, STONEYFORD,
CO. ANTRIM BT28 3SU
TEL: 028-9264 8313   FAX: 028-9264 8312
EMAIL: info@ballymachotel.ie

HOTEL ★★   MAP 15 O 18

The Ballymac is a new accommodation and conference development comprising of 15 en suite rooms with excellent facilities including satellite TV, tea/coffee making facilities, direct dial phone and hairdryer. Our grill bar and à la carte restaurants feature outstanding cuisine from award winning chefs. The Ballymac also boasts well-equipped function suites suitable for weddings, parties, trade shows and conferences. Extensive private parking available in our grounds.

WEB: www.ballymachotel.ie

B&B from £30.00 to £42.50

CATHY MULDOON
General Manager

American Express
Mastercard
Visa

15 15

Closed 25 December

HILTON TEMPLEPATRICK

CASTLE UPTON ESTATE,
TEMPLEPATRICK, CO. ANTRIM BT39 0DD
TEL: 028-9443 5500   FAX: 028-9443 5511
EMAIL: matthew_mullan@hilton.com

HOTEL ★★★★   MAP 15 O 18

Hilton Templepatrick, set in 220 acres of parkland, just 10 mins from Belfast International Airport is the perfect retreat for a short break. 130 en suite rooms offering views of the surrounding countryside. All rooms are equipped with satellite TV, phone, trouser press, hairdryer and hospitality tray. Dine in style in one of the hotel's restaurants or bars. Play a round of golf on the hotel's own 18 hole championship course or relax in the LivingWell Health Club.

WEB: www.hilton.com

B&B from £35.00 to £80.00

MATTHEW MULLAN

American Express
Diners
Mastercard
Visa

130 130

Open All Year

TEMPLETON HOTEL

882 ANTRIM RD, TEMPLEPATRICK,
BALLYCLARE, BT39 0AH CO. ANTRIM
TEL: 028-9443 2984   FAX: 028-9443 3406

HOTEL ★★★   MAP 15 O 18

This luxury hotel is in a prime location close to Belfast International Airport, Belfast City Centre and Larne Harbour. Mixing the best of modern facilities with the appeal of yesterday, the hotel offers total quality for all tastes and needs. Upton Grill Room serving lunch and dinner daily, Templeton à la carte restaurant, spacious lounge, 24 bedrooms including executive suites and family rooms, Sam's Bar with pub grub. Late bar on Friday and Saturday evenings.

B&B from £35.00 to £55.00

ALISON MCCOURT/CLAIRE KERR
Gen Manager/Mkt Manager

American Express
Diners
Mastercard
Visa

24 24

Closed 25 - 26 December

Room rates are Stg£ per room per night

ASHBURN HOTEL

81 WILLIAM STREET, LURGAN,
CO. ARMAGH BT66 6JB
TEL: 028-3832 5711 FAX: 028-3834 7194
EMAIL: info@theashburnhotel.com

HOTEL ★   MAP 15 O 17

Owned and managed by the McConaghy Family, the Ashburn Hotel is friendly and efficient. Conveniently situated with easy access to the motorway (M1), rail network and town centre. An ideal base for angling or golfing trips - 5 miles from the River Bann and 1 mile from local golf course. All bedrooms are en suite with colour TV, direct dial telephone and hospitality tray. Entertainment each weekend in our popular nightclub.

WEB: www.theashburnhotel.com

B&B from £29.00 to £29.00

JOHN F. MCCONAGHY

Mastercard
Visa

12 12

Closed 24 - 26 December

SILVERWOOD GOLF HOTEL AND COUNTRY CLUB

KILN ROAD, LURGAN, CRAIGAVON,
CO. ARMAGH
TEL: 028-3832 7722 FAX: 028-3832 5290

HOTEL ★   MAP 15 O 17

Silverwood Golf Hotel, situated in pleasant rural surroundings, is only 2 mins from the M1 motorway which links the hotel to Belfast and sea/airports within 20 minutes. The centre of business life at Craigavon is also close at hand. The hotel has a reputation for excellent food combined with friendly and efficient service in a relaxed and charming setting. Family owned. Golf course on doorstep; live entertainment at weekends; overlooks artificial ski slope (details available).

Member of Best Western Hotels

B&B from £20.00 to £35.00

SEAN HUGHES
Proprietor

American Express
Diners
Mastercard
Visa

Weekend specials from £55.00

28 28

Open All Year

SEAGOE HOTEL

22 UPPER CHURCH LANE, PORTADOWN,
CO. ARMAGH BT63 5JE
TEL: 028-3833 3076 FAX: 028-3835 0210
EMAIL: info@seagoe.com

HOTEL ★★★   MAP 14 N 17

Attractively situated in generous grounds with secure parking for 140 cars, the luxuriously appointed Seagoe Hotel is the Orchard County Of Armagh's best kept secret. Spectacularly reincarnated by its new owners, this innovative and contemporary designed 36 bedroom hotel, conference and entertainment complex combines style and sophistication with a casual elegance. The entire hotel has been thoughtfully designed for easy wheelchair access, featuring lifts and other disabled facilities.

WEB:www.seagoe.com

Room Rate from £60.00 to £90.00

TONY MCGANN
Manager

American Express
Diners
Mastercard
Visa

36 36

Closed 25 December

B&B rates are Stg£ per person sharing per night incl. Breakfast

ALDERGROVE HOTEL

BELFAST INTERNATIONAL AIRPORT,
CRUMLIN, BELFAST
TEL: 028-9442 2033   FAX: 028-9442 3500

HOTEL ★★★   MAP 15 P 18

Situated 50m from entrance to Belfast International Airport and 17 miles from Belfast City Centre. Fully air conditioned, this modern hotel has 108 rooms, fully equipped to the highest standard. Terrace Restaurant is open from 6am to 10pm daily. Fitness suite and sauna available free to all guests. Purpose built conference and banqueting facilities and free guest parking.

B&B from £32.50 to £37.50

CALUM MACLACHLAN
General Manager

American Express
Diners
Mastercard
Visa

108 108

Open All Year

CORR'S CORNER HOTEL

315 BALLYCLARE ROAD,
NEWTOWNABBEY, CO. ANTRIM BT36 4TQ
TEL: 028-9084 9221   FAX: 028-9083 2118
EMAIL: info@corrscorner.com

HOTEL ★★   MAP 15 P 18

Corr's Corner is a family-run business located 7 miles north of Belfast at the M2 and A8 junction, 14 miles from Larne Harbour and Belfast International Airport. The hotel has 30 en suite rooms with 2 rooms specifically designed for guests with disabilities. Meals are served all day in the Lady R Bar and the Corriander Room Restaurant. The Ballyhenry Lounge is open every evening and the Cedar Room caters for meetings and private parties up to 60 persons.

WEB: www.corrscorner.com

Room Rate from £45.00 to £55.00

EUGENE & CATHERINE McKEEVER

American Express
Diners
Mastercard
Visa

☺ Weekend specials from £69.00

30 30

Inet

Closed 25 - 27 December

DUKES HOTEL

65/67 UNIVERSITY STREET,
BELFAST BT7 1HL
TEL: 028-9023 6666   FAX: 028-9023 7177
EMAIL: info@dukes-hotel-belfast.co.uk

HOTEL ★★★   MAP 15 P 18

A bright new modern hotel constructed within one of Belfast's more distinguished Victorian buildings. Beside Queen's University, Ulster Museum, Botanic Gardens and less than 1 mile from the city centre. Golf courses only minutes away. 21 luxury en suite bedrooms, all with satellite TV, hairdryers and direct dial telephones. Gymnasium and saunas also available. Elegant restaurant serving local cuisine. Popular bar for the smart set. A friendly welcome and service is guaranteed.

WEB: www.dukes-hotel-belfast.co.uk

B&B from £36.00 to £55.00

MICHAEL CAFOLLA
General Manager

American Express
Diners
Mastercard
Visa

21 21

Open All Year

DUNADRY HOTEL AND COUNTRY CLUB

2 ISLANDREAGH DRIVE, DUNADRY,
CO. ANTRIM BT41 2HA
TEL: 028-9443 4343 FAX: 028-9443 3389
EMAIL: mooneyhotelgroup@talk21.com

HOTEL ★★★★ MAP 15 O 18

Truly the place to stay if you're looking for warm hospitality, comfort, charm, relaxation, imaginative gourmet cuisine. Millions of activities to choose from. Awarded Les Routiers Hotel of the year 1999. Luxurious bedrooms, beautiful food in Mill Race Bistro and fine dining restaurant, superb country club and swimming pool. Cycling, fishing, country walking, horse riding and golf available on site or on request. 5 minutes from Belfast Intl Airport. Central reservations @ 02890 385050.

WEB: www.mooneyhotelgroup.com

B&B from £42.50 to £80.00

ROBERT MOONEY
General Manager

American Express
Diners
Mastercard
Visa

😊 Weekend specials from £105.00

83 83

Closed 24 - 26 December

JURYS INN BELFAST

FISHERWICK PLACE,
GREAT VICTORIA ST, BELFAST BT2 7AP
TEL: 028-9053 3511   FAX: 028-9053 3500
EMAIL: belfast_inn@jurysdoyle.com

HOTEL ★★★ MAP 15 P 18

Modern attractive rooms capable of accommodating up to 3 adults or 2 adults and 2 children. All rooms are en suite with multi-channel TV, radio, direct dial phone, modem points and tea/coffee making facilities. Located in the centre of Belfast on Fisherwick Place, near Opera House, City Hall and business district. 2 minutes walk from major shopping areas of Donegal Place and Castlecourt Centre. Public car park close by. Jurys Doyle Hotel Group Central Reservations: Tel 01-607 0000; Fax 01-660 9625.

WEB: www.jurysdoyle.com

Room Rate from £67.00 to £69.00

MARGARET NAGLE
General Manager

American Express
Diners
Mastercard
Visa

190 190

Closed 24 - 26 December

LA MON HOTEL & COUNTRY CLUB

41 GRANSHA ROAD,
CASTLEREAGH, BELFAST BT23 5RF
TEL: 028-9044 8631 FAX: 028-9044 8026
EMAIL: info@lamon.co.uk

HOTEL ★★★ MAP 15 P 18

La Mon Hotel & Country Club is located 5 miles from Belfast City Centre in the heart of the County Down countryside. This warm & friendly family run hotel has been extensively refurbished. Guests can relax & unwind in the new La Mon Country Club. Facilities include a 15m pool, sauna, steam room, jacuzzi & fitness suites. Enjoy the best of both worlds, a rural retreat on the doorstep of the city.

WEB: www.lamon.co.uk

B&B from £32.50 to £40.00

FRANCIS BRADY
Managing Director

American Express
Mastercard
Visa

78 78

Open All Year

B&B rates are Stg£ per person sharing per night incl. Breakfast

MCCAUSLAND HOTEL

34-38 VICTORIA STREET,
BELFAST BT1 3GH
TEL: 028-9022 0200 FAX: 028-9022 0220
EMAIL: info@mccauslandhotel.com

HOTEL ★★★★ MAP 15 P 18

The McCausland Hotel, a magnificent classical Italianate building which exudes a style that follows through to a beautiful contemporary interior. Bedrooms offer luxury & comfort complete with Neutrogena® toiletries. Modern Irish dishes can be enjoyed in Merchants Brasserie & drinks in Cafe Marco Polo. Short stroll from museums, theatres, shopping & the Waterfront Hall. Sister to the Hibernian Hotel Dublin and Woodstock Hotel Ennis. GDS Acc code:LX. UK Toll free Access 00 800 525 48000.

WEB: www.mccauslandhotel.com

Member of Small Luxury Hotels of the World

Room Rate from £110.00 to £190.00

JOSEPH V. HUGHES
General Manager

American Express
Diners
Mastercard
Visa

😊 Weekend specials from £120.00

60 60

Closed 24 - 27 December

PARK AVENUE HOTEL

158 HOLYWOOD ROAD,
BELFAST BT4 1PB
TEL: 028-9065 6520 FAX: 028-9047 1417
EMAIL: frontdesk@parkavenuehotel.co.uk

HOTEL ★★★ MAP 15 P 18

Park Avenue Hotel has recently undergone a £2M refurbishment. *56 rooms, with en suite facilities, including TV with satellite channels. *Disabled facilities. *Free parking. Our new Griffin Restaurant offers an extensive menu to suit all tastebuds. Alternatively our bistro menu is served daily in Gelstons Corner Bar. *5 minutes from Belfast City Airport. *10 minutes from Belfast City centre. *Excellent links to the outer ring roads and all transport stations and ferry terminals.

WEB: www.parkavenuehotel.co.uk

B&B from £30.00 to £39.50

SHAW STEPHENS
General Manager/Director

American Express
Mastercard
Visa

56 56

Inet

Closed 25 December

POSTHOUSE PREMIER BELFAST

22 ORMEAU AVENUE,
BELFAST BT2 8HS
TEL: 0870 400 9005 FAX: 028-9062 6546

HOTEL ★★★★ MAP 15 P 18

A modern hotel situated in the heart of Belfast's City centre, and ideally located for city centre shops, restaurants, Odyssey Centre, Opera House, Belfast Zoo, Botanic Gardens/Ulster Museum, City Hall & the Waterfront Hall. This newly built hotel offers residents superior air-conditioned bedrooms, the contemporary Junction Restaurant and Bar, a superb Health and Leisure Centre (opening Spring 2001). There is also a Pay Car Park on site & an NCP car park behind the hotel.

WEB: www.posthouse-hotels.com

Member of Forte & Meridien

B&B from £42.00 to £71.00

ADRIAN MCLAUGHLIN
General Manager

American Express
Diners
Mastercard
Visa

😊 Weekend specials from £99.00

170 170

Open All Year

Room rates are Stg£ per room per night

WELLINGTON PARK HOTEL

21 MALONE ROAD,
BELFAST BT9 6RU
TEL: 028-9038 1111 FAX: 028-9066 5410
EMAIL: mooneyhotelgroup@talk21.com

HOTEL ★★★★ MAP 15 P 18

The ideal place to stay when you come to Belfast. Located 5 minutes from the city centre, in the fashionable area of South Belfast, the city's most popular venues are at our doorstep: King's Hall, Waterfront Hall, Odyssey complex, museums, theatres... Designed to international standards, the hotel is renowned for its elegant and relaxed atmosphere and its luxurious suites. You can also enjoy fine cuisine in the Piper's Bistro. Central Reservations 028-9038 5050.

WEB: www.mooneyhotelgroup.com

Member of Best Western Hotels

B&B from £40.00 to £75.00

ARTHUR MOONEY
General Manager

American Express
Diners
Mastercard
Visa

☺ Weekend specials from £95.00

75 75
 Inet FAX

Closed 24 - 26 December

BEECH HILL COUNTRY HOUSE HOTEL

32 ARDMORE ROAD,
DERRY BT47 3QP
TEL: 028-7134 9279 FAX: 028-7134 5366
EMAIL: info@beech-hill.com

HOTEL ★★★★ MAP 14 L 20

Beech Hill is a privately owned country house hotel, 2mls from Londonderry. It retains the elegance of country living, restored to create a hotel of charm, character and style. Its ambience is complemented by the surrounding grounds, planted with a myriad trees, including beech - after which the hotel is named. Winners of British Airways Best Catering - 1994. CMV & Associates 00353 1 295 8900. Best Kept Secrets of Northern Ireland. Sauna, Steamroom, jacuzzi & fitness suites.

WEB: www.beech-hill.com

Member of Manor House Hotels

B&B from £50.00 to £70.00

SEAMUS DONNELLY
Proprietor

American Express
Mastercard
Visa

☺ Weekend specials from £110.00

27 27
 inet

Closed 25 - 26 December

QUALITY HOTEL DA VINCIS

15 CULMORE ROAD,
DERRY BT48 8JB
TEL: 028-7127 9111 FAX: 028-7127 9222
EMAIL: davincis@god-group.com

HOTEL ★★★ MAP 14 L 20

Quality Hotel Da Vincis complex comprises of an award winning bar, à la carte restaurant, spirit bar, function room and 70 en suite rooms. Rates are on a room only basis with a maximum of four occupants. The complex is located just one mile from the centre of Derry and is the ideal base to explore the Maiden City and the North West.

WEB: www.davincishotel.com

Room Rate from £50.00 to £80.00

FINTAN KELLY
General Manager

American Express
Diners
Mastercard
Visa

70 70

 inet

Open All Year

B&B rates are Stg£ per person sharing per night incl. Breakfast

TRINITY HOTEL

22-24 STRAND ROAD, DERRY CITY,
CO. LONDONDERRY BT48 7AB
TEL: 028-7127 1271   FAX: 028-7127 1277
EMAIL: info@thetrinityhotel.com

HOTEL ★★★   MAP 14 L 20

Derry's premier city centre hotel provides the ideal meeting place for business/pleasure. It offers 40 en suite rooms which include 2 luxury suites and a standard of comfort and accommodation unrivalled in the area. Nolan's Bistro and Porter's Café Bar provide the ideal environment to pass many a pleasurable hour. For the conference organiser there are 3 dedicated meeting rooms with a maximum capacity of 150 theatre style. Rooms offer latest technology and full air-conditioning.

WEB: www.thetrinityhotel.com

B&B from £40.00 to £45.00

LORRAINE KERR
Hotel Manager

American Express
Diners
Mastercard
Visa

40 40

Closed 24 - 26 December

WHITE HORSE HOTEL

68 CLOONEY ROAD, CAMPSIE,
DERRY BT47 3PA
TEL: 028-7186 0606   FAX: 028-7186 0371
EMAIL: info@white-horse.demon.co.uk

HOTEL ★★   MAP 14 L 20

43 bedroom hotel, all en suite with colour TV, trouser press, tea/coffee making facilities. Located 5 miles from Derry City and on the main road to the Giant's Causeway. Ideal touring base for Donegal. Superb golf breaks and over 55s special breaks all year. Carvery lunch served every day, very popular tour stop. Large private car/coach park to rear of hotel, free of charge to guests. 5 minutes drive to City of Derry Airport. A perfect choice for both business and pleasure travellers.

Member of Best Western Hotels

B&B from £25.00 to £35.00

SHEILA HUNTER
General Manager

American Express
Diners
Mastercard
Visa

Weekend specials from £60.00

43 43

Open All Year

BROWN TROUT GOLF & COUNTRY INN

209 AGIVEY ROAD, AGHADOWEY,
COLERAINE, CO. DERRY BT51 4AD
TEL: 028-7086 8209   FAX: 028-7086 8878
EMAIL: bill@browntroutinn.com

HOTEL ★★★   MAP 14 N 20

The Brown Trout Golf and Country Inn nestles near the River Bann only 12.8km from the picturesque Causeway Coast. This old inn with 15 rooms, and four 5 star cottages, is Northern Ireland's first golf hotel. Bill, Gerry, Jane or Joanna will happily organise golf, horseriding and fishing packages with professional tuition if required or you can just enjoy a relaxing break and the crack with the locals. The warm hospitality and 'Taste of Ulster' restaurant will make your stay enjoyable.

WEB: www.browntroutinn.com

Member of Coast and Country Hotels

B&B from £30.00 to £42.50

BILL O'HARA
Owner

American Express
Diners
Mastercard
Visa

15 15

Open All Year

Room rates are Stg£ per room per night

BOHILL HOTEL & COUNTRY CLUB

69 CLOYFIN ROAD, COLERAINE, CO. LONDONDERRY
TEL: 028-7034 4406 FAX: 028-7035 2424
EMAIL: bohill@nildram.co.uk

HOTEL ★★★ MAP 14 N 21

In the heart of Co. Londonderry, just a few miles from the beautiful North Antrim coast stands the Bohill Hotel & Country Club bringing together the historic elegance of a country house with the best of today's international cuisine and facilities. Guests enjoy rooms whose furnishings include baby listening, trouser press, iron & tea/coffee facilities. To compliment these relaxing surroundings the Bohill boasts the largest private hotel pool & country club in the North West.

B&B from £40.00 to £55.00

DONAL MACAULEY
Managing Director

Diners

Mastercard

Visa

 Weekend specials from £90.00

🐾🏠☎️ⓉⒶⒸ♿CM❄️🚲🍴Ⓤ
🎵🎵🅿️🅰️alc ⌨️Inet
37 37

NIHF

Open All Year

EDGEWATER HOTEL

88 STRAND ROAD, PORTSTEWART, CO. DERRY
TEL: 028-7083 3314 FAX: 028-7083 2224
EMAIL: edgewater.hotel@virgin.net

HOTEL ★★ MAP 14 M 21

Adjacent to Portstewart Golf Club, the hotel is magnificently situated overlooking spectacular views of Portstewart Strand, Hills of Donegal and Atlantic Ocean. All 28 en suite rooms (incl 6 suites with sea views) contain colour TV, radio, direct dial phone and tea/coffee facilities. Indulge in dinner in O'Malleys split level restaurant or relax and enjoy a bar snack in the Inishtrahull lounge, both with picture windows capturing breathtaking views.

B&B from £30.00 to £45.00

KEVIN O'MALLEY
Proprietor

American Express

Diners

Mastercard

Visa

✓

 Weekend specials from £70.00

🐾🏠☎️ⓉⒸCMⓅⓈⒶ🍴
28 28

NIHF

Open All Year

CAIRN BAY LODGE

THE CAIRN, 278 SEACLIFF ROAD, BANGOR, CO. DOWN BT20 5HS
TEL: 028-9146 7636 FAX: 028-9145 7728
EMAIL: info@cairnbaylodge.com

GUESTHOUSE ★★★ MAP 15 Q 18

Award winning guesthouse set in extensive gardens directly overlooking Ballyholme Bay and National Trust property Ballymacormick Point. The Lodge is family run, offering the highest standards of food, accommodation and service in luxurious surroundings. An oasis of calm yet only 10 minutes walk from Bangor Town Centre and Marina. 50m from Ballyholme Yacht Club, 5 golf courses within 5 miles and resident beauty therapist. Perfect for business or pleasure.

WEB: www.cairnbaylodge.com

B&B from £25.00 to £27.50

CHRIS & JENNY MULLEN
Proprietor

Mastercard

Visa

 Weekend specials from £55.00

🐾🏠☎️ⓉⒸ♿CM❄️Ⓤ🅿️🅰️🍴
5 5
⌨️Inet

NIHF

Open All Year

B&B rates are Stg£ per person sharing per night incl. Breakfast

ROYAL HOTEL.

26/28 QUAY STREET, BANGOR,
CO. DOWN BT20 5ED
TEL: 028-9127 1866   FAX: 028-9146 7810
EMAIL: royalhotelbangor@cs.com

HOTEL ★★   MAP 15 Q 18

Overlooking Bangor marina this family run hotel is probably the best known landmark on Bangor's seafront. All 50 rooms are en suite and include 7 executive suites, satellite TV, direct dial phone, courtesy tray and hairdryer are all standard throughout. Renowned for superb food served in a variety of atmospheric restaurants and bars. Nightclub, conference and banqueting facilities. 15 minutes from Belfast City Airport. Direct rail link from Dublin and Derry.

WEB: www.the-royal-hotel.com

B&B from £37.50 to £42.50

PAUL DONEGAN
Proprietor

American Express
Diners
Mastercard
Visa

☺ Weekend specials from £70.00

🛏🕺☎🖥🔥📺T C M 🍷 🎵🛎 S 🅿 alc
50 50

NIHF

Closed 25 - 26 December

SHELLEVEN HOUSE

61 PRINCETOWN ROAD, BANGOR
BT20 3TA, CO. DOWN
TEL: 028-9127 1777   FAX: 028-9127 1777

GUESTHOUSE ★★★   MAP 15 Q 18

An end of terrace Victorian house set back from Princetown Road, with garden and private parking, convenient to the marina, seafront and shops. We have 11 rooms, all en suite. The front rooms have a view of Bangor Bay and the Irish Sea beyond. Train and bus station is 5 minutes away, with direct link to the Dublin train service, and the city airport. Tee off times can be arranged at several local golf courses.

B&B from £22.50 to £27.50

MARY WESTON

Mastercard
Visa

☺ Weekend specials from £60.00

🛏🕺☎T C 🔥 C M ❄ 🍷 J P S 🅿
11 11

NIHF

Open All Year

CHESTNUT INN

28/34 LOWER SQUARE, CASTLEWELLAN,
CO. DOWN BT31 9DW
TEL: 028-437 78247   FAX: 028-437 78247

GUESTHOUSE ★   MAP 12 P 16

In the old market town of Castlewellan the Chestnut Inn (King's) is ideally situated to take advantage of the Mournes, the seaside town of Newcastle and all the amenities of South Down. Royal County Down is only 5 minutes away as are the Forest Parks and the beaches of Dundrum Bay. The Inn is renowned for excellent bar food and also boasts a superb à la carte restaurant.

B&B from £25.00 to £35.00

JOHN & FIONNUALA KING
Proprietors

Mastercard
Visa

🛏🕺☎T C 🔥 C M 🍷 🎵 🎵🅿 alc 🍺
7 7

NIHF

Open All Year

Room rates are Stg£ per room per night

BURRENDALE HOTEL AND COUNTRY CLUB

51 CASTLEWELLAN ROAD, NEWCASTLE, CO. DOWN BT33 0JY
TEL: 028-4372 2599 FAX: 028-4372 2328
EMAIL: reservations@burrendale.com

HOTEL ★★★ MAP 12 P 16

At the foot of the Mournes, the Burrendale is the ideal location for your family, golfing holiday or short break. The hotel comprises of a Country Club, Beauty Salon, á la carte Vine Restaurant, bistro style Cottage Kitchen Restaurant, Cottage Bar and excellent banqueting / conference facilities. In close proximity are 15 golf courses including Royal County Down, golden beaches, nature walks, forest parks and pony trekking. Superb hospitality awaits you.

WEB: www.burrendale.com

B&B from £49.50 to £65.00

KEM AKKARI / SEAN SMALL
Manager/Proprietor

American Express
Diners
Mastercard
Visa

☺ Weekend specials from £97.00

69 69

Open All Year

SLIEVE DONARD HOTEL

DOWNS ROAD, NEWCASTLE, CO. DOWN BT33 0AH
TEL: 028-4372 3681 FAX: 028-4372 4830
EMAIL: res@sdh.hastingshotels.com

HOTEL ★★★★ MAP 12 P 16

Situated at the foot of the Mountains of Mourne, the Slieve Donard Hotel stands in 6 acres of private grounds leading to the world-famous Royal County Down Golf Course. Having completed a total refurbishment programme the Slieve Donard offers deluxe accommodation, Elysium Leisure Complex, restaurants and bars, including the Percy French, an informal pub restaurant in the hotel grounds, truly making it Northern Ireland's most popular holiday hotel.

WEB: www.hastingshotels.com

B&B from £60.00 to £75.00

RICHARD ROBINSON
General Manager

American Express
Diners
Mastercard
Visa

126 126

Open All Year

CANAL COURT HOTEL

MERCHANTS QUAY, NEWRY, CO. DOWN BT35 8HF
TEL: 028-3025 1234 FAX: 028-3025 1177
EMAIL: manager@canalcourthotel.com

HOTEL ★★★ MAP 12 O 15

British Airways award winning Canal Court Hotel. 51 en suite rooms with satellite TV, hospitality trays, hairdryer, direct dial phone and ironing facilities. The Old Mill Restaurant is one of the finest in the area, the Granary Bar has carvery and bar snacks served daily. Conference facilities for up to 300 people with superb suites for wedding receptions and private functions. Health and leisure complex incorporating gym, swimming pools, jacuzzi, sauna and steam room.

WEB: www.canalcourthotel.com

B&B from £50.00 to £65.00

MICHELLE BARRETT
General Manager

American Express
Diners
Mastercard
Visa

51 51

Closed 25 December

B&B rates are Stg£ per person sharing per night incl. Breakfast

Visit the Kingdoms

A wealth of leisure pursuits ...*of* Down

T: 0845 300 3393
Web: www.kingdomsofdown.com
Email: info@kingdomsofdown.com

Please Quote Ref: IR06

The Kingdoms of

South East Ulster

USEFUL TELEPHONE NUMBERS

Emergency	999	Air France	(01) 844 5633
(fire, Garda, (Police) & Ambulance)		Virgin Altantic	(01) 873 3388
Directory Enquiries	11811	Iberia/Viva Air	(01) 844 4939
(national)		(Dublin Airport)	
Directory Enquiries	11818	Irish Rail	(01) 836 6222
(to Great Britain)		(Passenger information)	
Operator Assistance	10	Connolly Station	(01) 836 3333
(Ireland/Northern Ireland/Great Britain)		Heuston Station	(01) 836 3333
Operator Assistance	114	Dart Information	(01) 836 3333
(international, excluding Great Britain)			
Dublin Airport	(01) 844 4131	Irish Bus (Bus Eireann)	(01) 836 1111
Shannon Airport	(061) 471 444	Dublin Bus	(01) 873 4222
Cork Airport	(021) 431 3131	(Bus Atha Cliath)	
Aer Lingus	(01) 886 6705	Irish Ferries (Enquiries)	1890 31 31 31
(flight enquiries)		Irish Ferries	(01) 855 2222
British Airways	1 800 62 67 47	General Post Office	(01) 705 7000
(enquiries)		(An Post)	
Ryanair	(01) 844 4411	Bord Fáilte	(01) 602 4000
(flight enquiries)			
Delta Airlines	(01) 844 4166		
(enquiries)			

NARROWS

8 SHORE ROAD, PORTAFERRY,
CO. DOWN BT22 1JY
TEL: 028-4272 8148   FAX: 028-4272 8105
EMAIL: reservations@narrows.co.uk

GUESTHOUSE ★★★   MAP 15 Q 17

In the four years since it opened, The Narrows has taken the Northern Ireland hospitality industry by storm. With numerous awards and reviews for its architecture, cuisine, accommodation, accessibility and conference facilities, you will see why our guests keep coming back. We have 13 rooms en suite with views of the Strangford Narrows and our restaurant won the British Airways Tourism Award 1999 for Best Catering in Northern Ireland. Sauna and walled garden for your relaxation.

WEB: www.narrows.co.uk

B&B from £39.00 to £42.50

WILL & JAMES BROWN

American Express
Mastercard
Visa

🐾🏠📞⚡T C🚗CM❄☂∪♪P
13 13

🅿🅰lc&

Open All Year

PORTAFERRY HOTEL

10 THE STRAND, PORTAFERRY,
CO. DOWN BT22 1PE
TEL: 028-4272 8231   FAX: 028-4272 8999
EMAIL: info@portaferryhotel.com

HOTEL ★★★   MAP 15 Q 17

Loughside Hotel in spectacular setting. Award winning cuisine and fine wines. Explore or simply relax and do nothing; just peace and tranquillity. BA Tourism Endeavour Award, RAC Restaurant of the Year Award, AA 2 rosettes, Taste of Ulster, Good Hotel Guide. 29 miles from Belfast.

WEB: www.portaferryhotel.com

B&B from £45.00 to £50.00

JOHN & MARIE HERLIHY
Proprietors

American Express
Diners
Mastercard
Visa

😊 Weekend specials from £89.00

🐾🏠📞T C🚗CM∪♪🅿🅰lc🏊
14 14

Open All Year

HOTEL CARLTON

2 MAIN STREET, BELLEEK,
CO. FERMANAGH
TEL: 028-6865 8282   FAX: 028-6865 9005
EMAIL: reception@hotelcarlton.co.uk

HOTEL ★★   MAP 13 I 17

The Hotel Carlton's setting on the banks of the River Erne in the heart of the Irish lake district is quite simply breathtaking. Also on the steps of one of Ireland's most famous landmarks, Belleek Pottery, Ireland's oldest pottery. Ideally situated for visitors who wish to tour the nearby counties of Donegal, Sligo, Tyrone and Leitrim. The Hotel Carlton has recently been completely rebuilt in a traditional style and boasts 19 luxurious well appointed en suite rooms.

WEB: www.hotelcarlton.co.uk

Member of MinOtel Ireland Hotel Group

B&B from £30.00 to £37.50

THE GALLAGHER & ROONEY
FAMILY

American Express
Mastercard
Visa

😊 Weekend specials from £75.00

🐾🏠📞T C🚗CM❄∪♪🅿🅰
19 19

🅰lc

Closed 24 - 25 December

B&B rates are Stg£ per person sharing per night incl. Breakfast

KILLYHEVLIN HOTEL

DUBLIN ROAD, ENNISKILLEN,
CO. FERMANAGH BT74 6RW
TEL: 028-6632 3481   FAX: 028-6632 4726
EMAIL: info@killyhevlin.com

HOTEL ★★★★   MAP 11 K 16

Killyhevlin Hotel and chalets are situated on the shores of beautiful Lough Erne, making it a terrific location at the gateway to the west and an ideal base for exploring the many sights of Fermanagh. All 43 bedrooms plus the Belmore Suite are fitted to a high standard, each has a bathroom / shower en suite, TV, direct dial phone, radio and tea facilities. Our scenic lounge and restaurant offer a wide variety of menus. Lunchtime buffet, bar snacks all day. Evenings, table d'hôte or à la carte.

WEB: www.killyhevlin.com

B&B from £42.50 to £52.50

RODNEY J. WATSON
Managing Director

American Express
Diners
Mastercard
Visa

43 43

Closed 24 - 26 December

MANOR HOUSE COUNTRY HOTEL

KILLADEAS, ENNISKILLEN,
CO. FERMANAGH BT94 1NY
TEL: 028-6862 2211   FAX: 028-6862 1545
EMAIL: manorhousehotel@lakelands.net

HOTEL ★★★★   MAP 14 K 16

This fine Victorian country mansion is beautifully situated in the Fermanagh countryside on the shores of lower Lough Erne. The hotel has been extensively refurbished to provide extreme comfort in splendid stately surroundings. All rooms are en suite with satellite TV, direct dial phone and tea making facilities. This is the ideal location for a break away where you can enjoy a range of activities in our ultra modern leisure complex including swimming pool.

WEB: www.lakelands.net/manorhousehotel

B&B from £45.00 to £55.00

DAVID BEGLEY
General Manager

American Express
Mastercard
Visa

😊 Weekend specials from £115.00

46 46

Open All Year

RAILWAY HOTEL.

34 FORTHILL STREET, ENNISKILLEN,
CO. FERMANAGH BT74 6AJ
TEL: 028-6632 2084   FAX: 028-6632 7480

HOTEL ★   MAP 11 K 16

James Crozier and Owen McKenna new owners of the Railway Hotel, are clearly succeeding in continuing the tradition of hospitality established through 150 years of family ownership. Guests have the choice of 19 well appointed bedrooms, all en suite, with Sky TV and telephone. A full range of meals is available, in style in the Dining Car Restaurant, which has an excellent reputation for food. Friendly staff and cosy atmosphere ensures a memorable breakaway for everyone.

B&B from £31.00 to £38.50

JAMES CROZIER/OWEN
MCKENNA Owners

Mastercard
Visa

19 19

Closed 25 - 26 December

MAHONS HOTEL

ENNISKILLEN ROAD, IRVINESTOWN,
CO. FERMANAGH
TEL: 028-6862 1656 FAX: 028-6862 8344
EMAIL: info@mahonshotel.co.uk

HOTEL ★★ MAP 13 K 17

Situated in the heart of the
Fermanagh Lakeland. Ideal base for
visiting all major tourist attractions -
Belleek Pottery 20 minutes, Marble
Arch Caves 30 minutes, Necarne
Equestrian Centre 5 minutes, Lough
Erne 5 minutes, Donegal 20
minutes. All rooms en suite, TV, tea
making facilities. Bushmills Bar of
the Year winner, entertainment at
weekends, private car park. Family
run from 1883. Visit us in our
second century. Cycling, horseriding,
tennis and golf all available.

WEB: www.mahonshotel.co.uk

Member of Fermanagh Lakeland Hotels

B&B from £32.00 to £35.00

JOE MAHON
Manager

American Express
Mastercard
Visa

Weekend specials from £69.00

18 18

Open All Year

CORICK HOUSE & LICENSED RESTAURANT

20 CORICK ROAD, CLOGHER,
CO. TYRONE
TEL: 028-8554 8216 FAX: 028-8554 9531

GUESTHOUSE ★★★ MAP 14 L 17

A warm welcome awaits you at
Corick House, a charming 17th
century 3*** approved country
residence, located in the heart of the
Clogher Valley, just off the main A4
Belfast to Enniskillen Road.
Attractively restored family home
offers 10 luxury rooms, licensed
restaurant, conference and wedding
facilities. Set in mature woodland
overlooking the Blackwater River it is
the ideal location for trout and
salmon fishing. Central to the
Fermanagh Lakelands and the Ulster
Way.

WEB: www.corickhousehotel@netscapeonline.co.uk

B&B from £28.00 to £35.00

JEAN BEACOM
Proprietor

American Express
Diners
Mastercard
Visa

Weekend specials from £70.00

10 10

Open All Year

SILVERBIRCH HOTEL.

5 GORTIN ROAD, OMAGH,
CO. TYRONE BT79 7DH
TEL: 028-8224 2520 FAX: 028-8224 9061
EMAIL: info@silverbirchhotel.com

HOTEL ★★ MAP 14 L 18

The hotel is situated on the outskirts
of Omagh on the B48 leading to the
Gortin Glens, Ulster History Park,
Sperrins and the Ulster American
Folk Park. Set in its own spacious
and mature grounds, the hotel now
has 40 new en suite bedrooms to
3*** standard. Other facilities
include Buttery Grill all day, newly
refurbished dining room, function
suite for 250 guests for weddings,
dinners or conferences. Award
winning leisure centre 300 metres
away.

WEB: www.silverbirchhotel.com

B&B from £36.00 to £45.00

JAMES DUNCAN
Manager

American Express
Diners
Mastercard
Visa

Weekend specials from £72.00

46 46

Closed 25 December

B&B rates are Stg£ per person sharing per night incl. Breakfast

MOTORING IN IRELAND

AND
THINK

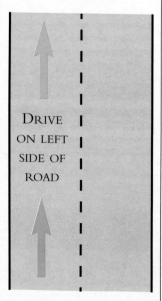

DRIVE ON LEFT SIDE OF ROAD

ENJOY YOUR HOLIDAY

INTERNATIONAL DIAL CODES

Emergency Services:
999 (freephone)

HOW TO DIAL
INTERNATIONAL
ACCESS CODE +
COUNTRY CODE +
AREA CODE +
LOCAL NUMBER

SAMPLE CODES:
E.G. UNITED KINGDOM
00 44 + Area Code + Local No.

U.S.A.	00	1	+
Italy	00	39	+
Spain	00	34	+
France	00	33	+
Germany	00	49	+
Iceland	00	354	+
Japan	00	81	+
Luxembourg	00	352	+
Netherlands	00	31	+

Operator (national)	1190
(G. Britain)	1197
(International)	1198

DUBLIN

As one of the oldest cities in Europe, Dublin provides the visitor with a multitude of cultural riches, from the ancient to the avant-garde: from history, architecture, literature, art and archaeology to the performing arts. Monuments in literature and in stone mark the history, writers, poets and people of Dublin. Medieval, Georgian and modern architecture provide a backdrop to a friendly, bustling port which can boast literary giants such as Wilde, Shaw, Joyce, Yeats, Beckett and O'Casey as native sons. Spawned by the need to ford the river Liffey, fortified by the Danes, developed by the Normans, adorned with fine buildings by the Anglo-Irish, the city has grown in stature and elegance over the century.

When it comes to entertainment, Dubliners with their natural friendly and fun-craving attitude, certainly know how to entertain. The quintessential 'Dublin Pub' provides the focal point of Dublin social life, illuminating the vibrant hues of Dubliners and their culture. It is a place where conversations and "craic" flow freely, unleashing the unique atmosphere that is at the heart of Dublin and its friendly people. Just a twenty-minute journey will bring the visitor from the bustling city centre to the charming coastal towns and villages of the

county. These towns and villages provide boundless opportunities for craft-shopping, watersports, seafood dining and picturesque walks against the spectacular background of Dublin Bay.

Whatever your heart desires, Dublin provides a superb location for all the above activities and many more besides.

Email: reservations@dublintourism.ie
http://www.visitdublin.com

Reservations and Information may be obtained by visiting one of our Information Centres:

- Dublin Tourism Centre, Suffolk St.,
- Arrivals Hall, Dublin Airport,
- Ferry Terminal,
  Dun Laoghaire Harbour,
- Baggot St Bridge.

St. Patrick's Day Festival, Dublin.
March

Dublin Film Festival
March / April

Kerrygold Horseshow, R.D.S. Dublin.
August

Guinness All-Ireland Hurling Championship Final, Croke Park, Dublin.
September

All-Ireland Football Championship Final, Croke Park, Dublin.
September

Dublin Theatre Festival, Dublin.
October

Event details correct at time of going to press

AARONMOR GUESTHOUSE

**1B/1C SANDYMOUNT AVENUE,
BALLSBRIDGE, DUBLIN 4
TEL: 01-668 7972   FAX: 01-668 2377
EMAIL: aaronmor@indigo.ie**

GUESTHOUSE ★★★ MAP 8 O 11

Welcome to Aaronmor, we trust your stay will have pleasant memories. Turn of century home in fashionable Ballsbridge. All rooms en suite, centrally heated, direct dial phones, fax, tea/coffee facilities. Private car park. Convenient R.D.S. showgrounds, Lansdowne Rugby Club, Point Depot, embassies, museums, car ferries, airport, bus/train service. 10 mins city centre. Enjoy our relaxed atmosphere. Traditional Irish breakfast. Lift to all floors. AA ◆◆◆◆

WEB: www.goirl.com/aaronmor

B&B from £25.00 to £45.00
€31.74 to €57.14

BETTY & MICHAEL DUNNE

American Express
Mastercard
Visa

Closed 24 - 26 December

ABBERLEY COURT HOTEL

**BELGARD ROAD, TALLAGHT,
DUBLIN 24
TEL: 01-459 6000   FAX: 01-462 1000
EMAIL: abberley@iol.ie**

HOTEL ★★★ MAP 8 O 11

The Abberley Court Hotel is a newly built hotel situated at the foothills of the Dublin Mountains, beside The Square towncentre in Tallaght. The facilities include 40 en suite bedrooms, Kilcawleys Traditional Irish pub, Court Restaurant. Conference/meeting/training facilities with private car parking. Activities in the locality include golf, pitch & putt, ten pin bowling, horse riding, pony trekking, fishing, watersports.

WEB: www.abberley.ie

B&B from £30.00 to £49.00
€38.09 to €62.22

**KAREN GARRY &
MAIREAD SLYE**

American Express
Diners
Mastercard
Visa

Closed 24 - 30 December

ABERDEEN LODGE

**53 PARK AVENUE, OFF AILESBURY ROAD,
BALLSBRIDGE, DUBLIN 4
TEL: 01-283 8155   FAX: 01-283 7877
EMAIL: aberdeen@iol.ie**

GUESTHOUSE ★★★★ MAP 8 O 11

Award-winning, 4★★★★, a luxurious combination of Edwardian grace, fine food, modern comforts, all that one expects of a private hotel, aircon suites with jacuzzi, executive facilities, landscaped gardens and guest carpark. Close to city centre, airport and car ferry terminals by DART or bus. Accolades - RAC AAA, Best Loved Hotels, Green Book, Johansens. Sister property of Merrion Hall and Halpins Hotel.
USA toll free 1800 223 6510.
Direct dial 353 1 283 8155.

WEB: www.halpinsprivatehotels.com

Member of Charming Hotels

B&B from £35.00 to £70.00
€44.44 to €88.88

PAT HALPIN
Proprietor

American Express
Diners
Mastercard
Visa

☺ Midweek specials from £115.00

Open All Year

ABRAE COURT

9 ZION ROAD, RATHGAR, DUBLIN 6
TEL: 01-492 2242 FAX: 01-492 3944
EMAIL: abrae@eircom.net

GUESTHOUSE ★★★ MAP 8 O 11

Built in 1864, family run, 3***
Victorian guesthouse is located in
the prestigious residential area of
Rathgar, just ten minutes from the
heart of Dublin City. Guestrooms are
furnished with en suite bathroom,
colour TV, direct dial phone and
coffee/tea making facilities. Laundry
service and a lock up car park are
available. Bus routes, a good
selection of restaurants, pubs, tourist
attractions and various sports.

B&B from £30.00 to £35.00
€38.09 to €44.44

NEVILLE KEEGAN
Owner

Mastercard
Visa

☺ Weekend specials from £100.00

14 14

Closed 22 - 28 December

ACADEMY HOTEL

FINDLATER PLACE, OFF O'CONNELL STREET, DUBLIN 1
TEL: 01-878 0666 FAX: 01-878 0600
EMAIL: stay@academy-hotel.ie

HOTEL N MAP 8 O 11

The natural choice for the discerning
visitor to Dublin, we offer the
ultimate in comfort & convenience.
Located off the city's main
thoroughfare, O'Connell Street, only
a short stroll from the very best of
international shopping, galleries,
theatres and the cosmopolitan area
of Temple Bar. Our beautifully
appointed en suite, air conditioned
rooms represent the perfect retreat
after a demanding meeting or a
hectic day of shopping or
sightseeing. Free parking.
GDS Access Code: HK

WEB: www.academy-hotel.ie

B&B from £35.00 to £70.00
€44.44 to €88.88

JOSEPH COMERFORD
General Manager

American Express
Diners
Mastercard
Visa

☺ Midweek Special from £99.00

98 98

Inet FAX

Closed 23 December - 02 January

ADAMS TRINITY HOTEL

28 DAME STREET, DUBLIN 2
TEL: 01-670 7100 FAX: 01-670 7101
EMAIL: reservationsadamstrinityhotel@indigo.ie

HOTEL ★★★ MAP 8 O 11

What better location in Dublin than
the Adams Trinity Hotel? Located
mid-way between Dublin Castle,
Grafton Street and Trinity College; it
faces the vibrant Temple Bar area.
Traditional style bedrooms are
finished to an exceptionally luxurious
standard. The hotel features the
Mercantile Bar and Restaurant and
O'Brien's Traditional Bar. The Adams
Trinity Hotel offers all guests that
same personal attention and
warmth, it has that little something
special.

B&B from £49.50 to £75.00
€62.85 to €95.23

FRAN RYDER/PETER HANAHOE
Proprietors

American Express
Diners
Mastercard
Visa

☺ Weekend specials from £99.00

28 28

Inet

Closed 24 - 27 December

B&B rates are IR£ per person sharing per night incl. Breakfast

AISHLING HOUSE

19/20 ST. LAWRENCE ROAD,
CLONTARF, DUBLIN 3
TEL: 01-833 9097   FAX: 01-833 8400
EMAIL: info@aishlinghouse.com

GUESTHOUSE ★★★   MAP 8 O 11

Elegant Grade II listed family-run Victorian residence. Situated in Clontarf, north Dublin's most exclusive suburb. Ideally located close to Point Theatre, city centre and Dublin Port, yet only 15 mins from airport. We offer superb luxury accommodation at affordable prices. Tranquil elegant lounge, half acre of well matured grounds, children's play area, private car park, fax facilities. A treasure of outstanding quality.

WEB: www.aishlinghouse.com

B&B from £25.00 to £35.00
€31.74 to €44.44

ROBERT & FRANCES ENGLISH
Owners

Mastercard

Visa

☺ Midweek specials from £75.00

9 9

IRISH HOTELS FEDERATION

Open All Year

ALEXANDER HOTEL

AT MERRION SQUARE,
DUBLIN 2
TEL: 01-607 3700   FAX: 01-661 5663
EMAIL: alexanderres@ocallaghanhotels.ie

HOTEL U   MAP 8 O 11

Contemporary style deluxe hotel ideally located in Dublin City Centre beside Trinity College, 5 mins walk from museums, shops and business districts. 102 air-conditioned guestrooms and suites with satellite TV, 3 telephones, high speed modem line, tea/coffee facilities, safe, trouser press, iron and board and 24 hour room service. Caravaggio's Restaurant specialises in European cuisine. Winners Bar pays tribute to world champions. Free private valet car parking and fitness room for residents. USA Toll Free Reservations 1800 569 9983

WEB: www.ocallaghanhotels.ie

Member of O'Callaghan Hotels

B&B from £94.00 to £142.00
€119.36 to €180.30

JOHN CLESHAM
General Manager

American Express

Diners

Mastercard

Visa

☺ Weekend specials from £180.00

102 102

Inet

IRISH HOTELS FEDERATION

Open All Year

ANCHOR GUEST HOUSE

49 LOWER GARDINER STREET,
DUBLIN 1
TEL: 01-878 6913   FAX: 01-878 8038
EMAIL: gtcoyne@gpo.iol.ie

GUESTHOUSE ★★★   MAP 8 O 11

The Anchor Guesthouse is located in the heart of the city centre. It is a tastefully refurbished Georgian house with a modern purpose built bedroom wing attached. Our location is a perfect base for city exploration. Temple Bar, Trinity College, Grafton Street, theatres, galleries and museums are but a stone's throw. We are 2 minutes walk from the central bus station, which has connections to the airport and ferry terminals.

WEB: www.anchorguesthouse.com

B&B from £22.50 to £40.00
€28.57 to €50.79

JOAN & GERRY COYNE
Proprietors

Mastercard

Visa

☺ Midweek specials from £67.50

21 21

IRISH HOTELS FEDERATION

Open All Year

Room rates are IR£ per room per night

ANGLESEA TOWN HOUSE

63 ANGLESEA ROAD, BALLSBRIDGE,
DUBLIN 4
TEL: 01-668 3877   FAX: 01-668 3461

GUESTHOUSE ★★★★   MAP 8 O 11

This is a world-renowned guesthouse of national breakfast award fame. It has been featured on TV in both Ireland and the UK and has won entry in British, Irish, European and American travel guides and journals. It is a fine Edwardian residence of 7 en suite rooms with phone and TV, offering quiet elegance to discerning guests who wish to combine country-style charm with convenience to town. A warm welcome awaits you from your hostess Helen Kirrane and her family.

B&B from £45.00 to £48.00
€57.14 to €60.95

HELEN KIRRANE
Owner

American Express
Mastercard
Visa

7 7

Closed 15 December - 08 January

ARDAGH HOUSE

NO.1 HIGHFIELD ROAD, RATHGAR,
DUBLIN 6
TEL: 01-497 7068   FAX: 01-497 3991
EMAIL: enquiries@ardagh-house.ie

GUESTHOUSE ★★★   MAP 8 O 11

Having been recently totally refurbished, Ardagh House is conveniently situated in a premier residential area. This imposing turn of the century premises contains many of the gracious and spacious features of a fine detached residence of that era and yet incorporating modern creature comforts. Within easy distance of the city centre, RDS, etc. This fine property stands on approximately 1/2 acre with ample off street car parking and good gardens.

WEB: www.ardagh-house.ie

B&B from £28.00 to £45.00
€35.55 to €57.13

WILLIE AND MARY DOYLE
Proprietors

Mastercard
Visa

19 19

Open All Year

ARIEL HOUSE

52 LANSDOWNE ROAD,
BALLSBRIDGE, DUBLIN 4
TEL: 01-668 5512   FAX: 01-668 5845
EMAIL: reservations@ariel-house.com

GUESTHOUSE ★★★★   MAP 8 O 11

Ariel House is a historic listed Victorian mansion that has recently been carefully restored to its former splendour. Classified 4★★★★ by Bord Failte, it offers an air of quiet luxury and elegant decor in a large variety of rooms, all with private bathroom. Situated in the fashionable tree-lined suburb of Ballsbridge only 3 minutes on the DART to the city centre and within easy access of the airport, ferryports and mainline rail stations.

WEB: www.ariel-house.com

Room Rate from £86.00 to £180.00
€109.20 to €228.55

MICHAEL O'BRIEN
Managing Director

Mastercard
Visa

Midweek specials from £99.00

40 40

Closed 23 December - 09 January

B&B rates are IR£ per person sharing per night incl. Breakfast

ARLINGTON HOTEL

23/25 BACHELORS WALK,
O'CONNELL BRIDGE, DUBLIN 1
TEL: 01-804 9100   FAX: 01-804 9112
EMAIL: arlington@eircom.net

HOTEL ★★★   MAP 8 O 11

Overlooking the River Liffey at O'Connell Bridge, the Arlington is Dublin's most central hotel. Nestled between Trinity College, Temple Bar, the Point Theatre and the Abbey Theatre; close to Jervis Street and Grafton Street shopping districts. 115 modern en suite rooms, private function and meeting room facilities, featuring a restaurant, lively Knightsbridge bars, nightclub and underground car parking. The perfect location for business or pleasure.

WEB: www.arlington.ie

B&B from £49.00 to £89.00
€62.22 to €113.01

PAUL KEENAN
General Manager

American Express
Diners
Mastercard
Visa

😊 Midweek specials from £129.00

115 115

HOTELS

Open All Year

ASHFIELD HOUSE

5 CLONSKEAGH ROAD,
DUBLIN 6
TEL: 01-260 3680   FAX: 01-260 4236

GUESTHOUSE U   MAP 8 O 11

One of Dublin's friendliest family run guesthouses. Providing comfort and service of a very high standard to the tourist and business sector. Rooms are en suite with TV, direct dial phones, tea/coffee facilities, hairdryer etc. A fax service is available. 10 mins from city centre, RDS, Lansdowne Road, Leopardstown Racecourse, ferry ports etc. Many top class pubs and restaurants adjacent to Ashfield House. We provide off street parking. There is an excellent bus service directly to city centre.

WEB: www.bftrade.travel.ie

B&B from £35.00 to £60.00
€44.44 to €76.18

FRANK AND OLIVE TAYLOR

Mastercard
Visa

10 10

Open All Year

Room rates are IR£ per room per night

AISHLING HOUSE

19/20 ST. LAWRENCE ROAD,
CLONTARF, DUBLIN 3
TEL: 01-833 9097   FAX: 01-833 8400
EMAIL: info@aishlinghouse.com

GUESTHOUSE ★★★   MAP 8 O 11

Elegant Grade II listed family-run Victorian residence. Situated in Clontarf, north Dublin's most exclusive suburb. Ideally located close to Point Theatre, city centre and Dublin Port, yet only 15 mins from airport. We offer superb luxury accommodation at affordable prices. Tranquil elegant lounge, half acre of well matured grounds, children's play area, private car park, fax facilities. A treasure of outstanding quality.

WEB: www.aishlinghouse.com

B&B from £25.00 to £35.00
€31.74 to €44.44

ROBERT & FRANCES ENGLISH
Owners

Mastercard

Visa

☺ Midweek specials from £75.00

🏠🚗☎️🖥️ⓉⒶⒸⒸⓂ❄️Ⓙ🅿️🔔
9 9

Open All Year

ASTON HOTEL

7/9 ASTON QUAY,
DUBLIN 2
TEL: 01-677 9300   FAX: 01-677 9007
EMAIL: stay@aston-hotel.com

HOTEL U   MAP 8 O 11

A warm welcome awaits you at the Aston Hotel, located in Temple Bar and overlooking the River Liffey. Friendly staff and pleasant surroundings will make your stay a memorable one. All our 27 rooms are en suite and offer every guest comfort including direct dial phone, colour TV, hairdryer and tea/coffee making facilities. A leisurely stroll from the Aston brings you to all Dublin's top attractions and amenities and makes it an ideal base for exploring the capital.

WEB: www.aston-hotel.com

B&B from £25.00 to £65.00
€31.74 to €82.53

ANN WALSH
Manager

American Express

Diners

Mastercard

Visa

🏠🚗☎️🖥️⑆Ⓣ ⒸⒸⓂ🔔
27 27

Closed 24 - 27 December

AUBURN GUESTHOUSE

NAVAN ROAD, CASTLEKNOCK, (AT AUBURN ROUNDABOUT), DUBLIN 15
TEL: 01-822 3535   FAX: 01-822 3550
EMAIL: auburngh@iol.ie

GUESTHOUSE ★★★   MAP 8 O 11

Auburn - set on its own grounds with ample car parking. Excellent accommodation with a varied breakfast menu. City centre 15 minutes, M50 adjacent, Dublin Airport 10 minutes. Ideal location for business or holiday. Blanchardstown Complex with shopping and many amenities 5 minutes. Numerous Golf Courses near by. Restaurants within walking distance.

Member of Premier Guesthouses

B&B from £28.00 to £35.00
€35.55 to €44.44

ELAINE COWLEY
Manageress

American Express

Mastercard

Visa

🏠🚗☎️🖥️ⓉⒸ❄️🔆ⓊⓅⓈ🔔
7 7

Closed 24 - 27 December

B&B rates are IR£ per person sharing per night incl. Breakfast

BARRY'S HOTEL

1-2 GREAT DENMARK STREET,
DUBLIN 1
TEL: 01-874 9407

HOTEL ★★ MAP 8 O 11

Barry's Hotel is one of Dublin's oldest hotels built in the later part of Georgian Period. Situated 300 yds off O'Connell Street. Barry's unique ambience friendly service assure visitors whether on business or pleasure the warmest of welcomes and special attention. The hotel is within walking distance of the Abbey and Gate Theatres, National Wax Museum, Croke Park and principal shopping districts and major tourist attractions.

B&B from £40.00 to £45.00
€50.79 to €57.14

NOELEEN DOYLE
Manager

Mastercard

Visa

32 32

Closed 24 - 27 December

BELGRAVE GUESTHOUSE

8-10 BELGRAVE SQUARE,
RATHMINES, DUBLIN 6
TEL: 01-496 3760 FAX: 01-497 9243

GUESTHOUSE ★★★ MAP 8 O 11

The Belgrave consists of three interconnecting early Victorian buildings overlooking a well matured square. While retaining all the character and charm of its era, the Belgrave has all the conveniences of a modern 3*** guesthouse, each room is en suite and has colour TV, direct dial telephone, tea making facilities. Private car park. Ideally located. We look forward to hosting you and according you a warm welcome for which we are renowned. AA ♦♦♦.

B&B from £25.00 to £50.00
€31.74 to €63.48

PAUL AND MARY O'REILLY
Owners

Mastercard

Visa

24 24

IRISH
HOTELS
FEDERATION

Closed 22 December - 04 January

BELVEDERE HOTEL

GREAT DENMARK STREET,
DUBLIN 1
TEL: 01-874 1413 FAX: 01-872 8631

HOTEL R MAP 8 O 11

Situated only three minutes walking distance from O'Connell Street, it is the ideal base for shopping and taking in the sights of this famous historic city. This area includes the National Wax Museum, major theatres, cinemas, sporting and concert venues, including the Point Theatre where most major acts perform. We are also the most convenient hotel to the new Croke Park, the main venue for all Gaelic Games.

B&B from £40.00 to £45.00
€50.79 to €57.14

MARION HENEGHAN
Manager

Mastercard

Visa

40 40

Closed 24 - 28 December

Room rates are IR£ per room per night

BERKELEY COURT

LANSDOWNE ROAD, BALLSBRIDGE, DUBLIN 4
TEL: 01-660 1711   FAX: 01-661 7238
EMAIL: berkeley_court@jurysdoyle.com

HOTEL ★★★★★ MAP 8 O 11

Renowned as one of Dublin's premier hotels and host to high-profile international dignitaries and celebrities. This hotel exudes an old-world, club-like aura which is nicely complimented by a broad range of modern-day facilities and exceptional services. Located in Dublin's most prestigous district, overlooking some of Dublin's famous Georgian residences, the hotel is just 5 minutes drive from the city centre and within 10 minutes drive from the International Financial Services Centre.

WEB: www.jurysdoyle.com

B&B from £105.00 to £160.00
€133.32 to €203.15

JOE RUSSELL
General Manager

American Express
Diners
Mastercard
Visa

188 188

Inet

Open All Year

BEWLEY'S HOTEL BALLSBRIDGE

MERRION ROAD, BALLSBRIDGE, DUBLIN 4
TEL: 01-668 1111   FAX: 01-668 1999
EMAIL: res@bewleyshotel.com

HOTEL N MAP 8 O 11

A new stylish concept in a prime location on Merrion Road combining the past with the present. Accommodating you in style with over 200 deluxe bedrooms and spacious suites. Enjoy an exciting dining experience in O'Connell's Restaurant. Bewley's Hotels Book on-line www.bewleyshotels.com

WEB: www.bewleyshotels.com

Room Rate from £69.00 to £138.00
€87.61 to €175.22

CLIO O'GARA
General Manager

American Express
Diners
Mastercard
Visa

220 220

Inet

Closed 24 - 26 December

BEWLEY'S HOTEL NEWLANDS CROSS

NEWLANDS CROSS, NAAS ROAD (N7), DUBLIN 22
TEL: 01-464 0140   FAX: 01-464 0900
EMAIL: res@bewleyshotels.com

HOTEL ★★★ MAP 8 O 11

A unique blend of quality, value and flexibility for independent discerning guests. Located just off the N7, minutes from the M50, Dublin Airport and the city centre. Our large spacious family size rooms are fully equipped with all modern amenities. Our Bewley's Restaurant offers you a range of dining options, from traditional Irish breakfast to full table service à la carte. Real time on line reservations and availability at www.bewleyshotels.com

WEB: www.bewleyshotels.com

Room Rate from £49.00 to £55.00
€62.22 to €69.84

DAMIEN MOLLOY
General Manager

American Express
Diners
Mastercard
Visa

258 258

Inet

Closed 24 - 26 December

B&B rates are IR£ per person sharing per night incl. Breakfast

USEFUL TELEPHONE NUMBERS

Emergency (fire, Garda, (Police) & Ambulance)	999
Directory Enquiries (national)	11811
Directory Enquiries (to Great Britain)	11818
Operator Assistance (Ireland / Northern Ireland / Great Britain)	10
Operator Assistance (International excluding Great Britain)	114
Dublin Airport	(01) 844 4131
Shannon Airport	(061) 471 444
Cork Airport	(021) 313131
Aer Lingus (flight enquiries)	(01) 886 6705
British Airways (enquiries)	1 800 62 67 47
Ryanair (flight enquiries)	(01) 844 4411
Delta Airlines	(01) 844 4166
(enquiries)	
Air France	(01) 844 5633
Virgin Altantic	(01) 873 3388
Iberia/Viva Air (Dublin Airport)	(01) 844 4939
Irish Rail (Passenger information)	(01) 836 6222
Connolly Station	(01) 836 3333
Heuston Station	(01) 836 3333
Dart Information	(01) 836 3333
Irish Bus (Bus Eireann)	(01) 836 1111
Dublin Bus (Bus Atha Cliath)	(01) 873 4222
Irish Ferries (Enquiries)	1890 31 31 31
Irish Ferries	(01) 855 2222
General Post Office (An Post)	(01) 705 7000
Bord Fáilte	(01) 602 4000

BEWLEY'S PRINCIPAL HOTEL

19/20 FLEET STREET, TEMPLE BAR, DUBLIN 2
TEL: 01-670 8122 FAX: 01-670 8103
EMAIL: bewleyshotel@eircom.net

HOTEL ★★★ MAP 8 O 11

Located in vibrant Temple Bar. Our location makes us an ideal base for both business and pleasure. We offer the finest traditions of quality and service from both Bewley's and Principal Hotels. All bedrooms have been completely refurbished, some with air conditioning and are equipped to the highest standards. A warm welcome awaits you.

WEB: bewleysprincipalhotel.com

B&B from £40.00 to £70.00
€50.79 to €88.88

CAROL MCNAMARA
General Manager

American Express
Diners
Mastercard
Visa

😊 Weekend specials from £90.00

70 70

Closed 24 - 27 December

BLOOMS HOTEL

6 ANGLESEA STREET, TEMPLE BAR, DUBLIN 2
TEL: 01-671 5622 FAX: 01-671 5997
EMAIL: blooms@eircom.net

HOTEL ★★★ MAP 8 O 11

Every city has one hotel that mirrors the life and humour of its people. Blooms is now at the centre of Dublin's cultural and artistic heart - Temple Bar. Being a small hotel, only 86 bedrooms, there is a feeling of intimacy and familiarity. The proximity of Blooms to both tourist and business locations makes it the ideal point for capturing the atmosphere and essence of Dublin City.

WEB: www.blooms.ie

B&B from £69.87 to £69.87
€88.72 to €88.72

MARTIN KEANE
Owner

American Express
Diners
Mastercard
Visa

😊 Midweek specials from £79.00

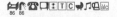
86 86

Closed 24 - 27 December

BROOKS HOTEL

DRURY STREET, DUBLIN 2
TEL: 01-670 4000 FAX: 01-670 4455
EMAIL: reservations@brookshotel.ie

HOTEL ★★★★ MAP 8 O 11

Located in the fashionable heart of Dublin City, 3 mins from Grafton St, Temple Bar, Dublin Castle & Trinity College. Brooks is a designer/ boutique hotel with high standards throughout, appealing in particular to the discerning international traveller. With superbly appointed air conditioned accommodation, the Butter Lane Bar, residents drawing room, Francesca's Restaurant & the Markets meeting room, Brooks is designed to cater for the sophisticated visitor. Secure parking available opposite the hotel.

WEB: www.sinnotthotels.com

Room Rate from £130.00 to £230.00
€165.07 to €292.04

ANNE MCKIERNAN
Resident Manager

American Express
Diners
Mastercard
Visa

75 75

Open All Year

B&B rates are IR£ per person sharing per night incl. Breakfast

BROWNES TOWNHOUSE & BRASSERIE

22 ST STEPHENS GREEN,
DUBLIN 2
TEL: 01-638 3939   FAX: 01-638 3900
EMAIL: info@brownesdublin.com

GUESTHOUSE ★★★★ MAP 12 O 11

Overlooking St. Stephen's Green, Brownes Brasserie and Townhouse has the most superb location in Dublin. Brownes - a rare find, striking the perfect balance between traditional comfort and a relaxed contemporary atmosphere. With 12 luxury rooms, it has all of the intimacy, warmth & character of a privately run townhouse, yet corporate guests have the convenience of ISDN, direct personal telephone and fax lines and cable TV and air conditioning.

WEB: www.brownesdublin.com

Member of Manor House Hotels

Room Rate from £120.00 to £350.00
€152.37 to €444.41

BARRY CANNY
Proprietor

American Express
Diners
Mastercard
Visa

12 12

Open All Year

BURLINGTON

UPPER LEESON STREET,
DUBLIN 4
TEL: 01-660 5222   FAX: 01-660 8496
EMAIL: burlington_hotel@jurysdoyle.com

HOTEL ★★★★ MAP 8 O 11

Dublin's largest, best known and liveliest hotel. Its popularity with local Dubliners who frequent its busy bars and restaurants, allows overseas guests experience the 'craic' that is synonymous with Dublin. Centrally located just 10 mins walk from the city centre. The Burlington offers the broadest range of facilities in Dublin.

WEB: www.jurysdoyle.com

B&B from £88.00 to £134.00
€111.74 to €170.14

JOHN CLIFTON
General Manager

American Express
Diners
Mastercard
Visa

504 504

Open All Year

BUSWELLS HOTEL

23/27 MOLESWORTH STREET,
DUBLIN 2
TEL: 01-614 6500   FAX: 01-676 2090
EMAIL: buswells@quinn-hotels.com

HOTEL U MAP 8 O 11

One of Dublin's best kept secrets, this gracious hotel has been recently refurbished to the highest standards, offering every modern amenity, yet retaining the charm of its Georgian era. Located in the quiet, elegant Molesworth Street, just minutes walk from St. Stephen's Green, Grafton Street, and easy reach of the city's major attractions. Toll-free: 1800-473-9527.

WEB: www.quinnhotels.com

Member of Quinn Hotels

B&B from £46.00 to £85.00
€58.41 to €107.93

PAUL GALLAGHER
General Manager

American Express
Diners
Mastercard
Visa

69 69

Closed 24 - 26 December

Room rates are IR£ per room per night

B&B rates are IR£ per person sharing per night incl. Breakfast

CARMEL HOUSE

16 UPPER GARDINER STREET,
DUBLIN 1
TEL: 01-874 1639   FAX: 01-878 6903

GUESTHOUSE ★★★   MAP 8 O 11

Carmel House is located in the heart of Dublin's historic north inner city. Adjacent to all shopping, theatre and cinema facilities and situated on the main bus route to the airport, this small exclusive guesthouse rivals the best in its comfortable ambience. All bedrooms are en suite, have TV, direct dial phone and tea and coffee making facilities. Secure on-premises parking is included. For an Irish welcome contact Tom or Anne Smyth. No agents please. For bookings Tel 353-1-8741639

B&B from £22.50 to £30.00
€28.57 to €38.09

TOM & ANNE SMYTH
Proprietors

Mastercard

Visa

IRISH HOTELS FEDERATION

Closed 23 - 31 December

CASSIDYS HOTEL

CAVENDISH ROW, UPPER
O'CONNELL ST., DUBLIN 1
TEL: 01-878 0555   FAX: 01-878 0687
EMAIL: rese@cassidys.iol.ie

HOTEL ★★★   MAP 8 O 11

A little gem in the heart of the city. Cassidys is a modern 88 bedroomed townhouse hotel located opposite the famous Gate Theatre in the city centre. Cassidys is a short walk from numerous museums, theatres, bars and shopping districts. The warm and welcoming atmosphere of Groomes Bar lends a traditional air to Cassidys and fine dining is assured in the stylish surroundings of Restaurant 6. Limited parking for guests. Conference facilities available.

WEB: www.cassidyshotel.com

B&B from £50.00 to £70.00
€63.49 to €88.88

MARTIN CASSIDY
General Manager

American Express

Diners

Mastercard

Visa

IRISH HOTELS FEDERATION

Closed 24 - 27 December

CASTLE HOTEL

2-4 GARDINER ROW,
DUBLIN 1
TEL: 01-874 6949   FAX: 01-872 7674
EMAIL: hotels@indigo.ie

HOTEL ★★   MAP 8 O 11

Elegant Georgian hotel close to Dublin's main shopping district, renowned for its friendly service. One of Dublin's oldest hotels. Authentically restored the decor and furnishings offer modern comfort combined with olde world features: crystal chandeliers, antique mirrors, marble fireplaces and period staircases. The individually decorated rooms offer private bathroom, satellite TV, direct dial phone and beverage making facilities. The hotel has an intimate residents bar and private parking.

Member of Castle Hotel Group

B&B from £35.00 to £45.00
€44.44 to €57.14

YVONNE EVANS
Manageress

Mastercard

Visa

☺ Midweek specials from £99.00

IRISH HOTELS FEDERATION

Closed 24 - 27 December

Room rates are IR£ per room per night

CEDAR LODGE

98 MERRION ROAD,
DUBLIN 4
TEL: 01-668 4410   FAX: 01-668 4533
EMAIL: info@cedarlodge.ie

GUESTHOUSE ★★★★   MAP 8 O 11

Cedar Lodge the luxurious alternative to a hotel. Modern comforts and Edwardian style combine to create a truly unique experience. Our beautifully furnished en suite bedrooms are of international standard. This jewel among guesthouses is located in Leafy Ballsbridge, adjacent to RDS, the British Embassy and the Four Seasons Hotel. 10 minutes from the city centre, close to airport and car ferriers. Private car park. AA Premier Selected ◆◆◆◆◆, RAC ◆◆◆◆◆.

WEB: www.cedarlodge.ie

B&B from £35.00 to £60.00
€44.44 to €76.18

GERARD & MARY DOODY
Owners

American Express
Mastercard
Visa

☺ Midweek specials from £115.00

15 15

Closed 22 - 28 December

CENTRAL HOTEL

1-5 EXCHEQUER STREET,
DUBLIN 2
TEL: 01-679 7302   FAX: 01-679 7303
EMAIL: reservations@centralhotel.ie

HOTEL ★★★   MAP 8 O 11

City centre location. Award winning library bar, 52 restaurants, numerous bars within walking distance. Temple Bar, Dublin's Left Bank, one block away. Trinity College, Grafton Street and Christchurch 5 mins from hotel. Rooms en suite include, direct dial phones, voicemail, hairdryers, tea/coffee making facilities, multi-channel TV. Private meeting rooms. Secure parking available nearby.

WEB: www.centralhotel.ie
Member of Best Western Hotels

B&B from £55.00 to £75.00
€69.84 to €95.23

JOHN-PAUL KAVANAGH
General Manager

American Express
Diners
Mastercard
Visa

70 70
inet

Closed 24 - 27 December

CHARLEVILLE LODGE

268-272 NORTH CIRCULAR ROAD,
PHIBSBORO, DUBLIN 7
TEL: 01-838 6633   FAX: 01-838 5854
EMAIL: charleville@indigo.ie

GUESTHOUSE ★★★   MAP 8 O 11

Charleville Lodge, (former home of Lord Charleville), is an elegant terrace of Victorian houses located mins. from the city centre, Trinity College & Temple Bar, en route to Dublin Airport and car ferry. The luxurious en suite bedrooms have direct dial phones and colour TV. Rated 4◆◆◆◆ by AA and RAC we are holders of the Sparkling Diamond award. Our car park is for guest use and is complimentary. Let us make your arrangements with local golf clubs. Visit our website.

WEB: www.charlevillelodge.ie
Member of Logis of Ireland

B&B from £25.00 to £55.00
€31.74 to €69.84

VAL & ANNE STENSON
Owners

American Express
Diners
Mastercard
Visa

☺ Midweek specials from £70.00

30 28

Closed 20 - 26 December

B&B rates are IR£ per person sharing per night incl. Breakfast

CHIEF O'NEILL'S HOTEL

**SMITHFIELD VILLAGE,
DUBLIN 7**
TEL: 01-817 3838   FAX: 01-817 3839
EMAIL: reservations@chiefoneills.com

HOTEL N   MAP 8 O 11

Chief O'Neill's Hotel is dedicated to the memory of Francis O'Neill, Chicago Chief of Police & one of the most important individual collectors of Irish traditional music this century. Its theme is Irish traditional music expressed through Ireland's finest contemporary design. Each of the 73 en suite luxury rooms is equipped with a CD/Hi-Fi system, multi-channel TV, direct dial phone & tea/coffee facility. A vibrant shopping area, restaurants & visitor attractions surround the hotel.

WEB: www.chiefoneills.com

Room Rate from £95.00 to £295.00
€120.63 to €374.57

RORY O'LEARY
General Manager

American Express
Diners
Mastercard
Visa

😊 Midweek specials from £47.50

Closed 23 - 28 December

CLARA HOUSE

**23 LEINSTER ROAD, RATHMINES,
DUBLIN 6**
TEL: 01-497 5904   FAX: 01-497 5904
EMAIL: clarahouse@eircom.net

GUESTHOUSE ★★★   MAP 8 O 11

Clara House is a beautifully maintained listed Georgian house with many original features skillfully combined with modern day comforts. Each bedroom has en suite bathroom, remote control colour TV, direct dial telephone, radio/alarm clock, tea/coffee making facilities, hair dryer and trouser press. Clara House is a mile from downtown with bus stops 100 metres away. Bus stop for Ballsbridge/RDS is 200 metres. Secure parking at rear of house.

B&B from £30.00 to £35.00
€38.09 to €44.44

PHIL & PAUL REID
Proprietors

Mastercard
Visa

Open All Year

CLARENCE HOTEL

**6-8 WELLINGTON QUAY,
DUBLIN 2**
TEL: 01-407 0800   FAX: 01-407 0820
EMAIL: reservations@theclarence.ie

HOTEL U   MAP 8 O 11

Built in 1852 and transformed into a contemporary boutique, design hotel in June 1996. Many of the hotel's original features have been revived. Antique panelling sets the backdrop for innovative furnishings. Located in the fashionable Temple Bar district and approx 30 mins from Dublin Airport. 50 rooms and suites, each one individually designed in contemporary, elegant style. The Tea Room and Octagon Bar provide a social focus for The Clarence and the Temple Bar area.

WEB: www.theclarence.ie

Member of Leading Small Hotels of the World

Room Rate from £210.00 to £225.00
€266.64 to €285.69

ROBERT VAN EERDE
General Manager

American Express
Diners
Mastercard
Visa

Closed 24 - 26 December

Room rates are IR£ per room per night

CLARION HOTEL DUBLIN IFSC

IFSC,
DUBLIN 1
TEL: 01-836 6404   FAX: 01-836 6522
EMAIL: bcurtis@choicehotelsireland.com

UNDER CONSTRUCTION OPENING FEB 2001

HOTEL P   MAP 8 O 11

New to City Centre the latest in stylish contemporary hotels in a cosmopolitan ambience. Bedrooms are comfortably appointed with modern features. Enjoy a choice of eating experiences - European Cuisine in our Restaurant, an exciting twist of Eastern fare in the Bar, and International style coffee bar. Well equipped meeting rooms for small and large conferences. Unwind at Sanovitae Health and Fitness Club including 18m indoor swimming pool, which is complimentary to guests.

Member of Choice Hotels International

B&B from £63.00 to £90.00
€79.99 to €114.28

BRENDAN CURTIS

American Express
Diners
Mastercard
Visa

Weekend specials from £145.00

147 147   aid Inet

Closed 24 - 27 December

CLARION STEPHENS HALL HOTEL AND SUITES

THE EARLSFORT CENTRE, LOWER
LEESON STREET, DUBLIN 2
TEL: 01-638 1111   FAX: 01-638 1122
EMAIL: stephens@premgroup.ie

HOTEL ★★★   MAP 8 O 11

Dublin's first all-suite hotel, beside St. Stephen's Green in the heart of Georgian Dublin. Tastefully furnished suites with separate living rooms and fax machines and CD players. Morel's at Stephens Hall, open all day, is popular locally as a great place to eat. Suites available for nightly or long-term occupancy. Free underground car parking. Toll Free USA for Clarion Hotels: 1800.CLARION (1800 252 7466).

WEB: www.premgroup.ie

Member of Choice Hotels Ireland

Room Rates from £155.00 to £195.00
€196.80 to €247.59

JIM MURPHY
Managing Director

American Express
Diners
Mastercard
Visa

37 37   Inet FAX

Open All Year

CLIFDEN GUESTHOUSE

32 GARDINER PLACE,
DUBLIN 1
TEL: 01-874 6364   FAX: 01-874 6122
EMAIL: bnb@indigo.ie

GUESTHOUSE ★★★   MAP 8 O 11

A refurbished city centre Georgian home. Our private car park provides security for guests cars, even after check-out, free. All rooms have shower, WC, WHB, TV, direct dial phone and tea making facilities. We cater for single, twin, double, triple and family occupancies. Convenient to airport, ferryports, Bus Aras (bus station) and DART. We are only 5 minutes walk from O'Connell Street. AA and RAC approved.

WEB: www.clifdenhouse.com

Member of Premier Guesthouses

Room Rate from £25.00 to £55.00
€31.74 to €69.84

JACK & MARY LALOR

Mastercard
Visa

Midweek specials from £80.00

14 14

Open All Year

B&B rates are IR£ per person sharing per night incl. Breakfast

CLIFTON COURT HOTEL

O'CONNELL BRIDGE,
DUBLIN 1
TEL: 01-874 3535   FAX: 01-878 6698
EMAIL: cliftoncourt@eircom.net

HOTEL ★★   MAP 8 O 11

Situated in the city centre overlooking the River Liffey at O'Connell Bridge. Beside Dublin's two premier shopping streets. The Abbey Theatre, Point Depot, Tara and Amien Street, Dart/Train stations and Bus Aras (airport terminal) are within 3 minutes walk. Our modern bedrooms are equipped with TV and tea/coffee making facilities. The hotel also incorporates one of Dublin's oldest and most famous pubs known as Lanigans (est 1822) which hosts Irish traditional music.

Room Rate from £43.45 to £100.00
€55.17 to €126.97

TIANA MCHALE
Manager

American Express
Mastercard
Visa

30 30

Closed 24 - 27 December

CLONTARF CASTLE HOTEL

CLONTARF,
DUBLIN 3
TEL: 01-833 2321   FAX: 01-833 0418
EMAIL: info@clontarfcastle.ie

HOTEL ★★★★   MAP 8 O 11

This historic castle, dating back to 1172, is today a luxurious 4**** deluxe, 111 room hotel. Ideally situated only 10 minutes from the city centre and 15 minutes from the airport. With superb facilities including uniquely designed rooms equipped with all the modern facilities. Templar's Bistro specialising in modern international cuisine, 2 unique bars, state of the art conference and banqueting facilities and stunning lobby. Complimentary carparking.

WEB: www.clontarfcastle.ie

B&B from £50.00 to £105.00
€63.49 to €133.32

ENDA O'MEARA
Managing Director

American Express
Diners
Mastercard
Visa

111 111

Closed 24 - 25 December

COMFORT INN, TALBOT STREET

95-98 TALBOT STREET,
DUBLIN 1
TEL: 01-874 9202   FAX: 01-874 9672
EMAIL: info@talbot.premgroup.ie

GUESTHOUSE ★★★   MAP 8 O 11

Talbot Street boasts the perfect location, just 2 minutes walk from O'Connell Street. In the surrounding area, you will find many shops, restaurants, pubs, theatres and nightclubs. Temple Bar and Trinity College are just a short stroll away. All rooms are en suite, with colourful modern decor. Full Irish Breakfast available every morning.

WEB: www.premgroup.ie

Member of Choice Hotels Ireland

Room Rate from £60.00 to £150.00
€76.18 to €190.46

JOANNA DOYLE
Manager

American Express
Diners
Mastercard
Visa

☺ Weekend Special 2 nights B&B
from £80.00

48 48

Closed 24 - 27 December

Room rates are IR£ per room per night

CONRAD INTERNATIONAL DUBLIN

EARLSFORT TERRACE, DUBLIN 2
TEL: 01-676 5555   FAX: 01-676 5424
EMAIL: info@conrad-international.ie

HOTEL ★★★★★   MAP 8 O 11

Just off St. Stephen's Green, the Conrad International is a short walk from the business, shopping and cultural centres of the city. 191 luxury rooms incl 9 suites with colour TV, free in-house movies, radio, direct dial phone, writing desk, trouser press, air conditioning, mini bar, 2 fluffy bathrobes and 24 hour room service. Two restaurants, the Alexandra and Plurabelle Brasserie and one of the most traditional Irish pubs in town, Alfie Byrnes. Fitness centre. Courtesy of Choice Member.

WEB: www.conrad-international.ie

Room Rate from £190.00 to £280.00
€241.25 to €355.53

MICHAEL GOVERNEY
General Manager

American Express
Diners
Mastercard
Visa

191 191

FAX

Open All Year

COPPER BEECH COURT GUEST HOUSE

16 HOLLYBROOK PARK, CLONTARF, DUBLIN 3
TEL: 01-833 3390   FAX: 01-853 2013

GUESTHOUSE ★★★   MAP 8 O 11

A Victorian building of historic interest, built for a wealthy merchant and carefully restored, offers an air of quiet luxury and elegant decor. All rooms en suite, equipped with multi-channel TV, direct dial phone and dressed with real Irish linen. Friendly staff ensure a superb standard of service. City centre shopping 15 minutes, airport 20 minutes. Choice of golf courses include Royal Dublin, Portmarnock and St. Margarets.

B&B from £30.00 to £60.00
€38.09 to €76.18

FRANCES CAMPBELL
Owner

Mastercard
Visa

9 9

Open All Year

DAVENPORT HOTEL

AT MERRION SQUARE, DUBLIN 2
TEL: 01-607 3500   FAX: 01-661 5663
EMAIL: davenportres@ocallaghanhotels.ie

HOTEL U   MAP 8 O 11

This elegant deluxe hotel is located at Merrion Square in Dublin City centre, beside Trinity College and just a 5 minute walk from the principal business, shopping and cultural districts. Fully air-conditioned with 115 deluxe guestrooms, state of the art conference and banqueting suites, discreet drawing room bar and fine dining restaurant; it offers that rare blend of the elegance of the 1800s combined with the high expectations of today's guests. Free private valet car parking. USA Toll Free Reservations 1800 569 9983.

WEB: www.davenporthotel.ie

Member of O'Callaghan Hotels

B&B from £94.00 to £142.00
€119.36 to €180.30

WELDON MATHER
General Manager

American Express
Diners
Mastercard
Visa

:) Weekend specials from £180.00

115 115
Inet

Open All Year

B&B rates are IR£ per person sharing per night incl. Breakfast

DERGVALE HOTEL

**4 GARDINER PLACE,
DUBLIN 1**
TEL: 01-874 4753   FAX: 01-874 8276
EMAIL: dergvale@indigo.ie

HOTEL ★★   MAP 8 O 11

The Dergvale Hotel is located within walking distance of all principal shopping areas, cinemas, museums, Trinity College, Dublin Castle and airport bus. Luxury bedrooms with showers en suite, colour TV and direct dial telephone. Fully licensed. A courteous and efficient staff are on hand to make your stay an enjoyable one. The hotel is under the personal supervision of Gerard and Nancy Nolan.

B&B from £28.50 to £40.00
€36.19 to €50.79

GERARD NOLAN
Owner

American Express
Mastercard
Visa

😊 Midweek specials from £70.00

20 17

Closed 24 December - 07 January

DONNYBROOK HALL

**6 BELMONT AVENUE,
DONNYBROOK, DUBLIN 4**
TEL: 01-269 1633 FAX: 01-269 1633

GUESTHOUSE ★★★   MAP 8 O 11

Situated in the fashionable Donnybrook district of Dublin, this beautifully restored Victorian residence retains many original features. Each of our en suite rooms are of international standard and are individually designed in elegant style. This guesthouse is ideally located just a short walk from the cultural, commercial and entertainment heart of the city. Nearby is the RDS, RTE, UCD, Lansdowne Road, St. Stephens Green and Trinity College.

WEB: www.donnybrookhall.com

B&B from £30.00 to £49.00
€38.09 to €62.22

DOROTHY GLENNON
Owner

Mastercard
Visa

6 6

Open All Year

DONNYBROOK LODGE

**131 STILLORGAN ROAD,
DONNYBROOK, DUBLIN 4**
TEL: 01-283 7333 FAX: 01-260 4770

GUESTHOUSE ★★★   MAP 8 O 11

Relax in comfortable surroundings in the heart of Dublin's most exclusive area. Ideally situated close to city centre, ferryports and adjacent to RDS, Lansdowne, UCD and RTE. A short stroll from a host of restaurants and entertainment. Recently refurbished, our well-appointed rooms feature en suites, direct dial phone and TV. Private parking available. Enjoy a leisurely breakfast in our elegant dining room, overlooking gardens. A relaxed atmosphere and warm welcome awaits you.

B&B from £27.50 to £47.50
€34.92 to €60.31

PAT BUTLER

Mastercard
Visa

7 7

Open All Year

Room rates are IR£ per room per night

DRURY COURT HOTEL

28-30 LOWER STEPHEN STREET, DUBLIN 2
TEL: 01-475 1988   FAX: 01-478 5730
EMAIL: druryct@indigo.ie

HOTEL U   MAP 8 O 11

Located in the heart of Dublin, beside Stephen's Green and Grafton Street. Convenient to the hotel are theatres, galleries, museums, Trinity College and Temple Bar. The Hotel comprises 32 luxurious bedrooms all en suite with direct dial phone, computer lines, multi-channel TV/Radio and tea/coffee facilities. There is also a restaurant and lively bar. The hotel is adjacent to secure public car parking. Just perfect for the leisure or business visitor.

WEB: drurycourthotel.com

Member of MinOtel Ireland Hotel Group

B&B from £45.00 to £85.00
€57.14 to €107.93

PAUL HAND
General Manager

American Express
Diners
Mastercard
Visa

32 32

Closed 23 - 27 December

EGAN'S GUESTHOUSE

7/9 IONA PARK, GLASNEVIN, DUBLIN 9
TEL: 01-830 3611   FAX: 01-830 3312
EMAIL: eganshouse@eircom.net

GUESTHOUSE ★★★   MAP 8 O 11

Egans house is a charming 3*** family run guesthouse situated away from the bustle of centre city yet convenient to the airport, ferryports, city centre and within walking distance of the Botanical Gardens. There are 23 rooms, all beautifully decorated, each with bathrooms, TV, phone, hair dryer and tea/coffee facilities. Our comfortable drawing rooms invite you to enjoy and relax in their pleasant, warm atmosphere. Car parking.

WEB: www.holiday/ireland.com

Member of Premier Guesthouses

B&B from £29.00 to £32.50
€36.82 to €41.27

SINEAD EGAN
Proprietor

Mastercard
Visa

23 23

Closed 24 - 27 December

EGLINTON MANOR

83 EGLINTON ROAD, DONNYBROOK, DUBLIN 4
TEL: 01-269 3273   FAX: 01-269 7527

GUESTHOUSE ★★★★   MAP 8 O 11

This gracious red-bricked Victorian Old House which has just been refurbished to the highest standard is situated in the very elegant suburb of Donnybrook. It is very close to the city centre and the RDS. All rooms have a bathroom and tea/coffee makers, TV, radio, and direct dial telephones. Private free car parking. 4**** premises with lovely garden. 48 hours is our cancellation policy.

B&B from £40.00 to £50.00
€50.79 to €63.49

ROSALEEN CAHILL O'BRIEN

American Express
Mastercard
Visa

9 9

Open All Year

B&B rates are IR£ per person sharing per night incl. Breakfast

ELIZA LODGE

23/24 WELLINGTON QUAY,
TEMPLE BAR, DUBLIN 2
TEL: 01-671 8044 FAX: 01-671 8362
EMAIL: info@dublinlodge.com

GUESTHOUSE ★★★ MAP 12 O 11

Eliza Lodge is superbly located at the foot of Dublin's new Millennium Bridge, offering luxury accommodation in the heart of vibrant Temple Bar. Every double, executive or penthouse bedroom has spectacular views of the River Liffey. All rooms are air conditioned with en suite bathrooms, direct dial phone, multi-channel TV, safes, hospitality trays and ironing facilities.

WEB: www.dublinlodge.com

B&B from £45.00 to £65.00
€57.14 to €82.53

SUSAN O'MAHONY

American Express
Mastercard
Visa

18 18

Closed 24 December - 29 December

FERRYVIEW HOUSE

96 CLONTARF ROAD, CLONTARF,
DUBLIN 3
TEL: 01-833 5893 FAX: 01-853 2141
EMAIL: ferryview@oceanfree.net

GUESTHOUSE ★★★ MAP 8 O 11

Situated on the coast road 2.5 miles from the City Centre on the 130 bus route, Ferryview House is conveniently located between Airport, Ferryport, Point Theatre and the City Centre. The house has been tastefully refurbished to provide 8 en suite bedrooms equipped with TV, direct dial phone, hairdryer, tea/coffee making facilities and free car parking. Local facilities include the famous Bull Island Bird Sanctuary, Dollymount Beach and 3 golf courses.

WEB: www.ferryviewhouse.com

B&B from £30.00 to £45.00
€38.09 to €57.14

MARGARET ALLISTER

Mastercard
Visa

8 8

Closed 22 December - 02 January

FITZSIMONS HOTEL

21-22 WELLINGTON QUAY, TEMPLE
BAR, DUBLIN 2
TEL: 01-677 9315 FAX: 01-677 9387
EMAIL: info@fitzsimons-hotel.com

HOTEL ★★ MAP 8 O 11

The Fitzsimons Hotel situated on the banks of the River Liffey beside the new Millenium Bridge, in the heart of the City's thriving left bank - Temple Bar. It's location offers the visitor doorstep access to this vibrant, colourful, exciting locale and all it has to offer. Theatres, Galleries, Studios, Bars, Restaurants, live music venues and alternative shops. Home to Dublins top entertainment venue with 3 floors of fun Fitzsimons Bar, Restaurant and the Ballroom Nite Club.

WEB: www.fitzsimonshotel.com

B&B from £45.00 to £75.00
€57.14 to €95.23

DARINA HOWARD
Manager

American Express
Mastercard
Visa

26 26

Closed 24 - 26 December

Room rates are IR£ per room per night

FITZWILLIAM

41 UPPER FITZWILLIAM STREET, DUBLIN 2
TEL: 01-662 5155 FAX: 01-676 7488

GUESTHOUSE ★★★ MAP 8 O 11

Centrally located in the heart of elegant Georgian Dublin, minutes walk from St. Stephen's Green, National Concert Hall and Galleries. Enjoy the charm of this spacious town house. Rooms with en suite facilities, colour TV, direct dial telephone, clock/radios and hair dryers. Overnight car parking available. Relax at our excellent restaurant. Our friendly staff will ensure your stay is a relaxed and memorable one.

B&B from £40.00 to £47.50
€50.79 to €60.31

DECLAN CARNEY
Manager

American Express
Diners
Mastercard
Visa

📠☎📺🅣🅒🅟🅢🅨alc
12 12

Closed 21 - 31 December

FITZWILLIAM HOTEL

ST. STEPHEN'S GREEN, DUBLIN 2
TEL: 01-478 7000 FAX: 01-478 7878
EMAIL: enq@fitzwilliam-hotel.com

HOTEL U MAP 8 O 11

A modern classic uniquely positioned on St. Stephen's Green, paces away from Grafton Street, Ireland's premier shopping location. Understated luxury, a fresh approach and impeccable service make it the perfect retreat for business and pleasure travelers. Dine in the highly acclaimed Restaurant Peacock Alley or the Mezzanine Café. Facilities include 3 conference rooms, free car parking for residents & Ireland's largest roof garden. Voted by Condé Nast Traveller Magazine as one of the Top 21 Hottest Hotels in the World.

WEB: www.fitzwilliam-hotel.com

Member of Summit Hotels

Room Rate from £205.00 to £475.00
€260.30 to €603.13

JOHN KAVANAGH
General Manager

American Express
Diners
Mastercard
Visa

☺ 2 Nights Bed & Breakfast from £160.00

📠☎📺🅣🅒CMP🅔alc
130 130

Open All Year

FORTE TRAVELODGE

AUBURN AVENUE ROUNDABOUT, NAVAN ROAD, DUBLIN 15
TEL: 1800-709709 FAX: 01-820 2151

HOTEL U MAP 8 O 11

Situated on the N3 route only 5 miles from Dublin City Centre, just off the M50 Dublin ring road and mins from the Airport, this superb hotel offers comfortable yet affordable accommodation. Each room is large enough to sleep up to three adults, a child under 12 and a baby in a cot. Price is fixed per room regardless of the number of occupants. Each room has en suite bathroom, colour satellite TV including Sky Sports and Sky Movies and direct dial phone. Sited next to Little Chef restaurant.

WEB: www.travelodge.co.uk

Room Rate from £49.95 to £69.95
€63.42 to €88.82

LINDA DAVIS-GRIMES
General Manager

American Express
Diners
Mastercard
Visa

📠☎📺🅣CMP🅟🛏🅘
60 60

Open All Year

B&B rates are IR£ per person sharing per night incl. Breakfast

GEORGE FREDERIC HANDEL HOTEL

16-18 FISHAMBLE STREET, CHRISTCHURCH,
TEMPLE BAR, DUBLIN 8
TEL: 01-670 9400   FAX: 01-670 9410
EMAIL: info@handelshotel.com

HOTEL U   MAP 8 O 11

A modern hotel, steeped in musical history, situated on the edge of Temple Bar, next to Christchurch Cathedral. Within easy walking distance of main tourist attractions and financial districts, our popular small hotel is built on the site where Handel's Messiah was first performed in 1742. We will offer you a warm welcome and a high standard of accommodation for your stay in Dublin.

WEB: www.handelshotel.com

B&B from £35.00 to £70.00
€44.44 to €88.88

JASON DELANEY
General Manager

American Express
Diners
Mastercard
Visa

40 40

Closed 24 - 27 December

GEORGIAN COURT GUESTHOUSE

77-79 LOWER GARDINER STREET,
DUBLIN 1
TEL: 01-855 7872   FAX: 01-855 5715

GUESTHOUSE U   MAP 8 O 11

Situated in the centre of Dublin City, 200m from O'Connell Street, Dublin's main shopping street, 50m from the city centre bus station. The 41 bus direct from Dublin Airport stops outside our door. 150m to Connolly rail station. 10 mins walk to Temple Bar. Secure car park available. Built in 1805 and located in a fine Georgian terrace. All rooms are en suite, colour TV, tea/coffee facilities, internal phones, hairdryer, electric iron available.

B&B from £25.00 to £35.00
€31.74 to €44.44

EILEEN CONROY
Owner

Mastercard
Visa

43 43

Closed 24 - 27 December

GEORGIAN HOTEL

18-22 BAGGOT STREET LOWER,
DUBLIN 2
TEL: 01-634 5000   FAX: 01-634 5100
EMAIL: hotel@georgianhouse.ie

HOTEL ★★★   MAP 8 O 11

This very comfortable 200 year old house with new extension in the heart of Georgian Dublin, next to St. Stephen's Green and a 5 minute walk to the major sites including Trinity College, galleries, museums, cathedrals, theatres and to fashionable shopping streets and pubs. Bathrooms en suite, TV, telephones. Perfect location for business or holiday travellers and offers all the amenities of an exclusive small hotel. Private car park.

Room Rate from £110.00 to £185.00
€139.67 to €234.90

ANNETTE O'SULLIVAN
Managing Director

American Express
Diners
Mastercard
Visa

47 47

Open All Year

Room rates are IR£ per room per night

GLEN GUESTHOUSE

**84 LOWER GARDINER STREET,
DUBLIN 1
TEL: 01-855 1374 FAX: 01-855 2506
EMAIL: theglen@eircom.net**

GUESTHOUSE ★★★   MAP 8 O 11

The Glen is a beautifully restored and maintained guesthouse. Located in the heart of Dublin City, adjacent to shops, theatres, cinemas, galleries, museums and Dublin's famous night spots. Close to bus and train stations en route to airport. Rooms en suite, TV, direct dial phones, tea and coffee facilities in all rooms.

WEB: homepage.eircom.net/~theglen

B&B from £23.00 to £37.00
€29.20 to €46.98

JOHN MURRAY
Manager

Mastercard

Visa

12 12

Open All Year

GLENOGRA HOUSE

**64 MERRION ROAD, BALLSBRIDGE,
DUBLIN 4
TEL: 01-668 3661   FAX: 01-668 3698
EMAIL: glenogra@indigo.ie**

GUESTHOUSE ★★★★   MAP 8 O 11

Located opposite the RDS and Four Seasons Hotel, close to city centre, bus, rail, embassies, restaurants, car ferries. Glenogra provides luxury and elegance in a personalised, family run environment. The cosy drawing room is perfect for a restoring afternoon tea. En suite bedrooms are decorated in harmony with a period residence, are all non-smoking with phone, TV, coffee making facilities. Private car parking. Attractive off season specials. AA, RAC ◆◆◆◆◆.

Member of Premier Guesthouses

Room Rate from £49.00 to £69.00
€62.22 to €87.61

CHERRY AND SEAMUS
MCNAMEE Proprietors

American Express

Mastercard

Visa

12 12

IRISH HOTELS FEDERATION

Closed 20 - 31 December

GRAFTON CAPITAL HOTEL

**STEPHENS STREET LOWER,
DUBLIN 2
TEL: 01-475 0888   FAX: 01-475 0908
EMAIL: info@graftoncapital-hotel.com**

HOTEL ★★★   MAP 8 O 11

Nestling in the heart of Dublin's most fashionable and cultural areas, the Grafton Capital Hotel presents the facade of a traditional Georgian townhouse while affording a wealth of comforts for the most discerning guest. The hotel provides the luxury of its superbly appointed en suite bedrooms, each designed to afford the highest levels of comfort. The hotel is just two minutes walk from Grafton Street.

WEB: www.capitalhotels.com

B&B from £75.00 to £79.50
€95.23 to €100.94

EIMEAR O'SHEA
General Manager

American Express

Diners

Mastercard

Visa

75 75

Inet

IRISH HOTELS FEDERATION

Closed 24 - 26 December

B&B rates are IR£ per person sharing per night incl. Breakfast

GRAFTON HOUSE

26-27 SOUTH GREAT GEORGES
STREET, DUBLIN 2
TEL: 01-679 2041   FAX: 01-677 9715
EMAIL: graftonguesthouse@eircom.net

GUESTHOUSE ★★★   MAP 8 O 11

This charming 3*** guesthouse
ideally located in the heart of the city
within 2 minutes walking distance of
Dublin's premier shopping centre
Grafton Street, St. Stephen's Green,
Trinity College and Dublin Castle. All
bedrooms newly decorated with
bathroom/shower, direct dial
telephone, TV, hairdryers, tea and
coffee making facilities. Public car
parking close by in enclosed car
parks. Grafton House is the ideal
location for business or holidays.

B&B from £35.00 to £50.00
€44.44 to €63.49

BRIDGET COLLINS

Mastercard
Visa

16 16

Closed 23 - 30 December

GRESHAM HOTEL

23 UPPER O'CONNELL STREET,
DUBLIN 1
TEL: 01-874 6881   FAX: 01-878 7175
EMAIL: ryan@indigo.ie

HOTEL ★★★★   MAP 8 O 11

Situated on Dublin's main
thoroughfare, The Gresham provides
the ultimate in luxury & service,
convenient to the capital's theatres,
galleries & shopping malls. Elegant
& eminently traditional, The Gresham
offers 288 luxury bedrooms
including 6 penthouse suites. Two
conference centres with 23 air-
conditioned meeting rooms & a
fitness centre complement the
spacious ground floor facilities,
which feature the Aberdeen
Restaurant, Toddy's Bar & the
Gresham Lounge. Multi-storey car
park £6/day.

WEB: www.ryan-hotels.com

B&B from £90.00 to £140.00
€114.28 to €177.76

SHAY LIVINGSTONE
General Manager

American Express
Diners
Mastercard
Visa

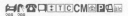

😊 2 B&B weekend from £130.00

288 288

Open All Year

HARCOURT HOTEL

60 HARCOURT STREET,
DUBLIN 2
TEL: 01-478 3677   FAX: 01-475 2013
EMAIL: reservations@harcourthotel.ie

HOTEL ★★★   MAP 8 O 11

Centrally located close to Grafton
Street and St. Stephen's Green,
convenient to the city's theatres,
museums and tourist attractions. Our
elegantly refurbished bedrooms are
fully equipped and include tea/coffee
making facilities. Once the home of
George Bernard Shaw, now the
home of traditional Irish music.

WEB: www.harcourthotel.ie

Member of Holiday Ireland Hotels

B&B from £35.00 to £80.00
€44.44 to €101.58

SALLY MCGILL
General Manager

American Express
Diners
Mastercard
Visa

94 94

Open All Year

Room rates are IR£ per room per night

HARDING HOTEL

COPPER ALLEY, FISHAMBLE STREET, DUBLIN 2
TEL: 01-679 6500   FAX: 01-679 6504
EMAIL: harding.hotel@usitworld.com

HOTEL ★★   MAP 8 O 11

Harding Hotel is a stylish city centre hotel located within Dublin's thriving left bank, Temple Bar. This historic area with its cobbled streets offers the visitor a variety of shops, restaurants, pubs and theatres. All 53 rooms are equipped to the highest standard with direct dial phone, TV, hairdryer and tea/coffee making facilities. The lively Darkey Kelly's Bar & Restaurant is the perfect setting for business or pleasure.

WEB: www.iol.ie/usitaccm

Member of USIT Accommodation Centres

Room Rate from £45.00 to £69.00
€57.14 to €87.61

EDEL KINSELLA
Manager

Mastercard
Visa

53 53

Closed 23 - 27 December

HARRINGTON HALL

70 HARCOURT STREET, DUBLIN 2
TEL: 01-475 3497   FAX: 01-475 4544
EMAIL: harringtonhall@eircom.net

GUESTHOUSE ★★★★   MAP 8 O 11

Harrington Hall with its secure private parking in the heart of Georgian Dublin, provides the perfect location for holiday and business visitors alike to enjoy the surrounding galleries, museums, cathedrals, theatres, fashionable shopping streets, restaurants and pubs. All rooms are equipped to today's exacting standards with en suite, direct dial phone, hospitality tray, trouser press and multi channel TV, access to fax facilities, e-mail and internet. All floors are serviced by elevator.

WEB: www.harringtonhall.com

B&B from £45.00 to £70.00
€57.14 to €88.88

HENRY KING
Proprietor

American Express
Mastercard
Visa

☺ Midweek specials from £50.00

28 28

Open All Year

HARVEY'S GUEST HOUSE

11 UPPER GARDINER STREET, DUBLIN 1
TEL: 01-874 8384   FAX: 01-874 5510
EMAIL: harveysguesthse@iol.ie

GUESTHOUSE ★★★   MAP 8 O 11

This fully restored family run Georgian guesthouse provides a friendly atmosphere. Located in the heart of Dublin City and only 500m from O'Connell Bridge and Temple Bar. Conveniently reached by the No 41 airport bus, first stop on our street by the church. Our en suite facilities include bath/shower and hairdryers. Our car park is free. All rooms have TV and telephone.

WEB: www.harveysguesthouse.com

B&B from £28.00 to £40.00
€35.55 to €50.79

EILISH FLOOD
Proprietor

Mastercard
Visa

☺ Midweek specials from £75.00

14 14

Open All Year

B&B rates are IR£ per person sharing per night incl. Breakfast

HAZELBROOK HOUSE

85 LOWER GARDINER STREET,
DUBLIN 1
TEL: 01-836 5003   FAX: 01-855 0310
EMAIL: homepage.eircom.net/~hazelbrook/

GUESTHOUSE U   MAP 8 O 11

Hazelbrook House offers superb accommodation with 34 en suite rooms including family rooms. All have remote control TV, iron, tea/coffee facilities and hairdryer. We provide a good Irish breakfast, cater for vegetarians and childrens special needs. Fax/phone on premises. For tourists there are attractions nearby: Trinity College, St Stephens Green and Dublin's trendy Temple Bar area. Our staff are always friendly and, most important, a warm welcome is assured.

WEB: www.hazelbrook@eircom.net

B&B from £30.00 to £40.00
€38.09 to €50.79

DOLORES BURNETT
Manager

Mastercard

Visa

34 34

Closed 23 - 28 December

HEDIGAN'S

TULLYALLAN HOUSE, 14 HOLLYBROOK
PARK, CLONTARF, DUBLIN 3
TEL: 01-853 1663   FAX: 01-833 3337
EMAIL: hedigans@indigo.ie

GUESTHOUSE ★★★   MAP 8 O 11

Hedigan's is a late Victorian listed residence in Clontarf located 15 mins from the airport, Dublin Port, Point Theatre 5 mins, city centre 10 mins. Local facilities include 3 golf courses, beach and Stann's Rose Gardens. This elegant house offers a choice of single, double and twin luxurious en suite rooms. Also available is a gracious drawing room and gardens. RAC Highly Acclaimed. AA selected ◆◆◆◆.

B&B from £30.00 to £40.00
€38.09 to €50.79

MATT HEDIGAN
Proprietor

Mastercard

Visa

9 9

IRISH
HOTELS
FEDERATION

Open All Year

HERBERT PARK HOTEL

BALLSBRIDGE,
DUBLIN 4
TEL: 01-667 2200   FAX: 01-667 2595
EMAIL: reservations@herbertparkhotel.ie

HOTEL ★★★★   MAP 8 O 11

Ideally located in Ballsbridge, adjacent to the RDS, conveniently central yet pleasantly secluded by Herbert Park. The hotel reflects the New Ireland in its unique style of contemporary art and architecture. 153 bedrooms and suites with air conditioning and modern facilities. Complimentary car parking for residents. The Pavilion Restaurant, Exhibition Bar and Terrace complete the luxury experience, which is the Herbert Park Hotel.

WEB: www.herbertparkhotel.ie

Member of UTELL International

B&B from £116.00 to £116.00
€147.29 to €147.29

EWAN PLENDERLEITH
· General Manager

American Express

Diners

Mastercard

Visa

2 nights B&B from £125.00

153 153

aid Inet FAX

IRISH
HOTELS
FEDERATION

Open All Year

Room rates are IR£ per room per night

HIBERNIAN HOTEL

**EASTMORELAND PLACE,
BALLSBRIDGE, DUBLIN 4**
TEL: 01-668 7666 FAX: 01-660 2655
EMAIL: info@hibernianhotel.com

HOTEL U   MAP 8 O 11

The Hibernian Hotel, a splendid city centre Victorian building. Bedrooms are elegant & luxurious offering every modern facility complete with Neutrogena® toiletries. Guests can enjoy gourmet delights in the hotel's restaurant. AA Courtesy & Care Award 1999/hotel of the year 1997 from Small Luxury Hotels. Close to museums, theatres, concert halls & Grafton Street. Sister property of McCausland Hotel, Belfast and Woodstock Hotel, Ennis. GDS Acc Code:LX.UK Toll free:00 800 525 48000

WEB: www.hibernianhotel.com

Member of Small Luxury Hotels of the World

Room Rate from £110.00 to £190.00
€139.67 to €241.25

NIALL COFFEY
General Manager

American Express
Diners
Mastercard
Visa

😊 Weekend specials from £130.00

 40 40

IRISH HOTELS FEDERATION

Closed 24 - 27 December

HILTON DUBLIN

**CHARLEMONT PLACE,
DUBLIN 2**
TEL: 01-402 9988 FAX: 01-402 9966
EMAIL: reservations_dublin@hilton.com

HOTEL U   MAP 8 O 11

The Hilton Dublin is a modern, superior hotel which opened in August '97. Overlooking the Grand Canal, the Hilton is centrally located for easy access to all of Dublin's major tourist attractions and road connections network. This excellent hotel has 189 bedrooms. Our Waterfront Restaurant serves the best in traditional and international cuisine. Champions Bar has a sports theme and beer garden. Private complimentary carpark for residents. Conference and banqueting for up to 300 people.

WEB: www.dublin.hilton.com

Room Rate from £140.00 to £225.00
€177.76 to €285.69

PATRICK STAPLETON
General Manager

American Express
Diners
Mastercard
Visa

😊 Weekend specials from £125.00

 189 189
Inet

IRISH HOTELS FEDERATION

Open All Year

HOLIDAY INN

**99-107 PEARSE STREET,
DUBLIN 2**
TEL: 01-670 3666 FAX: 01-670 3636
EMAIL: info@holidayinndublin.ie

HOTEL ★★★   MAP 8 O 11

Ireland's first Holiday Inn, located in the heart of the city centre. 88 superb en suite rooms with satellite TV, fax/modem line, hairdryer, trouser press and tea/coffee facilities. Executive rooms, disabled and designated non-smoking rooms are also available. Each room has either a king bed or two queen beds. Health and fitness centre. Esther Keogh's Traditional Irish Pub. Function rooms and conference facilities for up to 80 people. Secure private paid car park.

WEB: www.holidayinndublin.ie

B&B from £52.50 to £84.50
€66.66 to €107.29

JOHN R. MORAN
General Manager

American Express
Diners
Mastercard
Visa

88 88

IRISH HOTELS FEDERATION

Open All Year

B&B rates are IR£ per person sharing per night incl. Breakfast

HOTEL ISAACS

STORE STREET,
DUBLIN 1
TEL: 01-855 0067 FAX: 01-836 5390
EMAIL: hotel@isaacs.ie

HOTEL ★★★ MAP 8 O 11

Situated in the heart of Dublin City, 5 mins by foot from O'Connell Street Bridge, Hotel Isaacs, a converted wine-ware house, is the perfect location for the visitor to Dublin, at the perfect price, close to the shopping & financial centre. All rooms are tastefully furnished & are en suite with telephone, TV, tea/coffee making facilities & iron/ironing board. The restaurant, Il Vignardo, serves great tasting Italian food 7 days a week. Nearby overnight parking available at special rates.

WEB: www.isaacs.ie

B&B from £40.00 to £70.00
€50.79 to €88.88

EVELYN HANNIGAN
General Manager

American Express
Mastercard
Visa

58 58

Closed 23 - 27 December

HOTEL ST. GEORGE

7 PARNELL SQUARE,
DUBLIN 1
TEL: 01-874 5611 FAX: 01-874 5582
EMAIL: hotels@indigo.ie

HOTEL U MAP 8 O 11

The historical Hotel St. George is located on Parnell Square at the top of O'Connell Street, Dublin's principal thoroughfare. Within walking distance of the Abbey and the Gate Theatre, Municipal Art Gallery, Dublin's Writers Museum, Principal shopping district and other major tourist attractions. Each bedroom is en suite, individually decorated, every modern comfort, including direct dial phone, colour TV and tea/coffee making facilities. Private car park.

WEB: http://indigo.ie/~hotels

B&B from £40.00 to £50.00
€50.79 to €63.49

JIM STAUNTON
Proprietor

Mastercard
Visa

Midweek specials from £99.00

36 36

Closed 24 - 27 December

IONA HOUSE

5 IONA PARK, GLASNEVIN,
DUBLIN 9
TEL: 01-830 6217 FAX: 01-830 6732

GUESTHOUSE ★★★ MAP 8 O 11

Iona House is a popular 3*** guesthouse, near the city centre, in one of Dublin's unique Victorian quarters, full of charming red brick houses built around the turn of the century. Rooms with private shower and w.c. en suite, colour TV, self dial phone and central heating. A comfortable lounge and private patio round off the friendly atmosphere of Iona House. Listed with ADAC, AVD, ANWB, International Hotels - Restaurants - Tourisme, Beth Byrant and Fodors Guide.

B&B from £35.00 to £35.00
€44.44 to €44.44

CONRAD SHOULDICE
Manager

American Express
Mastercard
Visa

10 10

Closed 01 December - 31 January

JACKSON COURT HOTEL

**29/30 HARCOURT STREET,
DUBLIN 2**
TEL: 01-475 8777 FAX: 01-475 8793
EMAIL: info@jackson-court.ie

HOTEL ★★ MAP 8 O 11

Minutes walk from Grafton Street, Stephens Green and most of Dublin's historic landmarks. Enjoy the combination of local Dubliners and visitors from abroad in our hotel, busy bar and Dublin's hottest night spot, Copper Face Jacks. Rates include full Irish breakfast, night club admission, service and taxes. We look forward to welcoming you!

B&B from £47.50 to £47.50
€60.31 to €60.31

LESLEY-ANNE HAYES
Manager

American Express
Diners
Mastercard
Visa

☺ Midweek specials from £105.00

26 26

Closed 24 - 27 December

JURYS BALLSBRIDGE HOTEL

**PEMBROKE ROAD, BALLSBRIDGE,
DUBLIN 4**
TEL: 01-660 5000 FAX: 01-660 5540
EMAIL: ballsbridge_hotel@jurysdoyle.com

HOTEL ★★★★★ MAP 8 O 11

This 5***** hotel, with 300 large de luxe bedrooms, is situated in the city's prime residential and business district. Recently refurbished ground floor features 2 restaurants, traditional Dubliner bar and Library lounge, an indoor/outdoor pool, gym and ample car parking.

TOWERS

LANSDOWNE ROAD, DUBLIN 4
TEL: 01-667 0033 FAX: 01-660 5540
EMAIL: towers_hotel@jurysdoyle.com

5 Star Superior hotel adjacent to Jurys Ballsbridge Hotel.

WEB: www.jurysdoyle.com

B&B from £87.00 to £147.00
€110.46 to €186.65

RICHARD BOURKE
General Manager

American Express
Diners
Mastercard
Visa

300 300

Open All Year

JURYS GREEN ISLE HOTEL

**NAAS ROAD,
DUBLIN 22**
TEL: 01-459 3406 FAX: 01-459 2178
EMAIL: green_isle@jurysdoyle.com

HOTEL ★★★ MAP 8 O 11

Superior modern 3*** hotel offering high quality international service standards and friendly Irish service. Strategically located in Dublin south west, 12 miles from Dublin International Airport and 7 miles from Dublin City Centre. The hotel is within 5-10 mins drive from Dublin's most important multi-national business parks and 3 mins drive of major national routes leading to the south and west of Ireland.

WEB: www.jurysdoyle.com

B&B from £43.00 to £72.00
€54.73 to €91.42

JIM FLYNN
General Manager

American Express
Diners
Mastercard
Visa

90 90

Open All Year

B&B rates are IR£ per person sharing per night incl. Breakfast

JURYS INN CHRISTCHURCH

**CHRISTCHURCH PLACE,
DUBLIN 8**
TEL: 01-454 0000 FAX: 01-454 0012
EMAIL: christchurch_inn@jurysdoyle.com

HOTEL ★★★ MAP 8 O 11

Modern attractive rooms capable of accommodating up to 3 adults or 2 adults and 2 children. All rooms are en suite with multi-channel TV, tea/coffee making facilities, radio and direct dial phone. Located in the heart of Dublin City, opposite Christ Church, the Inn has an informal restaurant and a lively pub. It also has the added convenience of an adjoining public multi-storey car park (fee payable). Jurys Doyle Hotel Group central reservations Tel. 01-607 0000 Fax. 01-631 6999.

WEB: www.jurysdoyle.com

Room Rate from £66.00 to £70.00
€83.80 to €88.88

EDWARD STEPHENSON
General Manager

American Express
Diners
Mastercard
Visa

182 182

Closed 24 - 26 December

JURYS INN CUSTOM HOUSE

**CUSTOM HOUSE QUAY,
DUBLIN 1**
TEL: 01-607 5000 FAX: 01-829 0400
EMAIL:custom_house@jurysdoyle.com

HOTEL ★★★ MAP 8 O 11

Modern attractive rooms capable of accommodating up to 3 adults or 2 adults and 2 children. All rooms are en suite with multi-channel TV, radio, direct dial phone, tea/coffee making facilities. Located in the heart of Dublin City at the I.F.S. Centre, the Inn has an informal restaurant and lively pub, a business centre, conference rooms and a public multi-storey car park (fee payable). Jurys Doyle Hotel Group central reservations Tel. 01-607 0000 Fax. 01-660 9625.

WEB: www.jurysdoyle.com

Room Rate from £66.00 to £70.00
€83.80 to €88.88

MONICA FRIEL
General Manager

American Express
Diners
Mastercard
Visa

239 239

Closed 24 - 26 December

Room rates are IR£ per room per night

JURYS MONTROSE HOTEL

**STILLORGAN ROAD,
DUBLIN 4**
TEL: 01-269 3311 FAX: 01-269 1164
EMAIL: montrose_hotel@jurysdoyle.com

HOTEL ★★★ MAP 8 O 11

Quality, modern 3*** hotel, located just 2 miles from Dublin City Centre, 10 miles from Dublin International Airport and within 10-15 mins drive of all major southside business and entertainment districts. Overlooking the impressive grounds of University College Dublin and attractive residences, the hotel offers a warm, friendly atmosphere coupled with quality international standards.

WEB: www.jurysdoyle.com

B&B from £43.00 to £72.00
€54.73 to €91.42

**CONOR O'KANE
General Manager**

American Express
Diners
Mastercard
Visa

179 179

Open All Year

JURYS SKYLON HOTEL

**UPPER DRUMCONDRA ROAD,
DUBLIN 9**
TEL: 01-837 9121 FAX: 01-837 2778
EMAIL: skylon_hotel@jurysdoyle.com

HOTEL ★★★ MAP 8 O 11

Modern 3*** hotel offering a warm Irish ambience and high international service standards, located in a residential setting on the main link route between Dublin International Airport (3 miles) and Dublin City Centre (2 miles). Facilities include 88 de luxe rooms, bar, complimentary parking and full business services available.

WEB: www.jurysdoyle.com

B&B from £42.00 to £65.00
€53.32 to €82.53

**LOUIS LANGAN
General Manager**

American Express
Diners
Mastercard
Visa

88 88

Open All Year

JURYS TARA HOTEL

**MERRION ROAD,
DUBLIN 4**
TEL: 01-269 4666 FAX: 01-269 1027
EMAIL: tara_hotel@jurysdoyle.com

HOTEL ★★★ MAP 8 O 11

Modern 3*** hotel located just 2 miles from Dublin City Centre, 7 miles from Dublin International Airport and within 10-15 mins drive of all major southside business and entertainment districts. Commanding breathtaking view of Dublin Bay, this intimate hotel offers a warm, friendly Irish atmosphere combined with quality international service standards.

WEB: www.jurysdoyle.com

B&B from £44.00 to £73.00
€55.86 to €92.69

**MELISSA HYNES
General Manager**

American Express
Diners
Mastercard
Visa

113 113

Open All Year

B&B rates are IR£ per person sharing per night incl. Breakfast

KELLYS HOTEL

SOUTH GREAT GEORGES STREET,
DUBLIN 2
TEL: 01-677 9277 FAX: 01-671 3216
EMAIL: kellyhtl@iol.ie

HOTEL U MAP 8 O 11

Situated in the heart of Dublin beside
fashionable Grafton Street. A few
minutes walk to Trinity College.
Temple Bar and many of Dublin's
famous pubs and restaurants are on
our doorstep. Places of historical,
cultural and literary interest are close
by. Kelly's is a budget hotel of
unbeatable value for a city centre
location. There is no service charge
and our prices include breakfast.
Frommers recommended. Parking
available in adjacent public multi-
storey carpark (for fee).

WEB: www.kellyshtl.com

B&B from £29.00 to £40.00
€36.82 to €50.79

TERRY MOSER
General Manager

American Express
Mastercard
Visa

Midweek specials from £90.00

24 21

Closed 20 - 26 December

KILRONAN GUESTHOUSE

70 ADELAIDE ROAD,
DUBLIN 2
TEL: 01-475 5266 FAX: 01-478 2841
EMAIL: info@dublinn.com

GUESTHOUSE ★★★ MAP 8 O 11

This exclusive AA RAC ♦♦♦♦
recommended Georgian House is in
a secluded setting, walking distance
from St. Stephen's Green, Trinity
College, National Concert Hall,
Dublin Castle, Cathedrals, St.
Patrick's, Christchurch and most of
Dublin's historic landmarks. Well
appointed bedrooms with private
shower, direct dial phone, TV,
hairdryers, tea/coffee facilities and
quality orthopedic beds.
Commended by New York Times,
Beth Byrant, Michelin Guide, Fodors,
Frommer & Special Places to Stay.

WEB: www.dublinn.com

B&B from £35.00 to £48.00
€44.44 to €60.95

ROSE & TERRY MASTERSON
Owners

American Express
Diners
Mastercard
Visa

15 13

Open All Year

KINGSWOOD COUNTRY HOUSE

OLD KINGSWOOD, NAAS ROAD,
CLONDALKIN, DUBLIN 22
TEL: 01-459 2428 FAX: 01-459 2207
EMAIL: kingswoodhse@eircom.net

GUESTHOUSE ★★★ MAP 8 O 11

A warm and welcoming Country
House nestling within beautiful
walled gardens. Strategically located
3km from the M50 at the beginning
of the N7(Naas Road) the gateway
to the west and south west. Enjoy
the intimate atmosphere of the
restaurant which features open fires
and sophisticated Irish dishes with a
French influence. The seven tastefully
decorated bedrooms are all en suite
with TV, direct dial phone.
Recommended - Egon Ronay, Good
Hotel Guide, RAC, AA ♦♦♦♦.

B&B from £35.00 to £45.00
€44.44 to €57.14

SHEILA O'BRYNE
Manageress

American Express
Diners
Mastercard
Visa

1 Dinner, B&B from £65.00

7 7

Open All Year

Room rates are IR£ per room per night

LANSDOWNE HOTEL

**27-29 PEMBROKE ROAD,
BALLSBRIDGE, DUBLIN 4
TEL: 01-668 2522 FAX: 01-668 5585
EMAIL: lanhotel@iol.ie**

HOTEL ★★★ MAP 8 O 11

The Lansdowne Hotel is a 3***
Georgian hotel just minutes walk
from city centre. We combine olde
world charm with modern facilities.
Ideally located, with Lansdowne
Stadium, RDS, Point Theatre and
Dublin's business district just a short
stroll. You can relax and enjoy fine
Irish cuisine in our Celtic Restaurant
or savour the local atmosphere in
our Den Bar while enjoying mouth-
watering food from our bar menu.
We have a fully equipped conference
and banqueting hall. Private car
park.

WEB: www.lansdownehotel.com

Member of MinOtel Ireland Hotel Group

B&B from £35.00 to £75.00
€44.44 to €95.23

MARGARET ENGLISH
Assistant Manager

American Express
Diners
Mastercard
Visa

40 40

Closed 23 - 27 December

LANSDOWNE MANOR

**46-48 LANSDOWNE ROAD,
BALLSBRIDGE, DUBLIN 4
TEL: 01-668 8848 FAX: 01-668 8873
EMAIL: lansdownemanor@eircom.net**

GUESTHOUSE ★★★★ MAP 8 O 11

Lansdowne Manor, situated in
Ballsbridge, comprises of two early
Victorian mansions which maintain
the elegance of their original era. The
furnishings were specially
commissioned in the style of 18th
century France. Bedrooms range
from single to executive, each with
en suite, direct dial phone, multi
channel TV, trouser press and
tea/coffee making facilities. Laundry
service, private meeting room and
secretarial services are available. AA
Selected premises ◆◆◆◆.

WEB: lansdownemanor.com

B&B from £42.50 to £55.00
€53.96 to €69.84

BRENDA O'FLYNN
General Manager

American Express
Diners
Mastercard
Visa

😊 Midweek specials from £112.50

22 22

Closed 22 December - 03 January

LONGFIELDS

**9/10 FITZWILLIAM STREET LOWER,
DUBLIN 2
TEL: 01-676 1367 FAX: 01-676 1542
EMAIL: lfields@indigo.ie**

HOTEL ★★★ MAP 8 O 11

Longfield's, a charming and intimate
hotel in the heart of Ireland's capital
where, with its award winning
No. 10 Restaurant, one can relax in
oppulence reminiscent of times past.
Avid followers of good food guides
and well known accommodation
publications will have noted
numerous accolades bestowed upon
this renowned residence. Its central
location and its impeccable service
make it a must for discerning
travellers.

WEB: www.longfields.ie

Member of Manor House Hotels

B&B from £62.50 to £80.00
€79.36 to €101.58

PHILIP RYAN
Manager

American Express
Diners
Mastercard
Visa

😊 Weekend specials from £120.00

26 26

Closed 24 - 27 December

B&B rates are IR£ per person sharing per night incl. Breakfast

LYNAM'S HOTEL

63/64 O'CONNELL STREET, DUBLIN 1
TEL: 01-888 0886 FAX: 01-888 0890
EMAIL: lynams.hotel@indigo.ie

HOTEL P MAP 12 O 11

A boutique style 42 bedroom hotel located on O'Connell Street, close to the GPO and all of Dublin's many attractions. Decorated with elegance and individuality. All rooms are en suite, have direct dial phones and data port. 2 comfortable lounges are provided for guest use and our restaurant offers modern style cuisine. Lynam's Hotel is under the personal management of its owner Mr Gerard Lynam.

WEB: www.lynams-hotel.com

B&B from £50.00 to £65.00
€63.49 to €82.53

GERARD LYNAM

American Express
Diners
Mastercard
Visa

☺ Midweek specials from £150.00

42 42

Closed 24 - 28 December

LYNDON GUESTHOUSE

26 GARDINER PLACE, DUBLIN 1
TEL: 01-878 6950 FAX: 01-878 7420
EMAIL: lyndonh@gofree.indigo.ie

GUESTHOUSE ★★ MAP 8 O 11

Lyndon House is an extremely popular, beautifully restored, modernly designed, Georgian guesthouse. It is excellently located in the heart of Dublin's City Centre off Parnell Square at the top of O'Connell Street & is on 41/41c airport bus route. It is family run, so emphasis is on good value, warm atmosphere and friendly service. Rooms are bathroom en suite, with TV, internal telephone and hospitality tray. Highly Acclaimed AA ◆◆◆.

B&B from £25.00 to £35.00
€31.74 to €44.44

MICHAEL MOLONEY
Director

Mastercard
Visa

9 9

OPEN ALL YEAR

MAPLE HOTEL

LOWER GARDINER STREET, DUBLIN 1
TEL: 01-874 0225 FAX: 01-874 5239

HOTEL ★★ MAP 8 O 11

The Maple Hotel is situated in the heart of the city, just off O'Connell Street, beside all theatres, cinemas, main railway, bus and DART stations with a direct bus link to Dublin Airport. The hotel is owned and run by the Sharkey Family who have been welcoming guests here for over 37 years. All luxurious bedrooms en suite, colour TV, direct dial phones, hair dryer, coffee/tea facilities. Private car parking.

WEB: www.focus-irl.com/maplehotel

B&B from £25.00 to £45.00
€31.74 to €57.14

THE SHARKEY FAMILY

Mastercard
Visa

12 12

Closed 17 December - 11 January

Room rates are IR£ per room per night

MARIAN GUEST HOUSE

**21 UPPER GARDINER STREET,
DUBLIN 1
TEL: 01-874 4129**

GUESTHOUSE ★ MAP 8 O 11

Situated in Georgian Dublin, just off Mountjoy Square and five minutes walk from city centre and all principal shopping areas, cinemas, theatres, museums. All our rooms are tastefully decorated, with central heating and all usual amenities are available. There are tea/coffee making facilities. The Marian is family run and you are sure to get a warm welcome. On the 41 bus route from Dublin Airport. Open all year.

B&B from £20.00 to £22.00
€25.39 to €27.93

CATHRINE MCELROY
Owner

Mastercard
Visa

6 6

Open All Year

MERCER HOTEL

**MERCER STREET LOWER,
DUBLIN 2
TEL: 01-478 2179 FAX: 01-478 0328
EMAIL: stay@mercerhotel.ie**

HOTEL ★★★ MAP 8 O 11

The Mercer Hotel is ideally located in the heart of Dublin's most fashionable and cultural areas adjacent to the superb landscaped gardens of St. Stephens Green. The Mercer is a boutique style hotel with 21 superbly appointed en suite rooms. Discreetly blended into the decor is a full complement of modern amenities including individually controlled air conditioning, TV/video, CD player, trouser press, fax, modem points, direct dial phone, hairdryer. Conference and restaurant facilities.

WEB: www.mercerhotel.ie

B&B from £49.00 to £72.50
€62.22 to €92.06

CAROLINE FAHY
General Manager

American Express
Diners
Mastercard
Visa

21 21

Inet FAX

Open All Year

MERRION HALL

**54/56 MERRION ROAD,
BALLSBRIDGE, DUBLIN 4
TEL: 01-668 1426 FAX: 01-668 4280
EMAIL: merrionhall@iol.ie**

GUESTHOUSE ★★★★ MAP 8 O 11

The 4**** Award-winning Merrion Hall offers an elegant combination of Edwardian grace, fine food and modern comforts, all one expects of a private hotel, aircon suites, executive facilities, jacuzzis, 4-poster beds, private carpark & gardens. Adjacent to RDS, close to city centre, airport and car ferry terminals by DART or bus. Accolades, AAA ♦♦♦♦, RAC Property of Year, Times, Bestloved Hotels, Johansens. Sister property of adjoining Blakes Townhouse, Aberdeen Lodge & Halpins Hotel, Co. Clare.
US Toll Free 1800 223 6510.

WEB: www.halpinsprivatehotels.com

B&B from £35.00 to £70.00
€44.44 to €88.88

PAT HALPIN
Proprietor

American Express
Diners
Mastercard
Visa

Midweek specials from £115.00

30 30

FAX

Open All Year

B&B rates are IR£ per person sharing per night incl. Breakfast

MERRION HOTEL

UPPER MERRION STREET, DUBLIN 2
TEL: 01-603 0600 FAX: 01-603 0700
EMAIL: info@merrionhotel.com

HOTEL ★★★★★ MAP 8 O 11

The Merrion Hotel, Dublin's most luxurious 5***** hotel is situated in the city centre opposite the Irish Parliament on Upper Merrion Street. This hotel brings new standards of excellence to Ireland's capital by the nature of the discreet but friendly service offered to guests. With the meticulous restoration of four grade 1 listed Georgian town houses. The Merrion provides 145 beautifully appointed guest rooms and suites, many overlooking magnificent 18th century gardens.

WEB: www.merrionhotel.com

Member of Leading Hotels of the World

Room Rate from £220 to £285
€279.34 to €361.87

PETER MACCANN
General Manager

American Express
Diners
Mastercard
Visa

145 145

alc Inet FAX

Open All Year

MERRION LODGE

148 MERRION ROAD, BALLSBRIDGE, DUBLIN 4
TEL: 01-269 1565 FAX: 01-283 9998
EMAIL: merrionlodge@eircom.net

GUESTHOUSE N MAP 8 O 11

Luxurious accommodation located in prestigious Ballsbridge, convenient to embassies, RDS, Lansdowne RFC, St. Vincents Hospital, Elm Park, universities, restaurants, The Point and both ferry terminals. All tastefully decorated rooms are en suite with colour TV, direct dial phone, tea/coffee making facilities, hairdryer. Secure parking. While you are with us, relax or take a stroll in our beautiful secluded gardens. Our friendly and professional service ensure a memorable stay.
AA ◆◆◆◆.

WEB: www.merrionlodge.com

Member of AA Hotel Services

B&B from £30.00 to £45.00
€38.09 to €57.14

FENELLA MADIGAN
Proprietor

American Express
Diners
Mastercard
Visa

6 6

Closed 24 - 26 December

MERRION SQUARE MANOR

NO 31 MERRION SQUARE NORTH, DUBLIN 2
TEL: 01-662 8551 FAX: 01-662 8556
EMAIL: merrionmanor@eircom.ie

GUESTHOUSE ★★★ MAP 8 O 11

Merrion Square Manor is situated overlooking Dublin's most gracious Georgian square. Located a 5 minute stroll from the city centre this beautiful house has been tastefully restored and extends the welcome of Georgian days gone by. Bedrooms are individually designed and decorated, all are en suite and have been appointed to the highest standards. Private parking available. AA selected premises ◆◆◆◆.

WEB: www.merrionsquaremanor.com

B&B from £47.50 to £55
€60.31 to €69.84

VALERIE GANNON
Manager

American Express
Mastercard
Visa

20 20

Closed 22 December - 01 January

Room rates are IR£ per room per night

MESPIL HOTEL

MESPIL ROAD, DUBLIN 4
TEL: 01-667 1222 FAX: 01-667 1244
EMAIL: mespil@leehotels.ie

HOTEL ★★★ MAP 8 O 11

On the leafy banks of the Grand Canal, the Mespil offers an ideal city centre location. The emphasis throughout is on space and comfort and the modern stylish decor is reflected in Glaze Restaurant and the Terrace Bar. All 250 en suite rooms are bright, spacious and tastefully furnished. The Mespil provides the perfect base, close to all shopping and cultural amenities and offering excellent value for money. Private car parking.

WEB: www.leehotels.ie

Member of Lee Hotels

Room Rate from £90.00 to £130.00
€114.28 to €165.07

MARTIN HOLOHAN
General Manager

American Express
Diners
Mastercard
Visa

250 250

inet

Closed 24 - 27 December

MONT CLARE HOTEL

MERRION SQUARE, DUBLIN 2
TEL: 01-607 3800 FAX: 01-661 5663
EMAIL: montclareres@ocallaghanhotels.ie

HOTEL ★★★ MAP 8 O 11

Recently refurbished, the Mont Clare features 74 luxurious fully air conditioned bedrooms, traditional lounge bar, Goldsmith's Restaurant, convention facilities and free private valet parking. Overlooking Merrion Square the Mont Clare Hotel is the ideal city centre location, just a few minutes walk to all major attractions including Trinity College, museums, theatres, exhibition centres and shopping areas. Reservations via UTELL International Worldwide. USA Toll Free Reservations 1800 5699983.

WEB: www.ocallaghanhotels.ie

Member of O'Callaghan Hotels

B&B from £71.00 to £102.00
€90.15 to €129.51

COLM O'NEILL
General Manager

American Express
Diners
Mastercard
Visa

☺ Weekend specials from £125.00

74 74

Open All Year

MORGAN HOTEL

10 FLEET STREET, TEMPLE BAR, DUBLIN 2
TEL: 01-679 3939 FAX: 01-679 3946
EMAIL: sales@themorgan.com

HOTEL U MAP 8 O 11

The Morgan is a boutique contemporary style hotel with great emphasis on aesthetic detail. The rooms provide the ultimate in comfort and luxury for the discerning traveller. All rooms are equipped with TV/video, mini-hifi, voicemail and ISDN lines. Located in the vibrant Temple Bar area, The Morgan is in close proximity to theatres, shops, restaurants and the financial district of Dublin.

WEB: www.themorgan.com

Member of Design & Planet Hotels

Room Rate from £105.00 to £375.00
€133.32 to €476.15

MICHELLE MCKENNA
General Manager

American Express
Diners
Mastercard
Visa

☺ Midweek specials from £55.00

61 61

Closed 24 - 27 December

B&B rates are IR£ per person sharing per night incl. Breakfast

MORRISON

LOWER ORMOND QUAY,
DUBLIN 1
TEL: 01-887 2400 FAX: 01-878 3185
EMAIL: info@morrisonhotel.ie

HOTEL N MAP 8 O 11

Dublin's only designer hotel. Located between Millennium Bridge and Capel Street Bridge overlooking the River Liffey. With John Rocha as a design consultant, the hotel has 95 bedrooms that include 6 suites and a penthouse, all equipped with high tech efficiency to suit the modern traveller. Features include the Morrison Bar, a triumph of design and comfort, Halo Restaurant offering fusion cooking and Lobo Bar with an oriental theme.

WEB: www.morrisonhotel.ie

Member of Sterling & Resort Hotels

B&B from £75.00 to £150.00
€95.23 to €190.46

TRACEY DRISCOLL
General Manager

American Express
Diners
Mastercard
Visa

95 95

Closed 25 - 27 December

MOUNT HERBERT HOTEL

HERBERT ROAD, LANSDOWNE ROAD,
DUBLIN 4
TEL: 01-668 4321 FAX: 01-660 7077
EMAIL: info@mountherberthotel.ie

HOTEL U MAP 8 O 11

This Gracious Victorian residence is 5 mins south of the city centre in Ballsbridge, Dublin's most exclusive area, where most diplomatic embassies are based. Facilities include 185 modern bedrooms, restaurant, bar, coffee bar, sauna, gift shop, conference centre, private car park and picturesque gardens. The Loughran Family has been welcoming guests for over 45 years and it is renowned for its superb value and its warm and friendly atmosphere.

WEB: www.mountherberthotel.ie

B&B from £42.50 to £59.00
€53.96 to €74.91

MICHELLE SWEENEY
Manager

American Express
Diners
Mastercard
Visa

185 185

IRISH HOTELS FEDERATION

Open All Year

NORTHUMBERLAND LODGE

68 NORTHUMBERLAND ROAD,
BALLSBRIDGE, DUBLIN 4
TEL: 01-660 5270 FAX: 01-668 8679
EMAIL: info@northumberlandlodge.com

GUESTHOUSE ★★★ MAP 8 O 11

Luxurious Victorian house, built in the 1850s, situated in the prestigious embassy belt of Ballsbridge, Dublin 4. Close to the RDS, Shelbourne Park, bus and Dart station city centre. We offer executive accommodation - fully equipped rooms with multi channel TV, DD phone, hairdryer, etc. Secure car parking. A friendly welcome and service is guaranteed.

WEB: www.northumberlandlodge.com

B&B from £37.50 to £80.00
€47.62 to €101.58

AVRIL MORDAUNT

Mastercard
Visa

8 8

IRISH HOTELS FEDERATION

Open All Year

Room rates are IR£ per room per night

NUMBER 31

**31 LEESON CLOSE,
DUBLIN 2
TEL: 01-676 5011 FAX: 01-676 2929
EMAIL: number31@iol.ie**

GUESTHOUSE ★★★★ MAP 8 O 11

An award winning guest house right in the heart of Georgian Dublin. The former home of Ireland's leading architect Sam Stephenson just a few minutes walk from St. Stephen's Green and galleries. An oasis of tranquillity and greenery, where guests are encouraged to come back and relax and feel at home at any time of the day. Vast breakfasts in the dining room or in a sunny plant filled conservatory. Recommended by the Good Hotel Guide, Egon Ronay, Bridgestone 100 Best Places, Fodors.

WEB: www.number31.ie

B&B from £42.00 to £90.00
€53.33 to €114.27

DEIRDRE & NOEL COMER

American Express
Mastercard
Visa

18 18

OLD DUBLINER GUESTHOUSE

**62 AMIENS STREET,
DUBLIN 1
Tel: 01-855 5666 FAX: 01-855 5677
EMAIL: dublinerbb@hol.com**

GUESTHOUSE ★★★ MAP 8 O 11

In the heart of the City. A listed Georgian townhouse opened March 1999. New and fresh superb accommodation. Let our guest comments from our visitor book describe us: 19/4 Ian & Trish UK. "Immaculate, first class service, definitely recommendable." 18/8 Charlie Ward USA. "The very best in Ireland." 6/12 Emiko Suzuki, Japan. "Excellent." 30/4 Larjas, Sweden. "Absolutely smashing." All ensuite, direct dial telephone, t.v., coffee/tea, hair dryer.

Web: www.olddubliner.com

B&B from £35.00 to £40.00
€44.44 to €50.79

JOE NOLAN

Mastercard
Visa

14 14

IRISH HOTELS FEDERATION

ORMOND QUAY HOTEL

**7-11 UPPER ORMOND QUAY,
DUBLIN 7
TEL: 01-872 1811 FAX: 01-872 1362
EMAIL: ormondqh@indigo.ie**

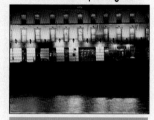

HOTEL U MAP 8 O 11

Overlooking the River Liffey and just minutes from Dublin's vibrant Temple Bar and bustling O'Connell St. The Ormond Quay Hotel is one of the city's best known. Alongside our 60 fully equipped en suite rooms, excellent conference and meeting facilities, food and entertainment in our acclaimed Sirens Bar and the unique Grosvenor Room art gallery. The Ormond Quay Hotel can proudly boast a friendly and welcoming atmosphere right at the heart of it.

WEB: www.ormondquayhotel.com

B&B from £27.50 to £75.00
€34.92 to €95.23

**VERONICA TIMLIN
General Manager**

American Express
Mastercard
Visa

60 60

IRISH HOTELS FEDERATION

B&B rates are IR£ per person sharing per night incl. Breakfast

ORWELL LODGE HOTEL

77A ORWELL ROAD, RATHGAR, DUBLIN 6
TEL: 01-497 7258 FAX: 01-497 9913
EMAIL: reception@orwelllodgehotel.ie

HOTEL ★ MAP 8 O 11

The Orwell is a comfortable hotel situated in the leafy garden suburb of Rathgar dating back to the elegant Victorian era. It enjoys a fine reputation for convivial atmosphere and good quality food of an international flavour. Under the personal management of Michael Lynch with friendly qualified staff who insure that your visit is enjoyable. We serve breakfast, lunch, dinner and bar food. Family and corporate functions are catered for. Off street parking available.

WEB: www.orwelllodgehotel.ie

B&B from £47.30 to £69.30
€60.06 to €87.99

MICHAEL LYNCH
Owner

American Express
Diners
Mastercard
Visa

10 10

Closed 24 - 26 December

OTHELLO HOUSE

74 LOWER GARDINER STREET, DUBLIN 1
TEL: 01-855 4271 FAX: 01-855 7460
EMAIL: othello1@eircom.net

GUESTHOUSE ★★ MAP 8 O 11

Othello is 150m from Abbey Theatre, 200m from Dublin's main O'Connell Street, 50m from centre bus station. 41 bus direct from Dublin Airport stops outside door. 150m to Connolly Railway Station, 1 mile to ferry terminal, 800m to Point Theatre. Lock up secure car park. All rooms en suite with TV, telephone, tea/coffee making facilities. Trinity College, National Museum, National Library all within walking distance.

B&B from £33.00 to £35.00
€41.90 to €44.44

JOHN GALLOWAY
Manager

American Express
Diners
Mastercard
Visa

22 22

Open All Year

PALMERSTOWN LODGE

PALMERSTOWN VILLAGE, DUBLIN 20
TEL: 01-623 5494 FAX: 01-623 6214
EMAIL: info@palmerstownlodge.com

GUESTHOUSE ★★★ MAP 8 O 11

Prime location adjacent to all amenities and facilities this superb purpose-built guesthouse adjoins the N4/M50 motorway. Minutes from the city centre and a mere 12 minutes drive to the airport we offer all the features and standards of a luxury hotel. Each elegant en suite bedroom has individual temperature control, ambient lighting, automated door locking system, phone, TV, etc. Separate tea/coffee and iron/trouser press facilities. Private car park. Golf Packages available.

WEB: www.palmerstownlodge.com

B&B from £25.00 to £40.00
€31.74 to €50.78

GERRY O'CONNOR
Owner

Mastercard
Visa

19 19

Open All Year

Room rates are IR£ per room per night

PARAMOUNT HOTEL

**PARLIAMENT STREET & ESSEX GATE,
TEMPLE BAR, DUBLIN 2
TEL: 01-417 9900 FAX: 01-417 9904
EMAIL: paramount@iol.ie**

HOTEL N MAP 8 O 11

Paramount Hotel, situated in Temple Bar, the very heart of one of Europe's most vibrant and exciting cities. The Paramount Hotel offers a warm and friendly atmosphere to today's traveller with 70 en suite bedrooms each appointed to the highest of international standards including multi channel TV, in house video, direct dial phone, hairdryer, trouser press, tea/coffee making facilities. The Paramount Bar & Bistro offers first class cuisine in an innovative & fashionable environment.

WEB: www.paramounthotel.ie

B&B from £46.00 to £70.00
€58.41 to €88.88

RITA BARCOE
General Manager

American Express
Diners
Mastercard
Visa

Weekend specials from £105.00

70 70

Closed 24 - 28 December

PARK LODGE HOTEL

**7 NORTH CIRCULAR ROAD,
DUBLIN 7
TEL: 01-838 6428 FAX: 01-838 0931**

HOTEL ★ MAP 8 O 11

A hotel with the unique situation of being right next to the Phoenix Park, with all its leisure facilities (including Dublin Zoo and horse riding) and at the same time being just a few minutes from Dublin City centre. All rooms with multi channel TV & direct dial phone. Ideal venue for people coming to Dublin for shopping. Lock up car park. Hotel German/Irish owned.

B&B from £24.50 to £38.00
€31.11 to €48.25

HORST FLIERENBAUM
Owner

Mastercard
Visa

20 20

Closed 23 - 28 December

PHOENIX PARK HOUSE

**38-39 PARKGATE STREET,
DUBLIN 8
TEL: 01-677 2870 FAX: 01-679 9769
EMAIL: info@dublinguesthouse.com**

GUESTHOUSE ★★ MAP 8 O 11

This friendly AA listed family run guesthouse directly beside the Phoenix Park with its many facilities is ideally located 2 minutes walk from Heuston Station with direct bus service to ferry ports, Dublin Airport, Connolly Train Station and central bus station. Close to the Guinness Brewery, Whiskey Corner, the re-located National Museum and Kilmainham Museum of Modern Art, the popular Temple Bar and numerous pubs and restaurants. Secure car parking available nearby.

WEB: www.dublinguesthouse.com

B&B from £19.50 to £35.00
€24.76 to €44.44

MARY SMITH & EMER SMITH
Proprietors

American Express
Mastercard
Visa
Diners Club

24 19

Closed 23 - 28 December

B&B rates are IR£ per person sharing per night incl. Breakfast

PLAZA HOTEL

BELGARD ROAD, TALLAGHT, DUBLIN 24
TEL: 01-462 4200 FAX: 01-462 4600
EMAIL: reservations@plazahotel.ie

HOTEL N MAP 8 O 11

AA 4**** hotel, 120 bedrooms, 2 suites. Convenient location on Belgard Road, just off the M50 motorway, 5 miles from the city centre. Secure underground car parking. Extensive conference & banqueting facilities for up to 220 people. The Olive Tree Restaurant (AA 2 rosettes) serving fine mediterranean food. The Vista Cafe overlooking the Dublin Mountains, ideal for informal snacks. Obar[1] stylish cafe bar. Grumpy McClafferty's traditional pub.

WEB: www.plazahotel.ie

Room Rate from £65.00 to £110.00
€82.53 to €139.67

CHARLES COSTELLOE
General Manager

American Express
Diners
Mastercard
Visa

122 122

Inet

PORTOBELLO HOTEL & BAR

33 SOUTH RICHMOND STREET, DUBLIN 2
TEL: 01-475 2715 FAX: 01-478 5010
EMAIL: portobellohotel@indigo.ie

HOTEL U MAP 8 O 11

This landmark building is located in the heart of Dublin City along the Grand Canal. First opened in 1793, the Portobello Hotel boasts a long tradition in hospitality and this new revival combines to provide all guests with comfortable accommodation, good food and a traditional Irish pub.

B&B from £39.50 to £44.50
€50.15 to €56.50

URSULA FOX
Manager

American Express
Diners
Mastercard
Visa

20 20

FAX

QUALITY CHARLEVILLE HOTEL AND SUITES

LOWER RATHMINES ROAD, DUBLIN 6
TEL: 01-406 6100 FAX: 01-406 6200
EMAIL: charleville@charleville.premgroup.ie

HOTEL ★★★ MAP 8 O 11

Ideally located for business or leisure, situated in the popular suburb of Rathmines Village, only a 15 min walk to Dublin's famous Grafton St, museums, galleries and theatres. Most rooms are suites offering sittingroom, kitchenette, separate bedrooms and bathroom. All equipped with fax machine, voice mail, CD player and modem point. Carmines Restaurant has an extensive European menu, also there is a multi-level themed bar. Free underground parking for residents.

WEB: www.premgroup.ie

Member of Choice Hotels Ireland

B&B from £75.00 to £100.00
€95.23 to €126.97

ANN BYRNE
General Manager

American Express
Diners
Mastercard
Visa

☺ Midweek specials from £135.00

51 51

Inet FAX

Room rates are IR£ per room per night

QUALITY HOTEL & SUITES

NAAS ROAD,
CO. DUBLIN
TEL: 01-458 7000 FAX: 01-458 7019
EMAIL: info@qualitycitywest.com

HOTEL ★★★ MAP 8 O 11

Located just 8 miles from Dublin City Centre and 20 minutes drive to Dublin Airport on the main N7 Dublin-Cork Route. A unique concept in hotel and suite accommodation, the hotel is comprised of 7 separate units. In addition to spacious bedrooms, the hotel offers one and two bedroom suites. Each suite offers the independence of a lounge, dining area and kitchenette. Free carparking for guests, hotel restaurant plus residents' bar.

WEB: www.premgroup.com

Member of Choice Hotels International

B&B from £57.00 to £65.00
€72.38 to €82.53

EVELYN HARAN
General Manager

American Express
Diners
Mastercard
Visa

144   144

Closed 24 - 28 December

RAGLAN LODGE

10 RAGLAN ROAD, BALLSBRIDGE,
DUBLIN 4
TEL: 01-660 6697 FAX: 01-660 6781

GUESTHOUSE ★★★★ MAP 8 O 11

Raglan Lodge is a magnificent Victorian residence dating from 1861. It is just ten minutes from the heart of Dublin in a most peaceful location. There are seven guest rooms, all of which have bathrooms en suite, colour TV, radio/alarm, telephone and tea/coffee facilities. Several of the rooms are noteworthy for their fine proportions and high ceilings. National winner of the Galtee Irish Breakfast Award. Secure car parking facilities. Recommended by RAC, AA and Egon Ronay.

B&B from £50.00 to £60.00
€63.49 to €76.18

HELEN MORAN
Proprietress

American Express
Diners
Mastercard
Visa

7   7

IRISH HOTELS FEDERATION

Closed 20 December - 06 January

RATHMINES CAPITAL HOTEL

LOWER RATHMINES ROAD,
DUBLIN 6
TEL: 01-496 6966 FAX: 01-491 0603
EMAIL: info@rathminescapital-hotel.com

HOTEL ★★★ MAP 8 O 11

The Rathmines Capital Hotel, located in a vibrant district of great character, abundant shopping and lively nightlife. Just ten minutes walk from the city centre. We offer a wealth of comforts for the most discerning guest including en suite facilities, remote control TV, direct dial phone and many other amenities. The hotel also features our "Savannah" café bar, the perfect place to enjoy a relaxing drink or coffee.

WEB: www.capital-hotels.com

B&B from £45.00 to £60.00
€57.14 to €76.18

FRANCES DEMPSEY
General Manager

American Express
Diners
Mastercard
Visa

54   54

IRISH HOTELS FEDERATION

Closed 24 - 26 December

B&B rates are IR£ per person sharing per night incl. Breakfast

RED COW MORAN HOTEL

RED COW COMPLEX, NAAS ROAD,
DUBLIN 22
TEL: 01-459 3650 FAX: 01-459 1588
EMAIL: reservations@morangroup.ie

HOTEL ★★★★ MAP 8 O 11

4**** Red Cow Moran Hotel combines classic elegance with modern design, situated at the Gateway to the Provinces, convenient to city centre, 15mins from Dublin Airport. Bedrooms are fully air-conditioned with colour teletext TV, direct dial phones/fax, hairdryer, trouser press & tea/coffee facilities. The complex boasts a choice of lively bars and features two superb restaurants and a carvery restaurant, conference facilities, baby sitting service on request. Night Club. Free carparking. AA 4 Star.

WEB: www.redcowhotel.com

B&B from £44.00 to £95.00
€55.87 to €120.63

TOM & SHEILA MORAN
Proprietors

American Express
Diners
Mastercard
Visa

Closed 24 - 26 December

RIVER HOUSE HOTEL

23/24 EUSTACE STREET, TEMPLE BAR,
DUBLIN 2
TEL: 01-670 7655 FAX: 01-670 7650
EMAIL: riverhousehotel@compuserve.com

HOTEL U MAP 8 O 11

A downtown Dublin hotel located in Dublin's colourful and exciting Temple Bar area. With its cobbled streets, shops, art galleries, bars, restaurants and lively night life, Temple Bar has become a tourist attraction itself. All our 29 bedrooms are en suite and have tea/coffee making facilities, remote control TV, radio, hairdryer and direct dial telephone. Hotel facilities include Danger Doyles Bar and the sound proofed The Zazu Nightclub.

WEB: www.visunet.ie/riverhouse

B&B from £34.50 to £75.00
€43.81 to €95.23

SHEELAGH CONWAY
Proprietor

American Express
Diners
Visa

Midweek specials from £93.00

Closed 24 - 27 December

ROYAL DUBLIN HOTEL

O'CONNELL STREET,
DUBLIN 1
TEL: 01-873 3666 FAX: 01-873 3120
EMAIL: enq@royaldublin.com

HOTEL ★★★ MAP 8 O 11

Located in the heart of the city on Dublin's most famous street, O'Connell Street. Perfect base from which to explore shops, theatres, museums and galleries. Guest rooms include hairdryer, tea/coffee making facilities, direct dial telephone and all are en suite. Relax in the elegant Georgian Room or enjoy the lively Raffles Bar. Excellent food available all day in the Cafe Royale Brasserie. Secure car park available.

WEB: www.royaldublin.com

Member of Best Western Hotels

B&B from £55.00 to £80.00
€69.84 to €101.58

DARRAGH BRADY
General Manager

American Express
Diners
Mastercard
Visa

Closed 24 - 26 December

Room rates are IR£ per room per night

SACHS HOTEL

19-29 MOREHAMPTON ROAD,
DONNYBROOK, DUBLIN 4
TEL: 01-668 0995 FAX: 01-668 6147

HOTEL ★★ MAP 8 O 11

Set in a quiet exclusive south city
location, yet only a short stroll from
the heart of Dublin. A unique blend
of Georgian excellence and modern
amenities. You will feel the warmth
of our welcome and the charm of the
traditional decor. Spacious
bedrooms individually designed and
with en suite, colour TV and direct
dial phone. Extensive conference
and banqueting facilities.

B&B from £42.50 to £75.00
€53.96 to €95.23

ANN BYRNE
Manager

American Express
Diners
Mastercard
Visa

20 20

Open All Year

SCHOOL HOUSE HOTEL

2-8 NORTHUMBERLAND ROAD,
BALLSBRIDGE, DUBLIN 4
TEL: 01-667 5014 FAX: 01-667 5015

HOTEL ★★★★ MAP 8 O 11

Situated in the heart of one of
Dublin's most fashionable districts
the hotel offers superb
accommodation, good food and
lively pub. All 31 bedrooms are
furnished to the highest international
standard, catering for both business
and leisure visitors to the capital.
Located just a short walk from the
commercial, cultural and
entertainment heart of the city, the
School House Hotel is poised to
become one of the city's leading new
hotels.

Member of Signature Hotels

B&B from £70.00 to £95.00
€88.88 to €120.63

BERTIE KELLY
General Manager

American Express
Diners
Mastercard
Visa

Weekend 2 Nights B&B £125.00

31 31

Closed 24 - 27 December

SHELBOURNE DUBLIN

27 ST. STEPHEN'S GREEN,
DUBLIN 2
TEL: 01-663 4500 FAX: 01-661 6006
EMAIL: shelbourneinfo@forte-hotels.com

HOTEL ★★★★★ MAP 8 O 11

Ireland's most distinguished
address, provides the ultimate in
luxury and service. In the heart of
Dublin, overlooking St. Stephen's
Green, within walking distance of
shopping areas and Dublin's social
and cultural life. The hotel has 190
rooms, 2 bars and 2 restaurants.
The Lord Mayor's Lounge is a must
for afternoon tea. The Shelbourne
Club offers exclusive surroundings
with fantastic choice of equipment,
18m pool, sauna, steam room,
jacuzzi and top class cardiovascular
equipment. Strictly over 18's only.
WAP: wap.shelbourne.ie

WEB: www.shelbourne.ie

Room Rate from £155.00 to £350.00
€196.81 to €444.41

JEAN RICOUX
General Manager

American Express
Diners
Mastercard
Visa

190 190

alc

Open All Year

B&B rates are IR£ per person sharing per night incl. Breakfast

SHELDON PARK HOTEL & LEISURE CENTRE

KYLEMORE ROAD,
DUBLIN 12
TEL: 01-460 1055 FAX: 01-460 1880
EMAIL: info@sheldonpark.ie

HOTEL ★★★ MAP 8 O 11

Warm and friendly, the Sheldon Park Hotel is ideally situated just 20 mins from Dublin Airport and 20 mins from the city centre. Just off the M50, we offer easy access to Ireland's most scenic country routes. Spend a relaxing day in our leisure centre, complete with swimming pool, sauna and jacuzzi and finish with a meal in our bistro style restaurant followed by live entertainment.

WEB: www.sheldonpark.ie

B&B from £35.00 to £55.00
€44.44 to €69.84

MAURA BISSETT
General Manager

American Express
Diners
Mastercard
Visa

72 72

Closed 24 - 26 December

ST. AIDEN'S GUESTHOUSE

32 BRIGHTON ROAD, RATHGAR,
DUBLIN 6
TEL: 01-490 2011 FAX: 01-492 0234
EMAIL: staidens@eircom.net

GUESTHOUSE ★★★ MAP 8 O 11

St. Aiden's charming family-run guesthouse is modernised to the highest standard of comfort and elegance while preserving its early Victorian character. Located in one of Dublin's most prestigious areas 15 mins from city centre on an excellent bus route, 10 mins from the M50 with its links to the airport and national routes, private parking at rear. Hospitality tray and books are provided in lovely drawing room. Under the personal care of Maura O'Carroll and recommended by AA ♦♦♦.

B&B from £27.50 to £40.00
€34.92 to €50.79

MAURA O'CARROLL
Proprietress

Mastercard
Visa

☺ Midweek specials from £60.00

8 8

Open All Year

ST. ANDREWS

1 LAMBAY ROAD, DRUMCONDRA,
DUBLIN 9
TEL: 01-837 4684 FAX: 01-857 0446
EMAIL: andrew@dublinn.com

GUESTHOUSE ★★★ MAP 8 O 11

Welcome to St Andrews, situated 10 mins from city centre, airport & car ferry. Refurbished to a Bord Failte Grade A standard we offer a variety of en suite rooms with direct dial phone, multi-channel TV, hairdryer. Hospitality trolley is provided in guests' lounge. Excellent base for exploring the famed attractions of Dublin - Temple Bar, Grafton St, Trinity College, museums, theatres, galleries, etc. Recommended by AA and RAC. Recently awarded the Sparkling Diamond accolade by RAC.

WEB: www.dublinn.com/andrew

Member of Premier Guesthouses

B&B from £25.00 to £35.00
€31.74 to €44.44

ROSE AND TERRY MASTERSON
Owners

American Express
Mastercard
Visa

13 13

Open All Year

Room rates are IR£ per room per night

STAIR CASE GUEST HOUSE

**21 AUNGIER STREET,
DUBLIN 1
TEL: 01-475 9759 FAX: 01-475 9760**

GUESTHOUSE P MAP 8 O 11

Location: No 21 Aungier Street provides attractive guest accommodation in one of Dublin's most historic houses. It is situated between St. Stephen's Green and Dublin Castle within walking distance of most of the city's main attractions including Temple Bar and Grafton Street.

**B&B from £37.00 to £40.00
€46.98 to €50.79**

**MARGARET JOHNSTONE
Manageress**

American Express
Visa

12 12

Closed 24 - 27 December

STAUNTONS ON THE GREEN

**83 ST. STEPHEN'S GREEN,
DUBLIN 2
TEL: 01-478 2300 FAX: 01-478 2263
EMAIL: hotels@indigo.ie**

GUESTHOUSE ★★★ MAP 8 O 11

Large Georgian house overlooking St. Stephen's Green, own private gardens. All rooms are en suite and fully equipped with direct dial telephone, TV and tea/coffee welcoming trays, trouser press and hairdryer. It is close to museums, galleries, Grafton Street shopping area and many other major tourist attractions. Stauntons On the Green occupies one of Dublin's most prestigious locations, close to many corporate headquarters and government buildings.

WEB: indigo.ie/~hotels

**B&B from £55.00 to £70.00
€69.84 to €88.88**

JOANNE NORMAN

American Express
Diners
Mastercard
Visa

30 30

Closed 24 - 27 December

STEPHEN'S GREEN HOTEL

**ST. STEPHEN'S GREEN,
DUBLIN 2
TEL: 01-607 3600 FAX: 01-661 5663
EMAIL: stephensgreenres@ocallaghanhotels.ie**

HOTEL N MAP 8 O 11

This deluxe boutique hotel enjoys a superb location on St. Stephen's Green, Dublin City Centre - in the heart of the business, cultural and shopping districts. Incorporating 2 historically listed Georgian houses, once home to famous Irish political leaders and writers, the hotel is a splendid craft of Georgian elegance and contemporary style with a 4 storey glass atrium overlooking St. Stephen's Green. 64 luxurious airconditioned guestrooms and 11 suites, restaurant, traditional bar, gym. Car parking. USA Toll Free Reservations 1800 5699983.

WEB: www.ocallaghanhotels.ie

Member of O'Callaghan Hotels

**B&B from £99.00 to £150.00
€125.70 to €190.46**

**SALLY HUGHES
General Manager**

American Express
Diners
Mastercard
Visa

Weekend specials from £180.00

75 75

Inet

IRISH HOTELS FEDERATION

Open All Year

B&B rates are IR£ per person sharing per night incl. Breakfast

TAVISTOCK HOUSE

64 RANELAGH ROAD, RANELAGH, DUBLIN 6
TEL: 01-496 7377 FAX: 01-496 7377
EMAIL: info@tavistockhouse.com

GUESTHOUSE ★★★ MAP 8 O 11

Magnificent Victorian house, tastefully converted retaining all its original plasterwork - very homely. Situated on the city side of Ranelagh Village, on the corner of Ranelagh / Northbrook Roads. We are only 7 mins walk from Stephen's Green in the heart of Dublin, near Helen Dillon's world famous garden. All rooms have colour TV, direct dial phone, hair dryer and tea/coffee making facilities. Private parking. There are a wide variety of restaurants locally. AA ♦♦♦. Internet facilities.

WEB: www.tavistockhouse.com

B&B from £25.00 to £60.00
€31.74 to €76.18

MAUREEN & BRIAN CUSACK
Co-Owners

American Express
Mastercard
Visa

☺ Midweek specials from £100.00

7 7

Open All Year

TEMPLE BAR HOTEL

FLEET STREET, TEMPLE BAR, DUBLIN 2
TEL: 01-677 3333 FAX: 01-677 3088
EMAIL: templeb@iol.ie

HOTEL ★★★ MAP 8 O 11

A Tower Group Hotel, located in the heart of Dublin's vibrant Temple Bar area, the Temple Bar Hotel is the ideal base from which to explore Dublin's cultural attractions, bars & restaurants, shops and theatres, Trinity College, Dublin Castle and the shopping districts of Grafton Street and Henry Street are just a short walk from our door. Within easy access from train stations, airport and Dublin Port, there is also a multi storey carpark nearby.

WEB: www.towerhotelgroup.ie

Member of Tower Hotel Group

B&B from £55.00 to £80.00
€69.84 to €101.58

DEIRDRE POWER
General Manager

American Express
Diners
Mastercard
Visa

☺ Weekend specials from £95.00

129 129

Closed 23 - 27 December

TRINITY CAPITAL HOTEL

PEARSE STREET, DUBLIN 2
TEL: 01-648 1000 FAX: 01-648 1010
EMAIL: info@trinitycapital-hotel.com

HOTEL P MAP 8 O 11

The Trinity Capital Hotel offers the perfect location to enjoy Dublin at its best. Designed with a full compliment of amenities the hotel presents a classic contemporary style with an art deco influence. Offering superb deluxe accommodation, a modern cafe style lobby bar, a Mediterranean style restaurant Siena and a themed bar and nightclub, Fireworks, our hotel offers an experience not to be missed.

WEB: www.capital-hotels.com

B&B from £75.00 to £79.50
€95.23 to €100.94

MARY RYAN

American Express
Diners
Mastercard
Visa

84 84

Closed 24 - 26 December

Room rates are IR£ per room per night

TRINITY LODGE

**12 SOUTH FREDERICK STREET,
DUBLIN 2**
TEL: 01-679 5044 FAX: 01-679 5223
EMAIL: trinitylodge@eircom.net

GUESTHOUSE ★★★ MAP 8 O 11

Situated in the heart of Dublin, Trinity Lodge offers superb en suite accommodation in a traditional Georgian townhouse. You will find all of Dublin's business, shopping and historic centres right on our doorstep and you are just steps away from Grafton Street, Trinity College and vibrant Temple Bar. Each room, from our singles to our 650sq' suites is equipped with air conditioning, personal safe, satellite TV, radio alarm, tea/coffee facilities and trouser press.

B&B from £50.00 to £100.00
€63.49 to €126.97

PETER MURPHY
Managing Director

American Express
Diners
Mastercard
Visa

10 10

Open All Year

UPPERCROSS HOUSE

**26-30 UPPER RATHMINES ROAD,
DUBLIN 6**
TEL: 01-497 5486 FAX: 01-497 5361
EMAIL: uppercrosshotel@ireland.com

HOTEL ★★★ MAP 8 O 11

Uppercross House is a hotel providing 49 bedrooms of the highest standard of comfort. All with direct dial phone, TV, tea/coffee maker, central heating and all en suite. Uppercross House has its own secure parking and is ideally situated in Dublin's south-side 2km from St. Stephen's Green and R.D.S., with excellent public transport from directly outside the door. A fully licensed restaurant and bar opens nightly with a warm and friendly atmosphere.

WEB: www.uppercrosshousehotel.com

B&B from £39.50 to £59.50
€50.15 to €75.55

DAVID MAHON
Proprietor

American Express
Diners
Mastercard
Visa

49 49

Inet

Closed 23 - 30 December

WATERLOO HOUSE

**8-10 WATERLOO ROAD,
BALLSBRIDGE, DUBLIN 4**
TEL: 01-660 1888 FAX: 01-667 1955
EMAIL: waterloohouse@eircom.net

GUESTHOUSE ★★★★ MAP 8 O 11

A warm welcome awaits you at this luxury guesthouse, in the heart of Georgian Dublin. It comprises 2 Georgian houses, refurbished to superb standard, retaining original features, offer unique atmosphere, style, elegance. Mins from; RDS, St. Stephen's Green, Grafton Street, city centre. Delicious breakfast is served in dining room, overlooking conservatory & gardens. Lift & carpark. Recommended: Bridgestone 100 Best Places, Alister Sawday's Special Places to Stay, Michelin Guide and AA ◆◆◆◆◆.

WEB: www.waterloohouse.ie

B&B from £32.50 to £55.00
€41.27 to €69.84

EVELYN CORCORAN
Proprietor

Mastercard
Visa

17 17

Closed 23 - 28 December

B&B rates are IR£ per person sharing per night incl. Breakfast

WATERLOO LODGE

**23 WATERLOO ROAD,
BALLSBRIDGE, DUBLIN 4
TEL: 01-668 5380 FAX: 01-668 5786
EMAIL: info@waterloolodge.com**

GUESTHOUSE ★★★ MAP 8 O 11

Waterloo Lodge is centrally located in Ballsbridge on the south side of Dublin City. Just minutes walk from the city centre, Stephen's Green, Temple Bar, museums, theatres, restaurants and pubs with a bus route outside our door. Our rooms are en suite, tastefully decorated, have direct dial phone, cable TV and hairdryer. Most are non-smoking. Fax and e-mail facilities are available. We assure you of a warm welcome and a pleasant stay.

WEB: www.waterloolodge.com

B&B from £29.50 to £45.00
€37.46 to €57.14

CATHAL DALY
Owner

Mastercard
Visa

☺ Midweek specials from £97.50

10 10

Closed 24 - 26 December

WEST COUNTY HOTEL

**CHAPELIZOD,
DUBLIN 20
TEL: 01-626 4011 FAX: 01-623 1378**

HOTEL ★★ MAP 8 O 11

The West County Hotel, an established hotel, situated on the main West Road and M50 motorway, convenient to city centre, airport and all main routes. Each of our en suite bedrooms is equipped with TV, direct dial phone, tea/coffee making facilities, ironing board and hairdryer. Our restaurant offers table d'hôte and à la carte menus and superb wines. 5 excellent golf courses within easy reach. Golf packages available. A warm and friendly welcome awaits you at the West County Hotel.

B&B from £43.50 to £50.00
€52.23 to €63.49

GERALD COLGAN
Proprietor

American Express
Diners
Mastercard
Visa

50 50

Closed 24 - 26 December

WESTBURY

**GRAFTON STREET,
DUBLIN 2
TEL: 01-679 1122 FAX: 01-679 7078
EMAIL: westbury_hotel@jurysdoyle.com**

HOTEL ★★★★★ MAP 8 O 11

Nestled in the heart of cosmopolitan Grafton Street, in the heart of Dublin's city centre. The Westbury can best be described as a truly international hotel which embraces the warmth and vitality of contemporary Dublin. Chic, modern and as popular with famous personalities from the arts and entertainment world, as with local Dubliners, the hotel is within 2 mins walk of central business districts, theatres, entertainment and cultural attractions.

WEB: www.jurysdoyle.com

B&B from £116.00 to £179.00
€147.29 to €227.28

PARAIC DOYLE
General Manager

American Express
Diners
Mastercard
Visa

☺ Weekend Specials from £190.00

204 204

Inet FAX

Open All Year

Room rates are IR£ per room per night

RADISSON SAS ST HELEN'S HOTEL

STILLORGAN ROAD, BLACKROCK, CO. DUBLIN
TEL: 01-218 6000 FAX: 01-218 6010
EMAIL: info@dubzh.rdsas.com

HOTEL U MAP 8 O 11

Conveniently located just 3 miles to the city centre, near to golf courses and Wicklow Gardens, we offer luxury accommodation and the highest international service standards. All spacious and air-conditioned rooms are equipped with safe, cable TV with in-house movie channels, minibar, trouser press, hairdryer, bathrobes, fax and modem as well as ice bucket and tea/coffee facilities. Italian and fine dining restaurants, bars, fitness room, beauty salon, snooker and free parking.

WEB: www.radisson.com/dublin.ie

Member of Radisson SAS Hotels

B&B from £125.00 to £125.00
€158.72 to €158.72

SUSANNE HAZENBERG
General Manager

American Express
Diners
Mastercard
Visa

151 151

a/c Inet

Open All Year

STILLORGAN PARK HOTEL

STILLORGAN ROAD, BLACKROCK, CO. DUBLIN
TEL: 01-288 1621 FAX: 01-283 1610
EMAIL: sales@stillorganpark.com

HOTEL ★★★ MAP 8 O 11

Dublin's premier hotel for the southside. After an investment of £12 million, this contemporary property now boasts 99 en suite fully air-conditioned bedrooms, a new fully equipped conference and banqueting centre catering for up to 500 delegates, a superb Mediterranean style restaurant and a comfortable bar. Located just a few minutes from Dublin's city centre on main N11, parking for 350 cars. 10 minutes from UCD/RDS. 20 mins. from Druids Glen Golf Course. AA 4****.

WEB: www.stillorganpark.com

B&B from £55.00 to £95.00
€69.84 to €120.62

RONAN DORAN
General Manager

American Express
Diners
Mastercard
Visa

Weekend specials from £120.00

99 99

a/c Inet

Open All Year

AIRPORT VIEW

COLD WINTERS, BLAKES CROSS, CO. DUBLIN
TEL: 01-843 8756 FAX: 01-807 1949
EMAIL: gerrybutterly@hotmail.com

GUESTHOUSE P MAP 8 O 11

Airport View newly built luxurious guesthouse situated 4.5 miles from Dublin Airport, on a 7 acre site. Incorporates 4 poster bedroom with jacuzzi, TV lounge, conference room, snooker room, restaurant. All rooms en suite, TV, tea/coffee, fax and computer outlet facilities. Private car park, golf packages available. Airport View is conveniently located 50 yds off the main Dublin-Belfast road. It has all the features of a luxury hotel.

WEB: www.airportviewguesthouse.com

B&B from £25.00 to £35.00
€31.74 to €44.44

GERARD BUTTERLY/
ANNEMARIE BEGGS Proprietors

Mastercard
Visa

Midweek specials from £75.00

10 10

P Y S Y Inet FAX

Open All Year

B&B rates are IR£ per person sharing per night incl. Breakfast

TUDOR HOUSE

DALKEY,
CO. DUBLIN
TEL: 01-285 1528 FAX: 01-284 8133
EMAIL: tudor@iol.ie

GUESTHOUSE ★★★★ MAP 08 P 11

An elegant listed manor house with secluded grounds in the heart of Dalkey. Period ambience and personal friendly service are the hallmarks of Tudor House. Bedrooms are individually decorated and enjoy views of Dublin Bay. Dalkey is a charming heritage town with Norman castles and quaint harbours. It has many excellent restaurants and pubs. It is 3km from Dun Laoghaire Ferry Port and offers rapid access to Dublin City.

WEB: www.iol.ie/tudor

B&B from £39.00 to £45.00
€49.52 to €57.14

KATIE HAYDON
Owner

Mastercard

Visa

6 6

Open All Year

DUNES HOTEL ON THE BEACH

DONABATE,
CO. DUBLIN
TEL: 01-843 6153 FAX: 01-843 6111

HOTEL R MAP 12 O 12

Occupying one of the best locations on the east coast on the beach at Donabate, our hotel is only 10 minutes north of Dublin Airport and 30 minutes from the city centre. Surrounded by 6 golf courses made up of links and parkland courses. Our en suite rooms have spectacular views of Lambay Island and Howth Head. Our bar and carvery offer the ideal ambience for a relaxing meal or drink. Breakfast served till noon.

B&B from £30.00 to £48.00
€38.09 to €60.95

PAULA BALDWIN
Proprietor

Mastercard

Visa

18 18

Closed 24 - 26 December

GREAT SOUTHERN HOTEL DUBLIN AIRPORT

DUBLIN AIRPORT,
CO. DUBLIN
TEL: 01-844 6000 FAX: 01-844 6001
EMAIL: res@dubairport.gsh.ie

HOTEL U MAP 12 O 11

Situated within the airport complex, just two minutes from the main terminal, the Great Southern Hotel provides a tranquil haven for the busy traveller. The guestrooms have every convenience and Potters Restaurant and Clancy's Bar allow guests unwind in stylish surroundings. The hotel has a wide range of conference rooms. Bookable worldwide through UTELL International or Central Reservations on 01-214 4800.

WEB: www.gsh.ie

Room Rate from £140.00 to £140.00
€177.76 to €177.76

EAMON DALY
General Manager

American Express

Diners

Mastercard

Visa

147 147

Closed 24 - 26 December

Room rates are IR£ per room per night

POSTHOUSE DUBLIN AIRPORT

DUBLIN AIRPORT, CO. DUBLIN
TEL: 01-808 0500 FAX: 01-844 6002
EMAIL: posthousedublin@hotmail.com

HOTEL ★★★★ MAP 12 O 11

A modern hotel located on the airport complex, offering a choice of standard and superior accommodation, and just 11.27km from the city centre. All 249 bedrooms are en suite with TV and pay movies, mini-bar, trouser press and hair dryer. 24 hour courtesy coach to and from the airport, 24 hour room service, superb choice of Sampans Oriental Restaurant and the Bistro Restaurant, traditional Irish Pub Bodhran Bar, with live music at weekends. Residents may use the ALSAA Leisure Centre (3 minutes walk) on a complimentary basis.

WEB: www.posthouse-hotels.com

Member of Forte & Meridien

B&B from £55.00 to £125.00
€69.84 to €158.71

BRIAN THORNTON
General Manager

American Express
Diners
Mastercard
Visa

☺ Weekend specials from £125.00

249 249

Closed 24 - 25 December

GLANDORE HOUSE

GLANDORE PARK, LWR MOUNTTOWN ROAD, DUN LAOGHAIRE, CO. DUBLIN
TEL: 01-280 3143 FAX: 01-280 2675
EMAIL: info@glandorehouse.com

GUESTHOUSE ★★★ MAP 8 P 11

Staying at Glandore House allows visitors to take a step back into a more gracious era while at the same time offering the most modern guesthouse facilities. All rooms are en suite with TV, direct dial phone, tea/coffee facilities. Trouser press/ironing centre. A 6 person lift and off street car parking is also available. Situated 5 min drive from Dun Laoghaire Ferry Terminal, DART station and bus terminals therefore offering easy accessibility to the city centre and surrounding areas.

WEB: www.glandorehouse.com

B&B from £30.00 to £45.00
€38.09 to €57.14

GRAINNE JACKMAN
Manager

Mastercard
Visa

12 12

Closed 22 December - 03 January

B&B rates are IR£ per person sharing per night incl. Breakfast

KINGSTON HOTEL

ADELAIDE ST., (OFF GEORGES ST.),
DUN LAOGHAIRE, CO. DUBLIN
TEL: 01-280 1810 FAX: 01-280 1237
EMAIL: reserve@kingstonhotel.com

HOTEL ★★ MAP 8 O 11

A delightful 38 bedroomed hotel with panoramic views of Dublin Bay, approximately 15 minutes from city centre. Beside ferryport and DART line. Situated convenient to R.D.S., Point Depot, Lansdowne Road and Leopardstown Racecourse. All rooms are en suite with direct dial phone, TV, tea/coffee making facilities. A family run hotel serving food all day in our lounge/bar and our Haddington Bistro opened nightly.

WEB: www.kingstonhotel.com

Member of MinOtel Ireland Hotel Group

B&B from £42.50 to £45.00
€53.96 to €57.14

JAMES J WALSH

American Express
Diners
Mastercard
Visa

38 38

Closed 25 December

PORT VIEW HOTEL

6/7 MARINE ROAD,
DUN LAOGHAIRE, CO. DUBLIN
TEL: 01-280 1663 FAX: 01-280 0447
EMAIL: portview@clubi.ie

HOTEL U MAP 8 P 11

The Port View Hotel, Dun Laoghaire, is ideally situated as a base for the social or serious golfer, within easy striking distance of several golf courses. Situated just 200 metres from Dun Laoghaire's high speed Ferry Port and 15 minutes by train to Dublin City. Why not relax after your long day by the open fire in our bar or sample some home produced food in a variety of surroundings.

B&B from £40.00 to £50.00
€50.79 to €63.49

DONOUGH DUIGNAN
Director

American Express
Mastercard
Visa

20 8

Closed 25 - 26 December

ROCHESTOWN LODGE HOTEL

ROCHESTOWN AVENUE,
DUN LAOGHAIRE, CO. DUBLIN
TEL: 01-285 3555 FAX: 01-285 3914

HOTEL ★★★ MAP 12 P 11

Located 2 miles from Dun Laoghaire Harbour and 5 miles from Dublin City centre. An excellent roads network leads to all areas of interest in Dublin and is a gateway to the sunny South East. The hotel boasts landscaped gardens and has 8 conference rooms, 68 en suite bedrooms, 3 bars and its own famous steak house restaurant. There are several championship golf courses in the area. During 2001 we will be adding a 5* leisure centre including 2 pools, jacuzzis, steam rooms and gym.

B&B from £40.00 to £60.00
€50.79 to €76.18

KEN FETHERSTON
Proprietor

American Express
Diners
Mastercard
Visa

68 68

Open All Year

Room rates are IR£ per room per night

ROYAL MARINE HOTEL

MARINE ROAD, DUN LAOGHAIRE,
CO. DUBLIN
TEL: 01-280 1911 FAX: 01-280 1089
EMAIL: ryan@indigo.ie

HOTEL ★★★ MAP 8 O 11

This elegant 19th century hotel, with panoramic views of Dublin Bay and the picturesque port of Dun Laoghaire, is set in its own landscaped gardens and features 103 bedrooms, including 8 Victorian four-poster suites. The elegant Bay Lounge, Toddy's Bar, and the Powerscourt Room Restaurant provide the ideal location to unwind. Only 20 mins to city centre by rapid rail or bus. Excellent conference facilities. Complimentary car parking. AA, RAC and Egon Ronay recommended.

WEB: www.ryan-hotels.com

B&B from £65.00 to £130.00
€82.53 to €165.07

PAUL MCCRACKEN
Operations Director

American Express
Diners
Mastercard
Visa

☺ Weekend specials from £100.00

103   103

Open All Year

BAILY COURT HOTEL

MAIN STREET, HOWTH,
CO. DUBLIN
TEL: 01-832 2691 FAX: 01-832 3730
EMAIL: info@bailycourthotel.com

HOTEL ★★ MAP 12 P 11

Located in the heart of the beautiful fishing village of Howth with 20 en suite rooms with TV, direct dial phone and tea/coffee making facilities. The city centre is 25 minutes away by DART and Dublin Airport 12km. A carvery lunch is served daily. Local amenities include golf, fishing and hill walking.

WEB: www.bailycourthotel.com

Member of Logis of Ireland

B&B from £35.50 to £37.50
€45.08 to €47.62

TOM MURPHY
Manager

American Express
Mastercard
Visa

20   20

Closed 24 - 26 December

DEER PARK HOTEL AND GOLF COURSES

HOWTH,
CO. DUBLIN
TEL: 01-832 2624 FAX: 01-839 2405
EMAIL: sales@deerpark.iol.ie

HOTEL ★★★ MAP 12 P 11

14km from Dublin City/Airport on a quiet hillside overlooking the bay, Deer Park enjoys spectacular elevated sea views. Featuring Ireland's largest golf complex (5 courses), 18m swimming pool, sauna and steam room and two all-weather tennis courts. Whether on a golfing holiday or a visit to Dublin you will find Deer Park the ideal choice.

WEB: www.deerpark-hotel.ie

Member of Coast and Country Hotels

B&B from £60.00 to £80.00
€76.18 to €101.58

DAVID & ANTOINETTE TIGHE
Managers

American Express
Diners
Mastercard
Visa

☺ Weekend specials from £105.00

80   80

Closed 23 - 27 December

B&B rates are IR£ per person sharing per night incl. Breakfast

KING SITRIC FISH RESTAURANT & ACCOMMODATION

EAST PIER, HOWTH,
CO. DUBLIN
TEL: 01-832 5235 FAX: 01-839 2442
EMAIL: info@kingsitric.ie

GUESTHOUSE N MAP 8 P 11

Est. 1971, Aidan and Joan MacManus have earned an international reputation for fresh seafood in their harbour-side restaurant in the picturesque fishing village of Howth. Now with 8 guest rooms, all with sea views. Wine lovers will enjoy browsing in the atmospheric wine cellar. For leisure pursuits, Howth is the perfect location for golfing, walking and sailing. Dublin City is 20 mins by DART; Dublin Airport 20 mins driving.

WEB: www.kingsitric.com

Member of Ireland's Blue Book

B&B from £45.00 to £75.00
€57.14 to €95.23

AIDAN AND JOAN MACMANUS

American Express
Diners
Mastercard
Visa

:/

Weekend specials from £110.00

8   8

Closed 21 January - 05 February

COURT HOTEL

KILLINEY BAY,
CO. DUBLIN
TEL: 01-285 1622 FAX: 01-285 2085
EMAIL: book@killineycourt.ie

HOTEL ★★★ MAP 8 P 10

Like a jewel in the crown, the Court Hotel, a Victorian mansion situated in Killiney, a magnificent seascape setting, south of Dublin. Features 86 en suite rooms, choice of Restaurants (Egon Ronay recommended). Cocktail Bar/Conservatory & Lounge - perfect place to relax and unwind in comfort. International state of the art conference centre with simultaneous interpreting equipment. Close to Leopardstown Racecourse and several golf courses. 100m to DART train serving Dublin, Howth & Bray.

WEB: www.killineycourt.ie

Member of Choice Hotels International

B&B from £49.50 to £76.50
€62.85 to €97.13

JOHN O'DOWD
Managing Director

American Express
Diners
Mastercard
Visa

:/

Weekend specials from £99.00

86   86

Open All Year

FITZPATRICK CASTLE DUBLIN

KILLINEY,
CO. DUBLIN
TEL: 01-230 5400 FAX: 01-230 5430
EMAIL: dublin@fitzpatricks.com

HOTEL ★★★★ MAP 8 P 10

Located in scenic Killiney with panoramic views of Dublin Bay Fitzpatrick Castle is ideally located 20 mins from Dublin City centre and close to the beauty of Wicklow County. Comprising of 113 newly refurbished Castle style rooms and suites, it boasts the renowned PJ's Restaurant, intimate Library Bar/Lounge, excellent health and fitness facilities and 22m pool. Our conference centre and banqueting suites cater for 4 to 400 people with state of the art communications and conference equipment.

WEB: www.fitzpatrickhotels.com

B&B from £84.50 to £92.00
€107.29 to €116.82

EOIN O'SULLIVAN
General Manager

American Express
Diners
Mastercard
Visa

Weekend specials from £140.00

113   113

Closed 24 - 26 December

Room rates are IR£ per room per night

BECKETTS COUNTRY HOUSE HOTEL

COOLDRINAGH HOUSE, LEIXLIP,
CO. KILDARE/DUBLIN
TEL: 01-624 7040 FAX: 01-624 7072
EMAIL: becketts@eircom.net

HOTEL ★★★ MAP 8 N 11

Becketts is situated in a quiet scenic area just off the N4 motorway at the Leixlip roundabout close to Dublin's new outer ring with easy access to Dublin Airport and all major road networks. Once home to the mother of Samuel Beckett the completely refurbished Cooldrinagh House is now home to Becketts. There are 4 suites and 6 luxury bedrooms and an elegant restaurant with a reputation for superb cuisine and full bar facilities.

B&B from £40.00 to £55.00
€50.79 to €69.84

JOHN O'BYRNE
Managing Director

American Express
Diners
Mastercard
Visa

10 10
Inet FAX

Open All Year

FINNSTOWN COUNTRY HOUSE HOTEL

NEWCASTLE ROAD, LUCAN,
CO. DUBLIN
TEL: 01-601 0700 FAX: 01-628 1088
EMAIL: manager@finnstown-hotel.ie

HOTEL ★★★ MAP 8 N 11

Finnstown Country House Hotel, although only 15 minutes drive by motorway from Dublin City Centre, it appears to lie in the very depths of the countryside, being surrounded as it is by imposing grounds and an immaculately maintained 18 hole putting course. A host of facilities includes an indoor heated swimming pool, tennis, gymnasium, Turkish bath and games room. The hotel offers 51 en suite bedrooms, each appointed with the latest in communication technology.

WEB: www.finnstown-hotel.ie
Member of Grand Heritage

B&B from £50.00 to £80.00
€63.48 to €101.58

PAULA SMITH
General Manager

American Express
Diners
Mastercard
Visa

 Weekend specials from £125.00

51 51

Open All Year

SPA HOTEL

LUCAN,
CO. DUBLIN
TEL: 01-628 0494 FAX: 01-628 0841
EMAIL: info@lucanspahotel.ie

HOTEL ★★ MAP 8 N 11

Situated on the N4, the gateway to the West, and 6km from M50, this elegant hotel is ideally located for convenience, comfort and is exceptionally well appointed with central heating, direct dial phone, colour TV, tea/coffee facilities and ironing board. Our restaurant offers a choice of 3 menus and superb wines. Ideal for conference and weddings alike. Special golf package available.

WEB: www.lucanspahotel.ie
Member of MinOtel Ireland Hotel Group

B&B from £43.50 to £50.00
€55.23 to €63.49

FRANK COLGAN
Director

American Express
Diners
Mastercard
Visa

70 70

Closed 25 December

B&B rates are IR£ per person sharing per night incl. Breakfast

WESTON WAY GUESTHOUSE

**2 WESTON PARK, LUCAN,
CO. DUBLIN WEST
TEL: 01-628 2855 FAX: 01-628 2855**

GUESTHOUSE ★★★ MAP 8 N 11

Near Castletown House, Japanese Gardens, National Stud, Kilmainham Gaol, Guinness Brewery, Christchurch, Trinity College. 20 minutes to city, 5 minutes to Ireland's biggest shopping centre, 15 minutes direct route to Dublin Airport.

B&B from £30.00 to £35.00
€38.09 to €44.44

ANGELA MCPARLAND & BILL DORTON Proprietors

6 6

Open All Year

CARRIAGE HOUSE

**LUSK (NEAR AIRPORT),
CO. DUBLIN
TEL: 01-843 8857 FAX: 01-843 8933
EMAIL: carrhous@iol.ie**

GUESTHOUSE U MAP 12 O 12

Carriage House is a family run, warm and friendly guesthouse conveniently situated 10 minutes from Dublin Airport, 20 minutes from city. On main Dublin bus route (33). Relax in our indoor heated swimming pool and sauna. Charming award winning gardens and putting green. All rooms en suite with direct dial phone and colour TV. Tea/coffee making facilities and secure car parking. Semi finalist in Leverclean accommodation awards. Breakfast menu.

WEB: www.iol.ie/~carrhous

B&B from £25.00 to £30.00
€31.74 to €38.09

ROBERT & GEMMA MCAULEY Proprietors

Mastercard

Visa

14 14

Open All Year

GRAND HOTEL

**MALAHIDE,
CO. DUBLIN
TEL: 01-845 0000 FAX: 01-816 8025
EMAIL: booking@thegrand.ie**

HOTEL ★★★★ MAP 12 O 12

The Grand Hotel is situated by the sea in the village of Malahide. Just 10 minutes drive from Dublin Airport and 20 minutes from the city centre, the hotel is ideally situated for guests staying for business or leisure. The conference and business centre is one of Ireland's largest and most successful. All 150 bedrooms have tea/coffee making facilities and fax/modem lines. Most bedrooms have spectacular sea views. Leisure centre includes a 21 metre swimming pool, jacuzzi and fully equipped gymnasium.

WEB: www.thegrand.ie

B&B from £97.50 to £165.00
€123.79 to €209.51

MATTHEW RYAN Operations Director

American Express

Diners

Mastercard

Visa

☺ 2 Nights Bed & Breakfast from £125.00

150 150

Closed 25 - 26 December

Room rates are IR£ per room per night

ISLAND VIEW HOTEL

**COAST ROAD, MALAHIDE,
CO. DUBLIN
TEL: 01-845 0099 FAX: 01-845 1498
EMAIL: info@islandviewhotel.ie**

HOTEL ★★ MAP 12 O 12

Island View Hotel is ideally located for comfort and convenience and just a 10 minute drive from Dublin Airport. Our rooms are all en suite and fully equipped with modern facilities. Oscar Taylors Restaurant is an exclusive 150 seater restaurant with a panoramic view of Lambay Island and Malahide coastline. The restaurant is noted for its excellent cuisine. The menu is extensive and moderately priced.

WEB: www.islandviewhotel.ie

B&B from £40.00 to £50.00
€50.79 to €63.49

PHILIP DARBY
Hotel Manager

American Express
Diners
Mastercard
Visa

✓

🖴☏📶⚡🇹🇨⚓CM∪🎵🅿🏧
10 10
☕

HOTELS

Open All Year

PORTMARNOCK HOTEL & GOLF LINKS

**STRAND ROAD, PORTMARNOCK,
CO. DUBLIN
TEL: 01-846 0611 FAX: 01-846 2442
EMAIL: reservations@portmarnock.com**

HOTEL ★★★★ MAP 12 O 11

.Once the home of the Jameson whiskey family, the Portmarnock Hotel and Golf Links is in a prime location reaching down to the sea, with views over the 18-hole Bernhard Langer designed links golf course. The 19th century character of the ancestral home is retained in the wood panelled walls, marble fireplaces and ornate ceilings of the Jameson Bar. Located just 15 minutes from Dublin Airport and 25 minutes from the city centre.

WEB: www.portmarnock.com
Member of Summit Hotels

B&B from £80.00 to £105.00
€101.58 to €133.32

SHANE COOKMAN
General Manager

American Express
Diners
Mastercard
Visa

✓🍴

😊 Weekend specials from £150.00

🖴☏📶⚡🇹🇨⚓CM✳∪🎵🅿
103 103
🍺alc🔥 ≡ inet

HOTELS

Open All Year

WHITE SANDS HOTEL

**COAST ROAD, PORTMARNOCK,
CO. DUBLIN
TEL: 01-846 0003 FAX: 01-846 0420
EMAIL: sandshotel@eircom.ie**

HOTEL ★★★ MAP 12 O 11

Ideally located facing the velvet strand. It is a 3*** family run Hotel. 10 minutes from Dublin Airport and 25 minutes from the City Centre with an abundance of golf courses nearby. The Hotel consists of 32 en suite tastefully decorated bedrooms, many with panoramic sea views. The Kingsford Smith Restaurant serves contemporary food with Irish flair. Carvery served daily. Private Function & Meeting rooms and the renowned Tamango Nightclub. Extensive Car Parking. Cead Mile Failte.

WEB: www.whitesandshotel.ie

B&B from £50.00 to £75.00
€63.49 to €95.23

GEORGINA HIGGINS
General Manager

American Express
Diners
Mastercard
Visa

🖴☏📶⚡🇹🇨⚓CM∪🎵🅿
32 32
alc ≡ inet

HOTELS

Closed 24 - 26 December

B&B rates are IR£ per person sharing per night incl. Breakfast

CITYWEST HOTEL, CONFERENCE, LEISURE & GOLF RESORT

SAGGART,
CO. DUBLIN
TEL: 01-401 0500 FAX: 01-458 8565
EMAIL: info@citywest-hotel.iol.ie

HOTEL ★★★★ MAP 8 N 11

Nestling peacefuly in its own private estate located within easy reach of the City centre and Dublin Airport, this luxury 332 bedroom hotel boasts a 5***** leisure club with 20m pool, two 18 hole golf courses, golf academy and state-of-the-art convention centre (6,500 delegates). The Terrace Restaurant, fashionable grill room and carvery offer fine dining, whilst our lively lounges and bars are a popular meeting place for locals and visitors alike.

WEB: www.citywesthotel-ireland.com

B&B from £47.50 to £65.00
€60.31 to €82.53

JOHN GLYNN
Chief Executive

American Express
Diners
Mastercard
Visa

☺ Weekend specials from £99.00

332 332

Open All Year

ABIGAIL HOUSE

COMMONS ROAD, LOUGHLINSTOWN,
SHANKILL, CO. DUBLIN
TEL: 01-282 4747 FAX: 01-272 1068
EMAIL: abigailsguesthouse@ireland.com

GUESTHOUSE U MAP 8 O 11

Nestled in woodlands on the banks of the Shanganagh River just off N11 is Abigail's Guesthouse. Irish Tourist Board approved. Large carpark. Beautiful gardens. TV lounge with tea/coffee facilities. 10 ground floor en suite rooms with direct dial phone, hairdryer, iron, etc. on request. City centre 30 minutes. Dun Laoire Ferryport 15 minutes. Convenient Shankill DART and city bus routes. Local amenities: golf, Druid's Glen, Woodbrook, Powerscourt, Leopardstown Races, bars and restaurants.

B&B from £22.50 to £30.00
€28.57 to €38.09

IMELDA REYNOLDS
Proprietor

Mastercard
Visa

11 10

Closed 16 December - 08 January

REDBANK HOUSE GUESTHOUSE & RESTAURANT

6 & 7 CHURCH STREET, SKERRIES,
CO. DUBLIN
TEL: 01-849 0439 FAX: 01-849 1598
EMAIL: redbank@eircom.net

GUESTHOUSE ★★★ MAP 12 P 12

Enjoy the extended hospitality of the McCoy's in Redbank House. The world famous seafood restaurant is the dining room of Redbank House. The seven en suite rooms have the McCoys sense of style and elegance. The area is particularly rich in golf courses and a wide variety of leisure activities includes sea fishing, boat trips, sailing and horse riding. The Chef Proprietor Terry McCoy cooks the catch of the day landed at Skerries Pier specialising in the world famous Dublin Bay prawns.

WEB: www.redbank.ie

Member of Logis of Ireland

B&B from £35.00 to £40.00
€44.44 to €50.79

TERRY MCCOY
Proprietor

American Express
Diners
Mastercard
Visa

☺ Weekend specials from £85.00

7 7

Closed 24 - 27 December

REDBANK LODGE & RESTAURANT

12 CONVENT LANE, SKERRIES,
CO. DUBLIN
TEL: 01-849 1005 FAX: 01-849 1598
EMAIL: redbank@eircom.net

GUESTHOUSE ★★★ MAP 12 P 12

Situated in the picturesque fishing port of Skerries, North County Dublin. Each of the five en suite double bedrooms are elegantly decorated with direct dial telephone and TV. Adjacent to the award winning Redbank Restaurant, with its famous reputation for superb cuisine (fish dishes our speciality) and a well stocked wine cellar. With easy access to Dublin City & Dublin Airport as well as enjoying local attractions such as Ardgillan Demesne, the nearby Boyne Valley & Newgrange.

WEB: www.guesthousesireland.com

Member of Logis of Ireland

B&B from £27.00 to £30.00
€34.28 to €38.09

TERRY MCCOY
Owner

American Express
Diners
Mastercard
Visa

Weekend specials from £85.00

5 5

Closed 24 - 28 December

MARINE HOTEL

SUTTON CROSS,
DUBLIN 13
TEL: 01-839 0000 FAX: 01-839 0442
EMAIL: info@marinehotel.ie

HOTEL ★★★ MAP 12 P 11

The Marine Hotel 3*** (AA***) overlooks the north shore of Dublin Bay. The two acres of lawn sweep down to the sea shore. All bedrooms are en suite and have trouser press, TV, Direct Dial phone and tea/coffee facilities. The city centre is 6km away and the airport 25 minutes drive. Close by is the DART rapid rail system. The hotel has a heated indoor swimming pool and sauna. Nearby are the Royal Dublin and Portmarnock championship golf courses.

WEB: www.marinehotel.ie

B&B from £60.00 to £90.00
€76.18 to €114.28

SHEILA BAIRD
General Manager

American Express
Diners
Mastercard
Visa

Weekend specials from £99.00

50 50

alc Inet

Closed 25 - 27 December

FORTE TRAVELODGE

PINNOCK HILL, SWORDS ROUNDABOUT,
BELFAST ROAD, CO. DUBLIN
TEL: 1800-709709 FAX: 01-840 9256

HOTEL U MAP 8 O 11

Situated only 12.8km from Dublin City centre on the Dublin to Belfast road and minutes from the airport, this superb modern hotel offers comfortable yet affordable, accommodation. Each room is large enough to sleep up to three adults, a child under 12 and a baby in a cot. Excellent range of facilities, from en suite bathroom to colour TV including Sky Sports and Sky Movies. Unbeatable value for business or leisure. Sited next to Little Chef restaurant.

WEB: www.travelodge.co.uk

Room Rate from £49.95 to £69.95
€63.42 to €88.82

BRIDGET AIKEN
Manager

American Express
Diners
Mastercard
Visa

100 100

Open All Year

B&B rates are IR£ per person sharing per night incl. Breakfast

GLENMORE HOUSE

AIRPORT ROAD, NEVINSTOWN, SWORDS, CO. DUBLIN
TEL: 01-840 3610 FAX: 01-840 4148
EMAIL: enquiries@glenmorehouse.com

GUESTHOUSE ★★★ MAP 12 O 12

Ideally situated just 1km from Dublin Airport and 20 minutes from the city centre, on the main airport/city bus routes, Glenmore House is a spacious family-run guesthouse set in 2 acres of gardens, lawns and private secure carparks. All rooms are beautifully decorated with bathroom, phone, TV, tea/coffee facilities and hairdryer. The warmest of welcomes at a very reasonable cost for business and leisure alike.

WEB: www.glenmorehouse.com

B&B from £25.00 to £35.00
€31.74 to €44.44

REBECCA GIBNEY
Proprietor

Mastercard

Visa

20 20

HOTELS FEDERATION

Closed 24 - 29 December

ASHVIEW HOUSE

THE WARD, ASHBOURNE ROAD, CO. DUBLIN
TEL: 01-835 0499

GUESTHOUSE ★★ MAP 12 O 11

A family run warm and friendly 2** guesthouse with guest sitting room, snooker room, private car park and landscaped gardens, golf, horse riding and swimming nearby. Situated on the main Dublin/Derry road, N2, 11km from Dublin City, 9km from Dublin Airport. Close to Fairyhouse Racecourse and Tattersalls Sales. Located 5km from Ashbourne it's an ideal touring centre for Newgrange, Slane Castle and the Boyne in Co. Meath. Clay pigeon shooting and fishing in the Boyne River.

B&B from £20.00 to £25.00
€25.39 to €31.74

JOSEPHINE FAY
Proprietor

8 3

HOTELS FEDERATION

Closed 24 - 28 December

BEAUFORT HOUSE

GHAN ROAD, CARLINGFORD, CO. LOUTH
TEL: 042-937 3879 FAX: 042-937 3878

GUESTHOUSE ★★★ MAP 12 O 5

Beaufort House, AA ♦♦♦♦♦, a magnificent shoreside residence with glorious sea and mountain views in medieval Carlingford village. Your hosts, Michael & Glynnis Caine, Bord Failte award winners of excellence, will ensure the highest standards. In-house activities include sailing school and yacht charter. Golfing arranged in any of five golf courses within 20 mins of Beaufort House. Helipad and private car parking. Dinner by prior arrangement.

B&B from £25.00 to £30.00
€31.74 to €38.09

MICHAEL & GLYNNIS CAINE

Mastercard

Visa

5 5

HOTELS FEDERATION

Open All Year

Room rates are IR£ per room per night

McKEVITT'S VILLAGE HOTEL

MARKET SQUARE, CARLINGFORD, CO. LOUTH
TEL: 042-937 3116 FAX: 042-937 3144

HOTEL ★★ MAP 12 O 15

McKevitts Village Hotel is family owned and personally supervised by Kay & Terry McKevitt. At the hotel, pride of place is taken in the personal attention given to guests by owners and staff. Carlingford is one of Ireland's oldest and most interesting medieval villages. Beautifully situated on the shores of Carlingford Lough and half way between Dublin and Belfast.

Member of Irish Family Hotels

B&B from £35.00 to £45.00
€44.44 to €57.14

TERRY & KAY McKEVITT
Owners

Mastercard
Visa

15 15

alc

IRISH HOTELS FEDERATION

Open All Year

BELLINGHAM CASTLE HOTEL

CASTLEBELLINGHAM, CO. LOUTH
TEL: 042-937 2176 FAX: 042-937 2766
EMAIL: bellinghamcastle@eircom.net

HOTEL ★★ MAP 12 O 14

Bellingham Castle Hotel is situated close by the pleasant little village of Castlebellingham, Co. Louth, resting in countryside enveloped in history, legend and engaged in beautiful scenery. In the hotel itself, which is an elegant refurbished 17th century castle, you will find all the facilities of a modern hotel, harmonising beautifully with the antique decor and atmosphere of old world splendour.

WEB: www.bellinghamcastle.com

B&B from £40.00 to £40.00
€50.79 to €50.79

PASCHAL KEENAN
Manager

American Express
Mastercard
Visa

20 20

alc

Closed 24 - 26 December

BOYNE VALLEY HOTEL & COUNTRY CLUB

DROGHEDA, CO. LOUTH
TEL: 041-983 7737 FAX: 041-983 9188
EMAIL: reservations@boyne-valley-hotel.ie

HOTEL ★★★ MAP 12 O 13

Gracious country house on 16 acres of gardens and woodlands, beside historic town of Drogheda, south on the N1. 40km from Dublin and 32km airport. Boyne Restaurant with daily supply of fresh fish. Nearby, historic sites of Newgrange, Dowth, Knowth and medieval abbeys Mellifont and Monasterboice. Leisure club, 18 hole pitch & putt on site. 2 tennis courts. 34 new bedrooms opening May 1st 2001.

WEB: www.boyne-valley-hotel.ie

B&B from £55.00 to £55.00
€69.84 to €69.84

MICHAEL McNAMARA
Proprietor/Manager

American Express
Diners
Mastercard
Visa

Weekend specials from £120.00

37 37

alc Inet FAX

IRISH HOTELS FEDERATION

Open All Year

B&B rates are IR£ per person sharing per night incl. Breakfast

WESTCOURT HOTEL

WEST STREET, DROGHEDA,
CO. LOUTH
TEL: 041-983 0965 FAX: 041-983 0970

HOTEL ★★★ MAP 12 O 13

At the Westcourt Hotel, our visitors will find the highest standard of courtesy and efficiency coupled with luxurious surroundings in the heart of the historical town of Drogheda. Our bedrooms are all en suite and decorated with television, direct dial phone, tea/coffee making facilities. Our restaurant and traditional Irish bar have the finest food, drink, and atmosphere for you to enjoy. We pride ourselves on a highly personalised service and look forward to welcoming you.

B&B from £35.00 to £45.00
€44.44 to €57.14

BARRY TIERNEY
Manager

American Express
Diners
Mastercard
Visa

27 27

Closed 25 December

BALLYMASCANLON HOUSE HOTEL

DUNDALK,
CO. LOUTH
TEL: 042-937 1124 FAX: 042-937 1598
EMAIL: info@ballymascanlon.com

HOTEL ★★★ MAP 12 O 14

Ballymascanlon Hotel is a Victorian mansion set in 130 acre demesne on the scenic Cooley Peninsula. The hotel while retaining its old world ambience has recently had its facilities modernised. Our leisure centre incorporates a 20m deck level pool, leisure pool, sauna, jacuzzi, steam room, gymnasium and tennis courts. Our 18 hole Parkland golf course surrounding the hotel is both a pleasurable challenge to play and exhilarating to view.

WEB: www.globalgolf.com/ballymascanlon

B&B from £52.00 to £55.00
€66.02 to €69.83

OLIVER QUINN

American Express
Diners
Mastercard
Visa

 Weekend specials from £130.00

43 43

Closed 24 - 27 December

CARRICKDALE HOTEL & LEISURE COMPLEX

CARRICKCARNON, RAVENSDALE,
DUNDALK, CO. LOUTH
TEL: 042-937 1397 FAX: 042-937 1740

HOTEL ★★★ MAP 12 O 14

This Hotel, Conference & swimming leisure complex is situated halfway between Dublin and Belfast on the main N1 route just 10km north of Dundalk, 8km south of Newry. All en suite bedrooms are tastefully decorated, the restaurant is the most popular in the area and carvery lunches are served daily. Entertainment each weekend. Ideal touring destination to the Mountains of Mourne, Cooley or Carlingford and Northern Ireland tourist areas.

B&B from £45.00 to £45.00
€57.14 to €57.14

JOHN MCPARLAND
Proprietor

American Express
Diners
Mastercard
Visa

Weekend specials from £115.00

50 50

Closed 25 - 26 December

Room rates are IR£ per room per night

CLANBRASSIL HOTEL

CLANBRASSIL STREET, DUNDALK, CO. LOUTH
TEL: 042-933 4141 FAX: 042-932 8779

HOTEL ★★ MAP 12 O 14

Ideally situated between the two capitals, Belfast and Dublin, in the heart of Dundalk Town, a heavenly location for shopaholics, with an abundance of superb shops. 18 hole golf course within 10km drive, Carlingford Lough, Mourne Mountains, Boyne Valley all a short drive away.

B&B from £27.50 to £35.00
€34.91 to €44.44

ANITA MCCANN

American Express
Diners
Mastercard
Visa

☺ Weekend specials from £67.00

15 15

Closed 25 - 26 December

DERRYHALE HOTEL

CARRICK ROAD, DUNDALK, CO. LOUTH
TEL: 042-933 5471 FAX: 042-933 5471
EMAIL: info@minotel.iol.ie

HOTEL ★★ MAP 12 O 14

Midway between Dublin and Belfast, Derryhale Hotel is an ideal base for touring the north east of Ireland, Mountains of Mourne, Carlingford, Cooley Peninsula. Bedrooms contain TV and direct dial telephone. Good quality food is a tradition at the hotel. Derryhale Hotel has wedding and conference facilities. Activities close by include fishing, water skiing, sailing, beaches, horse riding and golf.

Member of MinOtel Ireland Hotel Group

B&B from £40.00 to £50.00
€50.79 to €63.49

LIAM SEXTON
Managing Director

American Express
Diners
Mastercard
Visa

☺ Weekend specials from £90.00

19 19
alc

IRISH HOTELS FEDERATION

Open All Year

FAIRWAYS HOTEL

DUBLIN ROAD, DUNDALK, CO. LOUTH
TEL: 042-932 1500 FAX: 042-932 1511
EMAIL: info@fairways.ie

HOTEL ★★★ MAP 12 O 14

The Fairways Hotel and Conference Centre is a busy family-run hotel situated three miles south of Dundalk and approximately one hour's drive from either Dublin or Belfast. A wide range of food served throughout the day in the Carvery/Grill and Modi's Restaurant. Golf can be arranged by the Hotel on a choice of golf courses. Late 2001 additional facilities will include conference centre, 50 additional bedrooms and new leisure centre adjacent to hotel.

WEB: www.fairways.ie

B&B from £45.00 to £50.00
€57.14 to €63.49

BRIAN P. QUINN
Managing Director

American Express
Diners
Mastercard
Visa

44 44

Closed 24 - 25 December

B&B rates are IR£ per person sharing per night incl. Breakfast

HOTEL IMPERIAL

PARK STREET, DUNDALK, CO. LOUTH
TEL: 042-933 2241 FAX: 042-933 7909
EMAIL: info@imperialhoteldundalk.com

HOTEL ★★ MAP 12 O 14

Built in the 70's this is a modern hotel of high standard. There is an excellent bar, also a coffee shop which is open from 8am - 10pm. Dining room open all day serving à la carte menu and dinner from 6pm - 10pm. Secure parking can be arranged nearby at no extra charge. Rooms being refurbished at the moment to a high standard.

B&B from £35.00 to £42.50
€44.44 to €53.96

PETER QUINN
Managing Director
American Express
Diners
Mastercard
Visa

Weekend specials from £90.00

47 47

Closed 25 - 26 December

AISLING HOUSE

DUBLIN ROAD, ASHBOURNE, CO. MEATH
TEL: 01-835 0359 FAX: 01-835 1135
EMAIL: duke2@iol.ie

GUESTHOUSE ★★ MAP 12 O 12

Situated on one acre of landscaped gardens on the Dublin/Derry road N2 a mile from Ashbourne Village, only 20 minutes from Dublin City centre and Airport, convenient to Fairyhouse racecourse and Tattersalls sales. Rooms en suite with guest lounge, games room and private car park. Aisling House is an ideal base for business or holiday. Local amenities include golf, horse riding, clay pidgeon shooting and fishing in the Boyne River.

B&B from £25.00 to £25.00
€31.74 to €31.74

KATHLEEN DAVITT
Proprietor
Mastercard
Visa

9 9

Closed 24 - 28 December

BROADMEADOW COUNTRY HOUSE & EQUESTRIAN CENTRE

BULLSTOWN, ASHBOURNE, CO. MEATH
TEL: 01-835 2823 FAX: 01-835 2819
EMAIL: info@irelandequestrian.com

GUESTHOUSE ★★★★ MAP 12 O 12

This exceptional family-run country house is located near Ashbourne Village, only 12km from Dublin Airport and 20km from the city centre. It is set in 100 acres of farmland with a modern purpose-built equestrian centre. All rooms en suite and designed for maximum guest comfort. Private car parking, tennis court and landscaped gardens. Surrounded by numerous golf courses and restaurants. Ideal location for both tourist and business people. Specialists in equestrian packages.

WEB: www.irelandequestrian.com

Member of Equestrian Holidays Ireland

B&B from £36.00 to £40.00
€45.71 to €50.79

ELAINE DUFF
Manager
Mastercard
Visa

8 8

Closed 24 - 26 December

Room rates are IR£ per room per night

OLD DARNLEY LODGE HOTEL

MAIN STREET, ATHBOY,
CO. MEATH
TEL: 046-32283 FAX: 046-32255

HOTEL CR MAP 11 M 12

This 19th century hotel has just recently been refurbished to the very highest standards. The hotel is a haven of tranquillity and is ideally located. Dublin and Athlone are only one hour's drive away. All bedrooms are en suite and offer a variety of services including, direct dial phone, multi channel TV, trouser press, hair dryers and tea/coffee making facilities. There are plenty of historic landmarks to see and plenty of activities to enjoy, including golf, fishing, boating, horse riding.

B&B from £28.00 to £35.00
€35.55 to €44.44

MARY MURPHY

American Express
Diners
Mastercard
Visa

14 14

S alc

IRISH HOTELS FEDERATION

Open All Year

NEPTUNE BEACH

BETTYSTOWN,
CO. MEATH
TEL: 041-982 7107 FAX: 041-982 7412
EMAIL: info@neptunebeach.ie

HOTEL U MAP 12 O 13

Located 25 mins north of Dublin Airport with a spectacular setting overlooking Bettystown Beach. All 38 rooms are elegantly furnished to provide the comfort and facilities expected of a leading hotel. Enjoy fine dining in the restaurant, afternoon tea in the cosy Winter Garden or a relaxing drink in the Neptune Bar. The leisure club facilities include 20m swimming pool, jacuzzi, sauna and fitness suite. Local golf courses: Laytown & Bettystown, Seapoint and Co. Louth.

WEB: www.neptunebeach.ie

B&B from £55.00 to £100.00
€69.84 to €126.97

DENIS REDDAN
Proprietor

American Express
Mastercard
Visa

:) Weekend specials from £99.00

38 38

inet

IRISH HOTELS FEDERATION

Open All Year

HEADFORT ARMS HOTEL

KELLS,
CO. MEATH
TEL: 046-40063 FAX: 046-40587
EMAIL: headfortarms@eircom.net

HOTEL ★★ MAP 11 M 13

Situated in the historical town of Kells, it is 40km from Dublin on the main Derry/Donegal route. This traditional family hotel has 18 bedrooms, all have bath/shower, TV, video, etc. We at the Headfort offer a blend of homeliness, good taste and first class management. Conference facilities provided. Available locally: golf, fishing, tennis. Coffee shop / carvery open 7 days until 10pm.

WEB: www.headfortarms.com

B&B from £45.00 to £80.00
€57.14 to €101.58

VINCENT DUFF
General Manager

American Express
Mastercard
Visa

18 18

alc

IRISH HOTELS FEDERATION

Open All Year

B&B rates are IR£ per person sharing per night incl. Breakfast

STATION HOUSE HOTEL

**KILMESSAN,
CO. MEATH
TEL: 046-25239 FAX: 046-25588
EMAIL: stationhousehotel@eircom.net**

HOTEL U MAP 12 N 12

Old Railway Junction converted to a Country House Hotel & award-winning restaurant, 20 miles (35km) from Dublin Airport & City. Old signal cabin converted to bedroom suite. Set on 5 acres of woodland, gardens/lawns. 2.4km from Hill of Tara, 10km from Navan & Trim. Golf courses & angling close by. It is owned and run by Christy & Thelma Slattery. Professional and detailed service is provided in a relaxed rural setting. They pride themselves on hospitality & attention to detail.

WEB: www.thestationhousehotel.com

B&B from £25.00 to £50.00
€31.74 to €63.49

CHRIS & THELMA SLATTERY
Proprietors

American Express
Diners
Mastercard
Visa

☺ Weekend specials from £75.00

10 10 alc

IRISH HOTELS FEDERATION

Closed 24 December

ARDBOYNE HOTEL

**DUBLIN ROAD, NAVAN,
CO. MEATH
TEL: 046-23119 FAX: 046-22355
EMAIL: ardboyne-sales@quinn-hotels.com**

HOTEL ★★★ MAP 12 N 13

Having been recently refurbished, the Ardboyne Hotel is the newest member of the Quinn Hotel Group and is enjoying its attractive facelift. Situated in its own pleasant grounds, the hotel is conveniently located on the outskirts of Navan and is the perfect base for visiting the many places of interest. Our restaurant offers delicious food in cosy surroundings and our function rooms will cater for every occasion from the grand and gracious to the private and intimate.

WEB: www.quinnhotels.com

Member of Quinn Hotels

B&B from £42.00 to £45.00
€53.33 to €57.14

RITA GLEESON
General Manager

American Express
Diners
Mastercard
Visa

☺ Weekend specials from £90.00

29 29 alc

IRISH HOTELS FEDERATION

Closed 24 - 26 December

MA DWYERS GUESTHOUSE

**DUBLIN ROAD, NAVAN,
CO. MEATH
TEL: 046-77992 FAX: 046-77995**

GUESTHOUSE ★★★ MAP 12 N 13

Ma Dwyers newly opened guesthouse possesses many of the qualities of a high class hotel, along with a cosy homely feel which is so vitally important. 9 beautiful en suite rooms with a direct dial telephone, TV, hairdryer and tea/coffee facilities with fax and photocopying services available. Ideally located just minutes walk from the town centre and plenty of historic landmarks to see and activities to enjoy including golf, fishing, boating and horseriding.

B&B from £25.00 to £32.00
€31.74 to €40.63

MARY MURPHY

Mastercard
Visa

9 9

Closed 24 - 27 December

Room rates are IR£ per room per night

NEWGRANGE HOTEL

**BRIDGE STREET, NAVAN,
CO. MEATH**
TEL: 046-74100 FAX: 046-73977
EMAIL: info@newgrangehotel.ie

HOTEL ★★★ MAP 12 N 13

Centrally located in the heart of a typical Irish market town yet just 30 minutes from Dublin Airport, the Newgrange Hotel offers a perfect alliance of modern comforts, high standards of food and service. Set within a stylish Gothic design theme, 2 restaurants, 2 bars and a relaxing library lounge await you. (Conference & banqueting facilities to 550). Castles, gardens, craft shops, golfing, shopping, racing all nearby. Trim Castle and Newgrange burial tomb 20 minutes drive.

WEB: www.newgrangehotel.ie

B&B from £40.00 to £48.00
€50.79 to €60.95

MATT O'CONNOR
Managing Director

American Express
Diners
Mastercard
Visa

☺ Weekend specials from £94.50

Closed 24 - 25 December

FINCOURT

**OLIVER PLUNKETT STREET,
OLDCASTLE, CO. MEATH**
TEL: 049-8541153 FAX: 049-8542242
EMAIL: fincourt@hotmail.com

GUESTHOUSE N MAP 11 L 13

The Fincourt is a small family run pub and guesthouse situated in Oldcastle, the home of Loughcrew Passage Graves. You are guaranteed a warm welcome and good food. Bar food served all day. Restaurant: à la carte menu served weekend evening. Coffee shop open all day. Quality accommodation: Bed & breakfast or self catering. Full business facilities also available including meeting room. Coach groups catered for by prior appointment.

WEB: www.fincourt.com

B&B from £25.00 to £30.00
€31.74 to €38.09

JACKIE & GARRY O'NEILL

American Express
Diners
Mastercard
Visa

Open All Year

CONYNGHAM ARMS HOTEL

**SLANE,
CO. MEATH**
TEL: 041-988 4444 FAX: 041-982 4205
EMAIL: enquiry@conynghamarms.com

HOTEL ★★ MAP 12 N 13

Located in a lovely manor village built c. 1850, this traditional family hotel with 4 poster beds, where you can enjoy good food and friendly service, is an ideal base from which to tour the Boyne Valley - particularly the tomb of Knowth and Newgrange, various abbeys, and the birth place of Francis Ledwidge, all within 15 minutes drive. Available locally: 5 golf courses within 25km. Village Inn Hotels reservations: 353-1-295 8900.

WEB: www.conynghamarms.com

Member of Village Inn Hotels

B&B from £37.50 to £42.50
€47.62 to €53.96

GRAHAM & BERNIE CANNING
Proprietors

Diners
Mastercard
Visa

:/1

Closed 23 - 27 December

B&B rates are IR£ per person sharing per night incl. Breakfast

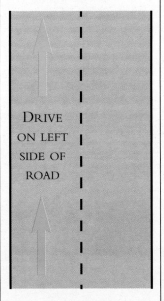

HIGHFIELD HOUSE

**MAUDLINS ROAD, TRIM,
CO. MEATH**
TEL: 046-36386 FAX: 046-38182
EMAIL: highfieldhouseaccom@eircom.net

GUESTHOUSE N MAP 11 M 12

Highfield House guest accommodation is a beautiful period residence. Historical building dates back to the early 18th century. It is situated overlooking Trim Castle and the River Boyne just off the main Dublin Road. Inside there are seven spacious en suite guest rooms with colour TV, direct dial phone, coffee/tea facilities. Beautiful view from all rooms. 2 mins walking distance to town. Newgrange 30km. Dublin Airport 30 km. Babysitting service & laundry service. Private car parking. We pride ourselves on a highly personalised service and look forward to welcoming you.

B&B from £20.00 to £22.50
€25.39 to €28.56

**EDWARD & GERALDINE
DUIGNAN Proprietors**

Mastercard
Visa

7 7

Closed 22 December - 05 January

WELLINGTON COURT HOTEL

**SUMMERHILL ROAD, TRIM,
CO. MEATH**
TEL: 046-31516 FAX: 046-36002
EMAIL: wellingtoncourt@eircom.net

HOTEL ★★ MAP 11 M 12

The Wellington Court Hotel is family owned and offers visitors a warm welcome and old fashioned courtesy along with excellent facilities. Our 18 rooms are all en suite with direct dial phone, colour TV, central heating. Also tea/coffee facilities. Superb accommodation, excellent food, set in Ireland's most historic surroundings with the magnificent medieval ruins of King John's Castle, one of the most enduring attractions in the area.
Additional Tel. No.: 01-821 3311

B&B from £30.00 to £39.00
€38.09 to €49.52

**M & C NALLY
Proprietors**

American Express
Mastercard
Visa

18 18

Closed 25 - 26 December

BLAINROE HOTEL

**COAST ROAD, WICKLOW,
CO. WICKLOW**
TEL: 0404-67500 FAX: 0404-69737
EMAIL: blainroehotel@oceanfree.net

HOTEL ★★★ MAP 8 P 9

The Blainroe Hotel is a haven of tranquillity in luxurious splendour with magnificent suites and bedrooms, 3 miles from Wicklow Town and a mere hour from Dublin. The Atrium Restaurant is open every evening at 6 pm for dinner. Food is served all day in the Garden Restaurant, Piano Lobby and Golfers Bar. Barbecues in the Terrace Restaurant (weather permitting). Two new conference rooms and the fitness club has a gymnasium, swimming pool, sauna, steam room, jacuzzi and Japanese showers. Music in the Piano Lobby at weekends.

WEB: www.blainroehotel.ie

B&B from £45.00 to £75.00
€57.14 to €95.23

**JOHANN ZALUD/DAVID ELLIS
Executive Chef/Owner**

American Express
Diners
Mastercard
Visa

Weekend specials from £79.00

13 13

Open All Year

GORMANSTOWN MANOR

FARM GUEST HOUSE, NEAR WICKLOW
TOWN (OFF N11), CO. WICKLOW
TEL: 0404-69432 FAX: 0404-61832
EMAIL: gormanstownmanor@eircom.net

GUESTHOUSE ★★ MAP 8 P 9

A warm welcome awaits you at this charming family guest house. Bright spacious en suite bedrooms. Peaceful relaxed atmosphere, spectacular surroundings. Golf driving range on farm, landscaped gardens, nature walks & superb personal services. Ideally located for golf and touring The Garden of Ireland. Breathtaking scenery, mountains, valleys, rivers, lakes & woodlands. Enjoy stunning sandy beaches of Brittas Bay. Sailing, fishing, gardens, heritage, horseriding, polo, golf.

B&B from £28.00 to £38.00
€35.55 to €48.25

MARGARET MURPHY
Proprietor
Mastercard
Visa

Open All Year

GRAND HOTEL

WICKLOW,
CO. WICKLOW
TEL: 0404-67337 FAX: 0404-69607
EMAIL: grandhotel@eircom.net

HOTEL ★★★ MAP 8 P 9

This charming hotel is the perfect base for touring the beautiful Garden of Ireland. Situated in Wicklow Town, it is only a 40 minute drive from Dublin on the N11. Enjoy golf, fishing, hill walking, sandy beaches and sight seeing locally. 33 large, bright, comfortable bedrooms all en suite with direct dial telephone, multi channel TV and tea/coffee making facilities. Fine food served in the restaurant and grill room all day. Lively lounge bar. Conference facilities.

WEB: www.grandhotel.ie

B&B from £33.00 to £50.00
€41.90 to €63.49

JOHN SULLIVAN
General Manager
Mastercard
Visa

 Weekend specials from £90.00

Open All Year

OLD RECTORY COUNTRY HOUSE

WICKLOW,
CO. WICKLOW
TEL: 0404-67048 FAX: 0404-69181

GUESTHOUSE ★★★★ MAP 8 P 9

Charming Victorian House in a peaceful setting with delightful enclosed gardens. A warm welcome awaits you at this family owned guesthouse. Our spacious bedrooms are en suite with bath and shower and are equipped with TV, direct dial phone, hairdryer and tea/coffee making facilities. Relax in our elegant Drawing Room or avail of our gym/sauna. Nearby attractions include Wicklow's Historic Goal, Mount Usher Gardens, Glendalough, Powerscourt and numerous golf courses.

B&B from £40.00 to £45.00
€50.79 to €57.14

PATRICK & CARMEL O'TOOLE
Proprietors
Mastercard
Visa

Closed 01 September - 01 May

Room rates are IR£ per room per night

ARKLOW BAY HOTEL

ARKLOW,
CO. WICKLOW
TEL: 0402-32309 FAX: 0402-32300
EMAIL: arklowbay@eircom.net

HOTEL ★★★ MAP 8 O 8

Nestled in the heart of Co. Wicklow, a warm welcome awaits your arrival. Set just outside scenic Arklow with panoramic views of The Garden of Ireland. State of the art Health and Leisure Centre recently opened. A lively bar, excellent cuisine, banqueting for 500 pax and extensive conference facilities in a range of suites. Enjoy golf, fishing, hovercrafting and quadracing, all available locally. Sister hotel to the Springhill Court in Kilkenny.

WEB: www.arklowbay.com

Member of Chara Hotel Group

B&B from £40.00 to £70.00
€50.79 to €88.88

ROBERT MCCARTHY
General Manager

American Express
Diners
Mastercard
Visa

55 55

Open All Year

BRIDGE HOTEL

BRIDGE STREET, ARKLOW,
CO. WICKLOW
TEL: 0402-31666 FAX: 0402-31666

HOTEL ★★ MAP 8 O 8

The Bridge Hotel is a family-run 15 bedroomed hotel situated at the bridge in Arklow beside the Avoca River and only 10 mins walk to the sea. Arklow has a strong seafaring heritage and is famous for its pottery. The town offers a great variety of holiday activities whether you swim, play golf, tennis, fish or walk. Arklow is an ideal base from which to see the beautiful scenery of Wicklow. Only 6.5km to Ballykissangel.

B&B from £30.00 to £38.00
€38.09 to €48.25

JIM HOEY
Proprietor

Mastercard
Visa

15 14

Closed 25 December

CLOGGA BAY HOTEL

CLOGGA, ARKLOW,
CO. WICKLOW
TEL: 0402-39299 FAX: 0402-91538

HOTEL ★★ MAP 8 O 8

Family owned and managed establishment situated 3km south of Arklow Town. Set on a 2 acre garden in the country by the sea, approx 60km from Rosslare and Dublin. A central location for touring Wicklow and Wexford. All rooms en suite with colour T.V. and direct dial telephone. Local attractions include golf, fishing and swimming. Our restaurant offers good traditional food.

B&B from £30.00 to £40.00
€38.09 to €50.79

FIOUNNUALA JAMESON
Proprietor

American Express
Mastercard
Visa

10 10

Open All Year

B&B rates are IR£ per person sharing per night incl. Breakfast

GLENART CASTLE HOTEL

**GLENART CASTLE, ARKLOW,
CO. WICKLOW**
TEL: 0402-31031 FAX: 0402-31032
EMAIL: glenart@eircom.net

HOTEL U MAP 8 O 8

The Hidden Castle of Glenart set amidst 63 acres of gardens and woodlands. Built circa. 1750 by the Earls of Carysfort, situated in the heart of the Avoca Valley. Only an hour's drive from Dublin, via N11. Local attractions include fishing, shooting, hillwalking and horse riding. A short drive to over 20 golf courses including Druid's Glen, Collattin, Woodenbridge and the Arklow Golf Course. Minutes away from the picturesque Ballykissangel (Avoca) Village.

B&B from £35.00 to £45.00
€44.44 to €57.14

DESMOND NAIK
Director

American Express
Mastercard
Visa

☺ Weekend specials from £85.00

28 28

alc

IRISH HOTELS FEDERATION

Open All Year

BALLYKNOCKEN HOUSE AND FARM

**GLENEALY, ASHFORD,
CO. WICKLOW**
TEL: 0404-44627 FAX: 0404-44696
EMAIL: cfulvio@ballyknocken.com

UNDER CONSTRUCTION OPENING MAR 2001

GUESTHOUSE P MAP 8 P 9

An 1850's romantic farmhouse, elegantly furnished with antiques and family memorabilia. Charming bedrooms, some with iron beds and claw feet baths offer lovely views over gardens and forest. Relax by the Drawing Room's log fire before the splendid dinner using garden and local produce including seafood. Superb breakfasts. Near to Wicklow Mountains, Glendalough, Powerscourt. Excellent golf, e.g. Druid's Glen. Own walking programmes. Dublin 29 miles. Frommers recommended.

WEB: www.ballyknocken.com

B&B from £25.00 to £29.50
€31.74 to €37.46

CATHERINE FULVIO
Proprietor

Mastercard
Visa

☺ Weekend specials from £66.00

8 8

Closed 01 December - 16 March

BEL-AIR HOTEL

**ASHFORD,
CO. WICKLOW**
TEL: 0404-40109 FAX: 0404-40188
EMAIL: belairhotel@eircom.net

HOTEL U MAP 8 P 9

Bel-Air Hotel is a family run hotel and equestrian centre, situated in the centre of 81 hectares of farm and parkland. Managed by the Murphy Freeman family since 1937. The lovely gardens have a breathtaking view to the sea. The traditional family atmosphere and rich history makes the hotel a popular venue, good restaurant, en suite with tea making facilities, T.V. and hairdryers. Bel Air Holiday village adjacent to hotel.

WEB: www.nci.ie

B&B from £34.00 to £45.00
€43.17 to €57.14

FIDELMA FREEMAN
Owner

American Express
Diners
Mastercard
Visa

10 10

alc

IRISH HOTELS FEDERATION

Closed 01 - 07 January

Room rates are IR£ per room per night

CHESTER BEATTY INN

**ASHFORD VILLAGE,
CO. WICKLOW
TEL: 0404-40206 FAX: 0404-49003
EMAIL: hotelchesterbeatty@eircom.net**

HOTEL U MAP 8 P 9

The Chester Beatty Inn is in the village of Ashford on the main N11 road, 35 mins south of Dublin. Ideally situated for touring, golf (adjacent to Druids Glen and many other golf courses), fishing, hill walking and gardens (opposite Mount Usher Gardens, 15 mins from Powerscourt Gardens). Charming country inn style family run hotel comprising 12 luxury en suite rooms, award-winning restaurant, lounge and traditional Irish bar all with open log fires. Secure private car park.

WEB: www.hotelchesterbeatty@eircom.net

B&B from £35.00 to £55.00
€44.44 to €69.84

KITTY & PAUL CAPRANI

American Express
Diners
Mastercard
Visa

😊 Mid week/weekend specials from £75.00

12 12

Closed 24 - 26 December

CULLENMORE HOTEL

**ASHFORD,
CO. WICKLOW
TEL: 0404-40187 FAX: 0404-40471
EMAIL: cullenmore@eircom.net**

HOTEL ★★ MAP 8 P 9

The Cullenmore hotel is a pleasant, friendly, family run hotel, located near Ashford in the garden of Ireland. All bedrooms are modern, en suite, with two designed for wheelchair users. TV (satellite) and direct dial phone are standard throughout. Extensive bar food menu served all day. Ideal venue for a relaxing break. Very reasonable rates.

Room Rate from £39.00 to £49.00
€49.52 to €62.22

OLIVE & DIRK VAN DER FLIER

American Express
Diners
Mastercard
Visa

17 17

Closed 24 - 27 December

BROOKLODGE

**MACREDDIN VILLAGE, (AUGHRIM),
CO. WICKLOW
TEL: 0402-36444 FAX: 0402-36580
EMAIL: brooklodge@macreddin.ie**

HOTEL N MAP 8 O 8

A welcome as warm as our real fires...an AA 4**** countryhouse hotel in spectacular countryside, yet only an hour from South Dublin...a relaxed drink in the charming waterside lounge or a creamy pint in Acton's Country Pub... sumptuous free range, organic and wild foods in the award winning Strawberry Tree Restaurant...deep baths and luxurious beds with breakfast until 11am...golf, horse riding, walks, field and clay shooting...food and wine shops.................perfection!

WEB: www.brooklodge.com

Member of Manor House Hotels

B&B from £70.00 to £85.00
€88.88 to €107.93

FREDA WOLFE & EVAN DOYLE
Hosts

American Express
Diners
Mastercard
Visa

40 40

alc Inet

Open All Year

B&B rates are IR£ per person sharing per night incl. Breakfast

LAWLESS'S HOTEL

**AUGHRIM,
CO. WICKLOW
TEL: 0402-36146 FAX: 0402-36384
EMAIL: lawhotel@iol.ie**

HOTEL ★★★ MAP 8 O 8

Lawless's Hotel, established in 1787, is a charming family run hotel which has been tastefully renovated. The award-winning restaurant enjoys a well established reputation for fine cuisine. Approximately one hour from Dublin, nestling in the Wicklow Hills, there is a wide choice of excellent golf courses nearby as well as scenic hill-walking, pony treking and trout fishing in the adjacent river. Other accommodation available in hotel grounds.

WEB: www.lawhotel.com

Member of Village Inn Hotels

B&B from £39.00 to £47.00
€49.52 to €59.68

SEOIRSE & MAEVE O'TOOLE
Proprietors

Diners
Mastercard
Visa

☺ Weekend specials from £97.50

14 14

Closed 24 - 26 December

VALE VIEW HOTEL

**AVOCA,
CO. WICKLOW
TEL: 0402-35236 FAX: 0402-35144
EMAIL: valeview@indigo.ie**

HOTEL ★★ MAP 8 O 8

Situated in the beautiful Vale of Avoca. All bedrooms en suite with tea/coffee making facilities, direct dial phone, TV. Function room to cater for different types of functions. Bar food, extensive à la carte and dinner menus.

WEB: indigo.ie/-valeview/

B&B from £30.00 to £45.00
€38.09 to €57.14

PETER AND MARY KING
Proprietors

American Express
Diners
Mastercard
Visa

10 10

Closed 24 - 26 December

DOWNSHIRE HOUSE HOTEL

**BLESSINGTON,
CO. WICKLOW
TEL: 045-865199 FAX: 045-865335
EMAIL: info@downshirehouse.com**

HOTEL ★★★ MAP 8 N 10

Downshire is a family run country hotel on Blessington's main street on route N81. Dublin 25km. Twenty five bedrooms all en suite, large garden, close to horse riding, fishing, hill walking, leisure centre on Blessington lakes. Shopping at The Square in Tallaght and twelve screen cinema. Fresh food is supplied daily and cooked under highly qualified supervision. Ideal location for touring the Wicklow Mountains or Midlands. RAC*** Award and RAC Dining Award in recognition of the overall dining experience..

WEB: www.downshirehouse.com

Member of Irish Family Hotels

B&B from £49.25 to £49.25
€62.53 to €62.53

JOAN FLYNN
Manager

Mastercard
Visa

25 25

Closed 22 December - 10 January

Room rates are IR£ per room per night

TULFARRIS GOLF & COUNTRY HOUSE HOTEL

BLESSINGTON LAKES, CO. WICKLOW
TEL: 045-867555 FAX: 045-867561

HOTEL ★★★★ MAP 8 N 10

Tulfarris House Hotel is located on the Wicklow/Kildare border, near Blessington, & within 50 minutes drive of Dublin City Centre & Airport. Built in 1760 Tulfarris nestles between the spectacular Wicklow Mountains & Blessington Lakes. It has 20 tastefully furnished en suite bedrooms, a courtyard bar, & an excellent restaurant. Facilities include an indoor heated swimming pool, gym, sauna, steam room, sunbed, massage, tennis courts, & a spectacular 18 hole championship golf course.

B&B from £55.00 to £75.00
€69.84 to €95.23

JIM & MAEVE HAYES
Managing Director & Prop

American Express
Diners
Mastercard
Visa

Open All Year

CROFTON BRAY HEAD INN

STRAND ROAD, BRAY, CO. WICKLOW
TEL: 01-286 7182 FAX: 01-286 7182

GUESTHOUSE ★★ MAP 8 P 10

This 130 year old building is situated on the seafront, under the Bray Head Mountain. A 10 minute walk away from an excellent commuter train to Dublin, but also ideally located for touring Wicklow - The Garden of Ireland. The Bray Head Inn has ample car-parking and is fully licensed. It has a lift, mostly en suite bedrooms with TV and Telephone. Our very reasonable prices include full Irish Breakfast.

B&B from £24.00 to £25.00
€30.47 to €31.74

NANCY REGAN

Mastercard
Visa

Closed 01 October - 01 June

WESTBOURNE HOTEL

QUINSBORO ROAD, BRAY, CO. WICKLOW
TEL: 01-286 2362 FAX: 01-286 8530

HOTEL ★★ MAP 8 P 10

The Westbourne Hotel is ideally located on the north east coast of the 'Garden of Ireland' in the charming town of Bray. Only minutes from exceptional scenery, beaches and has fast access to Dublin via the DART. Newly refurbished bedrooms en suite, direct dial phone, TV and tea/coffee making facilities. Dusty Millers Bar is a live music venue with music Wed-Sun. Clancy's Traditional Irish Bar, craic agus ceol. The Tube Nite Club open Thur-Sun. Food served all day.

B&B from £30.00 to £40.00
€38.09 to €50.79

SUSAN MC CARTHY
General Manager

Mastercard
Visa

☺ Midweek specials from £75.00

Closed 25 - 26 December

B&B rates are IR£ per person sharing per night incl. Breakfast

WOODLAND COURT HOTEL

SOUTHERN CROSS, BRAY,
CO. WICKLOW
TEL: 01-276 0258 FAX: 01-276 0298

HOTEL N MAP 8 P 10

Located just minutes from the N11 motorway and 12 miles from Dublin City Centre the Woodland Court Hotel has much to offer the tourist and business traveller. 65 well-appointed en suite rooms, state of the art conference/business centre and excellent value meals in our restaurant. An ideal venue for touring Dublin City and County Wicklow. Special group and business rates available on request.

Room Rate from £50.00 to £100.00
€63.49 to €126.97

EILEEN MURPHY
General Manager

American Express
Diners
Mastercard
Visa

65 65

Open All Year

RATHSALLAGH HOUSE, GOLF AND COUNTRY CLUB

DUNLAVIN,
CO. WICKLOW
TEL: 045-403112 FAX: 045-403343
EMAIL: info@rathsallagh.com

GUESTHOUSE ★★★★ MAP 8 N 9

Winner of the prestigious Country House of the Year Award 2000 and a member of Ireland's Blue Book, Rathsallagh is a large 4**** Grade A country house converted from Queen Anne stables in 1798. Rathsallagh, with its own 18 hole Championship Golf Course, is set in a peaceful oasis of 530 acres of rolling parkland with thousands of mature trees, lakes and streams. On the west side of the Wicklow Mountains close to Punchestown and The Curragh Racecourses, yet only 1 hour from Dublin Airport.

WEB: www.rathsallagh.com

Member of Ireland's Blue Book

B&B from £80.00 to £105.00
€101.58 to €133.32

THE O'FLYNN FAMILY
Proprietors

American Express
Diners
Mastercard
Visa

2 nights dinner, B&B and
2 rounds of golf from £259.00

29 29

Closed 23 - 28 December

POWERSCOURT ARMS HOTEL

ENNISKERRY,
CO. WICKLOW
TEL: 01-282 8903 FAX: 01-286 4909

HOTEL ★ MAP 8 O 10

Powerscourt Arms Hotel owned by the McTernan Family. Snuggling in the foothills of the Wicklow Mountains the Powerscourt Arms is an ideal base for touring expeditions, it is an intimate family run hotel with 12 bedrooms furnished to include direct dial telephone en suite bathrooms and multi channel TV, ample car parking facilities. The restaurant seats up to 45 people, our lounge with strong features of American white ash, serves bar food daily. The public bar also has its own atmosphere complete with an open fire.

B&B from £35.00 to £47.50
€44.44 to €60.31

CHARLES McTERNAN
General Manager

Mastercard
Visa

12 12

Closed 24 - 25 December

Room rates are IR£ per room per night

SUMMERHILL HOUSE HOTEL

ENNISKERRY,
CO. WICKLOW
TEL: 01-286 7928 FAX: 01-286 7929
EMAIL: res@summerhillhotel.iol.ie

HOTEL ★★★ MAP 8 O 10

This charming hotel is just a short walk to the quaint village of Enniskerry, and the famous Powerscourt Gardens. Located on the N11, 19km south of Dublin City & 15km to Dunlaoire Ferryport. 57 spacious bedrooms, private free car parking, traditional Irish breakfast, hill walking & nature trails, local golf courses, family rooms (2 adults and 3 children). Enjoy a rare blend of the Wicklow countryside close to Dublin City.

Member of Logis of Ireland

B&B from £40.00 to £60.00
€50.79 to €76.18

MICHAEL BLAKE
General Manager

American Express
Mastercard
Visa

57 57

Open All Year

GLENVIEW HOTEL

GLEN-O-THE-DOWNS, DELGANY,
CO. WICKLOW
TEL: 01-287 3399 FAX: 01-287 7511
EMAIL: glenview@iol.ie

HOTEL ★★★ MAP 8 O 10

Set idyllically in the garden of Ireland, the Glenview Hotel offers a relaxing atmosphere and discreet friendly service. The Woodlands Restaurant provides unrivalled views over the glen in which to sample its widely acclaimed cuisine & service. The new Conservatory Bar with live music & the state of the art leisure club complete the perfect base for a holiday. Golf, horse riding, shooting, hill walking within easy reach of the hotel. 25 mins from Dublin. Ideal for conferences.

WEB: www.glenviewhotel.ie

Member of Stafford Hotels

B&B from £68.00 to £85.00
€86.34 to €107.93

STEPHEN BYRNE
General Manager

American Express
Diners
Mastercard
Visa

74 74

☺ Weekend specials from £120.00

Closed 24 - 26 December

DERRYBAWN MOUNTAIN LODGE

DERRYBAWN, LARAGH,
GLENDALOUGH, CO. WICKLOW
TEL: 0404-45644 FAX: 0404-45645
EMAIL: derrybawnlodge@eircom.net

GUESTHOUSE ★★★ MAP 8 O 9

Derrybawn Mountain Lodge is a family-run guesthouse, situated on the slopes of Derrybawn Mountain. A walkers paradise close by famous Wicklow Way. Tranquil setting, mountain views, all rooms have bath & shower en suite, direct dial phone, coffee/tea making facilities, hairdryer. Spacious dining and lounge area to relax. Enjoy National Park, Glenmalure, historic Glendalough and Clara Vale. Members of local mountain rescue team. Excellent fresh food & wine. A warm welcome awaits you.

B&B from £30.00 to £30.00
€38.09 to €38.09

TERESA KAVANAGH
Proprietor

American Express
Mastercard
Visa

8 8

☺ Midweek specials from £80.00

Closed 24 - 27 December

B&B rates are IR£ per person sharing per night incl. Breakfast

GLENDALOUGH HOTEL

GLENDALOUGH,
CO. WICKLOW
TEL: 0404-45135 FAX: 0404-45142
EMAIL: info@glendaloughhotel.ie

HOTEL ★★★ MAP 8 O 9

The Glendalough Hotel, built in the early 1800s, is a family run hotel situated in the heart of Wicklow's most scenic valley and within the Glendalough National Park. The hotel has recently been extended offering 43 beautifully decorated en suite bedrooms with satellite TV and direct dial phone. The hotel's restaurant offers superb cuisine and wines in a tranquil environment overlooking the Glendasan River. The Tavern Bar serves good pub food and offers entertainment at weekends.

B&B from £44.00 to £60.00
€55.87 to €76.18

PATRICK CASEY

American Express
Diners
Mastercard
Visa

Midweek specials from £130.00

Closed 01 - 31 January

LA TOUCHE HOTEL

TRAFALGAR ROAD, GREYSTONES,
CO. WICKLOW
TEL: 01-287 4401 FAX: 01-287 4504
EMAIL: latouchehotel@hotmail.com

HOTEL ★★ MAP 8 P 10

Our hotel has a superb location overlooking the sea in the garden of Ireland. At our doorstep are Glendalough, Powerscourt and Mount Usher Gardens. All rooms are en suite with remote satellite TV, radio, tea/coffee facilities and DD phone. Our Captain's Lounge is the main meeting place for locals and visitors alike with a carvery 7 days a week. The Waterfront Conference Centre caters for parties up to 500. Also available are Bennigans Fun Bar and Club Life Night Club.

WEB: www.latouche.jumptravel.com

B&B from £45.00 to £65.00
€57.14 to €82.53

PAT TUFFY
General Manager

American Express
Diners
Mastercard
Visa

Open All Year

AVONBRAE GUESTHOUSE

RATHDRUM,
CO. WICKLOW
TEL: 0404-46198 FAX: 0404-46198

GUESTHOUSE ★★★ MAP 8 O 9

A small, long established, family run guesthouse, nestling in the Wicklow Hills. We pride ourselves in our good food and personal attention and extend a warm welcome to first time guests and to the many who return again and again. Horse riding, trekking, fishing and excellent golf available locally. We specialise in hill walking holidays and to relax - our own indoor heated pool and games room.

B&B from £24.00 to £24.00
€30.47 to €30.47

PADDY GEOGHEGAN
Proprietor

American Express
Mastercard
Visa

Closed 30 November - 28 February

Room rates are IR£ per room per night

MOUNT BRACKEN HOUSE

CUNNIAMSTOWN, RATHDRUM,
CO. WICKLOW
TEL: 0404-46311 FAX: 0404-46922

GUESTHOUSE ★★ MAP 8 O 9

Mount Bracken House is situated in beautiful countryside on a private estate on the road to Avoca. Wicklow Town is within easy driving distance. All rooms are modern and en suite with magnificent views of the countryside. Fishing, golf and equestrian facilities are nearby. Ideal for touring and walking and only a half hour from beautiful sandy beaches. Via the newly-built N11 Dublin City is less than an hour away.

B&B from £22.50 to £25.00
€28.57 to €31.74

PETER & CATHERINE VAN DIJK
Managers

Mastercard

Visa

🏠🚫TC❄♻UJP
6 6

Open All Year

HUNTERS HOTEL

NEWRATH BRIDGE, RATHNEW,
CO. WICKLOW
TEL: 0404-40106 FAX: 0404-40338
EMAIL: hunters@indigo.ie

HOTEL ★★★ MAP 8 P 9

One of Ireland's oldest coaching inns, its award winning gardens along River Vartry provide a haven from the world at large. Restaurant provides the very best of Irish food, fresh fish. Local amenities include golf, tennis, horseriding and fishing. Beautiful sandy beaches and sightseeing in the Garden of Ireland. Dublin 44.8km. Rosslare 115.2km. Off N11 at Rathnew or Ashford. Irish Country Houses and Restaurant Association. Refurbished 95-96. 1996 new Conference Room added.

WEB: www.hunters.ie

Member of Ireland's Blue Book

B&B from £65.00 to £80.00
€8.53 to €101.57

GELLETLIE FAMILY
Proprietors

American Express

Diners

Mastercard

Visa

🏠🚫🅿️☎T❄CM❄UJP🔲♿
16 16

Closed 24 - 26 December

TINAKILLY COUNTRY HOUSE AND RESTAURANT

WICKLOW, (RATHNEW),
CO. WICKLOW
TEL: 0404-69274 FAX: 0404-67806
EMAIL: reservations@tinakilly.ie

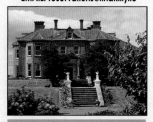

HOTEL ★★★★ MAP 8 P 9

This Victorian mansion was built for Captain Halpin, who laid the world's telegraph cables. The bedrooms, some with 4 posters, are furnished in period style and most overlook the Irish Sea. Award winning cuisine is prepared from garden vegetables, local fish and Wicklow lamb. The family welcome ensures a relaxing, memorable stay. Available locally - golf, horse riding, Powerscourt, Mount Usher Gardens and Wicklow Mountains. Dublin 46km. Awarded RAC Blue Ribbon for Excellence. Blue Book member.

WEB: www.tinakilly.ie

Member of Small Luxury Hotels

B&B from £74.00 to £104.00
€93.96 to €132.05

JOSEPHINE & RAYMOND
POWER Proprietors

American Express

Diners

Mastercard

Visa

☺ Midweek Off Peak Special from £138.00 (2 B&B and 1 Dinner)

🏠🚫🅿️♨TC❄❄🔲UJP🔲
52 52

♿♿

Open All Year

B&B rates are IR£ per person sharing per night incl. Breakfast

VALLEY HOTEL AND RESTAURANT

WOODENBRIDGE, VALE OF AVOCA, ARKLOW, CO. WICKLOW
TEL: 0402-35200 FAX: 0402-35542

HOTEL CR MAP 8 O 8

Quaint country family run hotel. Ideally located for touring County Wicklow. 1.5 miles from Ballykissangel. 1 hour to Dublin and Rosslare. Surrounded by woodlands and forest and gold miner stream running by hotel. Walking distance to Woodenbridge Golf Club. Our restaurant offers excellent food and our bars are lively with good atmosphere. Hill walking, fishing, beaches are all within minutes of the hotel.

B&B from £33.00 to £35.00
€41.90 to €44.44

DOREEN O'DONNELL
Proprietor

American Express
Diners
Mastercard
Visa

:/ ♪

😊 Weekend specials from £88.00

⌂🔥☎🖥TC⟲CM☀⌣♫🔊S
10 10

♿ alc

IRISH HOTELS FEDERATION

Open All Year

WOODENBRIDGE HOTEL

VALE OF AVOCA, ARKLOW, CO. WICKLOW
TEL: 0402-35146 FAX: 0402-35573
EMAIL: wbhotel@iol.ie

HOTEL ★★★ MAP 8 O 8

Family owned and run with 23 en suite bedrooms, rooms with balconies overlooking scenic 18 hole Woodenbridge Golf Course. Dating from 1608, the hotel is the oldest in Ireland. Our restaurant and bar serve the very best of food. Winner of tourism menu awards for 1998/'99. Bar food served all day. Horse riding, fishing, golfing, fine beaches and walking are all available locally. Near Avoca, film location for Ballykissangel. Adequate car parking.

B&B from £35.00 to £50.00
€44.44 to €63.49

ESTHER O'BRIEN & BILL O'BRIEN
Proprietors

American Express
Mastercard
Visa

:/ 🎿

⌂🔥☎🖥T⟍A⟍C⟲CM☀⌣♫P
23 23

 S⟍ alc

IRISH HOTELS FEDERATION

Closed 25 December

EMBASSIES & CONSULATES
ALL PREFIX (01)

AUSTRALIA
676 1517

AUSTRIA
269 4577

BELGIUM
269 2082

CANADA
478 1988

DENMARK
475 6404

FRANCE
260 1666

GERMANY
269 3011

ITALY
660 1744

JAPAN
269 4244

SPAIN
269 1640

UNITED KINGDOM
269 5211

UNITED STATES
668 8777

Room rates are IR£ per room per night

The East Coast and Midlands of Ireland offers a great diversity in scenery and a wealth of attractions to the visitor. Whether you are walking in the Wicklow Mountains or the Slieve Blooms, exploring the Shannon or the Cooley Peninsula or just relaxing on the sandy beaches,

this ancient Region has something for everybody. Catch the excitement of the Stradbally Steam Festival, the Wicklow Gardens Festival, Mullingar Bachelor's Festival and the Longford Summer Festival. In addition, there are many Summer Schools and other events, that take place throughout the Region.

MAJOR ATTRACTIONS

The Region is rich in archeological and historical sites of great interest, from the passage graves in the Boyne Valley, and the new Bru Na Boinne Visitor Centre, the early Christian settlements of Clonmacnoise and Glendalough to more recent wonders such as the Japanese Gardens at Tully; Wicklow Gaol, Wicklow Town; Avondale House in Rathdrum; Kilruddery House and Gardens, Bray; Russborough House in Blessington and Powerscourt Gardens and Waterfall, Enniskerry.

Other popular attractions include Newgrange Farm, Slane; Mosney; Crookstown Mill in Ballitore; Charleville Castle, Tullamore; Locke's Distillery, Kilbeggan; Athlone Castle Visitor Centre, Newtowncashel Heritage Centre and the designated Heritage towns of Athy, Kildare Town, Ardagh, Carlingford, Trim, Kells, Baltinglass, Abbeyleix and Tullamore; Heywood Gardens, Gash Gardens and Donaghmore Farm Museum in Co. Laois; Wineport Sailing Centre, Athlone; Holy Trinity Visitor Centre, Carlingford and the National Gardens

Exhibition Centre, Kilquade. In addition, Corlea Trackway Exhibition Centre, Kenagh; Ardagh Heritage Centre and the County Museum, Dundalk are also worth a visit as is the new Tullamore Dew Heritage Centre. Indeed there are many other interesting places to visit throughout the Region.

High quality golfing and equestrian facilities are widely available in the Region. Coarse, Game and Sea fishing is also available as is Cruising, Walking and other activities.

There is a great variety of accommodation from the most luxurious of Hotels to the more modest family run unit and other types of accommodation, each in their own way offering superb service to the visitor.

Full details on all festivals and events, heritage and special interest activities from angling to walking in the East Coast and Midlands Region are available from the local Tourist Information Office or from East Coast and Midlands Tourism, Market House, Mullingar, Co. Westmeath.
Tel: (00 353) 044-48650
Fax: (00 353) 044-40413
E-mail: midlandseasttourism@eircom.net
Web site: www.midlandseastireland.travel.ie

Budweiser Irish Derby Weekend, The Curragh, Co. Kildare.
June / July

Event details correct at time of going to press

CO. CAVAN
CAVAN TOWN / BAILIEBOROUGH / BALLINAGH

HOTEL KILMORE

DUBLIN ROAD, CAVAN
TEL: 049-433 2288 FAX: 049-433 2458
EMAIL: kilmore-sales@quinn-hotels.com

HOTEL ★★★   MAP 11 L 14

The Hotel Kilmore is ideally located in the heart of Ireland's Lakeland District. Recently refurbished, the hotel offers 39 luxuriously appointed rooms. Renowned for fine cuisine our AA Rosette Annalee Restaurant boasts a wide selection of dishes including local fish and game, complemented by an extensive wine list. Ideal venue for conferences and private functions the Hotel Kilmore is the perfect base for a business visit or to enjoy the varied leisure pursuits in the area.

WEB: www.quinnhotels.com
Member of Quinn Hotels

B&B from £41.00 to £45.00
€52.06 to €57.14

JIM BURKE
General Manager

American Express
Diners
Mastercard
Visa

Weekend specials from £95.00

39 39

Open All Year

BAILIE HOTEL

BAILIEBOROUGH, CO. CAVAN
TEL: 042-966 5334 FAX: 042-966 6506
EMAIL: mulbarton@eircom.net

HOTEL U   MAP 11 M 14

Friendly family run hotel. Rooms en suite. TV, direct dial phone. Excellent reputation for good food. Carvery lunches served daily. Also à la carte and evening dinner. Food served all day in lounge. Coarse fishing close by. Golf course and mountain climbing also close by. Newly opened swimming pool and leisure centre in town. Ideal for a relaxing break.

B&B from £25.00 to £30.00
€31.74 to €38.09

KEVIN MURPHY
Manager

American Express
Mastercard
Visa

Weekend specials from £60.00

18 17

Open All Year

LACKEN MILL HOUSE AND GARDENS

LACKEN LOWER, BALLINAGH, CO. CAVAN
TEL: 049-433 7592
EMAIL: info@lackenmillhouse.com

GUESTHOUSE P   MAP 11 K 14

Lacken Mill House, set amid four acres of mature woodlands, mill races, streams, developing gardens and 400 metres of River Erne frontage exudes exceptional beauty in natural surroundings. Fish the Erne on site or the myriad excellent local lakes. Enjoy various sporting activities or just relax in rural tranquillity. The stone built house offers Georgian elegance with open fires and all modern conveniences. Children welcome. Come and visit, you will return.

WEB: www.lackenmillhouse.com

B&B from £22.00 to £28.00
€27.93 to €35.55

NAOMI BRENNAN/ EAMON O'DONOGHUE

Mastercard
Visa

Weekend specials from £59.00

5 5

 Inet

Open All Year

Room rates are IR£ per room per night

MIDLANDS/LAKELANDS 151

KEEPERS ARMS

**BRIDGE STREET, BAWNBOY,
BALLYCONNELL, CO. CAVAN
TEL: 049-952 3318 FAX: 049-952 3008**

GUESTHOUSE ★★ MAP 11 K 15

Come taste our wares... in West Cavan. Enjoy the Shannon Erne Waterway on land or by water. Day or evening cruising, angling on our lakes and rivers, pet farms, Irish Music/Dancing Schools, horse riding, or try 18 Hole (Championship) golf all in our area. Explore to your heart's desire the maze of country roads adjoining the Cavan and Ulster Way. Delights on the Kingfisher Route with your bicycle. Unexpected pleasures await you in our peaceful & beautiful West Cavan.

B&B from £22.00 to £30.00
€27.93 to €38.09

SHEILA MCKIERNAN

Mastercard
Visa

11 11

Closed 24 - 26 December

SLIEVE RUSSELL HOTEL, GOLF & COUNTRY CLUB

**BALLYCONNELL,
CO. CAVAN
TEL: 049-952 6444 FAX: 049-952 6474
EMAIL: slieve-russell@quinn-hotels.com**

HOTEL ★★★★ MAP 11 K 15

The Slieve Russell Hotel, Golf and Country Club offers a unique experience in relaxation and leisure to our guests. Enjoy excellent cuisine, professional and friendly service and a range of leisure facilities. The 18 hole PGA championship golf course ensures a challenging game, whilst beginners will enjoy the 9 hole par 3 course. Country Club facilities include: a 20m leisure pool, saunas, steamroom, jacuzzi, fitness suite, tennis, squash, snooker, hair/beauty salon, crêche and games room.

WEB: www.quinnhotels.com

Member of Quinn Hotels

B&B from £75.00 to £110.00
€95.23 to €139.67

SHEILA GRAY
General Manager

American Express
Diners
Mastercard
Visa

😊 Special group rates available on request

151 151

98 18

Inet

Open All Year

CABRA CASTLE HOTEL

**KINGSCOURT,
CO. CAVAN
TEL: 042-966 7030 FAX: 042-966 7039
EMAIL: cabrach@iol.ie**

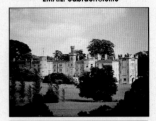

HOTEL U MAP 11 M 14

Follow in the footsteps of Oliver Cromwell and James II, and treat yourself to a stay in a Castle. Cabra Castle stands on 88 acres of gardens and parkland, with its own nine hole golf course. The bar and restaurant offer views over countryside famous for its lakes and fishing, as well as Dun a Ri Forest Park. An ideal venue for that holiday, specialising in golfing and equestrian holidays. Member of: Manor House Hotels Tel: 01-295 8900, GDS Access Code: UI Toll Free 1-800-44-UTELL.

WEB: www.cabracastle.com

Member of Manor House Hotels

B&B from £35.00 to £90.00
€44.44 to €114.28

HOWARD CORSCADDEN
Manager

American Express
Mastercard
Visa

67 67

Closed 23 - 27 December

PARK HOTEL

**VIRGINIA,
CO. CAVAN**
TEL: 049-854 7235   FAX: 049-854 7203
EMAIL: virginiapark@eircom.net

HOTEL ★★★   MAP 11 L 13

This beautifully restored hotel was built in 1750 as the hunting lodge of the Marquis De Headfort. Located on the shores of Lough Ramor and set in a 100 acre historic estate. Guests can avail of a 9 hole golf course, 15 miles of walking trails and beautiful gardens. Dine in the historic surroundings of The Marquis Restaurant, one of Ireland's top architecturally designed restaurants and take full advantage of the magnificent views over the gardens and lake.

WEB: www.bichotels.com

B&B from £45.00 to £70.00
€57.14 to €88.88

FRANK CLEVELAND

American Express
Diners
Mastercard
Visa

Midweek specials from £135.00

25 25

Open All Year

SHARKEYS HOTEL

**MAIN STREET, VIRGINIA,
CO. CAVAN**
TEL: 049-854 7561   FAX: 049-854 7761
EMAIL: sharkeys@destination-ireland.com

HOTEL ★★   MAP 11 L 13

Egon Ronay awardwinning family run hotel, situated in the heart of Virginia, 80km from Dublin, on the main route to Donegal. It is furnished to the highest standards, direct dial phone, TV in all rooms. Enjoy a day's fishing or travelling around the lake region and return to relax in the comfort of our restaurant and sample some of the delights of our awardwinning chef. It has both à la carte and dinner menu, carvery and extensive bar menu. Food served all day. 9 hole golf course 5 minutes walk.

WEB: www.destination-ireland.com/sharkeys

B&B from £37.50 to £40.00
€47.62 to €50.79

PAT AND GORETTI SHARKEY
Proprietors

Mastercard
Visa

Weekend specials from £75.00

13 13

Open All Year

CURRAGH LODGE HOTEL

**DUBLIN ROAD, KILDARE TOWN,
CO. KILDARE**
TEL: 045-522144   FAX: 045-521247

HOTEL ★★   MAP 7 M 10

The Curragh Lodge Hotel is situated in Kildare town on the N7 from Dublin going south. Steeped in history, Kildare is a must for tourists not only for its heritage but for its other attractions such as the Japanese Gardens and the Irish National Stud and Horse Museum. The Curragh Lodge Hotel offers excellent accommodation, food, drink, service and entertainment. Minutes away from the classic Curragh Racecourse and midway between Belfast and Cork. It is an ideal stopover.

B&B from £35.00 to £50.00
€44.44 to €63.49

LIAM MCLOUGHLIN
Manager

American Express
Diners
Mastercard
Visa

21 21

Open All Year

Room rates are IR£ per room per night

TONLEGEE HOUSE AND RESTAURANT

**ATHY,
CO. KILDARE**
TEL: 0507-31473 FAX: 0507-31473
EMAIL: tonlegeehouse@eircom.net

GUESTHOUSE ★★★★ MAP 7 M 9

Tonlegee House is situated on its own grounds, just outside Athy and only an hour from the bustle of Dublin. Our guests' relaxation is assured in the tranquil comfort of this lovingly restored Georgian Country House and Restaurant. With its antique furnishings and open fires it is an ideal place to stay for either an activity filled or leisurely break. Recommended by the Bridgestone Guide's Best 100 Places to Stay in Ireland.

Member of Premier Guesthouses

B&B from £40.00 to £40.00
€50.79 to €50.79

MARJORIE MOLLOY
Proprietor

American Express
Mastercard
Visa

Closed 01 - 14 November

ARDENODE HOTEL

**BALLYMORE EUSTACE,
CO. KILDARE**
TEL: 045-864198
EMAIL: ardenode@iol.ie

HOTEL ★★ MAP 8 N 10

Situated on the borders of Counties Wicklow and Kildare and just 20km from Dublin City, this hotel is a perfect base for touring. The Ardenode is a family run country house hotel, set in 7 acres of scenic gardens where personal attention, a warm welcome and friendly service awaits you. Enjoy fine dining in our gourmet restaurant. Relax in the scenic Garden Lounge. (Full leisure facilities available from Spring 2001.)

WEB: www.ardenode.hotel.ie

B&B from £37.50 to £100
€47.62 to €126.97

MICHELLE BROWNE
Manager

American Express
Mastercard
Visa

IRISH
HOTELS
FEDERATION

Closed 24 - 26 December

KILKEA CASTLE

**CASTLEDERMOT,
CO. KILDARE**
TEL: 0503-45156 FAX: 0503-45187
EMAIL: kilkea@iol.ie

HOTEL ★★★★ MAP 7 M 8

Kilkea Castle is the oldest inhabited Castle in Ireland. Built in 1180, offering the best in modern comfort while the charm and elegance of the past has been retained. The facilities include deluxe accommodation, a fine dining room, d'Lacy's Restaurant, restful bar/lounge area, full banqueting and conference facilities and full on site Leisure Centre with an indoor heated swimming pool, sauna, jacuzzi, steamroom and fully equipped gym. 18 hole golf course encircles the Castle.

WEB: www.kilkeacastle.ie

B&B from £80.00 to £130.00
€101.58 to €165.07

PAUL CORRIDAN
General Manager

American Express
Diners
Mastercard
Visa

IRISH
HOTELS
FEDERATION

Closed 23 - 27 December

STANDHOUSE HOTEL LEISURE & CONFERENCE CENTRE

**CURRAGH RACECOURSE,
THE CURRAGH, CO. KILDARE
TEL: 045-436177 FAX: 045-436180
EMAIL: standhse@indigo.ie**

HOTEL U   MAP 7 M 10

Standhouse Hotel has a tradition which dates back to 1700. Situated beside the Curragh Racecourse it has become synonymous with the classics. The premises has been restored to its former elegance and offers the discerning guest a fine selection of quality restaurants, bars, leisure facilities, including 20 metre pool, state of the art gym, jacuzzi, steam room, sauna and plunge pool. Conference facilities cater for 2 to 500 delegates.

B&B from £44.50 to £90.00
€56.50 to €114.28

ODHRAN LAWLOR
Manager

American Express
Mastercard
Visa

63 63

I R I S H
HOTELS
FEDERATION

Closed 25 - 26 December

AMBASSADOR HOTEL

**KILL,
CO. KILDARE
TEL: 045-877064 FAX: 045-877515
EMAIL: ambassador-sales@quinn-hotels.com**

HOTEL ★★★   MAP 8 N 10

Situated just 20km from Dublin City, this 36 bedroomed hotel is ideally located for those travelling from the south or west. Our restaurants boast excellent cuisine and our bar provides music 4 nights per week. Local amenities include 3 race courses, Curragh, Naas and Punchestown, four golf courses, Goffs Horse Sales, (just across the road) and plenty of horse riding. The Ambassador has something for everybody.

WEB: www.quinnhotels.com

Member of Quinn Hotels

B&B from £42.00 to £50.00
€53.33 to €63.49

NIALL CALLALY
General Manager

American Express
Diners
Mastercard
Visa

36 36

I R I S H
HOTELS
FEDERATION

Open All Year

Visit the

IRISH NATIONAL STUD
JAPANESE GARDENS
SAINT FIACHRA'S GARDEN

*"One visit...
...three different worlds"*

Opening Hours
12th Feb - 12th Nov.
9.30am to 6.00pm   7 Days
(last admission one hour before closing).

*Tully, Kildare Town,
Co. Kildare, Ireland.
Tel. +353-(0)45-521617 / 522963
Fax. +353-(0)45-522964*

*Email: stud@irish-national-stud.ie
Website: www.irish-national-stud.ie*

LEIXLIP HOUSE HOTEL

CAPTAIN'S HILL, LEIXLIP,
CO. KILDARE
TEL: 01-624 2268 FAX: 01-624 4177
EMAIL: manager@leixliphouse.com

HOTEL ★★★ MAP 8 N 11

A most elegant Georgian House Hotel built in 1772. Leixlip House is a mere 20 mins drive from Dublin City centre. The hotel has been lovingly restored and offers the discerning guest the highest standards of comfort and hospitality. It can cater for conferences of up to 70 people and our banqueting facilities can comfortably accommodate 120 people. Our signature restaurant The Bradaun has been awarded several accolades and offers varied and interesting menus & wine lists.

WEB: www.leixliphouse.com

Member of The Small Hotel Company

B&B from £60.00 to £75.00
€76.18 to €95.23

CHRISTIAN SCHMELTER
General Manager

American Express
Diners
Mastercard
Visa

15 15

Open All Year

GLENROYAL HOTEL, LEISURE CLUB & CONFERENCE CENTRE

STRAFFAN ROAD, MAYNOOTH,
CO. KILDARE
TEL: 01-629 0909 FAX: 01-629 0919
EMAIL: hotel@glenroyal.ie

HOTEL ★★★ MAP 8 N 11

Premier 3*** hotel with the finest of accommodation and leisure facilities 20 minutes from Dublin. Leisure facilities include 20m pool, aerobics studio, gym, sauna, jacuzzi and steamroom. Nancy Spain's Bar is always buzzing with conversation and laughter. Food is served here throughout the day, including carvery lunches and an extensive barfood menu. The restaurant has a fine reputation for its Irish and international cuisine. Entertainment a feature.

WEB: www.glenroyal.ie

B&B from £52.50 to £57.50
€66.66 to €73.01

HELEN COURTNEY
General Manager

American Express
Diners
Mastercard
Visa

Weekend specials from £115.00

52 52

Closed 25 December

STRAFFAN LODGE HOTEL

STRAFFAN ROAD, MAYNOOTH,
CO. KILDARE
TEL: 01-628 5002 FAX: 01-628 9781
EMAIL: bookings@straffanlodgehotel.com

HOTEL N MAP 8 N 11

The Straffan Lodge is a family owned and managed hotel situated in the heart of County Kildare. Ideally positioned close to the M4 and M50. 20 mins from the city centre. Our location is ideal for those interested in golf, racing, and all equestrian activities. Only a 5 min drive from the prestigious K Club. An 18-hole championship golf course designed by Arnold Palmer and venue for the Ryder Cup in 2005. It is an ideal haven for the golf enthusiast. Many golf courses nearby.

WEB: www.straffanlodgehotel.com

B&B from £35.00 to £39.50
€44.44 to €50.15

DEREK O'FARRELL &
MICHAEL FEATHERSTON

American Express
Diners
Mastercard
Visa

21 21

Closed 24 - 26 December

HAZEL HOTEL

**DUBLIN ROAD, MONASTEREVIN,
CO. KILDARE**
TEL: 045-525373 FAX: 045-525810
EMAIL: sales@hazelhotel.com

HOTEL ★★ MAP 7 N 10

The Hazel Hotel is a family run country hotel on the main Dublin/Cork/Limerick road (N7). All bedrooms have bath/shower, colour TV and international direct dial telephone. The hotel's restaurant has extensive à la carte and table d'hôte menus. Ample car parking. Entertainment is provided. Ideal base for going to the Curragh, Naas or Punchestown racecourses. Several golf courses close by. National Stud and Japanese Gardens only 7 miles from hotel. No service charge.

WEB: www.hazelhotel.com

Member of Logis of Ireland

B&B from £27.50 to £50.00
€34.92 to €63.48

MARGARET KELLY
Proprietor

American Express
Diners
Mastercard
Visa

15 15

Closed 25 - 26 December

HARBOUR HOTEL & RESTAURANT

**LIMERICK ROAD, NAAS,
CO. KILDARE**
TEL: 045-879145 FAX: 045-874002

HOTEL ★★ MAP 8 N 10

Looking after the needs of our guests and providing quality service is a priority in this family run hotel. All rooms have colour TV, direct dial telephone, hair dryer and teasmade. We offer superb home cooked food, extensive à la carte and table d'hôte menus and excellent wine list. Relax and enjoy a drink in our comfortable lounge. Conveniently situated to Dublin City, ferry, airport, Punchestown, The Curragh and Mondello.

B&B from £30.00 to £35.00
€38.09 to €44.44

MARY MONAGHAN
Proprietor

American Express
Diners
Mastercard
Visa

10 10

Closed 25 - 31 December

HILLVIEW HOUSE

**PROSPEROUS, NAAS,
CO. KILDARE**
TEL: 045-868252 FAX: 045-892305
EMAIL: hillview@eircom.net

GUESTHOUSE U MAP 8 N 11

Hillview House near Naas, is situated in golfers' paradise. 6 golf courses within 15 minutes, another 6 within 1/2 hour. 45 minutes to the airport and city centre. Between N4/N7 main routes south and west. Easy reach of Curragh, Punchestown, K-Club, Mondello. All rooms en suite, multi-channel TV, direct dial phone, tea/coffee facilities. Holistic centre on site, courses / workshops available. Whether touring, a golfer, race-goer, or just in need of a rest, we are here to welcome you.

WEB: www.kildare.ie/hillview

B&B from £25.00 to £39.00
€31.74 to €49.52

BRENDAN & MOIRA ALLEN
Proprietors

Mastercard
Visa

8 8

Closed 15 December - 5 January

Room rates are IR£ per room per night

ANNAGH LODGE GUESTHOUSE

NAAS ROAD, NEWBRIDGE,
CO. KILDARE
TEL: 045-433518 FAX: 045-433538
EMAIL: annaghlodge@eircom.net

GUESTHOUSE ★★★ MAP 7 M 10

New purpose-built guesthouse in peaceful setting, ideally located beside all town amenities, including hotels, restaurants and leisure centres. Facilities include private parking and sauna. Annagh Lodge provides the highest standard of comfort in superior rooms with all modern conveniences combined with excellent service. Dublin and the airport are 30 mins drive. Curragh, Naas and Punchestown racecourses, 8 golf courses and fishing are a short drive. Access for wheelchairs.

WEB: www.annaghlodge.ie

B&B from £30.00 to £45.00
€38.09 to €57.14

DERNA WALLACE
Proprietor

Mastercard

Visa

9 9

Closed 23 December - 02 January

GABLES GUESTHOUSE & LEISURE CENTRE

RYSTON, NEWBRIDGE,
CO. KILDARE
TEL: 045-435330   FAX: 045-435355

GUESTHOUSE ★★★ MAP 7 M 10

Set on the banks of the Liffey, our family run guesthouse has 10 bedrooms with bath/shower, multi channel TV, direct dial telephone, hairdryer and teas maid. Our leisure centre includes a 14 metre indoor swimming pool, jacuzzi, steam room, sauna and fully equipped gymnasium. Horse racing, golfing and fishing are well catered for locally. A warm and friendly welcome awaits you at the Gables. Brochures available on request.

B&B from £25.00 to £45.00
€31.74 to €57.14

RAY CRIBBIN
Proprietor

Mastercard

Visa

10 10

Closed 23 - 28 December

KEADEEN HOTEL

NEWBRIDGE,
CO. KILDARE
TEL: 045-431666 FAX: 045-434402
EMAIL: keadeen@iol.ie

HOTEL ★★★★ MAP 7 M 10

On 8 acres of award winning landscaped gardens, adjacent to the primary Dublin/Cork/Limerick road. This newly refurbished 4**** hotel containing The Keadeen Health and Fitness Club is only 40km from Dublin, 2km from The Curragh Racecourse and is easily accessible off the M7. All our luxurious en suite bedrooms are equipped to international standards. Our restaurant serves an extensive range of cuisine and has been awarded 2 red rosettes by The Automobile Association.

WEB: www.keadeenhotel.kildare.ie

B&B from £50.00 to £105.00
€63.49 to €133.32

ROSE O'LOUGHLIN
Proprietor

American Express

Diners

Mastercard

Visa

☺ Weekend specials from £105.00

55 55

Closed 24 December - 02 January

K CLUB

AT STRAFFAN,
CO. KILDARE
TEL: 01-601 7200 FAX: 01-601 7299
EMAIL: sales@kclub.ie

HOTEL ★★★★★ MAP 8 N 11

Ireland's only AA 5 Red Star hotel, located 30 minutes from Dublin Airport, invites you to sample its pleasures. Leisure facilities include an 18 hole championship golf course designed by Arnold Palmer, home to the Smurfit European Open and venue for the Ryder Cup in 2005. In addition, both river and coarse fishing are available with full health & leisure club and sporting activities. Meeting and private dining facilities also available.

WEB: www.kclub.ie

Member of Preferred Hotels & Resorts WW

Room Rate from £320.00 to £450.00
€406.31 to €1269.73

RAY CARROLL
Chief Executive

American Express
Diners
Mastercard
Visa

45 45

Open All Year

ABBEYLEIX MANOR HOTEL

ABBEYLEIX,
CO. LAOIS
TEL: 0502-30111 FAX: 0502-30220
EMAIL: info@abbeyleixmanorhotel.com

HOTEL N MAP 7 L 8

Already making a name for itself for its high standard of service, the recently opened Abbeyleix Manor Hotel with its fabulous bar and restaurant, is the perfect stop-off point halfway between Dublin and Cork on the N8. All the luxury bedrooms are en suite and food is available all day. Abbeyleix's friendly, rural atmosphere will revive the most jaded traveller and with golf, fishing and walking available locally, there is plenty to see and do.

WEB: www.abbeyleixmanorhotel.com

B&B from £30.00 to £40.00
€38.09 to €50.78

BILL O'CONNOR
Manager

American Express
Diners
Mastercard
Visa

23 23

Inet FAX

Closed 25 - 26 December

HIBERNIAN HOTEL

ABBEYLEIX,
CO. LAOIS
TEL: 0502-31252 FAX: 0502-31888

HOTEL ★★ MAP 7 L 8

Our family run hotel in Abbeyleix is the ideal place for a short break or holiday. We are situated on the main Dublin/Cork road (N8). Set in the finest Tudor style on the main street. Our excellent restaurant offers extensive à la carte and table d'hôte menus. All bedrooms are en suite with direct dial telephone. Scenic walks, 18 hole golf course, fishing and tennis also available.

B&B from £25.00 to £35.00
€31.74 to €44.44

MARY AND FRANK HARDING
Owners

Mastercard
Visa

Weekend specials from £65.00

10 10

Closed 25 - 27 December

Room rates are IR£ per room per night

CASTLE ARMS HOTEL

**THE SQUARE, DURROW,
CO. LAOIS
TEL: 0502-36117 FAX: 0502-36566**

HOTEL R   MAP 7 L 8

The Castle Arms Hotel is a family run hotel situated in the award winning picturesque village of Durrow. We are situated one and a half hours from Dublin, two hours from Cork and three hours from Belfast. Our reputation is for good food, service and friendliness. Local amenities include fishing, Granstown Lake is described as being the best Coarse fishing lake in Europe. Trout can be fished from the local rivers Erkina and Nore, horse trekking and many golf courses within easy reach.

B&B from £25.00 to £25.00
€31.74 to €31.74

SEOSAMH MURPHY
General Manager

Mastercard

Visa

🖥🅿☎🔒◻CMU♪🏛ald♨
10 10

⬛ IRISH HOTELS FEDERATION

Open All Year

MONTAGUE HOTEL

**EMO, PORTLAOISE,
CO. LAOIS
TEL: 0502-26154 FAX: 0502-26229**

HOTEL U   MAP 7 L 9

This attractive hotel is the perfect touring base to explore many parts of Ireland and our 70 comfortable bedrooms are en suite. Enjoy our de luxe carvery open daily for snacks, lunches and our Maple Room for evening meals. The Derries Bar with its relaxing atmosphere is ideal for the quiet drink. We have an excellent reputation for weddings, seminars and conferences. A warm friendly welcome awaits you at the Montague Hotel.

B&B from £35.00 to £45.00
€44.44 to €57.14

P. J. MCCANN
Group General Manager

American Express

Diners

Mastercard

Visa

🖥🅿☎◻TC✦CM✲U♪PS♨
70 70

ald👤♨

⬛ IRISH HOTELS FEDERATION

Open All Year

KILLESHIN HOTEL

**PORTLAOISE,
CO. LAOIS
TEL: 0502-21663 FAX: 0502-21976
EMAIL: killeshinhotel@eircom.net**

HOTEL ★★★   MAP 7 L 9

Centrally located just off the M7 approximately one and a half hours south of Dublin, you will find the ideal location for your weekend break. The Killeshin Hotel is the ideal stopover for the tourist or traveller. The location, cuisine and ambience together with our friendly relaxed style will ensure a memorable stay. Leisure centre which comprises 20 metre swimming pool, steam room, sauna, jacuzzi and state of the art gymnasium are now open.

B&B from £41.25 to £41.25
€52.38 to €52.38

P.J. MC CANN
Group General Manager

American Express

Diners

Mastercard

Visa

🖥🅿☎◻TC✦CM✲🛏◻♪PS
50 50

🅿ald👤♨

⬛ IRISH HOTELS FEDERATION

Open All Year

Room rates are IR£ per room per night

FOUR SEASONS HOTEL & LEISURE CLUB

COOLSHANNAGH,
MONAGHAN
TEL: 047-81888 FAX: 047-83131
EMAIL: info@4seasonshotel.ie

HOTEL ★★★   MAP 11 M 16

Elegance without extravagance! Enjoy the excellent service, warmth and luxury of this family run hotel. Relax by the turf fire in the Poitin Still Bar or savour the superb food and wine in the Range Restaurant. The bedrooms have all modern facilities and residents have unlimited use of the leisure club:- 18m pool, steamroom, jacuzzi, gymnasium and sunbed. Available locally:- 18 hole golf course, angling, equestrian centre and watersports.

B&B from £42.00 to £55.00
€53.32 to €69.83

FRANK MCKENNA
Managing Director

American Express
Diners
Mastercard
Visa

40 40

Closed 25 - 26 December

HILLGROVE HOTEL

OLD ARMAGH ROAD,
MONAGHAN
TEL: 047-81288 FAX: 047-84951
EMAIL: hillgrove@quinn-hotels.com

HOTEL U   MAP 11 M 16

This hotel combines comfort and genuine Irish hospitality, only 2 hours from Dublin, it offers 44 superbly appointed rooms, comfortable surroundings and a delightful restaurant. On the boundaries of the ecclesiastical capital of Ireland, the ancient seat of the Kings, the Hillgrove is perfectly situated for those who enjoy the rich tapestry of local history. There is a variety of activities offered by Monaghan, the most northerly town in the Lakeland region.

WEB: www.quinnhotels.com
Member of Quinn Hotels

B&B from £40.00 to £50.00
€50.79 to €63.49

ROSS MEALIFF
General Manager

American Express
Diners
Mastercard
Visa

Weekend specials from £98.00

44 44

Open All Year

NUREMORE HOTEL & COUNTRY CLUB

CARRICKMACROSS,
CO. MONAGHAN
TEL: 042 -966 1438 FAX: 042 -966 1853
EMAIL: nuremore@eircom.net

HOTEL ★★★★   MAP 12 N 14

A fine country hotel, Nuremore offers an unrivalled range of sporting and leisure facilities. Our parkland estate boasts a splendid 18 hole championship golf course. The superb country club has a swimming pool, whirlpool, sauna, steam room, gym, squash, tennis courts and snooker. Situated 1.5hrs from Dublin and Belfast. Extensive conference and banqueting facilities on site.

WEB: www.nuremore-hotel.ie

B&B from £70.00 to £100.00
€88.88 to €126.97

JULIE GILHOOLY
Proprietor

American Express
Diners
Mastercard
Visa

69 69

Open All Year

GLENCARN HOTEL AND LEISURE CENTRE

MONAGHAN ROAD,
CASTLEBLAYNEY, CO. MONAGHAN
TEL: 042-974 6666   FAX: 042-974 6521

HOTEL ★★★   MAP 11 M 15

Situated on the main Dublin route to the north west. This hotel has 27 bedrooms all en suite, with direct dial telephone, TV (family rooms available). Beside Lough Muckno Forest Park, great for fishing, water skiing, boating or a leisurely stroll. The Glencarn has established its name for quality food and efficient service. Music in the Temple Bar & night club. Our leisure centre boasts a jacuzzi, steam rooms, changing rooms, plunge pool, childrens pool, 21 metre swimming pool, gym.

B&B from £39.00 to £45.00
€49.52 to €57.14

PATRICK MCFADDEN
General Manager

American Express
Diners
Mastercard
Visa

:/♫♊

☺ Weekend specials from £90.00

🛏🍴☎📺TC📠CM❋✿♫PS
27 27

🔲alc

IRISH HOTELS FEDERATION

Closed 24 - 25 December

BROSNA LODGE HOTEL

BANAGHER-ON-THE-SHANNON,
CO. OFFALY
TEL: 0509-51350   FAX: 0509-51521
EMAIL: della@iolfree.ie

HOTEL ★★   MAP 7 J 10

A family owned country hotel, close to the River Shannon, welcomes guests with superb hospitality and relaxed elegance. Mature gardens surround the hotel. With unique peat bogs, mountains, the Shannon and Clonmacnois, you will delight in this gentle little known part of Ireland. Fishing, golf, pony trekking, nature and historical tours arranged locally. Enjoy beautiful food in our restaurant, The Fields and drinks in Pat's Olde Bar. Courtesy of Choice Programme.

WEB: www.brosnalodge.com

B&B from £26.00 to £28.00
€33.01 to €35.55

PAT & DELLA HORAN
Proprietors

American Express
Diners
Mastercard
Visa

:/♊

🛏🍴☎📺C📠CM❋♫PS
14 14

alc

IRISH HOTELS FEDERATION

Closed 25 - 26 December

COUNTY ARMS HOTEL

RAILWAY ROAD, BIRR,
CO. OFFALY
TEL: 0509-20791   FAX: 0509-21234
EMAIL: countyarmshotel@eircom.net

HOTEL ★★★   MAP 7 J 9

One of the finest examples of late Georgian architecture (C.1810), its well preserved interior features are outstanding. The atmosphere is warm, cosy & peaceful. Our hotel gardens and glasshouses provide fresh herbs, fruit and vegetables for our various menus. All our recently renovated bedrooms have private bathroom, telephone, colour TV & tea maker. 2 rooms adapted with facilities for disabled. Locally available golf, horseriding, fishing, tennis & heated indoor pool.

Member of MinOtel Ireland Hotel Group

B&B from £36.00 to £48.00
€45.71 to €60.95

WILLIE & GENE LOUGHNANE
Owners

American Express
Diners
Mastercard
Visa

:/♊

☺ Weekend specials from £92.00

🛏🍴☎TC📠CM❋♫JP
24 24

alc 🔲 Inet

Closed 24 - 28 December

Room rates are IR£ per room per night

DOOLYS HOTEL

EMMET SQUARE, BIRR,
CO. OFFALY
TEL: 0509-20032 FAX: 0509-21332
EMAIL: doolyshotel@esatclear.ie

HOTEL ★★★ MAP 7 J 9

An historic 250 year old coaching inn, this 3*** Bord Failte and AA hotel has been modernised to a very high standard of comfort and elegance. All bedrooms en suite, tastefully decorated with colour TV, video, radio, direct dial phone, tea/coffee making facilities. The Emmet Restaurant offers superbly cooked international dishes and is complemented by our modern Coachouse Grill and Bistro where you can obtain hot meals all day.

WEB: www.doolyshotel.com

B&B from £35.00 to £37.00
€44.44 to €46.98

SHARON GRANT/JO DUIGNAN
Proprietor/Manager

American Express
Diners
Mastercard
Visa

☺ Weekend specials from £85.00

18 18

Closed 25 December

KINNITTY CASTLE DEMESNE

KINNITTY, BIRR,
CO. OFFALY
TEL: 0509-37318 FAX: 0509-37284
EMAIL: kinnittycastle@eircom.net

HOTEL U MAP 7 J 9

The luxuriously refurbished Castle is situated 1.5 hrs from Dublin, Galway and Limerick, 37 magnificent en suite rooms, stately reception rooms in the main castle and excellent restaurant with gourmet food and fine wines. Conference & banqueting facilities are available. Moneyguyneen House on the estate with 12 en suite bedrooms is refurbished to exceptional country house standards. Facilities include an equestrian centre, clay pigeon shooting, walking, golf and fishing nearby.

WEB: www.kinnittycastle.com

B&B from £90.00 to £125.00
€114.28 to €158.72

FEARGHAL O'SULLIVAN
General Manager

American Express
Diners
Mastercard
Visa

☺ Weekend specials from £155.00

49 49

Open All Year

MALTINGS GUESTHOUSE

CASTLE STREET, BIRR,
CO. OFFALY
TEL: 0509-21345 FAX: 0509-22073

GUESTHOUSE ★★★ MAP 7 J 9

Secluded on a picturesque riverside setting beside Birr Castle, in the centre of Ireland's finest Georgian town. Built circa 1810 to store malt, for Guinness, and converted in 1994 to a 13 bedroom guesthouse with full bar and restaurant. All bedrooms are comfortably furnished with bath/shower en suite, colour TV and phones.

B&B from £22.50 to £25.00
€28.57 to €31.74

MAEVE GARRY
Manageress

Mastercard
Visa

☺ Midweek specials from £65.00

13 13

Open All Year

SPINNERS TOWN HOUSE

CASTLE ST, BIRR,
CO.OFFALY
TEL: 0509-21673   FAX: 0509-21672
EMAIL: spinners@indigo.ie

GUESTHOUSE ★★ MAP 7 J 9

With an outlook over the majestic walls of Birr Castle, the townhouse offers a modern revival of Georgian architecture and style. An enclosed courtyard garden and 13 spacious stylish bedrooms, thoughtfully designed for comfort and relaxation offering an hospitable oasis for the weary traveller. En suite rooms, direct dial phone and tour guide on request, French/German spoken. Our Bistro internationally renowned for food and wine...A complete hospitality package.

WEB: www.spinners-townhouse.com

B&B from £22.50 to £35.00
€28.57 to €44.44

LIAM F MALONEY
Managing Director

American Express
Diners
Mastercard
Visa

🛏🍴📺Ⓣ🅰Ⓒ♥CM✳☺ⒿⓈⓎalc
13 10
Inet FAX

IRISH
HOTELS
FEDERATION

Open All Year

BRIDGE HOUSE HOTEL & LEISURE CLUB

TULLAMORE,
CO. OFFALY
TEL: 0506-22000   FAX: 0506-25690
EMAIL: info@bridgehouse.com

HOTEL N MAP 7 K 10

The famous Bridge House, now a luxury 72 room hotel and leisure complex in the heart of Tullamore. Magnificent award winning bar, restaurant & coffee shop we are justifiably proud of our great tradition of hospitality, good food & service. The leisure complex, indoor swimming pool, spa pool, sauna, jacuzzi, gym & indoor world club golf driving range & simulator, 2 18 hole golf courses within 5 mins. Shopping centre & numerous attractions and activities locally.

WEB: www.bridgehouse.com

B&B from £55.00 to £65.00
€69.84 to €82.53

COLM MCCABE
Manager

American Express
Mastercard
Visa

✅

🛏🍴📺▯▯Ⓣ🅰Ⓒ♥CM✳🛴🐕👜
72 72
📷☺ⓊⒿ🎵ⓅⓈ🅰alc — Inet FAX

IRISH
HOTELS
FEDERATION

Closed 24 - 26 December

Room rates are IR£ per room per night

MOORHILL HOUSE HOTEL

MOORHILL, CLARA ROAD,
TULLAMORE, CO. OFFALY
TEL: 0506-21395 FAX: 0506-52424
EMAIL: info@moorhill.ie

HOTEL U   MAP 7 K 10

Mature chestnut trees and manicured lawns form a tranquil setting for the Victorian elegance of Moorhill. Superbly appointed bedrooms in the old house and garden mews, complement the softly furnished bar, with great atmosphere and open fires. Dining at Moorhill is special, with superb food, in surroundings that introduce the Victorian era to the New Millennium. Bookings through tourist office, travel agent or directly to Moorhill.

WEB: www.moorhill.ie

B&B from £30.00 to £40.00
€38.09 to €50.79

DAVID AND ALAN DUFFY

American Express
Mastercard
Visa

☺ Weekend specials from £90.00

Closed 24 - 26 December

SEA DEW GUESTHOUSE

CLONMINCH ROAD, TULLAMORE,
CO. OFFALY
TEL: 0506-52054 FAX: 0506-52054

GUESTHOUSE ★★★   MAP 7 K 10

Set in a mature garden of trees, Sea Dew is a purpose built guesthouse, providing guests with a high standard of comfort, located only 5 minutes walk from the town centre. The conservatory breakfast room will give you a bright start to the day, where there is an excellent selection of fresh produce. All bedrooms are spacious with en suite facilities, TV and direct dial telephones. Golfing, fishing, horse riding and shooting are available nearby. Access for wheelchairs.

B&B from £26.00 to £26.00
€33.01 to €33.01

CLAIRE & FRANK GILSENAN
Proprietors

Mastercard
Visa

Closed 23 December - 02 January

TULLAMORE COURT HOTEL

TULLAMORE,
CO. OFFALY
TEL: 0506-46666 FAX: 0506-46677
EMAIL: info@tullamorecourthotel.ie

HOTEL U   MAP 7 K 10

Situated in the heart of Ireland, the Tullamore Court Hotel is close to a range of amenities including golf courses, Clonmacnoise monastic settlement, the Slieve Bloom Mountains and the heritage town of Birr with its castle and gardens, making it the ideal location for a conference, special event or holiday break. The hotel offers 72 luxurious guest rooms, superb restaurant, lively bar, conference and banqueting facilities for up to 550 people and state of the art leisure facilities.

WEB: www.tullamorecourthotel.ie

B&B from £75.00 to £110.00
€95.23 to €139.67

JOE O'BRIEN
Managing Director

American Express
Diners
Mastercard
Visa

☺ Weekend specials from £120.00

Closed 24 - 26 December

CREGGAN COURT HOTEL

KILMARTIN N6 CENTRE, N6 ROUNDABOUT,
ATHLONE, CO. WESTMEATH
TEL: 0902-77777 FAX: 0902-77111
EMAIL: info@creggancourt.com

HOTEL P MAP 7 J 11

The Creggan Court Hotel located just off the N6 in Athlone, midway between Dublin & Galway. The ideal base to explore Clonmacnois, Ely O'Carroll country and the Shannon Basin, Athlone a golfer's paradise, surrounded by local championship golf courses including Glasson Golf Club. The Creggan Court Hotel offers spacious en suite family rooms, direct dial ISDN lines. Casual dining in our Granary Bar & Restaurant or a romantic dinner for two in our Lemon Tree Restaurant.

WEB: www.creggancourt.com

B&B from £35.00 to £50.00
€44.44 to €63.49

GERARD MOYLAN
General Manager

American Express
Diners
Mastercard
Visa

Weekend specials from £75.00

73 73

Inet FAX

Closed 25 December

HODSON BAY HOTEL

ATHLONE,
CO. WESTMEATH
TEL: 0902-80500 FAX: 0902-80520
EMAIL: info@hodsonbayhotel.com

HOTEL ★★★ MAP 11 J 11

Located on the lakeshore of Lough Ree, commanding breathtaking views of the neighbouring golf club and surrounding countryside. Offering sandy beaches and a modern marina with cruiser berthing, summer season daily lake cruise. The purpose built conference centre, leisure complex and award-winning bar and two rosette AA fish restaurant combine to make the hotel one of the finest in Ireland. Exit Athlone bypass, take the N61 Roscommon Road.

WEB: www.hodsonbayhotel.com

B&B from £40.00 to £60.00
€50.79 to €76.18

MICHAEL DUCIE
Director/General Manager

American Express
Diners
Mastercard
Visa

Weekend specials from £79.00

133 133

Open All Year

LAKESIDE HOTEL & MARINA

BALLYKEERAN, GLASSON, ATHLONE,
CO. WESTMEATH
TEL: 0902-85163 FAX: 0902-85431
EMAIL: info@lakesidehotel.ie

HOTEL ★★ MAP 7 J 11

Nestled on the shores of the inner lakes of Lough Ree, the Lakeside Hotel in its rich, tranquil surroundings provides the intimate location for your break. Local activities include golf, cruising, horseriding, walking or just relaxing….. Conference facilities for 10-500. Extensive carvery and à la carte bar food menu specialising in steak and locally produced seafood. Also home of the MV Goldsmith, Ireland's largest inland luxury ship cruising Lough Ree and the River Shannon with full bar and catering services on board for up to 120 guests.

WEB: www.lakesidehotel.ie

B&B from £25.00 to £45.00
€31.74 to €57.14

CHRIS MORAN & MAUREEN FLYNN
Managing Directors

American Express
Diners
Mastercard
Visa

10 10

Open All Year

Room rates are IR£ per room per night

PRINCE OF WALES HOTEL

**CHURCH STREET, ATHLONE,
CO. WESTMEATH
TEL: 0902-72626 FAX: 0902-75658**

HOTEL R   MAP 11 J 11

The Prince of Wales offers 69 tastefully refurbished en suite bedrooms. Situated in the heart of Athlone on the banks of the River Shannon, we are the ideal base to discover the unspoilt beauty of the midlands and west coast. Our facilities include superb restaurant, carvery and Preachers Bar. Local amenities: cruise of the River Shannon, bog tour, Clonmacnois, championship golf courses, pony riding and bowling.

WEB: www.pwh-athlone.com

B&B from £40.00 to £65.00
€50.79 to €82.53

**PAUL J RYAN
Managing Director**

American Express
Diners
Mastercard
Visa

:/T

Weekend specials from £99.00

69 69

Closed 24 - 26 December

ROYAL HOEY HOTEL

**ATHLONE,
CO. WESTMEATH
TEL: 0902-72924   FAX: 0902-75194**

HOTEL ★★   MAP 11 J 11

The Royal Hoey hotel offers comfort and cuisine. Today, the Royal is a modern hotel with all the services and comforts associated with today's travellers' needs. There are 38 luxuriously appointed bedrooms, colour TV, telephone, passenger lift to all floors, secure car parking, fully licensed bar and function room. Excellent restaurant. Fast food coffee dock. Restful lounge space, where you can relax and enjoy a slower pace of life.

B&B from £37.50 to £45.00
€47.62 to €57.14

**MARY HOEY
Proprietor**

American Express
Diners
Mastercard
Visa

✓/T

38 38

Closed 25 - 29 December

SHAMROCK LODGE HOTEL AND CONFERENCE CENTRE

**CLONOWN ROAD, ATHLONE,
CO. WESTMEATH
TEL: 0902-92601   FAX: 0902-92737**

HOTEL U   MAP 11 J 11

Extensive landscaped gardens form a tranquil setting for this elegant manor style country house. The hotel is situated in the heart of Ireland, just 5 minutes walk from Athlone Town centre, making it the ideal location for conferences or as a touring base for the rest of Ireland. Our superbly appointed en suite bedrooms are equipped with all modern facilities while still retaining their old world charm.

B&B from £40.00 to £50.00
€50.79 to €63.49

**PADDY MCCAUL
Proprietor**

American Express
Diners
Mastercard
Visa

:/T

Midweek (3 B&B and 2 Dinners) from £126.00

27 27

Closed 24 - 26 December

AUSTIN FRIAR HOTEL

AUSTIN FRIARS STREET, MULLINGAR,
CO. WESTMEATH
TEL: 044-45777 FAX: 044-45880

HOTEL U MAP 11 L 12

Offering warm hospitality in the best of Irish tradition, the Austin Friar Hotel provides a range of modern facilities and a dedicated professional and friendly service. Unique in its structural design, the hotel was built in an elliptical shape and features a central atrium. All rooms are en suite with interiors of warm natural colour and soft furnishing giving a modern, sophisticated appearance. Austins, the Californian-style restaurant, is the ideal place to enjoy good food.

WEB: www.globalgolf.com

B&B from £35.00 to £75.00
€44.44 to €95.23

JOHN VARLEY
General Manager

American Express
Diners
Mastercard
Visa

Weekend specials from £79.00

19 19

Closed 24 - 26 December

BLOOMFIELD HOUSE HOTEL & LEISURE CLUB

TULLAMORE ROAD, MULLINGAR,
CO. WESTMEATH
TEL: 044-40894 FAX: 044-43767
EMAIL: bloomfieldhouse@eircom.net

HOTEL ★★★ MAP 11 L 12

Situated 2 miles south of Mullingar on the shores of Lough Ennell, Bloomfield House is the perfect place to unwind and relax. Only 1 hour from Dublin, the hotel can boast 65 en suite rooms, a lake-view bar and restaurant and a full leisure centre including massage, aromatherapy and beauty therapies. It is adjacent to Mullingar Golf Club and Belvedere House & Gardens and a full range of activities can be arranged, from equestrian to fishing.

WEB: www.bloomfieldhouse.com

Member of Executive Club

B&B from £35.00 to £60.00
€44.44 to €76.18

SEAMUS LAFFAN
General Manager

American Express
Diners
Mastercard
Visa

65 65

Closed 24 - 26 December

Take a break at Glendeers 6 Acre Open Farm, sign-posted on the N6, just west of Athlone.Stretch your legs along the unspoilt nature walk where old horse drawn farm machinery can be viewed, Feed the pet animals which include deer, Vietnamese pot belly pigs, emu, ostrich, ponies, donkeys, Jersey cows, Jacob sheep, Anglo Nubian goats, peacocks and other rare birds and domestic fowl. A coffee shop, souvineer, craft & tuck shop, with soft drink, ice cream sweets etc.,picnic area, playground and toilet facilities are also provided. The farm has been designed so that visitors can mingle with all the pet animals.Groups catered for with guided tour by arrangement, also suitable for birthday parties.

For the month of December Glendeer is transformed into Irelands Lapland with Santa and his live deer, "Dancer" and Prancer". A crib with illuminated figures and live animals. A snow scene and lots more.

Glendeer Pet Farm
Phone: 00 353 902 37147
E-mail: glendeer@glendeer.com
web: www.glendeer.com

Room rates are IR£ per room per night

CROOKEDWOOD HOUSE

**MULLINGAR,
CO. WESTMEATH
TEL: 044-72165 FAX: 044-72166
EMAIL: cwoodhse@iol.ie**

GUESTHOUSE ★★★★ MAP 11 L 12

A crooked road winds you up the hill to Crookedwood House, a 200 year old rectory overlooking Lake Derravaragh, the home of the Children of Lir. This is a wonderful spot to relax and enjoy superb food cooked by Noel, one of Ireland's noted chefs. Crookedwood House is a member of Ireland's Blue Book and is listed in all major guides.

WEB: www.iol.ie/~cwoodhse

Member of Ireland's Blue Book

B&B from £45.00 to £55.00
€57.14 to €69.84

**NOEL & JULIE KENNY
Owners/Proprietors**

American Express
Diners
Mastercard
Visa

88

Open All Year

GREVILLE ARMS HOTEL

**MULLINGAR,
CO. WESTMEATH
TEL: 044-48563   FAX: 044-48052**

HOTEL ★★★ MAP 11 L 12

In the heart of Mullingar Town, the Greville Arms is a home from home with none of the packaged commerciality offered by so many modern hotels. Bedrooms all en suite, colour TV and direct dial phone. Most bedrooms look on to the unique garden and conservatory which is one of the finest gardens to be found in a town centre hotel. The new Greville Restaurant is noted for fine cuisine and wines. The Greville is the perfect centre for touring and action packed breaks.

B&B from £40.00 to £55.00
€50.79 to €69.84

**JOHN COCHRANE
General Manager**

American Express
Diners
Mastercard
Visa

 Weekend specials from £90.00

39 39

alc

IRISH
HOTELS
FEDERATION

Closed 25 December

AN TINTAIN GUESTHOUSE

**MAIN STREET, MULTYFARNHAM,
CO. WESTMEATH
TEL: 044-71411 FAX: 044-71434
EMAIL: milburns@gofree.indigo.ie**

GUESTHOUSE ★★★ MAP 11 K 12

Situated in a picturesque riverside setting with listed forge, in the quaint village of Multyfarnham. Behind the old world frontage lies a modern, luxurious, purpose built 3* guesthouse and restaurant, furnished to the highest standards, complete with TV, direct dial phone and hairdryer, all rooms en suite. Enjoy a relaxing drink and candlelit dining in our renowned fully licensed restaurant. Located in the heart of the country we are an ideal base for touring.

Member of Premier Guesthouses

B&B from £25.00 to £27.50
€31.74 to €34.92

**IAN & LIZ MILBURN
Proprietors**

Mastercard
Visa

88

Closed 02 - 26 January

SOUTH EAST
The Sunny South East

"River Valleys in an Ancient Land" - that's how best to summarise the very special appeal of Ireland's South East.

This is one of the best loved holiday regions among Irish people themselves. It combines the tranquil elegance of historic old towns and villages with the classic splendour of medieval Kilkenny and Waterford, the crystal city and regional capital.

There's a beautiful coastline too, dotted with sandy beaches and a mild warm climate which inspired the term "Sunny South East"

But it is the rivers which give uniqueness to the South East. The Slaney, Barrow, Nore, Suir and Blackwater carve a patchwork of fertile valleys and plains through Carlow, Kilkenny, South Tipperary, Waterford and Wexford as they wind their majestic way to the Celtic Sea.

They criss-cross the picturesque landscape past remnants of ancient times and older peoples, the Celts, Vikings, Normans and Anglo-Saxons. They were the early invaders, explorers, traders and missionaries. Their castles, abbeys, stone bridges and settlements lie scattered across the countryside as constant reminders of bygone times.

There's as much to do as to see in the South East. Golfers may enjoy the 'South East Sunshine Circuit' - 28 golf courses in all, mostly parkland, almost all uncluttered for free-and-easy golf.

Horse back lovers can choose between 29 registered centres. Anglers may enjoy sea, game or coarse fishing. Walkers and cyclists love the undulating countryside, the spectacular coastal ways.

Close to 60 visitor centres are open for visitors to explain the region's unique heritage more fully, e.g. Irish National Heritage Park.

Resorts like Courtown, Rosslare, Kilmore Quay, the Hook, Dunmore East, Tramore, Ardmore and Clonea lure families to the seaside in great numbers. They provide opportunities for endless fun and entertainment.

If you have not yet visited the South East, there's a special welcome in store.

For further details, contact South East Tourism, The Quay, Waterford.

Telephone: 051-875823.

Fax: 051-877388 or call to any of the South East's other year-round Tourist Offices at Carlow, Clonmel, Dungarvan, Kilkenny, Waterford, Wexford and Rosslare.

Kilkenny Arts Week, Kilkenny.
August

Wexford Opera Festival, Wexford.
October

Event details correct at time of going to press

CO. CARLOW
CARLOW TOWN

BALLYVERGAL HOUSE

DUBLIN ROAD,
CARLOW
TEL: 0503-43634 FAX: 0503-40386
EMAIL: ballyvergal@indigo.ie

GUESTHOUSE ★★ MAP 7 M 8

A large family run guesthouse conveniently located just outside Carlow Town on the Dublin Road (N9), adjacent to Carlow's 18 hole championship golf course. We offer our guests en suite rooms with TV, direct dial phone and hairdryer, a large residents' lounge and extensive private car parking. Most importantly you are assured of a warm friendly welcome. We are ideally located for golf (Carlow, Mount Wolseley, Kilkea Castle, Mount Juliet), angling, shooting, horseriding, and pitch & putt.

B&B from £20.00 to £25.00
€25.39 to €31.74

CON & ITA MARTIN
Proprietors

American Express
Mastercard
Visa

9 9

Open All Year

BARROWVILLE TOWN HOUSE

KILKENNY ROAD, CARLOW TOWN,
CO. CARLOW
TEL: 0503-43324 FAX: 0503-41953

GUESTHOUSE ★★★ MAP 7 M 8

"A Personal Guesthouse of Quality." A period listed residence in own grounds. 4 minutes to town centre. Well appointed rooms with most facilities. Antique furnishing. Traditional/buffet breakfast served in conservatory overlooking gardens. Ideal location for golf at Carlow, Kilkea, Mount Wolseley. Touring South East, Midlands, Glendalough, Kilkenny, Waterford and various gardens. Recommended AA, RAC, Travellers Guide, Bridgestone 100 Best and other good guide books. German spoken.

WEB: www.premier-guesthouses.ie

Member of Premier Guesthouses

B&B from £23.50 to £27.50
€29.84 to €34.92

RANDAL & MARIE DEMPSEY
Proprietors

American Express
Mastercard
Visa

7 7

Open All Year

CARLOW GUESTHOUSE

GREEN LANE, DUBLIN ROAD,
CARLOW
TEL: 0503-36033 FAX: 0503-36034
EMAIL: carlowguesthouse@eircom.net

UNDER CONSTRUCTION OPENING JAN 2001

GUESTHOUSE P MAP 7 M 8

Opening January 2001. Located on the N9, 5 minute walk from town centre approaching from Dublin. Our property is secluded on its own grounds with private gardens and car parks. Carlow Guest House offers an ideal setting to tour the South East during the day while enjoying Carlow's bustling nightlife in the evening including a wide selection of restaurants, music venues, etc to satisfy every taste. Room facilities include TV, trouser press, hair dryer, tea/coffee, and telephone.

WEB: www.carlowguesthouse.com

B&B from £23.00 to £28.00
€29.20 to €35.55

GER MCCORMACK

Mastercard
Visa

Weekend specials from £60.00

8 8

Open All Year

B&B rates are IR£ per person sharing per night incl. Breakfast

DOLMEN HOTEL AND RIVER COURT LODGES

KILKENNY ROAD,
CARLOW
TEL: 0503-42002   FAX: 0503-42375
EMAIL: reservations@dolmenhotel.ie

HOTEL ★★★   MAP 7 M 8

Nestled along the scenic banks of the River Barrow and set in 20 acres of landscaped beauty is the Dolmen Hotel, 1.5km from Carlow. Fishing, golf, shooting and horseriding are just some of the sporting facilities surrounding the hotel. With 40 beautifully appointed rooms including 3 luxury suites with en suite, TV, direct dial phone, trouser press and hairdryer. Our 1 bedroomed lodges are ideal for the sporting enthusiast. Largest conference and banqueting facilities in the South East.

WEB: www.dolmenhotel.ie

B&B from £39.50 to £52.50
€50.15 to €66.66

PADRAIG BLIGHE
General Manager

American Express
Diners
Mastercard
Visa

Weekend specials from £89.00

40 40

Closed 25 December

SEVEN OAKS HOTEL

ATHY ROAD,
CARLOW
TEL: 0503-31308   FAX: 0503-32155
EMAIL: sevenoak@eircom.net

HOTEL ★★★   MAP 7 M 8

A hotel of quality, standing in 2 acres of landscaped gardens offering you detailed personal service. We specialise in the best of Irish Foods in our award-winning Tudor Bar Carvery and intimate restaurant. Individually designed bedrooms are accessible by lift and have tea/coffee facilities, TV/Video, hairdryers, trousers press and telephone. 18 hole golf courses, shooting and fishing available locally. 20 metre pool and leisure club opening Spring 2001.

WEB: www.irelandhotels.com

B&B from £40.00 to £45.00
€50.79 to €57.14

MICHAEL MURPHY
Manager/Director

American Express
Diners
Mastercard
Visa

Special offers apply

38 38

Closed 25 December

LORD BAGENAL INN

MAIN STREET, LEIGHLINBRIDGE,
CO. CARLOW
TEL: 0503-21668   FAX: 0503-22629
EMAIL: info@lordbagenal.com

HOTEL N   MAP 7 M 8

Situated in the heritage village of Leighlinbridge along the River Barrow, with private marina and gardens, we are ideally located to explore the South East. Our en suite bedrooms are luxuriously furnished to the highest standards. Award winning restaurant reputed for fine food and excellent wines. Locals and visitors frequent our bar where carvery lunch and bar food are served daily. Children always welcome. Weddings, conferences, banquets catered for.

WEB: www.lordbagenal.com

B&B from £35.00 to £67.00
€44.44 to €85.07

JAMES & MARY KEHOE

Diners
Mastercard
Visa

12 12

Closed 25 - 26 December

Room rates are IR£ per room per night

MOUNT WOLSELEY HOTEL, GOLF AND COUNTRY CLUB

TULLOW,
CO. CARLOW
TEL: 0503-51674 FAX: 0503-52123
EMAIL: wolseley@iol.ie

HOTEL U MAP 8 N 8

Sensitive restoration of existing buildings, some dating back to the first half of the last century, coupled with additional construction work, have combined to provide a hotel with conference facilities, health centre and accommodation of exceptional standards with timeless elegance at Mount Wolseley Golf and Country Club. The hotel, itself an architectural delight, offering panoramic views of the golfcourse, featuring bars, lounges, restaurant and function rooms.

WEB: www.mountwolseley.ie

B&B from £45.00 to £55.00
€57.13 to €69.83

ANN MARIE MORRISSEY
Hotel Manager

Mastercard

Visa

2 nights B&B and 1 dinner from £95.00

40 40

Open All Year

BAMBRICKS TROYSGATE HOUSE

KILKENNY CITY,
CO. KILKENNY
TEL: 056-51000 FAX: 056-51200

GUESTHOUSE U MAP 7 L 7

Troysgate House formerly the Jailhouse of the old walled-in medieval City of Kilkenny. 20 en suite rooms newly constructed in 1994. Angling, swimming, horse riding nearby. Kilkenny Golf Course 1km away. It is an historic and charming old world inn which has retained its character while serving the needs of the modern world. Troysgate House incorporates Bambrick's renowned traditional pub which truly has an atmosphere all of its own. Winner of the Dining Pub of the Year 2000.

B&B from £20.00 to £45.00
€25.39 to €57.14

GREG FLANNERY
Manager

Mastercard

Visa

20 20

Open All Year

BERKELEY HOUSE

5 LOWER PATRICK STREET,
KILKENNY
TEL: 056-64848 FAX: 056-64829
EMAIL: berkeleyhouse@eircom.net

GUESTHOUSE ★★★ MAP 7 L 7

A warm and genuine welcome awaits you here at this charming owner operated period residence, uniquely situated in the very heart of medieval Kilkenny City. Berkeley House boasts ample private car parking, 10 spacious & tastefully decorated rooms, all en suite with multi channel TV, direct dial phone & tea/coffee facilities. We pride ourselves with a dedicated and professional team and ensure that every effort will be made to make your stay with us a most enjoyable one.

B&B from £27.50 to £37.50
€34.92 to €47.62

DECLAN CURTIS
Manager

Mastercard

Visa

10 10

Closed 22 - 26 December

B&B rates are IR£ per person sharing per night incl. Breakfast

BRANNIGANS GLENDINE INN

CASTLECOMER ROAD,
KILKENNY
TEL: 056-21069 FAX: 056-70714
EMAIL: branigan@iol.ie

GUESTHOUSE R MAP 7 L 7

The Glendine Inn has been a licensed tavern for over 200 years. It consists of 7 bedrooms (all en suite), a residents' lounge and dining room on 1st floor. Downstairs there are lounge and public bars serving snack or bar lunches. We are ideally located for golf (course 200m away), the railway station and the historic city of Kilkenny only 1.5km away. We assure you of a friendly welcome.

B&B from £22.00 to £30.00
€27.93 to €38.09

MICHAEL BRANNIGAN
Proprietor

American Express
Diners
Mastercard
Visa

7 7

Open All Year

BUTLER HOUSE

PATRICK STREET,
KILKENNY
TEL: 056-65707 FAX: 056-65626
EMAIL: res@butler.ie

GUESTHOUSE ★★★ MAP 7 L 7

Sweeping staircases, magnificent plastered ceilings, marble fireplaces and a walled garden are all features of this notable Georgian townhouse. Although secluded and quiet Butler House is located in the heart of the city, close to the castle. The house was restored by the Irish State Design Agency in the early 1970s. The combination of contemporary design and period elegance provides an interesting and unique experience. Suites and superior rooms available. Conference/ function facilities and private car park available. AA ◆◆◆◆.

WEB: www.butler.ie

Room Rate from £89.00 to £179.00
€113.01 to €227.28

GABRIELLE HICKEY
Manager (Acting)

American Express
Diners
Mastercard
Visa

Midweek specials from £145.00

13 13

inet

Closed 24 - 29 December

CLUB HOUSE HOTEL

PATRICK STREET,
KILKENNY
TEL: 056-21994 FAX: 056-71920
EMAIL: clubhse@iol.ie

HOTEL ★★ MAP 7 L 7

Situated uniquely in a cultural and artistic centre and against the background of Kilkenny's beautiful medieval city, the magnificent 18th century Club House Hotel maintains a 200 year old tradition of effortless comfort, hospitality and efficiency. The en suite rooms are decorated in both modern and period style with complimentary beverages, TV, hairdryer and phone. Food is locally sourced, cooked and presented to highest standards. Victors Bar old world charm and luxury.

WEB: www.clubhousehotel.com

Member of MinOtel Ireland Hotel Group

B&B from £33.00 to £70.00
€41.90 to €88.88

JAMES P. BRENNAN
Managing Director

American Express
Diners
Mastercard
Visa

Midweek specials from £90.00

28 28

Closed 24 - 27 December

Room rates are IR£ per room per night

FANAD HOUSE

CASTLE ROAD,
KILKENNY
TEL: 056-64126 FAX: 056-56001
EMAIL: fanadhouse@hotmail.com

GUESTHOUSE P MAP 7 L 7

Overlooking Kilkenny Castle Park, Fanad House is a five minute walk from the city centre. The newly built guesthouse offers all en suite rooms with complimentary beverages, multi-channel TV, hairdryer and direct dial phone. Extensive breakfast menu available. Private and secure parking provided. An ideal base for exploring the medieval city. We are adjacent to Kilkenny Tennis Club. Owner operated is your guarantee for an enjoyable stay.

B&B from £28.00 to £40.00
€35.55 to €50.79

PAT WALLACE
Proprietor
American Express
Diners
Mastercard
Visa

8 8

Open All Year

HIBERNIAN HOTEL

33 PATRICK STREET, KILKENNY,
CO. KILKENNY
TEL: 056-71888 FAX: 056-71877
EMAIL: info@hibernian.iol.ie

HOTEL N MAP 7 L 7

City centre location, designed to a 4 star standard incorporating restored Georgian Hibernian Bank building, creating a property with an abundance of character and old world charm. With 40 rooms, an intimate setting is provided with close attention to detail and personal service. Centrally located, just minutes walk from Kilkenny Castle, facilities include deluxe rooms, junior suites, penthouse suite, restaurant, bar and conference rooms.

WEB: www.thehibernian.com

B&B from £49.00 to £59.00
€62.22 to €74.91

JOE KELLY
General Manager
American Express
Diners
Mastercard
Visa

40 40

Inet FAX

Open All Year

HOTEL KILKENNY

COLLEGE ROAD,
KILKENNY
TEL: 056-62000 FAX: 056-65984
EMAIL: kilkenny@griffingroup.ie

HOTEL ★★★ MAP 7 L 7

Hotel Kilkenny is situated in landscaped gardens, just 10 minutes walk from medieval Kilkenny. It has completed a major development programme to include 24 new deluxe rooms, refurbishment of all existing rooms, a 5* health & fitness club with 20m pool, a stone conservatory to the front of the original Rosehill House, new stone entrance to the hotel and refurbishment of the bar & lobby areas. Excellent conference facilities. *The all new Hotel Kilkenny. Why resort to less?*

WEB: www.griffingroup.ie

Member of Griffin Hotel Group

B&B from £40.00 to £75.00
€50.79 to €95.23

RICHARD BUTLER
General Manager
American Express
Diners
Mastercard
Visa

103 103

Open All Year

B&B rates are IR£ per person sharing per night incl. Breakfast

KILFORD ARMS

JOHN STREET,
KILKENNY
TEL: 056-61018 FAX: 056-61018
EMAIL: kilfordarms@indigo.ie

GUESTHOUSE U MAP 7 L 7

The Kilford Arms is 50 yards from the bus/rail station and still in the city centre, offering you 3 luxury bars, luxury accommodation, entertainment nightly and a beautiful traditional Irish restaurant. Bar food is available all day. Late bar every night, games room. A new purpose built car park and state of the art nite club called Club Life all under one roof at a price hard to beat.

WEB: www.travel-ireland.com/irl/kilford.htm

B&B from £30.00 to £45.00
€38.09 to €57.14

PIUS PHELAN
Owner

Mastercard
Visa

30 30

alc

Open All Year

KILKENNY HOUSE

FRESHFORD ROAD,
KILKENNY
TEL: 056-70711 FAX: 056-70698

GUESTHOUSE ★★★ MAP 7 L 7

Located 1km from the city on the northside R693 near St. Lukes General Hospital. Set in 2 acres of gardens with ample private car parking. The conservatory breakfast room will give guests a bright start to the day. A full Irish and buffet breakfast is served. Home baking a speciality. All rooms en suite with pine furniture and oak floors. Guests have privacy and peace with their own entrance, reception, stairs and sitting-room. Owner operated guarantees 'rest for the tired'.

B&B from £25.00 to £25.00
€31.74 to €31.74

MICHELENE AND TED DORE
Proprietors

Mastercard
Visa

10 10

Closed 21 - 28 December

KILKENNY ORMONDE HOTEL

ORMONDE STREET,
KILKENNY
TEL: 056-23900 FAX: 056-23977
EMAIL: info@kilkennyormonde.com

HOTEL N MAP 7 L 7

The new Kilkenny Ormonde Hotel, RAC 4**** accredited, is designed to compliment its famous sister hotel, the Aghadoe Heights in Killarney, bringing the same level of service and excellence to Kilkenny City. The Kilkenny Ormonde is centrally located just off High Street and is adjacent to a secure 24 hour car park. With 118 large superior rooms, a conference centre with 10 meeting rooms and extensive leisure club, the Kilkenny Ormonde is ideal for both the leisure and corporate traveller.

WEB: www.kilkennyormonde.com

B&B from £55.00 to £85.00
€69.83 to €107.92

PATRICK CURRAN
General Manager/Director

American Express
Diners
Mastercard
Visa

118 118

alc Inet

Closed 24 - 25 December

Room rates are IR£ per room per night

KILKENNY RIVER COURT HOTEL

THE BRIDGE, JOHN STREET,
KILKENNY
TEL: 056-23388 FAX: 056-23389
EMAIL: krch@iol.ie

HOTEL U MAP 7 L 7

AA 4**** hotel, leisure club and conference centre. City centre location, stunning views of Kilkenny Castle and the River Nore. Ideal as a conference venue or simply sheer relaxation. Crystal chandeliers and antique furniture give a sense of old world grandeur and style. Leisure facilities which include a 17 metre swimming pool, sauna, geyser pool, jacuzzi, fully equipped gymnasium and beauty salon. Limited free car parking. Within easy access of Dublin, Rosslare, Waterford, Shannon and Cork.

WEB: www.kilrivercourt.com

Room Rate from £65.00 to £280.00
€82.53 to €355.53

PETER WILSON
General Manager

American Express
Mastercard
Visa

Weekend specials from £135.00

90 90

P S alc Inet

IRISH HOTELS FEDERATION

Closed 25 December

LACKEN HOUSE

DUBLIN ROAD,
KILKENNY
TEL: 056-61085 FAX: 056-62435
EMAIL: info@lackenhouse.ie

GUESTHOUSE ★★★ MAP 7 L 7

Stay at Lacken House and enjoy high quality accommodation, superb food and a friendly welcome. We are a family run guesthouse, situated in Kilkenny City, where you can enjoy exploring the medieval city. All bedrooms are en suite, central heating throughout, private car parking. Our house features the home cooking of our award winning restaurant, where fresh food is cooked to perfection. Full bar service is also available.

WEB: www.lackenhouse.ie

Member of Logis of Ireland

B&B from £35.00 to £40.00
€44.44 to €50.79

JACKIE & TREVOR TONER
Owners

Mastercard
Visa

9 9

IRISH HOTELS FEDERATION

Closed 22 - 28 December

LANGTON HOUSE HOTEL

69 JOHN STREET,
KILKENNY
TEL: 056-65133 FAX: 056-63693

HOTEL ★★★ MAP 7 L 7

Langton's Kilkenny, award-winning bar and restaurant; it has won National Pub of the Year 4 times. Now open, a wonderful new hotel extension with a 'five star' finish and the same standards of excellence that have made Langton's famous. Complete with executive, penthouse and art deco rooms the new Langton's Hotel completes the award-winning picture.

WEB: www.langtons.ie

B&B from £40.00 to £65.00
€50.79 to €82.53

EAMONN LANGTON
Proprietor

American Express
Diners
Mastercard
Visa

26 26

IRISH HOTELS FEDERATION

Closed 25 - 26 December

B&B rates are IR£ per person sharing per night incl. Breakfast

LAURELS

COLLEGE ROAD, KILKENNY,
CO. KILKENNY
TEL: 056-61501 FAX: 056-71334
EMAIL: laurels@eircom.net

UNDER CONSTRUCTION OPENING FEB 2001

GUESTHOUSE P   MAP 7 L 7

Located just 6 minutes from Kilkenny Centre and Castle. Private car parking. Breakfast menu is available. All our 8 bedrooms are en suite and 3 of them have whirlpool baths. TV, hairdryer in all rooms. Tea/coffee available at anytime. Central heating throughout. As our customers say, three musts in Kilkenny are, the Castle, the Cathedral and the Laurels.

WEB: thelaurelskilkenny.com

B&B from £20.00 to £27.00
€25.39 to €34.28

BRIAN AND BETTY MCHENRY

Mastercard
Visa

Open All Year

METROPOLE HOTEL

HIGH STREET,
KILKENNY
TEL: 056-63778 FAX: 056-63778

HOTEL ★   MAP 7 L 7

The Metropole Hotel is situated in the heart of Kilkenny City. Occupies a dominant position in Kilkenny's main shopping area (High Street). Within walking distance of all the city's medieval buildings e.g. Kilkenny Castle, Roth House and St. Canice's Cathedral. All bedrooms are en suite with multi channel TV, direct dial telephone and tea/coffee facilities. Live entertainment. Bord Failte approved.

B&B from £20.00 to £45.00
€25.39 to €57.14

ROBERT DELANEY
Proprietor

Mastercard
Visa

Open All Year

NEWPARK HOTEL

CASTLECOMER ROAD,
KILKENNY
TEL: 056-22122 FAX: 056-61111
EMAIL: info@newparkhotel.com

HOTEL ★★★   MAP 7 L 7

The recently refurbished Newpark Hotel (3***, AA***), set in 40 acres of parkland in Ireland's medieval city. 111 en suite rooms with TV, hairdryer, phone and tea/coffee making facilities. The executive leisure centre includes a 52 ft. pool, sauna, jacuzzi, steam room and gym. The new Scott Dove Bar and Bistro serves carvery lunch and a superb evening bar menu. Damask Restaurant specialises in fine dining. Live entertainment most nights. Excellent professional conference facilities.

WEB: www.newparkhotel.com

Member of Best Western Hotels

B&B from £49.50 to £69.00
€62.85 to €87.61

DAVID O'SULLIVAN
General Manager

American Express
Diners
Mastercard
Visa

Weekend specials from £120.00

Open All Year

Room rates are IR£ per room per night

O'MALLEY'S GUESTHOUSE

ORMONDE COURT,
ORMONDE ROAD, KILKENNY CITY
TEL: 056-71003   FAX: 056-71003

GUESTHOUSE N   MAP 7 L 7

O'Malley's Guesthouse is situated on the Ormonde Road in Kilkenny City. The house itself is in a quiet court with private parking. All rooms are tastefully decorated, en suite, multi-channel TV, direct dial phone, tea/coffee facilities. O'Malley's Guesthouse is just one minute's walk to Kilkenny Castle, Design Centre, Rothe House, St Canice's Cathedral and lots of shops, pubs and restaurants. You are assured of a Cead Mile Failte by hosts Ursula and Christy O'Malley.

WEB: o'malleys@eircom.net

B&B from £20.00 to £30.00
€25.39 to €38.09

URSULA & CHRISTY O'MALLEY

Mastercard
Visa

8   8

Closed 07 - 31 January

QUAYS HOTEL

JOHN STREET, KILKENNY CITY,
CO. KILKENNY
TEL: 056-70844   FAX: 056-23389
EMAIL: krch@iol.ie

HOTEL N   MAP 7 L 7

The Quays Hotel is situated in the centre of Kilkenny City, just a few minutes walk from Kilkenny Castle. An ideal location visiting the Kilkenny Design Centre, Craft Studios, Watergate Theatre, St. Canice's Cathedral and many of the small shopping boutiques, not to mention numerous fine restaurants and bars. Horse/dog racing, golf, fishing, cultural/heritage sites all available locally. All bedrooms are en suite with TV, tea/coffee and direct dial phone.

B&B from £25.00 to £55.00
€31.74 to €69.84

PETER WILSON

American Express
Diners
Mastercard
Visa

14   14

Closed 25 December

SPRINGHILL COURT HOTEL

WATERFORD ROAD,
KILKENNY
TEL: 056-21122   FAX: 056-61600
EMAIL: springhillcourt@eircom.net

HOTEL ★★★   MAP 7 L 7

The Springhill Court Hotel is situated only minutes from Kilkenny's vibrant and lively city centre. We have completed major developments throughout the hotel. We now offer 86 spacious en suite bedrooms, a dedicated business centre and excellent cuisine in our Claddagh Dining Room. The Paddock Bar offers weekend entertainment. The hotel is an ideal base for touring the Southeast. Car parking available. Sister Hotel: The Arklow Bay Hotel & Leisure Club, Wicklow.

WEB: www.springhillcourt.com

Member of Chara Hotel Group

B&B from £40.00 to £69.50
€50.79 to €88.25

JOHN HICKEY
General Manager

American Express
Diners
Mastercard
Visa

86   86

IRISH HOTELS FEDERATION

Open All Year

B&B rates are IR£ per person sharing per night incl. Breakfast

ZUNI

26 PATRICK STREET, KILKENNY
TEL: 056-23999 FAX: 056-56400
EMAIL: info@zuni.ie

HOTEL N   MAP 7 L 7

Zuni is a small, contemporary family run hotel and restaurant. We are located at 26 Patrick Street, Kilkenny City Centre. Ideally located for all Kilkenny's historic sights, great shopping, wonderful restaurants, bars and night clubs. Our restaurant at Zuni offers an unforgettable dining experience with excellent food prepared by our award winning chefs. Flawless friendly service in a relaxed atmosphere.

WEB: www.zuni.ie

B&B from £40.00 to £60.00
€50.79 to €76.18

PAULA BYRNE & SANDRA McDONALD Hosts
American Express
Mastercard
Visa

13 13

Closed 23 - 27 December

AVALON INN

THE SQUARE, CASTLECOMER, CO. KILKENNY
TEL: 056-41302 FAX: 056-41963
EMAIL: avalinn@eircom.net

GUESTHOUSE ★★★   MAP 7 L 7

The Avalon Inn, a Georgian building, set in the quiet town of Castlecomer, 16km from Kilkenny. A rural setting with quiet woodland walks nearby. The area has good trout and salmon fishing. 1km away there is a 9 hole golf course. There are many excellent golf courses nearby. Staying in Castlecomer offers you the best of both worlds with Kilkenny 15 minutes away and at your doorstep fishing, golfing, horseriding and leisurely walks.

B&B from £22.50 to £25.00
€28.57 to €31.74

PAT KEARNS Director
Mastercard
Visa

😊 Midweek specials from £55.00

7 7

Closed 24 - 25 December

WATERSIDE

THE QUAY, GRAIGUENAMANAGH, CO. KILKENNY
TEL: 0503-24246 FAX: 0503-24733
EMAIL: info@waterside.iol.ie

GUESTHOUSE ★★★   MAP 7 M 7

A beautifully restored 19th century cornstore with feature wooden beams and imposing granite exterior. Riverside location, all rooms have a view of the River Barrow. Excellent base for boating, fishing, hillwalking. 16km from Mount Juliet for golf. Nearby 13th century Duiske Abbey. 27km from historical Kilkenny. Superb restaurant features continental cuisine & international flavour wine list. Relaxed & friendly approach. Perfect for small groups. Guided hillwalking for groups.

WEB: www.watersideguesthouse.com

B&B from £27.50 to £38.00
€34.92 to €48.25

BRIAN & BRIGID ROBERTS Managers
Mastercard
Visa

10 10

Open All Year

Room rates are IR£ per room per night

CARROLLS HOTEL

KNOCKTOPHER,
CO. KILKENNY
TEL: 056-68082   FAX: 056-68290
EMAIL: info@carrollshotel.com

HOTEL N   MAP 7 L 6

Situated on the N10 between
Kilkenny and Waterford. Enjoy the
excellent service, warmth and luxury
of our newly opened family-run
hotel. All rooms en suite with TV,
and direct dial phone. Our Sionnach
St Restaurant has an excellent
reputation for good food. The hotel
provides live music 3 nights a week.
Golfing, karting, fishing, horse riding
and shooting are available nearby.

WEB: www.carrollshotel.com

B&B from £30.00 to £40.00
€38.09 to €50.79

WILLIAM CARROLL
Proprietor

American Express
Mastercard
Visa

Midweek specials from £70.00

Closed 25 December

RISING SUN

MULLINAVAT, VIA WATERFORD,
CO. KILKENNY
TEL: 051-898173   FAX: 051-898435

GUESTHOUSE ★★★   MAP 4 L 6

A family run guesthouse, 12.8km
from Waterford City on the main
Waterford - Dublin Road. It has 10
luxurious bedrooms all en suite with
D/D telephone and TV. The Rising
Sun Guesthouse is an ideal base for
sports enthusiasts, surrounded by
some beautiful golf courses within
15-30 minutes drive. The old world
charm of stone and timberwork sets
the tone of comfort and relaxation in
the bar and lounge. Traditional home
cooked lunches and bar food served
daily. Full à la carte menu and wine
list.

B&B from £26.00 to £30.00
€33.01 to €38.09

PATRICIA PHELAN
Manager

American Express
Mastercard
Visa

Closed 24 - 27 December

MOUNT JULIET ESTATE

THOMASTOWN,
CO. KILKENNY
TEL: 056-73000   FAX: 056-73019
EMAIL: info@mountjuliet.ie

HOTEL ★★★★   MAP 7 L 6

Mount Juliet, Ireland's premier hotel
and sporting estate offers several
styles of deluxe accommodation.
Guests can choose between the
elegance of the 18th century Mount
Juliet House or the more sporting
ambience of the Club Rooms or
Rose Garden Suites. Activities
include 18 hole Jack Nicklaus golf
course, fishing, shooting, archery,
Iris Kellet equestrian centre, tennis,
leisure centre, health & beauty
treatment rooms, 18-hole putting
course, cycling. Chauffeur driven
tours available. Awarded AA Hotel of
the Year 1999.

WEB: www.mountjuliet.com

Member of Small Luxury Hotels

Room Rate from £140.00 to £400.00
€177.76 to €507.90

RICHARD HUDSON
General Manager

American Express
Diners
Mastercard
Visa

Open All Year

B&B rates are IR£ per person sharing per night incl. Breakfast

ACH NA SHEEN GUESTHOUSE

CLONMEL ROAD, TIPPERARY, CO. TIPPERARY
TEL: 062-51298   FAX: 062-80467

GUESTHOUSE ★★   MAP 3 J 6

Family run guesthouse, 5 minutes from the town centre with a spacious sunlounge and diningroom overlooking gardens and the beautiful Galtee Mountains. Our 10 rooms, 5 are en suite, are all equipped with TV and tea/coffee making facilities on request. Ach-na-Sheen is adjacent to the picturesque Glen of Aherlow where fishing and hill walking can be arranged. Golf can be enjoyed at any one of 3 nearby championship courses. Ger & Sylvia Noonan offer you the utmost in Irish hospitality.

B&B from £20.00 to £30.00
€25.39 to €38.09

GER & SYLVIA NOONAN
Proprietors

Mastercard

Visa

10 5

Closed 10 December to 19 January

BALLYGLASS COUNTRY HOUSE HOTEL

GLEN OF AHERLOW ROAD, BALLYGLASS, TIPPERARY TOWN
TEL: 062-52104   FAX: 062-52229

HOTEL ★   MAP 3 J 6

Family run Ballyglass Country House Hotel is set in its own grounds. The Hotel is very comfortable with all facilities. There is a fine restaurant serving the best of local produce. The Forge Bar is adjacent to the Hotel for that quiet drink. We are just 2 miles from Tipperary Town at the entrance to the Glen of Aherlow where there are an abundance of superb walks.

B&B from £27.00 to £29.00
€34.28 to €36.82

JOAN AND BILL BYRNE
Proprietors

American Express

Mastercard

Visa

 Weekend specials from £60.00

10 10

alc

Closed 24 - 25 December

CAHIR HOUSE HOTEL

THE SQUARE, CAHIR, CO. TIPPERARY
TEL: 052-42727   FAX: 052-42727
EMAIL: cahirhousehotel@eircom.net

HOTEL ★★★   MAP 3 J 6

A Georgian building situated in the picturesque heritage town of Cahir nestled among some of Tipperary's most beautiful scenery surrounded by an abundance of leisure pursuits including golfing, horseriding, fishing, hunting etc. Our award winning restaurant The Butler's Pantry, serves only the best of local produce specialising in steaks, fish & poultry. Food served throughout the day in O'Briens Bar. Music sessions.

B&B from £35.00 to £45.00
€44.44 to €57.14

LIAM DUFFY M.I.H.C.I.

American Express

Mastercard

Visa

31 31

S alc

Closed 24 - 26 December

KILCORAN LODGE HOTEL

CAHIR,
CO. TIPPERARY
TEL: 052-41288   FAX: 052-41994
EMAIL: kilcoran@eircom.net

HOTEL ★★★   MAP 3 J 6

Kilcoran, a former hunting lodge set in spacious grounds overlooking beautiful countryside. An ideal holiday base located equal distance (15 min drive) between Tipperary, Cashel, Clonmel and Mitchelstown and 45 mins drive from Cork, Kilkenny and Limerick on the main Cork-Dublin road. The hotel has the charm of bygone days yet all the modern facilities of a 3 star hotel. Guests have free access to Shapes leisure centre with indoor pool etc. Golf, hillwalking, fishing, etc. locally.

WEB: www.tipp.ie/kilcoran.htm

B&B from £30.00 to £45.00
€38.09 to €57.13

JACQUELINE MULLEN
Managing Director

American Express
Diners
Mastercard
Visa

Open All Year

CARRAIG HOTEL

MAIN STREET, CARRICK-ON-SUIR,
CO. TIPPERARY
TEL: 051-641455   FAX: 051-641604
EMAIL: thecarraighotel@eircom.net

HOTEL ★★★   MAP 3 K 5

An ideal base from which to explore the South East's many attractions, walk or drive through the Knockmealdown and Comeragh mountain ranges, fish on the world famous River Suir, cycle the route of the Tour de France '98, horse riding or hunting, golf on one of the local courses, visit Tipperary Crystal, Waterford Crystal, the Ormonde Castle, the Rock of Cashel or simply enjoy Irish hospitality at its best.

WEB: www.tipp.ie/carraig~hotel.htm

B&B from £40.00 to £45.00
€50.79 to €57.14

WILLIAM HANRAHAN
General Manager

American Express
Diners
Mastercard
Visa

Closed 25 December

BAILEYS OF CASHEL

MAIN STREET, CASHEL,
CO. TIPPERARY
TEL: 062-61937   FAX: 062-62038
EMAIL: info@baileys-ireland.com

GUESTHOUSE ★★★   MAP 3 J 6

Built in 1703, this listed Pre-Georgian Townhouse has been restored to its original splendour yet offers modern day comfort with all bedrooms en suite. Now under new management, you are assured of a warm welcome at Bailey's of Cashel where you are sure of a memorable stay. With its own private car park, Bailey's is located in the centre of town just minutes away from the Rock of Cashel, Bru Boru Heritage Centre and many other places of interest in historical Cashel.

WEB: www.baileys-ireland.com

B&B from £25.00 to £35.00
€31.74 to €44.44

PHIL DELANEY
Manager

American Express
Diners
Mastercard
Visa

Closed 24 - 28 December

B&B rates are IR£ per person sharing per night incl. Breakfast

CASHEL PALACE HOTEL

MAIN STREET, CASHEL,
CO. TIPPERARY
TEL: 062-62707 FAX: 062-61521
EMAIL: reception@cashel-palace.ie

HOTEL ★★★ MAP 3 J 6

Built in 1730 as an Archbishop's Palace, the Cashel Palace has been restored as a hotel, complemented by tranquil walled gardens and a private walk to the famous Rock of Cashel. Our 23 rooms are all en suite with TV, phone, trouser press. Our Bishop's Buttery Restaurant is open for lunch and dinner, while the Guinness Bar is open for light snacks daily, both offering modern Irish cuisine at affordable prices. Sunday lunch served in our Three Sisters Restaurant.

WEB: www.cashel-palace.ie

B&B from £55.00 to £112.50
€69.84 to €142.85

SUSAN & PATRICK MURPHY
Proprietors

American Express
Diners
Mastercard
Visa

🖊🏊🏇

🛏🏠☎📠🖥T C 🚗CM✱☀️U J P S
23 23

📶 alc

Closed 24 - 26 December

DUNDRUM HOUSE HOTEL

DUNDRUM, CASHEL,
CO. TIPPERARY
TEL: 062-71116 FAX: 062-71366
EMAIL: dundrumh@iol.ie

HOTEL ★★★ MAP 3 J 7

A haven of peace and tranquillity, the hotel is surrounded by the manicured fairways of its own 18 hole championship course designed by Philip Walton. The Country Club features the Venue Clubhouse Bar/Restaurant, state of the art Health and Leisure centre with 20 mm deck level indoor pool, gym, jacuzzi, sauna. Beauty treatments by appointment. Elegant guest bedroom with antiques, and penthouse suites. Rossmore Restaurant is renowned fine foods and wines.

WEB: www.dundrumhousehotel.com

Member of Manor House Hotels

B&B from £45.00 to £70.00
€57.14 to €88.88

JOE KELLY
General Manager

American Express
Diners
Mastercard
Visa

🖊🏊🏇

🛏🏠☎📠🖥T C 🚗CM✱🍴🖥🔍
70 70

📶18 J 🎵P S 🛏 alc ♿ Inet

😊 Weekend specials from £105.00

Open All Year

LEGENDS TOWNHOUSE & RESTAURANT

THE KILN, CASHEL,
CO. TIPPERARY
TEL: 062-61292
EMAIL: info@legendsguesthouse.com

GUESTHOUSE ★★★ MAP 3 J 5

Legends Townhouse & Restaurant, graded AA ◆◆◆◆ is uniquely situated at the foot of the Rock of Cashel. Awarded Bridgestone 100 BEST PLACES TO STAY IN IRELAND 2000. At Legends a warm welcome with friendly and attentive service will help you to unwind & relax. Enjoy award winning cuisine prepared by chef/proprietor Michael. Wake up in comfortable surroundings to superb views of 'The Rock' and an extensive breakfast selection. Cashel is located 1 hour from all cities in Southern Ireland.

WEB: www.legendsguesthouse.com

B&B from £22.50 to £35.00
€28.56 to €44.44

ROSEMARY & MICHAEL O'NEILL

Mastercard
Visa

🛏🏠☎📠T✱U J P 🛏 alc 🚭

7 7

😊 Weekend specials from £59.00

Closed 24 - 28 December

Room rates are IR£ per room per night

BRIGHTON HOUSE

1 BRIGHTON PLACE, CLONMEL,
CO. TIPPERARY
TEL: 052-23665 FAX: 052-25210
EMAIL: brighton@iol.ie

GUESTHOUSE ★★ MAP 3 K 5

Family run 3 storey Georgian guest house, with a hotel ambience and antique furnishings. Clonmel Town centre - the largest inland town in Ireland bridging Rosslare Harbour (132km) with Killarney (160km) and the South West. Host to Fleadh Cheoil na hEireann 1993/94. Visit Rock of Cashel, Mitchelstown Caves, Cahir Castle etc. Golf, fishing and pony trekking arranged locally. All rooms direct dial phones, TV, radio, hairdryer and tea/coffee making facilities.

WEB: www.iol.ie/tipp/brighton.htm

B&B from £25.00 to £30.00
€31.74 to €38.09

BERNIE MORRIS
Proprietor

Mastercard

Visa

🖐️🚗🛏️T P S ♨️
6 4

IRISH HOTELS FEDERATION

Open All Year

CLONMEL ARMS HOTEL

CLONMEL,
CO. TIPPERARY
TEL: 052-21233 FAX: 052-21526
EMAIL: clonmelarms@iol.ie

HOTEL ★★★ MAP 3 K 5

Town centre hotel ideally situated either for business or pleasure. All 31 rooms en suite, direct dial telephone & colour TV. Full conference facilities available. The Paddock Restaurant open until 9.30pm each day provides the perfect setting for your personal or business requirements. The Paddock Bar is ideal for a quiet drink or alternatively a lively night out with the Paddock music sessions every weekend. Food in the Paddock is served daily.

WEB: www.tipp.ie/clonmelarms.htm

Member of Choice Hotels International

B&B from £35.00 to £70.00
€44.44 to €88.88

NEILUS MCDONNELL
Manager

American Express

Diners

Mastercard

Visa

🖐️🚗🛏️🅿️📺T C ♨️CM∪♪♫P S
♿️ aic ♨️
31 31

IRISH HOTELS FEDERATION

Closed 25 December

FENNESSY'S HOTEL

GLADSTONE STREET, CLONMEL,
CO. TIPPERARY
TEL: 052-23680 FAX: 052-23783

HOTEL ★★ MAP 3 K 5

Established old hotel. This beautiful Georgian building is newly restored and refurbished. Right in the centre of Clonmel, it is easily located by spotting from afar the green steeple of the town's main church, opposite which it stands. All bedrooms have direct dial phone, TV, en suite, some with jacuzzi. Family run hotel. Elegant and antique decor throughout. After your visit, you will wish to return.

B&B from £25.00 to £35.00
€31.74 to €44.44

RICHARD AND ESTHER
FENNESSY Proprietors

American Express

Mastercard

Visa

🖐️🚗🛏️📺T C ♨️CM∪♪♫🚗 aic
10 10

IRISH HOTELS FEDERATION

Open All Year

B&B rates are IR£ per person sharing per night incl. Breakfast

HEARNS HOTEL

PARNELL STREET, CLONMEL,
CO. TIPPERARY
TEL: 052-21611 FAX: 052-21135

HOTEL ★★ MAP 3 K 5

Situated in the centre of Clonmel Town, the historical Bianconi House, is ideal as a touring base for Cahir Castle, Rock of Cashel, Holycross Abbey, The Vee, Mitchelstown Caves and seaside resorts of Tramore and Clonea. All bedrooms are fully en suite with direct dial phone and TV. Ample parking, relaxing bar, live entertainment at weekends. Also available is our new restaurant, which serves continental food, new nightclub and attractive conference facilities.

B&B from £25.00 to £35.00
€31.74 to €44.44

VERONICA M BARRY
General Manager

American Express
Diners
Mastercard
Visa

25 25
a|c

Closed 25 - 26 December

HOTEL MINELLA & LEISURE CENTRE

CLONMEL,
CO. TIPPERARY
TEL: 052-22388 FAX: 052-24381
EMAIL: hotelminella@eircom.net

HOTEL ★★★ MAP 3 K 5

Magnificent country house hotel & 4**** leisure centre, on the banks of the Suir. Rooms throughout are elegantly furnished, 5 suites with jacuzzis, 3 with 4-poster beds & private steam rooms. Leisure centre: 20m pool, gym, aqua cruises, outdoor Canadian Hot Tub, sauna, steamroom, massage & therapys. Outdoor tennis court (all weather) and pleasure boats. Self catering apts to open July 2001. AA Rosette. Restaurant. Conference room for 500. Family owned/managed by the Nallen family.

WEB: www.hotelminella.ie

Member of Signature Hotels

B&B from £55.00 to £80.00
€69.84 to €101.58

ELIZABETH NALLEN
Managing Director

American Express
Diners
Mastercard
Visa

70 70

Closed 23 - 28 December

RECTORY HOUSE HOTEL

DUNDRUM,
CO. TIPPERARY
TEL: 062-71266 FAX: 062-71115
EMAIL: rectoryh@iol.ie

HOTEL ★★★ MAP 3 I 7

The Rectory House Hotel is a family run hotel standing amidst its tree lined grounds. It is a gracious country house providing an ideal haven for the country lover. Comfort and tranquillity are offered to our guests in tastefully decorated rooms en suite. Our candlelit restaurant and conservatory provides home cooking. Member of The Best Western International Group. 1km from 18-hole golf course.

WEB: www.rectoryhousehotel.com

Member of Best Western Hotels

B&B from £35.00 to £45.00
€44.44 to €57.13

JAMES SHEILS
Proprietor

Mastercard
Visa

10 10
a|c

Closed 23 - 27 December

Room rates are IR£ per room per night

CO. TIPPERARY South
GLEN OF AHERLOW

AHERLOW HOUSE HOTEL

**GLEN OF AHERLOW,
CO. TIPPERARY
TEL: 062-56153 FAX: 062-56212
EMAIL: aherlow@iol.ie**

HOTEL ★★★ MAP 316

Aherlow House Hotel and 4**** deluxe holiday homes The Lodges are set in the middle of a coniferous forest just 4 miles from Tipperary Town. Originally a hunting lodge now converted into an exquisitely furnished hotel. Aherlow House welcomes you to its peaceful atmosphere, enhanced by a fine reputation for hospitality, excellent cuisine and good wines. Overlooks the Glen of Aherlow and has beautiful views of the Galtee Mountains. Activities can be arranged.

WEB: www.aherlowhouse.ie

B&B from £49.00 to £57.00
€62.22 to €72.38

FRANCES FOGARTY
Manager
American Express
Diners
Mastercard
Visa

30 30

Open All Year

GLEN HOTEL

**GLEN OF AHERLOW,
CO. TIPPERARY
TEL: 062-56146 FAX: 062-56152**

HOTEL ★★ MAP 316

The Glen Hotel set in the shadows of the majestic Galtee Mountains, amidst the splendour of the Aherlow Valley is just 5 miles from Tipperary Town. To relax, dream, reminisce or plan this is the ideal haven. Our bedrooms are all en suite and have been recently tastefully redecorated. This family operated hotel has built up a fine reputation for excellent cuisine and offers friendly and efficient service. Hill walking, horse riding, fishing and golf.

B&B from £29.00 to £39.00
€36.82 to €49.52

MARGOT AND JAMES
COUGHLAN Proprietors
American Express
Diners
Mastercard
Visa

☺ Weekend specials from £75.00

24 24

Open All Year

WATCH FOR THE SYMBOL OF QUALITY

THIS SYMBOL OF QUALITY GUARANTEES YOU, THE VISITOR, A HIGH STANDARD OF ACCOMMODATION AND SERVICE WHICH IS EXPECTED OF IRISH HOTELS & GUESTHOUSES.

B&B rates are IR£ per person sharing per night incl. Breakfast

HORSE AND JOCKEY INN

HORSE AND JOCKEY, (NEAR CASHEL), CO. TIPPERARY
TEL: 0504-44192   FAX: 0504-44747
EMAIL: horseandjockeyinn@eircom.net

HOTEL ★★★   MAP 7 J 7

The Horse and Jockey Inn, located at the heartland of County Tipperary, midway between Cork and Dublin on the N8 holds great association with people from sporting, cultural and political walks of life. Our new refurbishment includes spacious lounge and bar facilities, a high quality restaurant, deluxe accommodation and a modern conference centre. Experience the atmosphere that's steeped in tradition and share with us the real Ireland, in the comfort of our new inn.

WEB: www.tipp.ie/horse-jockey-inn.htm

B&B from £40.00 to £45.00
€50.79 to €57.14

PAUL MEEHAN
General Manager

American Express
Diners
Mastercard
Visa

29   29

Inet FAX

Open All Year

ARDAGH HOUSE

KILLENAULE,
CO. TIPPERARY
TEL: 052-56224   FAX: 052-56224
EMAIL: ahouse@iol.ie

GUESTHOUSE ★   MAP 3 K 7

Fully licensed family guesthouse, piano lounge bar, residents' lounge, rooms en suite, home cooking. Set in the shadow of romantic Slievenamon, in the area of the Derrynaflan Chalice, the famous Coolmore Stud, in the heart of the Golden Vale. Near Holycross Abbey, Cashel and Kilkenny. Central for hunting, fishing, shooting, golf, horse riding and less strenuous walks through the hills of Killenaule. Finally, just one hour from the sea.

B&B from £20.00 to £22.00
€25.39 to €27.93

KATHLEEN & DAVID CORMACK
Proprietors

Mastercard
Visa

6   6

😊 Midweek specials from £50.00

Closed 25 December

TEMPLEMORE ARMS HOTEL

MAIN STREET, TEMPLEMORE,
CO. TIPPERARY
TEL: 0504-31423   FAX: 0504-31343
EMAIL: decor@iol.ie

HOTEL ★★   MAP 7 J 8

The Templemore Arms Hotel, located in the shadow of one of Ireland's most prominent landmarks, The Devil's Bit, in the centre of the town of Templemore. Recently rebuilt to match the demands of the most discerning guests, it boasts lounge bars, carvery, restaurant, banqueting suite and conference room, providing first class service. Visit the Templemore Arms Hotel and experience an enjoyable getaway.

WEB: www.tipp.ie/templeah.htm

B&B from £35.00 to £70.00
€44.44 to €88.88

DAN WARD

Mastercard
Visa

10   10

Closed 25 December

Room rates are IR£ per room per night

BELFRY HOTEL

CONDUIT LANE,
WATERFORD
TEL: 051-844800   FAX: 051-844814
EMAIL: info@belfryhotel.ie

HOTEL N   MAP 4 L 5

Opened June 2000, The Belfry is Waterford's newest city centre hotel. Family run, with a relaxing, friendly atmosphere, the hotel boasts 49 luxurious en suite rooms, an excellent restaurant, stylishly designed split level bar and a private function/meeting room facility. Located just off The Quay, the hotel is close to the shops and an abundance of local amenities. A perfect base for any individual traveller or leisure group.

WEB: www.belfryhotel.ie

B&B from £37.00 to £65.00
€46.98 to €82.53

TOM & MARY REID
Proprietors

American Express
Mastercard
Visa

Weekend specials from £79.00

49 49   Inet

Closed 24 - 26 December

BRIDGE HOTEL

NO 1 THE QUAY,
WATERFORD
TEL: 051-877222   FAX: 051-877229
EMAIL: bridgehotel@treacyhotelsgroup.com

HOTEL ★★★   MAP 4 L 5

Whether your stay in Waterford's Viking City is one of business or pleasure, you will quickly find that the Bridge Hotel, situated in the heart of this vibrant and exciting city, is exactly where you will want to stay. This 100 en suite bedroom hotel offers the finest traditions of quality & service expected from a modern 3*** hotel. Our restaurants specialise in local seafood & succulent steaks. Relax & enjoy a drink in our Timbertoes Bar. 2 minutes walk from bus & rail.

WEB: www.treacyhotelsgroup.com

Member of MinOtel Ireland Hotel Group

B&B from £38.00 to £60.00
€48.25 to €76.18

BRIDGET & JIM TREACY
Proprietors

American Express
Diners
Mastercard
Visa

Weekend specials from £89.00

100 100   Inet

Closed 24 - 26 December

COACH HOUSE

BUTLERSTOWN CASTLE, BUTLERSTOWN,
CORK ROAD, WATERFORD
TEL: 051-384656   FAX: 051-384751
EMAIL: coachhse@iol.ie

GUESTHOUSE ★★★   MAP 4 L 5

Surround yourself with comfort in this elegantly restored 19th century house. Situated 3 miles from Waterford City (Waterford Crystal 5 mins away) in an historic, tranquil, romantic setting (13th century castle in grounds). All rooms en suite. Private sauna available. 5 golf courses within 6 miles radius. Excellent pubs, restaurants nearby. 3*** Irish Tourist Board, AA ◆◆◆◆, Michelin recommended, Best Magazine's No.1 in Ireland. 'Crackling log fires and personal attention'.

WEB: homepages.iol.ie/~coachhse

B&B from £26.00 to £35.00
€33.01 to €44.44

DES O'KEEFFE
Proprietor

American Express
Diners
Mastercard
Visa

7 7

Closed 20 December - 20 January

B&B rates are IR£ per person sharing per night incl. Breakfast

DIAMOND HILL COUNTRY HOUSE

SLIEVERUE,
WATERFORD
TEL: 051-832855 FAX: 051-832254

GUESTHOUSE ★★★ MAP 4 L 5

Situated 1.2km from Waterford City off the Rosslare Waterford Road N25, this guesthouse has been refurbished to a Bord Failte 3 Star standard. Set in its own award winning gardens, all rooms en suite, direct dial phone, multi channel TV, tea/coffee making facilities. Recommended by Frommers, Foders, Michelin, AA, RAC. Member of Premier Guesthouses and Les Routiers. A warm welcome awaits you here at Diamond Hill.

B&B from £22.00 to £27.50
€27.93 to €34.92

MARJORIE SMITH LEHANE
Owner

Mastercard
Visa

17 17

HOTELS FEDERATION

Closed 25 - 26 December

DOOLEY'S HOTEL

THE QUAY,
WATERFORD
TEL: 051-873531 FAX: 051-870262
EMAIL: hotel@dooleys-hotel.ie

HOTEL ★★★ MAP 4 L 5

The waters of the River Suir swirl and eddy past the door of this renowned hotel, which is situated on The Quay at Waterford. With its high levels of comfort and very personal service Dooley's is an ideal choice for a centrally located hotel in the city. This family run hotel caters for the corporate/leisure traveller. The hotel has a purpose built conference centre with full facilities - "The Rita Nolan Suite". Stay at Dooley's and you won't be disappointed.

WEB: www.dooleys-hotel.ie

Member of Holiday Ireland Hotels

B&B from £55.00 to £70.00
€69.84 to €88.88

JUNE DARRER
Proprietor/Manager

American Express
Diners
Mastercard
Visa

113 113

Inet

HOTELS FEDERATION

Closed 25 - 27 December

FORTE TRAVELODGE

CORK ROAD (N25),
WATERFORD
TEL: 1800-709709 FAX: 051-358890

HOTEL U MAP 4 L O5

Situated on the N25 primary route from Rosslare Harbour to Cork, 1 mile from Waterford City and minutes from the Waterford Crystal Factory, this superb hotel offers comfortable yet affordable accommodation. Each room can sleep up to 3 adults, a child under 12 years and a baby in a cot. Price is fixed per room regardless of the number of occupants. Each room is en suite, has colour TV, Sky Sports and Movies. Sited next to Little Chef Restaurant.

WEB: www.travelodge.co.uk

Room Rate from £39.95 to £59.95
€50.73 to €76.12

MARY KELLY
General Manager

American Express
Diners
Mastercard
Visa

32 32

Open All Year

Room rates are IR£ per room per night

GRANVILLE HOTEL

MEAGHER QUAY, WATERFORD
TEL: 051-305555 FAX: 051-305566
EMAIL: stay@granville-hotel.ie

HOTEL ★★★ MAP 4 L 5

Waterford's most prestigious city centre hotel RAC**** overlooking the River Suir. This family run hotel is one of Ireland's oldest with significant historical connections. Justly proud of the Granville's heritage owners Liam and Ann Cusack today vigorously pursue the Granville's long tradition of hospitality, friendliness and comfort. It has been elegantly refurbished, retaining its old world Georgian character. Award winning Bianconi Restaurant, Thomas Francis Meagher Bar.

WEB: www.granville-hotel.ie

Member of Best Western Hotels

B&B from £50.00 to £75.00
€63.49 to €95.23

LIAM AND ANN CUSACK
Managers/Proprietors

American Express
Diners
Mastercard
Visa

☺ Weekend specials from £90.00

100 100

Closed 25 - 27 December

IVORY'S HOTEL

TRAMORE ROAD, WATERFORD
TEL: 051-358888 FAX: 051-358899
EMAIL: ivory@voyager.ie

HOTEL U MAP 4 L 5

A friendly, family-run hotel, Ivory's Hotel is Waterford's best value. Ideally located adjacent to Waterford Crystal Factory & city centre. Each en suite combines the convenience of direct dial phone, multi-channel TV with welcoming tea/coffee making facilities, in comfortable surroundings. The hotel boasts Una's Signature Restaurant, emphasising the best fresh local produce. Unwind in McGinty's Pub Carvery & allow us to arrange golf, fishing. Secure car-park. Groups welcome.

WEB: www.ivoryhotel@voyager.ie

B&B from £30.00 to £52.00
€38.09 to €66.03

DECLAN & NATALIE IVORY
Managing Proprietors

American Express
Diners
Mastercard
Visa

☺ Weekend or Midweek Specials from £79.00

40 40

Open All Year

JURYS WATERFORD HOTEL

FERRYBANK, WATERFORD
TEL: 051-832111 FAX: 051-832863
EMAIL: waterford_hotel@jurysdoyle.com

HOTEL ★★★ MAP 4 L 5

3*** hotel set in 38 acres of parkland with spectacular views of the city and River Suir, just half a mile from the city centre. Each spacious bedroom provides the extra amenity of tea/coffee making facilities. Enjoy a meal in Bardens, a relaxing drink in the Conor Bar, or the many activities available in the superb leisure centre. Ample car parking. Jurys Doyle Hotel Group central reservations.
Tel.: 01-607 0000
Fax.: 01-631 6999

WEB: www.jurysdoyle.com

B&B from £48.00 to £76.00
€60.95 to €96.50

STAN POWER
General Manager

American Express
Diners
Mastercard
Visa

98 98

Closed 24 - 28 December

B&B rates are IR£ per person sharing per night incl. Breakfast

MARSUCI COUNTRY HOUSE

OLIVER'S HILL, BUTLERSTOWN,
WATERFORD
TEL: 051-370429 FAX: 051-350983
EMAIL: marsuci@indigo.ie

GUESTHOUSE ★★★ MAP 4 L 5

Marsuci is a refreshingly different 3*** Irish Tourist Board approved guesthouse. Situated in a semi-rural area just 10 minutes drive from Waterford City, Marsuci is the perfect base for tourists, golfers and business people. All rooms are comfortable with en suite and tea/coffee facilities. A fax / e-mail service is available. Our extensive breakfast menu is second to none. Fluent English, French and Italian spoken.

B&B from £23.00 to £23.00
€29.20 to €29.20

J-PIERRE/CATHERINE OSTINELLI
Proprietors

Mastercard

Visa

6 6

Closed 22 December - 15 January

O'GRADY'S RESTAURANT & GUESTHOUSE

CORK ROAD,
WATERFORD
TEL: 051-378851 FAX: 051-374062
EMAIL: info@ogradyshotel.com

GUESTHOUSE U MAP 4 L 5

O'Gradys Restaurant and Guesthouse is ideally located on the main Cork Road adjacent to the Waterford Crystal factory and city centre. Family-run by Euro Toque chef Cornelius and his wife Sue; they offer the excellent combination of reasonably priced accommodation and a superb licensed Michelin recommended restaurant which specialises in fresh local seafood. Private off street parking. 4 championship golf courses nearby. Tennis, horseriding and fishing. French and Gaelic spoken.

WEB: www.ogradyshotel.com

B&B from £30.00 to £35.00
€38.09 to €44.44

CORNELIUS AND SUE
Proprietors

American Express

Diners

Mastercard

Visa

9 9

Closed 28 October - 12 November

RHU GLEN COUNTRY CLUB HOTEL

LUFFANY, SLIEVERUE,
WATERFORD
TEL: 051-832242 FAX: 051-832242
EMAIL: rhuglennhotel@ireland.com

HOTEL ★★ MAP 4 L 5

Built within its own grounds with parking for cars, coaches etc. the hotel is family run. Situated on the N25 Rosslare to Waterford Road, convenient to ferries, it offers a superb location whether your pleasure be golfing, fishing, or simply exploring the South East. All rooms are en suite with direct dial phone and multi-channel TV. The restaurant is renowned for its service of fine food. Relax and enjoy our lounge bars and ballroom with live entertainment provided by Ireland's top artistes.

B&B from £25.00 to £40.00
€31.74 to €50.79

LIAM MOONEY
Proprietor

American Express

Diners

Mastercard

Visa

☺ Weekend specials from £75.00

19 19

Closed 24 - 26 December

Room rates are IR£ per room per night

RICE GUESTHOUSE BATTERBERRY'S BAR

35 & 36 BARRACK STREET, WATERFORD
TEL: 051-371606 FAX: 051-357013
EMAIL: ricegh@eircom.net

GUESTHOUSE U   MAP 4 L 5

We are situated next to Mount Sion Christian Brothers school which Blessed Edmund Ignatius Rice founded in 1802. Tours of the shrine and museum may be arranged, so the name Rice Guesthouse. 20 en suite rooms have cable TV and direct dial phone. Ideally situated to the main shopping centre, Waterford Crystal and train and bus station. Ideal base for touring the South East or golf breaks. Tee times can be arranged and afterwards enjoy live entertainment most nights in our lounge.

B&B from £26.50 to £32.50
€33.65 to €41.27

JOHN & OLIVE O'DRISCOLL

Mastercard
Visa

21 21

Open All Year

ST. ALBANS GUESTHOUSE

CORK ROAD, WATERFORD
TEL: 051-358171 FAX: 051-358171

GUESTHOUSE ★★   MAP 4 L 5

St. Albans is a well established family run guesthouse. Ideally located minutes walk from Waterford City Centre and Waterford Crystal. Our very spacious superbly appointed rooms are all en suite with multi-channel TV, tea/coffee facilities and hairdryer. Secure parking at rear of premises. 4 championship golf courses in vicinity. Horse riding 3km. Tennis courts, swimming pool 2 minutes. Several local beaches and breathtaking scenery. Bus and train station a short distance.

B&B from £24.00 to £27.50
€30.47 to €34.92

TOM & HELEN MULLALLY
Proprietors

Mastercard
Visa

8 8

Closed 18 - 28 December

TOWER HOTEL & LEISURE CENTRE

THE MALL, WATERFORD
TEL: 051-875801 FAX: 051-870129
EMAIL: towerw@iol.ie

HOTEL ★★★   MAP 4 L 5

A Tower Group Hotel - located in the heart of Waterford, with 140 guest bedrooms it is the largest hotel in the South East and the flagship of the Tower Hotel Group. The Tower Hotel boasts extensive leisure facilities including a 20 metre pool and is the perfect base from which to explore the many scenic areas of the County Waterford.

WEB: www.towerhotelgroup.ie

Member of Tower Hotel Group

B&B from £35.00 to £66.00
€44.44 to €83.80

PAUL MCDAID
General Manager

American Express
Diners
Mastercard
Visa

☺ Weekend specials from £105.00

140 140

Closed 24 - 29 December

B&B rates are IR£ per person sharing per night incl. Breakfast

WATERFORD CASTLE HOTEL, GOLF & COUNTRY CLUB

THE ISLAND, BALLINAKILL,
WATERFORD
TEL: 051-878203   FAX: 051-879316
EMAIL: info@waterfordcastle.com

HOTEL U   MAP 4 L 5

3 miles from Waterford City. Waterford Castle luxury Hotel, Golf & Country Club is uniquely situated on 310 acres island overlooking the estuary of the River Suir. Access to the island is by a chain linked car ferry, which transfers you and your car across. The 15th century Castle combines the gracious living of an elegant past with every modern comfort, service, convenience. Dining at the Castle is an ultimate experience and is highly recognised. AA 2 Red Rosettes. Look forward to welcoming you.

WEB: www.waterfordcastle.com

Room Rate from £140.00 to £315.00
€177.76 to €399.97

NIALL EDMONDSON
General Manager

American Express
Diners
Mastercard
Visa

19 19

Closed 02 January - 01 February

WATERFORD MARINA QUALITY HOTEL

CANADA STREET,
WATERFORD
TEL: 051-856600   FAX: 051-856605
EMAIL: stay@irishcourthotels.com

HOTEL U   MAP 4 L 5

The Marina Hotel is located on the waterfront just 2 mins from the city centre. The hotel which has a distinctive art deco, incorporates superbly designed rooms. All rooms are en suite with multi-channel TV, direct dial phone, hairdryer, trouser press and tea/coffee making facilities. The Waterfront Bar & Bistro Restaurant offer an excellent choice of dishes. Guests have complimentary use of a secure indoor carpark, sauna.

WEB: www.irishcourthotels.com

Member of Irish Court Hotel Group

B&B from £35.00 to £85.00
€44.44 to €107.93

DECLAN MEAGHER
General Manager

American Express
Mastercard
Visa

81 81

Open All Year

WOODLANDS HOTEL

DUNMORE ROAD,
WATERFORD
TEL: 051-304574   FAX: 051-304575
EMAIL: woodhl@iol.ie

HOTEL N   MAP 4 L 5

This new hotel is located 3 miles from Waterford City Centre and yet has all the facilities of a countryside hotel with open spaces, a river view and parking for 150 cars. The hotel facilities include 47 en suite rooms with all modern amenities, a split level bar designed to generate a great pub atmosphere. Our restaurant offers the very best cuisine in an intimate setting, state of the art leisure centre plus full conference and banqueting facilities.

WEB: www.woodlandshotel.ie

B&B from £55.00 to £75.00
€69.83 to €95.23

MARGUERITE FITZGERALD
Sales & Marketing Manager

American Express
Diners
Mastercard
Visa

Weekend specials from £95.00

47 47

Open All Year

Room rates are IR£ per room per night

NEWTOWN FARM GUESTHOUSE

GRANGE, ARDMORE, VIA YOUGHAL, CO. WATERFORD
TEL: 024-94143   FAX: 024-94054
EMAIL: newtownfarm@eircom.net

GUESTHOUSE ★★★ MAP 3 K 3

Family-run farm guesthouse in scenic location, surrounded by its own farmland with dairying as main enterprise. With view of Atlantic Ocean, hills and cliff walks, comfortable spacious rooms, all en suite with direct dial phone, TV and tea/coffee facilities, some with balcony. Seafood award dishes a speciality. Hard tennis court, pony, games room, large garden, sandy beaches 4km. Signposted on N25 Rosslare Road, half way between Dungarvan/Youghal. Turn left at Flemings Pub.

WEB: homepage.eircom.net/~newtownfarm

Member of Premier Guesthouses

B&B from £22.00 to £28.00
€27.93 to €35.55

TERESA O'CONNOR
Proprietor
Mastercard
Visa

☺ Midweek specials from £68.00

Closed 20 - 31 December

ROUND TOWER HOTEL

COLLEGE ROAD, ARDMORE, CO. WATERFORD
TEL: 024-94494   FAX: 024-94254
EMAIL: rth@eircom.net

HOTEL U MAP 3 K 3

Situated within walking distance of Ardmore's award-winning beach, the Round Tower Hotel offers 10 well appointed en suite bedrooms. Fresh local produce feature prominently on both the bar and restaurant menus. The ancient monastic settlement of St. Declan & the Round Tower are situated behind the hotel. Ardmore also boasts some world famous cliff walks, & breathtaking scenery. Ardmore is 21 kms from Dungarvan & a 2hr drive from the port of Rosslare on the Primary N25 route.

WEB: www.waterfordtourism.org

B&B from £27.50 to £32.50
€34.92 to €41.27

AIDAN QUIRKE
Proprietor
Mastercard
Visa

Closed 01 November - 28 February

CLONANAV FARM GUESTHOUSE

NIRE VALLEY, BALLYMACARBRY, VIA CLONMEL, CO. WATERFORD
TEL: 052-36141   FAX: 052-36294
EMAIL: clonanav@iol.ie

GUESTHOUSE ★★★ MAP 3 K 5

Relax and enjoy the hospitality of the Ryan Family at award-winning Clonanav. Situated in the Nire Valley on a farm serving excellent home produced meals. Complimentary tea/coffee bar in conservatory, drying room, hard tennis/basketball court. French/Spanish spoken. Ireland's best dry fly fishing with guidance from Andrew on Rivers Suir, Nire & Tar. Permits, tuition, tackle hire and shop on premises. Explore the wonderful walking, mountain lakes and valley. 10 golf courses.

WEB: www.clonanav.com

Member of Great Fishing Houses of Ireland

B&B from £30.00 to £40.00
€38.09 to €50.79

EILEEN RYAN
Proprietor
American Express
Diners
Mastercard
Visa

Closed 01 November - 01 February

B&B rates are IR£ per person sharing per night incl. Breakfast

CO. WATERFORD
BALLYMACARBRY / CAPPOQUIN / CHEEKPOINT

HANORAS COTTAGE

**NIRE VALLEY, BALLYMACARBRY,
CO. WATERFORD
TEL: 052-36134 FAX: 052-36540
EMAIL: hanorascottage@eircom.net**

GUESTHOUSE ★★★★ MAP 3 K 5

Delightfully situated in the Comeragh Mountains, Hanoras Cottage has every comfort for discerning guests. Relax in the sheer bliss of an adult only house with spa tub and the soothing sounds of the Nire River running by. Spoil yourselves in our spacious rooms with jacuzzi baths. Superior rooms for that special occasion! Enjoy excellent cuisine from our Ballymaloe School chefs who cater for all diets. We specialise in walking holidays, golf, horse riding and just relaxing.

B&B from £45.00 to £65.00
€57.14 to €82.53

SEAMUS & MARY WALL
Proprietors

Mastercard

Visa

☺ Autumn/Spring Specials from
£120.00

10 10

Closed 20 - 28 December

RICHMOND HOUSE

**CAPPOQUIN,
CO. WATERFORD
TEL: 058-54278 FAX: 058-54988**

GUESTHOUSE ★★★★ MAP 3 J 4

Delightful 18th century Georgian Countryhouse and fully licenced award winning restaurant set in private grounds. Relax in total peace and tranquillity in front of log fires. Each room is a perfect blend of Georgian splendour combined with all modern comforts for the discerning guest. AA ◆◆◆◆◆ Recommended in the Bridgestone Guides; 100 Best Places to Stay and 100 Best Restaurants in Ireland. Recent Winner of the Gilbeys Gold Medal Award for Excellence.

WEB: www.amireland.com/richmond

B&B from £45.00 to £80.00
€57.14 to €101.58

PAUL & CLAIRE DEEVY
Proprietors

American Express

Diners

Mastercard

Visa

☺ Weekend specials from £120.00

9 9

Closed 23 December - 20 January

THREE RIVERS GUEST HOUSE

**CHEEKPOINT,
CO. WATERFORD
TEL: 051-382520 FAX: 051-382542
EMAIL: mail@threerivers.ie**

GUESTHOUSE ★★★ MAP 4 M 5

AA selected ◆◆◆◆ guesthouse overlooking scenic Waterford Estuary. Situated on the outskirts of the historic village, Cheekpoint, with its award winning pubs and seafood restaurants. Sample the delights of breakfast in our Estuary View dining room or relax over coffee in our spacious lounge. Ideal base for touring the sunny South East, close to Waterford, Dunmore East, Tramore and 2km from Faithlegg Golf Course. All rooms en suite with direct dial phone.

WEB: www.threerivers.ie

Member of Premier Guesthouses

B&B from £23.00 to £30.00
€29.20 to €38.09

TIM & AINE HAIER

American Express

Mastercard

Visa

☺ Stay 3 nights and 4th night is free

14 14

Closed 20 December - 10 January

Room rates are IR£ per room per night

CLONEA STRAND HOTEL, GOLF & LEISURE

CLONEA, DUNGARVAN,
CO. WATERFORD
TEL: 058-42416   FAX: 058-42880
EMAIL: info@clonea.com

HOTEL ★★★   MAP 3 K 4

Clonea Strand Hotel overlooking Clonea Beach. Family run by John and Ann McGrath. All rooms en suite with tea/coffee making facilities, hair-dryer and colour TV. Indoor leisure centre with heated pool, jacuzzi, sauna, Turkish bath, gymnasium and ten pin bowling alley. Situated close by is our 18 hole golf course bordering on the Atlantic Ocean with a scenic background of Dungarvan Bay and Comeragh Mountains. Our Bay Restaurant specialises in locally caught seafood.

WEB: www.clonea.com

B&B from £33.00 to £55.00
€41.90 to €69.84

MARK KNOWLES
Gen.Mgr.Group/Marketing

American Express
Diners
Mastercard
Visa

☺ Midweek specials from £90.00

58 58

Open All Year

GOLD COAST GOLF HOTEL & LEISURE CENTRE

BALLINACOURTY, DUNGARVAN,
CO. WATERFORD
TEL: 058-42249   FAX: 058-43378
EMAIL: info@clonea.com

HOTEL ★★★   MAP 3 K 4

Gold Coast Golf Hotel overlooking Dungarvan Bay, family run by John & Ann McGrath. All rooms en suite with tea/coffee making facilities, colour TV, direct dial telephone, leisure centre with heated pool and children's pool, sauna, gym, jacuzzi, bubble pool. Leisure centre with view of our 18 hole golf course. Our tower and bay restaurants specialises in locally caught seafood. Food available all day in bunker bar, with panoramic view of bay.

WEB: www.clonea.com

B&B from £33.00 to £55.00
€41.90 to €69.84

MAIRE MCGRATH
General Manager

American Express
Diners
Mastercard
Visa

☺ Weekend specials from £80.00

36 36

Open All Year

LAWLORS HOTEL

BRIDGE STREET, DUNGARVAN,
CO. WATERFORD
TEL: 058-41122   FAX: 058-41000
EMAIL: info@lawlors-hotel.ie

HOTEL ★★★   MAP 3 K 4

Lawlors Hotel is family run with 89 bedrooms, all en suite with tea/coffee making facilities, TV and direct dial phone. Lawlors is the ideal choice for your stay in the beautiful West Waterford countryside. Conferences, Weddings, Parties, Seminars are especially catered for. Good food is a speciality at Lawlors and the friendly atmosphere of Dungarvan Town is brought to life in the Old Worlde bar surroundings.

WEB: www.lawlors-hotel.ie

B&B from £32.00 to £50.00
€40.63 to €63.49

MICHAEL BURKE
Proprietor

American Express
Diners
Mastercard
Visa

89 89

Closed 25 December

B&B rates are IR£ per person sharing per night incl. Breakfast

PARK HOTEL

DUNGARVAN,
CO. WATERFORD
TEL: 058-42899 FAX: 058-42969
EMAIL: photel@indigo.ie

HOTEL ★★★ MAP 3 K 4

Overlooking the Colligan River Estuary, owned and run by the Flynn Family, whose experience in the hotel business is your best guarantee of an enjoyable and memorable stay. The hotel's spacious and comfortable bedrooms have been furnished with flair and imagination. All have private bathroom, direct dial telephone, 16 channel satellite TV. The hotel's leisure centre has a 20m swimming pool, sauna, steam room & gym.

B&B from £35.00 to £46.00
€44.44 to €58.41

PIERCE FLYNN
Manager

American Express
Diners
Mastercard
Visa

29 29

Open All Year

SEAVIEW

WINDGAP, N25/YOUGHAL ROAD,
DUNGARVAN, CO. WATERFORD
TEL: 058-41583 FAX: 058-41679
EMAIL: faheyn@gofree.indigo.ie

GUESTHOUSE N MAP 3 K 4

Want your vacation to never stop being a vacation? Enjoy breakfast overlooking the sea? Play one of Dungarvans three 18 hole golf courses or take a bus tour of the area and let someone else do the driving. How about dinner, entertained by traditional Irish musicians, at the nearby Marine Bar? Make every ounce of your vacation count. Try Seaview on N25 5km west of Dungarvan. Fax and e-mail facilities available. Continental and Full Irish breakfast served. Laundry service available.

WEB: www.amireland.com/seaview/

B&B from £20.00 to £25.00
€25.39 to €31.74

NORA & MARTIN & MEALLA
FAHEY

Mastercard
Visa

8 8

Open All Year

HAVEN HOTEL

DUNMORE EAST,
CO. WATERFORD
TEL: 051-383150 FAX: 051-383488

HOTEL ★★ MAP 4 M 5

The Haven Hotel is family owned and managed. Situated in Dunmore East, one of Ireland's most beautiful seaside resorts. The restaurant is renowned for its first class food and specialises in prime rib beef, steaks and locally caught seafood. The Haven is an ideal location for day trips to the many surrounding golf clubs. Children are also made especially welcome with our motto being - the children of today are the customers of tomorrow.

WEB: www.thehavenhotel.com

B&B from £35.00 to £40.00
€44.44 to €50.79

JEAN & JOHN KELLY
Managers/Owners

Mastercard
Visa

24 24

Closed 01 November - 28 February

Room rates are IR£ per room per night

OCEAN HOTEL

**DUNMORE EAST,
CO. WATERFORD**
TEL: 051-383136 FAX: 051-383576
EMAIL: oceanhotel@ireland.com

HOTEL ★★ MAP 4 M 5

The Ocean Hotel 15 minutes drive from Waterford City, is situated in one of Ireland's most picturesque villages. The Jewel of the sunny South East. We offer you the personal attention & service, only a family run hotel can provide. Our extensive à la carte menu is available in both dining room and bar with a strong emphasis on seafood dishes. Our menu is reasonably priced. Golf packages arranged. Our new Alfred D Snow Bar is air conditioned with decor depicting a nautical theme.

B&B from £30.00 to £40.00
€38.09 to €50.79

BRENDAN GALLAGHER
Proprietor

American Express
Diners
Mastercard
Visa

12 12

Closed 25 December

FAITHLEGG HOUSE HOTEL

**FAITHLEGG,
CO. WATERFORD**
TEL: 051-382000 FAX: 051-382010
EMAIL: faithleg@iol.ie

HOTEL U MAP 4 M 5

A Tower Group Hotel - The restoration of Faithlegg House has returned one of Waterford's finest estates to its former elegance and created a luxury hotel. Faithlegg House Hotel is an 18th century mansion with 14 master bedrooms in the original house and an additional 68 in the new wing. An extensive range of health, fitness and beauty treatments are available including the on-site 18-hole championship golf course and new 17 metre pool.

WEB: www.towerhotelgroup.ie

Member of Tower Hotel Group

B&B from £70.00 to £125.00
€88.88 to €158.72

MADGE BARRY
General Manager

American Express
Diners
Mastercard
Visa

☺ Weekend specials from £135.00

82 82

Closed 03 January - 07 February

LISMORE HOTEL

**MAIN STREET, LISMORE,
CO. WATERFORD**
TEL: 058-54555 FAX: 058-53068

HOTEL ★★ MAP 3 J 4

Situated in the heart of historical Lismore, on the Munster Blackwater River, this newly refurbished hotel is the ideal location for a relaxing break. Take a walk back through time and enjoy Lismore with its majestic castle and gardens, historical cathedral and peaceful river walks. Horse riding, fishing and golf are all available locally. Our warm and friendly staff await your arrival and we look forward to serving you in our award winning restaurant.

B&B from £35.00 to £40.00
€44.44 to €50.79

JAMES J KELLY
Manager

Mastercard
Visa

20 20

Closed 25 December

B&B rates are IR£ per person sharing per night incl. Breakfast

BELAIR GUEST HOUSE

**RACECOURSE ROAD, TRAMORE,
CO. WATERFORD**
TEL: 051-381605 FAX: 051-386688

GUESTHOUSE ★★ MAP 4 L 5

Belair is a beautiful Georgian house built in 1797 featuring delightful enclosed gardens. The house, which overlooks Tramore Bay and miles of sandy beach, has been newly refurbished throughout. All rooms en suite, TV, phone, tea/coffee facilities. It is quiet and peaceful for that restful break and offers safe parking. Fishing, tennis, horseriding, surfing, golfing and Splashworld all at hand. Waterford Crystal and six excellent golf courses within an eight mile radius.

B&B from £25.00 to £35.00
€31.74 to €44.44

MARY CURRAN
Manager

Mastercard

Visa

Open All Year

MAJESTIC HOTEL

**TRAMORE,
CO. WATERFORD**
TEL: 051-381761 FAX: 051-381766
EMAIL: info@majestic-hotel.ie

HOTEL ★★★ MAP 4 L 5

A warm welcome awaits you at the newly refurbished Majestic Hotel overlooking Tramore Bay, and only 10km from Waterford City. Family owned and managed, all 60 bedrooms are en suite with TV, phone, hairdryer, & tea/coffee facilities. Full leisure facilities (incl. steam room, swimming pool and gym) available to guests at Splashworld Health and Fitness Club adjacent to hotel. Gold Key Award 1999. Les Routiers. Golf packages our speciality on choice of 6 golf courses.

WEB: www.majestic-hotel.ie

Member of Les Routiers Ireland

B&B from £35.00 to £49.50
€44.44 to €62.85

ANNETTE & DANNY DEVINE
Proprietors

American Express

Mastercard

Visa

Open All Year

O'SHEA'S HOTEL

**STRAND STREET, TRAMORE,
CO. WATERFORD**
TEL: 051-381246 FAX: 051-390144
EMAIL: info@osheas-hotel.com

HOTEL ★★ MAP 4 L 5

O'Shea's is an intimate family run hotel, newly refurbished and extended, situated beside Tramore's famous 5km safe sandy beach and just a few minutes from Splashworld. Sample our seafood and steak restaurant, full bar food menu available. Entertainment every night during Summer. Golfing holiday packages are our speciality - we will organise your tee times at any of the surrounding golf courses. We look forward to meeting you.

WEB: www.osheas-hotel.com

B&B from £27.50 to £47.50
€34.91 to €60.31

NOREEN & JOE O'SHEA
Proprietors

American Express

Diners

Mastercard

Visa

☺ Weekend specials from £70.00

Closed 22 - 31 December

Room rates are IR£ per room per night

SANDS HOTEL

STRAND ROAD, TRAMORE,
CO. WATERFORD
TEL: 051-381355 FAX: 051-393869

HOTEL P MAP 4 L 5

The Sands Hotel, newly refurbished and extended. All rooms en suite, TV, direct dial telephone, tea/coffee facilities. Situated in the heart of Tramore tourist area, a minute's walk from the beach and Splashworld. A choice of 3 bars with entertainment to suit all ages. Carvery lunches, evening grill menu, full bar food menu. Friendly atmosphere and homely welcome.

B&B from £27.50 to £45.00
€34.28 to €57.13

PAUL CUSACK Gen. Manager
FREDDIE PIPER Owner

Mastercard
Visa

20 20

Closed 20 - 29 December

FAYTHE GUEST HOUSE

THE FAYTHE, SWAN VIEW,
WEXFORD
TEL: 053-22249 FAX: 053-21680
EMAIL: faythhse@iol.ie

GUESTHOUSE ★★★ MAP 4 0 6

Family run guesthouse in quiet part of town centre, is built on the grounds of a former castle of which one wall remains today. All rooms refurbished in 2000, some overlook our gardens and Wexford Harbour. Due to all improvements we are now graded to 3***. All rooms have bathroom en suite, colour TV, direct dial phone, clock radio and tea/coffee making facilities. Rosslare Ferry Port is only 15 minutes drive (early breakfast on request). We also have a large private car park.

WEB: www.faytheguesthouse.com

B&B from £18.00 to £25.00
€22.86 to €31.74

DAMIAN AND SIOBHAN LYNCH
Proprietors

Mastercard
Visa

10 10

Closed 24 - 28 December

FERRYCARRIG HOTEL

FERRYCARRIG BRIDGE,
WEXFORD
TEL: 053-20999 FAX: 053-20982
EMAIL: ferrycarrig@griffingroup.ie

HOTEL ★★★ MAP 4 N 6

Ferrycarrig Hotel (AA & RAC 4****) boasts one of the most inspiring locations of any hotel in Ireland, with sweeping views across the River Slaney Estuary. The hotel has completed a development programme to include the refurbishment of all of the original rooms of the hotel and the development of 13 extra rooms. Facilities include a 5***** health and fitness club with 20m pool, 2 award winning waterfront restaurants, 103 rooms/suites and conference centre. Part owners St Helen's Bay Golf Club.

WEB: www.griffingroup.ie

Member of Griffin Hotel Group

B&B from £45.00 to £95.00
€57.14 to €120.63

MARK BROWNE
General Manager

American Express
Diners
Mastercard
Visa

103 103

Open All Year

B&B rates are IR£ per person sharing per night incl. Breakfast

Room rates are IR£ per room per night

TALBOT HOTEL CONFERENCE AND LEISURE CENTRE

TRINITY STREET,
WEXFORD
TEL: 053-22566   FAX: 053-23377
EMAIL: talbotwx@eircom.net

HOTEL ★★★ MAP 4 0 6

Located in the heart of Wexford Town is the Talbot Hotel Conference & Leisure Centre. Our Quay Leisure Centre offers extensive leisure facilities for the fitness enthusiast and for those who just want pure pampering. Award winning Slaney Restaurant offers fresh Wexford fayre and an extensive wine list. Evening entertainment in the Trinity Bar at weekends. Bedrooms are fully equipped with direct dial phone, satellite TV and are tastefully decorated for your comfort and relaxation.

WEB: www.talbothotel.ie

B&B from £49.00 to £55.00
€62.22 to €69.84

URSULA SINNOTT
General Manager

American Express
Diners
Mastercard
Visa

Weekend specials from £115.00

99 99

IRISH HOTELS FEDERATION

Open All Year

WESTGATE HOUSE

WESTGATE,
WEXFORD
TEL: 053-22167   FAX: 053-22167
EMAIL: westgate@wexmail.com

GUESTHOUSE ★★ MAP 4 0 6

Westgate House stands in a charming, traditional area across the road from the famed Selskar Abbey and Westgate Castle. It is an historic house formerly Westgate Hotel in 1812. It has been refurbished in period style with taste and elegance, with beautifully furnished bedrooms which create a sense of ease and timelessness matching this it offers full modern amenities. Situated in the exciting town centre with superb shops, pubs and restaurants. A secure lock-up car park is provided.

WEB: www.wexford-online.com/westgate

B&B from £20.00 to £25.00
€25.39 to €31.74

M & D ALLEN
Owners

Mastercard
Visa

10 10

IRISH HOTELS FEDERATION

Open All Year

WHITES HOTEL

GEORGE STREET,
WEXFORD
TEL: 053-22311   FAX: 053-45000
EMAIL: info@whiteshotel.iol.ie

HOTEL ★★★ MAP 4 0 6

Est. 1779, this charming 3*** hotel is centrally located in the historic and picturesque town of Wexford. The hotel's facilities include a health & fitness club, Harpers superb brasserie restaurant offering the finest local and international dishes for lunch & dinner and the immensely popular Harpers Bar where carvery lunches and bar food is served daily and which is open late Thurs-Sun. The hotel is 5 mins walk from the bus and train station and only 20 mins drive from Rosslare Europort.

WEB: www.wexfordirl.com/accommodation/whites/

Member of Best Western Hotels

B&B from £37.50 to £47.50
€47.62 to €60.31

MICHAEL CONNOLLY
General Manager

American Express
Diners
Mastercard
Visa

Midweek 3 B&B and 3 Dinners from £89.00

82 82

IRISH HOTELS FEDERATION

Open All Year

B&B rates are IR£ per person sharing per night incl. Breakfast

WHITFORD HOUSE HOTEL

NEW LINE ROAD,
WEXFORD
TEL: 053-43444 FAX: 053-46399
EMAIL: whitford@indigo.ie

HOTEL ★★★ MAP 4 N 5

One of the leading family run tourist establishments in the South East. Footprints award winning restaurant receives constant accolades for excellence, presentation and value. Seafood a speciality. Standard and Superior de luxe accommodation. Entertainment at weekends. Unwind in our indoor swimming pool (Mar/mid Nov) or serve an ace on our tennis court. For younger members we boast a children's playground. Locally there is golf, fishing, horse riding and excellent beaches.

WEB: www.whitford.ie

B&B from £36.00 to £43.00
€45.71 to €54.60

KAY WHITTY
Proprietor

American Express
Mastercard
Visa

2 B&B and 1 Dinner from £90.00

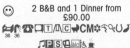
36 36

Closed 23 December - 13 January

DUNBRODY COUNTRY HOUSE HOTEL & RESTAURANT

ARTHURSTOWN,
CO. WEXFORD
TEL: 051-389600 FAX: 051-389601
EMAIL: info@dunbrodyhouse.com

HOTEL ★★★★ MAP 4 M 5

Set in 200 acres of beautiful parkland, Dunbrody is an enchantingly intimate 1830s Georgian manor. Spacious and elegantly decorated rooms overlook the magnificent gardens and create a distinctive atmosphere of pure relaxation and luxurious comfort. With an award-winning restaurant and a choice of fine wines to complement master chef Kevin Dundon's innovative culinary creations, guests return again and again to relish the unique ambience that is Dunbrody Country House.

WEB: www.dunbrodyhouse.com

Member of Ireland's Blue Book

B&B from £59.00 to £120.00
€74.91 to €152.36

KEVIN & CATHERINE DUNDON
Owners

American Express
Diners
Mastercard
Visa

Closed 24 December - 31 January

CRANDONNELL LODGE HOTEL

BARNTOWN,
CO. WEXFORD
TEL: 053-34300

HOTEL U MAP 4 N 6

Choice restaurant facilities with widest selection menus and an elegant lounge bar. Located a few miles outside the Viking town of Wexford and just off the national motorway network linking the country with all major centres on the Wexford/New Ross Road. 5 mins drive from the international award-winning Irish National Heritage Park and the ideal centre for horse riding, riding lessons, trekking, golf and driving range, watersports and major Wexford attractions.

B&B from £25.00 to £30.00
€31.74 to €38.09

GEORGE CARROLL

Mastercard
Visa

12 12

Open All Year

Room rates are IR£ per room per night

BAYVIEW HOTEL

COURTOWN HARBOUR, GOREY,
CO. WEXFORD
TEL: 055-25307 FAX: 055-25576
EMAIL: bayview@iol.ie

HOTEL ★★ MAP 8 O 7

The Bayview is owned and run by the McGarry Family. The hotel is overlooking the marina at Courtown Harbour. It is renowned for its good food and friendly atmosphere. All rooms are en suite with TV, video channel and direct dial telephone. Self catering apartments in hotel. Enjoy the Squash & Tennis centre free to guests. Courtown's 18 hole golf course 2km. It is an ideal setting for weddings and parties.

WEB: www.courtown.com/page4

B&B from £38.00 to £40.00
€48.25 to €50.79

BRIAN MCGARRY
Manager
American Express
Diners
Mastercard
Visa

13 13

Closed 01 November - 01 March

HARBOUR HOUSE GUESTHOUSE

COURTOWN HARBOUR, COURTOWN,
GOREY, CO. WEXFORD
TEL: 055-25117 FAX: 055-25117

GUESTHOUSE ★★ MAP 8 O 7

Harbour House just off the main Rosslare/Dublin N11 route and only 6.4km from Gorey is ideally located in the renowned seaside resort of Courtown Harbour. Harbour House is the ideal base for both business and holiday travellers and is central to all amenities and only three minutes from Courtown's sandy beaches. All rooms are en suite with your own private car park. Your holiday here is under the personal supervision of the O'Gorman Family.

B&B from £23.00 to £25.00
€29.20 to €31.74

DONAL & MARGARET O'GORMAN
Proprietors
American Express
Diners
Mastercard
Visa

 Midweek Special from £65.00
excl. July & August

15 15

Closed 31 October - 10 April

BORRMOUNT LODGE

BORRMOUNT, ENNISCORTHY,
CO. WEXFORD
TEL: 054-47122 FAX: 054-47133
EMAIL: borrmountlodge@eircom.net

GUESTHOUSE ★★★ MAP 4 N 6

Charming country house with the comfort of a hotel and the warmth of a home. At dinner silver and crystal shine in the candlelight. Gourmet evening meals. Extensive wine list hand picked from Burgundy. Breakfast served until noon. Free salmon fishing. Golf and beautiful walks near by. Central location for touring in the South East.

B&B from £25.00 to £34.00
€31.74 to €43.17

NOREEN & GUY KING-URBIN
Owners
Mastercard
Visa

6 6

Open All Year

B&B rates are IR£ per person sharing per night incl. Breakfast

LEMONGROVE HOUSE

BLACKSTOOPS, ENNISCORTHY,
CO. WEXFORD
TEL: 054-36115   FAX: 054-36115
EMAIL: lemongrovehouse@iolfree.ie

GUESTHOUSE ★★★   MAP 4 N 6

Spacious luxury home 1km north of
Enniscorthy just off roundabout on
Dublin/Rosslare Road (N11).
Lemongrove house is set in mature
gardens with private parking. All
rooms en suite with direct dial
phone, TV, hairdryer and tea/coffee
making facilities. Recommended by
Guide du Routard, AA, and other
leading guides. Within walking
distance of a choice of restaurants,
pubs and new pool and leisure
centre. Locally we have beaches,
golf, horseriding, walking and quad
track.

B&B from £19.00 to £23.00
€24.13 to €29.20

COLM & ANN MCGIBNEY
Owners

Mastercard

Visa

🛢🅿🔥🕿🖵TC☀♣UJP🚶S⚓
6   6

Open All Year

MURPHY - FLOODS HOTEL

MARKET SQUARE, ENNISCORTHY,
CO. WEXFORD
TEL: 054-33413   FAX: 054-33413
EMAIL: mfhotel@indigo.ie

HOTEL ★★   MAP 4 N 6

Overlooking Market Square of
historic 6th century Enniscorthy
Town on Slaney salmon River.
Package rates for golf breaks,
midweek and weekends. Elegant
restaurant, in Georgian style,
presents menus of quality and
variety. Room service, excellent bar
food, packed lunches available, cots
provided, night porter service.
Central for touring lovely Slaney
Valley and sunny South East.
Rosslare Ferry 43km, Waterford
56km, Dublin 120km, Shannon
240km. 1km from National 1798
Centre.

WEB: www.murphyfloods.com

B&B from £30.00 to £45.00
€38.09 to €57.14

MICHAEL J WALL
Proprietor

American Express

Diners

Mastercard

Visa

🙂 Weekend specials from £65.00

🛢🅿🕿🖵TC CM🍴alc⚓
19 17

Closed 24 - 28 December

PINES COUNTRY HOUSE HOTEL

CAMOLIN, ENNISCORTHY,
CO. WEXFORD
TEL: 054-83600   FAX: 054-83588
EMAIL: thepineshotel@eircom.net

HOTEL N   MAP 4 N 6

Beautifully located amongst the
woods of Camolin Park. The Pines is
within easy reach of the local
village, with its choice of pubs and
restaurants. The hotel's leisure
facilities include a state of the art
gymnasium, relaxing sauna,
steamroom and plunge pool. With
pony trekking on site plus lots more.
A relaxed and uniquely warm
atmosphere combined with superb
Mediterranean cuisine makes The
Pines the perfect place to relax and
unwind.

WEB: www.pinescountryhousehotel.com

B&B from £25.00 to £38.00
€31.74 to €48.25

FRANK MURHILL
Director Manager

Mastercard

Visa

🛢🅿🔥🕿🖵🖵🛁🕶UJP alc⚓
12 11

Open All Year

RIVERSIDE PARK HOTEL

THE PROMENADE, ENNISCORTHY,
CO. WEXFORD
TEL: 054-37800 FAX: 054-37900
EMAIL: riversideparkhotel@eircom.net

HOTEL ★★★ MAP 4 N 6

Located on the banks of the picturesque River Slaney, the hotel is a welcome addition to the bustling Enniscorthy. Comprising 60 delightfully furnished rooms offering every modern convenience, facilities include the Moorings Restaurant, newly opened Alamo Tex-Mex Restaurant, the Promenade & Mill House bars. 30 mins drive from Rosslare it is the perfect base for touring historic Vinegar Hill, the 1798 Visitor Centre, the Castle Museum as well as golf courses and beaches.

WEB: www.riversideparkhotel.com

B&B from £45.00 to £52.50
€57.14 to €66.66

JIM MAHER
General Manager

American Express
Diners
Mastercard
Visa

Closed 24 - 26 December

TREACYS HOTEL

TEMPLESHANNON, ENNISCORTHY,
CO. WEXFORD
TEL: 054-37798 FAX: 054-37733
EMAIL: treacyshotel@treacyhotelsgroup.com

HOTEL ★★★ MAP 4 N 6

Treacys Hotel is situated in the town centre. Just 30 minutes from Rosslare Ferryport and 1 hour 20 minutes from Dublin City. Boasting 48 de-luxe bedrooms with bath/power shower, satellite TV, direct dial phone, hairdryer, tea/coffee. Serving à la carte and table d'hôte menus. Our very own Temple Bar is known to be one of the finest in the South East. New adjacent cineplex and leisure centre (25m swimming pool, gym, sauna, steam room) opened July '99.

B&B from £34.00 to £49.00
€43.17 to €62.22

ANTON & YVONNE TREACY

American Express
Diners
Mastercard
Visa

☺ Weekend specials from £89.00

Closed 24 - 26 December

HORSE AND HOUND INN

BALLINABOOLA, FOULKSMILLS,
CO. WEXFORD
TEL: 051-428323 FAX: 051-428471
EMAIL: mur40@iol.ie

GUESTHOUSE ★★★ MAP 4 N 5

The Horse and Hound Inn, Ballinaboola, Co. Wexford is owned and run by the Murphy Family. Situated six miles from New Ross on the N25 from Rosslare. It is a convenient venue for a meal and a rest. Best Irish produce is used in preparing specialities of fish and beef dishes. There are twelve bedrooms should you wish to stay. Catering for all needs - from private parties, weddings to conferences.

B&B from £27.00 to £30.00
€34.28 to €38.09

CHRISTY MURPHY

Mastercard
Visa

Open All Year

B&B rates are IR£ per person sharing per night incl. Breakfast

ASHDOWN PARK HOTEL

**GOREY,
CO. WEXFORD**
TEL: 055-80500 FAX: 055-80500
EMAIL: info@ashdownparkhotel.ie

UNDER CONSTRUCTION OPENING MAY 2001

HOTEL P MAP 8 O 7

This stylish new hotel has been designed to a superior 3*** standard. 60 highly comfortable bedrooms, including 6 suites offer all modern conveniences. Enjoy a drink by the cosy fire in the lounge followed by a splendid dinner in the elegant restaurant. The magnificent leisure centre sports a swimming pool, jacuzzi, children's pool, gym, sauna and sunroom. Centrally located close to Dublin and Rosslare, Ashdown Park is ideally located for touring Counties Wexford/Wicklow.

WEB: www.ashdownparkhotel.com

B&B from £39.00 to £65.00
€49.52 to €82.53

REDMOND FAMILY
Proprietors

American Express
Diners
Mastercard
Visa

☺ Weekend specials from £98.00

60 60

S 🅐alc

Open All Year

MARLFIELD HOUSE HOTEL

**GOREY,
CO. WEXFORD**
TEL: 055-21124 FAX: 055-21572
EMAIL: info@marlfieldhouse.ie

HOTEL ★★★★ MAP 8 O 7

Formerly the residence of the Earls of Courtown, Marlfield has been renovated by your hosts the Bowe Family. Enjoy this Regency period house filled with antiques and set amidst 36 acres of woodland walks and flower gardens. The kitchen garden provides fresh produce for its award winning restaurant. Five minutes to an 18 hole golf course and sandy beaches. Very highly rated by Michelin, AA and RAC. Member of Ireland's Blue Book and Relais et Châteaux.

WEB: www.marlfieldhouse.com

Member of Relais & Châteaux

B&B from £83.00 to £90.00
€105.38 to €114.27

MARY BOWE
Proprietor

American Express
Diners
Mastercard
Visa

☺ Weekend specials from £220.00

20 20

Closed 15 December - 25 January

HOTEL SALTEES

**KILMORE QUAY,
CO. WEXFORD**
TEL: 053-29601 FAX: 053-29602

HOTEL ★★ MAP 4 N 5

Hotel Saltees, is situated in the picturesque fishing village of Kilmore Quay. Renowned for its thatched cottages and maritime flavour, it is located just 22km from Wexford Town and 19km from the international port of Rosslare. Offering excellent value accommodation, with all rooms en suite, TV, telephone and all well designed to cater for families. The Coningbeg Seafood Restaurant, specialises in serving the freshest seafood. Shore and deep-sea fishing available locally.

B&B from £25.00 to £32.00
€31.74 to €40.63

TOMMY AND NED BYRNE
Proprietors

Mastercard
Visa

☺ Weekend specials from £69.00

10 10

Closed 25 December

Room rates are IR£ per room per night

QUAY HOUSE

KILMORE QUAY,
CO. WEXFORD
TEL: 053-29988 FAX: 053-29808
EMAIL: kilmore@esatclear.ie

GUESTHOUSE ★★★   MAP 4 N 5

3*** Guesthouse. AA Selected
♦♦♦. Quay House is located in the
centre of Kilmore Quay; famous for
its thatched cottages, marina, sea
angling, nature trails and walks
along the Wexford Coast. Quay
House offers you a stay that will
bring you back again and again.
Good food and wine served in our
restaurant Quay Plaice. All inclusive
mini breaks available excluding July
& August. Private car park to rear.

WEB: www.quayhouseguesthouse.com

B&B from £22.50 to £28.00
€28.57 to €35.55

SIOBHAN MCDONNELL
Proprietor

Mastercard

Visa

☺ Weekend specials from £60.00

10 10

Open All Year

CEDAR LODGE HOTEL & RESTAURANT

CARRIGBYRNE, NEWBAWN, (NEAR
NEW ROSS), CO. WEXFORD
TEL: 051-428386 FAX: 051-428222
EMAIL: cedarlodge@eircom.net

HOTEL ★★★   MAP 4 N 6

Charming 3*** country hotel located
in a picturesque setting, 30 minutes
drive from Rosslare Port on the N25
New Ross Road. All bedrooms en
suite with direct dial phone and TV.
The restaurant which concentrates
on freshly prepared produce, is
noted for its good food.
Recommended by Michelin, Good
Hotel Guide, RAC. Forest walks
nearby. Golf, horse riding, JF
Kennedy Park, county museum,
heritage park and sandy beaches
within easy driving distance.

WEB: www.prideofeirehotels.com

B&B from £45.00 to £60.00
€57.14 to €76.18

TOM MARTIN
Proprietor

American Express

Diners

Mastercard

Visa

☺ 3 B&B and 3 Dinners
from £195.00

28 28

Closed 20 December - 01 February

CLARION BRANDON HOUSE HOTEL & LEISURE CENTRE

NEW ROSS,
CO. WEXFORD
TEL: 051-421703 FAX: 051-421567
EMAIL: brandonhouse@eircom.net

HOTEL ★★★   MAP 4 M 6

A deluxe country manor house set in
landscaped grounds with panoramic
views overlooking the River Barrow.
Dine in the AA awardwinning
restaurant or relax in the Library Bar.
All rooms are elegantly furnished.
Luxurious health & leisure club with
20m pool, kiddies pool, fully
equipped gym, sauna, steam room,
jacuzzi, solarium and thalasso
treatment rooms. Nearby golf,
angling, horseriding & gardens. An
ideal base for touring the sunny
South East.

WEB: www.brandonhousehotel.ie

Member of Choice Hotels Ireland

B&B from £45.00 to £70.00
€57.14 to €88.88

GERARD M. DUGGAN
General Manager

American Express

Diners

Mastercard

Visa

☺ Weekend specials from £99.00

60 60

Closed 24 - 25 December

B&B rates are IR£ per person sharing per night incl. Breakfast

CREACON LODGE HOTEL

CREACON, NEW ROSS,
CO. WEXFORD
TEL: 051-421897 FAX: 051-422560
EMAIL: creacon@indigo.ie

HOTEL ★★★ MAP 4 M 6

Set amidst the peace and tranquillity of the countryside. 45 minutes drive from Rosslare, 2 hours from Dublin and only a short scenic drive to the Hook Peninsula and JFK Park. Relax and enjoy our beautiful gardens, comfy sofas and log fires and sample the delights of our restaurant and bar. All bedrooms are en suite with D.D. phone, colour TV. Local amenities include golf, angling, horse-riding water sports and sandy beaches.

WEB: www.creaconlodge.com

B&B from £30.00 to £40.00
€38.09 to €50.79

JOSEPHINE FLOOD & NICK CROSBIE

Mastercard
Visa

😊 Weekend specials from £85.00

10 10

Open All Year

OLD RECTORY HOTEL

ROSBERCON, NEW ROSS,
CO. WEXFORD
TEL: 051-421719 FAX: 051-422974
EMAIL: oldrectorynewross@eircom.net

HOTEL ★★ MAP 4 M 6

Owner-managed country house hotel combining historic charm and modern comfort. Set in 2.5 acres of beautiful gardens overlooking the River Barrow and New Ross Town. All bedrooms en suite with TV, phone and tea/coffee facilities. The intimate restaurant is renowned for its tempting dishes and fine wines. Centrally located between Wexford, Waterford and Kilkenny. Ideal base for touring the South East. Dublin 85 miles; Rosslare 30 miles. Ample off street car parking. Golf, fishing and horse riding nearby.

WEB: www.amireland.com/oldrectory

Member of Irish Family Hotels

B&B from £27.50 to £32.50
€34.92 to €41.27

GERALDINE & JAMES O'LEARY
Proprietors

American Express
Diners
Mastercard
Visa

😊 Weekend specials from £79.00

12 12

Open All Year

ASSALY LODGE

KILLINCK, ROSSLARE,
CO. WEXFORD
TEL: 053-58300 FAX: 053-58300
EMAIL: sales@wexfordirl.com

GUESTHOUSE P MAP 4 O 5

Assaly Lodge is located on two acres of landscaped gardens on the N25. It is a family-run country house with a cosy ambience, antique furniture, open fires, super king size beds all combine to make your stay very special. Bedrooms are luxurious and spacious with direct dial telephone, television and large en-suite. Conveniently located close to Rosslare Harbour, there are numerous restaurants, sandy beaches and golf clubs nearby. Assaly Lodge combines luxury and elegance with a genuine welcome and hospitality.

WEB: www.wexfordirl.com

B&B from £25.00 to £30.00
€31.74 to €38.09

ALBERT & HELEN MURPHY
Owner

Mastercard
Visa

😊 Weekend specials available

6 6

Closed 20 December - 10 January

Room rates are IR£ per room per night

CHURCHTOWN HOUSE

TAGOAT, ROSSLARE,
CO. WEXFORD
TEL: 053-32555 FAX: 053-32577
EMAIL: churchtown.rosslare@indigo.ie

GUESTHOUSE ★★★★ MAP 405

AA Guesthouse of the Year 1998. AA & RAC ◆◆◆◆◆. Churchtown is a period house c.1703 where peace and tranquillity together with country house hospitality combine with modern comforts to make it 'A SPECIAL PLACE TO STAY'. A rural setting in mature gardens, 0.5 mile off the N25 and 5 mins from Rosslare Ferryport/Strand. Explore Wexford's 'Land of Living History', gardens, golf, beaches, birdwatching, fishing and riding. Evening meals served Tues-Sat. Please pre-book.

WEB: www.churchtown-rosslare.com

Member of Manor House Hotels

B&B from £45.00 to £69.00
€57.14 to €87.61

AUSTIN AND PATRICIA CODY
Owners

American Express
Mastercard
Visa

☺ Weekend specials from £105.00

12 12

IRISH HOTELS FEDERATION

Closed 30 November - 01 March

CROSBIE CEDARS HOTEL

ROSSLARE,
CO. WEXFORD
TEL: 053-32124 FAX: 053-32243
EMAIL: info@crosbiecedars.iol.ie

HOTEL ★★★ MAP 405

The Crosbie Cedars Hotel is an AA*** deluxe hotel situated in the heart of Rosslare. The hotel provides elegant and tastefully designed en suite rooms, restaurant and bars, ensuring a comfortable and relaxing stay for all. A haven of outstanding quality, offering true Irish warmth and hospitality. Ideal golf centre within easy reach of 3 excellent courses, Rosslare, St. Helens and Wexford. Golf rates and packages available.

WEB: www.crosbiecedarshotel.com

B&B from £30.00 to £50.00
€38.09 to €63.48

LIZ SINNOTT
General Manager

American Express
Diners
Mastercard
Visa

34 34

IRISH HOTELS FEDERATION

Open All Year

DANBY LODGE HOTEL

ROSSLARE ROAD, KILLINICK,
ROSSLARE, CO. WEXFORD
TEL: 053-58191 FAX: 053-58191
EMAIL: danby@eircom.net

HOTEL U MAP 405

Nestling in the heart of South County Wexford, Danby Lodge Hotel has rightfully earned for itself a reputation for excellence in cuisine and accommodation. Once the home of the painter Francis Danby, 1793-1861, this hotel bears all the hallmarks of a charming country residence. Conveniently located on main Rosslare to Wexford Road (N25). Danby Lodge Hotel offers the visitor a quiet country getaway yet just minutes drive from the port of Rosslare and the town of Wexford. RAC and AA recommended.

Room Rate from £49.00 to £69.00
€62.22 to €87.61

RAYMOND & MARGARET PARLE
Owners

American Express
Diners
Mastercard
Visa

24 24

IRISH HOTELS FEDERATION

Closed 22 - 30 December

KELLY'S RESORT HOTEL

ROSSLARE,
CO. WEXFORD
TEL: 053-32114 FAX: 053-32222
EMAIL: kellyhot@iol.ie

HOTEL ★★★★ MAP 4 O 5

Since 1895 the Kelly Family have created a truly fine resort hotel. Good food, wine and nightly entertainment are very much part of the tradition. Amenities include tennis, squash, snooker, bowls, croquet and an excellent choice of local golf courses. Pamper and relax in our Health & Beauty Centre. 7-day break (July/August): 5-day midweek & 2-day weekend (Spring/Autunm). Special Activity Midweeks in Spring & Autunm - wine tasting, cooking demonstrations, gardening, painting, etc.

WEB: www.kellys.ie

B&B from £55.00 to £77.00
€69.84 to €97.77

WILLIAM J KELLY
Manager/Director
American Express
Mastercard
Visa

Special Autumn & Spring Offer:
5 Days Full Board from £407.00

99 99

Closed 10 December - 23 February

AILSA LODGE

ROSSLARE HARBOUR,
CO. WEXFORD
TEL: 053-33230 FAX: 053-33581
EMAIL: ailsalodge@eircom.net

GUESTHOUSE ★★ MAP 4 O 5

Ailsa Lodge a family run guesthouse in the town of Rosslare Harbour. Positioned in a quiet location with private grounds and spacious parking, it overlooks the Irish Sea, the beach and the ferryport. 5 minutes walk from the bus/rail/ferry terminal. All rooms en suite with TV and direct dial phone. Early breakfasts served. A short walk from all shops, pubs and restaurants. Excellent beaches, fishing, walks and golf courses locally.

WEB: www.ailsalodge.com

Member of Premier Guesthouses

B&B from £18.00 to £24.00
€22.86 to €30.47

DOMINIC SHEIL
Proprietor
Mastercard
Visa

10 10

Closed 24 December - 01 January

CORAL GABLES

TAGOAT, ROSSLARE HARBOUR,
CO. WEXFORD
TEL: 053-31213 FAX: 053-31414
EMAIL: coralgables@eircom.net

GUESTHOUSE ★★ MAP 4 O 5

Coral Gables is situated on a hilltop in quiet secluded surroundings overlooking the Wexford/Rosslare N25, just 3km from the ferry. Good food and friendly atmosphere provides the perfect stopover for visitors arriving and departing through Rosslare Port or for golfing, fishing, horseriding or relaxing on our safe sandy beaches. Our guesthouse has 15 en suite rooms with direct dial phone, tea/coffee facilities, hairdryer, TV, central heating, private car parking. TV lounge.

B&B from £20.00 to £30.00
€25.39 to €38.09

SARAH & PAUL HASLAM
Proprietors
Mastercard
Visa

15 15

Open All Year

Room rates are IR£ per room per night

EURO LODGE

ROSSLARE HARBOUR,
CO. WEXFORD.
TEL: 053-33118   FAX: 053-33910
EMAIL: eurolodge@eircom.net

GUESTHOUSE ★★★ MAP 4 0 5

A new luxury lodge conveniently located beside Rosslare Europort (600m). All 20 rooms have bathroom en suite with colour TV, tea/coffee facilities, phone and private car parking. Twin and family rooms available. An ideal location to stay while touring the South East. Close to all amenities. With two 18-hole golf courses, sandy beaches, fishing, horse riding and leisure centre nearby.

WEB: www.wexford-online.com/eurolodge

Room Rate from £49.00 to £59.00
€62.22 to €74.91

HELEN SINNOTT
Manager

Mastercard

Visa

20 20

Closed 01 December - 15 March

FERRYPORT HOUSE

ROSSLARE HARBOUR,
CO. WEXFORD
TEL: 053-33933   FAX: 053-33033
EMAIL: thh@iol.ie

GUESTHOUSE ★★★ MAP 4 0 5

A new luxury guesthouse conveniently located close to Rosslare Ferryport (400m). The last guesthouse when leaving Ireland and the first on your return. It has 17 en suite bedrooms with direct dial phone, colour TV, central heating, tea/coffee making facilities, hairdryer and private car parking. Local amenities include golf, fishing, horse riding and safe sandy beaches.

WEB: www.tuskarhousehotel.com

B&B from £19.00 to £32.50
€24.13 to €41.27

BILLY & PATRICA ROCHE
Proprietors

Mastercard

Visa

17 17

Open All Year

HOTEL ROSSLARE

ROSSLARE HARBOUR,
CO. WEXFORD
TEL: 053-33110   FAX: 053-33386
EMAIL: info@hotelrosslare.ie

HOTEL ★★★ MAP 4 0 5

Hotel Rosslare, the longest established hotel in Rosslare Harbour, enjoys spectacular views over the harbour and Europort. Enjoy a meal in the Anchorage Bistro overlooking the bay or spend some time in the historic Portholes Bar. Relax in our en suite rooms, most with sea views, direct dial phone, satellite TV and tea/coffee making facilities. Superbly located, we are only a short drive from 6 golf courses, magnificent beaches, angling, horse riding and Wexford Town.

WEB: www.hotelrosslare.ie

B&B from £29.00 to £45.00
€36.82 to €57.14

GEORGE LEAHY
General Manager

American Express

Diners

Mastercard

Visa

25 25

Closed 24 - 25 December

B&B rates are IR£ per person sharing per night incl. Breakfast

ROSSLARE GREAT SOUTHERN HOTEL

ROSSLARE HARBOUR,
CO. WEXFORD
TEL: 053-33233 FAX: 053-33543
EMAIL: res@rosslare.gsh.ie

HOTEL ★★★ MAP 4 0 5

In Rosslare, a favourite resort, the Great Southern Hotel provides a warm welcome with traditional hospitality. The hotel is beautifully situated on a clifftop overlooking Rosslare Harbour. All rooms are en suite with direct dial phone, TV, radio, hairdryer, in-house movie channel and tea/coffee facilities. Enjoy the leisure centre with indoor swimming pool, jacuzzi, steam room, the comfortable lounges and excellent food of the Mariner's Restaurant. Central reservations Tel: 01-214 4800 or UTELL.

WEB: www.gsh.ie

B&B from £50.00 to £65.00
€63.49 to €82.53

PAT CUSSEN
General Manager

American Express
Diners
Mastercard
Visa

☺ Weekend specials from £89.00

99 99

Closed 02 January - 02 February

ST. MARTINS

ST. MARTINS ROAD, ROSSLARE
HARBOUR, CO. WEXFORD
TEL: 053-33133 FAX: 053-33133
EMAIL: thh@iol.ie

GUESTHOUSE P MAP 4 0 5

St Martins Guesthouse is situated only 500 metres from Rosslare Europort providing the ideal base for ferry and train travel but also for touring the South East. Local activities include golf, horse-riding, angling and watersports as well as visitor attractions such as Yola Farmstead and the Heritage Park. All rooms are en suite with TV, tea/coffee making facilities, direct dial phone and hairdryer. Some rooms also available with 4 poster beds.

WEB: www.tuskarhousehotel.com

B&B from £18.00 to £26.00
€22.86 to €33.01

ORLA ROCHE/PATRICK PEARE
Hosts

Mastercard
Visa

8 8

Closed 24 - 27 December

TUSKAR HOUSE HOTEL

ROSSLARE HARBOUR,
CO. WEXFORD
TEL: 053-33363 FAX: 053-33033
EMAIL: thh@iol.ie

HOTEL ★★★ MAP 4 0 5

Family run hotel enjoying panoramic views of Rosslare Bay, just 219m from ferry and train terminals. It has all en suite bedrooms with telephone, TV, central heating and some with balconies. Dinner served nightly until 11pm and Sunday lunch 12.30/2.30, with local seafood a speciality. Regular entertainment in the lively Punters Bar. Local amenities include: golf, fishing, horse riding and safe beaches. Michelin recommended.

WEB: www.tuskarhousehotel.com

B&B from £30.00 to £38.00
€38.09 to €48.25

ORLA ROCHE
General Manager

American Express
Diners
Mastercard
Visa

30 30

Closed 25 - 26 December

Room rates are IR£ per room per night

Located in the south-west corner of Ireland, the Cork and Kerry region offers its visitors a great diversity of scenery, culture and leisure activities. Cork and Kerry claims some of the most varied and spectacular scenery in the country.

The Queenstown Story, Cobh, Co. Cork

Natural attractions abound, from the West Cork coast, the Beara and Dingle peninsulas and the Ring of Kerry to the Lakes of Killarney and the Bandon, Lee and Blackwater valleys.

With its remarkable charm, bumpy bridges, hilly streets and distinctive continental air the city of Cork will not fail, like the rest of the Region, to captivate and welcome all visitors, young and old. Cobh, situated on the southern short of the Great Island, lies in one of the world's largest natural harbours. The Queenstown Story in Cobh tells the story of emigration and the history of sail and steam in Cork Harbour. Cobh was the last port of call for the ill-fated Titanic.

The coast road from Kinsale to Skibbereen passes through many attractive villages and towns giving breath-taking views of the south west coastline. Kinsale, a town which has retained its old world charm and character is firmly established as one of Ireland's leading gourmet centres. Passing onto Clonakilty, Ireland's 1999 national Tidy Towns winners, one of Cork's many picturesque and colourful towns.There are many amenities in the area, with places of interest to visit, sporting and leisure activities and festivals.

The unspoilt coastal and inland waters of Cork and Kerry offer numerous water sports, from fishing to sailing, diving and windsurfing.

The Ring of Kerry is a journey through some of the country's most outstanding scenery. It is not only one of great natural beauty - it is enhanced by the influence of both ancient folklore and local traditions. With its three famous lakes and great mountain ranges Killarney has been

the inspiration of poets and painters over many centuries. A spectacular attraction is the Skellig Experience Centre at Valentia Island which imaginatively tells the story of the history of the Skelligs.

The Dingle Peninsula has some of the most intersting antiquities, historic sites and varied scenery in the whole country. Dingle, the most westerly town in Europe is an excellent centre for the visitor. It still retains much of its old-world atmosphere with its many shops and restaurants.

For further information contact:
Cork Kerry Tourism, Aras Failte,
Grand Parade, Cork.
Tel. (021) 273251. Fax. (021) 273504
email: user@cktourism.ie

Killarney Tourist Office, Beech Road,
Killarney, Co. Kerry.
Tel. (064) 31633. Fax (064) 34506.

The Skellig Experience Visitor Centre,
Valentia Island, Co. Kerry

Guinness Puck Fair, Killorglin, Co. Kerry
August

Rose of Tralee Festival, Tralee,
Co. Kerry.
August

Guinness Cork Jazz Festival, Cork.
October

Event details correct at time of going to press

ACHILL HOUSE

WESTERN ROAD,
CORK CITY
TEL: 021-427 9447 FAX: 021-427 9447
EMAIL: info@achillhouse.com

GUESTHOUSE P MAP 2 H 3

Stay in luxury and style at Achill House. This elegant period house is ideally located opposite UCC and in the heart of Cork City centre. Achill House is convenient to ferry, airport, and bus termini, the perfect base for exploring Cork and Kerry. All rooms have deluxe en suite bathrooms with optional jacuzzi. An extensive breakfast menu caters for all tastes from hearty Irish breakfasts to lighter options. A warm and relaxed atmosphere awaits you whether on business or pleasure.

WEB: www.achillhouse.com

B&B from £25.00 to £50.00
€31.74 to €63.48

HELENA MCSWEENEY
Proprietor

Mastercard

Visa

Sunday - 10% discount

Open All Year

ACORN HOUSE

14 ST. PATRICK'S HILL,
CORK
TEL: 021-450 2474 FAX: 021-450 2474
EMAIL: info@acornhouse-cork.com

GUESTHOUSE ★★★ MAP 2 H 3

Acorn House is a comfortable refurbished listed Georgian house of architectural merit dating back to 1810. It is a 3 minute walk to St. Patrick Street, Cork City's principal thoroughfare with theatres and excellent choice of restaurants. 5 minutes walk to bus and rail stations; 15 minutes drive to airport and car ferry. Rooms en suite with TV, phone and tea/coffee facilities. Michelin and Stilwell recommended. Children over 12 welcome.

WEB: www.acornhouse-cork.com

B&B from £23.00 to £30.00
€29.20 to €38.09

JACKIE BOLES
Proprietor

Mastercard

Visa

Closed 22 December - 10 January

AIRPORT LODGE

FARMERS CROSS, KINSALE ROAD,
CORK AIRPORT, CORK
TEL: 021-431 6920 FAX: 087-349 8100
EMAIL: airlodge@indigo.ie

GUESTHOUSE U MAP 2 H 3

Located at the gates of Cork Airport, 15 minutes drive from Ringaskiddy Ferryport and adjacent to all major roads around Cork City, we are ideal as a first/last night stop. Cork City is only 8km away, Kinsale 30km. We have extensive free car parking and provide a welcome break before you continue your journey.

WEB: www.corkairportlodge.com

B&B from £20.00 to £35.00
€25.39 to €44.44

MARY & MAURICE BERGIN
Proprietors

Mastercard

Visa

Room Only from £25.00 to £50.00

Closed 24 - 29 December

Room rates are IR£ per room per night

AMBASSADOR HOTEL

MILITARY HILL, ST. LUKES,
CORK
TEL: 021-455 1996 FAX: 021-455 1997
EMAIL: info@ambassadorhotel.ie

HOTEL U MAP 2 H 3

The Ambassador Hotel has already received excellent reviews since opening in June '97. This historic building of striking architectural design dates back to 1872. Situated on its own private grounds in a quiet central location with breathtaking views over the city, guests can relax in the Cocktail Lounge or Embassy Bar or enjoy gourmet dining in the Seasons Restaurant. 60 spacious bedrooms luxuriously decorated to the highest standards and professional service ensure a memorable stay.

WEB: www.ambassadorhotel.ie

Member of Best Western

B&B from £35.00 to £70.00
€44.44 to €88.88

DUDLEY FITZELL

American Express
Diners
Mastercard
Visa

2 Nights B&B + 1 Dinner
from £95.00

60 60

alc

Closed 24 - 26 December

ANTOINE HOUSE

WESTERN ROAD,
CORK
TEL: 021-427 3494 FAX: 021-427 3092
EMAIL: antoinehouse@eircom.net

GUESTHOUSE ★★ MAP 2 H 3

Located at gateway to West Cork and Kerry for business or pleasure. An ideal base from which to explore, less than one mile from city centre and in close proximity to airport, train, ferry, Blarney and Fota. All rooms en suite with direct dial phones, Satellite TV, hairdryer, tea/coffee facilities. Private lock up car park at rear, golf, shooting, fishing, horse-riding, flying can be arranged. Children welcome. Frommers recommended and AA listed.

B&B from £20.00 to £30.00
€25.39 to €38.09

KEVIN CROSS
Proprietor

American Express
Diners
Mastercard
Visa

10 10

Open All Year

ARBUTUS LODGE HOTEL

MONTENOTTE,
CORK
TEL: 021-450 1237 FAX: 021-450 2893
EMAIL: info@arbutuslodge.net

HOTEL ★★★ MAP 2 H 3

Elegant townhouse built in the late 18th century, set in its own gardens, overlooking the River Lee and Cork City. There are 16 rooms all individually decorated. An imaginative fusion of French influence and Irish produce combined with an impressive wine list ensures that Arbutus Lodge has one of the best restaurants in Ireland. There is a delightful bar and patio where meals are served all day and also a traditional bar where there is traditional music at weekends. The hotel is family owned and John and family look forward to meeting you.

WEB: www.arbutuslodge.net

B&B from £47.50 to £65.00
€60.32 to €82.54

CARMODY FAMILY

American Express
Diners
Mastercard
Visa

Weekend Specials from £105.00

16 16

alc

Closed 23 - 27 December

B&B rates are IR£ per person sharing per night incl. Breakfast

CO. CORK
CORK CITY

ASHLEY HOTEL

COBURG STREET,
CORK
TEL: 021-450 1518 FAX: 021-450 1178
EMAIL: ashleyhotel@eircom.net

HOTEL U MAP 2 H 3

The Ashley Hotel is family-owned, run by Anita Coughlan and her enthusiastic staff, with all the benefits of the city centre location to shops and other attractions. It is the perfect place to relax and have fun. The Ashley has plenty to offer you with a secure lock-up car park, 27 rooms with bathroom en suite, tea/coffee making facilities and direct dial phone with a lively bar and restaurant.

WEB: www.ashleyhotel.com

B&B from £29.50 to £38.50
€37.46 to €48.88

ANITA COUGHLAN

American Express
Diners
Mastercard
Visa

27 27

Open All Year

BRAZIER'S WESTPOINT HOUSE

WESTERN ROAD, (OPP. UCC),
CORK
TEL: 021-427 5526 FAX: 021-425 1955
EMAIL: westpoint@eircom.net

GUESTHOUSE U MAP 2 H 3

A warm welcome and friendly service awaits you at the family run Brazier's Westpoint House which is located less than 10 minutes walk from Cork City centre and opposite University College Cork. Tastefully decorated, all rooms are en suite with colour TV, direct dial phone, tea/coffee facilities and we have a private lock-up carpark at the rear. An ideal base to visit Cork and tour the beautiful South West.

WEB: www.braziersguesthouse.com

B&B from £22.50 to £27.50
€28.57 to €34.92

JOY BRAZIER
Proprietor

American Express
Mastercard
Visa

8 8

Closed 23 December - 02 January

EAST CORK TOURISM

Call us on **1850 504040**
for your free guide to East Cork

A visit to the Old Midleton Distillery will take you right to the heart of the cherished Whiskey making tradition. The Jameson tour commences with an audio visual presentation, followed by a guided walking tour of the Old Distillery. The tour ends in the Jameson Bar where all visitors are invited to sample the world's largest selling Irish Whiskey, Jameson. After the tour you can visit the Distillery Shop or relax in the traditional style restaurant.

Opening Times

March to October
Tours Daily (7 days)
10.00 am to 6.00 pm
Last tour commencing
at 4.30 pm
November to February
2 tours daily Monday to Friday
at 12.00 & 3.00 pm
Saturday & Sunday
2.00 & 4.00 pm
Admission Charge

Old midleton distillery
Distillery Walls
Midleton Co. Cork
Phone: 021 - 4613594
Fax: 021 - 4613642
www.irish-whiskey-trail.com

East Cork Tourism,
Market Square, Youghal,
East Cork, Ireland.
Tel: +353 24 92 592
Fax: +353 24 92 602
email: ect@tinet.ie

Room rates are IR£ per room per night

BROOKFIELD HOTEL

**BROOKFIELD HOLIDAY VILLAGE,
COLLEGE ROAD, CORK
TEL: 021-434 4032 FAX: 021-434 4327**

HOTEL ★★★ MAP 2 H 3

Brookfield Hotel, College Road is just 1 mile from Cork City centre. Set on 10 acres of rolling parkland, it is truly a rural setting. *24 bright, modern bedrooms. *Family rooms. *Interconnecting rooms. *Complimentary use of our leisure and fitness centre which incorporates 25m indoor pool. Kiddies pool, water slide, saunas, steam room, spa jacuzzi, outdoor hot tub, massage, gym, sunbeds, outdoor tennis courts.

**B&B from £40.00 to £75.00
€50.79 to €95.23**

MIRIAM RYAN
Reservations Manager

American Express
Mastercard
Visa

CLARION HOTEL & SUITES MORRISONS ISLAND

**MORRISON'S QUAY,
CORK
TEL: 021-427 5858 FAX: 021-427 5833
EMAIL: morisons@iol.ie**

HOTEL ★★★ MAP 2 H 3

Clarion Hotel & Suites Morrisons Island is Cork's premier business hotel, located in the financial services district. Each of our 56 contemporary styled studio guestrooms, suites and penthouses offer luxury to the highest standard. The Clarion Hotel & Suites meets all accommodation requirements for the individual business traveller, as well as for the family holiday.

WEB: www.choicehotelsireland.com

Member of Choice Hotels Ireland

**Room Rate from £65.00 to £170.00
€82.53 to €215.86**

FRANK CASHMAN
General Manager

American Express
Diners
Mastercard
Visa

CRAWFORD HOUSE

**WESTERN ROAD,
CORK
TEL: 021-427 9000 FAX: 021-427 9927
EMAIL: crawford@indigo.ie**

GUESTHOUSE ★★★ MAP 3 H 3

A Fresh Approach to Bed & Breakfast: Crawford House is one of Cork's most recent additions. All rooms come equipped with quality features and include Irish oak-wood furniture and orthopaedic king-size beds. Deluxe en suites include Jacuzzi baths with power showers. Fax/modem points in all rooms. Located directly across from Cork University and a short walk to the City Centre. Crawford House is also convenient to ferry, airport and bus termini. Car Parking available.
AA ◆◆◆◆

WEB: www.crawfordhouse.com

**B&B from £25.00 to £40.00
€31.74 to €50.79**

CECILIA O'LEARY
Manager

American Express
Mastercard
Visa

Closed 23 December - 04 January

Closed 24 - 27 December

Closed 23 - 27 December

B&B rates are IR£ per person sharing per night incl. Breakfast

CO. CORK
CORK CITY

CO. CORK
CORK CITY

D'ARCYS

7 SIDNEY PLACE, WELLINGTON ROAD, CORK
TEL: 021-450 4658 FAX: 021-450 2791
EMAIL: accommodation@darcysguesthouse.com

GUESTHOUSE ★ MAP 2 H 3

Not until you enter 7 Sidney Place do you realise what a large building it is. High ceilings and large spacious rooms. The front rooms have views over the city. Rooms are uncluttered, calm, cool places, very peaceful in the centre of the city. Children are welcome. Breakfast is not to be missed. Try freshly squeezed fruit juices, smoked salmon and scrambled eggs and home made preserves.

WEB: www.darcysguesthouse.com

B&B from £25.00 to £35.00
€31.74 to €44.44

CLARE D'ARCY
Proprietor

American Express
Diners
Mastercard
Visa

6 2

Closed 23 - 27 December

DOUGHCLOYNE HOTEL

DOUGHCLOYNE, CORK
TEL: 021-431 2535 FAX: 021-431 6086

HOTEL ★★★ MAP 2 H 3

The Doughcloyne Hotel is situated 2 miles from the city centre, close to the University Hospital in Wilton and Cork Airport, south link N28 exit Doughcloyne Sarsfields Road roundabout. Our restaurant presents bonne cuisine with friendly service. The lounge bar is noted for its lunch-time barfood and live music at the weekends. Guests have complimentary use of Brookfield Leisure Centre with a 25m swimming pool located near by.

B&B from £25.00 to £35.00
€31.74 to €44.44

DAVID HARNEY
General Manager

American Express
Diners
Mastercard
Visa

☺ Weekend specials from £65.00

50 50

Closed 24 December - 02 January

FOTA WILDLIFE PARK
conservation - because we care

Wild Experience!

Enjoy a great family day out.
Come face-to-face with over 90 species of exotic wildlife and see conservation in action.

Situated just 10 miles from Cork City, off the N25. Access by road or rail.
Monday - Saturday 10am-6pm,
Sunday 11am-6pm,
last admissions at 5pm
Open Daily 17 Mar. - 28 Oct. 2001
Weekends 3 Nov. - Dec. 2001
& 5 Jan. - 15 Mar. 2002

For more details
telephone **021-481 2678**

EAGLE LODGE GUEST HOUSE

1 WILLOWBROOK, WESTERN ROAD,
CORK
TEL: 021-427 7380 FAX: 021-427 6432
EMAIL: nora_murray@hotmail.com

GUESTHOUSE ★★★   MAP 2 H 3

Eagle Lodge is a 10 minute walk from city centre and close to bus and train stations. All rooms en suite with TV, tea/coffee making facilities, hair dryer and ironing facilities. An ideal base from which to tour West Cork and Kerry. Situated opposite University College. Eagle Lodge is within a short walk of many traditional Irish pubs and a variety of restaurants to suit all tastes.

WEB: http://eaglelodge.foundmark.com

B&B from £20.00 to £35.00
€25.39 to €44.44

NORA MURRAY
Proprietor

American Express
Diners
Mastercard
Visa

3 nights B&B from £60.00

7 7

Open All Year

FAIRY LAWN

WESTERN ROAD,
CORK
TEL: 021-454 3444 FAX: 021-454 4337
EMAIL: fairylawn@holidayhound.com

GUESTHOUSE ★★★   MAP 3 H 3

Fairy Lawn, newly restored and beautifully extended, this luxury guesthouse, with open fires, is tastefully decorated throughout. Bedrooms provide comfort with orthopaedic 6 ft king size beds (optional), satellite TV, direct dial phones, hairdryers and hospitality trays. Deluxe en suites with power showers. This family-run guesthouse, where a warm welcome awaits you and breakfast is not to be missed. Opposite UCC. Close to City Centre with ample private car parking to the front. AA ♦♦♦♦. RAC ♦♦♦♦ and Sparkling Diamond Award 2000. Ideal touring base for the South of Ireland.

WEB: www.holidayhound.com/fairylawn.htm

B&B from £24.00 to £34.00
€30.47 to €43.17

TONY & JOAN McGRATH
Proprietors

American Express
Mastercard
Visa

14 14

Open All Year

FORTE TRAVELODGE

BLACKASH, KINSALE ROAD,
CORK
TEL: 1800-709709 FAX: 021-431 0723

HOTEL U MAP 3 H 3

Situated a couple of miles from Cork City Centre, minutes from the Airport and on the direct routes to/from the car ferry, beautiful Kinsale and West Cork, this superb modern hotel offers comfortable yet affordable accommodation. Each room is large enough to sleep up to three adults, a child under 12 and a baby in a cot. Excellent range of facilities from en suite bathroom to colour TV including Sky Sports and Sky Movies. Sited next to Little Chef Restaurant.

WEB: www.travelodge.co.uk

Room Rate from £39.95 to £59.95
€50.73 to €76.12

CAROLINE WALSH
Manager

American Express
Diners
Mastercard
Visa

40 40

Open All Year

B&B rates are IR£ per person sharing per night incl. Breakfast

GARNISH HOUSE

WESTERN ROAD,
CORK
TEL: 021-427 5111 FAX: 021-427 3872
EMAIL: garnish@iol.ie

GUESTHOUSE ★★★ MAP 3 H 3

A stay in Garnish House is a memorable one. Tastefully appointed rooms, with optional en suite jacuzzi and our extensive gourmet breakfast is certain to please. 24 hr reception for enquiries. Situated opposite UCC. Convenient to ferry, airport, bus terminal and City centre. Ideal base to visit Southern Ireland. Open all year. Recommended by AA, RAC and Bridgestone Best Places to stay, Award's Sparkling Diamond & Warm Welcome. Suites & studios accommodation also available.

WEB: www.garnish.ie

B&B from £25.00 to £45.00
€31.74 to €57.14

JOHANNA LUCEY
Manageress

American Express
Diners
Mastercard
Visa

14 14

IRISH
HOTELS
FEDERATION

Open All Year

GLENVERA HOTEL

WELLINGTON ROAD,
CORK
TEL: 021-450 2030   FAX: 021-450 8180
EMAIL: glenvera@eircom.net

HOTEL U MAP 3 H 3

Glenvera Hotel is a Victorian mansion in the heart of Cork City. Glenvera Hotel has 34 bedrooms en suite with colour TV, radio, direct dial phone and personally controlled central heating. Glenvera Hotel is only 3 minutes from bus and rail. It is convenient to car ferry and airport. Glenvera Hotel is fully licensed and has a private locked car park. Groups specially catered: rugby, soccer, golf, fishing. A special full arrangements made for groups e.g. Golfers, Rugby or Soccer teams.

WEB: homepage.eircom.net/~mainags

B&B from £30.00 to £60.00
€38.09 to €76.18

JOHN O'CONNOR
Proprietor

American Express
Diners
Mastercard
Visa

34 34

IRISH
HOTELS
FEDERATION

Closed 22 December - 03 January

CORK CITY GAOL

CORK CITY GAOL
Sunday's Well, Cork.

A step back in time to see what 19th and early 20th Century life was like in Cork – inside and outside prison walls. Amazingly lifelike figures, furnished cells, sound effects and fascinating exhibitions.

Also at the same location new attraction "Radio Museum Experience" which deals not alone with the early days of Irish & International Radio Broadcasting but with the impact of its invention on all our lives. Open daily throughout the year.

Tel: (021) 4305022.
Admission Charge.

Room rates are IR£ per room per night

GREAT SOUTHERN HOTEL

**CORK AIRPORT,
CORK CITY**
TEL: 021-494 7500 FAX: 021-494 7501
EMAIL: res@corkairport.gsh.ie

UNDER CONSTRUCTION OPENING MAR 2001

HOTEL P   MAP 2 H 3

Opening in March 2001 the Great Southern Hotel Cork Airport is a stylish contemporary hotel conveniently located within walking distance of the terminal at Cork Airport. With a wide range of meeting rooms, a business centre and a leisure centre with gymnasium, steam room and jacuzzi, it is the perfect base for business meetings or for first or last night stays. Bookable worldwide through UTELL International or Central Reservations 01-214 4800.

WEB: www.gsh.ie

Room Rate from £110.00 to £110.00
€139.67 to €139.67

FREDA DARCY
General Manager

American Express
Diners
Mastercard
Visa

81 81
Inet FAX

Open All Year

HAYFIELD MANOR HOTEL

**PERROTT AVENUE, COLLEGE ROAD,
CORK**
TEL: 021-431 5600 FAX: 021-431 6839
EMAIL: enquiries@hayfieldmanor.ie

HOTEL ★★★★★ MAP 2 H 3

Cork's premier 5***** hotel ideally located 5 mins from the city and 7km from Cork Airport. As a family owned hotel we endeavour to bring warm and homely touches to our rooms whilst retaining the traditional feel of a country house hotel. Our rooms are spacious and elegant with direct access to our private leisure facilities. Hayfield retains a serene atmosphere combining the elegance of an earlier age with every luxury the modern traveller could wish for. Conference facilities for up to 80 delegates. A member of Small Luxury Hotels of The World.

WEB: www.hayfieldmanor.ie

Member of Small Luxury Hotels of the World

B&B from £105.00 to £200.00
€133.32 to €253.94

MARGARET NAUGHTON

American Express
Diners
Mastercard
Visa

 Weekend Specials from £175.00

87 87

Open All Year

HOTEL ISAACS

**48 MAC CURTAIN STREET,
CORK**
TEL: 021-450 0011 FAX: 021-450 6355
EMAIL: cork@isaacs.ie

HOTEL ★★★ MAP 3 H 3

A homely city centre hotel set in its own courtyard garden and Greene's Restaurant even overlooks a waterfall! Our comfortable en suite rooms with an Irish literary theme have phone, TV, tea/coffee making facilities and hairdryers. We are 5-10 minutes from all amenities (commercial or leisure) including bus and train stations with nearby limited free carparking. Hotel Isaacs Cork is simply an oasis within Cork City centre.

WEB: www.isaacs.ie

B&B from £35.00 to £60.00
€44.44 to €76.18

PAULA LYNCH
General Manager

American Express
Mastercard
Visa

36 36

Closed 23 - 26 December

B&B rates are IR£ per person sharing per night incl. Breakfast

IMPERIAL HOTEL

SOUTH MALL,
CORK
TEL: 021-427 4040 FAX: 021-427 5375
EMAIL: imperial@iol.ie

HOTEL ★★★ MAP 3 H 3

Located in the heart of the business and shopping district, this historic city centre hotel was acquired by Flynn Hotels in 1998. Since then the Imperial has undergone extensive renovations. South's Bar is one of the most popular in Cork and the new French style coffee shop is a must for all visitors. Conference facilities for up to 450 delegates are available. Free car parking for residents.

WEB: www.flynnhotels.com

B&B from £40.00 to £70.00
€50.79 to €88.88

JOHN FLYNN
Proprietor

American Express
Diners
Mastercard
Visa

88 88

Inet FAX

IRISH HOTELS FEDERATION

Closed 24 - 27 December

JOHN BARLEYCORN HOTEL

RIVERSTOWN, GLANMIRE,
CORK
TEL: 021-482 1499 FAX: 021-482 1221
EMAIL: johnbarleycorn@eircom.net

HOTEL ★★ MAP 3 H 3

This fine 18th century residence retains all the atmosphere and charm of a rustic coach stop. Nestling in its own grounds of river and trees, just a short 6km jaunt from Cork City, just off the R639 (alternative Cork/Dublin Road). Ideal base for trips to Blarney, Kinsale, Fota and Cobh Heritage Centre. We welcome all guests with enthusiasm and attention. A Village Inn Hotel, Central reservations tel: 01-295 8900, fax: 01-295 8940.

Member of Village Inn Hotels

B&B from £27.00 to £40.00
€34.28 to €50.79

OLIVIA LOFTUS
Manageress

American Express
Diners
Mastercard
Visa

14 14

IRISH HOTELS FEDERATION

Closed 24 - 25 December

JURYS CORK HOTEL

WESTERN ROAD,
CORK
TEL: 021-427 6622 FAX: 021-427 4477
EMAIL: cork_hotel@jurysdoyle.com

HOTEL ★★★★ MAP 2 H 3

Centrally located on the banks of the River Lee. Just 5 minutes walk from the city centre. Renowned for its distinctly warm welcome, friendly staff and efficient and professional service. The newly refurbished ground floor comprises the Glandore Restaurant with its wide menu selection, a lively atmosphere in Kavanagh's traditional Irish Pub and the Library Lounge, perfect for a relaxing drink. Jurys Doyle Hotel Group central reservations Tel. 01-607 0000 Fax. 01-631 6999.

WEB: www.jurysdoyle.com

B&B from £67.00 to £112.00
€85.28 to €142.21

FERGAL SOMERS
General Manager

American Express
Diners
Mastercard
Visc

188 188

IRISH HOTELS FEDERATION

Closed 24 - 26 December

Room rates are IR£ per room per night

JURYS INN CORK

**ANDERSON'S QUAY,
CORK**
TEL: 021-4276 444 FAX: 021-4276 144
EMAIL: cork_inn@jurysdoyle.com

HOTEL ★★★ MAP 2 H 3

Modern attractive rooms capable of accommodating up to 3 adults or 2 adults and 2 children. All rooms are en suite with multi-channel TV, radio, direct dial phone and tea/coffee making facilities. Located in the centre of Cork City, overlooking the River Lee, it has an informal restaurant and a lively pub, business centre, conference rooms and an adjoining public multi-storey car park (fee payable). Jurys Doyle Hotel Group central reservations Tel. 01-607 0000 Fax. 01-631 6999.

WEB: www.jurysdoyle.com

Room Rate from £55.00 to £62.00
€49.52 to €54.60

JULIEANN BRENNAN
General Manager

American Express
Diners
Mastercard
Visa

133 133

Closed 24 - 26 December

KILLARNEY GUEST HOUSE

**WESTERN ROAD, (OPP. UCC),
CORK**
TEL: 021-427 0290 FAX: 021-427 1010
EMAIL: killarneyhouse@iol.ie

GUESTHOUSE ★★★ MAP 2 H 3

The Killarney House is a 3*** guest house situated opposite University College Cork - a short drive from Cork Airport and Ferry. Registered with the AA, RAC and featured in many travel guides it offers exceptional style and comfort within walking distance of Cork City. All the rooms are en suite with direct dial phones, TV and tea/coffee making facilities. Room with jacuzzi bath available. It is ideally situated for touring in the Cork/Kerry region. Large car park at rear of house.

WEB: www.killarneyhouse.com

B&B from £25.00 to £35.00
€31.74 to €44.44

MARGARET O'LEARY
Manageress

American Express
Mastercard
Visa

19 19

Closed 23 - 26 December

KINGSLEY HOTEL

**VICTORIA CROSS,
CORK**
TEL: 021-480 0500 FAX: 021-480 0527
EMAIL: resv@kingsleyhotel.com

HOTEL U MAP 2 H 3

This de luxe Hotel is nestled on the River Lee, located only minutes from Cork's Airport. State of the art facilities, an elegant atmosphere and tranquil surroundings. The Sabrona Lounge and Library with open fires are havens of tranquillity. Otters Brasserie is a creative dining experience. Poachers Bar is a distinctly different hotel bar. For business clients a customised business centre and conference facilities. The Kingsley Club allows guests unwind at leisure.

WEB: www.kingsleyhotel.com

B&B from £80.00 to £100.00
€101.58 to €126.97

MICHAEL ROCHE
General Manager

American Express
Diners
Mastercard
Visa

69 69

OPEN ALL YEAR

B&B rates are IR£ per person sharing per night incl. Breakfast

LANCASTER LODGE

**WESTERN ROAD,
CORK**
TEL: 021-425 1125 FAX: 021-425 1126
EMAIL: info@lancasterlodge.com

GUESTHOUSE ★★★★ MAP 2 H 3

Lancaster Lodge is a purpose-built 39 roomed en suite guesthouse including two luxury suites with jacuzzi baths. Located alongside Jurys Hotel and only five minutes from the city centre, the guesthouse provides private parking, 24-hour reception, an extensive breakfast menu, spacious rooms including wheelchair facilities and lift to each floor. For comfort and convenience Lancaster Lodge awaits you.

WEB: www.lancasterlodge.com

B&B from £35.00 to £60.00
€44.44 to €76.18

SUSAN LEAHY
Manageress

American Express
Diners
Mastercard
Visa

🚗📷☎️📠🅃🄲♿🆄🄿🅂📧 inet
39 39

Closed 24 - 25 December

LOTAMORE HOUSE

**TIVOLI,
CORK**
TEL: 021-482 2344 FAX: 021-482 2219
EMAIL: lotamore@iol.ie

GUESTHOUSE ★★★★ MAP 3 H 3

A beautiful house with 20 en suite rooms, 4★★★★, and all the amenities of a hotel. 9 mins drive from the city centre but having a quiet location surrounded by 4 acres. Cobh Heritage Centre, Fota Island, many golf courses. Blarney, Kinsale within easy reach. Situated 3 mins from the Lee Tunnel. Ideally situated for travelling to the airport, ferry terminals, west Cork, Killarney and the Ring of Kerry.

B&B from £25.00 to £30.00
€31.74 to €38.09

MAIREAD HARTY
Proprietor/Manager

American Express
Mastercard
Visa

😊 Midweek Specials from £75.00

🚗📷☎️🅃🄲♿🄲🄼✳️🄿♿🅂📧
20 20

Closed 20 December - 07 January

LOUGH MAHON HOUSE

**TIVOLI,
CORK**
TEL: 021-450 2142 FAX: 021-450 1804
EMAIL: info@loughmahon.com

GUESTHOUSE ★★★ MAP 3 H 3

Family run comfortable Georgian house with private parking. Convenient to city centre, bus and rail station. En suite bedrooms are decorated to a high standard with every comfort for our guests. TV, direct dial phone, tea/coffee maker, hair dryer, trouser press and ironing facilities available. Near to Fota Wildlife Park, Cobh Heritage Centre, golf clubs and fishing. Ideal base for trips to Blarney Castle, Kinsale and Killarney. Open all year.

WEB: www.loughmahon.com

Member of Premier Guesthouses

B&B from £22.50 to £35.00
€28.57 to €44.44

MARGOT MEAGHER
Proprietor

American Express
Mastercard
Visa

🚗📷☎️🅃🄲♿🆄🄿♿🅂📧
6 6

Closed 24 - 27 December

Room rates are IR£ per room per night

MARYBOROUGH HOUSE HOTEL

MARYBOROUGH HILL, DOUGLAS, CORK
TEL: 021-436 5555   FAX: 021-436 5662
EMAIL: maryboro@indigo.ie

HOTEL ★★★★   MAP 3 H 3

Distinctive, delightful and different. Maryborough is set on 24 acres of listed gardens and woodland, located only 10 minutes from Cork City. This charming 18th Century house with its creatively designed extension features exquisite conference, banqueting and leisure facilities. 79 spacious rooms, some with balconies overlooking the magnificent gardens and orchards. Zing's Restaurant, contemporary relaxed design is an exciting mix of modern flavours and styles. 4 mins from Lee Tunnel.

WEB: www.maryborough.ie

B&B from £50.00 to £65.00
€63.49 to €82.53

JUSTIN MCCARTHY
General Manager

American Express
Diners
Mastercard
Visa

79 79

Closed 24 - 27 December

METROPOLE RYAN HOTEL AND LEISURE CENTRE

MACCURTAIN STREET, CORK
TEL: 021-450 8122   FAX: 021-450 6450
EMAIL: ryan@indigo.ie

HOTEL ★★★   MAP 3 H 3

Located in the heart of Cork overlooking the Lee, the Metropole has been recently refurbished to the highest international standards. The hotel features the Riverview Restaurant, Met Bar and Waterside Cafe. The superb leisure centre includes three main pool areas, a whirlpool spa, sauna, steam room, aerobics studio and gym. Complimentary parking for guests.

WEB: www.ryan-hotels.com

B&B from £50.00 to £85.00
€63.49 to €107.93

JOE KEARNEY
General Manager

American Express
Diners
Mastercard
Visa

☺ Weekend Specials from £90.00

113 113

Open All Year

QUALITY SHANDON COURT HOTEL

SHANDON, CORK
TEL: 021-455 1793   FAX: 021-455 1665
EMAIL: qualshan@indigo.ie

HOTEL U   MAP 2 H 3

Located in the heart of the city centre, close to all amenities and points of interest the Quality Shandon Court Hotel offers the elegance of old world splendour with the facilities of a modern day hotel. Recently refurbished Bells Bar and Bistro offers an exciting yet reasonably priced menu as well as a regular entertainment schedule.

WEB: ww.choicehotelsireland.com

Member of Choice Hotels Ireland

B&B from £30.00 to £55.00
€38.09 to €69.84

RICHARD COLLINS
General Manager

American Express
Diners
Mastercard
Visa

☺ Midweek specials from £59.00

64 64

Closed 24 - 27 December

B&B rates are IR£ per person sharing per night incl. Breakfast

REDCLYFFE GUEST HOUSE

WESTERN ROAD,
CORK
TEL: 021-427 3220   FAX: 021-427 8382
EMAIL: redclyffe@eircom.net

GUESTHOUSE ★★   MAP 2 H 3

Redclyffe is a charming Victorian red brick guesthouse, family run and decorated to the highest standard. Opposite University, museum, consultants clinic and Jury's hotel. 13 luxurious bedrooms, all en suite with direct dial phone, satellite TV, hairdryer & tea/coffee making facilities. 10 minutes walk to city centre, No 8 bus at door. Easy drive to airport & car ferry. AA approved. Spacious car park front & rear. Be assured of a warm welcome.

B&B from £22.50 to £27.50
€28.57 to €34.92

MICHAEL SHEEHAN
Proprietor

American Express
Diners
Mastercard
Visa

13 13

Closed 24 - 25 December

ROCHESTOWN PARK HOTEL

ROCHESTOWN ROAD, DOUGLAS,
CORK
TEL: 021-489 2233 FAX: 021-489 2178
EMAIL: info@rochestownpark.com

HOTEL ★★★★   MAP 3 H 3

The Rochestown Park Hotel is a manor style hotel set in mature gardens on the south side of the city. Facilities include an award winning leisure centre and Ireland's Premier Thalasso Therapy Centre. A large proportion of our 104 bedrooms are air-conditioned and overlook our gardens and Mahon Golf Club. We cater for weekend breaks, conferences, meetings as well as groups and families. Future plans include the development of 45 more bedrooms to be completed next year.

WEB: www.rochestownpark.com
Member of Conference Connections

B&B from £40.00 to £70.00
€50.78 to €88.86

LIAM LALLY
General Manager

American Express
Diners
Mastercard
Visa

104 104

Open All Year

ROSERIE VILLA GUEST HOUSE

MARDYKE WALK, OFF WESTERN ROAD, CORK
TEL: 021-427 2958 FAX: 021-427 4087
EMAIL: info@roserievilla.com

GUESTHOUSE ★★★   MAP 2 H 3

Roserie Villa is a 10 minute walk from city centre and close to bus and train stations. 16 en suite bedrooms with direct dial telephone, TV, tea/coffee making facilities, hairdryer and ironing facilities. An ideal base for the busy executive or holiday maker to explore the south west. Airport and ferry 15 minutes drive. Golf, tennis, cricket, fishing nearby and just minutes from university college.

WEB: www.roserievilla.com

B&B from £20.00 to £35.00
€25.39 to €44.44

PADDY MURPHY
Proprietor

American Express
Mastercard
Visa

16 16

Open All Year

Room rates are IR£ per room per night

SAINT KILDA GUESTHOUSE

WESTERN ROAD,
CORK
TEL: 021-427 3095 FAX: 021-427 5015
EMAIL: gerald@stkildas.com

GUESTHOUSE ★★★ MAP 2 H 3

Exclusive overnight accommodation just a 10 minutes walk to city centre. Directly opposite university with long-established tennis and cricket clubs at rear. Magnificent swimming and leisure centre nearby. Killarney 1 hour, Kinsale 30 minutes, airport and Blarney Castle 20 minutes. Registered with RAC and recommended by Frommers, Stilwells and Lonely Planet guides. A short pleasant drive to numerous golf courses including Old Head of Kinsale, Fota Island, Lee Valley and Monkstown.

WEB: www.cork-guide.ie/st-kilda/index.htm

B&B from £20.00 to £30.00
€25.39 to €38.09

GERALD COLLINS
Proprietor

Mastercard

Visa

T C P S
20 20

Closed 18 December - 10 January

SEVEN NORTH MALL

7 NORTH MALL,
CORK
TEL: 021-439 7191 FAX: 021-430 0811
EMAIL: sevennorthmall@eircom.net

GUESTHOUSE ★★★★ MAP 2 H 3

Comfortable 240 year old listed house on tree lined mall, facing south, overlooking River Lee. Adjacent to all sites including theatres, art galleries, Shandon, the University and some of Ireland's best restaurants. Individually decorated en suite bedrooms include direct dial telephone, cable TV, trouser press and hair dryer. Small conference room, private car park and accommodation for disabled guests. Children over 12 welcome. ITB Graded 4★★★★.

B&B from £35.00 to £45.00
€44.44 to €57.14

ANGELA HEGARTY
Proprietor

Mastercard

Visa

T P
5 5

Closed 17 December - 08 January

SILVERSPRINGS MORAN HOTEL

TIVOLI,
CORK
TEL: 021-450 7533 FAX: 021-450 7641
EMAIL: silversprings@morangroup.ie

HOTEL ★★★★ MAP 3 H 3

This 4★★★★ hotel is 5 minutes drive from city centre. 109 rooms with cable TV, hairdryer, trouserpress & tea/coffee maker. PJ's has a relaxed atmosphere and exciting, well-priced menu. The adjoining Gallery Lounge is an art-themed modern trendy cafe. Enjoy daily carvery in Thady Quill's. Leisure centre & 9 hole golf course in the grounds. Excellent base from which to tour many visitor attractions. 4 18-hole championship courses 30 mins drive from the Hotel. A Moran Hotel.

WEB: www.morangroup.ie

B&B from £39.00 to £69.00
€49.52 to €87.61

TOM & SHEILA MORAN
Proprietors

American Express

Diners

Mastercard

Visa

Weekend Specials from £104.00

T C CM
109 109

P alc

Closed 25 - 26 December

B&B rates are IR£ per person sharing per night incl. Breakfast

VICTORIA HOTEL

PATRICK STREET, COOK STREET, CORK
TEL: 021-427 8788 FAX: 021-427 8790
EMAIL: vicgeneral@eircom.net

HOTEL ★★ MAP 3 H 3

The Victoria Hotel is situated in Cork City Centre. All rooms have bath & shower, direct dial phone, TV and hair dryer. Family suites available. Built in 1810, it was frequented by European Royalty and was home to some of our own great political leaders, including Charles Stewart Parnell who made his major speeches from its upper balcony. James Joyce recounts his stay in one of his novels. The James Joyce suite is available for bookings (IR£50 Supplement).

WEB: www.victoriahotel.com

Member of MinOtel Hotel Group

B&B from £25.00 to £50.00
€31.74 to €63.49

KING FAMILY

Mastercard
Visa

29 29

Open All Year

VICTORIA LODGE

VICTORIA CROSS, CORK
TEL: 021-454 2233 FAX: 021-454 2572

GUESTHOUSE ★★★★ MAP 2 H 3

This newly renovated monastery located just minutes from city centre, yet standing in mature gardens, has 28 luxury bedrooms with private bath and shower, colour TV, orthopaedic beds, computerised fire detection, direct dial telephone, central heating, tea making facilities, secure car parking, lift to each floor. Convenient to tennis village, golf clubs, museum and fishing facilities. Light snacks, cold meals and drinks served.

B&B from £30.00 to £35.00
€38.09 to €44.44

BRENDAN & MARION LONG
Proprietors

American Express
Mastercard
Visa

28 28

Closed 24 - 28 December

VIENNA WOODS HOTEL

GLANMIRE, CORK
TEL: 021-482 1146 FAX: 021-482 1120
EMAIL: vienna@iol.ie

HOTEL U MAP 3 H 3

An 18th century mansion set in 20 acres of woodland just 5 minutes from Cork City. Located near the mouth of the Jack Lynch Tunnel, the hotel is within easy reach of all Cork's finest golf courses and leisure destinations. The hotel boasts well appointed en suite rooms and extensive conference and banqueting facilities.

WEB: www.viennawoodshotel.com

B&B from £35.00 to £50.00
€44.44 to €63.49

JOHN GATELY/DARINA O'DRISCOLL Proprietors

American Express
Diners
Mastercard
Visa

50 50

Closed 24 - 26 December

Room rates are IR£ per room per night

SEA VIEW GUEST HOUSE

CLUIN VILLAGE, ALLIHIES, BEARA,
CO. CORK
TEL: 027-73004   FAX: 027-73211
EMAIL: seaviewg@iol.ie

GUESTHOUSE ★★★   MAP 1 C 2

Sea View Guest House is a family run concern in the remote and unspoilt Beara Peninsula. All bedrooms are en suite with TV and telephone. Situated in the village of Allihies it is within walking distance of a beach, playground and tennis court. The nearby hills afford excellent opportunities for walking, offering breathtaking views. Traditional Irish music and a friendly welcome can be found in the village pubs.

WEB: www.bearatourism.com

Member of Premier Guesthouses

B&B from £21.00 to £25.00
€26.66 to €31.74

JOHN AND MARY O'SULLIVAN
Proprietors

Mastercard

Visa

10 10   FAX

Closed 31 October - 01 March

BAYVIEW HOTEL

BALLYCOTTON,
CO. CORK
TEL: 021-464 6746   FAX: 021-464 6075
EMAIL: info@bayviewhotel.net

HOTEL ★★★★   MAP 3 J 3

The Bayview Hotel is a luxury 35 bedroom hotel, magnificently situated overlooking Ballycotton Bay and fishing harbour. Private gardens with steps lead to the sea and bathing spot. The Capricho Restaurant produces innovative Irish cuisine and was awarded 2 rosettes by the AA. There are 6 superb golf courses in the area, sea angling, heritage centres and many other activities available. GDS Access Code: UI Toll Free 1-800-44-UTELL

WEB: www.bayviewhotel.net

Member of Manor House Hotels

B&B from £56.50 to £69.00
€71.74 to €87.61

STEPHEN BELTON
General Manager

American Express

Diners

Mastercard

Visa

35 35

Closed 31 October - 31 March

SPANISH POINT SEAFOOD RESTAURANT & GUEST HOUSE

BALLYCOTTON,
CO. CORK
TEL: 021-464 6177   FAX: 021-464 6179
EMAIL: spanishp@indigo.ie

GUESTHOUSE ★★★   MAP 3 J 3

Spanish Point Seafood Restaurant & Guest accommodation is situated on a cliff face overlooking Ballycotton Bay. The conservatory restaurant specialises in seafood which is caught from our own trawler. Mary Tattan, Chef/Owner, trained at Ballymaloe Cookery School. We have recently built on a new lounge and sun deck for our residents and guests to enjoy.

B&B from £25.00 to £30.00
€31.74 to €38.09

MARY TATTAN
Chef/Owner

Diners

Mastercard

Visa

5 5

Closed 02 January - 13 February

B&B rates are IR£ per person sharing per night incl. Breakfast

BALLYLICKEY MANOR HOUSE

BALLYLICKEY, BANTRY BAY, CO. CORK
TEL: 027-50071   FAX: 027-50124
EMAIL: ballymh@eircom.net

GUESTHOUSE ★★★★   MAP 2 E 2

Overlooking beautiful Bantry Bay in 4 hectares of parkland and ornamental gardens, bordered by the Ouvane River, Ballylickey, a 17th century manor house together with cottages around the swimming pool, offers both standard and luxury suite accommodation, an outdoor heated swimming pool, private fishing, 2 golf courses (3 and 8km) and riding nearby. Ballylickey is a member of the Irish Country House and Restaurant Association and of Relais and Châteaux International.

WEB: http://homepage.eircom.net/~ballymh

Member of Ireland's Blue Book

B&B from £66.00 to £82.50
€83.80 to €104.75

MR AND MRS GRAVES
Owners

American Express
Diners
Mastercard
Visa

11 11

Closed 05 November - 01 April

SEA VIEW HOUSE HOTEL

BALLYLICKEY, BANTRY, CO. CORK
TEL: 027-50073   FAX: 027-51555
EMAIL: seaviewhousehotel@eircom.net

HOTEL ★★★★   MAP 2 E 2

Delightful comfortable country house hotel and restaurant, set back in extensive grounds on main Bantry/Glengarriff Road. All bedrooms en suite, D.D. telephone and colour TV. Ideal for touring West Cork and Kerry. Two golf courses nearby. Recommended Egon Ronay, Good Hotel Guide etc. For the restaurant, AA Rosettes and Bord Failte Awards of Excellence. Seafood a speciality. Member Manor House Hotels, Tel: 01-295 8900 Fax: 01-295 8940. GDS Access Code: UI Toll Free 1-800-44-UTELL.

WEB: www.cmvhotel.com

Member of Manor House Hotels

B&B from £45.00 to £55.00
€57.14 to €69.84

KATHLEEN O'SULLIVAN
Proprietor

American Express
Diners
Mastercard
Visa

16 16

Closed 15 November - 14 March

ABBEY HOTEL

BALLYVOURNEY, CO. CORK
TEL: 026-45324   FAX: 026-45449

HOTEL U MAP 2 F 3

Family run hotel nestles in the valley of the Sullane River among the Cork and Kerry Mountains on the N22. It combines a friendly atmosphere and excellent catering. An ideal base for touring Kerry and Cork. A wide range of activities are available to you at the hotel including fishing, mountaineering, nature walks and golfing. 39 bedrooms with private facilities, direct dial phone & colour TV. Within 20 minutes drive are two 18 hole golf courses and trout fishing on the Sullane River.

B&B from £25.00 to £35.00
€31.74 to €44.44

CORNELIUS CREEDON
Proprietor

American Express
Diners
Mastercard
Visa

☺ Weekend specials from £59.00

39 39

Closed 01 November - 16 March

BALTIMORE BAY GUEST HOUSE

THE SQUARE, BALTIMORE,
CO. CORK
TEL: 028-20600 FAX: 028-20495
EMAIL: baltimorebay@youenjacob.com

GUESTHOUSE ★★★ MAP 2 E 1

Baltimore Bay Guest House is a superbly appointed new guesthouse with 8 spacious bedrooms. 5 bedrooms have a magnificent view on the sea. Two restaurants are attached to the guesthouse, La Jolie Brise budget restaurant, Egon Ronay listed, and Chez Youen, Egon Ronay Best Irish Fish Restaurant of the Year in 1994 and listed as one of the best 100 restaurants in the Bridgestone Guide. Youen & Mary Jacob and sons, Proprietors. Sailing facilities. In Bridgestone's 100 Best Places to Stay.

WEB: www.youenjacob.com

B&B from £25.00 to £40.00
€31.74 to €50.79

YOUEN & MARY JACOB
Owner-Managers

American Express
Mastercard
Visa

Weekend special £70.00
1st Sept to 1st July

8 8

Open All Year

BALTIMORE HARBOUR HOTEL & LEISURE CENTRE

BALTIMORE,
CO. CORK
TEL: 028-20361 FAX: 028-20466
EMAIL: info@bhrhotel.ie

HOTEL ★★★ MAP 2 E 1

The hotel is situated overlooking the Harbour & Islands in the charming coastal village of Baltimore. It is the ideal haven from which to explore the beauty and wonders of West Cork and the sea and to enjoy the many varied activities available locally, including sailing, golfing, angling, diving, horse-riding, walking, cycling and of course the Islands. We are especially suited for families and offer children's entertainment during peak season. Enjoy our superb indoor leisure centre.

WEB: www.bhrhotel.ie

Member of Best Western Hotels

B&B from £41.00 to £55.00
€52.06 to €69.84

ANTHONY PALMER
General Manager

American Express
Diners
Mastercard
Visa

Weekend specials from £80.00

64 64

Closed 03 January - 11 February

CASEY'S OF BALTIMORE

BALTIMORE,
CO. CORK
TEL: 028-20197 FAX: 028-20509
EMAIL: caseys@eircom.net

HOTEL ★★★ MAP 2 E 1

A warm welcome awaits you at Casey's of Baltimore. Situated at the entrance to Baltimore with its lovely views overlooking the bay, this superb family run hotel is the perfect place to spend some time. All rooms feature en suite bathrooms, satellite TV, tea/coffee facility, direct dial phone, hairdryer and trouser press. The traditional pub and restaurant feature natural stone and wood decor, a spectacular view, extensive menu - seafood is our speciality. Activities can be arranged.

WEB: www.baltimore-ireland.com/caseys

A Member of Coast & Country Hotels

B&B from £39.00 to £55.00
€49.52 to €69.84

ANN & MICHAEL CASEY
Owners

American Express
Diners
Mastercard
Visa

Midweek Specials from £90.00

14 14

Closed 5-20 November

B&B rates are IR£ per person sharing per night incl. Breakfast

MUNSTER ARMS HOTEL

OLIVER PLUNKETT STREET, BANDON,
CO. CORK
TEL: 023-41562   FAX: 023-41562
EMAIL: info@munsterarmshotel.com

HOTEL ★★★   MAP 2 G 2

Set at the gateway to West Cork, 30
high quality en suite bedrooms with
tea/coffee facilities, direct dial
telephone, remote control T.V. radio
and hairdryer. Set in beautiful scenic
West Cork accessible by the N71
route from Cork City. Renowned for
its homely atmosphere and superb
quality. Ideal touring base and easily
accessible to Kinsale, Cork City,
Blarney, Killarney and West Cork.
Relax and be pampered!

WEB: www.munsterarmshotel.com

B&B from £30.00 to £35.00
€38.09 to €44.44

JOHN COLLINS/DON
O'SULLIVAN

American Express
Diners
Mastercard
Visa

☺ Weekend specials from £75.00

🖥️🛏️📺Ⓣ🅒⛄CM✼♪♫Ⓢ🔒alc
30 30

HOTELS
FEDERATION

Closed 25 - 26 December

ATLANTA HOUSE

MAIN STREET, BANTRY,
CO. CORK
TEL: 027-50237   FAX: 027-50237
EMAIL: atlantaguesthouse@eircom.net

GUESTHOUSE ★★★   MAP 2 E 2

Atlanta House is a long established
family run guesthouse situated in the
centre of Bantry. It is an ideal base
from which to tour West Cork and
Kerry if you are walking cycling or
driving. Golf, fishing and horseriding
are all close by. Rooms are en suite
with TV, D.D phone & tea/coffee
making facilities. We assure you of
a warm welcome and we look
forward to seeing you in Bantry.

B&B from £18.00 to £20.00
€22.86 to €25.39

RONNIE & ESTHER O'DRISCOLL
Owners

American Express
Mastercard
Visa

🖥️🛏️📺Ⓣ🅒⛄♪🔒
9 9

HOTELS
FEDERATION

Closed 19 - 31 December

BANTRY BAY HOTEL

WOLFE TONE SQUARE, BANTRY,
CO. CORK
TEL: 027-50062   FAX: 027-50261
EMAIL: bantrybay@eircom.net

HOTEL ★★   MAP 2 E 2

The Bantry Bay has been operated
by the O'Callaghan family for 53
years in the centre of historic Bantry.
Extensively refurbished since 1995,
the premises consists of a choice of
family, tourist and commercial
accommodation. All rooms are en
suite with satellite TV, direct dial
phone, teamaker and hairdryer. They
are complimented by our beautiful
maritime themed bar and restaurant.
Carvery in operation daily. Guests
assured of a hearty O'Callaghan
welcome.

WEB: www.bantrybayhotel.com

B&B from £33.00 to £36.30
€41.90 to €46.09

VIVIAN O'CALLAGHAN
SNR/JNR Proprietor/Manag

American Express
Diners
Mastercard
Visa

🖥️🛏️📺Ⓣ🅒⛄CM♪♫Ⓢ🔒alc
14 14
🖨️ Inet

HOTELS
FEDERATION

Closed 24 - 27 December

Room rates are IR£ per room per night

VICKERY'S INN

NEW STREET, BANTRY,
CO. CORK
TEL: 027-50006 FAX: 027-20002
EMAIL: vickerys_inn@westcork.com

GUESTHOUSE ★ MAP 2 E 2

Originally a coaching inn established 1850. Most bedrooms en suite. All with TV, tea/coffee facilities. An extensive bar and grill menu is available all day, reasonably priced lunches and dinner in the restaurant. Guide du Routard recommended. Traditional music in the bar during season. Ideally situated to explore scenic West Cork/Kerry. Golf, river, lake, seafishing and horseriding close by. Groups catered in separate dining room, seating 40. Internet access available.

WEB: www.westcork.com/vickerys-inn

B&B from £23.00 to £25.00
€29.20 to €31.74

HAZEL VICKERY
Proprietor

American Express
Diners
Mastercard
Visa

Closed 23 - 29 December

WESTLODGE HOTEL

BANTRY,
CO. CORK
TEL: 027-50360 FAX: 027-50438
EMAIL: reservations@westlodgehotel.ie

HOTEL ★★★ MAP 2 E 2

3*** hotel beautifully situated in the scenic surroundings of Bantry Bay. Super health and leisure centre including indoor heated swimming pool, children's pool, toddlers pool, sauna, steam room, jacuzzi, gym, aerobics, squash. Outdoor amenities include tennis, pitch & putt, wooden walks. The Westlodge specialise in family holidays with organised activities during June, July & August. A warm and friendly welcome awaits you at the Westlodge. Self-catering cottages available.

WEB: www.westlodgehotel.ie

B&B from £40.00 to £60.00
€50.79 to €76.18

EILEEN M O'SHEA MIHCI
General Manager

American Express
Diners
Mastercard
Visa

Closed 23 - 28 December

BLARNEY CASTLE HOTEL

BLARNEY,
CO. CORK
TEL: 021-438 5116 FAX: 021-438 5542
EMAIL: castlehb@iol.ie

HOTEL ★★ MAP 2 H 3

Established in 1837, still run by the Forrest family. Picturesque inn on peaceful village green, 5 miles from Cork City. Tastefully appointed bedrooms, unspoilt traditional bar and restaurant specialising in finest local produce. Killarney, Kenmare, West Cork, Kinsale, Cobh, Fota Wildlife and numerous golf courses all an easy drive. Immediately to the right Blarney Woollen Mills, to the left the magnificent gardens of Blarney Castle guarding that famous stone. Private carpark for hotel guests. Quality entertainment nightly in village.

WEB: www.blarney-castle-hotel.com

B&B from £28.00 to £40.00
€35.55 to €50.79

IAN FORREST
Manager

American Express
Diners
Mastercard
Visa

☺ Weekend specials from £65.00

Closed 25 - 26 December

B&B rates are IR£ per person sharing per night incl. Breakfast

BLARNEY PARK HOTEL

BLARNEY,
CO. CORK
TEL: 021-438 5281 FAX: 021-438 1506
EMAIL: info@blarneypark.com

HOTEL ★★★ MAP 2 H 3

Located in the heart of picturesque Blarney, famous for it's castle and stone, this modern hotel enjoys a relaxed atmosphere and offers a wide range of facilities. Award winning leisure centre (and 40-meter slide), you can truly unwind after a hard day discovering Cork and the majestic Lee Valley. Well situated to visit Blarney Woollen Mills, or for day trips to the Ring of Kerry and Waterford Crystal. Children will love our supervised playroom. Callsave 1850 50 30 10.

WEB: www.blarneypark.com

B&B from £55.00 to £70.00
€69.84 to €88.88

GERRY O'CONNOR
Managing Director

American Express
Diners
Mastercard
Visa

Weekend specials from £100.00

91 91

Open All Year

CHRISTY'S HOTEL

BLARNEY,
CO. CORK
TEL: 021-438 5011 FAX: 021-438 5350
EMAIL: christys@blarney.ie

HOTEL ★★★ MAP 2 H 3

Located in Blarney, Christy's Hotel is a 3 star hotel with 49 beautifully appointed bedrooms each en suite with D.D. phone, TV/Radio and tea/coffee making facilities. Blarney is situated 9.6kms from Cork City and just 22.4kms from Cork Airport. In addition to our all day Self Service restaurant the award winning Weaving Room has a reputation for fine foods at reasonable prices. The hotel has a full Health and Sports Centre. Blarney Woollen Mills Shopping Complex adjoins.

WEB: www.blarney.ie

B&B from £36.50 to £49.00
€46.35 to €62.22

FRANK KELLEHER

American Express
Diners
Mastercard
Visa

49 49

Closed 24 - 26 December

SUNSET RIDGE HOTEL

KILLEENS, BLARNEY,
CO. CORK
TEL: 021-438 5271

HOTEL ★ MAP 2 H 3

Situated on main Cork/Limerick road, Cork City 4.8km / Blarney Village 3.2km. All rooms en suite, TV, direct dial phone. Fully licensed bar, complimentary entertainment Wed/Sat/Sun, bar food available. Our restaurant offers a selection of lunch, dinner and à la carte menus daily. Local amenities include horse riding, golf and fishing. A scenic nature trail walk links our hotel with Blarney Village. Special rates for group bookings. Bus tours catered for.

B&B from £25.00 to £32.00
€31.74 to €40.63

DENIS CRONIN
Manager

American Express
Diners
Mastercard
Visa

28 28

Closed 25 - 26 December

Room rates are IR£ per room per night

WATERLOO INN

**WATERLOO, BLARNEY,
CO. CORK**
TEL: 021-438 5113   FAX: 021-438 2829
EMAIL: waterlooinn@eircom.net

GUESTHOUSE ★★ MAP 2 H 3

Enjoy a holiday in an old country inn located just 1.5 miles from Blarney Castle and 6 miles from Cork City. Set in a peaceful location this riverside inn offers comfortable rooms with tea/coffee making facilities. Relax in our conservatory, have a drink in the bar or walk up to the old round tower of Waterloo. All leisure activities nearby (golf, horse riding etc). This is an ideal centre to tour the south of Ireland. Secure parking available.

WEB: www.thewaterlooinn.com

B&B from £20.00 to £25.00
€25.39 to €31.74

PATRICIA DORAN/MARY
DUGGAN Proprietors

Mastercard

Visa

😊 Midweek Specials from £55.00

5   3

Closed 15 November - 15 February

CARRIGALINE COURT HOTEL

**CARRIGALINE,
CO. CORK**
TEL: 021-485 2100   FAX: 021-437 1103
EMAIL: carrigcourt@eircom.net

HOTEL U MAP 3 H 3

Cork's newest luxury hotel, situated only minutes from the city centre, airport and ferryport. Our 52 rooms offer the finest in modern comforts including ISDN phone, satellite TV and radio. A distinguished menu of classic and traditional Irish dishes will ensure superb dining in our restaurant. An Carrig Leisure Centre, luxurious and stress-free facilities include a 20m pool. Local facilities include golf, sailing and a host of other events in this beautiful area.

WEB: www.carrigcourt.com

B&B from £60.00 to £70.00
€76.18 to €88.88

JOHN O'FLYNN
General Manager

American Express

Diners

Mastercard

Visa

😊 Weekend specials from £95.00

52 52

Closed 25 December

FERNHILL GOLF & COUNTRY CLUB

**FERNHILL, CARRIGALINE,
CO. CORK**
TEL: 021-437 2226   FAX: 021-437 1011
EMAIL: fernhill@iol.ie

GUESTHOUSE ★★★ MAP 3 H 3

Fernhill Golf & Country is the ideal venue for your relaxing holiday; 18 hole golf course (free to residents), indoor swimming pool, sauna, tennis, horse riding and fishing. 10 mins from Cork City and Airport, 5 mins from Ringaskiddy Ferries, 15 mins from Kinsale. All rooms en suite, TV, direct dial phone, tea/coffee making facilities, full bar and restaurant all day in clubhouse. Music at weekends. Also new luxurious 3 bedroom holiday homes on site.

WEB: www.fernhillgolfhotel.com

B&B from £35.00 to £55.00
€44.44 to €69.84

MICHAEL BOWES
Owner/Manager

American Express

Diners

Mastercard

Visa

😊 Weekend specials from £99.00

18 18

Closed 25 December

B&B rates are IR£ per person sharing per night incl. Breakfast

GLENWOOD HOUSE

BALLINREA ROAD, CARRIGALINE,
CO. CORK
TEL: 021-437 3878 FAX: 021-437 3878
EMAIL: glenwoodhouse@eircom.net

GUESTHOUSE ★★★★ MAP 3 H 3

Close to Ringaskiddy Ferryport (5 mins) and Cork Airport (10 mins) Glenwood House is a modern bungalow style guesthouse incorporating all modern facilities including accommodation for disabled guests. All rooms en suite, satellite TV, radio, tea making facilities, direct dial phone, 10 mins from Cork City. We are ideally situated for touring the South of Ireland. Private and secure carpark. Deep sea fishing can be arranged, 10 golf course nearby. Egon Ronay, AA & Michelin Guides recommended. Kinsale 15 minutes, Crosshaven 3 miles.

WEB: www.glenwoodhouse.ie

Member of Premier Guesthouses

B&B from £29.00 to £39.00
€31.74 to €44.44

CATHERINE MAYE
Proprietor

Diners
Mastercard
Visa

☺ Midweek specials from £75.00

16 16

Inet FAX

Closed 25 - 31 December

CASTLE

CASTLETOWNSHEND,
CO. CORK
TEL: 028-36100 FAX: 028-36166

GUESTHOUSE ★ MAP 2 F 1

18th century Townshend family home overlooking Castlehaven Harbour. Set in own grounds at waters edge with access to small beach and woods. Most bedrooms en suite on second floor with excellent sea views. Panelled hall/sitting room with TV and open fire. Breakfast in elegant dining room. Mary Ann's Restaurant close by. Ideal for touring Cork and Kerry. Also self catering apartments and cottages. For illustrated brochure please apply.

B&B from £25.00 to £55.00
€31.74 to €69.83

MRS COCHRANE-TOWNSHEND

Mastercard
Visa

7 6

Closed 15 December - 15 January

DEERPARK HOTEL

LIMERICK ROAD, CHARLEVILLE,
CO. CORK
TEL: 063-81581 FAX: 063-81581

HOTEL ★★ MAP 2 G 5

The Deerpark Hotel is the ideal centre for your stay in North Cork, South Limerick, South Tipperary area. Convenient to Blarney, Cork, Adare, Shannon and the Glen of Aherlow. Horse riding, bicycle hire, fishing, pitch & putt special green fees at one of Munsters finest inland 27 hole courses (18 & 9) are all available locally to our guests. Extensive à la carte menu throughout the day. Site on 9 acres with mature gardens. The Sheehan Family welcome you to the Deerpark Hotel.

WEB: www.charleville.com

Room Rate from £39.00 to £70.00
€49.52 to €88.88

ROSARIO & MARK SHEEHAN
Proprietor

Mastercard
Visa

20 20

alc

Open All Year

DUNMORE HOUSE HOTEL

MUCKROSS, CLONAKILTY, CO. CORK
TEL: 023-33352 FAX: 023-34686
EMAIL: dunmorehousehotel@eircom.net

HOTEL ★★★ MAP 2 G 2

Situated on the southwest coast of Ireland, Dunmore House Hotel is family owned. Rooms are beautifully decorated, all with spectacular views of the Atlantic Ocean. Sample a true taste of West Cork with our home-cooked local produce and seafood. Private foreshore available for sea angling. Green fees at the on-site golf club are free to residents. Wheelchair access throughout hotel. Interesting collection of local and modern Irish art.

WEB: www.cork-guide.ie/clonakilty/dunmorehousehotel

Member of Green Book of Ireland

B&B from £48.00 to £52.00
€60.95 to €66.03

DERRY & MARY O'DONOVAN
Proprietors

American Express
Diners
Mastercard
Visa

☺ Midweek specials from £115.00

24 24

Closed 01 February - 01 March

EMMET HOTEL

EMMET SQUARE, CLONAKILTY, CO. CORK
TEL: 023-33394 FAX: 023-35058
EMAIL: emmethotel@eircom.net

HOTEL U MAP 2 G 2

Ideally located in a Georgian square within two minutes walk of the main street and a five minute drive to beautiful beaches, the Emmet offers old fashioned courtesy, a personal service with a very friendly ambience. Our Bistro has established itself as having the best food in West Cork using fresh organic seasonal produce. Leisure centre, golf, riding and angling available locally. Conference facilities. Participants in 'Ireland's Best Service Plus'.

B&B from £35.00 to £45.00
€44.44 to €57.14

TONY & MARIE O'KEEFFE
Manager

American Express
Diners
Mastercard
Visa

20 20

Open All Year

FERNHILL HOUSE HOTEL

CLONAKILTY, CO. CORK
TEL: 023-33258 FAX: 023-34003
EMAIL: info@fernhillhousehotel.com

HOTEL ★★ MAP 2 G 2

Fernhill House is a family run old Georgian style hotel located on picturesque grounds 0.8km from Clonakilty. All bedrooms en suite with tea/coffee making facilities, phone, TV and hairdryer. Conference and function facilities available, Par 3 golf 18 hole Pitch & Putt course. Our hotel offers intimate homely atmosphere, excellent food and comfortable bar. Holiday with us and enjoy scenic West Cork from centrally situated Fernhill House Hotel. Use of local leisure facility available.

WEB: www.fernhillhousehotel.com

B&B from £35.00 to £40.00
€44.44 to €50.79

MICHAEL & TERESA O'NEILL
Proprietors

American Express
Diners
Mastercard
Visa

☺ Midweek specials from £100.00

11 11

Closed 23 December - 01 January

B&B rates are IR£ per person sharing per night incl. Breakfast

LODGE & SPA AT INCHYDONEY ISLAND

**CLONAKILTY,
CO. CORK
TEL: 023-33143   FAX: 023-35229
EMAIL: reservations@inchydoneyisland.com**

HOTEL ★★★★   MAP 2 G 2

Situated on the idyllic island of Inchydoney, between two EU blue flag beaches, the hotel offers de luxe rooms, a fully equipped thalassotherapy (seawater) spa, restaurant, Dunes Pub and function and meeting facilities. Within a short distance guests can enjoy sailing, golf at the Old Head of Kinsale, riding and deep sea fishing. The style of cooking in the Gulfstream Restaurant reflects the wide availability of fresh seafoods and organically grown vegetables.

WEB: www.inchydoneyisland.com

Members of Concorde Hotels

B&B from £99.00 to £124.75
€125.70 to €158.40

MICHAEL KNOX-JOHNSTON

American Express
Diners
Mastercard
Visa

😊 Midweek specials from £330.00

67 67

Open All Year

O'DONOVAN'S HOTEL

**PEARSE STREET, CLONAKILTY,
WEST CORK
TEL: 023-33250   FAX: 023-33250
EMAIL: odhotel@iol.ie**

HOTEL ★   MAP 2 G 2

Charles Stewart Parnell, Marconi and Gen Michael Collins found time to stop here. This fifth generation, family run hotel is located in the heart of Clonakilty Town. Abounding in history, the old world charm has been retained whilst still providing the guest with facilities such as bath/shower en suite, TV etc. Our restaurant provides snacks and full meals and is open to non-residents. Ideal for conferences, private functions, meetings etc., with lock up car park.

WEB: www.odonovanshotel.com

B&B from £35.00 to £40.00
€44.44 to €50.79

O'DONOVAN FAMILY
Proprietors

American Express
Mastercard
Visa

26 26

Closed 24 - 27 December

Clonakilty

Entente Florale winner – 2000
Ireland's tidiest Town – 1999

Seeing is Believing

Craic

Culture

Beaches

For Information and Special Offers in recommended accommodation B&B's, Hotels, Selfcatering etc.

Clonakilty & District Chamber of Tourism-
"In existence to care for you"
Callsave: 1850 230 730
E-mail: tourism@clonakilty.ie
Site: www.clonakilty.ie

Room rates are IR£ per room per night

QUALITY HOTEL AND LEISURE CENTRE

CLONAKILTY,
CO. CORK
TEL: 023-35400 FAX: 023-35404
EMAIL: qualityhotel@eircom.net

HOTEL ★★★ MAP 2 G 2

Clonakilty is a thriving and busy attractive town with a wealth of musical and artistic cultural activities. Excellent visitor attractions include model railway village, Lisselan Gardens plus access to superb sandy beaches, makes Clonakilty the perfect gateway to West Cork. This new hotel complex with award winning leisure centre, exciting themed restaurant and bar is completed with a 3 screen multiplex cinema. Your value for money choice.

WEB: www.qualityhotelclon.com

B&B from £25.00 to £45.00
€31.74 to €57.14

DAVID HENRY
General Manager

American Express
Diners
Mastercard
Visa

☺ Weekend Specials from £66.00

58 58

Closed 24 - 27 December

COMMODORE HOTEL

COBH,
CO. CORK
TEL: 021-481 1277 FAX: 021-481 1672
EMAIL: commodorehotel@eircom.net

HOTEL R MAP 3 13

The Commodore Hotel newly refurbished, owned by the O'Shea family for 30 years overlooks Cork Harbour. 25 minutes from city centre. Facilities: indoor pool, snooker, entertainment, roof garden. Available locally free golf and pitch & putt. Ideal for visiting Fota, Blarney, The Jameson and Queenstown Heritage Centres. All 42 rooms have full facilities, 21 overlook Cork Harbour. Ringaskiddy Ferryport 15 mins via river car ferry.

WEB: www.commodorehotel.ie

Member of Logis of Ireland

B&B from £30.00 to £60.00
€38.09 to €76.18

PATRICK O'SHEA
General Manager

Mastercard
Visa

☺ Weekend specials from £85.00

42 42

Closed 24 - 27 December

ROBIN HILL HOUSE & RESTAURANT

LAKE ROAD, RUSHBROOKE,
COBH, CO. CORK
TEL: 021-481 1395 FAX: 021-481 4680
EMAIL: robinhillhse@eircom.net

GUESTHOUSE ★★★ MAP 3 13

Robin Hill House is a former Rectory built by the Rushbrooke Family in 1866. Set in mature gardens high above Cork Harbour. It has been completely yet tastefully renovated, restoring it to its former glory. Our 50 seater restaurant, since its opening has gained wide acclaim for its classical dining and extensive wine list. All rooms have en suite facilities and a complimentary snipe of champagne on arrival. The Island of Cobh is only 20 min drive from Cork City and Airport.

WEB: www.dragnet-systems.ie/dira/robinhill

B&B from £35.00 to £45.00
€44.44 to €57.14

COLIN PIELOW
Proprietor

Mastercard
Visa

☺ Weekend specials from £95.00

6 6

Closed 01 January - 01 February

B&B rates are IR£ per person sharing per night incl. Breakfast

WATERSEDGE HOTEL

**YACHT CLUB QUAY, COBH,
CO. CORK
TEL: 021-481 5566 FAX: 021-481 2011
EMAIL: watersedge@eircom.net**

HOTEL N MAP 313

Situated on the waterfront overlooking Cork Harbour. All rooms en suite with satellite TV, tea making facilities, direct dial phone, modem, hairdryer, trouser press. Our restaurant, Jacobs Ladder, is renowned for its seafood, steaks, ambience and friendly staff. Local activities and sightseeing include Cobh Heritage Centre (next door), Cathedral, Titanic Trail, Fota Wildlife Park, golf, sailing, angling, tennis, horseriding. Ideal touring base for Cork City, Kinsale & Blarney.

WEB: www.watersedgehotel.ie

B&B from £35.00 to £70.00
€44.44 to €88.88

MARGARET & MIKE WHELAN
Proprietors

American Express
Diners
Mastercard
Visa

☺ Weekend Specials from £89.00

19 19 alc Inet FAX

Open All Year

WHISPERING PINES HOTEL

**CROSSHAVEN,
CO. CORK
TEL: 021-483 1843 FAX: 021-483 1679**

HOTEL ★★ MAP 313

Whispering Pines, personally run by the Twomey Family is a charming hotel sheltered by surrounding woodland & overlooking the Owenabue River. In this idyllic setting one can enjoy good company, quality homecooked food & a host of amenities to ensure your stay is a restful & memorable experience. All rooms with direct dial phone, tea/coffee facilities & TV. Our 3 angling boats fish daily from April-Oct. Ideal base for touring Cork/Kerry Region. Cork Airport 12kms & Cork City 19km. AA approved.

B&B from £25.00 to £35.00
€31.74 to €44.44

NORMA TWOMEY
Proprietor

American Express
Diners
Mastercard
Visa

15 15

Closed 01 December - 01 January

DUN-MHUIRE HOUSE

**KILBARRY ROAD, DUNMANWAY,
CO. CORK
TEL: 023-45162 FAX: 023-45162
EMAIL: hayesdunmhuire@eircom.net**

GUESTHOUSE ★★★ MAP 2 F 2

Dun Mhuire is a small exclusive family run guesthouse with award winning restaurant, noted for its excellent cuisine. Situated in the heart of West Cork. It has a lot to offer the holiday maker who will appreciate its relaxed atmosphere and high standards. Ideal base from which to tour Cork and Kerry. Luxury bedrooms, all with bathroom, TV, direct dial telephone. Local amenities include swimming, golf, tennis, fishing, pony riding. Scenic walks nearby.

Member of Premier Guesthouses

B&B from £25.00 to £30.00
€31.74 to €38.09

CARMEL & LIAM HAYES
Proprietors

Mastercard
Visa

☺ Week Partial Board from £280.00

6 6 alc

Closed 24 - 26 December

CASTLEHYDE HOTEL

CASTLEHYDE, FERMOY,
CO. CORK
TEL: 025-31865 FAX: 025-31485
EMAIL: cashyde@iol.ie

HOTEL U MAP 314

Country house hotel accommodation in a fully restored Georgian house and courtyard. Gracious hospitality in gracious surroundings. Only 35 minutes from Cork, a world apart from its bustle! All outdoor pursuits catered for. Heated outdoor pool. Exquisite cuisine served in Mermaids Restaurant, perfect peace in the library. The ideal base in the beautiful North Cork region, be it for leisure or for business.

WEB: www.castlehydehotel.com

Member of Best Loved Hotels Of The World

B&B from £52.50 to £75.00
€66.66 to €95.23

HELEN & ERIK SPEEKENBRINK

American Express
Diners
Mastercard
Visa

14 14

Open All Year

GLANWORTH MILL COUNTRY INN

GLANWORTH,
CO. CORK
TEL: 025-38555 FAX: 025-38560
EMAIL: glanworth@iol.ie

GUESTHOUSE ★★★★ MAP 314

A water mill, a Norman castle, a river, an ancient bridge, gorgeous rooms, a gourmet restaurant, tea rooms, library, courtyard garden and river walk... you'll find it here at Glanworth Mill. Unwind in this 1790 water mill with its sense of history & love of literature. There is a wealth of activities nearby - fishing, horse-riding, golf, hill walking, historic trails & houses & gardens to visit. Hidden Gem Award 2000. All in the lush Blackwater Valley of North Cork.

WEB: www.iol.ie/glanworth

B&B from £45.00 to £50.00
€57.14 to €63.49

EMELYN HEAPS & LYNNE GLASSCOE

Diners
Mastercard
Visa

10 10

Closed 24 - 28 December

CASEY'S HOTEL

THE VILLAGE, GLENGARRIFF,
CO. CORK
TEL: 027-63010 FAX: 027-63072

HOTEL ★★ MAP 1D2

Casey's Hotel has been run by the same family since 1884. Recently refurbished to cater for the expectations of the modern traveller. All rooms en suite with direct dial phones and TV. The hotel offers personal, friendly service with old fashioned courtesy, private car park and gardens. Casey's Hotel is the perfect base for day trips to Barley Cove, Gougane Barra, Killarney and the Ring of Kerry. Come and discover the unspoilt beauty of the Beara Peninsula. Hill walking tours arranged.

B&B from £27.00 to £33.00
€34.28 to €41.90

DONAL & EILEEN DEASY
Owners

American Express
Diners
Mastercard
Visa

☺ Midweek Specials from £70.00

19 19

Closed 15 November - 01 March

B&B rates are IR£ per person sharing per night incl. Breakfast

GLENGARRIFF ECCLES HOTEL

GLENGARRIFF,
CO. CORK
TEL: 027-63003   FAX: 027-63319
EMAIL: eccleshotel@iol.ie

HOTEL R   MAP 2 D 2

Located in beautiful Bantry Bay, the Glengarriff Eccles Hotel is one of the oldest established hotels in Ireland. The hotel contains 80 recently refurbished en suite bedrooms, new restaurant, bar and function room. An excellent base for touring West Cork/Kerry region. The hotel is situated directly opposite the world famous Garnish Island. Boating, fishing, golf, sailing, pony trekking and hill walking are all catered for nearby.

WEB: www.eccleshotel.com

B&B from £30.00 to £75.00
€38.09 to €95.23

GERARD AND CARL HANRATTY

American Express
Mastercard
Visa

IRISH HOTELS FEDERATION

Closed 23 - 27 December

GOUGANE BARRA HOTEL

GOUGANE BARRA, BALLINGEARY,
CO. CORK
TEL: 026-47069   FAX: 026-47226
EMAIL: gouganebarrahotel@eircom.net

HOTEL ★★   MAP 2 E 3

Situated on its own grounds overlooking Gougane Barra Lake, the source of the River Lee. Most bedrooms enjoy fine views of the lake, glens and hills beyond. Ideally situated for touring the beauty spots of Cork and Kerry, 72km west of Cork City and Airport. A walk along the banks of the Lee through the forest park which covers 162 hectares, will take you through varied scenery of mystic beauty. We are members of CMV marketing group. GDS Access Code UI Toll Free: 1-800-44-UTELL

WEB: www.cork-guide.ie

Member of Coast and County Hotels

B&B from £36.00 to £42.00
€45.71 to €53.33

BREDA & CHRISTOPHER LUCEY

American Express
Diners
Mastercard
Visa

IRISH HOTELS FEDERATION

Closed 15 October - 23 April

CREEDON'S HOTEL

INCHIGEELA, MACROOM,
CO. CORK
TEL: 026-49012   FAX: 026-49265

HOTEL ★   MAP 2 F 3

The story of Creedon Hotel is one of great continuity and change. At the hub of the village, it has been a family hotel for 3 generations. The simplicity and comfort reflects the natural, relaxed atmosphere of an inn where the spirit is renewed in tranquil surroundings and where people always come first. It is ideal for small group getaways where the complicated luxuries of modern life are replaced by simplicity. Experience the real 'Hidden Ireland'.

Member of Irish Family Hotels

B&B from £20.00 to £25.00
€25.39 to €31.74

JOSEPH & ANNE CREEDON
Proprietors

Mastercard
Visa

IRISH HOTELS FEDERATION

Open All Year

Room rates are IR£ per room per night

INNISHANNON HOUSE HOTEL

INNISHANNON,
CO. CORK
TEL: 021-477 5121 FAX: 021-477 5609
EMAIL: innishannonhotel@eircom.net

HOTEL ★★★ MAP 2 G 2

The most romantic hotel in Ireland built in 1720 in the Petit Château style on the banks of the River Bandon. All rooms en suite with TV, radio, direct dial, etc. Award winning restaurant (AA**, RAC, Egon Ronay) serving fresh fish and lobster daily. Superb wine cellar, stunning views, boating and free salmon and trout fishing from the grounds. Horse riding and golf nearby. GDS Code: UI Toll Free 1-800-44 Utell.

WEB: www.iol.ie/hotels

Member of Manor House Hotels

B&B from £40.00 to £69.50
€50.79 to €88.25

SIOBHAN MCGRATH
Operations Manager

American Express
Diners
Mastercard
Visa

13 13

Closed 24 - 26 December

ACTONS HOTEL

PIER ROAD, KINSALE,
CO. CORK
TEL: 021-477 2135 FAX: 021-477 2231
EAIL: info@actonshotelkinsale.com

HOTEL ★★★ MAP 2 H 2

Located in private gardens overlooking picturesque Kinsale Harbour and Yachting Marina. This attractive hotel, renowned for its cuisine and atmosphere, features a modern health and leisure centre including heated pool, sauna, gym, and solarium. Kinsale is famous as the gourmet capital of Ireland and the hotel's Captain's Table Restaurant is a member of Kinsale's Good Food Circle. All bedrooms have multi-channel T.V., hair dryer and tea/coffee making facilities.

WEB: www.actonshotelkinsale.com

B&B from £45.00 to £65.00
€57.14 to €82.53

JACK WALSH
General Manager

American Express
Diners
Mastercard
Visa

Mid-Week 3 B&B and 2 Dinners from £165.00

76 76

Open All Year

INTERNATIONAL DIAL CODES

Emergency Services: 999 (freephone)

HOW TO DIAL INTERNATIONAL
ACCESS CODE + COUNTRY CODE + AREA CODE + LOCAL NUMBER

SAMPLE CODES:
E.G. UNITED KINGDOM
00 44 + Area Code + Local No.

U.S.A.	00	1	+
Italy	00	39	+
Spain	00	34	+
France	00	33	+
Germany	00	49	+
Iceland	00	354	+
Japan	00	81	+
Luxembourg	00	352	+
Netherlands	00	31	+
Operator (national)			1190
(G. Britain)			1197
(International)			1198

B&B rates are IR£ per person sharing per night incl. Breakfast

BLINDGATE HOUSE

BLINDGATE, KINSALE,
CO. CORK
TEL: 021-477 7858 FAX: 021-477 7868
EMAIL: info@blindgatehouse.com

GUESTHOUSE P MAP 2 H 2

Overlooking the town, Blindgate House caters for the discerning traveller, combining traditional Irish hospitality with modern facilities and imaginative cuisine. All rooms are ensuite, airy and bright and have satellite TV, telephone, fax and modem connections. Our kitchen is run to an extremely high standard, using fresh local produce and breakfast is quite a treat. No better way to start the day! There is a large private car park adjacent to the house and a south facing quiet garden for relaxing. We promise to make your stay a memorable one.

WEB: www.blindgatehouse.com

Room Rate from £90.00 to £110.00
€114.28 to €139.67

MAEVE COAKLEY

American Express
Diners
Mastercard
Visa

🏠🍴☎🅿C➤CM✳♦UJ🅿⛴ Inet
11 11

FAX

IRISH HOTELS FEDERATION

Closed 02 January - 16 March

BLUE HAVEN HOTEL

3/4 PEARSE STREET, KINSALE,
CO. CORK
TEL: 021-477 2209 FAX: 021-477 4268
EMAIL: bluhaven@iol.ie

HOTEL ★★★ MAP 2 H 2

The perfect place to stay in Kinsale - Ireland's Gourmet capital and centrally located on the site of the old fish market. Awarded Ireland Hotel of the Year 1996 by Egon Ronay and Jameson Guide. Renowned for its fresh seafood and shellfish cuisine, ambience, atmosphere and friendly staff. Seventeen rooms with an old town house style and all mod cons. The Blue Haven epitomises what a small owner-run hotel should be. Reservations advised.

B&B from £55.00 to £85.00
€69.84 to €107.93

THE GREENE FAMILY

American Express
Diners
Mastercard
Visa

😊 Weekend Specials from £125.00 to £200.00
🏠🍴☎🅃C➤CMUJ♫🅟aid⛴
17 17

IRISH HOTELS FEDERATION

Closed 24 - 26 December

CAPTAINS QUARTERS

5 DENIS QUAY, KINSALE,
CO. CORK
TEL: 021-477 4549 FAX: 021-477 4944
EMAIL: captquarters@eircom.net

GUESTHOUSE ★★★ MAP 2 H 2

This Georgian period townhouse is situated close to the yacht club marina and in easy walking distance of all restaurants and town centre amenities. It offers quality accommodation in a maritime ambience. The spacious and tranquil lounge overlooks the harbour. The wheelchair accessible groundfloor rooms (1 twin / 1 single, sharing shower / toilet) are also very convenient for the elderly. TV, direct dial phone, tea/coffee making facilities, hairdryer in all rooms. German and French spoken.

WEB: http://captains-kinsale.webjump.com

B&B from £19.00 to £29.00
€24.13 to €36.82

BERNY & CAPT. RUDI
TEICHMANN Co-Owners

Mastercard
Visa

🏠🍴☎C U J☕
6 4

IRISH HOTELS FEDERATION

Closed 28 January - 15 March

Room rates are IR£ per room per night

COLNETH HOUSE

CAPPAGH, KINSALE,
CO. CORK
TEL: 021-477 2824 FAX: 021-477 3357
EMAIL: colnethhouse@eircom.net

GUESTHOUSE ★★★ MAP 3 H 2

We welcome you to relax in the comfort of our home. Colneth House is a newly built guesthouse with very high standards maintained throughout. Ideally situated in a tranquil scenic location, rooms en suite, multi channel TV, direct dial phone, complimentary tray, hairdryer, canopied beds, breakfast menu, private car parking, landscaped gardens, rooms with beautiful views. Suite available, tastefully decorated to make our guests' stay enjoyable, comfortable and memorable.

WEB: www.euroka.com/cork/colneth

B&B from £25.00 to £35.00
€31.74 to €44.44

LORRAINE O'BRIEN
Proprietress
Mastercard
Visa

88

Closed 20 - 29 December

COTTAGE LOFT

6 MAIN STREET, KINSALE,
CO. CORK
TEL: 021-477 2803 FAX: 021-477 2803

GUESTHOUSE ★★ MAP 2 H 2

Located in the heart of Kinsale, the 200 year old town house has an old world charm. Decorated in rich deep tones giving a warm and welcoming ambience. All rooms are en suite with direct dial telephone and TV. Tea & Coffee making facilities in all rooms. Our restaurant, a member of Kinsale's Good Food Circle is noted for its excellent cuisine. All Michael's dishes are created using the finest and freshest ingredients available locally.

B&B from £22.50 to £27.50
€28.57 to €34.92

MICHAEL & CAROLANNE
BUCKLEY Owners
American Express
Mastercard
Visa

66

Closed 23 - 27 December

KIERANS FOLKHOUSE INN

GUARDWELL, KINSALE,
CO. CORK
TEL: 021-477 2382 FAX: 021-477 4085
EMAIL: folkhse@indigo.ie

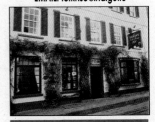

GUESTHOUSE ★★★ MAP 2 H 2

Charming 250 year old Country Inn, personally managed by Denis and Geraldine Kieran for 13 years. Awarded Irish Inn of the Year 1999. 27 en suite rooms, the Bacchus Niteclub and spanish themed Cordoba Bar awarded Dining Pub of the Year 2000 & features live music nightly. Shrimps Seafood Bistro member of The Kinsale Good Food Circle. An attractive and bright restaurant featuring a unique stained glass wall and many contemporary paintings, including works by artist Geraldine.

Member of Logis of Ireland

B&B from £25.00 to £37.50
€31.74 to €47.62

GERALDINE & DENIS KIERAN
Owners
American Express
Mastercard
Visa

Weekend specials from £65.00

27 27

Closed 25 December

B&B rates are IR£ per person sharing per night incl. Breakfast

KILCAW HOUSE

KINSALE, SITUATED ON R600,
CO. CORK
TEL: 021-477 4155 FAX: 021-477 4755
EMAIL: kilcawhouse@hotmail.com

GUESTHOUSE ★★★ MAP 2 H 2

Kilcaw House is a newly built guest house set on 7 acres with magnificent views. It is built with a traditional flair, yet is modern and luxurious. Open fires, wooden floors and striking colours all add to a feeling of warmth and character. The bedrooms are spacious, furnished in antique pine, en suite with TV, direct dial phone and tea/coffee making facilities. Guests comfort is an absolute priority at this family run guest house.

WEB: http://homepage.eircom.net/~kilcawhouse/

B&B from £22.50 to £30.00
€28.57 to €38.09

HENRY & CHRISTINA
MITCHELL Owners

American Express
Mastercard
Visa

7 7

Open All Year

LONG QUAY HOUSE

LONG QUAY, KINSALE,
CO. CORK
TEL: 021-477 3201 FAX: 021-477 4563

GUESTHOUSE ★★★ MAP 2 H 2

Long Quay House is a Georgian residence which typifies its era with rooms of splendid dimensions, furnished to afford the greatest possible guest comfort. Bedrooms are en suite (majority with bath), TV, direct dial phone, tea making facilities and hair dryer. Located centrally overlooking inner harbour, yacht marina and within walking distance of all Kinsale's gourmet restaurants and many tourist attractions. Sea angling trips by local skippers arranged. AA recognised establishment ♦♦♦♦.

B&B from £25.00 to £40.00
€31.74 to €50.79

JIM & PETER DEASY
Hosts

Mastercard
Visa

7 7

Closed 01 - 27 December

MOORINGS

SCILLY, KINSALE,
CO. CORK
TEL: 021-477 2376 FAX: 021-477 2675
EMAIL: mooring5@indigo.ie

GUESTHOUSE ★★★★ MAP 2 H 2

This superbly appointed guesthouse has private car parking. The en suite spacious bedrooms have balconies overlooking the harbour, TV, direct dial phone, tea/coffee making, hairdryers. The elegantly furnished residents' lounge and dining room open onto a large conservatory which houses exotic cacti and has panoramic views of the harbour and yacht marina. The golfing proprietors can arrange tee times for guests at preferential green fees.
Recommended by all major guides.

WEB: http://indigo.ie/~mooring5

B&B from £37.50 to £75.00
€47.62 to €95.23

BRIAN & MARY BENNETT
Proprietors

American Express
Diners
Mastercard
Visa

8 8

Closed 02 - 29 December

Room rates are IR£ per room per night

OLD BANK HOUSE

11 PEARSE STREET, NEXT TO POST
OFFICE, KINSALE, CO. CORK
TEL: 021-477 4075 FAX: 021-477 4296
EMAIL: oldbank@indigo.ie

GUESTHOUSE ★★★★ MAP 2 H 2

The Old Bank House is a Georgian
residence of great character & charm
providing luxurious accommodation
in the historic harbour town of
Kinsale. Each bedroom has super
King or Twin beds, antique furniture
and original art, whilst bathrooms are
beautifully appointed with tub and
shower, top quality toiletries and
Egyptian cotton towels and
bathrobes. Gourmet breakfast by
award winning Master Chef Michael
Riese. Golf friendly and tee times
arranged. Voted one of the "Top 100
Places to Stay in Ireland" every year
since 1990. RAC ◆◆◆◆ AA ◆◆◆◆.

WEB: http://indigo.ie/~oldbank

B&B from £60.00 to £90.00
€76.18 to €114.28

MICHAEL & MARIE RIESE
Proprietors

American Express

Mastercard

Visa

🖐🛏📶♨🛜T🚗U♨
17 17

Closed 23 - 26 December

QUAYSIDE HOUSE

THE PARK, KINSALE,
CO. CORK
TEL: 021-477 2188 FAX: 021-477 2664
EMAIL: quaysidehouse@eircom.net

GUESTHOUSE ★★★ MAP 2 H 2

A family run guesthouse ideally
located in a picturesque setting
overlooking the Kinsale Harbour
adjacent to town centre, yachting
marina and all amenities. All
bedrooms are en suite with direct
dial telephone, TV and tea/coffee
making facilities. Kinsale's famous
gourmet restaurants are all within
walking distance and Kinsale's golf
club is just a five minute drive. Sea
angling trips can be arranged.

B&B from £20.00 to £35.00
€25.39 to €44.44

MARY COTTER

Mastercard

Visa

🖐🛏📶🅿T🅲🚿♨U♨🍴🐾
6 6

Open All Year

TIERNEYS GUEST HOUSE

MAIN STREET, KINSALE,
CO. CORK
TEL: 021-477 2205 FAX: 021-477 4363
EMAIL: mtierney@indigo.ie

GUESTHOUSE ★★ MAP 2 H 2

Tierney's Guest House. A well
established guest house perfectly
situated in the heart of magnificent
award winning Kinsale. Our guest
house offers all amenities, TV, en
suite, hair dryers, tea/coffee on
request. Tastefully decorated and a
warm welcome guaranteed. Stay in
Tierney's and be in the centre of
Kinsale and enjoy the Gourmet
Restaurants, various bars & music
lounges, breathtaking scenery, water
sports, golf & etc.

WEB: www.dragnet-systems.ie/dira/tierneys.htm

B&B from £22.00 to £25.00
€27.93 to €31.74

MAUREEN TIERNEY
Owner

American Express

Mastercard

Visa

🖐🛏📶🅲U🚗S
9 9

Closed 23 - 28 December

B&B rates are IR£ per person sharing per night incl. Breakfast

TRIDENT HOTEL

WORLD'S END, KINSALE,
CO. CORK
TEL: 021-477 2301 FAX: 021-477 4173
EMAIL: info@tridenthotel.com

HOTEL ★★★ MAP 2 H 2

The hotel enjoys a superb waterfront location. All rooms en suite with sea views. Award winning Savannah Waterfront Restaurant is a member of the 'Good Food Circle', the popular Wharf Tavern provides bar food daily & weekend entertainment in summer. Leisure facilities include sauna, gym, steam room & jacuzzi. Meetings for large/small groups are in the high-tech conference suites. Golf, sailing, fishing, tours & cruises available locally. Private parking & wheelchair access.

WEB: www.tridenthotel.com

B&B from £40.00 to £75.00
€50.79 to €95.23

HAL MCELROY
Managing Director

American Express
Mastercard
Visa

3 nights B&B and 2 Dinners from £119.00

 58 58

Closed 25 - 26 December

WHITE HOUSE

PEARSE ST. & THE GLEN, KINSALE,
CO. CORK
TEL: 021-477 2125 FAX: 021-477 2045
EMAIL: whitehse@indigo.ie

GUESTHOUSE ★★★ MAP 2 H 2

The White House epitomises Kinsale hospitality with 3*** accommodation, Chelsea's Bistro, Le Restaurant D'Antibes and a thoroughly modern bar where all the old values of guest satisfaction, comfort and value for money prevail. We have welcomed both visitors and locals since the 1850s and from its earliest days has enjoyed a reputation for fine food, drinks of good cheer and indulgent service. Today we pride ourselves on enhancing that tradition. A member of Kinsale's Good Food Circle.

WEB: www.whitehouse-kinsale.ie

Member of Premier Guesthouses

B&B from £35.00 to £55.00
€44.44 to €69.84

MICHAEL & ROSE FRAWLEY
Proprietors

American Express
Diners
Mastercard
Visa

3 B&B and 3 Dinners from £175.00

 10 10

Closed 24 - 25 December

WHITE LADY HOTEL

LOWER O'CONNELL ST, KINSALE,
CO. CORK
TEL: 021-477 2737 FAX: 021-477 4641
EMAIL: wlady@indigo.ie

HOTEL ★★ MAP 2 H 2

Looking after your needs and making you feel at home is the priority in this 10 bedroom hotel. All rooms have en suite facilities, TV and direct dial phone. Our Paddy Garibaldis Restaurant provides you with a very varied and reasonably priced menu, while it also offers a selection of fresh seafood. Our on-site nite club ensures a lively atmosphere at weekends. Golf and sea angling trips can be arranged at your request.

B&B from £30.00 to £40.00
€38.09 to €50.79

ANTHONY COLLINS/ROMAN
MINIHANE Owners

American Express
Mastercard
Visa

 10 10

Closed 24 - 26 December

Room rates are IR£ per room per night

CASTLE HOTEL & LEISURE CENTRE

MAIN STREET, MACROOM,
CO. CORK
TEL: 026-41074 FAX: 026-41505
EMAIL: castlehotel@eircom.net

HOTEL ★★★ MAP 2 F3

Nestled between Blarney and Killarney the Castle Hotel is the ideal centre for your stay in the scenic south west. Guided walks, horse-riding, bicycle hire, coarse & game fishing, free pitch & putt and half-price green fees on one of Ireland's finest parklands 18 hole golf courses are all available locally to our guests. Hotel facilities include - our award winning restaurant (AA Rosette 92/00), new health & leisure club with 16m pool, kiddies pool, steam room and gymnasium.

WEB: www.castlehotel.ie

Member of Village Inn Hotels

B&B from £39.00 to £46.50
€49.52 to €59.04

DON & GERARD BUCKLEY
Proprietors
American Express
Diners
Mastercard
Visa

3 B&B, 2 Dinner, 2 Golf from £145.00

 42 42

Closed 24 - 28 December

COOLCOWER HOUSE

COOLCOWER, MACROOM,
CO. CORK
TEL: 026-41695 FAX: 026-42119
EMAIL: coolcowe@gofree.indigo.ie

GUESTHOUSE ★★ MAP 2 F3

Coolcower House is a large country residence on picturesque grounds. The house is ideally located within easy driving distance of all the tourist attractions in the Cork-Kerry region including Killarney, Kenmare, Kinsale, Blarney and Bantry. Located on the river's edge for coarse fishing and boating. Also outdoor tennis court. Restaurant offers the best of home produce on its à la carte and dinner menus. Fully licensed bar. TV's and Tea/Coffee making facilities in all rooms.

B&B from £22.00 to £24.50
€27.93 to €31.11

EVELYN CASEY
Mastercard
Visa

Midweek specials from £60.00

12 12

Closed 14 December - 06 March

VICTORIA HOTEL

THE SQUARE, MACROOM,
CO. CORK
TEL: 026-41082 FAX: 026-42148
EMAIL: hotelvictoria@eircom.net

HOTEL ★★ MAP 2 F3

Situated in the centre of Macroom Town, the Victoria is a small friendly hotel, family owned and managed. An ideal base for your visit to the beautiful Lee Valley or the scenic south west. Local amenities include fishing, local 18 hole golf course, hiking, walking and horse riding. All our rooms are en suite with telephone, TV and tea/coffee facilities. A la carte and full dinner menu available. Bar meals served all day.

WEB: www.thevictoria-hotel.com

B&B from £28.00 to £35.00
€35.55 to €44.44

ENDA LINEHAN
Manageress
American Express
Mastercard
Visa

Midweek specials from £90.00

16 16

Open All Year

B&B rates are IR£ per person sharing per night incl. Breakfast

CORTIGAN HOUSE

GOLF COURSE ROAD, MALLOW,
CO. CORK
TEL: 022-22770 FAX: 022-22732
EMAIL: info@cortiganhouse.com

GUESTHOUSE ★★★ MAP 2 G 4

A warm welcome awaits you at our 18th century home, overlooking Mallow Castle & River Blackwater, renowned for salmon & trout angling. Just a 25 minute drive from Cork City & Blarney. Cortigan House is ideally based for touring Kinsale, Killarney and South West. We are adjacent to Mallow Golf Club and within easy drive of ten other courses. 5 min walk to excellent restaurants, traditional pubs and genealogy centre. Recommended by Le Guide du Routard. AA selected ♦♦♦♦.

WEB: www.cortiganhouse.com

Member of Premier Guesthouses

B&B from £23.00 to £33.00
€29.20 to €41.90

LIONEL & SHEILA BUCKLEY
Proprietors
American Express
Mastercard
Visa

9 9

Closed 22 - 30 December

HIBERNIAN HOTEL

MAIN STREET, MALLOW,
CO. CORK
TEL: 022-21588 FAX: 022-22632

HOTEL ★★★ MAP 2 G 4

The Hibernian Hotel blends olde-world surroundings with modern conveniences and comforts in a warm, friendly atmosphere. Situated in the heart of Munster, the Hibernian is an ideal base for touring Cork and Kerry. All rooms are equipped with multi-channel TV, hairdryer, tea/coffee making facilities, trouser press and phone. ISDN lines available. A choice of restaurants and lounge bars are available. Decorated to high standards. A warm welcome awaits you.

B&B from £35.00 to £40.00
€44.44 to €50.79

DAIRE MANNION
General Manager
American Express
Diners
Mastercard
Visa

55 55

Closed 25 - 26 December

LONGUEVILLE HOUSE & PRESIDENTS' RESTAURANT

MALLOW,
CO. CORK
TEL: 022-47156 FAX: 022-47459
EMAIL: info@longuevillehouse.ie

HOTEL ★★★★ MAP 2 G 4

Longueville stands on a wooded eminence in a 500 acre private estate, overlooking the Blackwater Valley, itself famous for its game fishing and private walks. The aim at Longueville is peace and relaxation and for guests to partake only of its own fresh produce, superbly prepared by William O'Callaghan. Longueville is an ideal base for touring the scenic south-west, to laze by the fire in the drawing room, or to enjoy the peace and serenity of the estate. Member of Relais et Châteaux and Ireland's Blue Book.

WEB: www.longuevillehouse.ie

Member of Ireland's Blue Book

B&B from £62.50 to £125.00
€79.36 to €158.72

WILLIAM O'CALLAGHAN
Chef/Proprietor
American Express
Diners
Mastercard
Visa

Week partial board from £615.00

20 20

Closed 16 December - 02 March

MALLOW PARK HOTEL

MALLOW,
CO. CORK
TEL: 022-21527 FAX: 022-51222
EMAIL: info@mallowparkhotel.com

HOTEL ★★ MAP 2 G 4

The Mallow Park Hotel, situated in the centre of Mallow, is a handsome structure with an excellent and historical façade. The hotel interior has recently been completely refurbished and is decorated to the highest standard with a warm and welcoming foyer lounge, coffee dock, bistro, and An Sibín traditional bar which provides the best of music entertainment every Friday, Saturday and Sunday. The Wedgewood Ballroom provides a great location for weddings, anniversaries and birthday parties. Mallow is an ideal location for touring the South West, Killarney, the Ring of Kerry and West Cork.

B&B from £35.00 to £40.00
€44.44 to €50.79

SEAN GLEESON
General Manager

American Express
Mastercard
Visa

 Weekend specials from £65.00

🚬🅿️🐾☎️T|C♨CM♪♫P|S🅰️
20 20
alc☕

IRISH
HOTELS
FEDERATION

Closed 25 December

SPRINGFORT HALL HOTEL

MALLOW,
CO. CORK
TEL: 022-21278 FAX: 022-21557
EMAIL: stay@springfort-hall.com

HOTEL ★★★ MAP 2 G 4

Springfort Hall 18th century Georgian manor house, owned by the Walsh Family. Highly recommended restaurant, fully licensed bar, bedrooms en suite, coloured TV and direct outside dial. 6km from Mallow off the Limerick Road, N20. Ideal for touring the southwest, Blarney, Killarney, Ring of Kerry. Local amenities, 18-hole golf course, horse riding, angling on river Blackwater. Gulliver Central Reservations.

WEB: www.springfort-hall.com

Member of Green Book of Ireland

B&B from £40.00 to £60.00
€50.79 to €76.18

WALSH FAMILY
Proprietors

American Express
Diners
Mastercard
Visa

 Weekend specials from £80.00

🚬🅿️🐾☎️T|C♨CM❄️☀️P|S🅰️
49 49
alc

IRISH
HOTELS
FEDERATION

Closed 23 December - 02 January

BARNABROW COUNTRY HOUSE

CLOYNE, MIDLETON,
EAST CORK
TEL: 021-465 2534 FAX: 021-465 2534
EMAIL: barnabrow@eircom.net

GUESTHOUSE ★★★ MAP 3 I 3

17th century family-run country house set in 35 acres of parkland adjacent to the historic village of Cloyne (580AD). The house has been extensively refurbished to offer a perfect blend of old world charm & new world comfort. Trinity Rooms our new restaurant provides a unique venue for that special celebration. This is the perfect setting to relax and soak up an atmosphere of peaceful unhurried living with log fires and candlelit dinners. Nearby: Ballymaloe & Stephen Pearse.

WEB: www.barnabrow.com

B&B from £33.00 to £47.50
€41.90 to €60.31

GERALDINE O'BRIEN
Proprietor

Diners
Mastercard
Visa

🚬🅿️🐾T|C♨CM❄️☀️U|P|🍴
20 20
S🅰️alc

IRISH
HOTELS
FEDERATION

Closed 21 - 28 December

B&B rates are IR£ per person sharing per night incl. Breakfast

MIDLETON PARK HOTEL

OLD CORK ROAD, MIDLETON, CO. CORK
TEL: 021-463 1767 FAX: 021-463 1605
EMAIL: info@midletonparkhotel.ie

HOTEL ★★★ MAP 3 I 3

Midleton Park Hotel is situated in scenic East Cork on the N25, only 16km from Cork City. Our friendly professional staff offer attentive service and traditional hospitality which, when combined with its reputation for award-winning cuisine, makes Midleton Park Hotel an ideal choice for business or pleasure. Egon Ronay and AA recommended. Our recently refurbished guest rooms are tastefully furnished. Adjacent to blue flag beaches, championship golf courses, heritage trails and wildlife sanctuary.

WEB: www.kingsleyhotel.com

Member of Signature Hotels

B&B from £35.00 to £67.50
€44.44 to €85.71

CLODAGH DUNWORTH
General Manager

American Express
Diners
Mastercard
Visa

Midweek Specials from £99.00

 40 40

Closed 25 December

FIR GROVE HOTEL

CAHIR HILL, MITCHELSTOWN, CO. CORK
TEL: 025-24111 FAX: 025-84541

HOTEL ★★ MAP 3 I 5

The Fir Grove Hotel is a modern hotel, set in its own grounds beneath the Galtee Mountains. Situated on the main Cork/Dublin Road, we are central to most of Munster's large towns and cities. We have a restaurant that serves good local food with a friendly service. All bedrooms are en suite with central heating and TV. Local facilities include golf, fishing, hill walks and pony trekking.

B&B from £24.00 to £25.00
€30.47 to €31.74

PAT & BRENDA TANGNEY
Proprietors

American Express
Diners
Mastercard
Visa

15 15

Closed 24 - 25 December

CELTIC ROSS HOTEL CONFERENCE & LEISURE CENTRE

ROSSCARBERY, WEST CORK
TEL: 023-48722 FAX: 023-48723
EMAIL: info@celticrosshotel.com

HOTEL ★★★ MAP 2 F 1

The Celtic Ross is a new 3*** luxury hotel, set in Rosscarbery Bay. West Cork is renowned for its beautiful scenery and fresh food. The hotel truly captures this uniqueness. Come and relax in this oasis of peace and allow us to pamper you. Facilities include 67 guest rooms, many overlooking the bay, Druids Restaurant, Library & Tower, traditional Old Forge Pub & Eaterie with regular entertainment, leisure centre including pool, gym, steam room and sauna. Reservations: 1800-272737

WEB: www.celticrosshotel.com

B&B from £45.00 to £75.00
€57.14 to €95.23

NOLLAIG HURLEY
Assistant General Manager

American Express
Diners
Mastercard
Visa

Weekend specials from £99.00

67 67

Open All Year

Room rates are IR£ per room per night

COLLA HOUSE HOTEL

COLLA, SCHULL,
CO. CORK
TEL: 028-28105   FAX: 028-28497
EMAIL: collahousehotels@eircom.net

HOTEL ★   MAP 2 D 1

An attractive family run hotel situated in a magnificent position overlooking the sea, with panoramic views of the Atlantic Ocean, Cape Clear and Carbery's Hundred Isles. It is surrounded by its own pitch & putt course running direct to the sea. Colla House also has its own horse-riding school on its grounds. All bedrooms en suite with direct dial telephone and TV. Local amenities include 18 hole golf course, deep sea angling and boat trips to islands.

WEB: www.cork-guide.ie

B&B from £25.00 to £35.00
€31.74 to €44.44

MARTIN O'DONOVAN
Proprietor

American Express
Diners
Mastercard
Visa

10 10

Open All Year

EAST END

SCHULL,
CO. CORK
TEL: 028-28101   FAX: 028-28012

HOTEL ★★   MAP 2 D 1

A family run hotel overlooking Schull Harbour and within walking distance of the numerous amenities in this cosmopolitan village. The hotel's kitchen uses fresh produce and provides quality food all day. TV and direct dial phone in all bedrooms. Dine alfresco in our new patio garden. We especially welcome families with young children.

Member of Irish Family Hotels

B&B from £27.50 to £37.50
€34.92 to €47.62

DERRY & DOROTHY ROCHE
Proprietors

American Express
Diners
Mastercard
Visa

17 15

Closed 23 - 27 December

BALLYMALOE HOUSE

SHANAGARRY, MIDLETON,
CO. CORK
TEL: 021-465 2531   FAX: 021-465 2021
EMAIL: res@ballymaloe.ie

GUESTHOUSE ★★★★   MAP 3 I 3

A large country house on a 400 acre farm. Home and locally grown produce is served in the award winning restaurant. Small golf course, tennis court and outdoor pool. Sea and river fishing and riding can be arranged. The Allen Family also run a craft and kitchen shop, the cafe at the Cork Municipal Art Gallery and the Ballymaloe Cookery School. Take the N25 from Cork City for approx 13 miles. Go right at roundabout towards Ballycotton. Ballymaloe House is 2 miles beyond Cloyne.

WEB: www.ballymaloe.ie

Member of Ireland's Blue Book

B&B from £67.50 to £95.00
€85.71 to €120.63

MYRTLE ALLEN
Proprietor

American Express
Diners
Mastercard
Visa

Reduced Winter 2-day rates available, November-March

32 32

Closed 24 - 26 December

B&B rates are IR£ per person sharing per night incl. Breakfast

GARRYVOE HOTEL

SHANAGARRY, MIDLETON,
CO. CORK
TEL: 021-464 6718 FAX: 021-464 6824

HOTEL ★★ MAP 3 J 3

Situated on Ballycotton Bay, miles of Blue Flag sandy beach, deep sea fishing at Ballycotton (4 miles), own tennis courts. 6 golf courses in the area. All bedrooms en suite with TV and direct dial telephone. The restaurant offers high quality Irish foods, featuring a daily selection of locally caught fish. Midleton 13km, Cork 32km.

B&B from £45.00 to £45.00
€57.14 to €57.14

CARMEL & JOHN O'BRIEN
Proprietors

American Express
Diners
Mastercard
Visa

Closed 25 December

ELDON HOTEL

BRIDGE STREET, SKIBBEREEN,
WEST CORK
TEL: 028-22000 FAX: 028-22191
EMAIL: welcome@eldon-hotel.ie

HOTEL U MAP 2 E 1

Our aim is to provide the best of the simple things in life, good food, good drink and good company. Michael Collins found these when he visited the Eldon in the 1920's, our guests say they still find them today! Extracts of Collins' love letters to Kitty Kiernan and photos of his visits to the Eldon can be found in our new Porch Bar. Our award winning Bistro-Restaurant will complete your experience.

WEB: www.eldon-hotel.com

Member of Logis of Ireland

B&B from £25.00 to £55.00
€31.74 to €69.84

ARTHUR LITTLE/LYDIA
O'FARRELL Managers

Diners
Mastercard
Visa

2 B&B & 1 Dinner & 1 Round of Golf from £99.00

Closed 24 - 28 December

WEST CORK HOTEL

ILEN STREET, SKIBBEREEN,
CO. CORK
TEL: 028-21277 FAX: 028-22333

HOTEL ★★★ MAP 2 E 1

The West Cork Hotel offers one of the warmest welcomes you will find in Ireland, and combines old-fashioned courtesy with the comfort of tastefully decorated and well-equipped accommodation. Guests can enjoy the friendly bar atmosphere or dine in the elegant restaurant. However long your stay the West Cork Hotel is the perfect base from which to discover and explore the glorious surroundings and activities available in West Cork.

B&B from £35.00 to £50.00
€44.44 to €63.49

JOHN MURPHY
General Manager

American Express
Diners
Mastercard
Visa

Midweek specials from £141.00

Closed 22 - 28 December

Room rates are IR£ per room per night

AHERNE'S TOWNHOUSE & SEAFOOD RESTAURANT

163 NORTH MAIN STREET, YOUGHAL, CO. CORK
TEL: 024-92424 FAX: 024-93633
EMAIL: ahernes@eircom.net

GUESTHOUSE ★★★★ MAP 3 J 3

Open turf fires and the warmest of welcomes await you in this family run hotel in the historic walled port of Youghal. Our rooms exude comfort and luxury, stylishly furnished with antiques and paintings. Our restaurant and bar food menus specialise in the freshest of locally landed seafood. Youghal is on the N25, 35 mins from Cork Airport and is a golfers' paradise. There are 18 golf courses within 1 hours drive. Find us in Ireland's Blue Book and other leading guides.

WEB: www.ahernes.com

Member of Ireland's Blue Book

B&B from £55.00 to £65.00
€69.84 to €82.53

THE FITZGIBBON FAMILY

American Express
Diners
Mastercard
Visa

☺ Reduced Winter 2 Day packages available

12 12

IRISH HOTELS FEDERATION

Closed 24 December - 03 January

DEVONSHIRE ARMS HOTEL & RESTAURANT

PEARSE SQUARE, YOUGHAL, CO. CORK
TEL: 024-92827 FAX: 024-92900
EMAIL: reservations@dev.arms.ie

HOTEL ★★ MAP 3 J 3

Luxurious old world family run hotel. Centrally located in the town of Youghal with Blue Flag Beach, 18 hole golf course, riding and historical walking tours. All bedrooms individually decorated, TV, direct dial telephone, hair dryer and valet cleaning unit service. Our restaurant (AA2 Rosettes) offers fresh seafood and a wide range of dishes to suit all tastes, also à la carte bar menu. Half an hour from Cork, two hour drive from Rosslare N25.

B&B from £35.75 to £40.00
€45.39 to €50.79

STEPHEN & HELEN O'SULLIVAN
Proprietors

American Express
Diners
Mastercard
Visa

10 10

alc

IRISH HOTELS FEDERATION

Closed 24 - 31 December

CLIFF HOUSE HOTEL

CLIFF ROAD, BALLYBUNION, CO. KERRY
TEL: 068-27777 FAX: 068-27783
EMAIL: cliffhousehotel@eircom.net

HOTEL ★★★ MAP 5 D 6

Overlooking Ballybunion's sandy beaches, the modern 3*** Cliff House Hotel, with 45 de luxe guest bedrooms, is a golfer's paradise. The region boasts 7 championship golf courses. Ballybunion's famous links are no more than a four-iron away, while Tralee, Killarney, Lahinch and Waterville Golf Clubs are all within easy reach. Every aspect of your golfing vacation is catered for - concession green fees are available at Ballybunion and tee times can be reserved for you.

WEB: www.cliffhousehotel.net

B&B from £35.00 to £75.00
€44.44 to €95.23

KEVIN O'CALLAGHAN
Director

American Express
Diners
Mastercard
Visa

45 45

IRISH HOTELS FEDERATION

Closed 24 - 26 December

B&B rates are IR£ per person sharing per night incl. Breakfast

EAGLE LODGE

BALLYBUNION,
CO. KERRY
TEL: 068-27224

GUESTHOUSE U   MAP 5 D 6

Owner managed, delightful guesthouse situated in town centre. All bedrooms with bathrooms and central heating throughout. A beautiful lounge and private car park for guests. Local amenities include two championship golf courses, sea fishing, tennis, pitch and putt, swimming and boating. Extra value reduced green fees at Ballybunion Golf Club. Cliff walks and surfing also available.

B&B from £25.00 to £35.00
€31.74 to €44.44

MILDRED GLEASURE

Open All Year

HARTY COSTELLO TOWN HOUSE

MAIN STREET, BALLYBUNION,
CO. KERRY
TEL: 068-27129   FAX: 068-27489
EMAIL: hartycostello@eircom.net

GUESTHOUSE ★★★★   MAP 5 D 6

8 luxury bedrooms en suite, in a Townhouse style, all modern conveniences. Elegant dining with traditional high standards of fresh food and wine in our Seafood Restaurant and Bar. Table d'hôte and extensive à la carte menus available. Local amenities, two championship golf links, cliff walks, hot seaweed baths, fishing, four golden beaches and bird watching. Ideal base for golfers or touring and horse riding.

B&B from £35.00 to £55.00
€44.44 to €69.84

DAVNET & JACKIE HOURIGAN
Owners

American Express
Mastercard
Visa

☺ Weekend special from £80.00

Closed 30 October - 01 April

MANOR INN

DOON ROAD, BALLYBUNION,
CO. KERRY
TEL: 068-27577   FAX: 068-27757
EMAIL: drao@ballybunion-manorinn.com

GUESTHOUSE N   MAP 5 D 6

The purpose built Manor Inn offers luxury accommodation overlooking the Atlantic at the mouth of the Shannon River. 1km from town centre, 2kms from world famous Ballybunion Golf Club. Bedrooms all en suite, TV, alarm radio, direct dial phone, hairdryer, tea/coffee facilities and central heating. Antique bedroom a feature. Private car parking. Local amenities: 2, 18 hole links courses, seaweed bath, sea angling, pony trekking, surfing, swimming, cliff walking and Shannon Ferry.

WEB: www.ballybunion-manorinn.com

B&B from £24.00 to £40.00
€30.47 to €50.78

THE MANAGEMENT

American Express
Mastercard
Visa

Closed 15 November - 14 March

Room rates are IR£ per room per night

MARINE LINKS HOTEL

SANDHILL ROAD, BALLYBUNION,
CO. KERRY
TEL: 068-27139 FAX: 068-27666
EMAIL: marinelinkshotel@eircom.net

HOTEL ★★ MAP 5 D 6

A small intimate owner-managed
hotel with 10 rooms overlooking the
mouth of the Shannon which
welcomes golfers and
holidaymakers from all over the
world who enjoy the local amenities
of golf, Blue Flag sandy beaches,
hot seaweed baths, cliff walks,
fishing, cycling and pony trekking.
The restaurant is recognised in the
area for fine dining with a table
d'hôte and extensive à la carte menu
served nightly.

WEB: www.marinelinksballybunion.com

B&B from £28.00 to £45.00
€35.55 to €57.14

R. RAFTER & S. WILLIAMSON
Proprietors

American Express
Diners
Mastercard
Visa

10 10

Closed 01 January - 15 March

SOUTHERN HOTEL

SANDHILL ROAD, BALLYBUNION,
CO. KERRY
TEL: 068-27022 FAX: 068-27085
EMAIL: southotel@eircom.net

HOTEL U MAP 5 D 6

The Southern Hotel overlooks
Ballybunion's spacious beaches and
the 9th hole of Ballybunion Golf
Course. Residents qualify for a
special reduction in green fees from
October to May. All rooms have, in
addition to standard facilities,
elegant designer furniture and many
have stunning sea views. The hotel
is family owned and its size allows
a level of personal attention not often
possible in larger hotels.

WEB: www.kerry-insight.com/southern

Member of Ballybunion Marketing Group

B&B from £30.00 to £50.00
€38.09 to €63.49

THOMAS O'BRIEN

American Express
Mastercard
Visa

15 15

Closed 01 November - 20 April

TEACH DE BROC

LINK ROAD, BALLYBUNION,
CO. KERRY
TEL: 068-27581 FAX: 068-27919
EMAIL: teachdebroc@eircom.net

GUESTHOUSE ★★★★ MAP 5 D 6

The simple gift of a quality time will
be awarded to you when you stay at
Teach de Broc Country House. This
4**** 10 bedroomed property has
an enviable location, where a 2
minutes walk finds you on the 1st
tee and is located a mere 10yds
from the practice ground. The
intricacy of Ballybunion requires a
head start. To put you in fine
swinging form we serve a wide
choice of breakfast including freshly
baked scones from 6am.
Concession green fees available.
Tea to Tee in 2 minutes.

WEB: www.ballybuniongolf.com

B&B from £35.00 to £55.00
€44.44 to €69.83

SEAMUS AND AOIFE BROCK
Owners

Mastercard
Visa

10 10

Open All Year

B&B rates are IR£ per person sharing per night incl. Breakfast

DERRYNANE HOTEL

CAHERDANIEL, RING OF KERRY,
CO. KERRY
TEL: 066-947 5136   FAX: 066-947 5160
EMAIL: info@derrynane.com

HOTEL ★★★   MAP 1 C 2

Amidst the most spectacular scenery in Ireland, halfway round the famous Ring of Kerry (on the N70) lies the Derrynane 3*** Hotel with 75 en suite bedrooms. Facilities include 15m outdoor heated pool, steamroom, sauna, gym and tennis court. We are surrounded by beautiful beaches and hills, lovely walks and Derrynane House and National Park. Deep sea angling, lake fishing, golf, horseriding, seasports, boat trips to Skellig Rock all within a short distance. Newly published hotel walking guide to the area.

WEB: www.derrynane.com

Member of Best Western Hotels

B&B from £38.50 to £49.50
€48.88 to €62.85

MARY O'CONNOR
Manager/Director

American Express
Diners
Mastercard
Visa

☺ Weekend specials from £89.00

75 75

Closed 15 October - 15 April

SCARRIFF INN

CAHERDANIEL,
CO. KERRY
TEL: 066-947 5132   FAX: 066-947 5425
EMAIL: scarriff@aol.com

GUESTHOUSE ★★   MAP 1 C 3

This family-run guesthouse overlooks the best view in Ireland, with majestic views of Derrynane, Kenmare and Bantry Bay, situated halfway round the Ring of Kerry. All our rooms have sea views. Dine in our seafood restaurant and enjoy outstanding cuisine as recommended by Sir Andrew Lloyd Webber or relax in our Vista Bar and enjoy scenery and ambience. The area is varied in activities, the Kerry Way, several beautiful beaches within walking distance. Day trips to Skellig Rocks.

WEB: www.caherdaniel.net

B&B from £22.95 to £26.95
€29.14 to €34.22

KATIE O'CARROLL
Proprietor

American Express
Mastercard
Visa

6 6

Closed 30 October - 05 March

BARNAGH BRIDGE
COUNTRY GUEST HOUSE

CAMP, TRALEE,
CO. KERRY
TEL: 066-713 0145   FAX: 066-713 0299
EMAIL: bbguest@eircom.net

GUESTHOUSE ★★★   MAP 1 C 5

Between mountains & sea on the Dingle Peninsula. In landscaped grounds, architect's guesthouse combines modern character with traditional cooking and friendly atmosphere. Family run with delightful breakfasts. Local golfing, fishing, walking & horse riding. AA RAC ♦♦♦♦ & Frommers listed as stunning house offering exceptional value. Peaceful retreat with a friendly welcome, a good bed & beauty all around. Leave N86 at Camp, follow Conor Pass Road R560, 1 mile.

WEB: www.barnaghbridge.com

Member of Premier Guesthouses

B&B from £16.00 to £26.00
€20.32 to €33.01

HEATHER WILLIAMS
Host

American Express
Mastercard
Visa

☺ Reduced rate for 3 nights or more

5 5

Closed 31 October - 01 March

Room rates are IR£ per room per night

ARD-NA-SIDHE

CARAGH LAKE, KILLORGLIN,
CO. KERRY
TEL: 066-976 9105 FAX: 066-976 9282
EMAIL: sales@kih.liebherr.com

HOTEL ★★★★ MAP 1 D 4

20 bedroom 4**** de luxe Victorian mansion delightfully located in its own park on Caragh Lake. Highest standards of comfort. Tastefully furnished with antiques and open fireplaces. Luxurious lounges and restaurant. Cosy spot for a quiet holiday. Free boating, fishing and facilities of sister hotels - Hotel Europe and Hotel Dunloe Castle - available to guests. 11 major golf courses nearby. Special green fees. Central Reservations
Tel: 064-31900 Fax: 064-32118.

WEB: www.iol.ie/khl

B&B from £63.00 to £88.00
€79.99 to €111.74

KATHLEEN DOWLING

American Express
Diners
Mastercard
Visa

20 20

Closed 01 October - 30 April

CARAGH LODGE

CARAGH LAKE,
CO. KERRY
TEL: 066-976 9115 FAX: 066-976 9316
EMAIL: caraghl@iol.ie

GUESTHOUSE ★★★★ MAP 1 D 4

A Victorian fishing lodge standing in 7.5 acres of parkland containing many rare and subtropical trees and shrubs. Winner of the National Garden Award. The gardens sweep down to Caragh Lake, ideal for trout fishing. The lounges and dining room are very comfortably furnished and overlook the gardens and lake. Excellent cuisine includes local lamb and wild salmon. Golf and beaches within 5 minutes.

WEB: www.caraghlodge.com

Member of Ireland's Blue Book
B&B from £62.50 to £110.00
€79.36 to €139.67

MARY GAUNT
Owner

American Express
Diners
Mastercard
Visa

15 15

Closed 16 October - 12 April

CRUTCH'S HILLVILLE HOUSE HOTEL

CONOR PASS ROAD, CASTLEGREGORY,
DINGLE PENINSULA, CO. KERRY
TEL: 066-713 8118 FAX: 066-713 8159
EMAIL: macshome@iol.ie

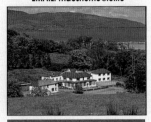

HOTEL ★★ MAP 1 C 5

Delightful country house owned and managed by Ron & Sandra. Situated near Fermoyle Beach on Kerry's scenic Dingle Peninsula. Close to the highest mountain pass in Ireland - The Conor Pass, Slea Head, Dingle & Killarney. The Fermoyle Room Restaurant offers traditional home cooking using fresh local produce, vegetarians, special diets catered for on request. A friendly country house atmosphere, generously sized rooms, some with four poster beds & sea views, cosy bar and open fires. Celebrating 30 years.

Member of Coast and Country Hotels
B&B from £35.00 to £46.50
€44.44 to €59.04

RON & SANDRA
Proprietors

American Express
Diners
Mastercard
Visa

19 19

alc

Open All Year

B&B rates are IR£ per person sharing per night incl. Breakfast

TRALEE BAY HOTEL

**CASTLEGREGORY,
CO. KERRY**
TEL: 066-713 9033   FAX: 066-713 9034
EMAIL: traleebayhotel@hotmail.com

HOTEL N   MAP 1 C 5

Family run hotel in a very scenic location in the heart of the Dingle Peninsula. 100 metres from miles of unspoilt beaches, nestled at the base of the Sliabh Mish Mountains. Restaurant facilities offer good food for good value, seafood specialities, very family friendly. Nightly entertainment in the summer season in the lounge. Great walking routes nearby, excellent base for angling, horse riding, water sports and golf.

B&B from £25.00 to £35.00
€31.74 to €44.44

BARRIE & DONNA O'BRIEN

American Express
Mastercard
Visa

17 17
alc

Open All Year

O'CONNOR'S GUESTHOUSE

**CLOGHANE, DINGLE PENINSULA,
CO. KERRY**
TEL: 066-713 8113   FAX: 066-713 8270
EMAIL: oconnorsguesthouse@eircom.net

GUESTHOUSE R   MAP 1 B 5

A long established, spacious country home with spectacular views of sea and mountains, overlooking Brandon Bay and within easy reach of Dingle on the Dingle Way. Private car park, guest lounge, open fire, home cooked meals, pub and a warm welcome are just some of the things awaiting our guests.

B&B from £19.00 to £25.00
€24.13 to €31.74

MICHEAL & ELIZABETH O'DOWD
Owners

Mastercard
Visa

9 9

Closed 01 November - 28 February

ALPINE HOUSE

**MAIL ROAD, DINGLE,
CO. KERRY**
TEL: 066-915 1250   FAX: 066-915 1966
EMAIL: alpinedingle@eircom.net

GUESTHOUSE ★★★   MAP 1 B 4

Superb guesthouse run by the O'Shea Family. AA ◆◆◆◆ and RAC ◆◆◆◆ highly acclaimed. Elegant en suite bedrooms with TV, direct dial phone, hairdryers, central heating and tea/coffee facilities. Spacious dining room with choice of breakfast. Delightful guest lounge. 2 minutes walk to town centre, restaurants, harbour and bus stop. Local amenities include Slea Head Drive and Blasket Islands, also pony trekking, angling and boat trips to Fungi the dolphin.

WEB: www.alpineguesthouse.com

B&B from £18.50 to £28.00
€23.49 to €35.55

PAUL O'SHEA
Manager

American Express
Mastercard
Visa

10 10

Open All Year

Room rates are IR£ per room per night

BAMBURY'S GUEST HOUSE

MAIL ROAD, DINGLE,
CO. KERRY
TEL: 066-915 1244   FAX: 066-915 1786
EMAIL: bamburysguesthouse@eircom.net

GUESTHOUSE ★★★   MAP 1 B 4

AA selected ♦♦♦♦, new house, excellent location, 2 minutes walk to town centre. Offering peaceful accommodation in spacious, double, twin or triple rooms all with en suite, direct dial telephone and satellite TV. Attractive guest lounge to relax in. Private car parking, choice of breakfast in spacious dining room. Local attractions, Dingle Peninsula, horse riding, angling and golf on local 18 hole golf links. Reduced green fees can be arranged. Listed in all leading guides.

B&B from £18.00 to £30.00
€22.86 to €38.09

BERNIE BAMBURY
Proprietor

Mastercard

Visa

12 12

| IRISH HOTELS FEDERATION |

Open All Year

BARR NA SRAIDE INN

UPPER MAIN STREET, DINGLE,
CO. KERRY
TEL: 066-915 1331   FAX: 066-915 1446
EMAIL: barrnasraide@eircom.net

GUESTHOUSE ★★★   MAP 1 B 4

Family run bar/guesthouse. Located in the town centre. The Barr na Sraide Inn has been recently refurbished to a very high standard. An extensive menu awaits our guests for breakfast. End each day with a relaxing drink in our comfortable bar amongst the locals. Private enclosed car park. Ideal base for your stay in the South West. Golf, fishing, sailing, cycling, horse riding and trips to Fungi the dolphin available nearby.

WEB: http://homepage.eircom.net/~barrnasraide/

B&B from £25.00 to £40.00
€31.74 to €50.79

PATRICIA GEANEY

Mastercard

Visa

22 22

| IRISH HOTELS FEDERATION |

Closed 17 - 26 December

BENNERS HOTEL

MAIN STREET, DINGLE,
CO. KERRY
TEL: 066-915 1638   FAX: 066-915 1412
EMAIL: benners@eircom.net

HOTEL ★★★   MAP 1 B 4

A 300 year old hotel with young ideas. Benners is a timeless part of Kerry's proud holiday tradition. It is part of the emotional experience that lingers on... long after a visit to the magnificent Dingle Peninsula. Benners is synonymous with excellence in comfort and cuisine, specialising in a daily fresh Atlantic catch. Our rooms are all en suite with antique furniture, hairdryer, TV, direct dial phone and tea/coffee facilities. Open all year. Special weekend and midweek packages available.

WEB: www.bennershotel.com

Member of Best Western Hotels

B&B from £35.00 to £75.00
€44.44 to €95.23

PAT GALVIN
General Manager

American Express

Diners

Mastercard

Visa

51 51

| IRISH HOTELS FEDERATION |

Closed 25 - 26 December

B&B rates are IR£ per person sharing per night incl. Breakfast

BOLAND'S GUESTHOUSE

GOAT STREET, DINGLE,
CO. KERRY
TEL: 066-915 1426

GUESTHOUSE ★★ MAP 1 B 4

A warm welcome awaits you in our family run guesthouse. Situated in Dingle Town with panoramic views of Dingle Bay. All our rooms are en suite with direct dial phones, TV, hairdryers, tea/coffee making facilities. Full breakfast menu in our conservatory dining room. Relax and enjoy the magnificent views of Dingle Bay from our guest lounge. Boland's is A.A. selected and R.A.C. listed.

B&B from £18.00 to £27.50
€22.86 to €34.92

BREDA BOLAND
Owner

Mastercard
Visa

7 7

Closed 01 December - 31 January

CAPTAINS HOUSE

THE MALL, DINGLE,
CO. KERRY
TEL: 066-915 1531   FAX: 066-915 1079
EMAIL: captigh@eircom.net

GUESTHOUSE ★★★ MAP 1 B 4

A welcome awaits you at the Captains House situated in Dingle Town. Approached by foot bridge over the Mall Stream and through award winning gardens our three star family run guest house is tastefully furnished with items collected on the Captains voyages. All rooms are en suite with direct dial telephones and TV. A breakfast menu featuring home made bread and preserves is served in the conservatory overlooking the garden.

WEB: homepage.eircom.net/~captigh/

B&B from £25.00 to £30.00
€31.74 to €38.09

MARY & JIM MILHENCH
Proprietors

American Express
Diners
Mastercard
Visa

8 8

Closed 01 December - 16 March

CLEEVAUN COUNTRY HOUSE

LADYS CROSS, MILLTOWN, DINGLE,
CO. KERRY
TEL: 066-915 1108   FAX: 066-915 2228
EMAIL: cleevaun@iol.ie

GUESTHOUSE ★★★ MAP 1 B 4

Galtee Regional Breakfast Winner 1994. Cleevaun is set in landscaped gardens overlooking Dingle Bay, 1 mile from Dingle Town. Rooms with private bathrooms, TVs, hairdryers, tea/coffee facilities. Relax and enjoy the magnificent views of Dingle Bay from our breakfast room while you choose from our award winning menu. Often described as an oasis of peace and tranquillity. Cleevaun is commended by AA, RAC, and Karen Browne. Local amenities golf, walking, pony trekking.

WEB: www.cleevaun.com

B&B from £25.00 to £32.50
€31.74 to €41.27

CHARLOTTE CLUSKEY
Host

Mastercard
Visa

8 8

Closed 15 November - 15 March

Room rates are IR£ per room per night

COASTLINE GUESTHOUSE

THE WOOD, DINGLE,
CO. KERRY
TEL: 066-915 2494 FAX: 066-915 2493
EMAIL: coastlinedingle@eircom.net

GUESTHOUSE ★★★ MAP 1 B 4

Beautiful new guesthouse on the water's edge of Dingle Bay. All rooms are en suite with direct dial phone, TV, hairdryer, tea/coffee making facilities and many have panoramic views of the harbour. Ground floor rooms available. Enjoy our excellent breakfast and relax in our sitting room in the evening and watch the fishing fleet return with their catch. Private car park. 5 minutes walk to town centre. Ideal base to enjoy all Dingle has to offer - excellent restaurants and pubs.

WEB: www.coastlinedingle.com

B&B from £20.00 to £27.00
€25.39 to €34.28

VIVIENNE O'SHEA
Proprietor

Mastercard
Visa

6 6

CONNORS

DYKEGATE STREET, DINGLE,
CO. KERRY
TEL: 066-915 1598 FAX: 066-915 2376

GUESTHOUSE ★★ MAP 1 B 4

Welcome to our newly refurbished guesthouse. All rooms en suite with TV, clock radio, hairdryer, direct dial phone, tea/coffee making facilities, central heating, orthopaedic beds. We are situated in the heart of Dingle Town. Within walking distance to all restaurants and pubs. Recommended Guide Du Routard, Rick Steves Guide to Ireland and Stilwells Guide. Breakfast menu available in our spacious dining room. Packed lunches available on request.

B&B from £18.00 to £27.50
€22.86 to €34.92

CAROL CONNOR

American Express
Mastercard
Visa

15 15

DINGLE SKELLIG HOTEL

DINGLE,
CO. KERRY
TEL: 066-915 0200 FAX: 066-915 1501
EMAIL: dsk@iol.ie

HOTEL ★★★★ MAP 1 B 4

Renowned hotel situated on the beautiful harbour of Dingle Bay. Luxurious leisure club & pool; jacuzzi, geyser pool, children's pool, steamroom, gymnasium. Ki-massage, reflexology & aromatherapy. Fungi Kids Club and Creche available weekends and holidays. Excellent cuisine specialising in locally caught seafood. Established conference & banqueting centre with stunning views for up to 250 people. Reduced green fees & guaranteed tee times (including weekends) at Ceann Sibeal.

WEB: www.dingleskellig.com

B&B from £42.50 to £97.50
€53.96 to €123.80

PHILIP GAVIN
General Manager

American Express
Diners
Mastercard
Visa

Midweek specials 3 B&B and 2 Dinners from £135.00

116 116

B&B rates are IR£ per person sharing per night incl. Breakfast

DOYLES SEAFOOD BAR & TOWN HOUSE

JOHN STREET, DINGLE,
CO. KERRY
TEL: 066-915 1174 FAX: 066-915 1816
EMAIL: cdoyles@iol.ie

GUESTHOUSE ★★★★ MAP 1 B 4

Eight bedrooms all generous in size, warm with comfortable furniture, full bathroom attached, direct dial telephone and TV. The restaurant has an old range, sugan chairs, kitchen tables. Natural stone and wood combined give Doyle's a cosy country atmosphere. Lobster our speciality, is chosen from a tank in the bar. The menu consists only of fresh food and is chosen on a daily basis from the fish landed by the Dingle boats.

WEB: www.doylesofdingle.com

Member of Ireland's Blue Book

B&B from £38.00 to £45.00
€48.25 to €57.13

SEAN CLUSKEY
Host

Diners
Mastercard
Visa

Closed 15 November - 15 February

GORMANS CLIFFTOP HOUSE AND RESTAURANT

GLAISE BHEAG, BALLYDAVID, DINGLE
PENINSULA, TRALEE, CO KERRY
TEL: 066-915 5162 FAX: 066-915 5162
EMAIL: gormans@eircom.net

GUESTHOUSE P MAP 1 B 5

Enjoy the best in Irish hospitality. Good food, comfortable surroundings and a warm welcome. Wonderful location looking out over Smerwick Harbour and the Atlantic Ocean. AA ◆◆◆◆◆, member of Besl Loved Hotels.

WEB: www.gormans-clifftophouse.com

Member of Best Loved Hotels of the World

B&B from £35.00 to £60.00
€44.44 to €76.18

VINCENT AND SILE O'GORMAIN
Proprietors

Mastercard
Visa

Closed 10 January - 01 March

GREENMOUNT HOUSE

UPPER JOHN STREET, DINGLE,
CO. KERRY
TEL: 066-915 1414 FAX: 066-915 1974
EMAIL: mary@greenmounthouse.com

GUESTHOUSE ★★★★ MAP 1 B 4

Greenmount House is the proud recipient of the 1997 RAC Guest House of the Year for Ireland. A charming 4**** country house yet centrally located. Spacious lounges to relax in and take advantage of its magnificent scenic location overlooking Dingle Town & Harbour. Each bedroom has private bathroom TV/radio & direct dial phone. Award winning buffet breakfasts served in conservatory with commanding views of Dingle. Luxurious, peaceful retreat. Recognised by all leading guides.

WEB: www.greenmounthouse.com

B&B from £25.00 to £45.00
€31.74 to €57.14

JOHN & MARY CURRAN
Owners

Mastercard
Visa

Closed 20 - 26 December

Room rates are IR£ per room per night

HALF DOOR WATERFRONT GUESTHOUSE

MAIL ROAD, DINGLE,
CO. KERRY
TEL: 066-915 1883   FAX: 066-915 1297
EMAIL: halfdoor@iol.ie

UNDER CONSTRUCTION OPENING MAY 2001

GUESTHOUSE P   MAP 1 B 4

Newly refurnished guesthouse opening in May 2001. All our bedrooms are spacious and appointed with a view of Dingle Bay. All bedrooms have king size beds dressed in crispy white linen. We are approx 1/4 mile from Dingle town centre. Enjoy your breakfast overlooking Dingle Bay prepared by Chef Denis. Dine in our sister restaurant the Half Door in Dingle centre.

WEB: www.halfdoor@iol.ie

B&B from £25.00 to £45.00
€31.74 to €57.14

TERESA O'CONNOR

American Express
Mastercard
Visa

🛏🍴🏛📷🅣CM☼∪🅟🅨alc🍴 FAX
9 9

Closed 01 January - 01 February

HEATON'S GUESTHOUSE

THE WOOD, DINGLE,
CO. KERRY
TEL: 066-915 2288   FAX: 066-915 2324
EMAIL: heatons@iol.ie

GUESTHOUSE ★★★★   MAP 1 B 4

Superb new family run guesthouse situated on the shore of Dingle Bay, 5 minutes walk from the town. All rooms are en suite (pressure shower and bath), with TV, direct dial phone and tea/coffee welcome tray. Breakfast is our speciality. Local amenities include golf, sailing, fishing, surfing, cycling, walking, horse riding and the renowned gourmet restaurants.

WEB: www.euroka.com/dingle/heatons

B&B from £25.00 to £40.00
€31.74 to €50.79

NUALA & CAMERON HEATON
Proprietors

Mastercard
Visa

🛏🍴🏛📷🅣C☼∪🅟🍴
12 12

Open All Year

MILLTOWN HOUSE

MILLTOWN, DINGLE,
CO. KERRY
TEL: 066-915 1372   FAX: 066-915 1095
EMAIL: milltown@indigo.ie

GUESTHOUSE ★★★★   MAP 1 B 4

Award winning family run Milltown House is ideally located overlooking Dingle Bay and Town from our private gardens. All rooms which retain the character of the 130 year old house are en suite, have tea/coffee making facilities, direct dial phone, TVs, trouser press and hairdryer. Some rooms are wheelchair friendly. Assistance in planning your day. One of the most scenic and quiet locations in the town area, walking 15 minutes, driving 2 minutes!

WEB: www://indigo.ie/~milltown/

B&B from £30.00 to £45.00
€38.09 to €57.13

ANNE AND MARK KERRY
Proprietors

American Express
Mastercard
Visa

🛏🍴🏛📷🅒☼∪🅟🅨🍴
10 10

Closed 01 December - 31 January

B&B rates are IR£ per person sharing per night incl. Breakfast

OLD PIER

AN FHEOTHANACH, BALLYDAVID,
DINGLE, CO. KERRY
TEL: 066-915 5242
EMAIL: info@oldpier.com

GUESTHOUSE ★★★ MAP 1 B 4

Situated in the heart of the West
Kerry Gaeltacht on the Dingle
Peninsula overlooking beautiful
Smerwick Harbour and the Atlantic
Ocean. This family run establishment
offers 3★★★ accommodation with
beautiful sea and mountain vistas.
The Old Pier Restaurant offers a
broad range of locally caught
seafood, prime steak and meat
dishes. Adjacent activities include 18
hole golf course, deep sea angling,
mountain walking and archaeology
sites. A warm welcome awaits you.

WEB: www.oldpier.com

B&B from £20.00 to £30.00
€25.39 to €38.09

JACQUI & PADRAIG O CONNOR

Mastercard

Visa

6 6

Open All Year

PAX HOUSE

UPPER JOHN STREET, DINGLE,
CO. KERRY
TEL: 066-915 1518   FAX: 066-915 2461
EMAIL: paxhouse@iol.ie

GUESTHOUSE ★★★★ MAP 1 B 4

Pax House has undeniably one of
the most spectacular views in the
Peninsula. Guestbook quote Peace
Perfect Peace. 1km from Dingle
Town. Bedrooms including suites
beautifully appointed. Breakfast is a
major event, with fish, meats,
cheese, homemade breads,
preserves and yoghurt. We offer
guests charm, tranquillity and
unequalled hospitality. Enjoy a drink
on the balcony and watch the boats
return with their catch. Voted one of
the top ten places to stay in Ireland.
AA ◆◆◆◆.

WEB: www.kerrygems.ie/pax/

Member of Premier Guesthouses

B&B from £23.50 to £40.00
€29.83 to €50.79

RON & JOAN BROSNAN WRIGHT
Owners

Mastercard

Visa

12 12

FAX

Closed 01 December - 31 January

SMERWICK HARBOUR
HOTEL

BALLYFERRITER, DINGLE,
CO. KERRY
TEL: 066-915 6470   FAX: 066-915 6473
EMAIL: info@smerwickhotel.com

HOTEL ★★★ MAP 1 B 5

Smerwick Harbour Hotel, Seafood
Restaurant with its old world bar, is
located on Slea Head Drive, 2km
from Gallarus Oratory. Our local 18
hole golf course is on your doorstep,
4km away, reduced green fees for
guests. All rooms en suite (family
rooms also) with TV, direct dial
phone, tea/coffee facilities. Spacious
lounge. Enjoy excellent cuisine in
our seafood restaurant, specialising
in local seafood and char grilled
steaks. Quality barfood also
available. Old world ambience. The
best sandy beaches in Ireland
nearby.

WEB: www.smerwickhotel.com

B&B from £25.00 to £50.00
€31.74 to €63.49

FIONNBAR WALSH
Manager

American Express

Mastercard

Visa

32 32

☺ Weekend Specials from £70.00

Open All Year

Room rates are IR£ per room per night

TOWERS HOTEL

GLENBEIGH,
CO. KERRY
TEL: 066-976 8212 FAX: 066-976 8260
EMAIL: towershotel@eircom.net

HOTEL ★★★ MAP 1 C 4

The family run Towers Hotel, on the Ring of Kerry, is an ideal place to relax and enjoy the splendours of Kerry. The hotel is a short distance from sandy beaches and dramatic mountains. Paradise for golfers, walkers, fishermen and anyone interested in the Kerry landscape. The Towers internationally known restaurant is renowned for its excellent seafood and distinguished atmosphere. Its traditional pub provides a chance to mingle with the people of Glenbeigh in a real Kerry atmosphere.

Member of Coast & Country Hotels

B&B from £39.00 to £48.00
€49.52 to €60.95

DOLORES SWEENEY
Proprietor

American Express
Mastercard
Visa

28 28

Closed 01 December - 01 April

GLENCAR HOUSE HOTEL

GLENCAR,
CO. KERRY
TEL: 066-976 0102 FAX: 066-976 0167
EMAIL: info@glencarhouse.com

HOTEL ★★ MAP 1 C 4

The Glencar House Hotel, built in 1732, lies framed by the McGillycuddy Reeks Mountains and is 2km from Caragh Lake. Declared an area of Special Conservation in 1997, it is the perfect base for a relaxing or activity holiday. Local golf courses include Dooks, Beaufort and Killarney. Traditional Irish cuisine is served in our restaurant. Salmon and trout fishing is available on the Caragh Fishery and boats are for hire on Caragh Lake. All bedrooms have private bath/shower and TV.

WEB: www.glencarhouse.com

Member of Great Fishing Houses of Ireland

B&B from £40.00 to £55.00
€50.79 to €69.84

KEVIN FACTOR
Manager

American Express
Diners
Mastercard
Visa

One week's partial board from
£371.00

18 18

HOTELS
FEDERATION

Closed 16 October - 18 February

ASHBERRY LODGE

SNEEM ROAD, N70, KENMARE,
CO. KERRY
TEL: 064-42720

GUESTHOUSE P MAP 1 D 3

Welcome to our new family-run guesthouse which offers friendly comfortable accommodation with spacious en suite bedrooms, central heating, excellent showers, colour TV, direct dial phones and a breakfast menu. We are situated on the Ring of Kerry Road, N70, which is within a short walking distance to the town centre. It is an ideal homebase to tour the Ring of Beara, Ring of Kerry, Gap of Dunloe, Healy's Pass, and much more! Also available are two 18 hole golf courses.

WEB: www.kenmare.com/ashberry

B&B from £20.00 to £25.00
€25.39 to €31.74

FRANCIE & REGINA MURPHY

Mastercard
Visa

8 8

HOTELS
FEDERATION

Open All Year

B&B rates are IR£ per person sharing per night incl. Breakfast

BRASS LANTERN

**OLD RAILWAY ROAD, KENMARE,
CO. KERRY
TEL: 064-42601 FAX: 064-42600
EMAIL: thebrasslantern@eircom.net**

GUESTHOUSE ★★★ MAP 1 D 3

The Brass Lantern is ideally located just beyond Kenmare Town Green. Each of the rooms has beautiful custom-made ash furniture, en suite bathroom, TV and phone. The two ground-floor rooms are ideal for anyone who has difficulty with stairs. It's a two minute walk to Kenmare's famous gourmet restaurants and speciality shops. Local amenities include golf courses, fishing, watersports, pony-trekking and cycling. Ideal base from which to explore South Kerry and West Cork.

WEB: www.kenmare-insight.com/brasslantern

**B&B from £20.00 to £35.00
€25.39 to €44.44**

PADRAIG JONES
Manager

Mastercard

Visa

6 6

Open All Year

DROMQUINNA MANOR HOTEL

**BLACKWATER BRIDGE P.O.,
KENMARE, CO. KERRY
TEL: 064-41657 FAX: 064-41791
EMAIL: info@dromquinna.com**

HOTEL ★★★ MAP 1 D 3

Breathtaking south facing views, of sea, islands and mountains. 29 delightful rooms, four-posters, suites & Ireland's only Tree House. Conservatory dining room, Intl cuisine, informal atmosphere. Coach House Annexe with 18 charming rooms including family rooms. 40 acres of grounds, marina, jetty, slipway, small beach. Amenities: Water Sports, Children's Playground, Boathouse Restaurant. Golf Courses: Ring of Kerry 3 minutes, Kenmare 5 minutes. Well placed for sight seeing in Kerry.

WEB: www.dromquinna.com

**B&B from £40.00 to £90.00
€50.79 to €114.28**

MIKE & SUE ROBERTSON
Proprietors

American Express

Diners

Mastercard

Visa

29 29

Closed 31 October - 01 March

FOLEYS SHAMROCK

**HENRY STREET, KENMARE,
CO. KERRY
TEL: 064-42162 FAX: 064-41799
EMAIL: foleyest@iol.ie**

GUESTHOUSE ★★★ MAP 1 D 3

Foleys is situated in Kenmare, Kerry Heritage town, ten very comfortable centrally heated en suite rooms with colour TV, phone & tea making facilities. Our chef owned restaurant & pub bistro serves Irish & international cuisine. Traditional sessions in the pub. Foleys is within walking distance of Kenmare 18 hole golf course, horse riding & fishing trips can be arranged. One of Ireland's Best - Fodors. Also recognised by Routard & Michelin.

**B&B from £20.00 to £27.50
€25.39 to €34.92**

MARGARET FOLEY
Owner/Manager

Mastercard

Visa

10 10

Open All Year

Room rates are IR£ per room per night

KENMARE BAY HOTEL

KENMARE,
CO. KERRY
TEL: 064-41300 FAX: 064-41541
EMAIL: kenmare@leehotels.ie

HOTEL ★★★ MAP 1 D 3

We offer a quiet hospitality with panoramic views of both the Cork and Kerry Mountains. By day you can choose from golfing, walking, fishing, touring and cycling; by night we offer quality cuisine followed by traditional Irish music in our lounge. Located in acres of parkland, we are only half a km from Ireland's most colourful heritage town - Kenmare.

WEB: www.leehotels.ie

Member of Lee Hotels

B&B from £35.00 to £50.00
€44.44 to €63.49

TERRY O'DOHERTY
General Manager

American Express
Diners
Mastercard
Visa

☺ Weekend specials from £95.00

136 136

Closed 01 November - 01 April

LANSDOWNE ARMS HOTEL

WILLIAM STREET, KENMARE,
CO. KERRY
TEL: 064-41368 FAX: 064-41114
EMAIL: info@lansdownearms.com

HOTEL ★★★ MAP 1 D 3

Located in a prominent position in the town, the Lansdowne Arms was established as Kenmare's first hotel in the 1790s by the First Marquis of Lansdowne, Earl of Shelbourne. Kenmare, a heritage town, is unique in that it is among the few select planned towns in Ireland. Situated in the heart of the south coast Kenmare is the ideal touring base for the Ring of Kerry and the South West. The Lansdowne Arms Hotel has a long tradition of hospitality and is the ideal location for golfers.

WEB: www.lansdownearms.com

B&B from £30.00 to £40.00
€38.09 to €50.79

RICHARD VOKE/PATRICK
GEOGHEGAN Owner/Manager

American Express
Diners
Mastercard
Visa

☺ Midweek and Weekend Specials

26 26

Open All Year

LODGE

KILGARVAN ROAD, KENMARE,
CO. KERRY
TEL: 064-41512 FAX: 064-42724
EMAIL: thelodgekenmare@eircom.net

GUESTHOUSE P MAP 1 D 3

Newly-built luxury guesthouse directly opposite Kenmare's 18 hole golf course. Within 3 minutes walk of some of the finest restaurants in Ireland. All rooms are elegantly furnished with en suite bathrooms, kingsize beds, safes and central heating. Private parking. An ideal location for the activist with walking, horseriding and bikes for hire nearby. 4 of the bedrooms are on ground level with one especially equipped for wheelchair use.

B&B from £30.00 to £40.00
€38.09 to €50.79

ROSEMARIE QUILL
Proprietor

Mastercard
Visa

11 11

Closed 01 November - 01 March

B&B rates are IR£ per person sharing per night incl. Breakfast

O'DONNABHAIN'S

**HENRY STREET, KENMARE,
CO. KERRY**
TEL: 064-42106 FAX: 064-42321
EMAIL: info@odonnabhain-kenmare.com

GUESTHOUSE P MAP 1 D 3

Conviently located in the centre of Kenmare Town, providing affordable accommodation with lashings of old world charm. Spacious en suite rooms (direct dial phone, TV 6 channels, parking), some with king size beds, finished with the comfort of the guests in mind. Rooms are located away from the bar, so as to ensure no sleepless nights, quietness in the centre of town. Ideal base to discover the South's attractions.

WEB: www.odonnabhain-kenmare.com

B&B from £22.00 to £30.00
€27.93 to €38.09

JEREMIAH FOLEY
Owner

Mastercard

Visa

Midweek Specials from £66.00

10 10

Open All Year

PARK HOTEL KENMARE

**KENMARE,
CO. KERRY**
TEL: 064-41200 FAX: 064-41402
EMAIL: info@parkkenmare.com

HOTEL ★★★★★ MAP 1 D 3

Built in 1897, this Victorian Hotel overlooks the Kenmare Estuary. Set in 11 acres of natural gardens it is a 2 minute walk from Kenmare Town. Staff lace attentiveness with an attractive friendliness that makes guests feel really welcome. 18 hole golf course, tennis, croquet on property. Renowned for outstanding cuisine featuring the best local seafood. Recognised by all major guides AA Red Star, Michelin, Egon Ronay, Small Luxury Hotels of the World, Ireland's Blue Book.

WEB: www.parkkenmare.com

Member of Ireland's Blue Book

B&B from £132.00 to £262.00
€167.61 to €332.67

FRANCIS BRENNAN
Proprietor

American Express

Diners

Mastercard

Visa

49 49

Closed 02 January - 13 April

RIVERSDALE HOUSE HOTEL

**KENMARE,
CO. KERRY**
TEL: 064-41299 FAX: 064-41075
EMAIL: riversdale@eircom.net

HOTEL ★★★ MAP 1 D 3

Located on the scenic shores of Kenmare Bay and backed by the McGillycuddy Reeks and Caha Mountains the hotel is the ideal choice to tour the famous Ring of Kerry and beautiful West Cork. Recently refurbished, the hotel boasts 4 luxurious suites, each with panoramic views of the scenery beyond our seven acre garden. Our Waterfront Restaurant is renowned for its fine cuisine while local activities include an 18 hole golf course, deep sea angling, hill walking, cycling and water-skiing.

WEB: www.kenmare.com/riversdale

Member of Best Western Hotels

B&B from £30.00 to £65.00
€38.09 to €82.53

PEGGY O'SULLIVAN
Proprietor

American Express

Diners

Mastercard

Visa

Weekend Specials from £75.00

64 64

Closed 06 November - 22 March

Room rates are IR£ per room per night

ROSEGARDEN GUESTHOUSE

SNEEM RD (N70), KENMARE,
CO. KERRY
TEL: 064-42288 FAX: 064-42305
EMAIL: rosegard@iol.ie

GUESTHOUSE ★★★ MAP 1 D 3

The Rosegarden Guesthouse and Restaurant is situated within walking distance of Kenmare Town, Ring of Kerry (N70). Set in 1 acre of landscaped garden with 350 roses. Private car park. All rooms en suite, power showers, centrally heated. Restaurant open from 6.30 pm. Menu includes lamb, steaks, salmon, stuffed crab, mussels and wine list. Enjoy our peaceful and relaxed ambience. We are looking forward to your visit. Ask for our 3 and 7 day specials.

WEB: www.euroka.com/rosegarden

B&B from £22.50 to £27.50
€28.57 to €34.92

INGRID & PETER RINGLEVER

American Express
Diners
Mastercard
Visa

8 8

Closed 01 November - 31 March

SEA SHORE FARM

TUBRID, KENMARE,
CO. KERRY
TEL: 064-41270 FAX: 064-41270
EMAIL: seashore@eircom.net

GUESTHOUSE ★★★ MAP 1 D 3

Our setting on the Bay is uniquely peaceful and private yet only 1 mile from town. Our farm extends to the shore affording unspoilt field walks in natural habitat with plentiful bird/wildlife. Large en suite rooms with panoramic seascapes, king beds, phone, tea facilities, etc. AA ◆◆◆◆ Selected, Recommended Guide du Routard, Los Angeles Times. Sign posted 300m from Kenmare by Esso Station - junction N71/N70 Killarney/Ring of Kerry Sneem Road.

WEB: www.seashorefarm.com

B&B from £27.50 to £40.00
€34.92 to €50.79

MARY PATRICIA O'SULLIVAN
Proprietor

Mastercard
Visa

6 6

Closed 01 November - 28 February

SHEEN FALLS LODGE

KENMARE,
CO. KERRY
TEL: 064-41600 FAX: 064-41386
EMAIL: info@sheenfallslodge.ie

HOTEL ★★★★★ MAP 1 D 3

The lodge presides over a dramatic 300 acre estate above the Sheen Waterfalls and the Kenmare Bay. Superb dining is available in either La Cascade Restaurant or Oscars Bistro. Facilities on the estate include horseriding, tennis, clay shooting, salmon fishing, heli-pad and two 18 hole golf courses nearby; within the lodge, health and fitness centre, swimming pool, library, billiard room, wine cellar and conference facilities available for up to 120 delegates.

WEB: www.sheenfallslodge.ie

Member of Relais et Châteaux

Room Rate from £180.00 to £285.00
€228.55 to €361.88

ADRIAAN BARTELS
General Manager

American Express
Diners
Mastercard
Visa

61 61

Closed 03 - 23 December

B&B rates are IR£ per person sharing per night incl. Breakfast

19TH GREEN

LACKABANE, FOSSA, KILLARNEY,
CO. KERRY
TEL: 064-32868 FAX: 064-32637
EMAIL: 19thgreen@eircom.net

GUESTHOUSE ★★★ MAP 2 E 4

Family run guesthouse 3km from Killarney Town. Ring of Kerry Road; adjacent to Killarney's 3 x 18 hole championship courses. Ideal for golfers playing Killarney, Beaufort, Dooks, Waterville, Tralee or Ballybunion. All tee times arranged. Putting green for guests' use. Tours arranged: Gap of Dunloe, Ring of Kerry and Dingle Peninsula. All rooms en suite with direct dial phone and TV. Whether you are sightseeing, fishing, rambling or golfing, the 19th Green will suit you to a tee.

WEB: www.19thgreen-bb.com

B&B from £22.00 to £30.00
€27.93 to €38.09

TIMOTHY AND BRIDGET FOLEY
Proprietors

Mastercard

Visa

10 10

| Closed 01 November - 01 March |

ABBEY LODGE

MUCKROSS ROAD, KILLARNEY,
CO. KERRY
TEL: 064-34193 FAX: 064-35877
EMAIL: abbeylodgekly@eircom.net

GUESTHOUSE P MAP 2 E 4

Abbey Lodge, newly refurbished to a very high standard with all rooms en suite, TV, tea/coffee, direct dial phone and central heating, is located on the Muckross Road (N71) a three minute walk to town centre. Private car park for guests. The King family invites you to experience the delights of Killarney and Kerry from this ideal location where genuine recommendations for tours and sightseeing is gladly provided. Cead Mile Failte.

B&B from £22.50 to £35.00
€28.57 to €44.44

JOHN G KING
Owner

Mastercard

Visa

15 15

| Closed 20 - 30 December |

AGHADOE HEIGHTS HOTEL

AGHADOE, KILLARNEY,
CO. KERRY
TEL: 064-31766 FAX: 064-31345
EMAIL: aghadoeheights@eircom.net

HOTEL ★★★★★ MAP 2 E 4

Recently refurbished, this luxury 5***** hotel enjoys panoramic views of Killarney's lakes and mountains. From the luxuriously furnished bedrooms to the highly acclaimed Fredrick's Restaurant this hotel is renowned for outstanding comfort and hospitality. Perfect for sports, rest and relaxation with a superb leisure centre including an indoor swimming pool. Within easy reach of the south west championship golf courses and breathtaking scenery.

WEB: www.aghadoeheights.com

B&B from £90.00 to £130.00
€114.27 to €165.07

PAT CHAWKE
General Manager

American Express

Diners

Mastercard

Visa

☺ Weekend Specials from £165.00

75 75

| Open All Year |

Room rates are IR£ per room per night

AISLING HOUSE

COUNTESS ROAD, KILLARNEY,
CO. KERRY
TEL: 064-31112 FAX: 064-30079
EMAIL: aislinghouse@eircom.net

GUESTHOUSE ★★★ MAP 2 E 4

Aisling House located in peaceful surroundings just 800 meters off Muckross Road and 8 minutes walk from the centre of Killarney. All bedrooms are en suite, with tea/coffee facilities, TV and central heating. There is private car park and garden for guests. Aisling House is well within walking distance of Killarney National Park, Ross Castle and Muckross House. Tours of the Ring of Kerry/Dingle may be arranged. Nearby facilities include golf, horse riding, angling.

Member of Premier Guesthouses

B&B from £18.00 to £25.00
€22.86 to €31.74

PADDY O'DONOGHUE
Owner

Mastercard
Visa

🏨🚗📞🅲✽🅤🅿💷
10 10

Closed 20 - 27 December

ARBUTUS HOTEL

COLLEGE STREET, KILLARNEY,
CO. KERRY
TEL: 064-31037 FAX: 064-34033
EMAIL: arbutushotel@eircom.net

HOTEL ★★★ MAP 2 E 4

To get a taste of the real Ireland, stay at a family run hotel with turf fires, good food, personal service with spacious rooms en suite. Oak panelled bar where the best Guinness is filled while traditional music weaves its magic through the air. If you're coming to sightsee, golf, fish or relax, the Arbutus is where you'll find a home away from home.

WEB: www.arbutuskillarney.com

B&B from £40.00 to £65.00
€50.79 to €82.53

SEAN BUCKLEY
Proprietor

American Express
Diners
Mastercard
Visa

🏨🚗📞🅣🅲⚫🅒🅜🎵🆂🅖ald💷
38 38

Inet FAX

Closed 17 - 30 December

ASHVILLE GUESTHOUSE

ROCK ROAD, KILLARNEY,
CO. KERRY
TEL: 064-36405 FAX: 064-36778
EMAIL: ashvillehouse@eircom.net

GUESTHOUSE ★★★ MAP 2 E 4

Ashville is a spacious family run guesthouse, 2 mins walk from town centre, on main Tralee Road (N22). Private car park. Comfortably furnished en suite rooms include orthopaedic beds, direct dial phone, multi channel TV, hairdryer. Sample our varied breakfast menu. Convenient to Killarney National Park, pony trekking, golf and fishing. Ideal touring base for Ring of Kerry, Dingle and Beara. Declan and Elma assure you of a warm welcome at Ashville. Awarded AA ♦♦♦, RAC highly acclaimed.

WEB: www.ashvillekillarney.com

B&B from £20.00 to £28.00
€25.39 to €35.55

ELMA & DECLAN WALSH
Proprietors

American Express
Mastercard
Visa

🏨🚗📞🅣🅲🅤🅿💷
12 12

Closed 18 - 30 December

B&B rates are IR£ per person sharing per night incl. Breakfast

BEAUFIELD HOUSE

PARK ROAD, KILLARNEY,
CO. KERRY
TEL: 064-34440   FAX: 064-34663

GUESTHOUSE ★★★ MAP 2 E 4

Beaufield House is a family run guesthouse, 2km from Killarney Town Centre on main Cork Road (N22). 14 modern centrally heated bedrooms all with bath/shower en suite, direct dial telephone, radio and TV. Spacious visitors' lounge. Relax and enjoy local amenities which include golf, fishing, Killarney's famous lakes, mountains, National Park, tour the Ring of Kerry and Dingle Peninsula. You will be made welcome when you stay at Beaufield House.

Member of Premier Guesthouses

B&B from £20.00 to £25.00
€25.39 to €31.74

MOYA BOWE
Proprietor

American Express
Diners
Mastercard
Visa

☺ Midweek specials from £57.00

🛏️🅿️☎️📺TC❄️
14 14

IRISH HOTELS FEDERATION

Closed 20 - 28 December

BROOK LODGE HOTEL

HIGH STREET, KILLARNEY,
CO. KERRY
TEL: 064-31800   FAX: 064-35001
EMAIL: brooklodgekillarney@eircom.net

HOTEL N MAP 2 E 4

Brook Lodge Hotel is a new hotel, family-run, situated in the heart of Killarney Town, set back from the street on over an acre of landscaped garden with private parking. Our large and tastefully decorated bedrooms are all en suite, including tea/coffee, direct dial phone, hairdryer, multichannel TV. Wheelchair facilities. Lift. Excellent cuisine in Brook Restaurant with wine licence and residents' bar.

WEB: www.brooklodgekillarney.com

B&B from £30.00 to £50.00
€38.09 to €63.49

JOAN COUNIHAN
Owner

American Express
Diners
Mastercard
Visa

☺ Midweek/Weekend Specials available

🛏️🅿️☎️♿️☂️TC📺CM♨️♪🅿️S♿️
18 18

a|c 🖥️ Inet

IRISH HOTELS FEDERATION

Closed 01 November - 15 March

CASTLE OAKS

MUCKROSS ROAD, KILLARNEY,
CO. KERRY
TEL: 064-34154   FAX: 064-36980

GUESTHOUSE ★★★ MAP 2 E 4

At the gateway to Killarney National Park and only minutes from the lively town centre, you are always assured of a warm and friendly welcome at this luxury, family-run guesthouse. Enjoy the comfort of the spacious rooms, including large family rooms, all en suite with direct dial phone, colour TV, hair dryer and power shower; or relax in the guest lounge with our complimentary tea/coffee whilst absorbing breathtaking views of Killarney's lakes and mountains. Private parking.

B&B from £28.00 to £32.00
€35.55 to €40.63

EAMON & VALERIE COURTNEY
Proprietors

Mastercard
Visa

🛏️🅿️☎️📺TC❄️☀️♨️🅿️
17 17

IRISH HOTELS FEDERATION

Closed 10 - 27 December

CASTLELODGE GUESTHOUSE

**MUCKROSS ROAD, KILLARNEY,
CO. KERRY**
TEL: 064-31545 FAX: 064-32325
EMAIL: castlelodge@eircom.net

GUESTHOUSE U MAP 2 E 4

Conveniently located, just two minutes walk from Killarney Town Centre. Open all year round, our Guesthouse offers very friendly staff, a homely atmosphere and easy access to all the major attractions and magnificent scenery in Killarney. Good restaurants and Live Music will be recommended, come and see the sights, hear the Music and taste the atmosphere.

WEB: homepage.eircom.net/~castlelodge/

B&B from £20.00 to £28.00
€25.39 to €35.55

TONY O'SHEA

American Express
Diners
Mastercard
Visa

25 25

Open All Year

CASTLEROSSE HOTEL & LEISURE CENTRE

**KILLARNEY,
CO. KERRY**
TEL: 064-31144 FAX: 064-31031
EMAIL: castler@iol.ie

HOTEL ★★★ MAP 2 E 4

A Tower Group Hotel - situated right on the lakeside, between the golf course and the National Park and a little over a mile from Killarney Town Centre, the Castlerosse commands magnificent views of the lakes and mountains, especially from the restaurant and panoramic bar. The impressive range of leisure facilities, including the new on-site golf course, 20m swimming pool and 2 floodlit tennis courts makes the Castlerosse the perfect location for a holiday or leisure break.

WEB: www.towerhotelgroup.ie

Member of Tower Hotel Group

B&B from £35.00 to £50.00
€44.44 to €63.49

DANNY BOWE
General Manager

American Express
Diners
Mastercard
Visa

Weekend specials from £75.00

121 121

9 18

Closed 01 November - 07 March

COFFEY'S LOCH LEIN HOUSE HOTEL

**GOLF COURSE ROAD, FOSSA,
KILLARNEY, CO. KERRY**
TEL: 064-31260 FAX: 064-36151
EMAIL: ecoffey@indigo.ie

UNDER CONSTRUCTION OPENING MAR 2001

HOTEL P MAP 2 E 4

Superb family run hotel, uniquely situated by the shores of Killarney's Lower Lake. Magnificent views of lakes & mountains. Ideally located on the Ring/Dingle roads, near the Gap of Dunloe. Tours personally arranged. Nearby four 18 hole championship golf courses, horseriding & fishing.
While you will be surprised by the delightful new building, you will be pleased that the hospitality, grade A service & relaxed atmosphere have not changed. A warm welcome awaits you here.

WEB: www.lochlein.com

B&B from £20.00 to £40.00
€25.39 to €50.79

EITHNE COFFEY
Proprietor

Mastercard
Visa

10 10

Closed 10 November - 10 March

B&B rates are IR£ per person sharing per night incl. Breakfast

DARBY O'GILLS COUNTRY HOUSE HOTEL

LISSIVGEEN, MALLOW ROAD,
KILLARNEY, CO. KERRY
TEL: 064-34168   FAX: 064-36794
EMAIL: darbyogill@eircom.net

HOTEL U   MAP 2 E 4

Darby O'Gills Country House Hotel is a charming family run hotel located in an excellent position on the edge of Killarney Town in a quiet rural setting only 5 minutes from Killarney Town Centre. Guest comfort is foremost in our mind and our comfortable rooms reflect this. This is a family friendly hotel where we hope to make your stay a relaxing and memorable occasion.

WEB: www.kerry-insight.com/darbyogills/

Member of MinOtel Ireland Hotel Group

B&B from £30.00 to £50.00
€38.09 to €63.49

PAT & JOAN GILL & FAMILY

American Express
Diners
Mastercard
Visa

🖐🚗🛏🍽TC✻CM❄☾♩🎵PS
13 13
☕♿

Closed 25 - 26 December

DROMHALL HOTEL

MUCKROSS ROAD, KILLARNEY,
CO. KERRY
TEL: 064-31431   FAX: 064-34242
EMAIL: info@dromhall.com

HOTEL U   MAP 2 E 4

The newly rebuilt, family owned and managed Dromhall Hotel is ideally located minutes from Killarney. The elegant marbled lobby affords the guest the perfect introduction to the high standard of accommodation, which they will enjoy during their stay. Choose between the Abbey Restaurant or Kaynes Bistro for dining. A choice of Kaynes lively pub or the residents' intimate bar will suit all. Banquet & Conference facilities catering for 300 available. Leisure facilities available.

WEB: www.dromhall.com

B&B from £35.00 to £55.00
€44.44 to €69.84

BERNADETTE RANDLES
Managing Director

American Express
Mastercard
Visa

😊 Weekend specials from £80.00

🖐🚗🛏TC✎CM▨⌂☾♩
70 70
PS♿☕

Closed 23 - 29 December

EARLS COURT HOUSE

WOODLAWN JUNCTION, MUCKROSS ROAD, KILLARNEY, CO. KERRY
TEL: 064-34009   FAX: 064-34366
EMAIL: earls@eircom.net

GUESTHOUSE ★★★★   MAP 2 E 4

RAC Small Hotel of the Year for Ireland 1998. A magical 4**** hideaway, 5 mins walk to town centre. Traditional country house ambience, antique furnishings, log fires, fresh flowers, home baking and fine wines. Here keynotes are charm, tranquillity and unparalleled hospitality afforded to each discerning guest. Breakfast is special - a feast offering tempting choices. Superior rooms with individual themes, full bathroom, TV, ice, phone and individual balconies. Private parking. AA ◆◆◆◆◆.

WEB: www.killarney-earlscourt.ie

B&B from £32.00 to £48.00
€40.63 to €60.95

EMER & RAY MOYNIHAN
Owners

Mastercard
Visa

🖐🚗🛏TC✻☾UJP♟inet
11 11

Closed 13 November - 16 February

Room rates are IR£ per room per night

EVISTON HOUSE HOTEL

NEW STREET, KILLARNEY,
CO. KERRY
TEL: 064-31640 FAX: 064-33685
EMAIL: evishtl@eircom.net

HOTEL ★★★ MAP 2 E 4

Eviston House Hotel is located in the centre of Killarney yet only a few minutes away from the National Park and championship golf courses. All our luxurious bedrooms are complete with private bathroom, direct dial telephone, tea/coffee facilities, hair dryer and satellite TV. The elegant Colleen Bawn Restaurant offers fine food in intimate surroundings. Afterwards visit our famous pub, the Danny Mann, for the best in traditional music and great 'craic'.

WEB: www.killarney-hotel.com

Member of Best Western Hotels

B&B from £27.00 to £49.00
€34.28 to €62.22

EDWARD EVISTON
Proprietor

American Express
Diners
Mastercard
Visa

Weekend Specials from £75.00

75 75

Open All Year

FAILTE HOTEL

COLLEGE STREET, KILLARNEY,
CO. KERRY
TEL: 064-33404 FAX: 064-36599
EMAIL: failtehotel@eircom.net

HOTEL ★★ MAP 2 E 4

The Failte Hotel was recently refurbished to a very high standard is owned and managed by the O'Callaghan family. Sons Dermot and Donal run the award winning restaurant. It is internationally known for its high standard of cuisine. Paudie supervises the award winning bar. It is situated in the town centre, adjacent to railway station, new factory outlet, shopping complex. Also close by are many local cabarets & night clubs. Local amenities include golfing, fishing, walking.

WEB: www.kerry-insight.com

B&B from £30.00 to £45.00
€38.09 to €57.14

DERMOT & EILEEN
O'CALLAGHAN Proprietors

American Express
Mastercard
Visa

Midweek Special from £85.00

12 12

Closed 24 - 26 December

FOLEY'S TOWNHOUSE

23 HIGH STREET, KILLARNEY,
CO. KERRY
TEL: 064-31217 FAX: 064-34683

GUESTHOUSE ★★★★ MAP 2 E 4

Originally a 19th Century Coaching Inn, this old house has hosted generations of travellers. Newly refurbished, this is a 4**** family-run town centre located guesthouse. Luxury bedrooms are individually designed for comfort complete with every modern amenity. Downstairs is our award-winning seafood and steak restaurant. Chef/owner Carol provides meals from fresh local produce. Choose from approx 200 wines. Personal supervision. Private parking. Awarded AA ♦♦♦♦, RAC highly acclaimed.

B&B from £45.50 to £45.50
€57.77 to €57.77

CAROL HARTNETT
Proprietor

American Express
Mastercard
Visa

28 28

Closed 01 November - 04 April

B&B rates are IR£ per person sharing per night incl. Breakfast

FRIARS GLEN

MANGERTON ROAD, MUCKROSS,
KILLARNEY, CO. KERRY
TEL: 064-37500   FAX: 064-37388
EMAIL: fullerj@indigo.ie

GUESTHOUSE ★★★★   MAP 2 E 4

This 4**** Guesthouse, built in a
traditional style, offers a haven of
peace and tranquillity; set in its own
28 acres of wood & pastureland and
located in the heart of Killarney
National Park. Reception rooms
have a rustic feel, with a warm and
friendly atmosphere, finished in
stone and wood with open fires and
antiques. Bedrooms & bathrooms
are finished to the highest standards.
The dining room, patio & garden
have a terrific mountain view. An
ideal base in the Southwest.

WEB: www.indigo.ie/~fullerj

B&B from £25.00 to £40.00
€31.74 to €50.79

MARY & JOHN FULLER
Proprietors

Mastercard

Visa

🖐🐾📞🗎©❄♻🅿🛎
10 10

IRISH HOTELS FEDERATION

Closed 01 November - 28 February

FUCHSIA HOUSE

MUCKROSS ROAD, KILLARNEY,
CO. KERRY
TEL: 064-33743   FAX: 064-36588
EMAIL: fuchsiahouse@eircom.ie

GUESTHOUSE ★★★★   MAP 2 E 4

We invite you to enjoy the affordable
luxury of Fuchsia House which is set
well back from the road in mature,
leafy gardens yet is only 7 minutes
walk from Killarney Town Centre.
Purpose built to combine the
amenities of a modern 4**** guesthouse with the elegance of an earlier
age, Fuchsia House offers orthopaedic
beds dressed in crisp cotton & linen,
private bath with power shower, direct
dial phone. Conservatory. Irish &
vegetarian menu. Winner 1999 "Best
Guesthouse" in Killarney Looking
Good Competition. RAC Sparkling
Diamond Award.

WEB: www.fuchsiahouse.com

B&B from £30.00 to £42.00
€38.09 to €53.33

MARY TREACY
Owner

Mastercard

Visa

🖐🐾📞🗎Ⓣ🅰©❄♻🅿🆂🛎
8 8

IRISH HOTELS FEDERATION

Closed 15 December - 28 February

GLEANN FIA COUNTRY HOUSE

DEERPARK, KILLARNEY,
CO. KERRY
TEL: 064-35035   FAX: 064-35000
EMAIL: gleanfia@iol.ie

GUESTHOUSE ★★★   MAP 2 E 4

Set in a secluded 30 acre wooded
river valley, 1 mile from Killarney -
Gleann Fia is the perfect holiday
setting. Our Victorian style country
house offers tasteful en suite rooms,
each with phone, TV and
orthopaedic beds. Stroll along the
river walk admiring the wild flowers
and Autumn colours. Relax by the
peat fire or enjoy tea/coffee in the
conservatory. Wholesome breakfasts
include freshly squeezed juice and
homemade preserves. Friendly
personal attention assured. 300yds
from bypass, N22 on Kilcummin
Road.

WEB: ireland.iol.ie/kerry-insight/gleannfia

B&B from £25.00 to £35.00
€31.74 to €44.44

JERRY AND NORA GALVIN
Owners

American Express

Mastercard

Visa

🖐🐾📞🗎Ⓣ🅰©❄♻🅿🛎
17 17

IRISH HOTELS FEDERATION

Closed 01 December - 01 March

Room rates are IR£ per room per night

GLENA GUESTHOUSE

**MUCKROSS ROAD, KILLARNEY,
CO. KERRY
TEL: 064-32705 FAX: 064-35611
EMAIL: glena@iol.ie**

GUESTHOUSE U MAP 2 E 4

Glena House award-winning guesthouse, AA ◆◆◆◆, RAC acclaimed, Les Routier recommended. It's the simple things that make it right; in a great location, a bed to rest in, a shower/bath to invigorate, tea/coffee when you want. A bowl of ice for a bedroom drink, homebaking and a breakfast as individual as you are. Glena House where memories are made, 5 minutes walk from town centre. Parking.

WEB: www.kerry-insight/glena.com

B&B from £25.00 to £35.00
€31.74 to €44.44

MARINA & TIM BUCKLEY
Owners/Managers

American Express
Diners
Mastercard
Visa

26 26

Closed 25 December

GLENEAGLE HOTEL

**KILLARNEY,
CO. KERRY
TEL: 064-36000 FAX: 064-32646
EMAIL: gleneagl@iol.ie**

HOTEL ★★★ MAP 2 E 4

Ireland's leading leisure and conference/convention hotel, adjacent to Killarney's National Park with beautifully furnished rooms. The newly opened 2000 seat National Events Centre, ideally suited for conventions, conferences, exhibitions, sporting events, concerts and theatrical productions. Our award winning chefs will delight you in both our restaurants. We have a great line-up of entertainment all year round. Relax and unwind using our indoor/outdoor leisure facilities.

WEB: www.gleneagle-hotel.com

B&B from £40.00 to £68.00
€50.79 to €86.34

O'DONOGHUE FAMILY
Proprietors

American Express
Diners
Mastercard
Visa

250 250

Open All Year

HOLIDAY INN KILLARNEY

**MUCKROSS ROAD, KILLARNEY,
CO. KERRY
TEL: 064-33000 FAX: 064-33001
EMAIL: holidayinnkillarney@eircom.net**

HOTEL N MAP 2 E 4

Holiday Inn Killarney enjoys a quiet but central location close to Killarney Town Centre. Its 24 suites and spacious en suite rooms are tastefully decorated to the highest standard. Our fully-equipped leisure centre is the perfect place to relax and unwind. Our Library Point Restaurant serves the finest of local cuisine while Saddlers Pub serves food daily and has entertainment nightly. A haven for all seasons!

WEB: www.holidayinnkillarney.com

Member of Signature Hotels

B&B from £33.00 to £63.00
€41.90 to €79.99

DAVID HENNESSY
General Manager

American Express
Diners
Mastercard
Visa

☺ Weekend Specials from £79.00

104 104

Open All Year

B&B rates are IR£ per person sharing per night incl. Breakfast

HOTEL DUNLOE CASTLE

KILLARNEY,
CO. KERRY
TEL: 064-44111 FAX: 064-44583
EMAIL: sales@kih.liebherr.com

HOTEL ★★★★★ MAP 2 E 4

100 bedroomed resort near Killarney, facing the famous Gap of Dunloe. Historical park and botanic gardens with ruins of castle. Elegant decor with many valuable antiques. Luxurious lounges, cocktail bar, gourmet restaurant. Extensive leisure facilities: pool, sauna, gym, riding, putting green, tennis, jogging track. 10 championship courses nearby. Sister hotels: Ard-na-Sidhe and Hotel Europe. Central Reservations: Tel: 064-31900, Fax: 064-32118.

WEB: www.iol.ie/khl

B&B from £66.00 to £93.00
€83.80 to €118.09

MICHAEL BRENNAN
Manager

American Express
Diners
Mastercard
Visa

100 100

Closed 01 October - 15 April

HOTEL EUROPE

KILLARNEY,
CO. KERRY
TEL: 064-31900 FAX: 064-32118
EMAIL: sales@kih.liebherr.com

HOTEL ★★★★★ MAP 2 E 4

De luxe resort known internationally for its spectacular location on the Lakes of Killarney. 200 spacious bedrooms and suites of highest modern standards, many with lake view. Elegant lounges, cocktail bar, panorama restaurant. Boutique. Health/fitness centre, 25m indoor pool, sauna, gym. Tennis, horseriding, fishing, boating, cycling. 6 championship courses nearby. Sister hotels: Hotel Dunloe Castle and Ard-na-Sidhe.

WEB: www.iol.ie/khl

B&B from £62.00 to £88.00
€78.72 to €111.74

American Express
Diners
Mastercard
Visa

200 200

Closed 01 November - 15 March

HUSSEYS TOWNHOUSE & BAR

43 HIGH STREET, KILLARNEY,
CO. KERRY
TEL: 064-37454 FAX: 064-33144
EMAIL: husseys@iol.ie

GUESTHOUSE ★★★ MAP 2 E 4

Centrally located, within walking distance of Killarney National Park, the principal shopping areas & the best restaurants in town. This family owned house offers peaceful accommodation in tastefully decorated rooms, equipped to a high standard. Enjoy a choice of breakfast in our delightful dining room, relax in our comfortable guest lounge or cosy friendly bar. For walkers, cyclists, golfers or touring Kerry this is the discerning traveller's perfect choice. Private parking.

B&B from £20.00 to £30.00
€25.39 to €38.09

GERALDINE O'LEARY
Owner

American Express
Mastercard
Visa

5 5

Closed 31 October - 23 March

Room rates are IR£ per room per night

INTERNATIONAL BEST WESTERN HOTEL

KENMARE PLACE, KILLARNEY,
CO. KERRY
TEL: 064-31816 FAX: 064-31837
EMAIL: inter@iol.ie

HOTEL ★★★ MAP 2 E 4

A warm welcome awaits you at the International. This town centre hotel has been brought into the 21st Century with carefully planned refurbishment. 80 luxurious bedrooms all with the modern facilities you expect to make your stay a memorable one. Excellent cuisine served daily. Traditional music in our award winning Hannigans Pub. Nearby are Killarney's 3 18 hole Championship Golf Courses, Ballybunion, Dooks, Tralee and Waterville within easy reach. Bus/Train Station 200m.

WEB: www.killarney-inter.com

Member of Best Western Hotels

B&B from £29.00 to £60.00
€36.82 to €76.18

TERENCE MULCAHY
Manager

American Express
Diners
Mastercard
Visa

☺ Weekend specials from £78.00

80 80

S ℗ alc

Closed 22 - 29 December

INVERARAY FARM GUESTHOUSE

BEAUFORT, KILLARNEY,
CO. KERRY
TEL: 064-44224 FAX: 064-44775
EMAIL: inver@indigo.ie

GUESTHOUSE ★★ MAP 2 E 4

A luxury farm guesthouse in a quiet sylvan setting. Views of Killarney lakes, mountains and Gap of Dunloe. 9km west of Killarney, 1km off N72, left over bridge at Shop. Free private trout and salmon fishing on River Laune. Angling, walking and golfing tours arranged. Tea-room, games-room, playground and pony for children. Singing pubs, horse-riding locally. Home-baking, seafood and dinner a speciality with good, wholesome home cooking. Recommended Le Guide du Routard 2000.

B&B from £19.00 to £24.00
€24.13 to €30.47

EILEEN & NOEL SPILLANE
Proprietors

10 10

Closed 01 November - 10 March

KATHLEENS COUNTRY HOUSE

TRALEE ROAD, KILLARNEY,
CO. KERRY
TEL: 064-32810 FAX: 064-32340
EMAIL: info@kathleens.net

GUESTHOUSE ★★★★ MAP 2 E 4

Kathleen's is a delightful family run guesthouse. ITB 4****,AA ♦♦♦♦♦ and RAC Small Hotel/Guesthouse of the Year for Ireland are amongst its many awards. Set on 3 acres of mature gardens in peaceful rural surrounds only 3km from town centre. Rooms furnished in antique pine with; bath/power shower, tea/coffee facilities, hairdryer, phone, orthopaedic beds. Art lovers will enjoy the many paintings. Non-smoking house. Easy to get to! Hard to leave! Cancellation policy 14 days.

WEB: www.kathleens.net

B&B from £32.00 to £50.00
€40.63 to €63.49

KATHLEEN O'REGAN SHEPPARD
Proprietor

American Express
Mastercard
Visa

☺ 3 nights stay 10% discount/direct bookings

17 17

Closed 07 November - 10 March

B&B rates are IR£ per person sharing per night incl. Breakfast

KILLARNEY AVENUE HOTEL

KENMARE PLACE, KILLARNEY,
CO. KERRY
TEL: 064-32522 FAX: 064-33707
EMAIL: kavenue@odonoghue-ring-hotels.com

HOTEL R MAP 2 E 4

Killarney Avenue Hotel is a new hotel in the centre of Killarney Town. All 66 bedrooms are air-conditioned and also feature TV, radio, direct dial phone, hairdryer and tea/coffee making facilities. Guests are welcome to use the leisure facilities of our sister hotel (Killarney Towers Hotel), 100m away. Underground garage parking is available to guests. An excellent hotel in an excellent location in downtown Killarney.

WEB: www.odonoghue-ring-hotels.com

B&B from £50.00 to £90.00
€63.49 to €114.28

LIAM KEALY
General Manager

American Express
Mastercard
Visa

66 66

Closed 01 December - 31 January

KILLARNEY COURT HOTEL

TRALEE ROAD, KILLARNEY,
CO. KERRY
TEL: 064-37070 FAX: 064-37060
EMAIL: stay@irishcourthotels.com

HOTEL ★★★ MAP 2 E 4

Opened in April '98 the Killarney Court Hotel is a 5 minute walk from Killarney Town Centre, only 15km from Kerry International Airport and close to 3 world famous golf courses. Our 100 en suite bedrooms boast a tasteful neo-gothic style decor. Enjoy a meal in our Seasons Restaurant with traditional Irish and international cuisine or a drink in McGillicuddys traditional Irish pub with its wonderful 'ceol, ol agus craic' atmosphere. We assure you your stay will be enjoyable.

WEB: www.irishcourthotel.com

Member of Irish Court Hotel Group

B&B from £35.00 to £85.00
€44.44 to €107.93

ROBERT LYNE
Proprietor

American Express
Diners
Mastercard
Visa

100 100

Open All Year

KILLARNEY GREAT SOUTHERN HOTEL

KILLARNEY,
CO. KERRY
TEL: 064-31262 FAX: 064-31642
EMAIL: res@killarneygsh.ie

HOTEL ★★★★ MAP 2 E 4

Experience bygone charm with modern comfort set in scenic gardens in the heart of Killarney. This hotel has extensive leisure facilities - indoor heated swimming pool, sauna, steamroom, plunge pool, gym, jacuzzi, outdoor tennis courts and children's playground. Other facilities - hair & beauty salons, cocktail bar, main dining room and Peppers À la Carte Restaurant. Conference facilities for 800 delegates. Bookable worldwide through UTELL Intl or Central Res., Tel 01-214 4800.

WEB: www.gsh.ie

B&B from £82.00 to £92.00
€104.11 to €118.64

CONOR HENNIGAN
General Manager

American Express
Diners
Mastercard
Visa

Weekend specials from £99.00

180 180

Open All Year

KILLARNEY HEIGHTS HOTEL

CORK ROAD, KILLARNEY, CO. KERRY
TEL: 064-31158 FAX: 064-35198
EMAIL: khh@iol.ie

HOTEL U MAP 2 E 4

Situated 1km from Killarney Town Centre on the Cork Road, this beautiful 70 bedroomed hotel overlooks the majestic Torc & Mangerton Mountains. Open fires, olde world flagstone floors and pitch pine furnishings create a unique nostalgic atmosphere in the bars, restaurants and bistro. The hotel is easily accessed by mainline rail or by flying into Kerry Airport, just 14km away. The Killarney Heights Hotel, the perfect venue for the perfect holiday.

Member of Logis of Ireland

B&B from £42.00 to £60.00
€53.33 to €76.18

BERNARD O'RIORDAN

Mastercard
Visa

Weekend Special from £85.00

70 70

Open All Year

KILLARNEY LODGE

COUNTESS ROAD, KILLARNEY, CO. KERRY
TEL: 064-36499 FAX: 064-31070
EMAIL: klylodge@iol.ie

GUESTHOUSE ★★★★ MAP 2 E 4

Killarney Lodge, a purpose built guesthouse set in private walled-in gardens, only 2 minutes walk from the town centre. The guesthouse provides private parking, spacious en suite air conditioned bedrooms with all modern amenities including wheelchair facilities. Enjoy an extensive breakfast menu in the spacious dining room and relax in comfortable lounges with open fires. The Lodge has already gained an outstanding reputation for quality of service, relaxed atmosphere and friendliness.

WEB: www.kerry-insight.com/killarney-lodge

B&B from £28.00 to £45.00
€35.55 to €57.14

CATHERINE TREACY
Owner

American Express
Diners
Mastercard
Visa

16 16

Closed 15 November - 14 February

INTERNATIONAL DIAL CODES

Emergency Services: 999 (freephone)

HOW TO DIAL INTERNATIONAL
ACCESS CODE +
COUNTRY CODE +
AREA CODE +
LOCAL NUMBER

SAMPLE CODES:
E.G. UNITED KINGDOM
00 44 + Area Code + Local No.

U.S.A.	00	1	+
Italy	00	39	+
Spain	00	34	+
France	00	33	+
Germany	00	49	+
Iceland	00	354	+
Japan	00	81	+
Luxembourg	00	352	+
Netherlands	00	31	+
Operator (national)			1190
(G. Britain)			1197
(International)			1198

B&B rates are IR£ per person sharing per night incl. Breakfast

KILLARNEY PARK HOTEL

KENMARE PLACE, KILLARNEY,
CO. KERRY
TEL: 064-35555 FAX: 064-35266
EMAIL: info@killarneyparkhotel.ie

HOTEL ★★★★★ MAP 2 E 4

Superbly located in the heart of Killarney Town, this family owned luxury hotel offers the quietness, intimacy and privacy associated with times past. In addition to a country house style lobby, library, drawing room and billiard room, the hotel also offers a magnificent 20m swimming pool, sauna, jacuzzi, outdoor hot tub, fitness suite and treatment room. Dining options include a candlelit dinner in the Park Restaurant or an appetising snack in the Garden Bar.

WEB: www.killarneyparkhotel.ie

B&B from £85.00 to £125.00
€107.93 to €158.72

DONAGH DAVERN
General Manager

American Express
Diners
Mastercard
Visa

Weekend specials from £170.00

76 76

Closed 24 - 27 December

KILLARNEY ROYAL

COLLEGE STREET, KILLARNEY,
CO. KERRY
TEL: 064-31853 FAX: 064-34001
EMAIL: royalhot@iol.ie

HOTEL U MAP 2 E 4

The Killarney Royal is not like anywhere else. Family-run and situated in the heart of Killarney, Joe and Margaret Scally have anticipated your needs. Each room has been individually and personally re-designed to meet your comforts with air conditioning throughout, 24 hour personal service, parking facilities available, elegant dining room, local bar atmosphere. Meticulously high standards of service ensure that you can make the most of the charming and graceful surroundings.

WEB: www.killarneyroyal.ie

B&B from £45.00 to £90.00
€57.14 to €114.28

JOE SCALLY
Proprietor

American Express
Diners
Mastercard
Visa

29 29

inet

Closed 22 - 28 December

KILLARNEY RYAN HOTEL & LEISURE CENTRE

CORK ROAD, KILLARNEY,
CO. KERRY
TEL: 064-31555 FAX: 064-32438
EMAIL: ryan@indigo.ie

HOTEL ★★★ MAP 2 E 4

Just 2km from Killarney Town centre and ideally located for exploring Kerry, this hotel offers the perfect leisure break. Savour a meal in the Ross and Herbert Rooms, unwind in the Lobby Lounge or enjoy nightly entertainment in the bar. The extensive leisure centre features an 18m pool, steam rooms, sauna, jacuzzi and sports hall. An award winning creche and a children's activity programme during school holidays ensure a fun filled stay. Car park. AA, RAC and Egon Ronay recommended.

WEB: www.ryan-hotels.com

B&B from £45.00 to £85.00
€57.14 to €107.93

PAT GALVIN
General Manager

American Express
Diners
Mastercard
Visa

Weekend specials from £90.00

168 168

Open All Year

Room rates are IR£ per room per night

KILLARNEY TOWERS HOTEL & LEISURE CENTRE

COLLEGE SQUARE, KILLARNEY,
CO. KERRY
TEL: 064-31038 FAX: 064-31755
EMAIL: towersky@iol.ie

HOTEL ★★★ MAP 2 E 4

3*** hotel in the centre of Killarney with underground car park, 182 superb en suite bedrooms, satellite TV and video channels, direct dial phone, hairdryers and tea/coffee facilities. Other guest facilities include a 20m indoor heated pool, sauna, steam room and fully equipped gymnasium. Live music entertainment nightly and green fees reserved at all Kerry courses through our golf department. A great hotel in downtown Killarney.

WEB: www.odonoghue-ring-hotels.com

B&B from £55.00 to £80.00
€69.84 to €101.58

FRANK MC CARTHY

American Express
Diners
Mastercard
Visa

182 182
IRISH HOTELS FEDERATION

Closed 30 November - 01 February

KILLARNEY TOWN HOUSE

31 NEW STREET, KILLARNEY,
CO. KERRY
TEL: 064-35388 FAX: 064-35259

GUESTHOUSE ★★ MAP 2 E 4

Comfortable family-run 10 roomed guesthouse situated in the heart of Killarney Town - within easy walking distance of rail/bus stations. Rooms complete with every modern amenity. Outdoor activities arranged through reception - fishing, golfing and sightseeing.

B&B from £22.00 to £26.00
€27.93 to €33.01

AILISH HALLISSEY

Mastercard
Visa

10 10

Open All Year

KILLEEN HOUSE HOTEL

AGHADOE, LAKES OF KILLARNEY,
CO. KERRY
TEL: 064-31711 FAX: 064-31811
EMAIL: charming@indigo.ie

HOTEL ★★★ MAP 2 E 4

The Killeen House is truly a charming little hotel. With only 23 rooms, 8 of them deluxe, it is the ideal base for touring 'God's own country', the magical Kingdom of Kerry. With our DIY GolfPub and an elegant award-winning dining room you are assured a memorable experience. Go on, do the smart thing and call us now! We look forward to extending the 'hospitality of the house' to you!

WEB: www.killeenhousehotel.com

B&B from £40.00 to £75.00
€50.79 to €95.23

MICHAEL & GERALDINE ROSNEY
Owners

American Express
Diners
Mastercard
Visa

23 23

IRISH HOTELS FEDERATION

Closed 01 November - 31 March

B&B rates are IR£ per person sharing per night incl. Breakfast

KINGFISHER LODGE GUESTHOUSE

LEWIS ROAD, KILLARNEY,
CO. KERRY
TEL: 064-37131 FAX: 064-39871
EMAIL: kingfisherguesthouse@eircom.net

GUESTHOUSE N MAP 2 E 4

A warm welcome awaits you at Kingfisher Lodge, a family run luxury Irish Tourist Board approved guesthouse, 3 minutes walk from Killarney Town Centre with its excellent pubs, restaurants, entertainment and shopping. Our spacious bedrooms are beautifully decorated with TV, direct dial phone and hairdryers. Relaxing guest lounge with tea/coffee facilities and channel TV. Varied breakfast menu. Private parking. Tackle, drying rooms available for anglers, walkers and golfers. Tours arranged.

WEB: www.kerry-insight.com/kingfisher

B&B from £20.00 to £30.00
€25.39 to €38.09

ANN & DONAL CARROLL

Mastercard
Visa

Midweek Specials from £60.00

9 9

Closed 14 December - 14 January

LAKE HOTEL

ON LAKE SHORE, MUCKROSS
ROAD, KILLARNEY, CO. KERRY
TEL: 064-31035 FAX: 064-31902
EMAIL: lakehotel@eircom.net

HOTEL ★★★ MAP 2 E 4

Stunning location on Killarney's Lake Shore. Built in 1820. Open log fires, relaxed and friendlly atmosphere. Spacious rooms. Luxury lakeside suites with jacuzzi, balcony & some 4 poster beds. New for 2001 Season, *unique to Ireland Incredible Fantasy Theme Suites with large beds, huge jacuzzi/rock pool and stunning imaginative decor*. Superb Lakeside Castlelough Restaurant. New Devils Punch Bowl Bar with traditional music during busy season. "A little bit of heaven on earth."

WEB: www.lakehotel.com

Member of Irish Family Hotels

B&B from £35.00 to £90.00
€44.44 to €114.28

TONY HUGGARD
Managing Director

American Express
Diners
Mastercard
Visa

Special Half Board Rates

64 64

Closed 04 December - 12 February

LIME COURT

MUCKROSS ROAD, KILLARNEY,
CO. KERRY
TEL: 064-34547 FAX: 064-34121
EMAIL: limecrt@iol.ie

GUESTHOUSE ★★★ MAP 2 E 4

Lime Court has the perfect location, 3*** quality and superb standards. Just 5 minutes walk from town, easy off-street parking, on the main entrance route to Killarney National Park (over 26,000 acres) and on the Ring of Kerry Road. All room types available, singles, doubles, twins, triples and family rooms. Lime Court is a purpose-built guesthouse and family run to ensure you have a relaxing and pleasurable stay.

WEB: www.lime-court.com

B&B from £20.00 to £30.00
€25.39 to €38.09

GERALDINE & ALAN COURTNEY
Owners/Managers

American Express
Mastercard
Visa

10% discount on 3 or more nights

16 16

Closed 23 - 27 December

Room rates are IR£ per room per night

LINDEN HOUSE HOTEL

NEW ROAD, KILLARNEY,
CO. KERRY
TEL: 064-31379 FAX: 064-31196

HOTEL ★★ MAP 2 E 4

Situated in a quiet tree lined avenue 2 minutes walk from the town centre. Linden House is under the personal supervision of Peter and Ann Knoblauch. The Linden Restaurant has an enviable reputation for good food prepared by owner chef. Year after year, guests return to Linden House, ample proof that you, too, will be made welcome and comfortable during your stay in beautiful Killarney.

B&B from £26.00 to £32.00
€33.01 to €40.63

ANN & PETER KNOBLAUCH
Owners/Chef

Mastercard

Visa

☺ Special Offer: 3 nights B&B and 2 Dinners from £112.00 to £130.00

20 19

HOTELS

Closed 15 November - 01 February

MCCARTHY'S TOWN HOUSE

19 HIGH STREET, KILLARNEY,
CO. KERRY
TEL: 064-35655 FAX: 064-35745
EMAIL: mcth@eircom.net

GUESTHOUSE ★★★ MAP 2 E 4

McCarthy's Townhouse is the combination of everything you would expect during a visit to Killarney. Crock O'Gold Pub, live traditional music, splendid bedrooms, great restaurant, breakfast room, guests lounge, direct dial telephone, TV and hairdryer. The twenty five years experience of Con & May McCarthy is reflected in the warm, comfortable and welcoming atmosphere you feel in the McCarthy's Townhouse. Positively enjoy a visit to Killarney. Secure private car park.

WEB: www.iol.ie/kerry-insight/mccarthys

B&B from £25.00 to £30.00
€31.74 to €38.09

CORNELIUS & MAY MCCARTHY
Owners/Managers

American Express

Mastercard

Visa

8 8

HOTELS

Open All Year

MCSWEENEY ARMS HOTEL

COLLEGE STREET, KILLARNEY,
CO. KERRY
TEL: 064-31211 FAX: 064-34553
EMAIL: sales@mcsweeneyarms.com

HOTEL ★★★ MAP 2 E 4

The McSweeney Arms Hotel is situated in the heart of Killarney Town. Small, cosy and run to a very high standard by your hosts Tony and Pauline McSweeney. There are 28 bedrooms with private bathroom, direct dial telephone, colour TV and hairdryer. Our bar and restaurant caters for all tastes with emphasis on traditional Irish food. Local amenities are four 18 hole championship golf courses also two 9 hole courses and the Killarney National Park.

WEB: www.mcsweeneyarms.com

B&B from £40.00 to £60.00
€50.79 to €76.18

TONY MCSWEENEY
Proprietor

American Express

Diners

Mastercard

Visa

28 28

HOTELS

Closed 05 January - 28 February

B&B rates are IR£ per person sharing per night incl. Breakfast

MOUNTAIN VIEW GUEST HOUSE

MUCKROSS ROAD, KILLARNEY, CO. KERRY
TEL: 064-33293 FAX: 064-37295
EMAIL: tguerin@indigo.ie

GUESTHOUSE ★★ MAP 2 E 4

Mountain View Guest House offers the highest standard of accommodation by friendly and efficient staff. All rooms are en suite with direct dial phone, tea/coffee making facilities, multi channel televisions and hairdryers. Mountain View Guest House is located only 6 minutes walk from Killarney Town Centre and 3 minutes from the Gleneagle Country Club on the famous Ring of Kerry scenic route close to Ross Castle, Ross Golf Club, Muckross House, Torc Waterfall.

B&B from £18.00 to £28.00
€22.86 to €35.56

TIMOTHY GUERIN
Owner

American Express
Mastercard
Visa

66

Closed 03 January - 10 March

MUCKROSS PARK HOTEL

MUCKROSS VILLAGE, KILLARNEY, CO. KERRY
TEL: 064-31938 FAX: 064-31965
EMAIL: muckrossparkhotel@eircom.net

HOTEL ★★★★ MAP 2 E 4

Muckross Park Hotel is set in the heart of Killarney's National Park, comprising of 27 superior rooms, including suites. Molly Darcy's, our award winning, traditional Irish pub and restaurant is an experience not to be missed. Situated 4km outside Killarney, and adjacent to Muckross House and Abbey. Local amenities include golf, boating, fishing, horse riding and hillwalking.

WEB: www.muckrosspark.com

B&B from £49.00 to £85.00
€62.22 to €107.93

PATRICIA SHANAHAN
General Manager

American Express
Diners
Mastercard
Visa

 Special Offers Available

27 27

Closed 20 November - 12 February

OAKLAND HOUSE

CORK ROAD, KILLARNEY, CO. KERRY
TEL: 064-37286 FAX: 064-37991
EMAIL: oakland@eircom.net

GUESTHOUSE ★★ MAP 2 E 4

Oakland House is a new family run guesthouse on the main Cork Road. 1km from town centre, bus and train stations. All rooms en suite with TV, direct dial phone. Golf, fishing, pony trekking, leisure centres nearby. All scenic tours arranged. Guest lounge with tea/coffee making facilities. Launderette, supermarket, post office, bureau de change approximately 100 metres. Visa, Amex, MasterCard, vouchers. Personal attention and a warm welcome awaits you at Oakland House.

B&B from £20.00 to £22.00
€25.39 to €27.93

DAVID & NOREEN HEGARTY
Proprietors

American Express
Mastercard
Visa

8 8

Closed 24 - 26 December

Room rates are IR£ per room per night

OLD WEIR LODGE

MUCKROSS ROAD, KILLARNEY,
CO. KERRY
TEL: 064-35593 FAX: 064-35583
EMAIL: oldweirlodge@eircom.net

GUESTHOUSE ★★★★ MAP 2 E 4

A purpose built, family-run, Tudor designed, magnificent house, conveniently located 500m from the centre of Killarney Town, within 1km of Killarney National Park. Set in landscaped garden with 30 en suite king sized bedrooms, with bath and power shower, direct dial phone, orthopaedic beds, multi-channel TV, hairdryer, tea/coffee facilities. 2 spacious lounges, private parking, with home baking a speciality. Friendly, relaxed atmosphere ensures an enjoyable stay. Ground floor rooms.

WEB: www.oldweirlodge.com

B&B from £25.00 to £35.00
€31.74 to €44.44

MAUREEN & DERMOT
O'DONOGHUE Proprietors
American Express
Diners
Mastercard
Visa

30 30

Closed 23 - 26 December

RANDLES COURT CLARION HOTEL

MUCKROSS ROAD, KILLARNEY,
CO. KERRY
TEL: 064-35333 FAX: 064-35206
EMAIL: randles@iol.ie

HOTEL ★★★★ MAP 2 E 4

On main road to Killarney National Park & Lakes 5 minutes from town close to championship golf courses fishing etc. Formerly a residential rectory, built in 1906, it was elegantly developed into a superior 49 roomed 4**** deluxe hotel in 1992 by the Randles Family. Warm friendly welcome, renowned & exquisite cuisine. Grandly spacious, luxurious rooms. Fine art, antique collections and relaxing atmosphere are just a few reasons why our guests return again. Special car hire rates available.

WEB: www.randleshotels.com

Member of Choice Hotels Ireland

B&B from £40.00 to £80.00
€50.79 to €101.58

TOM RANDLES
General Manager
American Express
Diners
Mastercard
Visa

 Weekend special from £99.00

49 49

Closed 20 - 28 December

RIVERMERE

MUCKROSS ROAD, KILLARNEY,
CO. KERRY
TEL: 064-37933 FAX: 064-37944
EMAIL: rivermereguesthouse@eircom.net

GUESTHOUSE ★★★★ MAP 2 E 4

Rivermere is a custom built, family run 4**** guesthouse within walking distance of Lakes and National Park and only 7 minutes walk from town centre. All rooms are spacious with TV, radio, direct dial phone, orthopaedic beds, bath, power showers, hairdryer. Rivermere is in a delightful setting and combines luxury with charm, elegance and serenity, walkers and golfers paradise. Drying room available. Private parking. Choose from our delicious breakfast menu. A warm welcome awaits you.

B&B from £25.00 to £42.00
€31.74 to €53.33

HANNAH & ANDREW KISSANE
Proprietors
Mastercard
Visa

8 8

Closed 01 November - 09 March

B&B rates are IR£ per person sharing per night incl. Breakfast

RIVERSIDE HOTEL

MUCKROSS ROAD, KILLARNEY, CO. KERRY
TEL: 064-39200   FAX: 064-39202
EMAIL: stay@riversidehotelkillarney.com

HOTEL P   MAP 2 E 4

Located on the Muckross Road, the main road to Killarney National Park and Lakes. Just 5 minutes from town. The hotel boasts a choice of deluxe rooms and suites. All bedrooms are equipped with state of the art interactive TVs with movie channels, computer points and direct dial telephones. Our fashionable Bacchus Restaurant serves both traditional and international cuisine. A warm welcome awaits you.

WEB: www.irishcourthotel.com

Member of Irish Court Hotel Group

B&B from £30.00 to £80.00
€38.09 to €101.58

UNA YOUNG
General Manager

American Express
Diners
Mastercard
Visa

☺ Weekend specials from £89.00

69 69

alc Inet

IRISH
HOTELS
FEDERATION

Open All Year

ROSS HOTEL

KENMARE PLACE, KILLARNEY, CO. KERRY
TEL: 064-31855   FAX: 064-31139
EMAIL: ross@kph.iol.ie

HOTEL ★★★   MAP 2 E 4

A warm and friendly welcome awaits you at the family owned Ross Hotel, established since 1929. Located directly within the town of Killarney, this elegant hotel has a perfect combination of old world character, superb cuisine and friendly attentive service. Private car parking and leisure facilties are available at our sister hotel, the Killarney Park Hotel. We are pleased to arrange for you golf on Kerry's premier courses, fishing, horseriding or guided walks.

B&B from £36.00 to £48.00
€45.71 to €60.95

JANET & PADRAIG TREACY
Proprietors

American Express
Diners
Mastercard
Visa

☺ Weekend Specials from £85.00

32 32

IRISH
HOTELS
FEDERATION

Closed 07 December - 28 February

Room rates are IR£ per room per night

SCOTTS GARDENS HOTEL

KILLARNEY,
CO. KERRY
TEL: 064-31060 FAX: 064-36656

HOTEL U   MAP 2 E 4

Newly refurbished town centre hotel with private carpark facilities. 52 3*** standard bedrooms with direct dial phone, hairdryer, satellite TV, tea/coffee facilities. Adjacent to shops, restaurants, pubs, churches and Killarney National Park. Tours, cruises, golf, and fishing arranged. Entertainment nightly July/August and on weekends during the rest of the year.

B&B from £30.00 to £55.00
€38.09 to €69.84

MAURICE EOIN O'DONOGHUE
Proprietor

American Express
Mastercard
Visa

52 52

Closed 24 - 26 December

SLIEVE BLOOM MANOR GUESTHOUSE

MUCKROSS ROAD, KILLARNEY,
CO. KERRY
TEL: 064-34237 FAX: 064-35055
EMAIL: slievebloomanor@eircom.net

GUESTHOUSE ★★★   MAP 2 E 4

This charming 3*** guesthouse has a premier location on Muckross Road only 7 minutes walk to Killarney Town and gateway to Killarney's world famous National Park and lakes. Rooms are tastefully furnished with all facilities, varied breakfast menu available, private parking and store for bicycles etc. Local amenities include superb golf at Killarney's 2 renowned courses, horse riding and fishing. Leisure centre close by. All tours arranged. Looking forward to your visit.

B&B from £18.00 to £25.00
€22.86 to €31.74

TERESA CLERY
Proprietor

Mastercard
Visa

11 11

Closed 15 December - 01 February

TORC GREAT SOUTHERN HOTEL

KILLARNEY,
CO. KERRY
TEL: 064-31611 FAX: 064-31824
EMAIL: res@torc.gsh.ie

HOTEL ★★★   MAP 2 E 4

A 3*** modern hotel situated in beautiful gardens, just 5 minutes from Killarney Town. 94 rooms, all en suite, with direct dial phone, hairdryer, radio, tea/coffee making facilities and colour TV. Leisure facilities include indoor heated swimming pool, steamroom, jacuzzi. Outdoor tennis courts. Superbly located for golfing at Killarney's championship courses. An ideal base from which to tour the Kerry region. Bookable worldwide through UTELL International or Central Reservations 01-214 4800.

WEB: www.gsh.ie

Room Rate from £69.00 to £103.50
€87.61 to €131.42

FREDA DARCY
General Manager

American Express
Diners
Mastercard
Visa

Weekend specials from £89.00

94 94

Closed 10 October - 10 April

B&B rates are IR£ per person sharing per night incl. Breakfast

TUSCAR LODGE

GOLF COURSE ROAD, FOSSA,
KILLARNEY, CO. KERRY
TEL: 064-31978   FAX: 064-31978
EMAIL: tuscar-lodge@ireland.com

GUESTHOUSE ★★ MAP 2 E 4

Tuscar Lodge is a family run guest house. The proprietress Mrs Fitzgerald and her family always ensure that the guests have an enjoyable stay. Situated in scenic surroundings overlooking Loch Lein, with a magnificent view of the Magillycuddy Reeks. With its own car park, it is very central for touring the beauty spots of West Cork and Kerry. Pony trekking, boating, fishing and mountain climbing, all within easy range. Very near Killarney's three championship golf courses.

B&B from £18.00 to £25.00
€22.85 to €31.74

EILEEN FITZGERALD
Proprietor

🛏️🚶🕿TC☀☼U🅟
10 10

Closed 01 November - 28 February

WOODLAWN HOUSE

WOODLAWN ROAD, KILLARNEY,
CO. KERRY
TEL: 064-37844   FAX: 064-36116
EMAIL: awrenn@eircom.net

GUESTHOUSE ★★★ MAP 2 E 4

Old style charm and hospitality. Family run. Relaxed atmosphere. All modern conveniences. Ideally located 5 minutes walk from town centre. Near leisure centre, lakes and golf courses. Tours arranged. Private parking. Decorated with natural pine wood. Orthopaedic beds dressed in white cotton and linen. Irish and vegetarian menus. Our wholesome breakfasts include freshly squeezed orange juice, homemade preserves and bread. Early bird breakfast also available. A warm welcome assured.

WEB: www.kerry-insight.com/woodlawnhouse

B&B from £25.00 to £35.00
€31.74 to €44.44

JAMES & ANNE WRENN

| Mastercard |
| Visa |

🛏️🚶🕿TC☀☼U🅟🅟S
9 9

Closed 01 - 29 December

BIANCONI

KILLORGLIN, RING OF KERRY,
CO. KERRY
TEL: 066-976 1146   FAX: 066-976 1950

GUESTHOUSE ★★★ MAP 1 D 4

Family run inn on the Ring of Kerry. Gateway to Dingle Peninsula, Killarney 18km. On the road to Glencar - famous for its scenery, lakes, hill walking and mountain climbing. Famous for its table. High standard of food in bar. Table d'hôte and à la carte available. 50 minutes to Waterville, Tralee & Ballybunion golf courses. 15 minutes to Dooks & Beaufort courses. 5 minutes to Killorglin Course. 15 mins to Killarney Course. Private access to Caragh Lake. Own boat. Mentioned by many guides.

B&B from £35.00 to £40.00
€44.44 to €50.78

RAY SHEEHY
Owner

| American Express |
| Diners |
| Mastercard |
| Visa |

🛏️🚶🕿TCCM☀U🎵🎮alc
15 15

IRISH HOTELS FEDERATION

Closed 23 - 29 December

Room rates are IR£ per room per night

GROVE LODGE GUESTHOUSE

KILLARNEY ROAD, KILLORGLIN,
CO. KERRY
TEL: 066-976 1157 FAX: 066-976 2330
EMAIL: info@grovelodge.com

GUESTHOUSE ★★★ MAP 1 D 4

Ideally located for all your holiday activities; golfing, fishing, hill walking, sightseeing, beaches, Ring of Kerry/Ring of Dingle, with local gourmet restaurants & pub entertainment. (5 min walk from town centre). We invite you to share your holiday with us in our newly refurbished, spacious & luxurious accommodation, situated on 3 acres of mature gardens & woodlands, fronted by the River Laune & McGillycuddy Reeks Mountains & savour our speciality gourmet breakfasts. RAC, AA ◆◆◆◆.

WEB: www.grovelodge.com

B&B from £28.00 to £36.00
€35.55 to €45.71

DELIA & FERGUS FOLEY
Owners & Managers

American Express
Diners
Mastercard
Visa

Closed 22 - 29 December

WESTFIELD HOUSE

KILLORGLIN,
CO. KERRY
TEL: 066-976 1909 FAX: 066-976 1996
EMAIL: westhse@iol.ie

GUESTHOUSE ★★★ MAP 1 D 4

Westfield House is a family run guesthouse. All rooms are bright & spacious en suite, orthopaedic beds, direct dial telephone, TV, tea/coffee maker. Extra large family room available. We are situated on the Ring of Kerry in a quiet peaceful location only 5 minutes walk from town with panoramic views of MacGillycuddy Reeks. There are five 18 hole golf courses within 20 minutes drive. Recognised stop for many weary cyclists. Ideal location for the hillwalker and climber.

B&B from £22.50 to £25.00
€28.57 to €31.74

LEONARD CLIFFORD
Proprietor

Mastercard
Visa

Open All Year

LISTOWEL ARMS HOTEL

THE SQUARE, LISTOWEL,
CO. KERRY
TEL: 068-21500 FAX: 068-22524

HOTEL ★★★ MAP 2 E 6

In a tranquil corner of Listowel's old square, the Listowel Arms Hotel is a haven of comfort and hospitality, an establishment with a proud tradition of fine food, and discreet service, a quiet retreat, a warm and intimate meeting place. Famous for its annual race meeting, Listowel is an ideal location to explore the famous Ring of Kerry, Dingle Peninsula and Lakes of Killarney. Tee times can be reserved at nearby world famous Ballybunion Golf Club along with Listowel Golf Club.

B&B from £35.00 to £75.00
€44.44 to €95.23

KEVIN O'CALLAGHAN
Director

American Express
Diners
Mastercard
Visa

Closed 24 - 26 December

B&B rates are IR£ per person sharing per night incl. Breakfast

MOORINGS

PORTMAGEE,
CO. KERRY
TEL: 066-947 7108   FAX: 066-947 7220
EMAIL: moorings@iol.ie

GUESTHOUSE ★★★   MAP 1 B 3

The Moorings is a family owned guesthouse & restaurant overlooking the picturesque fishing port in Portmagee. Excellent cuisine, specialising in locally caught seafood. Adjacent to the Moorings is the Bridge Bar, also run by the family, here you can enjoy a wonderful night of music, song & dance. The Moorings is central to all local amenities including angling, diving, watersports, 18 hole golf course etc. Trips to Skellig Michael can be arranged. Recently awarded RAC ◆◆◆◆.

WEB: www.moorings.ie

B&B from £25.00 to £35.00
€31.74 to €44.44

GERARD & PATRICIA KENNEDY
Proprietors

Mastercard

Visa

14 14

Closed 01 November - 01 March

PARKNASILLA GREAT SOUTHERN HOTEL

SNEEM,
CO. KERRY
TEL: 064-45122   FAX: 064-45323
EMAIL: res@parknasilla.gsh.ie

HOTEL ★★★★   MAP 1 C 3

Acknowledged as one of Ireland's finest hotels, Parknasilla is a 19th century house set in 300 acres of grounds. A classically individual hotel with 84 bedrooms equipped with every modern amenity. Leisure facilities include indoor heated swimming pool, sauna, steam room, jacuzzi, hydrotherapy baths, outdoor hot tub, pony trekking, clay pigeon shooting, archery, water skiing, private 9 hole golf course - special green fees for guests. UTELL International or Central Reservations 01-214 4800

WEB: www.gsh.ie

B&B from £103.00 to £120.00
€130.78 to €152.37

JIM FEENEY
General Manager

American Express
Diners
Mastercard
Visa

☺ Weekend special from £145.00

84 84

Open All Year

TAHILLA COVE COUNTRY HOUSE

TAHILLA, NEAR SNEEM,
CO. KERRY
TEL: 064-45204   FAX: 064-45104
EMAIL: tahillacove@eircom.net

GUESTHOUSE ★★★   MAP 1 D 3

Travel writers have described this family-run, fully licensed seashore guesthouse as the most idyllic spot in Ireland - the haunt of Irish/British dignitaries. Located on the Ring of Kerry seashore. 14 acre estate boasts mature gardens & private pier. Ideal place for a relaxing holiday/touring centre. Each room has en suite facilities, phone, TV, radio, hairdryer, iron and tea/coffee facilities. Log fires, superb views, home cooking. Take Sneem Road from Kenmare (N70).

WEB: www.sneem.com/tahillacove.html

B&B from £38.00 to £43.00
€48.25 to €54.60

JAMES/DEIRDRE/CHAS
WATERHOUSE Owners

American Express
Diners
Mastercard
Visa

☺   7 B&B and 6 Dinners from £360.00

9 9

Closed 15 October - 01 April

Room rates are IR£ per room per night

ABBEY GATE HOTEL

MAINE STREET, TRALEE,
CO. KERRY
TEL: 066-712 9888   FAX: 066-712 9821
EMAIL: abbeygate@iol.ie

HOTEL ★★★   MAP 1 D 5

Welcome, the Abbey Gate Hotel is located in the heart of Tralee. All 100 rooms are spacious with full facilities. The Old Market Place pub is Tralee's liveliest venue with great pub grub served all day and casual dining in Bistro Marché at night. Or try our intimate Vineyard Restaurant for the best of Irish and continental dishes. The Abbey Gate Hotel is your gateway to the delights of Kerry!

B&B from £30.00 to £55.00
€38.09 to €69.84

PATRICK DILLON
General Manager

American Express
Diners
Mastercard
Visa

Weekend specials from £75.00

100 100

Closed 24 - 26 December

BALLYGARRY HOUSE HOTEL

KILLARNEY ROAD, TRALEE,
CO. KERRY
TEL: 066-712 1233   FAX: 066-712 7630

HOTEL ★★★★   MAP 1 D 5

Ballygarry House Hotel invites you to relax by open fires and experience an air of wellbeing. Ideally situated for Kerry's magnificent golf courses, we can be found less than 1.5km from Tralee en route to Kerry Airport and Killarney (N22). This country house hotel boasts 30 luxurious rooms overlooking beautiful landscaped gardens. Our Riverside Restaurant offers modern and traditional cuisine in an intimate atmosphere. A warm welcome awaits you.

Member of Signature Hotels Collection

B&B from £45.00 to £65.00
€57.14 to €82.53

OWEN MCGILLICUDDY
Proprietor

American Express
Mastercard
Visa

30 30

Closed 20 - 28 December

BALLYSEEDE CASTLE HOTEL

BALLYSEEDY, TRALEE,
CO. KERRY
TEL: 066-712 5799   FAX: 066-712 5287

HOTEL ★★★   MAP 1 D 5

Ballyseede Castle Hotel is a casual, almost cosy 15th century castle on 35 hectares of parkland. The castle boasts a fine selection of continental cuisine as well as many traditional Irish dishes. Located on the main Tralee/Killarney Road within easy reach of Kerry's five magnificent golf courses, Ballybunion, Waterville, Killarney, Dooks and Barrow, the recently designed course for Tralee by Arnold Palmer. Ideally situated for touring the Ring of Kerry and Dingle Peninsula.

B&B from £70.00 to £100.00
€88.88 to €126.97

BART W O'CONNOR
Managing Director

Mastercard
Visa

12 12

Open All Year

B&B rates are IR£ per person sharing per night incl. Breakfast

BARROW HOUSE

WEST BARROW, TRALEE,
CO. KERRY
TEL: 066-713 6437   FAX: 066-713 6402
EMAIL: info@barrowhouse.com

GUESTHOUSE U   MAP 1 D 5

Built in 1723, Barrow House, located on Barrow Harbour next to the superb Arnold Palmer Tralee Golf Club (R558). Set on 4.5 acres of land with magnificent views of Slieve Mish Mountains and Dingle Peninsula. Elegantly refurbished to superior standards with luxurious suites and deluxe rooms. Personal attention and the tranquillity and serenity of our setting, yet minutes away from golf, angling, bird watching, sailing & golden beaches. Award-winning restaurants and pubs close by.

WEB: www.barrowhouse.com

B&B from £30.00 to £60.00
€38.09 to €76.18

NOELLE CROSBIE
Manager

Mastercard
Visa

14 14
FAX

Closed 20 December - 14 February

BRANDON COURT HOTEL

JAMES STREET, TRALEE,
CO. KERRY
TEL: 066-712 9666   FAX: 066-712 9690
EMAIL: louise@brandonhotel.ie

HOTEL U   MAP 1 D 5

The concept - quality at a fixed price. Bright, modern and spacious rooms, each with its own bathroom, colour TV, direct dial telephone and tea/coffee making facilities. The price remains fixed when a room is occupied by 1, 2 or 3 adults or up to 2 adults and 2 children. Bright, spacious public areas, cosy bar facilities and restaurant serving breakfast and light evening meals. Located in Tralee's old quarter, adjacent to Siamsa Tire, Aqua Dome and Kerry County Museum.

WEB: www.brandonhotel.ie

B&B from £32.50 to £60.00
€41.27 to €76.18

MARY ROSE STAFFORD
General Manager

American Express
Diners
Mastercard
Visa

49 49

Closed 01 January - 31 May

Kerry County Museum

Kerry County Museum at the Ashe Memorial Hall is the ideal starting point for tours of County Kerry. It consists of 3 superb attractions which tell the story of Kerry and Ireland over 8,000 years:

Kerry in Colour - a panoramic multi-image audio-visual tour of County Kerry featuring scenery, historic sites, people and traditions.

Kerry County Museum - a museum with a difference. Interactive media and reconstructions stand side-by-side with priceless treasures dating from the Stone and Bronze Age to the Present Day. The Museum also hosts major international temporary exhibitions.

Geraldine Tralee - This is well worth a detour on its own! Imagine being transported 600 years back in time to the Middle Ages and experiencing a day in the life of an Irish medieval town. Visitors are seated in time cars and brought on a fascinating journey through the reconstructed streets, houses, Abbey and Castle of Geraldine Tralee complete with sounds and smells. Commentaries in 7 languages.

Opening Hours: 9.30 - 18.00 hrs (12.00 noon - 16.30 Nov 1st - Dec 23rd) March 17 - December 23. Closed Dec. 24-26, Jan. 1 - March 16.

GROUP BOOKINGS - Kerry County Museum,

Ashe Memorial Hall, Denny Street, Tralee, Co. Kerry, Ireland.

Telephone: **066 7127777**
Facsimile: **066 7127444**

Room rates are IR£ per room per night

CO. KERRY
TRALEE

BRANDON HOTEL

PRINCES STREET, TRALEE,
CO. KERRY
TEL: 066-712 3333   FAX: 066-712 5019
EMAIL: louise@brandonhotel.ie

HOTEL ★★★   MAP 1 D 5

This renowned, privately owned premises is located in the heart of Tralee Town, close to shopping and cultural interests. The hotel offers a wide range of accommodation - standard, superior and deluxe rooms - and a choice of bars and restaurants. It is also equipped with full leisure centre incorporating swimming pool, sauna and steamroom and has extensive conference facilities. The Brandon Hotel is easily reached by mainline rail or flying to Kerry County Airport just 10 miles away.

WEB: www.brandonhotel.ie

B&B from £35.00 to £70.00
€44.44 to €88.88

MARY ROSE STAFFORD
General Manager

American Express
Diners
Mastercard
Visa

Closed 22 - 29 December

BROOK MANOR LODGE

FENIT ROAD, TRALEE,
CO. KERRY
TEL: 066-712 0406   FAX: 066-712 7552
EMAIL: brookmanor@eircom.net

GUESTHOUSE ★★★★   MAP 1 D 5

A warm welcome awaits you at our new 4**** luxurious, family-run lodge. Only minutes drive from Tralee, golden beaches and Arnold Palmer designed golf course. 30 minutes from Killarney. 40 minutes from Ballybunion. The Lodge is situated in acres of meadowlands and surrounded by a babbling brook. All our rooms are en suite with full facilities. Brook Manor Lodge is the ideal place for the perfect holiday.

Member of Premier Guesthouses

B&B from £30.00 to £45.00
€38.09 to €57.14

MARGARET & VINCENT
O'SULLIVAN Owners

American Express
Mastercard
Visa

Open All Year

GLENDUFF HOUSE

KIELDUFF, TRALEE,
CO. KERRY
TEL: 066-713 7105   FAX: 066-713 7099
EMAIL: glenduffhouse@eircom.net

GUESTHOUSE ★★★   MAP 1 D 5

Enter the old world charm of the 19th century in our family run period house set on 6 acres with mature gardens. Refurbished to give the comforts of the modern day, yet keeping its original character with antiques & paintings. Personal attention assured. Evening meals by pre-arrangement. Relax & enjoy a drink in our friendly bar. Also self catering cottages in courtyard. Ideally situated for golf and sports amenities. From Tralee take route to racecourse off N21 at Clash roundabout, continue for 4 1/2 miles. RAC ◆◆◆◆

WEB: www.tralee-insight.com/glenduff

B&B from £26.00 to £40.00
€33.01 to €50.79

SHEILA SUGRUE
Owner

Mastercard
Visa

Closed 01 November - 14 March

B&B rates are IR£ per person sharing per night incl. Breakfast

GRAND HOTEL

**DENNY STREET, TRALEE,
CO. KERRY**
TEL: 066-712 1499   FAX: 066-712 2877
EMAIL: info@grandhoteltralee.com

HOTEL ★★★   MAP 1 D 5

The Grand Hotel is a 3*** hotel situated in Tralee Town centre. Established in 1928, its open fires, ornate ceilings & mahogany furnishings offer guests old world charm in comfortable surroundings. All our rooms are equipped with direct dial phone, computer point, satellite TV and tea/coffee welcoming trays. Residents can avail of green fee reductions at Tralee Golf Club. Also reduced rates to the fabulous Aqua Dome Waterworld complex. Family rooms are available at discounted rates.

WEB: www.grandhoteltralee.com

B&B from £30.00 to £55.00
€38.09 to €69.84

DICK BOYLE
General Manager
American Express
Mastercard
Visa

☺ Weekend specials from £79.00

44 44

alc inet

Closed 24 - 27 December

MEADOWLANDS HOTEL

**OAKPARK, TRALEE,
CO. KERRY**
TEL: 066-718 0444   FAX: 066-718 0964
EMAIL: medlands@iol.ie

HOTEL ★★★★   MAP 1 D 5

A charming and intimate hotel, set in a tranquil corner of Tralee, on its own 3 acres with beautiful landscaped gardens. This small luxurious hotel comprises of 27 superbly appointed rooms including suites. Our gourmet restaurant specialises in the freshest of locally-caught seafood and shellfish cuisine. The Meadowlands is an ideal base for golfing enthusiasts and touring the Dingle Peninsula, Ring of Kerry, Killarney and West Cork. Experience an experience!

Member of MinOtel Ireland Hotel Group

B&B from £45.00 to £60.00
€57.14 to €76.18

JOHN PALMER
Manager
Mastercard
Visa

☺ Weekend specials from £100.00

27 27

S alc

Closed 24 - 26 December

OAKLEY HOUSE

**BALLYMULLEN, TRALEE,
CO. KERRY**
TEL: 066-712 1727   FAX: 066-712 1727

GUESTHOUSE ★★   MAP 1 D 5

Spacious period house with old world charm and character. Situated on main road (N70) to Dingle Peninsula, Killorglin and Ring of Kerry. Overlooking Slieve Mish Mountains. Ideal touring base. 8 minutes walk from town centre, National Folk Theatre, Medieval Experience. 10 minutes walk from Aqua Dome. Private car park, convenient to beaches, angling, golf, horseriding and pony trekking. Complementary Tea/Coffee available in our spacious TV lounge. A cead mile failte awaits you.

B&B from £20.00 to £22.00
€25.39 to €27.93

MICHAEL & PHILOMENA BENNIS
Proprietors
Mastercard
Visa

☺ Midweek Special from £57.00

7 7

Open All Year

Room rates are IR£ per room per night

TRALEE TOWNHOUSE

HIGH STREET, TRALEE,
CO. KERRY
TEL: 066-718 1111   FAX: 066-718 1222

GUESTHOUSE P   MAP 1 D 5

Centrally located beside all of Tralee's visitor attractions; - Siamsa Tire, Aqua Dome, Tralee Superbowl, Geraldine Experience, Kerry County Museum, Blennerville Windmill, Steam Train and the new Tralee Marina. Local amenities include - for the golf enthusiast, the world renowned Tralee & Ballybunion Golf Courses are only a few miles away. 2 excellent 9 hole courses are within 1 mile of the town centre. Fishing, horse riding, hillwalking, sports centre with indoor pool, etc.

B&B from £23.00 to £40.00
€29.20 to €50.79

ELEANOR COLLINS
Manager

Mastercard

Visa

20   20

Open All Year

BAY VIEW HOTEL

WATERVILLE,
CO. KERRY
TEL: 066-947 4122 FAX: 066-947 4504
EMAIL: bayviewwaterville@eircom.net

HOTEL CR   MAP 1 B 3

The Bay View Hotel has old world charm with beautiful spacious bedrooms with front rooms facing the Atlantic. On the Ring of Kerry in the middle of the village of Waterville the hotel is an ideal location for exploring the peninsula with its breathtaking scenery and archaeological sites. Make sure you visit the Sceilig Rock.

WEB: www.bayviewwaterville.com

B&B from £25.00 to £45.00
€31.74 to €57.14

MICHAEL O'SHEA
Manager

American Express

Mastercard

Visa

69   69

Closed 01 November - 01 March

BROOKHAVEN GUESTHOUSE

NEW LINE ROAD, WATERVILLE,
CO. KERRY
TEL: 066-947 4431 FAX: 066-947 4724
EMAIL: brookhaven@esatclear.ie

GUESTHOUSE ★★★   MAP 1 B 3

New, purpose built guesthouse, located on the scenic Ring of Kerry Route. Luxury spacious en suite rooms decorated to a high standard with all modern amenities. Rooms overlook the Atlantic Ocean and the renowned Waterville Golf Course. It is within easy reach of other scenic and challenging courses and to all local amenities; golfing, fishing, pony treking, sandy beaches, walking, cycling and gourmet restaurants. AA ◆◆◆. RAC Highly Acclaimed. Sparkling diamond accolade 1999.

WEB: www.euroka.com/waterville/brookhaven

B&B from £23.00 to £40.00
€29.20 to €50.79

MARY CLIFFORD
Proprietor

5   5

Closed 01 January - 01 March

B&B rates are IR£ per person sharing per night incl. Breakfast

BUTLER ARMS HOTEL

WATERVILLE,
CO. KERRY
TEL: 066-947 4144   FAX: 066-947 4520
EMAIL: reservations@butlerarms.com

HOTEL ★★★   MAP 1 B 3

This charming hotel, on the scenic Ring of Kerry, has been run by 4 generations of the Huggard Family. Tastefully furnished bedrooms, many with magnificent seaviews, cosy lounges, specializing in local seafood (AA 2 Red Rosettes) and the Fishermens Bar with its cosmopolitan ambience. Only 1mile from Waterville's Championship Golf Llinks. Renowned salmon & seatrout fishing, sandy beaches, horseriding, hill-walking.

WEB: www.butlerarms.com

Member of Manor House Hotels

B&B from £56.50 to £80.00
€71.74 to €101.58

MARY & PETER HUGGARD
Proprietors

American Express
Diners
Mastercard
Visa

Weekend specials from £99.00

30 30

Closed 20 October - 11 April

LAKELANDS FARM GUESTHOUSE

LAKE ROAD, WATERVILLE,
CO. KERRY
TEL: 066-947 4303   FAX: 066-947 4678
EMAIL: lakelands@eircom.net

GUESTHOUSE ★★★   MAP 1 B 3

Luxury family run guesthouse in unique location set on 100 acre estate on the south shore of Europe's best free salmon and sea trout lake. Smoking and non smoking lounges. Comfortable spacious en-suite bedrooms with all mod cons, some with balcony or jacuzzi. Proprietor professional angler with 10 motor boats. Private pools on River Inny. Convenient to Waterville Golf Course. For the golf enthusiast we have a complimentary 250 yards practice range.

WEB: www.kerrygems.ie/lakelands/

B&B from £22.00 to £32.00
€27.93 to €40.63

ANNE & FRANK DONNELLY
Proprietors

Mastercard
Visa

10 10

Closed 25 December

SMUGGLERS INN

CLIFF ROAD, WATERVILLE,
CO. KERRY
TEL: 066-947 4330   FAX: 066-947 4422

GUESTHOUSE ★★★   MAP 1 B 3

The Smugglers Inn, a family run inn with old world charm and character, quiet location on 2km sandy beach. Adjacent to Waterville Golf Course, near lake and sea fishing facilities and sporting activities. Very high standard in our gourmet seafood restaurant, meals prepared by chef proprietor Harry Hunt and son Henry. Dining room under supervision of his wife Lucille. Exceptional accommodation. Recommended by many good food guides. Breathtaking sea views and spectacular sunsets.

B&B from £25.00 to £40.00
€31.74 to €50.79

LUCILLE & HARRY HUNT
Proprietors

American Express
Diners
Mastercard
Visa

3 B&B and 3 Dinners from £145.00

14 14

Closed 31 October - 01 March

Room rates are IR£ per room per night

SHANNON
Romantic and Exciting

Your holiday in the Shannon Region can be as active or as placid as you choose. Whichever you choose, you are guaranteed relaxation and enjoyment. All the ingredients are there: the towering cliffs and golden beaches of Clare and North Kerry; the enigmatic rockscapes of the Burren; the gentle beauty of the rolling Slieve Bloom Mountains in South Offaly; Tipperary's fertile pastures and the woodland estates in the heart of County Limerick. And, of course, the mighty Shannon River, which has bestowed its riches on the surrounding countryside and glories in its beauty.

This is one of the few remaining places on earth where clean, unpolluted air is taken for granted.

You have the space to breathe, to refresh your spirit a universe away from frenetic and crowded cities.

There is a sense of timelessness aided by the many physical reminders of Ireland's turbulent past. Castles, forts and ancient churches, spanning centuries of history, abound. many have been lovingly restored.

At the famous Bunratty Castle, visitors can slip back in time and take part in a 15th century Mediaeval Banquet of romance and merriment. The Bunratty Folk Park, in the castle grounds, accurately recreates Irish village life at the turn of the century.

Sporting facilities, in contrast, are very much up to date. Imagine golfing in a magnificent, scenic setting or fishing some of the most productive and versatile fishing waters in Europe. Take to the saddle on horse-back and the countryside is yours.

If boating is your pleasure, the possibilities are, literally, limitless.

There are many elements to a really memorable holiday and the Shannon Region can provide them all. One of the most important is the feeling of being really welcome, of being valued. This intangible but very real feature of a Shannon holiday will be immediately evident in the sense of fun which you will encounter and an eagerness to treat you as an honoured guest.

In Ireland, enjoyment is an art form. Go to one of the many festivals in the Shannon Region and you will experience the art at its best. Entertainment, spontaneous or organised, is everywhere, so too is good food and good company. For further information contact: Tourist Information Office, Arthur's Quay, Limerick. Tel: 061 317522. Fax: 061 317939. Visit our website: www.shannon-dev.ie/tourism

BALLYVAUGHAN LODGE

BALLYVAUGHAN,
CO. CLARE
TEL: 065-707 7292 FAX: 065-707 7287
EMAIL: ballyvau@iol.ie

GUESTHOUSE ★★★ MAP 6 F 10

Located in the heart of Ballyvaughan, a small fishing village overlooking Galway Bay. A custom built modern guesthouse, dedicated to the comfort and relaxation of our guests. Each room en suite having TV, direct dial phone, tea/coffee making facilities, etc. Allow us to plan your carefree days in the most unspoilt natural environment imaginable, the Burren, including Neolithic caves, sea fishing, hill walking, cycling, Cliffs of Moher and the Aran Islands.

B&B from £20.00 to £28.00
€25.39 to €35.55

PAULINE BURKE
Owner

Mastercard

Visa

♿🛏🚗©♨CM✿∪🅿🅢⚓
8 8

IRISH HOTELS FEDERATION

Closed 25 - 26 December

CAPPABHAILE HOUSE

BALLYVAUGHAN,
CO. CLARE
TEL: 065-707 7260 FAX: 065-707 7300
EMAIL: cappabhaile@oceanfree.net

GUESTHOUSE ★★★ MAP 6 F 10

Relax, enjoy the peace & quiet, luxury & comfort and a warm family welcome at Cappabhaile House. All rooms generously sized with private bathrooms. We have scenic views of the Burren Mountains, Newtown Castle & Ailwee Cave. We have a private carpark, pitch & putt course, games room & the Burren Gallery, all FREE to our guests. Courtesy bus to facilitate hill walking, beaches, nature trails, pubs & restaurants. Perfect base for touring the Burren, Aran Islands and Connemara.

WEB: www.cappabhaile.com

B&B from £20.00 to £28.00
€25.39 to €35.55

MARGARET & CONOR FAHY
Proprietors

Mastercard

Visa

😊 Walks and archaeological tours from £50.00

♿🛏🚗🅣🅐©♨CM✿∪✓

IRISH HOTELS FEDERATION

Closed 05 November - 01 March

DRUMCREEHY HOUSE

BALLYVAUGHAN,
CO. CLARE
TEL: 065-707 7377 FAX: 065-707 7379
EMAIL: b&b@drumcreehyhouse.com

GUESTHOUSE ★★★ MAP 6 F 10

Delightful country style house overlooking Galway Bay and the surrounding Burren landscape. Open fires, antique furnishings plus a friendly and personal service by conscientious hosts Armin and Bernadette help to make your stay both enjoyable and memorable. Tastefully decorated rooms, all en suite and equipped with TV and direct dial phone. Extensive breakfast menu and simple country style cooking in a relaxed and homely atmosphere. Ideally located for touring Clare, Kerry and Galway.

WEB: www.drumcreehyhouse.com

B&B from £20.00 to £30.00
€25.39 to €38.09

A & B MOLONEY-GREFKES
Proprietors

Mastercard

Visa

😊 Weekend specials from £57.00

♿🛏🚗🅣©♨CM✿∪🅟🅢
10 10
♀

IRISH HOTELS FEDERATION

Open All Year

Room rates are IR£ per room per night

CO. CLARE
BALLYVAUGHAN

GREGANS CASTLE HOTEL

BALLYVAUGHAN,
CO. CLARE
TEL: 065-707 7005 FAX: 065-707 7111
EMAIL: res@gregans.ie

HOTEL ★★★★   MAP 6 F 10

4**** luxury hotel amid splendid Burren mountain scenery, overlooking Galway Bay. Country house comforts, turf fires, tranquillity, no TV in rooms. Award winning gardens, food, service, accommodations. Individually designed superior rooms/suites. Nearby ocean swimming, horse riding, hillwalking. Golf at Lahinch. Halfway between Kerry and Connemara using ferry. RAC Blue Ribbon winner. AA Red Stars award. 1 hour to Shannon Airport. Excellence of private ownership for 25 years.

WEB: www.gregans.ie

Member of Ireland's Blue Book

B&B from £55.00 to £73.00
€69.84 to €92.69

SIMON HADEN
Manager & Director

Mastercard

Visa

⌂♨☎🅣🅒♣CM✹⋃🅟🅟🅐🅓ℹ🚹
22 22

Closed 01 November - 27 March

HYLAND'S HOTEL

BALLYVAUGHAN,
CO. CLARE
TEL: 065-707 7037 FAX: 065-707 7131
EMAIL: hylands@eircom.net

HOTEL ★★★   MAP 6 F 10

A charming family run hotel whose present owners are 7th and 8th generation proudly carrying on the tradition for hospitality and good food. Experience bygone charm with modern day facilities, open turf fires, informal bars and restaurants specialising in the finest local seafood. An ideal base for the golfing and walking enthusiasts, exploring the unique Burren landscape, visiting the Aran Islands, touring the unspoilt Clare, Connemara and Kerry countrysides, truly an artist's haven.

WEB: www.iol.ie/hotels

Member of Village Inn Hotels

B&B from £39.00 to £46.50
€49.52 to €59.04

MARIE GREENE
Inn Keeper

American Express

Diners

Mastercard

Visa

☺ Weekend specials from £80.00

⌂♨☎🅣🅒CM⋃🎵🅟🅐🅐ℹ
30 30

Closed 06 January - 01 March

RUSHEEN LODGE

BALLYVAUGHAN,
CO. CLARE
TEL: 065-707 7092 FAX: 065-707 7152
EMAIL: rusheenl@iol.ie

GUESTHOUSE ★★★★   MAP 6 F 10

Rusheen Lodge is a superb 4**** family run guesthouse, nestling in a valley surrounded by the Burren Limestone Mountains noted for their rock formations and unique flora. A previous winner of the Small Hotel & Guesthouse of the Year award. The Lodge provides elegant and tastefully designed en suite bedrooms, dining room and residents' lounge ensuring a comfortable and relaxing stay. Excellent location for touring Clare, Kerry and Connemara.

WEB: www.rusheenlodge.com

B&B from £30.00 to £35.00
€38.09 to €44.44

JOHN & RITA MC GANN
Proprietors

American Express

Mastercard

Visa

☺   Stay 6 nights B&B and
7th night free

⌂♨☎🅣🅒✹⋃🅟🅢■
8 8

Closed 30 November - 01 February

B&B rates are IR£ per person sharing per night incl. Breakfast

BUNRATTY CASTLE HOTEL

BUNRATTY,
CO. CLARE
TEL: 061-707034 FAX: 061-364891
EMAIL: info@bunrattycastlehotel.iol.ie

HOTEL ★★★   MAP 6 G 7

The new Bunratty Castle Hotel is a 3*** Georgian hotel. Situated in the centre of Bunratty Village overlooking the historic Bunratty Castle and just across the road from Ireland's oldest pub, Durty Nellies. The rooms have been tastefully decorated in the traditional style. All rooms have air conditioning, satellite TV and have every modern comfort. Relax in Kathleens Irish Pub and Restaurant and enjoy great food. We welcome you to experience the warmth and hospitality here.

B&B from £50.00 to £60.00
€63.49 to €76.18

KATHLEEN MCLOUGHLIN
Director

American Express
Diners
Mastercard
Visa

59 59

álc   Inet

IRISH HOTELS FEDERATION

Closed 25 December

BUNRATTY GROVE

CASTLE ROAD, BUNRATTY,
CO. CLARE
TEL: 061-369579 FAX: 061-369561
EMAIL: bunrattygrove@eircom.net

GUESTHOUSE ★★★   MAP 6 G 7

Bunratty Grove is a purpose built luxurious guest house. This guesthouse is located within 3 minutes drive from Bunratty Castle and Folk Park and 10 minutes from Shannon Airport. Fishing, golfing, historical interests within a short distance. Ideally located for tourists arriving or departing Shannon Airport. Bookings for Bunratty and Knappogue Banquets taken on request. All rooms en suite with multi-channel TV, hair dryer, tea/coffee facilities and direct dial phone.

WEB: http://homepage.eircom.net/~bunrattygrove/

B&B from £22.50 to £30.00
€28.57 to €38.09

PETER & PATSY GOLDEN
Owners

Mastercard
Visa

9 9

IRISH HOTELS FEDERATION

Closed 30 October - 01 April

BUNRATTY MANOR HOTEL

BUNRATTY,
CO. CLARE
TEL: 061-707984 FAX: 061-360588
EMAIL: bunrattymanor@eircom.net

HOTEL P   MAP 6 G 7

A Manor House hotel designed to reflect the ambience and comforts associated with elegant living. Beautiful gardens, superb classical Italian cuisine prepared by David (including vegetarian), renowned for friendliness, comfort, tranquillity and hospitality. Bunratty Village - excellent restaurants, fun pubs, the Castle and shopping - is two minutes walk! Within easy reach of eleven Championship golf courses and breathtaking scenery. Tea/coffee facilities, ice, TV and ISDN.

WEB: www.bunrattymanor.net

B&B from £38.50 to £49.50
€48.88 to €62.85

GERRY HUGHES
Host

American Express
Diners
Mastercard
Visa

14 14

álc   Inet

IRISH HOTELS FEDERATION

Closed 24 - 27 December

Room rates are IR£ per room per night

BUNRATTY VIEW GUESTHOUSE

CRATLOE, NEAR BUNRATTY, CO. CLARE
TEL: 061-357352 FAX: 061-357491
EMAIL: bunrattyview@eircom.net

GUESTHOUSE ★★★ MAP 6 G 7

Bunratty View is a 3*** guesthouse located 10 minutes from Shannon Airport, 2 km from Bunratty Castle. Bedrooms have private bathroom, satellite TV, direct dial telephone, hair dryer, tea/coffee facilities, orthopaedic beds. Ideal for tourists arriving or departing Shannon Airport. Excellent location for touring Cliffs of Moher, Ailwee Caves, Lakes of Killaloe. Banquets for Bunratty and Knappogue booked on request. Recommended by leading guides for accommodation and hospitality.

B&B from £20.00 to £26.00
€25.39 to €33.01

JOE & MAURA BRODIE
Proprietors

Mastercard

Visa

Open All Year

BUNRATTY WOODS COUNTRY HOUSE

LOW ROAD, BUNRATTY, CO. CLARE
TEL: 061-369689 FAX: 061-369454
EMAIL: bunratty@iol.ie

GUESTHOUSE ★★★ MAP 6 G 7

Bunratty Woods is a 3*** luxurious guesthouse situated in the old grounds of Bunratty Castle (2 minutes drive) to Bunratty Castle and Folk Park and the renowned Durty Nellies Pub. All rooms are en suite with direct dial phone, TV, tea/coffee making facilities and hair dryer. Magnificent mountain views. Bunratty Woods is furnished with style and taste of a bygone era - featuring items such as a settle bed and a famine pot and many, many other items from yesteryear.

WEB: http://ireland.iol.ie/~bunratty

B&B from £22.50 to £27.50
€28.57 to €34.92

MAUREEN & PADDY O'DONOVAN
Owners

Diners

Mastercard

Visa

Closed 21 - 28 December

CRATLOE LODGE

SETRIGHTS CROSS, CRATLOE, NEAR BUNRATTY, CO. CLARE
TEL: 061-357168

GUESTHOUSE ★★★ MAP 6 G 7

Cratloe Lodge is a 3*** luxury guesthouse purpose built to a high standard. Bedrooms are all en suite with satellite TV, direct dial phone and trouser press. Complimentary tea/coffee available on arrival. This guesthouse is located 10 minutes from Shannon Airport and 5 minutes from Bunratty Castle. Excellent location for those arriving or departing Shannon Airport. Ideal as starting point for touring Cliffs of Moher, Ailwee Caves and the Lakes of Killaloe.

B&B from £19.00 to £25.00
€24.13 to €31.74

TOM & MAURA GALVIN

Mastercard

Visa

Open All Year

B&B rates are IR£ per person sharing per night incl. Breakfast

FITZPATRICK BUNRATTY

BUNRATTY,
CO. CLARE
TEL: 061-361177 FAX: 061-471252
EMAIL: bunratty@fitzpatricks.com

HOTEL U MAP 6 G 7

Situated in wooded grounds in Bunratty Village against the backdrop of the medieval castle and folk park. Discover village life with lively pubs, colourful restaurants and shops. 4 miles from Shannon. Hotel facilities include excellent bar and restaurant, fitness centre and rooms with bath, satellite TV and direct dial phone. Four 18 hole championship golf courses within easy drive. Horse riding available locally. The ideal choice for your stay in the Mid-West.

WEB: www.fitzpatrickhotels.com

B&B from £64.00 to £70.00
€81.26 to €88.88

SANDRA DOYLE
General Manager

American Express
Diners
Mastercard
Visa

3 B&B and 3 Dinners from £220.00

115 115

Closed 24 - 26 December

ARAN VIEW HOUSE HOTEL & RESTAURANT

COAST ROAD, DOOLIN,
CO. CLARE
TEL: 065-707 4061 FAX: 065-707 4540
EMAIL: bookings@aranview.com

HOTEL ★★★ MAP 5 E 9

A Georgian house built in 1736, has a unique position commanding panoramic views of the Aran Islands, the Burren region and the Cliffs of Moher. Situated on 100 acres of farmland, Aran View echoes spaciousness, comfort and atmosphere in its restaurant and bar. Menus are based on the best of local produce, fish being a speciality. All rooms with private bathroom, colour TV and direct dial phone. Visitors are assured of a warm and embracing welcome at the Aran View House Hotel.

WEB: www.aranview.com

B&B from £35.00 to £50.00
€44.44 to €63.49

THERESA & JOHN LINNANE
Proprietors

American Express
Diners
Mastercard
Visa

Weekend specials from £90.00

19 19

Closed 31 October - 01 April

BALLINALACKEN CASTLE COUNTRY HOUSE & RESTAURANT

COAST ROAD, DOOLIN,
CO. CLARE
TEL: 065-707 4025 FAX: 065-707 4025
EMAIL: ballinalackencastle@eircom.net

HOTEL ★★★ MAP 5 E 9

A romantic peaceful oasis steeped in history and ambience offering the most spectacular views of the Cliffs of Moher, Aran Islands, Atlantic Ocean and Connemara Hills. Built in 1840 as the home of Lord O'Brien. Family members radiate a warm friendly welcome. Award winning chef Frank Sheedy (son-in-law) makes dining here an experience to remember. Peat and log fires add to the cosy atmosphere. Ideal base for exploring Clare. Recommended by Egon Ronay, Michelin, Fodor, Frommer, RAC. Charming Hotels of Ireland.

WEB: www.ballinalackencastle.com

B&B from £36.00 to £50.00
€45.71 to €63.49

MARY AND DENIS
O'CALLAGHAN Proprietors

American Express
Diners
Mastercard
Visa

12 12

Closed 05 October - 31 March

Room rates are IR£ per room per night

CULLINAN'S RESTAURANT & GUESTHOUSE

DOOLIN,
CO. CLARE
TEL: 065-707 4183 FAX: 065-707 4239
EMAIL: cullinans@eircom.net

GUESTHOUSE ★★★ MAP 5 E 9

Cullinan's Restaurant and Guesthouse, centrally located in the heart of Doolin provides spacious and elegant bedrooms, all en suite with tea/coffee making facilities, direct dial phone, hairdryers and a comfortable TV lounge. Idyllic setting with highly acclaimed restaurant overlooking the Aille River. Imaginative menus are carefully chosen by the chef/owner, specialising in the freshest of locally caught seafood. Natural stone and wood combined gives Cullinan's a cozy, comfortable atmosphere.

B&B from £18.00 to £25.00
€22.86 to €31.74

CAROL & JAMES CULLINAN
Owners
Mastercard
Visa

Closed 24 - 25 December

DOONMACFELIM HOUSE

DOOLIN,
CO. CLARE
TEL: 065-707 4503 FAX: 065-707 4129

GUESTHOUSE ★★★ MAP 5 E 9

Doonmacfelim House is a 3*** guesthouse, situated on our farm in the village of Doolin, famous for traditional Irish music. Excellent location for visiting Cliffs of Moher, boat to Aran Islands, visiting prehistoric ruins. Its geology, flora, caves, archaeology and history set it apart as a place of mystery and beauty. All rooms en suite, with hairdryers, direct dial telephone. Shannon Airport & Killimer Car Ferry 70km. Hard tennis court, rackets supplied.

WEB: www.kingsway.ie/doonmacfelim

B&B from £18.00 to £23.50
€22.86 to €29.84

MAJELLA & FRANK MOLONEY
Owners
Mastercard
Visa

Closed 24 - 28 December

CLARE INN GOLF & LEISURE HOTEL

DROMOLAND,
CO. CLARE
TEL: 065-682 3000 FAX: 065-682 3759
EMAIL: reservations@lynchotels.com

HOTEL ★★★ MAP 6 G 8

Located on Dromoland's 18-hole Golf Course with stunning views of the Shannon Estuary. Just 5 mins from Ennis, 10 mins from Shannon, 10 mins from Limerick. 183 well furnished en suite rooms, inc. Presidential Suite, each with satellite TV & free movies; good food and superb outdoor and indoor leisure facilities inc. pool, gym & sauna. Poacher's Pub. Conference facilities for up to 400, parking 300. KidsPlus playcentre/Summer kidscamp. Free ValuPass to 25 local attractions. A leading wedding venue.

WEB: www.clareinnhotel.com

Member of Lynch Hotels

B&B from £25.00 to £65.00
€31.74 to €82.53

MICHAEL B LYNCH GROUP MD
Noel Mulhaire Gen Mgr
American Express
Diners
Mastercard
Visa

Weekend specials from £96.00

Open All Year

B&B rates are IR£ per person sharing per night incl. Breakfast

ARDILAUN GUESTHOUSE

GALWAY ROAD, ENNIS,
CO. CLARE
TEL: 065-682 2311 FAX: 065-684 3989
EMAIL: purcellsennis@eircom.net

GUESTHOUSE ★★★ MAP 6 F 8

Ardilaun is Gaelic for high island. This is a modern architect-designed 3*** guesthouse overlooking the River Fergus and Ballyallia Lake amenity area. Most rooms have panoramic views of the river and all are superbly decorated with en suite, phone, TV, and hairdryer. Our gymnasium sauna facility also overlooks the river and is available to guests only. Ardilaun is just 20 minutes drive from Shannon Airport on the N18 and is the ideal touring base for Clare, Limerick and Galway.

B&B from £22.50 to £24.00
€28.57 to €30.47

ANNE PURCELL
Proprietress

Mastercard
Visa

10 10 FAX

Open All Year

AUBURN LODGE HOTEL

GALWAY ROAD, ENNIS,
CO. CLARE
TEL: 065-682 1247 FAX: 065-682 1232
EMAIL: stay@irishcourthotels.com

HOTEL ★★★ MAP 6 F 8

Located in the historic town of Ennis, the 100 bedroom Auburn Lodge Hotel is the ideal base for the Golf or Fishing Holiday. Convenient to Lahinch, Shannon, Dromoland, Woodstock and Ennis. It offers a wide choice of rolling parkland or links courses - with golf to suit everyone. Within a few miles drive, are the Cliffs of Moher, Scenic Burren, Ailwee Caves and Bunratty Castle and Folkpark. Enjoy nightly traditional music in Tailor Quigleys Pub and re-live the day's golf. Shannon International Airport 15km.

WEB: www.irishcourthotels.com

Member of Irish Court Hotel Group

B&B from £35.00 to £85.00
€44.44 to €107.93

BARRY DEANE
General Manager

American Express
Diners
Mastercard
Visa

100 100

HOTELS

Closed 25 December

BANNER LODGE

MARKET STREET, ENNIS,
CO. CLARE
TEL: 065-682 4224 FAX: 065-682 1670
EMAIL: noelcarrennis@eircom.net

GUESTHOUSE P MAP 6 F 8

Located in the heart of Ennis Town within easy reach of shops and restaurants. 10 miles from Shannon International Airport and within 30 minutes drive of all county tourist attractions. Downstairs Henry J's Bar provides nightly entertainment. All bedrooms are en suite with TV, phone and tea/coffee facilities. Local attractions include the Aran Islands, the Burren, Cliff of Moher and Bunratty Castle.

WEB: homepage.eircom.net/~bannerlodge

B&B from £22.00 to £25.00
€27.93 to €31.74

NOEL CARR

Mastercard
Visa

8 8

Closed 23 - 31 December

Room rates are IR£ per room per night

CILL EOIN HOUSE

KILDYSERT CROSS, CLARE ROAD,
ENNIS, CO. CLARE
TEL: 065-684 1668 FAX: 065-684 1669
EMAIL: cilleoin@iol.ie

GUESTHOUSE ★★★ MAP 6 F 8

Cill Eoin, named after the nearby 13th Century Abbey, is a 3*** guesthouse on the main tourist route to the west coast of Clare, with its unparalleled beauty in the scenery of the desolate Burren and the majestic vistas, that are the Cliffs of Moher. Golf, with a links and three courses nearby, is abundantly available. Horse riding, fishing and many other pastimes are well provided for in the area. Call and see us soon, you will feel at home.

WEB: www.euroka.com/cilleoin

B&B from £22.00 to £25.00
€27.93 to €31.74

PAT & BRIDGET GLYNN LUCEY

American Express
Diners
Mastercard
Visa

😊 Weekend specials from £59.00

14 14

Closed 24 December - 08 January

CLAREHILLS GUESTHOUSE

CLAUREEN, LAHINCH ROAD, ENNIS,
CO. CLARE
TEL: 065-684 3355 FAX: 065-684 4755
EMAIL: guests@clarehills.com

GUESTHOUSE ★★ MAP 6 G 7

Situated on the N85 (Lahinch Rd), we are located just 1km from the historic town of Ennis. All rooms are en suite: - direct dial phone, TV, tea/coffee making facilities & hairdryer. Ideal for golfing enthusiasts as we are near Lahinch, Shannon, Dromoland, Woodstock and Ennis golf courses. Within a few miles drive are the Cliffs of Moher, magnificent Burren, Ailwee Caves, and Bunratty Castle and Folkpark. Enjoy traditional music, good food and plenty of craic nightly in town. Shannon 15km.

WEB: www.clarehills.com

B&B from £20.00 to £25.00
€25.39 to €31.74

KATHLEEN RYNNE
Proprietor/Manager

Mastercard
Visa

7 7

Open All Year

FOUNTAIN COURT

LAHINCH ROAD, ENNIS,
CO. CLARE
TEL: 065-682 9845 FAX: 065-684 5030
EMAIL: kyran@fountain-court.com

GUESTHOUSE ★★★ MAP 6 F 8

Peaceful rural setting yet only 4 minutes drive to Ennis. Superb bedrooms with king sized beds, TV, tea making facilities, Hi Fi bath and power shower. Family run with delicious breakfasts. Beautiful reception rooms and the personal service of the owners make Fountain Court the ideal base to tour the Burren National Park, Cliffs of Moher and Bunratty Castle and Folk Park. Golf, fishing and horse riding all within easy reach. Shannon Airport 15km.

WEB: www.fountain-court.com

Member of Premier Guesthouses

B&B from £22.00 to £30.00
€27.93 to €38.09

KYRAN & BREED CARR

American Express
Diners
Mastercard
Visa

😊 Midweek specials from £70.00

12 12

Closed 20 December - 07 January

B&B rates are IR£ per person sharing per night incl. Breakfast

GLENCAR GUESTHOUSE

GALWAY ROAD, ENNIS,
CO. CLARE
TEL: 065-682 2348 FAX: 065-682 2885
EMAIL: glencar.ennis@eircom.net

GUESTHOUSE ★★★ MAP 6 F 8

Glencar Guesthouse is a newly-refurbished 12 bedroomed 3*** accommodation. Situated on the N18 (Galway Road), 1km from Ennis Town and 20m from Auburn Lodge Hotel. Shannon Airport 20 minutes drive. Glencar is an ideal base for golfing, cycling, fishing or walking holidays. Special attractions: Bunratty Castle, Cliffs of Moher, the Burren and the Ailwee Caves all easily accessible. Ennis is the home of traditional Irish music.

WEB: www.glencar.ennis.ie

B&B from £20.00 to £25.00
€25.39 to €31.74

PETER & LIZ HOULIHAN

Mastercard
Visa

12 12

inet

Closed 23 - 27 December

KELLORNA HOUSE

GALWAY ROAD, ENNIS,
CO. CLARE
TEL: 065-682 1519 FAX: 065-684 1079
EMAIL: kellorna.ennis@eircom.net

GUESTHOUSE N MAP 6 G 8

Situated on the main Galway Road and within walking distance from Ennis Town centre, Kellorna House is a charming purpose built guesthouse. It captures the beauty of old world interior design while incorporating modern facilities that one expects when visiting Ireland's Information Age Town. Eleven bedrooms (all en suite) including wheelchair access and ground floor accommodation with full facilities.

WEB: www.kellorna.com

B&B from £25.00 to £40.00
€31.74 to €50.79

MARTIN AND CONNIE GUERIN

Mastercard
Visa

11 11

Open All Year

MAGOWNA HOUSE HOTEL

INCH, KILMALEY, ENNIS,
CO. CLARE
TEL: 065-683 9009 FAX: 065-683 9258
EMAIL: info@magowna.com

HOTEL ★★★ MAP 6 F 8

We are a beautifully located, family managed, country house hotel with extensive gardens and lovely views. Ideal for an active or purely relaxing break. Close to excellent golf courses, angling and walks. (Mid-Clare Way 1.5km) Shannon Airport, Cliffs of Moher, the Burren, Doolin, Bunratty Castle, Killimer Car Ferry to Kerry within easy reach. Conference room (capacity 200). Enjoy hospitality, comfort, good food and a genuine welcome in the heart of County Clare.

WEB: www.magowna.com

Member of Irish Family Hotels

B&B from £32.00 to £36.00
€40.63 to €45.71

GAY MURPHY
Proprietor

American Express
Diners
Mastercard
Visa

Weekend specials from £77.00

10 10

alc

Closed 24 - 26 December

OLD GROUND HOTEL

O'CONNELL STREET, ENNIS,
CO. CLARE
TEL: 065-682 8127 FAX: 065-682 8112
EMAIL: oghotel@iol.ie

HOTEL ★★★ MAP 6 F 8

Ivy clad manor house dates to the 18th century. Has recently been imaginatively extended and renovated to provide 83 deluxe rooms & superior suites with king beds. The elegant formal dining room is renowned for excellent cuisine. A new bistro opened in August 2000. The hotel is in the centre of the historic town of Ennis, 30 minutes from Shannon Airport, a few miles from The Cliffs of Moher, The Burren, Bunratty Castle and many superb challenging golf courses.

WEB: www.flynnhotels.com

Member of Flynn Hotels

B&B from £35.00 to £60.00
€44.44 to €76.18

ALLEN FLYNN-MANAGING DIR
Mary Gleeson-Gen Manager

American Express
Diners
Mastercard
Visa

:/ T

☺ Weekend specials from £79.00

83 83

S Ⓐ alc

HOTELS

Closed 24 - 25 December

QUEENS HOTEL

ABBEY STREET, ENNIS,
CO. CLARE
TEL: 065-682 8963 FAX: 065-682 8628
EMAIL: stay@irishcourthotels.com

HOTEL ★★★ MAP 6 F 8

The Queen's Town Centre Hotel is an ideal base for touring Bunratty Castle and Folk Park, Cliffs of Moher and the Burren. All bedrooms are en suite, with satellite TV, video, radio, phone, hairdryer, tea/coffee. Overlooking the 13th century Franciscan Abbey from which Ennis takes its origin. Adjoins the famous Cruise's Pub and Restaurant built circa 1658. Renowned for its authentic old world charm, superb home cooked Fayre and traditional music nightly. Shannon International Airport 15km.

WEB: www.irishcourthotels.com

Member of Irish Court Hotel Group

B&B from £35.00 to £85.00
€44.44 to €107.93

MAURICE WALSH
General Manager

American Express
Diners
Mastercard
Visa

30 30

alc

HOTELS

Closed 25 December

TEMPLE GATE HOTEL

THE SQUARE, ENNIS,
CO. CLARE
TEL: 065-682 3300 FAX: 065-682 3322
EMAIL: templegh@iol.ie

HOTEL ★★★ MAP 6 F 8

Resting on the site of a 19th century Convent, the Gothic style combines with luxurious charm in this town house hotel. Sharing the grounds with the Clare Museum and set back from the centre of historic, yet progressive, Information Age town of Ennis. Exceptional bedrooms, AA Rosettes for JM's Bistro 4 consecutive years and acclaimed bar menu in James Joyce award-winning Preachers Pub. Near Shannon Airport, Bunratty Castle & Lahinch golf course.

WEB: www.templegatehotel.com

B&B from £45.00 to £75.00
€57.14 to €95.23

VERA & JOHN MADDEN
Proprietors

American Express
Diners
Mastercard
Visa

:/ T

70 70

S Ⓐ alc

HOTELS

Open All Year

B&B rates are IR£ per person sharing per night incl. Breakfast

WEST COUNTY CONFERENCE & LEISURE HOTEL

CLARE ROAD, ENNIS,
CO. CLARE
TEL: 065-682 3000 FAX: 065-682 3759
EMAIL: reservations@lynchotels.com

HOTEL ★★★ MAP 6 F 8

Centrally located, the West County boasts well furnished en suite rooms, superb food & easy access to Clare's attractions. 5 mins walk from historic Ennis & its shopping, 15 mins from Bunratty & Shannon. Conference facilities for 1,650. Health & leisure club with 3 pools, gym, sauna, steamroom, a KidsPlus playcentre, ideal for families, beauty salon. Boru's Porterhouse, award winning traditional Irish pub/carvery. Summer KidsCamp. Free ValuPass to 25 local attractions. A leading wedding venue.

WEB: www.westcountyhotel.com

Member of Lynch Hotels

B&B from £25.00 to £65.00
€31.74 to €82.53

MICHAEL B LYNCH GROUP MD
Brian Harrington Group Operations Manager

American Express
Diners
Mastercard
Visa

😊 Weekend specials from £96.00

152 152

Open All Year

WESTBROOK HOUSE

GALWAY ROAD, ENNIS,
CO. CLARE
TEL: 065-684 0173 FAX: 065-686 7777
EMAIL: westbrook.ennis@eircom.net

GUESTHOUSE ★★★ MAP 6 F 8

Westbrook House is the most recently built luxury accommodation in Ennis. All rooms are fitted to exceptionally high standards. Within walking distance of the centre of historic Ennis, with its friendly traditional pubs and fantastic shopping. Ideal base for golfing holidays, special discounts with local golf courses. A short drive to the majestic Cliffs of Moher, the Burren or Bunratty Castle and Folk Park. Only 15 minutes from Shannon Airport.

WEB: www.westbrookhouse.net

B&B from £20.00 to £30.00
€25.39 to €38.09

SHEELAGH & DOMHNALL
LYNCH Proprietors

Mastercard
Visa

10 10

Closed 23 - 26 December

WOODSTOCK HOTEL

SHANAWAY ROAD, ENNIS,
(NEAR SHANNON), CO. CLARE
TEL: 065-684 6600 FAX: 065-684 6611
EMAIL: info@woodstockhotel.com

HOTEL N MAP 6 F 8

Woodstock Hotel is an exclusive property in a magnificent setting. The hotel offers 67 luxury bedrooms complete with Neutrogena® toiletries. Conference facilities for up to 200 and banqueting for up to 180. Contemporary dishes and a relaxing drink can be enjoyed in Spikes Brasserie & Bar. Facilities include 18 hole golf course, health and fitness spa. Sister property of Hibernian Hotel, Dublin and McCausland Hotel, Belfast. GDS Access LX. UK Toll free: 00 800 525 48000.

WEB: www.woodstockhotel.com

Member of Small Luxury Hotels of the World

B&B from £51.00 to £107.50
€64.76 to €136.50

SIOBHAN MAHER
General Manager

American Express
Diners
Mastercard
Visa

😊 Weekend specials from £133.00

67 67

Closed 25 December

Room rates are IR£ per room per night

FALLS HOTEL

ENNISTYMON,
CO. CLARE
TEL: 065-707 1004 FAX: 065-707 1367
EMAIL: falls@iol.ie

HOTEL ★★★ MAP 5 E 9

A 3*** - 130 bedroom hotel, overlooking the cascades of the River Inagh, the Falls Hotel is located in 50 acres of parkland, close to the centre of the busy market town, Ennistymon. Relax and unwind in renowned Dylan Thomas Bar. The Falls is an ideal base to explore the Burren National Park, The Cliffs of Moher and the Ailwee Caves. For the sportsman - there is the World Famous Lahinch Golf Club close by.

WEB: www.iol.ie/~falls

B&B from £35.00 to £50.00
€44.44 to €63.49

JOE LEONARD
Manager

American Express
Mastercard
Visa

Weekend specials from £90.00

130 130

Open All Year

GROVEMOUNT HOUSE

LAHINCH ROAD, ENNISTYMON,
CO. CLARE
TEL: 065-707 1431 FAX: 065-707 1823
EMAIL: grovmnt@gofree.indigo.ie

GUESTHOUSE ★★★ MAP 5 E 9

Grovemount House, the Golfers' Paradise. What better than to return to luxurious tranquillity after a refreshing day on Lahinch's championship Golf Course, just 5 minutes drive from here. Or perhaps you would like a rejuvenating sauna in Lahinch's leisure centre before retiring for the night. We offer easy access to the famous Cliffs of Moher and Burren region. Whatever is your pleasure, be it fishing, golfing or traditional music, this is the place for you.

Member of Premier Guesthouses

B&B from £20.00 to £25.00
€25.39 to €31.74

SHEILA LINNANE
Owner

Mastercard
Visa

Midweek specials from £50.00

8 8

Closed 29 October - 30 April

WATCH FOR THE SYMBOL OF QUALITY

THIS SYMBOL OF QUALITY GUARANTEES YOU, THE VISITOR, A HIGH STANDARD OF ACCOMMODATION AND SERVICE WHICH IS EXPECTED OF IRISH HOTELS & GUESTHOUSES.

B&B rates are IR£ per person sharing per night incl. Breakfast

HALPIN'S HOTEL & VITTLES RESTAURANT

ERIN STREET, KILKEE, CO. CLARE
TEL: 065-905 6032 FAX: 065-905 6317
EMAIL: halpins@iol.ie

HOTEL ★★★ MAP 5 D 7

Highly acclaimed 3*** hotel & award winning Vittles Restaurant. Combination of old world charm, fine food, vintage wines & modern comforts - overlooking old Victorian Kilkee, near Shannon Airport - Killimer car ferry - Cliffs of Moher - the Burren & Loop drive. Nearby golf courses- Lahinch/Ballybunion. Accolades- RAC, AA, Times, Best Loved Hotels, Johansens. Sister property of Aberdeen Lodge and Merrion Hall.
USA Toll Free 1800 223 6510, direct dial 353 65 905 6032.

WEB: www.halpinsprivatehotels.com

Member of Green Book of Ireland

B&B from £30.00 to £47.50
€38.09 to €60.31

PAT HALPIN
Proprietor

American Express
Diners
Mastercard
Visa

☺ Midweek specials from £90.00

12 12

Closed 15 November - 15 March

KILKEE BAY HOTEL

KILRUSH ROAD, KILKEE, CO. CLARE
TEL: 065-906 0060 FAX: 065-906 0062
EMAIL: info@kilkee-bay.com

HOTEL ★★★ MAP 5 D 7

A superb location - 3 minutes walk from Kilkee's renowned Blue Flag beach and town centre. This modern hotel has 41 spacious en suite bedrooms with direct dial phone, tea/coffee facilities and TV. On site tennis court, multiplex cinema, nite club, bar and seafood bistro. The perfect base for touring the Cliffs of Moher, Burren and Ailwee Caves. Shannon Airport/Limerick City within an hour's drive. Reduced rates at local dolphin watching, golf, diving centre, thalassotherapy, pony trekking and waterworld.

WEB: www.kilkee-bay.com

B&B from £25.00 to £35.00
€31.74 to €44.44

TONY LYNCH
General Manager

American Express
Mastercard
Visa

☺ Weekend specials from £69.00

41 41

Open All Year

OCEAN COVE GOLF AND LEISURE HOTEL

KILKEE BAY, CO. CLARE
TEL: 065-682 3000 FAX: 065-682 3759
EMAIL: reservations@lynchotels.com

HOTEL N MAP 5 D 7

Newly built hotel overlooking Kilkee's sandy bay. 50 en suite rooms, including seaview and family rooms; PanAsian's à la carte Restaurant, Boru's traditional Irish pub/carvery; Sports club gym free to residents; KidsPlus play centre; adjacent to Kilkee Waterworld and dive centre; 18 hole golf course also nearby. Ideal for touring Kerry and North Clare. Meeting facilities for 70. Parking 100 cars. Free ValuPass to 25 local attractions.

WEB: www.oceancovehotel.com

Member of Lynch Hotels

B&B from £25.00 to £65.00
€31.74 to €82.53

MICHAEL B LYNCH GROUP MD
Damian Caldwell Gen Mgr

American Express
Diners
Mastercard
Visa

☺ Weekend specials from £86.00

50 50

Open All Year

STELLA MARIS HOTEL

KILKEE,
CO. CLARE
TEL: 065-905 6455 FAX: 065-906 0006
EMAIL: stellamaris@eircom.net

HOTEL ★★ MAP 5 D 7

The Stella Maris is a small family-run hotel in the heart of Kilkee. Its attractions are open peat fires, friendly staff and a veranda overlooking the bay and town of Kilkee. Traditional music in the bar and a variety of home-cooked food all go to make your stay a very memorable and pleasant experience.

Member of Logis of Ireland

B&B from £25.00 to £40.00
€31.74 to €50.79

ANNE HAUGH

American Express
Mastercard
Visa

😊 Weekend specials from £60.00

🖼️ 10 10

Open All Year

STRAND GUEST HOUSE

THE STRAND LINE, KILKEE,
CO. CLARE
TEL: 065-905 6177 FAX: 065-905 6177
EMAIL: thestrandkilkee@eircom.net

GUESTHOUSE ★★★ MAP 5 O 7

Situated on the seafront in Kilkee, one of the most westerly seaside resorts in Europe. Kilkee is built around a 1.5km beach, considered one of the best and safest bathing places in the west with breathtaking coastal walks. The Strand makes an ideal touring base - visit the Burren, Cliffs of Moher, Ailwee Caves. For golf enthusiasts there is a local 18 hole course, Kilrush 13km, Lahinch 42km or Ballybunion 40km (via car ferry). Restaurant fully licenced, specialises in local seafood.

WEB: www.countyclareguesthouse.com

B&B from £22.50 to £35.00
€28.57 to €44.44

JOHNNY & CAROLINE
REDMOND

Mastercard
Visa

🖼️ 6 6

Open All Year

THOMOND GUESTHOUSE & KILKEE THALASSOTHERAPY CENTRE

GRATTAN STREET, KILKEE,
CO. CLARE
TEL: 065-905 6742 FAX: 065-905 6762
EMAIL: mulcahype@eircom.net

GUESTHOUSE ★★★ MAP 5 D 7

Thomond Guesthouse is a magnificent new premises with 5 en suite rooms coupled with Kilkee Thalassotherapy Centre, offering natural seaweed baths, algae body wraps, beauty salon and other thalassotherapy treatments. Ideal get-away for those looking for a totally unique and relaxing break. Situated in beautiful Kilkee with golfing (18), scuba diving, deep sea angling, dolphin watching, swimming, pony trekking and spectacular cliff walks, all within walking distance. Specials available.

B&B from £27.00 to £37.00
€34.28 to €46.98

EILEEN MULCAHY
Proprietor

Mastercard
Visa

😊 2 B&B & Treatment packages from £210.00

🖼️ 5 5

Closed 31 January - 28 February

B&B rates are IR£ per person sharing per night incl. Breakfast

KINCORA HALL HOTEL

KILLALOE,
CO. CLARE
TEL: 061-376000 FAX: 061-376665
EMAIL: kincora@iol.ie

HOTEL ★★★   MAP 6 H 8

Kincora Hall Hotel in Killaloe (Ancient capital of Ireland) is a comfortable 31 bedroomed hotel on the banks of the River Shannon. This oasis of calm provides a true County Clare welcome combined with friendly service and a wide selection of food in our carvery and restaurant which overlook our marina and the River Shannon.

B&B from £45.00 to £50.00
€57.14 to €63.49

JOHN O'CONNOR
General Manager

American Express
Diners
Mastercard
Visa

☺ Mid-week only – 2 B&Bs
and 1 Dinner from £90.00

31 31

Open All Year

LAKESIDE HOTEL & LEISURE CENTRE

KILLALOE,
CO. CLARE
TEL: 061-376122 FAX: 061-376431
EMAIL: lakesidehotelkillaloe@eircom.net

HOTEL ★★★   MAP 6 H 8

On the banks of the River Shannon, overlooking Lough Derg, the Lakeside is the ideal base for touring Counties Clare, Limerick and Tipperary. Enjoy our fabulous indoor leisure centre with its 40 metre water-slide, swimming pools, sauna and steam rooms, jacuzzi, gym, snooker and creche rooms. Our 3*** hotel has 46 en suite bedrooms, including 10 superior family suites. Fully licensed restaurant and conference facilities available.

WEB: www.dirl.com/clare/lakeside.htm

Member of Coast and Country Hotels

B&B from £35.00 to £45.00
€44.44 to €57.14

CHRISTOPHER BYRNES
General Manager

American Express
Diners
Mastercard
Visa

46 46

Closed 23 - 26 December

LANTERN HOUSE

OGONNELLOE, KILLALOE,
CO. CLARE
TEL: 061-923034 FAX: 061-923139

GUESTHOUSE ★★★   MAP 6 H 8

Ideally situated overlooking Lough Derg in a beautiful part of East Clare, 6 miles north of historic Killaloe and 45 minutes drive from Shannon Airport. Our en suite rooms are non-smoking, have semi-orthopaedic beds, direct dial phone. TV and radio, residents' lounge, homely atmosphere and safe car parking. Enjoy the wonderful views from our fully licenced restaurant. Owner chef. Local activities include golf, watersports, fishing, pony trekking and walking.

B&B from £22.00 to £25.00
€27.93 to €31.74

ELIZABETH COPPEN/PHILIP HOGAN
Owners

American Express
Mastercard
Visa

6 6

Closed 01 November - 03 March

WATERMAN'S LODGE COUNTRY HOUSE HOTEL

BALLINA, KILLALOE,
CO. CLARE
TEL: 061-376333 FAX: 061-375445
EMAIL: info@watermanslodge.ie

HOTEL ★★★ MAP 6 H 8

Perched on a hill overlooking the River Shannon, Watermans Lodge Country House Hotel offers with simplicity and taste, the attractions of high ceilings and large comfy beds and open fires. Less that 2 hours from Dublin and Cork it is an ideal venue for business and pleasure (only 15 minutes from Limerick). It boasts one of the finest restaurants in Killaloe - The Courtyard and a relaxing bar - The Derg Lounge. Fishing, golf, shooting all on our doorstep.

WEB: www.watermanslodge.ie

Member of C.M.V.

B&B from £50.00 to £70.00
€63.49 to €88.88

TOM REILLY
Manager

American Express
Mastercard
Visa

😊 Weekend specials from £99.00

🖥🚗☎📺 ⚘ ∪ ♪ 🅿 🆂 🅰 ♿
10 10

Inet

HOTELS FEDERATION

Closed 22 December - 15 January

CENTRAL GUESTHOUSE

46 HENRY STREET, KILRUSH,
CO. CLARE
TEL: 065-905 1332 FAX: 065-905 1332

GUESTHOUSE P MAP 5 E 7

Family run attractive Georgian town house on N67 route (Kilrush-Heritage town). Close to Shannon Airport - Killimer Car Ferry - Cliffs of Moher - the Burren and Loop Head Drive. Major golf courses nearby - Kilrush/Kilkee/Doonbeg/Lahinch/Ballybunion. Attractive woodlands with walled gardens and walks. Marina within walking distance, boat trips to Slattery Island. Also, Dolphin watching on Shannon River. Close to all restaurants and amenities.

B&B from £17.00 to £25.00
€21.59 to €31.74

SEAN & MARY COTTER
Owners

Mastercard
Visa

😊 Midweek specials from £50.00

🖥🚗📺 ♪ 🆂 Inet
6 6

Open All Year

B&B rates are IR£ per person sharing per night incl. Breakfast

KILLIMER/TARBERT CAR FERRY

M.V. "Shannon Willow" (44 cars) loading at Killimer.

From Killimer, Co. Clare
DEPARTURE ON THE HOUR

		FIRST SAILING	LAST SAILING
APRIL/SEPTEMBER.	Weekdays	7.00 a.m.	9.00 p.m.
	Sundays	9.00 a.m.	9.00 p.m.
OCTOBER/MARCH.	Weekdays	7.00 a.m.	7.00 p.m.
	Sundays	10.00 a.m.	7.00 p.m.

From Tarbert, Co. Kerry
DEPARTURE ON THE HALF HOUR

APRIL/SEPTEMBER.	Weekdays	7.30 a.m.	9.30 p.m.
	Sundays	9.30 a.m.	9.30 p.m.
OCTOBER/MARCH.	Weekdays	7.30 a.m.	7.30 p.m.
	Sundays	10.30 a.m.	7.30 p.m.

SAILINGS
Every day of the year except Christmas Day.

TWO FERRY SERVICE
During the peak holiday period both Ferry Boats operate to give half-hourly sailings from each side.

Scenic and Direct
Routes via
Drive-on/Drive-off
Car Ferry Service

m.v. "Shannon Breeze" (60 cars)
m.v. "Shannon Willow" (44 cars)

SHANNON FERRY LTD.
KILLIMER, KILRUSH, CO. CLARE

Telephone   Fax
065 9053124   065 9053125
Email:enquiries@shannonferries.com
www.shannonferries.com

AILLWEE CAVE

In The West. In The Burren.
Ireland's premier showcave.

Add to the holiday experience by taking a stroll underground with one of our expert guides.

Ballyvaughan, Co. Clare. Tel: (065) 7077067

ABERDEEN ARMS HOTEL

LAHINCH,
CO. CLARE
TEL: 065-708 1100 FAX: 065-708 1228
EMAIL: aberdeenarms@eircom.net

HOTEL ★★★ MAP 5 E 9

A haven for the discerning traveller who will appreciate its relaxed and friendly atmosphere. Mackensies Restaurant offers excellent cuisine. The Aberdeen Grill serves imaginative and tempting fair. Lahinch's Golden Strand and Golf Course are about 5 minutes from the hotel which is just 51.2km from Shannon Airport on the beautiful Clare Coast. Whatever your preference, golf, fishing, horse riding, sightseeing all are within easy reach. Conference facilities available.

WEB: www.aberdeenarms.ie

B&B from £25.00 to £55.00
€31.74 to €69.84

BRIAN HEGARTY
General Manager

American Express
Diners
Mastercard
Visa

55 55

Closed 22 - 28 December

ATLANTIC HOTEL

MAIN STREET, LAHINCH,
CO. CLARE
TEL: 065-708 1049 FAX: 065-708 1029
EMAIL: atlantichotel@eircom.net

HOTEL ★★★ MAP 5 E 9

The Atlantic Hotel is a family run hotel where comfort and friendliness is our priority. Intimate dining room offering the very best in local seafood. All rooms are en suite and have direct dial phone, TV, hairdryer and tea/coffee making facilities. 51km from Shannon Airport, 5 minutes from the famous Lahinch championship golf courses, Cliffs of Moher and the Burren. Recently refurbished and upgraded, this charming little hotel has much to offer our special guests. A warm welcome awaits you.

B&B from £35.00 to £40.00
€44.44 to €50.79

SEAMUS & ALAN LOGUE
Your Hosts

Diners
Mastercard
Visa

14 14

Closed 24 - 26 December

DOUGH MOR LODGE

STATION ROAD, LAHINCH,
CO. CLARE
TEL: 065-708 2063 FAX: 065-707 1384
EMAIL: dough@gofree.indigo.ie

GUESTHOUSE N MAP 5 E 9

Purpose-built family run guesthouse with residents' lounge and dining room. Private car parking and large garden. You can see Lahinch's famous golflinks from the house. Tee times can be booked and arranged for guests. This is an ideal location for golfing, touring the Burren or visiting the Cliffs of Moher. The beach is within 5 mins walk. Lahinch Sea World has a fine heated indoor swimming pool. The ideal place to unwind and enjoy your holiday.

B&B from £27.00 to £27.00
€34.28 to €34.28

JIM FOLEY
Proprietor

Mastercard
Visa

6 6

Closed 31 October - 31 March

GREENBRIER INN GUESTHOUSE

LAHINCH,
CO. CLARE
TEL: 065-708 1242 FAX: 065-708 1247
EMAIL: gbrier@indigo.ie

GUESTHOUSE ★★★   MAP 5 E 9

Luxurious 3*** guesthouse with 14 guest rooms, our diningroom and guest lounge are overlooking Lahinch Golf Course and the Atlantic Ocean. Totally renovated and extended in '99. Within a short walk of Lahinch Village. All rooms are en suite with antique pine furnishings, direct dial phone, TV, tea/coffee making facilities. An excellent base from which to visit the Cliffs of Moher, the Burren, Aran Islands and Galway or play golf on the nearby Lahinch Championship Course. Enjoy our home while away from your own.

WEB: www.greenbrierinn.com

B&B from £25.00 to £42.50
€31.74 to €53.96

MARGARET & VICTOR MULCAHY
Proprietors

Mastercard

Visa

14 14

IRISH HOTELS FEDERATION

Closed 03 January - 20 February

MOY HOUSE

LAHINCH,
CO. CLARE
TEL: 065-708 2800 AX: 065-708 2500
EMAIL: moyhouse@eircom.net

GUESTHOUSE ★★★★   MAP 5 E 9

Moy House prevails over the breathtaking seascape of Lahinch Bay, set on 15 acres of grounds, adorned by mature woodland and a picturesque river. Major restoration has transformed this 18th century country house in keeping with present day expectations of superior standards, yet preserving its unique character style and period ambience. Personal attention and the relaxation of a sanctuary, yet minutes away from the many amenities available, are the hallmarks that distinguish us.

Member of Irish Country Houses & Restaurants

B&B from £60.00 to £85.00
€76.18 to €107.93

BERNADETTE MERRY
General Manager / Director

American Express

Mastercard

Visa

7 7

IRISH HOTELS FEDERATION

Open All Year

SANCTA MARIA HOTEL

LAHINCH,
CO. CLARE
TEL: 065-708 1041 FAX: 065-708 1529

HOTEL ★★   MAP 5 E 9

The McInerney Family have welcomed holiday makers to the Sancta Maria for over 40 years. Many of the attractive bedrooms overlook the famous Lahinch golf links and golden beach, which are within 100 metres of the hotel. Our restaurant specialises in fresh produce and special emphasis is placed on local seafoods and home baking. The Sancta Maria is the ideal base for touring the Burren or visiting the Cliffs of Moher and Aran Islands.

B&B from £25.00 to £30.00
€31.74 to €38.09

THOMAS MCINERNEY
Proprietor

Mastercard

Visa

😊 Weekend specials from £64.00

24 24

alc

IRISH HOTELS FEDERATION

Closed 30 October - 03 March

Room rates are IR£ per room per night

SHAMROCK INN HOTEL

MAIN STREET, LAHINCH,
CO. CLARE
TEL: 065-708 1700 FAX: 065-708 1029
EMAIL: atlantichotel@eircom.net

HOTEL ★★ MAP 5 E 9

Situated right in the heart of charming Lahinch. All tastefully decorated rooms have direct dial phone, TV, hairdryer and tea/coffee making facilities. Our restaurant is renowned for its warm and intimate atmosphere offering a choice of excellent cuisine, catering for all tastes. Delicious home cooked bar food is served daily and by night the bar comes to life with the sound of music. Whatever your interest, golf, fishing or horseriding, we can arrange it for you.

B&B from £35.00 to £40.00
€44.44 to €50.79

SEAMUS & ALAN LOGUE
Your Hosts

Mastercard
Visa

10 10

Closed 24 - 26 December

CARRIGANN HOTEL

LISDOONVARNA,
CO. CLARE
TEL: 065-707 4036 FAX: 065-707 4567
EMAIL: carrigannhotel@eircom.net

HOTEL ★★★ MAP 5 E 9

Small, quiet, friendly and relaxing hotel, set in its own landscaped grounds, just two mins from the village square. Rockeries, rose gardens and lawns can be viewed from our recently refurbished restaurant. Relax and enjoy fresh local produce expertly cooked and served. Ground floor rooms. Laundry/drying facilities. Walking holiday specialists - providing our own maps and notes of the unique Burren region. Logis of Ireland, Tel: 01-668 9743.

WEB: www.gateway-to-the-burren.com

Member of Logis of Ireland

B&B from £29.00 to £39.00
€36.82 to €49.52

MARY & GERARD HOWARD
Proprietors

Mastercard
Visa

☺ Weekend specials from £72.00

20 20

Closed 01 November - 28 February

KINCORA HOUSE

LISDOONVARNA,
CO. CLARE
TEL: 065-707 4300 FAX: 065-707 4490
EMAIL: kincorahotel@eircom.net

GUESTHOUSE ★★★ MAP 5 E 9

A warm welcome awaits you at our award-winning Country Inn. AA ◆◆◆◆. Built in 1860 the house exudes charm and character. Recently refurbished, individually designed rooms offer every modern comfort. Enjoy excellent cuisine in our dining room/art gallery, set in gardens with a National Award of Merit. Old athmospheric pub. Ideally situated in the Burren region near the Cliffs of Moher and Lahinch Golf Course.

WEB: www.kincora-hotel.com

Member of Les Routiers Ireland

B&B from £25.00 to £40.00
€31.74 to €50.79

DOREEN & DIARMUID
DRENNAN, Proprietors

Mastercard
Visa

11 11

Closed 31 October - 01 March

B&B rates are IR£ per person sharing per night incl. Breakfast

LYNCH'S HOTEL

**LISDOONVARNA,
CO. CLARE**
TEL: 065-707 4010 FAX: 065-707 4611
EMAIL: lynchshotel@eircom.net

HOTEL ★ MAP 5 E 9

Family-owned and run hotel, (currently fifth generation). Comprises 10 bedrooms with all usual facilities. Extensive à la carte menu available till 9.30pm. Located in centre of village with easy access to Burren, Cliffs of Moher and North Clare Atlantic Coast. Enjoyable for botanists, bird watchers, anglers, cavers, walkers, swimmers. Most musical tastes catered for nightly in village.

WEB: http://homepage.eircom.net/~joelynch

B&B from £20.00 to £26.00
€25.39 to €33.01

MAUREEN LYNCH
Owner

Mastercard

Visa

10 10

Closed 10 October - 10 May

RATHBAUN HOTEL

**LISDOONVARNA,
CO. CLARE**
TEL: 065-707 4009 FAX: 065-707 4009

HOTEL ★★ MAP 5 E 9

Rathbaun Hotel on the main street in the centre of Lisdoonvarna is a unique hotel for special guests. Quality accommodation, excellent food served all day, personal service and brilliant value for money are the hallmarks of our hotel. We are also renowned for our bar music and unusual gift shop. We offer maps and helpful information to all our guests on the Burren area. Cead mile failte.

B&B from £18.00 to £25.00
€22.86 to €31.74

JOHN CONNOLLY
Owner

Mastercard

Visa

3 B&B £50.00

12 12

alc Inet

IRISH
HOTELS
FEDERATION

Closed 08 October - 31 March

BELLBRIDGE HOUSE HOTEL

**SPANISH POINT, MILTOWN MALBAY,
CO. CLARE**
TEL: 065-708 4038 FAX: 065-708 4830
EMAIL: bellbridge@eircom.net

HOTEL ★★★ MAP 5 E 8

Situated on the West Clare Coastline, this new hotel offers excellent accommodation and cuisine. Adjacent to Spanish Point golf course, sandy beaches, horse riding, fishing, tennis and water sports. Ideal base for touring the Burren, Cliffs of Moher, Aillwee Caves, Bunratty Castle and Folk Park. A family run hotel with friendly and efficient staff whose aim is to make your stay enjoyable and memorable. All rooms have hairdryer, tea/coffee making facilities, direct dial phone and colour TV.

WEB: www.westireland.com/bellbridge

B&B from £30.00 to £40.00
€38.09 to €50.79

PAT O'MALLEY
Proprietor

American Express

Mastercard

Visa

60 60

IRISH
HOTELS
FEDERATION

Closed 04 January - 10 March

Room rates are IR£ per room per night

CO. CLARE

BURKES ARMADA HOTEL

SPANISH POINT, MILTOWN MALBAY,
CO. CLARE
TEL: 065-708 4110 FAX: 065-708 4632
EMAIL: armada@iol.ie

UNDER CONSTRUCTION OPENING APR 2001

HOTEL R   MAP 5 E 8

The redeveloped Burkes 62 bedroom Armada Hotel commands a superb oceanfront setting in the beautiful seaside resort of Spanish Point. All rooms are furnished to a very high standard with satellite TV, tea/coffee facilities, hairdryer etc. The spectacularly located and Clare Good Food Circle recognised Cape Restaurant serves local and international cuisine in a relaxed environment. From the luxurious foyer to the olde world Flagship Bar Burkes Armada Hotel has something for everyone. Conference and banqueting facilities for 350 guests.

WEB: www.iol.ie/~armada/index.htm

Member of MinOtel Ireland Hotel Group

B&B from £25.00 to £40.00
€38.09 to €50.79

JUNE AND CLAIRE BURKE
Hosts

Mastercard
Visa

24 24

Open All Year

MOUNTSHANNON HOTEL

MOUNTSHANNON,
CO. CLARE
TEL: 061-927162 FAX: 061-927272

HOTEL ★★   MAP 6 H 9

The Mountshannon Hotel, situated in the rural and peaceful village of Mountshannon, offers you first class accommodation in friendly surroundings. All bedrooms are en suite with direct dial phone, TV, tea/coffee making facilities and hairdryer. Our continental style restaurant, which is known for excellent and reasonably priced cuisine, overlooks our garden and Lough Derg. Private car park. Mountshannon Harbour is four minutes walk away. Fishing, pony trekking and golf are available.

Member of Irish Family Hotels

B&B from £25.00 to £35.00
€31.74 to €44.44

PAULINE AND MICHAEL
MADDEN Director/Owner

American Express
Mastercard
Visa

14 14

Closed 25 December

DROMOLAND CASTLE

NEWMARKET-ON-FERGUS,
CO. CLARE
TEL: 061-368144 FAX: 061-363355
EMAIL: sales@dromoland.ie

HOTEL ★★★★★   MAP 6 G 8

Located 13km from Shannon Airport. Stately halls, elegant public areas & beautifully furnished guest rooms are steeped in a timeless atmosphere that is unique to Dromoland. The international reputation for excellence is reflected in the award-winning cuisine in the castle's Earl of Thomond & The Fig Tree Restaurant in the Dromoland Golf & Country Club. A meticulously maintained 18-hole golf course, fishing, horse-riding, clay shooting, health & beauty clinic & much more.

WEB: www.dromoland.ie

Member of Preferred Hotels & Resorts WW

Room Rate from £146.00 to £328.00
€185.38 to €416.47

MARK NOLAN
General Manager

American Express
Diners
Mastercard
Visa

☺ Weekend specials from £250.00

100 100

Open All Year

B&B rates are IR£ per person sharing per night incl. Breakfast

GOLF VIEW

LATOON, QUIN ROAD, NEWMARKET-ON-FERGUS, CO. CLARE
TEL: 061-368095 FAX: 065-682 8624
EMAIL: mhogangolfviewbandb@eircom.net

GUESTHOUSE ★★★ MAP 6 G 8

New purpose built family run 3*** guesthouse, overlooking Dromoland Castle and Clare Inn Golf Course, one hundred metres off N18 on Quin Road at the entrance to the Clare Inn Hotel. Non smoking en suite rooms on the ground floor with phone, multi-channel TV and hair dryers. Local tourist attractions include Bunratty and Knappogue Castles, many 18 hole golf courses and horse riding schools. Castle banquets can be arranged. Shannon Airport 10 minutes. Private car park.

WEB: www.clarelive.com/golfview

B&B from £25.00 to £30.00
€31.74 to €38.09

MAUREEN HOGAN
Proprietor

Mastercard

Visa

🛏🚗🐾📺☀♿🅿 Inet
6 6

IRISH HOTELS FEDERATION

Closed 23 - 28 December

HUNTERS LODGE

THE SQUARE, NEWMARKET-ON-FERGUS, CO. CLARE
TEL: 061-368577 FAX: 061-368057

GUESTHOUSE ★★★ MAP 6 G 8

Ideally situated for visitors arriving or departing from Shannon Airport (12km). We offer 6 comfortable bedrooms en suite with telephone and TV. Our olde worlde pub and restaurant specialises in good quality fresh food served in a relaxed atmosphere with a friendly and efficient service. Local tourist attractions include Bunratty Folk Park, castle banquets and many 18 hole golf courses. Ideal stopover for touring Co. Clare or commencing your trip to the west of Ireland.

B&B from £22.50 to £25.00
€28.57 to €31.74

ROBERT & KATHLEEN HEALY
Proprietors

American Express

Diners

Mastercard

Visa

🛏🚗🐾📺TCMU♿alc
6 6

Open All Year

CARRYGERRY COUNTRY HOUSE

SHANNON AIRPORT, NEWMARKET-ON-FERGUS, CO. CLARE
TEL: 061-363739 FAX: 061-363823
EMAIL: carrygerry-hotel@hotmail.com

HOTEL ★★★ MAP 6 G 7

Traditional Irish hospitality is alive and well in our 205 year old Country House, set on 15 acres of woodlands and gardens overlooking the Fergus River. Ideally situated for golf, horseriding and fishing. 10 minutes from Shannon Airport. Good Food Circle 3 Toques - outstanding cuisine - seafood specialities. Enchanting courtyard - sylvan setting. Weddings/private parties/banquets/ conference facilities. Coach House Bar. Ample parking. Languages F/G/E/D.

Member of Logis of Ireland

B&B from £47.50 to £57.50
€60.31 to €73.00

ANGELA & MARINUS VAN KOOYK
Proprietors

American Express

Diners

Mastercard

Visa

☺ Weekend specials from £116.00

🛏🚗🐾📺T☎♿C♥CM☀U♿🅿🎿
12 12

S♿alc🎣

IRISH HOTELS FEDERATION

Closed 01 January - 01 March

Room rates are IR£ per room per night

OAK WOOD ARMS HOTEL

SHANNON,
CO. CLARE
TEL: 061-361500 FAX: 061-361414
EMAIL: reservations@oakwoodarms.com

HOTEL ★★★ MAP 6 G 7

The Oak Wood Arms Hotel located on the airport road. With its eye-catching tower clock, the hotel retains an unusual charm and character. Sophie's lounge, with its delightful hand carved solid oak panels and old brass, has won national awards for its bar service and food. Also attracting a large following, the Spruce Goose Restaurant is cosy and intimate, offering a variety of dishes at a very high standard.

WEB: www.oakwoodarms.com

B&B from £40.00 to £49.00
€50.79 to €62.22

STEPHEN KEOGH
General Manager

American Express
Diners
Mastercard
Visa

100 100

alc

Closed 24 - 26 December

QUALITY HOTEL SHANNON

BALLYCASEY, SHANNON,
CO. CLARE
TEL: 061-364588 FAX: 061-364045
EMAIL: sales@qualityshannon.com

HOTEL N MAP 6 G 7

The Quality Hotel, Shannon, located 3 miles from the airport, opened in June 1999. This 54 roomed hotel has all rooms en suite with direct dial phone and multi channel TV. The Old Lodge Bar serves food all day. There is also an all day carvery. Enjoy à la carte meals every evening in the Lodge Restaurant. This lodge style hotel has a fine brick finish throughout.

WEB: www.choicehotelsireland.com

B&B from £35.00 to £50.00
€44.44 to €63.48

SHANE MCSHORTALL
General Manager

American Express
Diners
Mastercard
Visa

54 54

alc

Closed 24 - 25 December

SHANNON GREAT SOUTHERN HOTEL

SHANNON AIRPORT, SHANNON,
CO. CLARE
TEL: 061-471122 FAX: 061-471982
EMAIL: res@shannon.gsh.ie

HOTEL ★★★ MAP 6 G 7

Shannon Great Southern is a hotel with exceptional style and comfort within walking distance of the terminal building at Shannon Airport. All 115 rooms are en suite with direct dial phone, TV, tea/coffee making facilities, hairdryer and trouser press. Leisure facilities include a gym and steam room. Bookable worldwide through Utell International or central reservations 01-2144800.

WEB: www.gsh.ie

Room Rate from £100.00 to £100.00
€126.97 to €126.97

PAT DOOLEY
General Manager

American Express
Diners
Mastercard
Visa

☺ Weekend specials from £85.00

115 115

alc

Closed 24 - 26 December

B&B rates are IR£ per person sharing per night incl. Breakfast

ALEXANDRA GUEST HOUSE

5-6 O'CONNELL AVENUE,
LIMERICK
TEL: 061-318472 FAX: 061-400433
EMAIL: info@alexandra.iol.ie

GUESTHOUSE ★★ MAP 6 H 7

Elegant Victorian house, 5 mins walk to the heart of the city centre and located on the Angela's Ashes trail. Many beautifuly architecturally renowned churches nearby. Comfortable spacious rooms, en suite with multi channel TV, direct dial phone. Relaxing guest lounge with tea/coffee facilities provided. Conveniently located for bus and rail stations and 20 mins drive to Shannon and Bunratty. We can organise a taxi to pick up and drop off at Shannon etc. Multi guide recommendations.

B&B from £25.00 to £30.00
€31.74 to €38.09

AGNES DONOVAN
General Manager

Mastercard
Visa

10 7

Closed 23 December - 06 January

CASTLETROY PARK HOTEL

DUBLIN ROAD,
LIMERICK
TEL: 061-335566 FAX: 061-331117
EMAIL: sales@castletroy-park.ie

HOTEL ★★★★ MAP 6 H 7

Limerick's finest 4★★★★ hotel, the Castletroy Park Hotel, stands on 14 acres of beautifully landscaped gardens overlooking the Clare Hills, 3.2km from Limerick City. Our traditionally styled hotel offers McLaughlin's fine dining restaurant, the Merry Pedlar Irish pub and an outstanding health and fitness club. The 101 rooms and 6 suites have been furnished and equipped to the highest international standards, ideally suited to today's discerning traveller.

WEB: www.castletroy-park.ie

B&B from £47.00 to £80.00
€59.68 to €101.58

DARAGH O'NEILL
General Manager

American Express
Diners
Mastercard
Visa

Weekend specials from £110.00

107 107

Open All Year

CLIFTON HOUSE GUEST HOUSE

ENNIS ROAD,
LIMERICK
TEL: 061-451166 FAX: 061-451224
EMAIL: cliftonhouse@eircom.net

GUESTHOUSE ★★★ MAP 6 H 7

Set in 1 acre of landscape gardens. All sixteen rooms en suite, with multi-channel TV, trouser press, hair dryers, direct dial telephone. Complimentary tea/coffee available in our spacious TV lounge. We are situated on the main Limerick/Shannon Road. Within 15 minutes walk of city centre. 22 space car park. AA listed. Friendly welcome awaits you.

B&B from £22.50 to £25.00
€28.57 to €31.74

MICHAEL & MARY POWELL
Proprietor

Mastercard
Visa

16 16

Closed 24 December - 06 January

Room rates are IR£ per room per night

CLONMACKEN HOUSE GUEST HOUSE

**CLONMACKEN, OFF ENNIS ROAD,
(AT IVANS), LIMERICK
TEL: 061-327007 FAX: 061-327785
EMAIL: clonmac@indigo.ie**

GUESTHOUSE ★★★ MAP 6 H 7

A purpose built, family run guest house, built to the highest standards, with multi-channel TV, direct dial phone, tea/coffee making facilities and hair dryer in each of its ten en suite superbly decorated bedrooms. Limerick City and King John's Castle are 5 minutes drive, Bunratty and Shannon Airport are situated nearby. Golf outings, coach tours, car hire & Bunratty Banquet can be arranged. Private secure car parking on our own 1 acre site. Home to the Cranberries and Frank McCourt.

WEB: www.euroka.com/limerick/clonmacken

Member of Premier Guesthouses

B&B from £22.50 to £25.00
€28.57 to €31.74

BRID AND GERRY MCDONALD
Proprietors

American Express
Diners
Mastercard
Visa

10 10

Closed 21 December - 07 January

CRUISES HOUSE

**DENMARK STREET,
LIMERICK
TEL: 061-315320 FAX: 061-316995
EMAIL: cruiseshouse@eircom.net**

GUESTHOUSE ★★★ MAP 6 H 7

Limerick's largest guesthouse, situated in the heart of the city centre. Offering luxurious en suite accommodation with direct dial phone, satellite TV, tea/coffee making facilities and hairdryer in each room. Convenient to Limerick's finest restaurants, pubs and shops. Additional facilities include a business meeting room, bringing a whole new concept to the guesthouse market.

Member of Premier Guesthouses

B&B from £20.00 to £30.00
€25.39 to €38.09

CAROLE KELLY
Manager

American Express
Diners
Mastercard
Visa

29 27

Closed 24 - 28 December

INTERNATIONAL DIAL CODES

Emergency Services:
999 (freephone)

HOW TO DIAL INTERNATIONAL ACCESS CODE + COUNTRY CODE + AREA CODE + LOCAL NUMBER

SAMPLE CODES:
E.G. UNITED KINGDOM
00 44 + Area Code + Local No.

U.S.A.	00	1	+
Italy	00	39	+
Spain	00	34	+
France	00	33	+
Germany	00	49	+
Iceland	00	354	+
Japan	00	81	+
Luxembourg	00	352	+
Netherlands	00	31	+
Operator (national)			1190
(G. Britain)			1197
(International)			1198

B&B rates are IR£ per person sharing per night incl. Breakfast

FORTE TRAVELODGE

COONAGH ROUNDABOUT,
ENNIS ROAD, LIMERICK
TEL: 1800-709709   FAX: 061-457009

HOTEL P   MAP 6 H 7

This superb modern hotel offers comfortable yet affordable, accommodation. Each room is large enough to sleep up to three adults, a child under 12 and a baby in a cot. Excellent range of facilities, from en suite bathroom to colour TV including Sky Sports and Sky Movies. Unbeatable value for business or leisure. From UK call free: 0800 850950 or from Ireland Freephone 1800 709709.

WEB: www.travelodge.co.uk

Room Rate from £39.95 to £59.95
€50.73 to €76.12

GILLIAN NAUGHTON
General Manager

American Express
Diners
Mastercard
Visa

40 40

Open All Year

GLENTWORTH HOTEL

GLENTWORTH STREET,
LIMERICK
TEL: 061-413822 FAX: 061-413073
EMAIL: glentworthhotel@oceanfree.net

HOTEL R   MAP 6 H 7

The Glentworth Hotel established in 1878 and situated in the city centre is the perfect location for entertainment & shopping. Our hotel features 42 newly refurbished en suite rooms with multi channel TV, hairdryer, tea/coffee facilities & trouser press. Superb restaurant, coffee shop, lounge bar, banqueting & conference facilities. 5 mins walk from bus/train, 25 mins from Shannon and private lock-up carpark. The Glentworth where people matter - Limerick's friendliest hotel.

Member of UTELL / Robert Reid

B&B from £30.00 to £45.00
€38.09 to €57.14

JEREMIAH FLYNN
Director/General Manager

American Express
Diners
Mastercard
Visa

42 42

IRISH
HOTELS
FEDERATION

Open All Year

GREENHILLS HOTEL
CONFERENCE/LEISURE

ENNIS ROAD,
LIMERICK
TEL: 061-453033 FAX: 061-453307

HOTEL ★★★   MAP 6 H 7

This hotel is set in 3.5 acres of gardens, is 5 minutes from Limerick City, 15 minutes from Shannon International Airport. Enjoy our popular theme bar the Jockey club, award winning Bay Leaf Restaurant. Lamb a speciality - hotel's own farm. Also Brasserie Grill and residents' lounge. Super leisure centre, 18m swimming pool. Resident beautician / masseuse. Local amenities include horseriding, bowling and golf.

B&B from £40.00 to £55.00
€50.79 to €69.84

SARAH GREENE
Hospitality Manager

American Express
Diners
Mastercard
Visa

☺ Weekend specials from £90.00

57 57

IRISH
HOTELS
FEDERATION

Closed 25 - 26 December

Room rates are IR£ per room per night

HANRATTY'S HOTEL

**5 GLENTWORTH STREET,
LIMERICK
TEL: 061-410999 FAX: 061-411077**

HOTEL ★★ MAP 6 H 7

Compact, cosy and convenient, our 22 en suite rooms are decorated to a high standard to ensure comfort. Each room has TV, hairdryer and tea/coffee facilities and direct dial phone. Hanrattys, being Limerick's oldest hotel, retains its character in a modern world. Traditional bar with music most nights. City centre location, near all facilities. Overnight lock-up carpark.

Member of Irish Family Hotels

B&B from £25.00 to £32.50
€31.74 to €41.27

JOHN LIKELY
Proprietor

American Express
Diners
Mastercard
Visa

22 22

Closed 24 - 26 December

JURYS INN LIMERICK

**LOWER MALLOW STREET,
LIMERICK
TEL: 061-207000 FAX: 061-400966
EMAIL: limerick_inn@jurysdoyle.com**

HOTEL ★★★ MAP O6 H O7

Modern attractive rooms capable of accommodating up to 3 adults or 2 adults and 2 children. All rooms are en suite with multi-channel TV, radio, modem points, direct dial phone and tea/coffee making facilities. Located in the centre of Limerick City, the Inn has an informal restaurant and lively pub and an adjoining public multi-storey car park (fee payable). Jurys Doyle Hotel Group Central Reservations Tel. 01-607 0000 Fax. 01-631 6999.

WEB: www.jurysdoyle.com

Room Rate from £49.00 to £55.00
€62.21 to €69.83

DEREK McDONAGH
General Manager

American Express
Diners
Mastercard
Visa

151 151

Closed 24 - 26 December

JURYS LIMERICK HOTEL

**ENNIS ROAD,
LIMERICK
TEL: 061-327777 FAX: 061-326400
EMAIL: limerick_hotel@jurysdoyle.com**

HOTEL ★★★★ MAP 6 H 7

Enjoy 4**** service on a quiet 5 acre garden site situated on the banks of the River Shannon, just a short stroll to the city centre. Our Sorrels Restaurant offers superb international cuisine while the Limericks Bar invites you to experience the local culture in comfortable surroundings. The extensive leisure facilities provide you with a choice of ways to relax during your stay. Jurys Doyle Hotel Group Central Reservations:
Tel: 01-607 0000
Fax: 01-631 6999

WEB: www.jurysdoyle.com

B&B from £54.00 to £104.00
€68.57 to €132.05

AILEEN PHELAN
General Manager

American Express
Diners
Mastercard
Visa

95 95

Closed 24 - 27 December

B&B rates are IR£ per person sharing per night incl. Breakfast

LIMERICK INN HOTEL

ENNIS ROAD,
LIMERICK
TEL: 061-326666 FAX: 061-326281
EMAIL: limerick-inn@limerick-inn.ie

HOTEL ★★★★ MAP 6 H 7

15 mins from Shannon Airport and 5 from the centre of Historical Limerick, it is set in landscaped gardens with free car park. All the luxuries of a modern 4**** hotel, spacious guestrooms, excellent Irish and Intl Cuisine in the Burgundy Room Restaurant. Visit MacEee's Pub for good food and drink in traditional surroundings. Health and Leisure Centre has facilities to unwind or for the more energetic to work out. Full Conference Facilities. GDS code UI Free 1800 44 UTELL.

WEB: limerick-inn.ie

B&B from £63.00 to £78.00
€79.99 to €99.04

JOHN FAHEY
General Manager

American Express
Diners
Mastercard
Visa

Weekend specials from £100.00

153 153
UPS

Closed 24 - 26 December

LIMERICK RYAN HOTEL

ARDHU HOUSE, ENNIS ROAD,
LIMERICK
TEL: 061-453922 FAX: 061-326333
EMAIL: ryan@indigo.ie

HOTEL ★★★ MAP 6 H 7

The original house of the Limerick Ryan Hotel dates back to 1780. Restored to enhance the original architecture, this hotel combines the grace and spaciousness of an earlier age with the comforts of today. 179 en suite bedrooms, 2 suites, the award winning Ardhu Restaurant, gymnasium, superior meeting rooms, Toddy's Bar, Cocktail Bar, business centre and complimentary car parking. 2km from the city and 15 minutes from Shannon Airport. AA, RAC and Egon Ronay recommended.

WEB: www.ryan-hotels.com

B&B from £40.00 to £65.00
€50.79 to €82.53

DERMOT FEHILY
General Manager

American Express
Diners
Mastercard
Visa

Weekend specials from £79.00

181 181
P

Open All Year

RAILWAY HOTEL

PARNELL STREET,
LIMERICK
TEL: 061-413653 FAX: 061-419762
EMAIL: sales@railwayhotel.ie

HOTEL ★★ MAP 6 H 7

Family run hotel, owned and managed by the McEnery/Collins Family, this hotel offers Irish hospitality at its best. Personal attention is a way of life, along with an attractive lounge/bar, comfortable en suite accommodation and good home cooked food, one can't ask for more. Ideally situated, opposite rail/bus station, convenient to city centre, it is the perfect stop for the tourist and businessman alike. All major credit cards accepted.

WEB: www.railwayhotel.ie

B&B from £27.00 to £30.00
€34.28 to €38.09

PAT & MICHELE MCENERY
Owners/Managers

American Express
Diners
Mastercard
Visa

20 20

Closed 25 - 26 December

Room rates are IR£ per room per night

CO. LIMERICK
LIMERICK CITY

ROYAL GEORGE HOTEL

O'CONNELL STREET, LIMERICK
TEL: 061-414566 FAX: 061-317171
EMAIL: royalgeorgehotel@eircom.net

HOTEL R   MAP 6 H 7

This family run 3*** hotel is ideally suited for business or pleasure situated in the heart of Limerick City. Enjoy a night in our traditional Irish pub of distinction, The Sibin, with nightly entertainment. 15 mins drive from Shannon International Airport. Local attractions include St. Johns Castle, Bunratty Folk Park, the Hunt Museum, Cliffs of Moher and Adare. Secure lock-up carpark.

WEB: www.royalgeorge.com

Room Rate from £39.00 to £64.00
€49.52 to €81.26

SEAN LALLY

American Express
Diners
Mastercard
Visa

⌨🏠🅿️⬆️T©♥CMU♪♫P S
52 52
☕🍴

Closed 25 - 26 December

SHANNON GROVE GUESTHOUSE

ATHLUNKARD, CORBALLY ROAD, LIMERICK
TEL: 061-345756 FAX: 061-343838
EMAIL: noreenmarsh@eircom.net

GUESTHOUSE ★★★   MAP 6 H 7

Shannon Grove Guesthouse is a charming, family-managed, registered 3*** guesthouse, within 5 mins of Limerick City, yet away from the bustle of city noise and traffic. With 10 beautifully decorated en suite bedrooms, multi channel TV, direct dial phone and secure car parking, Shannon Grove is the ideal location for your stay in Limerick, being in close proximity to a wide range of leisure activities, university, Shannon Airport, Bunratty and King John's Castle, and Lough Derg. Route R463, from Limerick.

B&B from £25.00 to £30.00
€31.74 to €38.09

NOREEN MARSH
Owner

Mastercard
Visa

⌨🏠🅿️T❀U♪P
10 10

Closed 15 December - 06 January

SOUTH COURT BUSINESS AND LEISURE HOTEL

RAHEEN ROUNDABOUT, ADARE ROAD, LIMERICK
TEL: 065-682 3000 FAX: 065-682 3759
EMAIL: reservations@lynchotels.com

HOTEL U   MAP 6 H 7

Few hotels compare to this impressive RAC 4* hotel, 65 large en suite rooms with satellite TV, latest pay per view movies, fax/modem point; executive rooms have fax, mini bar, trouser press, writing desk etc. Seasons fine dining à la carte restaurant & Boru's Porterhouse traditional Irish pub/bistro. Polo Lifestyle Club incl gym, sauna, massage, 3 indoor pools due 2001. Business/office support. Parking 250 cars. Limerick 5 mins, Shannon 15 mins. 60 new rooms designed with Paul Costelloe, plus International Convention Centre for 1,250.

WEB: www.southcourthotel.com

Member of Lynch Hotels

B&B from £40.00 to £65.00
€50.79 to €82.53

MICHAEL B LYNCH GROUP MD
David Byrne Gen Mgr

American Express
Diners
Mastercard
Visa

☺ Weekend specials from £96.00

⌨🏠🅿️⬆️T S©♥CM🐕🍴📷
65 65
U♪♫P S☕🍴alc Inet FAX

Open All Year

B&B rates are IR£ per person sharing per night incl. Breakfast

TWO MILE INN HOTEL

ENNIS ROAD,
LIMERICK
TEL: 061-326255 FAX: 061-453783

HOTEL R MAP 6 H 7

123 bedroomed 3*** hotel situated outside Limerick City on the main Limerick/Shannon/Galway Road, 15 minutes drive from Shannon International Airport, and 6.44km from Bunratty Castle and Folk Park. All bedrooms have private bathroom, TV, radio & tea/coffee making facilities. À la carte and table d'hôte restaurant and Thady O'Neills old world Pub and Restaurant with traditional music. Ideal base for scenic tours to the Cliffs of Moher, Galway and Killarney. Toll Free 1800 528 1234.

Member of Best Western Hotels

B&B from £35.00 to £55.00
€44.44 to €69.84

BRENDAN DUNNE
Proprietor

American Express
Diners
Mastercard
Visa

☺ Weekend specials from £75.00

123 123

Open All Year

WOODFIELD HOUSE HOTEL

ENNIS ROAD,
LIMERICK
TEL: 061-453022 FAX: 061-326755
EMAIL: woodfieldhotel@eircom.net

HOTEL ★★★ MAP 6 H 7

Reminiscent of days gone by, the stylish Woodfield House Hotel welcomes you with traditional family hospitality. Over the years it has earned a reputation for quality, service and fine cuisine, creating a memorable experience. A combination of convenient ground floor and upper story en suite rooms offers a high standard of comfort to ensure a relaxed stay. All bedrooms include direct dial phone, multi-channel TV, trouser press and hair dryer.

WEB: www.woodfieldhousehotel.com

Member of MinOtel Ireland Hotel Group

B&B from £42.50 to £49.50
€53.96 to €62.85

AUSTIN GIBBONS
Proprietor

American Express
Diners
Mastercard
Visa

☺ Weekend specials from £90.00

26 26

Closed 25 December

LEENS HOTEL

MAIN STREET, ABBEYFEALE,
CO. LIMERICK
TEL: 068-31121 FAX: 068-32550
EMAIL: leenshotelabbeyfeale@eircom.net

HOTEL ★★ MAP 5 E 6

Leens Hotel is located in the Square, Abbeyfeale in the heart of West Limerick. It has been recently refurbished to the highest standard and is under the personal supervision of Maurice and Olive Sheehan. It has 19 new bedrooms, tastefully finished to a very high standard. There is a carvery lunch served daily and a wide selection of barfood available throughout the day. There is a very warm atmosphere in the Oak Bar and a very intimate restaurant offering the best in local produce.

B&B from £25.00 to £37.50
€31.74 to €47.62

OLIVE AND MAURICE SHEEHAN

American Express
Mastercard
Visa

☺ Weekend specials from £70.00

19 19

Closed 24 - 26 December

ADARE MANOR HOTEL & GOLF RESORT

ADARE,
CO. LIMERICK
TEL: 061-396566 FAX: 061-396124
EMAIL: reservations@adaremanor.com

HOTEL ★★★★★ MAP 6 G 7

Located 20 miles from Shannon Airport. Adare Manor Hotel & Golf Resort, set on the banks of the River Maigue, boasts splendour in its luxuriously finished rooms. The Oak Room Restaurant provides haute cuisine laced with Irish charm. Indoor facilities include heated pool, fitness centre, sauna and massage therapy. Outdoor pursuits include fishing, horseriding, clay pigeon shooting and the Robert Trent Jones Senior championship golf course. New clubhouse with state of the art conference centre.

WEB: www.adaremanor.ie

Member of Small Luxury Hotels

B&B from £75.00 to £250.00
€95.23 to €317.43

FERGHAL PURCELL
Managing Director

American Express
Diners
Mastercard
Visa

74 74

Open All Year

CARRABAWN HOUSE

KILLARNEY ROAD (N21), ADARE,
CO. LIMERICK
TEL: 061-396067 FAX: 061-396925
EMAIL: carrabaw@indigo.ie

GUESTHOUSE ★★★ MAP 6 G 7

Beside Adare Manor Golf Course, multi recommended Carrabawn Guesthouse is a luxury establishment situated in the picturesque village of Adare, renowned for its Tidy Town awards. The Lohan Family offer you first class accommodation in friendly surroundings and assure you a most memorable stay. Colour TV, direct dial phone, tea/coffee making facilities and hairdryer in all rooms. Only 30 mins Shannon Airport / Bunratty Folk Park. Equestrian centre 1km, golf courses too numerous to mention.

WEB: www.carrabawnhouseadare.com

Member of Premier Guesthouses

B&B from £22.50 to £32.50
€28.57 to €41.27

BRIDGET LOHAN
Proprietor

Mastercard
Visa

7 7

Closed 24 - 26 December

DUNRAVEN ARMS HOTEL

ADARE,
CO. LIMERICK
TEL: 061-396633 FAX: 061-396541
EMAIL: reservations@dunravenhotel.com

HOTEL ★★★★ MAP 6 G 7

Established in 1792 a 4★★★★ old world hotel surrounded by ornate thatched cottages, in Ireland's prettiest village. Each bedroom, including twelve suites, is beautifully appointed with antique furniture, dressing room and bathroom en suite. Award-winning restaurant, AA Three Red Rosettes. Leisure centre comprised of a 17m pool, steam room and gym studio. Equestrian and golf holidays a speciality. 30 mins from Shannon Airport. GDS Access Code UI Toll Free 1-800-44 UTELL

WEB: www.dunravenhotel.com

Member of Manor House Hotels

B&B from £72.50 to £89.50
€92.06 to €113.64

LOUIS MURPHY
Resident Manager

American Express
Diners
Mastercard
Visa

76 76

Open All Year

B&B rates are IR£ per person sharing per night incl. Breakfast

FITZGERALDS WOODLANDS HOUSE HOTEL AND LEISURE CLUB

KNOCKANES, ADARE,
CO. LIMERICK
TEL: 061-605100 FAX: 061-396073
EMAIL: reception@woodlands-hotel.ie

HOTEL ★★★ MAP 6 G 7

Luxurious 94 bedroom hotel located in the Splendour of Adare, Co. Limerick on its own grounds of 44 acres. Superior and Executive Suites available boasting Jacuzzi baths. Award winning Brennan Room Restaurant, Timmy Mac's Traditional Bar and Bistro, Trad sessions and storytelling. Reva's Hair, Beauty & Relaxation Spa boasting Balneotherapy & Yonka. State of the art Health & Leisure Club. Golf & Pamper Packages a speciality. Excellent Wedding and Conference Facilities.

WEB: www.woodlands-hotel.ie

Member of Village Inn Hotels

B&B from £45.00 to £65.00
€57.14 to €82.53

DICK, MARY & DAVID FITZGERALD Hosts

American Express
Diners
Mastercard
Visa

94 94

Closed 24 - 26 December

CASTLE OAKS HOUSE HOTEL & COUNTRY CLUB

CASTLECONNELL,
CO. LIMERICK
TEL: 061-377666 FAX: 061-377717
EMAIL: info@castle-oaks.com

HOTEL ★★★ MAP 6 H 7

The Castle Oaks Country Hotel and its superb country club leisure centre, including indoor pool, are set on a 26 acre estate on the banks of the River Shannon. All our lavishly furnished bedrooms are en suite. Our luxurious suites contain jacuzzis. The Castle Oaks is renowned for its superb cuisine and ambience. We welcome you to experience the warmth and hospitality of our Georgian mansion. Fishing and golfing available locally. Logis of Ireland member.
Tel: 01-668 9743.

WEB: www.castle-oaks.com

Member of Logis of Ireland

B&B from £39.60 to £71.50
€50.28 to €90.78

FRANCIS MURPHY/AILEEN KENNEDY Hosts

American Express
Diners
Mastercard
Visa

20 20

Closed 24 - 26 December

KILMURRY LODGE HOTEL

DUBLIN ROAD, CASTLETROY,
LIMERICK
TEL: 061-331133 FAX: 061-330011
EMAIL: manager@kilmurry.com

HOTEL ★★★ MAP 6 H 7

Opened in 1995, the Kilmurry Lodge Hotel boasts 43 beautiful bedrooms, landscaped gardens, extensive parking & great location. Close to the University & National Technology Park - this is an excellent venue for business or pleasure. The restaurant is very popular & serves breakfast, lunch & dinner daily, whilst Nelligan's Bar is famous for a great carvery lunch or pint. 5 well appointed conference rooms also available. A friendly hotel providing comfort & value for money.

B&B from £45.00 to £60.00
€57.14 to €76.18

SIOBHAN & PAT HOARE Proprietors

American Express
Diners
Mastercard
Visa

Weekend specials from £89.00

43 43

Closed 25 - 26 December

Room rates are IR£ per room per night

COURTENAY LODGE HOTEL

NEWCASTLE WEST,
CO. LIMERICK
TEL: 069-62244 FAX: 069-77184
EMAIL: res@courtenaylodge.iol.ie

HOTEL ★★★ MAP 2 F 6

A warm welcome awaits you at the Courtenay Lodge Hotel situated on the main Limerick to Killarney Road and only 15 mins from the picturesque village of Adare. The newly-built, tastefully decorated, en suite rooms complete with TV, direct dial phone, power showers, trouser press, tea/coffee facilities, etc. ensure a level of comfort second to none. The ideal base for touring the Shannon and South West region and the perfect location for golfers to enjoy some of the most renowned courses.

B&B from £30.00 to £45.00
€38.09 to €57.14

DECLAN O'GRADY
General Manager

American Express
Diners
Mastercard
Visa

22 22

Closed 25 December

DEVON INN HOTEL

TEMPLEGLANTINE,
NEWCASTLEWEST, CO. LIMERICK
TEL: 069-84122 FAX: 069-84255
EMAIL: devoninnhotel@eircom.net

HOTEL ★★★ MAP 6 F 6

The newly refurbished Devon Inn Hotel offers a superb base to explore the wonderful attractions of the South West. Situated midway between Limerick City and Killarney in the heart of West Limerick. The hotel features 40 excellent bedrooms, a superb restaurant featuring the best of local produce, a choice of two bars and conference and banqueting for up to 400 guests. Private car park. Just over an hour's drive from Shannon Airport and under an hour to Killarney.

Member of Irish Family Hotels

B&B from £30.00 to £40.00
€38.09 to €50.79

WILLIAM SHEEHAN
Manager

American Express
Diners
Mastercard
Visa

Weekend specials from £75.00

40 40

Closed 24 - 26 December

RATHKEALE HOUSE HOTEL

RATHKEALE,
CO. LIMERICK
TEL: 069-63333 FAX: 069-63300
EMAIL: rhh@iol.ie

HOTEL ★★★ MAP 6 G 6

Rathkeale House Hotel, located just off the N21 Limerick to Killarney route and 4 miles West of Ireland's prettiest village, Adare. 26 superior en suite rooms, O'Deas Bistro open each evening 6-9:30pm. Chestnut Tree Bar where carvery lunch is available each day. Conference & banqueting facilities for 300 guests. Golf packages a speciality. Local courses, Adare, Adare Manor, Newcastlewest (Ardagh), Charleville. Spacious gardens for your relaxation. A warm welcome awaits you.

B&B from £35.00 to £45.00
€44.44 to €57.14

GERRY O'CONNOR
General Manager

American Express
Diners
Mastercard
Visa

3 nights Dinner, B&B, 3 rounds of Golf from £169.00

26 26

Closed 25 December

B&B rates are IR£ per person sharing per night incl. Breakfast

ABBEY COURT HOTEL

DUBLIN ROAD, NENAGH,
CO. TIPPERARY
TEL: 067-41111 FAX: 067-41022
EMAIL: abycourt@indigo.ie

HOTEL ★★★ MAP 6 I 8

Located on the main Dublin Road (N7) and within easy walking distance of Nenagh Town, the Abbey Court Hotel boasts 46 lavishly appointed rooms decorated to suit the most discerning guests with direct dial phone, multi-channel TV, tea/coffee making facilities, trouser press/iron centre, etc. Superb conference and banqueting facilities with secretarial back-up. Award winning Rosette Cloister Restaurant, Abbots Bar and daily carvery lunch. Golf packages available. State of the art leisure facilities opening for 2001 season.

WEB: www.nenagh-abbeycourt.ie

B&B from £39.00 to £49.00
€49.52 to €62.22

TOM WALSH
Managing Director

American Express
Diners
Mastercard
Visa

46 46

Open All Year

DROMINEER BAY HOTEL

DROMINEER, NENAGH,
CO. TIPPERARY
TEL: 067-24114 FAX: 067-24444
EMAIL: stay@dromineer.com

HOTEL ★★★ MAP 6 I 8

Family run hotel on the shores of Lough Derg near Nenagh in County Tipperary. Beautiful lake views and a high level of comfort and service. Facilities include Captains Deck Bar serving extensive à la carte menu and Moorings Restaurant. Coarse and game fishing, canoeing, yachting, pony trekking, shooting, walking and golf. Conference facilities available.

WEB: www.dromineer.com

Member of Coast and Country Hotels

B&B from £35.00 to £45.00
€44.44 to €57.14

GERRY CALLANAN
Owner

American Express
Diners
Mastercard
Visa

23 23

Open All Year

GRANT'S HOTEL

CASTLE STREET, ROSCREA,
CO. TIPPERARY
TEL: 0505-23300 FAX: 0505-23209
EMAIL: grantshotel@eircom.net

HOTEL ★★★ MAP 7J9

Located on the main link road from Dublin to Kerry, Limerick and Clare (N7). Visit Grant's Hotel, 3*** Hotel in the heart of the heritage town of Roscrea. The hotel features 25 en suite bedrooms pleasantly furbished in warm toned colours. Lunch and evening meals served in Kitty's Tavern daily. The award-winning Lemon Tree Restaurant is the ideal place to relax after a day's golfing, fishing or exploring Ely O'Carroll country. Special golf packages available.

WEB: www.grantshotel.com

B&B from £35.00 to £45.00
€44.44 to €57.14

SHARON GRANT
Proprietor

American Express
Diners
Mastercard
Visa

Weekend specials from £90.00

25 25

Closed 24 - 27 December

RACKET HALL COUNTRY HOUSE HOTEL

DUBLIN ROAD, ROSCREA,
CO. TIPPERARY
TEL: 0505-21748 FAX: 0505-23701
EMAIL: racketh@iol.ie

HOTEL U MAP 7 J 9

Charming family-run olde world country residence set in the heart of the monastic midlands. Situated on the busy N7 just outside the heritage town of Roscrea, this is the ideal location for the avid golfer, fishing enthusiast or those who wish to explore the abundant historic sites in the area. The Slieve Bloom Mountains are also only a stone's throw away. This is a very convenient stopping off point from Dublin to Limerick, Clare or Kerry. Lily Bridges Bar, Willow Tree Restaurant.

B&B from £24.50 to £29.50
€31.11 to €37.46

MICHAEL COSTELLO
Proprietor

American Express
Mastercard
Visa

☺ Weekend specials from £69.00

10 10

alc

IRISH HOTELS FEDERATION

Closed 25 December

TOWER

CHURCH STREET, ROSCREA,
CO. TIPPERARY
TEL: 0505-21774 FAX: 0505-22425
EMAIL: thetower@eircom.net

GUESTHOUSE ★★★ MAP 7 J 9

The Tower is a unique 3*** guest house offering the facilities of a fully licensed restaurant and bar with à la carte and dinner menus. The 10 bedrooms are furnished to a very high standard. It is situated in the town centre and golfing, pitch & putt, angling and hill-walking are available nearby. Special golf weekends available on request. Members of Premier Guest Houses and Automobile Association.

Member of Premier Guesthouses

B&B from £20.00 to £25.00
€25.39 to €31.74

GERARD & BRIDIE COUGHLAN
Proprietors

American Express
Diners
Mastercard
Visa

✓

10 10

IRISH HOTELS FEDERATION

Closed 25 - 26 December

ANNER HOTEL & LEISURE CENTRE

DUBLIN ROAD, THURLES,
CO. TIPPERARY
TEL: 0504-21799 FAX: 0504-22111

HOTEL ★★★ MAP 7 J 7

The Anner Hotel is situated on its own private grounds with beautiful landscaped gardens. We offer our guests a warm welcome, excellent food and a friendly service in comfortable surroundings. Each room is spaciously furnished and fully fitted with direct dial phone, cable TV, tea/coffee making facilities, trouser press and hairdryer. Our luxurious newly-opened health & leisure centre has an 18m pool, kiddies pool, jacuzzi, sauna, steam room, solarium and gym. On the outskirts of Thurles.

WEB: www.iol.ie/annerhtl.htm

B&B from £39.50 to £55.00
€50.15 to €69.84

FRANK MULCAHY

American Express
Diners
Mastercard
Visa

✓

☺ Weekend specials from £75.00

64 64

Open All Year

B&B rates are IR£ per person sharing per night incl. Breakfast

Galway, Mayo and Roscommon

There is a special quality about these three counties in the West of Ireland which is unique in Europe. The welcome is heartwarming, the quality of life, people and landscapes are all there for the visitor to enjoy.

The spectaculury beautiful countryside, the coast that has been etched by the Atlantic, the rambling hills and mountains and the lovely lakes and bays that mirror that special light from the clear skies over the countryside. Each county has its own special attractions and rich in all that is best in Irish folklore, music and song. There is something here for everyone. You will not be disappointed

MAJOR ATTRACTIONS

Galway City has a host of attractions on offer, including Galway Irish Crystal Heritage Centre,Royal Tara China, Lynch's Castle, the Spanish Arch, Nora Barnacle House and the Talbhdhearc – Ireland's only Irish-speaking theatre. In Co. Galway you have Thoor Ballylee, the home of the poet W.B. Yeats, and Coole Park Visitor Centre, former home of Lady Gregory, both located just north of Gort. The Battle of Aughrim Interpretative Centre near Ballinasloe gives a fascinating account of one of the most decisive battles in European history. Other major attractions include Aughnanure Castle in Oughterard, Dan O'Hara's Pre-Famine Farm near Clifden, Leenane Cultural Centre, Kylemore Abbey in Letterfrack, Connemara, Glengowla Mines near Oughterard and Ionad Arann, Aran's Heritage Centre on Inishmore.

Amongst the attractions worth a visit in Co. Mayo are the Ceide Fields in Ballycastle, Foxford Woollen Mills,Turlough Park House, Knock Shrine and Folk Museum, Ballintubber Abbey and the Westport Heritage Centre.

While Roscommon can boast the County Heritage and Genealogical centre in Strokestown, Strokestown Park House, Gardens and Famine Museum, Clonalis House in Castlerea, Douglas Hyde Interpretative Centre in Porthard, King House and Boyle Abbey in Boyle and the magnificent Lough Key Forest Park.

For information and accommodation bookings in Counties Galway, Mayo and Roscommon contact:

Ireland West Tourism,
Aras Fáilte, Forster Street, Galway.
Tel: 00353 91 563081
Fax: 00353 565201
Email: info@irelandwest.ie

Tourist Information Office,
James Street, Westport, Co. Mayo.
Tel: 00353 98 25711
Fax: 00353 98 26790
Email: westport@irelandwest.ie

Tourist Information Office,
Boyle, Co. Roscommon.
Tel: 00353 79 62145.

Galway Arts Festival, Co. Galway.
July

Guinness Galway Races, Co. Galway.
July / August

Galway International Oyster Festival, Co. Galway.
September

Guinness Ballinasloe International October Fair & Festival, Co. Galway.
September / October

Event details correct at time of going to press

A STAR OF THE SEA

125 UPPER SALTHILL,
SALTHILL, GALWAY
TEL: 091-525900   FAX: 091-589563
EMAIL: astarsea@iol.ie

GUESTHOUSE P   MAP 6 F 10

Luxury family managed guesthouse overlooking Galway Bay, within walking distance of Galway's medieval city and Salthill's sandy beach. An ideal base for holiday makers and business people, offering a very high standard of accommodation. All rooms have en suite, cable TV, hairdryers, tea/coffee. Some of our rooms have stunning views of the sea with balconies. Convenient to Leisureland, tennis, windsurfing, fishing, horseriding and golf. Safe facilities and carpark available.

WEB: www.astarofthesea.com

B&B from £20.00 to £35.00
€25.39 to €44.44

LORRAINE MCEVADDY
Owner

American Express
Mastercard
Visa

8 8

ABBEY HOUSE

113 UPPER NEWCASTLE,
GALWAY
TEL: 091-524394   FAX: 091-528217
EMAIL: johndarby@eircom.net

GUESTHOUSE ★★   MAP 6 F 10

Family run guest house located on the N59 leading to Connemara. Convenient to city centre. Rooms are en suite with cable TV, and direct dial phones. Private car parking. Close to golf, fishing, tennis, swimming pool, horse riding, seaside and city centre. Excellent location for touring Connemara, Aran Islands and the Burren. A warm welcome awaits you from the Darby family.

WEB: homepage.eircom.net/~johndarby/

B&B from £18.00 to £30.00
€22.86 to €38.09

JOHN DARBY

Mastercard
Visa

12 11

IRISH
HOTELS
FEDERATION

ABBINGTON GUEST HOUSE

CUAN GLAS, 12 BISHOP O'DONNELL'S
ROAD, TAYLORS HILL, GALWAY
TEL: 091-525530
EMAIL: abbingtonguesthouse@eircom.net

GUESTHOUSE ★★★   MAP 6 F 10

New luxurious, purpose-built guesthouse within walking distance of Salthill Promenade and 5 minutes drive from city centre. All rooms interior designed with power shower, bath, direct dial phone, cable TV, hairdryer, iron press and complimentary tea/coffee facilities. Private car parking. Convenient to Leisureland, tennis, wind surfing, fishing and horseriding. Ground floor rooms available.

WEB: www.galway.net/pages/abbington

B&B from £17.00 to £40.00
€21.59 to €50.79

COLETTE NUGENT
Proprietor

Mastercard
Visa

8 8

B&B rates are IR£ per person sharing per night incl. Breakfast

CO. GALWAY
GALWAY CITY

ACORN GUESTHOUSE

19 DUBLIN ROAD, GALWAY
TEL: 091-770990   FAX: 091-770173
EMAIL: acorn1@eircom.net

GUESTHOUSE ★★★   MAP 6 F 10

Acorn Guesthouse is a family run registered guesthouse. Within walking distance of Galway City. An ideal base for holiday makers and business people. Bedrooms contain en suite bathrooms, orthopaedic beds, direct dial phones, hairdryers, remote control multi-channel TV, complimentary tea and coffee. Private car park. Acorn Guesthouse is adjacent to Ryan's Hotel and Corrib Great Southern.

WEB: www.homepage.eircom.net/~acorn

B&B from £20.00 to £40.00
€25.39 to €50.79

GARRY & CAROL McKEON
Owners

Mastercard
Visa

7 5

Closed 23 - 27 December

ADARE GUEST HOUSE

9 FATHER GRIFFIN PLACE, GALWAY
TEL: 091-582638   FAX: 091-583963
EMAIL: adare@iol.ie

GUESTHOUSE ★★★   MAP 6 F 10

Adare Guesthouse is a family managed guesthouse, within 5 minutes of city centre (train/bus). Refurbished with old time pine furniture & floors, you can enjoy your multi choice breakfast in our dining room overlooking our beautiful patio area. All bedrooms have en suite, direct dial phones, cable TV & hairdryers. Tea/coffee & ironing facilities are available. 2 new suites built to a high standard with baths, direct dial fax phone, trouser press/iron, tea/coffee/cable TV/radio. Safe facilities available.

B&B from £22.50 to £35.00
€28.57 to €44.44

GRAINNE & PADRAIC CONROY
Proprietors

American Express
Mastercard
Visa

12 12

Closed 24 - 27 December

ANNO SANTO HOTEL

THREADNEEDLE ROAD, SALTHILL, GALWAY
TEL: 091-523011   FAX: 091-522110
EMAIL: annosant@iol.ie

HOTEL ★★   MAP 6 F 10

Small family run hotel located in quiet residential area. Galway's major tennis/badminton and squash club lies opposite the hotel. The golf club is also close by (1km), while Galway City and beaches are within easy reach. We are also on a main bus route. All rooms are en suite, TV, tea/coffee and direct dial telephone. Your hosts, the Vaughan Family, provide high class service in comfortable bedrooms at budget prices.

B&B from £25.00 to £42.50
€31.74 to €53.96

GERARD & JOANNA VAUGHAN
Proprietors

American Express
Diners
Mastercard
Visa

14 14

Closed 20 December - 20 January

Room rates are IR£ per room per night

WEST 343

ARDAWN HOUSE

31 COLLEGE ROAD,
GALWAY
TEL: 091-568833 FAX: 091-563454
EMAIL: ardawn@iol.ie

GUESTHOUSE ★★★★   MAP 6 F 10

Ardawn House is a luxurious haven
for the discerning visitor to Galway.
Located within five minutes walking
of city centre, train & bus. Antiques,
fresh flowers, silver and china help
to make our multi choice home
cooked breakfast famous. All
bedrooms have en suite, direct dial
phones, cable TV & hairdryers.
Tea/coffee & ironing facilities are
also available. Highly recommended
in Guide du Routard, AA and many
other guide books.

WEB: www.galway.net/pages/ardawn-house/

B&B from £25.00 to £45.00
€31.74 to €57.14

MIKE & BREDA GUILFOYLE
Proprietors

American Express
Mastercard
Visa

🛏🅿☎🖵T🅿S
6 6

HOTELS FEDERATION

Closed 22 - 26 December

ARDILAUN HOUSE HOTEL, CONFERENCE CENTRE & LEISURE CLUB

TAYLOR'S HILL,
GALWAY
TEL: 091-521433 FAX: 091-521546
EMAIL: ardilaun@iol.ie

HOTEL ★★★★   MAP 6 F 10

The Ardilaun is a privately owned 89
bedroomed 4**** hotel, in 5 acres
of beautiful grounds. All rooms en
suite with *direct dial phone *TV
*Trouser press *Tea and coffee
making facilities *Hairdryer *Award
winning restaurant *New leisure club
*Deck level pool *Hydro-spa
*Jacuzzi *Sauna *Steamroom
*Aerobics *Hi-tech gym *Sun-room
therapy suites *Billiard room *Golf
*Tennis *Beach & city within 5
minutes drive. Conference centre for
25-500 persons. Bookable
worldwide UteLL International.

WEB: www.ardilaunhousehotel.ie

Member of Signature Hotels

B&B from £50.00 to £90.00
€63.49 to €114.28

T.A. MACCARTHY O'HEA
General Manager

American Express
Diners
Mastercard
Visa

🎿🍴

😊 Weekend specials from £95.00

🛏🅿☎🖵🅱T🅲🚲CM❋🕭🛏🆑
U🅿🅿🖪🆂🅰alc🔥☎ Inet

HOTELS FEDERATION

Closed 22 - 28 December

ASHFORD MANOR

NO 7 COLLEGE ROAD,
GALWAY
TEL: 091-563941 FAX: 091-563941
EMAIL: ashfordmanor@esatclear.ie

GUESTHOUSE U MAP 6 F 10

Centrally located in the heart of
Galway's City centre, Ashford Manor
offers a unique combination of
stylish en suite accommodation in a
prestigious location at affordable
prices. All rooms include multi-
channel TV, radio, direct dial phone,
professional hairdryer and tea/coffee
facilities. Ideal base for touring
Connemara, the Burren and the Aran
Islands. AA selected ♦♦♦♦ and as
featured in Bon Voyage. Credit cards
accepted.

WEB: www.galway.net/page/ashfordmanor

B&B from £20.00 to £35.00
€25.39 to €44.44

CORINNE MANNION
Proprietor

American Express
Mastercard
Visa

🛏🅿☎🖵T🅲🚲CMU🅿🔔
5 5

Closed 24 - 25 December

B&B rates are IR£ per person sharing per night incl. Breakfast

ATLANTIC VIEW HOUSE

**4 OCEAN WAVE,
GALWAY**
TEL: 091-582109 FAX: 091-528566
EMAIL: jennifertreacy@ireland.com

GUESTHOUSE ★★★ MAP 6 F 10

Atlantic View House is a luxurious haven overlooking Galway Bay with a large sun balcony. Some of our rooms have stunning views of the sea, with balconies. The house overlooks the beach with spectacular views of the Aran Islands and the Burren Mountains. We are only a short walk from the medieval city of Galway and the seaside resort of Salthill. Our rooms are luxuriously decorated with direct dial phone, satellite TV, trouser press, hair dryer, hospitality tray and clock-radio.

B&B from £19.00 to £50.00
€24.13 to €63.49

BREDA & JENNIFER TREACY
Proprietors

Mastercard
Visa

5 5

IRISH HOTELS FEDERATION

Closed 23 - 28 December

BRENNANS YARD HOTEL

**LOWER MERCHANTS ROAD,
GALWAY**
TEL: 091-568166 FAX: 091-568262
EMAIL: brennansyard@eircom.net

HOTEL ★★★ MAP 6 F 10

A refurbished city centre hotel, Brennans Yard is a charming, intimate hotel with excellent standards of accommodation, food and service. Our en suite bedrooms have been individually designed and are furnished with antique pine furniture. In our restaurant, you can dine in discreet elegance, choose from a wide range of dishes prepared from the freshest ingredients. The Spanish Bar offers an intimate, warm and lively atmosphere, or join us in the new Terry's Restaurant. Bookable worldwide through UTELL International.

B&B from £37.50 to £52.50
€47.62 to €66.66

CONNIE FENNELL
General Manager

American Express
Diners
Mastercard
Visa

45 45

IRISH HOTELS FEDERATION

Closed 24 - 29 December

CORRIB GREAT SOUTHERN HOTEL

**RENMORE,
GALWAY**
TEL: 091-755281 FAX: 091-751390
EMAIL: res@corrib.gsh.ie

HOTEL ★★★★ MAP 6 F 10

This 4**** hotel overlooks Galway Bay. It has 180 rooms, all en suite with radio, TV, direct dial phone, hairdryer, tea/coffee making facilities and trouser press. Leisure facilities include indoor heated swimming pool, steam room, jacuzzi, gym. Evening entertainment and children's play centre during summer months. Currach Restaurant and O'Malley's Bar. Convention centre accommodates up to 800 delegates. Bookable through central reservations 01-214 4800 or UTELL International.

WEB: www.gsh.ie

B&B from £56.00 to £98.00
€71.11 to €124.43

MICHEAL CUNNINGHAM
General Manager

American Express
Diners
Mastercard
Visa

☺ Weekend specials from £99.00

180 180

IRISH HOTELS FEDERATION

Closed 24 - 26 December

B&B rates are IR£ per person sharing per night incl. Breakfast

CORRIB HAVEN

107 UPPER NEWCASTLE, GALWAY
TEL: 091-524171 FAX: 091-524171
EMAIL: corribhaven@eircom.net

GUESTHOUSE ★★★ MAP 6 F 10

Corrib Haven's motto is quality hospitality for discerning people. AA Selected ◆◆◆◆. It is new, purpose built, located in Galway City on the N59 leading to Connemara. All rooms en suite, power showers, posture sprung beds, cable TV, video, direct dial phones. Tea/coffee facility, breakfast menu, private parking. Convenient to city centre, good restaurants, nightly entertainment. Ideal for touring Connemara, Aran Islands. Smooth professionalism with personal warmth to our visitors. Non-smoking.

B&B from £18.00 to £30.00
€22.86 to €38.09

FRANK KELLY
Owner

Mastercard
Visa

9 9

EGLINTON HOTEL

THE PROMENADE, SALTHILL, GALWAY
TEL: 091-526400 FAX: 091-526495
EMAIL: eglintonhotel@europe.com

HOTEL U MAP 6 F 10

Located right in the centre of Salthill. 48 brand new top quality bedrooms, sleeping up to 4 people. Entertainment on premises most nights; 100 metres from Leisureland swimming and entertainment complex. Galway Golf Course nearby. Free private car park. Groups and parties welcome any time. (Special rates available). Enjoy comfortable accommodation at keen rates in a lovely seafront location.

WEB: www.geocities.com/eglintonhotel

B&B from £30.00 to £57.50
€38.09 to €73.01

PATRICK MCGOVERN
Manager

American Express
Diners
Mastercard
Visa

48 48

EYRE SQUARE HOTEL

FORSTER STREET, OFF EYRE SQUARE, GALWAY
TEL: 091-569633 FAX: 091-569641
EMAIL: eyresquarehotel@eircom.net

HOTEL ★★★ MAP 6 F 10

The Eyre Square Hotel is situated right in the heart of Galway adjacent to both bus and rail stations. The Eyre Square Hotel caters for both the tourist and business person offering a very high standard of accommodation, rooms en suite with direct dial phone, satellite TV and tea/coffee making facilities. Enjoy excellent cuisine in our Red's Bistro or visit the lively Red Square pub. A warm and friendly welcome awaits you at the Eyre Square Hotel.

WEB: www.byrne-hotels-ireland.com

Member of Byrne Hotel Group

B&B from £35.00 to £80.00
€44.44 to €101.58

JOHN HUGHES
General Manager

American Express
Diners
Mastercard
Visa

☺ Weekend specials from £85.00

45 45

Inet FAX

Closed 24 - 27 December

Closed 20 - 29 December

Closed 25 - 26 December

Room rates are IR£ per room per night

FLANNERYS HOTEL

**DUBLIN ROAD,
GALWAY**
TEL: 091-755111 FAX: 091-753078
EMAIL: flanneryshotel@eircom.net

HOTEL ★★★ MAP 6 F 10

Flannerys Hotel is long established in Galway as an hotel offering comfort and style within relaxed surroundings. A welcome choice for business traveller or leisure guest. We take pride in ensuring that a special emphasis is placed on guest comfort enhanced by a genuinely caring and efficient service. Recently refurbished, the interior features tasteful decor, excellent restaurant and relaxing cocktail bar. Sample a selection of 136 rooms and suites. Member of Best Western.

Member of Best Western Hotels

B&B from £35.00 to £70.00
€44.44 to €88.88

MARY FLANNERY
Proprietor

American Express
Diners
Mastercard
Visa

Closed 20 - 30 December

FORSTER COURT HOTEL

**FORSTER STREET,
GALWAY**
TEL: 091-564111 FAX: 091-539839
EMAIL: sales@forstercourthotel.com

HOTEL P MAP 6 F 10

This new hotel is excellently located in Galway City centre and is easily accessed by all major approach roads. The hotel is impeccably finished incorporating every comfort for our guests. It comprises of 48 stylish en suite guest rooms, all designed to cater for your every need. Enjoy dining in the intimacy of Elwood's Restaurant or why not relax in our extensive bar. The Forster Court Hotel gives you Freedom of the City.

WEB: www.forstercourthotel.com

B&B from £35.00 to £70.00
€44.44 to €88.88

JONATHAN MURPHY
General Manager

American Express
Mastercard
Visa

Inet FAX

Closed 24 - 26 December

GALWAY BAY HOTEL, CONFERENCE & LEISURE CENTRE

**THE PROMENADE, SALTHILL,
GALWAY**
TEL: 091-520520 FAX: 091-520530
EMAIL: info@galwaybayhotel.net

HOTEL U MAP 6 F 10

This AA**** Hotel situated on Galway's City Seafront at the Promenade, Salthill, has all the advantages of a city location while being situated on a beautiful beach overlooking the famous Galway Bay. All bedrooms are designed for maximum guest comfort. The hotel has a fully equipped leisure centre and swimming pool. Enjoy dining in The Lobster Pot Restaurant which offers modern style cuisine with strong emphasis on fresh fish and lobster from the lobster tank.

WEB: www.galwaybayhotel.net

B&B from £35.00 to £80.00
€44.44 to €101.58

DAN MURPHY
General Manager

American Express
Diners
Mastercard
Visa

☺ Weekend specials from £89.00

Open All Year

B&B rates are IR£ per person sharing per night incl. Breakfast

GALWAY GREAT SOUTHERN HOTEL

EYRE SQUARE,
GALWAY
TEL: 091-564041   FAX: 091-566704
EMAIL: res@galway.gsh.ie

HOTEL ★★★★   MAP 6 F 10

A blend of 19th century elegance & modern amenities, Galway Great Southern (built in 1845) overlooks Eyre Square in Galway City. It offers a wide range of facilities including The Oyster Room Restaurant, cocktail bar & O'Flaherty's Pub. Rooftop leisure facilities include indoor heated swimming pool, steamroom, sauna. Accommodation includes well appointed en suite bedrooms plus level 5, a range of luxurious suites. Bookable worldwide through UTELL International or Central Res. 01-214 4800

WEB: www.gsh.ie

B&B from £74.00 to £120.00
€86.34 to €135.86

ROBERT BYRNE
General Manager

American Express
Diners
Mastercard
Visa

☺ Weekend specials from £115.00

114 114

Closed 24 - 26 December

GALWAY HARBOUR HOTEL

THE HARBOUR,
GALWAY
TEL: 091-569466   FAX: 091-569455
EMAIL: info@galwayharbourhotel.com

UNDER CONSTRUCTION OPENING MAR 2001

HOTEL P   MAP 6 F 10

Opening March 2001, this hotel is located on Galway Harbour, in the heart of Galway City. This is the only city centre hotel in Galway to offer guests secure, on-site, complimentary parking. 96 bedrooms, sleeping 3 adults or 2 adults and 2 children, restaurant, bar and 4 syndicate rooms for 2-50 people. The location, parking and competitive room only rates make this hotel an attractive venue to all visitors to Galway.

WEB: www.galwayharbourhotel.com

Room Rate from £59.00 to £75.00
€74.91 to €95.23

JOHN BRODERICK
General Manager

American Express
Diners
Mastercard
Visa

96 96

Closed 24 - 27 December

GALWAY RYAN HOTEL & LEISURE CENTRE

DUBLIN ROAD, GALWAY CITY EAST,
GALWAY
TEL: 091-753181   FAX: 091-753187
EMAIL: ryan@indigo.ie

HOTEL ★★★   MAP 6 F 10

This hotel offers the ultimate in relaxation and leisure facilities. 96 en suite rooms, the air-conditioned Oranmore Room, 2 air-conditioned meeting rooms, Toddy's Bar and a relaxing lobby lounge. A magnificent leisure centre with a 2,500 sq ft. pool incorporating 60ft. swimming lanes, lounger, geyser and toddlers' pools, steam room, jacuzzi, sauna, multi purpose sports hall, aerobics studio, a state of the art gym and floodlit tennis courts. Parking. AA, RAC & Egon Ronay recommended.

WEB: www.ryan-hotels.com

B&B from £45.00 to £90.00
€57.14 to €114.28

PAUL COLLERAN
General Manager

American Express
Diners
Mastercard
Visa

☺ Weekend specials from £90.00

96 96

Open All Year

GLENLO ABBEY HOTEL

BUSHYPARK,
GALWAY
TEL: 091-526666 FAX: 091-527800
EMAIL: glenlo@iol.ie

HOTEL ★★★★★ MAP 6 F 10

Glenlo Abbey Hotel - an 18th century country residence, is located on a 138 acre lake side golf estate just 4km from Galway City. Now a Bord Failte rated 5***** hotel, Glenlo Abbey is a haven for all discerning travellers. All 46 rooms have a marbled bathroom, personal safe, direct dial phone, trouser press, cable TV, radio and 24 hour room service. The Pullman Restaurant, two unique Orient Express carriages, offers a totally new dining experience. Other activities include fishing, etc.

WEB: www.glenlo.com

Member of Small Luxury Hotels

Room Rate from £147.00 to £235.00
€186.65 to €298.39

PEGGY & JOHN BOURKE
Proprietors

American Express
Diners
Mastercard
Visa

46 46

Open All Year

HOLIDAY HOTEL

181 UPPER SALTHILL, SALTHILL,
GALWAY
TEL: 091-523934 FAX: 091-527083

HOTEL U MAP 6 F 10

Holiday Hotel is in close proximity to beaches, amusements, a new state of the art aquarium, and nightly entertainment. A Bord Failte approved hotel, with all rooms en suite, direct dial phone, multi-channel TV, hairdryer and trouser-press. Ideally located for golfing, fishing, family holidays and relaxing breaks. The Holiday Hotel offers a recently renovated bar, where you can be guaranteed a relaxing time following a tough day at the office.

B&B from £28.00 to £35.00
€35.55 to €44.44

DAVID FINAN
General Manager

American Express
Mastercard
Visa

10 10

Open All Year

HOTEL SACRE COEUR

LENABOY GARDENS, SALTHILL,
GALWAY
TEL: 091-523355 FAX: 091-523553

HOTEL ★★ MAP 6 F 10

Hotel Sacre Coeur is a family owned and managed hotel where a Cead Mile Failte awaits you. All of our 40 rooms are en suite, direct dial telephone, with colour TV and tea/coffee making facilities. Within five minutes walk of the hotel we have Salthill's magnificent promenade, tennis club and a wonderful 18 hole golf course. Renowned for its friendly service and excellent food you will enjoy your stay at the Sacre Coeur.

B&B from £30.00 to £36.00
€38.09 to €45.71

SEAN OG DUNLEAVY
Manager

Mastercard
Visa

40 40

Closed 22 - 30 December

B&B rates are IR£ per person sharing per night incl. Breakfast

HOTEL SPANISH ARCH

**QUAY STREET,
GALWAY
TEL: 091-569600   FAX: 091-569191
EMAIL: emcdgall@iol.ie**

HOTEL ★★   MAP 6 F 10

Situated in the heart of Galway this is a 20 roomed boutique style hotel. Rooms of unsurpassed elegance created and individually designed by Easter McDonagh. Our unique Victorian bar which has original wooden panelled walls from the home of Lilly Langtree, confidante to King Edward VII. A 16th Century stone wall was uncovered and can be found in the back bar where locals and visitors mingle - where late nightly music can be enjoyed and various functions/weddings. Bistro. Carpark.

WEB: www.irishholidays.com/sp-indexs.html

Room Rate from £50.00 to £85.00
€63.49 to €107.93

**EASTER MCDONAGH GALLAGHER
Managing Director**

American Express

Mastercard

Visa

20 20

FAX

IRISH HOTELS FEDERATION

Closed 25 - 26 December

IMPERIAL HOTEL

**EYRE SQUARE,
GALWAY
TEL: 091-563033   FAX: 091-568410
EMAIL: imperialhtl@hotmail.com**

HOTEL ★★★   MAP 6 F 10

A bustling hotel in the centre of Galway City with modern comfortable 3 star bedrooms. Located in the main shopping area surrounded by a large choice of restaurants, pubs and quality shops. Five minutes walk from the new Galway Theatre, main bus and rail terminals. Beside main taxi rank with multi storey parking nearby. Full service hotel; friendly and informative staff. No service charge. R.A.C. 3 star.

B&B from £40.00 to £62.50
€50.79 to €79.36

**KEVIN FLANNERY
General Manager**

American Express

Diners

Mastercard

Visa

84 84

IRISH HOTELS FEDERATION

Closed 24 - 27 December

INISHMORE GUESTHOUSE

**109 FR. GRIFFIN ROAD, LOWER
SALTHILL, GALWAY
TEL: 091-582639   FAX: 091-589311
EMAIL: inishmorehouse@eircom.net**

GUESTHOUSE ★★★   MAP 6 F 10

A charming family residence with secure carpark within 5 minutes walk of city and beach. All rooms contain direct dial phone, multi-channel TV and hairdryers. Tea/coffee and ironing facilities available. German spoken. An ideal base for touring the Aran Islands, Burren and Connemara. Golf holidays, sea angling trips and coarse or game fishing arranged. Recommended by many leading travel guides. Specialise in Golf Package Holidays.

WEB: www.galway@pop.galway.net

B&B from £20.00 to £35.00
€25.39 to €44.44

**MARIE & PETER
Proprietors**

Mastercard

Visa

7 6

IRISH HOTELS FEDERATION

Closed 23 December - 07 January

Room rates are IR£ per room per night

JAMESONS HOTEL

SALTHILL,
GALWAY
TEL: 091-528666 FAX: 091-528626
EMAIL: jamesons@iol.ie

HOTEL ★★★ MAP 6 F 10

Jamesons Hotel is located in the heart of Salthill, overlooking Galway Bay. All rooms are en suite with special jacuzzi suites available. We offer excellent cuisine in the pleasant surroundings of our restaurant. Live entertainment 7 nights a week in summer and at weekends over the winter period. Conference suites facilitating up to 60 people. Private car parking. Special weekend rates available.

WEB: www.galway.net/pages/jamesons

B&B from £30.00 to £100.00
€38.09 to €126.97

JONATHAN POWELL
General Manager

American Express
Diners
Mastercard
Visa

☺ Midweek specials from £75.00

Open All Year

JURYS INN GALWAY

QUAY STREET,
GALWAY
TEL: 091-566444 FAX: 091-568415
EMAIL: galway_inn@jurysdoyle.com

HOTEL ★★★ MAP 6 F 10

Modern attractive rooms capable of accommodating up to 3 adults or 2 adults and 2 children. All rooms are en suite with multi-channel TV, radio, direct dial phone and tea/coffee making facilities. Located in the heart of Galway City, Jury's Inn has an informal restaurant and a lively pub, a business centre, conference rooms and an adjoining public multi-storey car park (fee payable). Jurys Doyle Hotel Group Central Reservations:
Tel. 01-607 0000
Fax. 01-631 6999.

WEB: www.jurysdoyle.com

Room Rate from £48.00 to £72.00
€60.94 to €91.42

KAREN CREMINS
General Manager

American Express
Diners
Mastercard
Visa

Closed 24 - 26 December

KNOCKREA GUEST HOUSE

55 LOWER SALTHILL,
GALWAY
TEL: 091-520145 FAX: 091-529985
EMAIL: knockrea@eircom.net

GUESTHOUSE ★★★ MAP 6 F 10

A 3*** family run guesthouse established 1950. Refurbished to a high standard with pine floors throughout. Car park at rear. 1km from city centre on bus route. 300 metres from Salthill Promenade. Restaurants, theatres, golf, tennis, horseriding close by. Perfect base for touring Connemara, Burren and Aran Islands. Within walking distance of Spanish Arch and Quay Street. Irish pub music entertainment available locally. All rooms en suite, TV and direct dial phone. Frommers Guide recommended.

WEB: www.galway.net/pages/knockrea/

B&B from £20.00 to £30.00
€25.39 to €38.09

EILEEN STORAN
Proprietor

Mastercard
Visa

Closed 23 - 26 December

B&B rates are IR£ per person sharing per night incl. Breakfast

LOCHLURGAIN HOTEL

22 MONKSFIELD, UPPER SALTHILL, GALWAY
TEL: 091-529595 FAX: 091-522399
EMAIL: lochlurgain@eircom.net

HOTEL U MAP 6 F 10

Welcome to Lochlurgain. Completely refurbished elegant Town House Hotel, AA***. Beside church off Main St, 5 minutes beach and leisure centre. City centre 5 minutes. Fresh home cooked food served. Seafood also featured. Enjoy comfort, peace, tranquillity and relaxation. Lochlurgain is 62 miles/100km north of Shannon Airport. One hour from the Burren and Connemara. On parle français. Bed, breakfast and dinner breaks, please ask for details. Peadar and Joan Cunningham welcome you.

WEB: www.failte.com/salthill/loch.htm

B&B from £27.50 to £55.00
€34.92 to €69.84

PEADAR & JOAN
CUNNINGHAM Proprietors

Mastercard

Visa

2 B&B & 2 Dinners from £100.00

10 10

Closed 31 October - 10 March

MARIAN LODGE GUESTHOUSE

KNOCKNACARRA ROAD, SALTHILL UPPER, GALWAY
TEL: 091-521678 FAX: 091-528103
EMAIL: celine@iol.ie

GUESTHOUSE ★★★ MAP 6 F 10

Family-run, adjacent to Promenade and beach in Salthill Upper. Private parking. On bus route/city centre/Aran Islands/Connemara. Home baking. Lounge with rustic fireplace displaying pots and pans of old. Bedrooms en suite, cable TV, direct dial phone, clock radios, orthopaedic beds, hairdryers, tea/coffee facilities. Ironing facilities & trouserpress available. Convenient to Leisureland, tennis, wind surfing, fishing, horseriding. Beside golf course, driving range, restaurant, pubs, shops.

WEB: www.marian-lodge.com

B&B from £19.00 to £28.00
€24.13 to €35.55

CELINE MOLLOY

Mastercard

Visa

6 6

Closed 23 - 28 December

MENLO PARK HOTEL AND CONFERENCE CENTRE

TERRYLAND, HEADFORD ROAD, GALWAY
TEL: 091-761122 FAX: 091-761222
EMAIL: menlopkh@iol.ie

HOTEL ★★★ MAP 6 F 10

Situated near Galway's City centre the Menlo Park offers the best of modern facilities with old fashioned hospitality. All rooms have TV/teletext, welcome tray, power showers, rich colour schemes. Executive rooms also feature king beds, sofas, trouser press/iron. Contemporary chic but casual restaurant; MP's Bar. Easy access to main roads. Free car parking. Redevelopment for 2001 includes new Conference Centre plus 20 bedrooms.

WEB: www.menloparkhotel.com

B&B from £37.50 to £80.00
€47.62 to €101.58

DAVID KEANE
General Manager

American Express

Diners

Mastercard

Visa

Midweek specials from £75.00

44 44

S alc Inet FAX

Closed 24 - 26 December

Room rates are IR£ per room per night

OCEAN CREST HOUSE

**OCEAN WAVE, SEAPOINT
PROMENADE, SALTHILL, GALWAY
TEL: 091-589028   FAX: 091-529399
EMAIL: oceanbb@iol.ie**

GUESTHOUSE ★★★   MAP 6 F 10

We chose this site and built this guesthouse to provide what our guests love, a taste of subtropical elegance, overlooking Galway Bay and beaches with panoramic views of the Burren Mountains. We are walking distance from the bustling medieval city of Galway and across the road we have the Promenade. Our bedrooms are beautifully appointed with multi channel TV, en suite facilities, phone, trouser press, hair dryers, hospitality tray and armchairs.

WEB: www.oceanbb.com

B&B from £18.00 to £30.00
€22.86 to €38.09

American Express
Mastercard
Visa

TCP
6 6

Closed 24 - 28 December

PARK HOUSE HOTEL & PARK ROOM RESTAURANT

**FORSTER STREET, EYRE SQUARE,
GALWAY
TEL: 091-564924   FAX: 091-569219
EMAIL: parkhousehotel@eircom.net**

HOTEL ★★★★   MAP 6 F 10

An oasis of luxury and hospitality in the heart of Galway City centre. We are Bord Failte 4****, AA 4 star and RAC 4 star. All 57 rooms are en suite with bath and shower, direct dial phone, ISDN line, multi channel TV, tea/coffee making facilities, trouser press, awards of excellence winning restaurant over many years. Les Routiers Restaurant of the Year Ireland 1998-1999. Our high standards are your guarantee. Private residents' car park on hotel grounds.

B&B from £45.00 to £90.00
€57.14 to €114.28

EAMON DOYLE & KITTY CARR
Proprietors

American Express
Diners
Mastercard
Visa

TC CMP aid
57 57

IRISH HOTELS FEDERATION

Closed 24 - 28 December

RADISSON SAS HOTEL

**LOUGH ATALIA ROAD,
GALWAY
TEL: 091-539300   FAX: 091-539380
EMAIL: sales_galway@radissonsas.com**

UNDER CONSTRUCTION OPENING APRIL 2001

HOTEL P   MAP 6 F 10

The Radisson SAS Hotel is ideally located on the waterfront on Lough Atalia Road, near the railway station. The hotel has 206 well appointed rooms featuring The Radisson SAS room style concepts Maritime and Scandinavian. The hotel has one main all day restaurant and bar, 12 meeting rooms (largest up to 1,000 guests for a standing reception), spa and health centre with gym, sauna, beauty treatments and a swimming pool.

WEB:www.radissonsas.com/hotel/gwyzh

Member of Radisson SAS Hotels and Resorts

Room rate from £150.00 to £150.00
€190.46 to €190.46

ULLA VIRKKULA
Project Director of Sales

American Express
Diners
Mastercard
Visa

TC CM
206 206
PS aid Inet FAX

Open All Year

B&B rates are IR£ per person sharing per night incl. Breakfast

ROCKBARTON PARK HOTEL

ROCKBARTON PARK, SALTHILL,
GALWAY
TEL: 091-522286 FAX: 091-527692
EMAIL: tyson'shotel@eircom.net

HOTEL ★★ MAP 6 F 10

Owned and managed by the Tyson Family, fully licensed, in a quiet residential cul de sac. 200 metres from seafront and Leisureland Centre. Golf, tennis, badminton and squash just 5 minutes walk. Tyson's Restaurant offers a homely comfortable atmosphere noted for fresh local fish and prime steaks, prepared and cooked delightfully by chef/proprietor Terry. Bar food also available. Friendly service.

WEB: www.travel-ireland.com/ire/rckbrton.htm

Member of Logis of Ireland

B&B from £25.00 to £45.00
€31.74 to €57.14

PATRICIA AND TERRY TYSON
Proprietors

American Express
Diners
Mastercard
Visa

  Weekend specials from £68.00

10 10

Closed 24 - 31 December

ROCKLAND HOTEL

SALTHILL,
GALWAY
TEL: 091-522111 FAX: 091-526577

HOTEL ★ MAP 6 F 10

Overlooking the scenic splendour of Galway Bay, the Rockland Hotel is ideally situated to capture all the charm of the rugged beauty of Connemara. All bedrooms are en suite with TV, direct dial phone, tea/coffee making facilities and many with panoramic views of Galway Bay. Enjoy our good food, comfortable bar, nightly entertainment during high season and of course our friendly staff.

B&B from £20.00 to £45.00
€25.39 to €57.14

BRIAN MURPHY
Manager

Mastercard
Visa

14 14

Closed 22 - 29 December

SALT LAKE GUESTHOUSE

4 LOUGH ATALIA ROAD,
GALWAY
TEL: 091-564572 FAX: 091-567037
EMAIL: oceanbb@iol.ie

GUESTHOUSE ★★★ MAP 6 F 10

Salt Lake House is a beautifully purpose-built guesthouse with exquisite views of Lough Atalia (inlet of Galway Bay). We offer luxurious accommodation within easy reach of Galway City centre, only minutes from bus/train station. Each room is beautifully appointed with en suite facilities, multi-channel TV (12 channels), armchairs and table, hospitality tray, iron and board and hairdryer.

WEB: www.oceanbb.com

B&B from £18.00 to £30.00
€22.86 to €38.09

American Express
Mastercard
Visa

8 8

Closed 24 - 30 December

Room rates are IR£ per room per night

SALTHILL COURT HOTEL

**SALTHILL,
GALWAY**
TEL: 091-522711 FAX: 091-521855
EMAIL: salthillhotel@eircom.net

HOTEL ★★★ MAP 6 F 10

A Byrne Hotel, 50m from Salthill's sandy beach. Live entertainment most nights, every night from June to Sept (Thu-Sun rest of year). All rooms en suite, direct dial phone, tea making facilities, hair dryer. Excellent cuisine and service. 100m from Leisureland and indoor swimming pool. Overlooking Galway Bay with large car park. Ideal location for family holidays and over 55s in off season. Less than 2 miles from the medieval city of Galway. Many sporting activities nearby.

WEB: www.byrne-hotels-ireland.com

Member of Byrne Hotel Group

B&B from £35.00 to £70.00
€44.44 to €88.88

JOEY HALLINAN
General Manager

American Express
Diners
Mastercard
Visa

75 75

Closed 23 - 26 December

SKEFFINGTON ARMS HOTEL

**EYRE SQUARE,
GALWAY**
TEL: 091-563173 FAX: 091-561679
EMAIL: info@skeffington.ie

HOTEL ★★★ MAP 6 F 10

The Skeffington Arms Hotel has been caring for guests for over 100 years. Overlooking Eyre Square, within walking distance of rail and bus terminal, it enjoys an enviable position in the heart of Galway. This privately owned hotel is justifiably proud of its new bars and à la carte menu which is very popular with both locals and guests alike. The bedrooms, which are newly refurbished have multi-channel TV, direct dial phone and bath/shower en suite.

WEB: www.skeffington.ie

B&B from £35.00 to £80.00
€44.44 to €101.58

JULIE-ANNE KEANE
Reservations Manager

American Express
Mastercard
Visa

23 23

Closed 25 - 26 December

SPINNAKER HOUSE HOTEL

**KNOCKNACARRA, SALTHILL,
GALWAY**
TEL: 091-525425 FAX: 091-526650
EMAIL: spinnakerhousehotel@eircom.net

HOTEL ★★ MAP 6 F 10

The newly refurbished Spinnaker Hotel is a family run hotel overlooking Galway Golf Course and has spectacular views of Galway Bay and the Burren. All 20 rooms, most with private balconies, are newly built with en suite facilities, telephone, TV and tea/coffee maker. Within 2km of the hotel we have beaches, fishing, horse riding, golf and tennis clubs, Leisureland complex and the ferry port to the Aran Islands.

B&B from £27.50 to £45.00
€34.92 to €57.14

SEAN DIVINEY

American Express
Mastercard
Visa

20 20

Closed 25 - 26 December

B&B rates are IR£ per person sharing per night incl. Breakfast

VICTORIA HOTEL

VICTORIA PLACE, EYRE SQUARE,
GALWAY
TEL: 091-567433 FAX: 091-565880
EMAIL: victoriahotel@eircom.net

HOTEL ★★★ MAP 6 F 10

The Victoria Hotel is centrally located just 100 yards off Eyre Square, within walking distance of all shops, theatres, pubs and cinemas. Each of the 57 spacious en suite rooms are beautifully appointed with direct dial phone, trouserpress and hairdryer. A hotel restaurant serving à la carte dinner along with a lively bar serving lunches will all add up to make your stay at the Victoria as enjoyable as possible. The Victoria is your enclave in the city, dedicated to pleasing you.

WEB: www.byrne-hotels-ireland.com

Member of Byrne Hotel Group

B&B from £37.50 to £70.00
€47.62 to €88.88

OWEN MCCARTHY
General Manager

American Express
Diners
Mastercard
Visa

57 57

Closed 24 - 26 December

WATERFRONT HOTEL

SALTHILL,
GALWAY
TEL: 091-588100 FAX: 091-588107
EMAIL: info@waterfront.ie

HOTEL N MAP 6 F 10

Located on Salthill's Promenade, all of our 64 modern and spacious rooms have a panoramic view of Galway Bay. All rooms are furnished with kitchenette or lounge and have direct dial phone, cable TV, tea/coffee making facilities, trouser press and hairdryer. Family rooms available. Secure parking and only 5 minutes for city centre. Incorporating Kitty O'Shea's Bar and Restaurant, featuring regular live entertainment. Reservations Callsave 1850 588 488.

WEB: www.waterfront.ie

Room Rate from £45.00 to £85.00
€57.14 to €107.93

KEN BERGIN
General Manager

American Express
Mastercard
Visa

☺ Weekend specials from £75.00

64 64

alc Inet

Closed 24 - 31 December

WEST WINDS

5 OCEAN WAVE, SALTHILL,
GALWAY
TEL: 091-520223 FAX: 091-520223
EMAIL: westwinds@eircom.net

GUESTHOUSE ★★★ MAP 6 F 10

Westwinds is a charming family-managed guesthouse overlooking Galway Bay, 10 minutes walk from Galway City, an ideal base for all travellers wishing to explore the Burren, Connemara and the Aran Islands. We are situated at the city end of Salthill Promenade, restaurants, nightly entertainment and all other amenities 5-10 minutes walk. All rooms have en suite bathrooms with power shower, hairdryer, cable TV, tea/coffee making facility. Our hospitality awaits!

WEB: www.travelaccommodation.co.uk/westwind.htm

B&B from £18.00 to £35.00
€22.86 to €44.44

RITA & PATRICK JOYCE
Proprietors

American Express
Mastercard
Visa

10 10

Closed 12 December - 01 April

Room rates are IR£ per room per night

WESTWOOD HOUSE HOTEL

DANGAN, UPPER NEWCASTLE,
GALWAY
TEL: 091-521442   FAX: 091-521400
EMAIL: westwoodhotel@eircom.net

HOTEL N   MAP 6 F 10

The Westwood House Hotel, commands a prime location on the edge of Galway City and at the gateway to Connemara. Tastefully designed to international standards and air conditioned throughout, the Westwood boasts 58 superbly appointed bedrooms which include 6 junior suites, 8 executive rooms, 44 deluxe bedrooms, the award winning Meridian Restaurant, a themed bar along with Conference/Banqueting facilities with ample car parking.

WEB: www.westwoodhousehotel.com

Member of Signature Hotels

B&B from £40.00 to £89.50
€50.79 to €113.64

RACHAEL COYLE
General Manager

American Express
Diners
Mastercard
Visa

58 58
inet FAX

Closed 24 - 26 December

WHITE HOUSE

2 OCEAN WAVE,
GALWAY CITY
TEL: 091-529399   FAX: 091-529399
EMAIL: oceanbb@iol.ie

GUESTHOUSE ★★★   MAP 6 F 10

New and beautiful purpose-built guest house in Galway's finest location, overlooking Galway Bay and the Burren Mountains, minutes walk to Galway's medieval city and Salthill's new hotel, the Galway Bay. Large bedrooms with armchairs and tables, iron and board, multi-channel TV, hospitality tray and hairdryer.

B&B from £18.00 to £30.00
€22.86 to €38.09

American Express
Mastercard
Visa

6 6

Open All Year

ARD EINNE GUESTHOUSE

INISMOR, ARAN ISLANDS,
CO. GALWAY
TEL: 099-61126   FAX: 099-61388
EMAIL: ardeinne@eircom.net

GUESTHOUSE ★★   MAP 5 D 10

A few days on historical Inismor (Aran Islands) is an essential part of an Irish holiday. Enjoy the stress-free experience in the relaxed atmosphere of spectacularly situated and high quality Ard Einne, with sweeping panoramic views of Galway/Clare Coastlines, Mountains and Galway Bay. Earth has not anything to show more fair. Walks, tours, cycle trips organised. Artists, writers, groups, clubs, societies offered very attractive rates. Convenient to air-sea services, beach and pub.

WEB: www.dragnet-systems.ie/dira/ardeinne/

B&B from £18.00 to £23.00
€22.86 to €29.20

KEVIN AND ENDA GILL
Proprietors

Mastercard
Visa

☺ Weekend specials from £56.00

15 12

Closed 10 December - 01 February

B&B rates are IR£ per person sharing per night incl. Breakfast

KILMURVEY HOUSE

KILRONAN, INISMOR,
ARAN ISLANDS, CO. GALWAY
TEL: 099-61218 FAX: 099-61397
EMAIL: kilmurveyhouse@eircom.net

GUESTHOUSE ★★★ MAP 5 D 10

Kilmurvey House is a 150 year-old country house situated at the foot of Dun Aonghus, beside Dun Aongusa visitor centre. 3 minutes walk from a Blue Flag beach in one of the more peaceful locations on the island. We are the ideal setting for cyclists, walkers, botanists and those that just want to relax. Special group rates available.

B&B from £25.00 to £25.00
€31.74 to €31.74

BRIDGET HERNON/TREASA
JOYCE Proprietors

Mastercard

Visa

12 12

HOTELS

Closed 31 October - 01 April

PIER HOUSE GUESTHOUSE

LOWER KILRONAN, INISMOR,
ARAN ISLANDS, CO. GALWAY
TEL: 099-61417 FAX: 099-61122
EMAIL: pierh@iol.ie

GUESTHOUSE ★★★ MAP 5 D 10

Pier House is perfectly located less than 100m from Kilronan Harbour and Village, within walking distance of sandy beaches, pubs, restaurants and historical remains. This modern house is finished to a very high standard, has a private gym for guest use and many other extra facilities. Its bedrooms are well appointed and have perfect sea and landscape views. If it is comfort and old fashioned warmth and hospitality you expect, then Pier House is the perfect location to enjoy it.

B&B from £25.00 to £40.00
€31.74 to €50.79

MAURA & PADRAIG JOYCE
Proprietors

Mastercard

Visa

12 12

HOTELS

Closed 01 November - 01 March

TIGH FITZ

KILLEANY, KILRONAN, INISMOR,
ARAN ISLANDS, CO. GALWAY
TEL: 099-61213 FAX: 099-61386

GUESTHOUSE ★★★ MAP 5 D 10

Tigh Fitz, a family run guest house, bar, lounge, is in Killeany, Inishmore. Offering a luxurious accommodation in this unspoilt area of the Aran Isles. Tigh Fitz is unique in its situation, in its spaciousness and proximity to beaches and areas of archaeological and historical remains. In this area are the tall cliffs of Aran and the magnificent pre-historic forts. Tigh Fitz is 1.6km from the Island capital Kilronan and close to the Aer Arann Airstrip.

B&B from £25.00 to £30.00
€31.74 to €38.09

PENNY MAHON
Proprietor/Owner

Mastercard

Visa

11 11

HOTELS

Closed 01 November - 01 March

Room rates are IR£ per room per night

NEWPARK HOTEL

CROSS STREET, ATHENRY,
CO. GALWAY
TEL: 091-844035   FAX: 091-844921

HOTEL ★   MAP 6 G 10

The Newpark Hotel under the management of Alacoque Feeney and family since Feb '99. The hotel is situated in a quiet part of this medieval heritage town surrounded by the famed 'Fields of Athenry' and only 15 minutes drive from Galway City. Our rooms are tastefully decorated and furnished to enhance your stay. Our dining room menu offers the guest an excellent choice of Irish and international cuisine in warm relaxed surroundings. Unwind and enjoy a drink in our warm comfy bar. Music each weekend.

B&B from £25.00 to £45.00
€31.74 to €57.14

ALACOQUE FEENEY
Proprietor

Mastercard

Visa

11 7

Closed 23 - 31 December

AANDERS GUESTHOUSE

13 SOCIETY STREET, BALLINASLOE,
CO. GALWAY
TEL: 0905-44937   FAX: 0905-44937

GUESTHOUSE P   MAP 6 I 11

Superior quality guesthouse decorated in old world Georgian charm, situated in the heart of Ballinasloe. Spacious en suite rooms; power shower, TV, direct dial phone, hairdryer plus the added facilities of the renowned Elle Room Hair & Beauty Salon offering a professional hair & beauty service. Special group rates. Ideally based to enjoy a host of other activities locally including golf, fishing, horse riding, kayaking and scenic walks. Gourmet restaurants and bars just a walk away.

B&B from £25.00 to £35.00
€31.74 to €44.44

MARGARET CAMPBELL
Proprietor

Mastercard

Visa

5 5

Closed 24 December - 02 January

HAYDEN'S GATEWAY BUSINESS & LEISURE HOTEL

DUNLO STREET, BALLINASLOE,
CO. GALWAY
TEL: 065-6823000   FAX: 065-6823759
EMAIL: reservations@lynchotels.com

HOTEL ★★★   MAP 6 I 11

Ideal location off main Dublin-Galway Road, famous for hospitality, award winning coffee shop and à la carte restaurant. 48 recently refurbished en suite rooms incl. Exec rooms with spa bath and 1 mini-suite. 40 mins Galway, 15 mins Athlone. Award winning traditional pub, Planet Nite Club, free to residents. Conference facilities for 300. Car parking for 150. 6 championship golf courses & excellent angling nearby. Leading wedding venue. Free ValuPass to 25 leading attractions. Member of Best Western Hotels.

WEB: www.haydenshotel.com

Member of Lynch Hotels

B&B from £25.00 to £65.00
€31.74 to €82.53

MICHAEL B LYNCH Group MD
Joe Melody Gen Mgr

American Express

Diners

Mastercard

Visa

☺ Weekend specials from £86.00

48 48

Open All Year

B&B rates are IR£ per person sharing per night incl. Breakfast

BALLYNAHINCH CASTLE HOTEL

BALLYNAHINCH, RECESS,
CONNEMARA, CO. GALWAY
TEL: 095-31006   FAX: 095-31085
EMAIL: bhinch@iol.ie

HOTEL ★★★★   MAP 5 D 11

Once home to the O'Flaherty Chieftains, pirate queen Grace O'Malley, Humanity Dick Martin and Maharajah Ranjitsinji, Ballynahinch is now a 4★★★★ hotel. With casual country elegance overlooking the river and ringed by mountains, Ballynahinch offers an unpretentious service and is an ideal centre from which to tour the west. Log fires and a friendly fisherman's pub complement a restaurant offering the best in fresh game, fish and produce. Ballynahinch, the Jewel in Connemara's Crown.

WEB: www.commerce.ie/ballynahinch/

Member of Manor House Hotels

B&B from £57.20 to £110.00
€72.63 to €139.67

PATRICK O'FLAHERTY
General Manager

American Express
Diners
Mastercard
Visa

☺ Winter specials from £108.90

40 40
 Inet FAX

Closed 01 - 28 February

SILVERSEAS

CAPPAGH ROAD, BARNA,
CO. GALWAY
TEL: 091-590575   FAX: 091-590575
EMAIL: silverseas@eircom.net

GUESTHOUSE ★★★   MAP 5 F 10

Newly built ultra modern luxury residence, 1.6km from Salthill overlooking Galway Bay, unsurpassed view and landscaped gardens. AA selected ◆◆◆. Family run guesthouse with high standard of accommodation, all bedrooms en suite with power showers, TV, radio clock, hairdryer, trouser press, guest sitting room with tea/coffee making facilities, large private car park. Riding stables, golf, surfing, beach nearby, cycling, nature walks and historical tours, Aran Island trips arranged.

B&B from £19.00 to £27.00
€24.13 to €34.28

GEULAH MCGRATH
Proprietor

Mastercard
Visa

8 8

Open All Year

CARNA BAY HOTEL

CARNA, CONNEMARA,
CO. GALWAY
TEL: 095-32255   FAX: 095-32530
EMAIL: carnabay@iol.ie

HOTEL ★★★   MAP 9 D 11

Are you looking for somewhere special? Allow us to plan your carefree days in the most magical scenery in Ireland. Connemara, unique landscape, flora and fauna, unspoilt beaches, mountain ranges. Beautiful Western Way walking routes. Cycling, bicycles provided free. Our kitchen offers the finest fresh Irish produce. 26 well appointed rooms, most with sea or mountain views. Locally: St. McDara's Island, Connemara National Park, Kylemore Abbey, Aran and Inisbofin Ferry 40 mins drive.

WEB: www.carnabay.com

Member of Village Inn Hotels

B&B from £35.00 to £60.00
€44.44 to €76.18

PARAIC & MARY CLOHERTY
Proprietors

American Express
Mastercard
Visa

☺ Midweek specials from £100.00

26 26

Open All Year

Room rates are IR£ per room per night

HOTEL CARRAROE BEST WESTERN

**CARRAROE,
CO. GALWAY
TEL: 091-595116 FAX: 091-595187**

HOTEL ★★ MAP 5 D 10

The Best Western Hotel Carraroe is a 25 bedroomed en suite family run hotel situated in the heart of the Connemara Gaeltacht. The village of Carraroe itself is renowned for its traditional values and music. Daily boat trips to the Aran Islands are from nearby Rossaveal Harbour. Our local friendly staff will provide information on where to fish, play golf, horse ride or tour beautiful Connemara.

Member of Best Western Hotels

B&B from £30.00 to £45.00
€38.09 to €57.14

PAT & EILEEN MURRAY
Owners

American Express
Mastercard
Visa

🐾🏨📷T🛗⚠️♨️C CM✱🔍🕊️♪♫
25 25

P S 🛗 🅿️ 🚿

CASHEL HOUSE HOTEL

**CASHEL,
CO. GALWAY
TEL: 095-31001 FAX: 095-31077
EMAIL: info@cashel-house-hotel.com**

HOTEL ★★★★ MAP 5 D 11

Elegance in a wilderness on the shores of the Atlantic. It is set amidst the most beautiful garden in Ireland. Enjoy long walks, bicycle or horseback rides, and fishing. Later, relax in front of a peat fire in this elegant residence appointed with antique furniture and period paintings. Most guestrooms look onto the gardens and some onto the sea. Dine on bounty from the sea and garden - enjoy vintage wine. Also member of Ireland's Blue Book.

WEB: www.cashel-house-hotel.com

Member of Relais & Châteaux

B&B from £66.37 to £95.62
€84.27 to €121.41

MCEVILLY FAMILY
Proprietors

American Express
Diners
Mastercard
Visa

🐾🏨📷T🛗C✳️CM✱🔍U🅿️📮
32 32

🅰️🍴🛗☕

IRISH
HOTELS
FEDERATION

GLYNSK HOUSE HOTEL

**CASHEL BAY, CONNEMARA,
CO. GALWAY
TEL: 095-32279 FAX: 095-32342
EMAIL: glynsk@iol.ie**

HOTEL ★★ MAP 5 D 11

Overlooking Cashel Bay and Twelve Bens Mountains, this small family-run hotel is the ideal location for touring Connemara. Enjoy the best of local seafood and Connemara lamb in our restaurant, à la carte and bar menu also available. Local attractions: Connemara National Park, Kylemore Abbey, safe white sandy beaches, Aran and Inisbofin Ferry 40 minutes drive. Golf and pitch & putt also a short drive away. Bicycles free. Western Way Walking Route close by.

WEB: www.glynsk.com

B&B from £25.00 to £35.00
€31.74 to €44.44

PARAIC & MARY CLOHERTY
Proprietors

American Express
Mastercard
Visa

😊 Midweek specials from £80.00

🐾🏨📷T🛗C✳️CM✱🔍U🅿️🎾🅂
12 12

🍴🅰️🅰️c 📶inet

IRISH
HOTELS
FEDERATION

B&B rates are IR£ per person sharing per night incl. Breakfast

ZETLAND COUNTRY HOUSE HOTEL

CASHEL BAY, CONNEMARA,
CO. GALWAY
TEL: 095-31111 FAX: 095-31117
EMAIL: zetland@iol.ie

HOTEL ★★★★ MAP 5 D 11

Overlooking Cashel Bay this 19th century manor house is renowned for its peace and commanding views. The bedrooms and superb seafood restaurant overlook the gardens and Cashel Bay. Facilities include tennis court and billard room and there are many activities, hill walking and golf in the surrounding area. Good Hotel Guide recommended '98, AA Courtesy of Care Award '98 and Gilbeys Gold Medal Winner '97. 4**** Manor House Hotel, GDS Access Code, US 1-800-44-UTELL

WEB: www.connemara.net/zetland/

Member of Manor House Hotels

B&B from £61.00 to £73.00
€77.45 to €92.69

JOHN & MONA PRENDERGAST
Proprietors

American Express
Diners
Mastercard
Visa

Weekend specials from £129.00

19 19

Closed 01 November - 01 April

OYSTER MANOR HOTEL

CLARENBRIDGE,
CO. GALWAY
TEL: 091-796777 FAX: 091-796770
EMAIL: reservation@oystermanorhotel.com

HOTEL ★★★ MAP 6 F 10

Located in the famous oyster village of Clarenbridge the Oyster Manor Hotel was opened in May 1996. The building dates back some 150 years and has been tastefully redecorated in mature grounds. The hotel is family run which adds to its relaxing and friendly atmosphere. The hotel boasts a wide reputation for excellent cuisine in the Pearl Restaurant. Music and craic every weekend in the Leanach Bar.

WEB: www.oystermanorhotel.com

B&B from £30.00 to £70.00
€38.09 to €88.88

NED & JULIANNE FORDE
Proprietors

American Express
Diners
Mastercard
Visa

26 26

Closed 24 - 26 December

ABBEYGLEN CASTLE HOTEL

SKY ROAD, CLIFDEN,
CO. GALWAY
TEL: 095-21201 FAX: 095-21797
EMAIL: info@abbeyglen.ie

HOTEL ★★★★ MAP 9 C 12

Abbeyglen Castle Hotel was built in 1832 in the heart of Connemara by John D'Arcy of Clifden Castle. It is romantically set in beautiful gardens with waterfalls and streams, has a panoramic view of Clifden and the bay with a backdrop of the Twelve Bens. Abbeyglen provides a long list of indoor/outdoor facilities, cuisine of international fame, unique qualities of peace, serenity and ambience. Complimentary afternoon tea a speciality. AA 2 rosettes for good food and service.

WEB: www.abbeyglen.ie

Member of Manor House Hotels

B&B from £57.00 to £69.00
€72.38 to €87.61

BRIAN/PAUL HUGHES
Manager/Proprietor

American Express
Diners
Mastercard
Visa

29 29

Closed 10 January - 01 February

Room rates are IR£ per room per night

ALCOCK AND BROWN HOTEL

CLIFDEN, CONNEMARA,
CO. GALWAY
TEL: 095-21206 FAX: 095-21842
EMAIL: alcockandbrown@eircom.net

HOTEL ★★★ MAP 9 C 12

Alcock and Brown Hotel is family owned and operated. Situated in the centre of Clifden Village, featuring Brownes Restaurant with AA Rosette and 2 RAC ribbons for food and service. Ideal base for touring Connemara. Pursuits to be enjoyed are pony trekking, golfing on Connemara championship links course. Sea angling, guided heritage walks and mountain climbing. Numerous sandy beaches nearby. Member of Best Western Hotels - Central Reservations 01-6766776.

WEB: www.alcockandbrown-hotel.com

Member of Best Western Hotels

B&B from £35.00 to £44.00
€44.44 to €55.87

DEIRDRE KEOGH
Manager

American Express
Diners
Mastercard
Visa

☺ Weekend specials from £85.00

19 19

Closed 22 - 26 December

ARDAGH HOTEL & RESTAURANT

BALLYCONNEELY ROAD, CLIFDEN,
CO. GALWAY
TEL: 095-21384 FAX: 095-21314
EMAIL: ardaghhotel@eircom.net

HOTEL ★★★ MAP 9 C 12

A quiet family-run 3*** hotel, 2km from Clifden on Ardbear Bay, AA and RAC recommended. Bedrooms individually decorated with television, telephone and tea/coffee facilities. Award-winning restaurant specialises in lobsters, salmon, oysters and Connemara lamb with homegrown vegetables and a wide selection of wines. Local amenities: golf, fishing and beaches. Reservations by post, phone, fax. Superior suites with bay view available.

WEB: www.commerce.ie/ardaghhotel

Member of Coast and Country Hotels

B&B from £45.00 to £59.00
€57.14 to €74.91

STEPHANE & MONIQUE BAUVET
Proprietor/Manager/Chef

American Express
Diners
Mastercard
Visa

☺ Week partial board from £450.00

17 17

Closed 01 November - 31 March

BARRY'S HOTEL

MAIN STREET, CLIFDEN,
CO. GALWAY
TEL: 095-21287 FAX: 095-21499
EMAIL:nkbarry@yahoo.com

HOTEL ★★ MAP 9 C 12

We are a family run hotel that offers the discerning visitor food, accommodation and drinks of the highest standard.Traditional music sessions most nights in the bar also the ideal location to explore Connemara and the islands, pony tracking, walks, fishing , shopping and golf nearby.

B&B from £25.00 to £45.00
€31.74 to €57.14

KEVIN & NOREEN BARRY
Owners

American Express
Mastercard
Visa

20 20

Closed 5 January - 15 March

B&B rates are IR£ per person sharing per night incl. Breakfast

BEN VIEW HOUSE

**BRIDGE STREET, CLIFDEN,
CONNEMARA, CO. GALWAY
TEL: 095-21256 FAX: 095-21226
EMAIL: benvuehouse@ireland.com**

GUESTHOUSE ★★ MAP 9 C 12

Charming mid 19th century town house of immense character. Owned and managed by our family since 1926. We have been extending traditional family hospitality to our guests since then. Recommended by Frommer and Le Petit Fute Guides. Enjoy all the modern comforts and special ambience of this elegant guesthouse, surrounded by antiques and old world atmosphere. Wishing all our guests a pleasant and safe journey.

WEB: www.connemara.net/benviewhouse

B&B from £18.50 to £24.00
€23.49 to €30.47

EILEEN MORRIS
Proprietor

American Express

Mastercard

Visa

☺ Midweek specials from £55.50

Closed 24 - 26 December

BENBAUN HOUSE

**LYDONS, WESTPORT ROAD,
CLIFDEN, CO. GALWAY
TEL: 095-21462 FAX: 095-21462
EMAIL: benbaunhouse@eircom.net**

GUESTHOUSE P MAP 9 C 12

We invite you to enjoy the affordable luxury of Benbaun, set well back from the road in mature, leafy gardens, 3 mins walk from Clifden Town Centre. Newly refurbished to a high standard. We offer a variety of en suite rooms with TV, phone, hairdryers and a hospitality trolley in the study. Breakfast is special, a feast offering tempting choices. Whether you're sightseeing, fishing, rambling, golfing, Benbaun House is where you'll find a home away from home.

WEB: www.connemara.net/benbaunhouse

B&B from £20.00 to £25.00
€25.39 to €31.74

DR BRENDAN LYDON
Proprietor

American Express

Mastercard

Visa

Closed 01 November - 01 April

BUTTERMILK LODGE

**WESTPORT ROAD, CLIFDEN,
CO. GALWAY
TEL: 095-21951 FAX: 095-21953
EMAIL: buttermilk@anu.ie**

GUESTHOUSE ★★★ MAP 9 C 12

A warm friendly home from home, 400m from Clifden Town Centre (5 minutes walk). Our spacious en suite rooms have satellite TV, direct dial phone, radio/alarm clock and hairdryer. Your warm welcome includes tea/coffee and home baking by the turf fire where there is always a cuppa available. Our breakfast options, tasteful decor and many extra touches bring our guests back. Internet access for guests. Irish Tourist Board 3***, AA ♦♦♦♦ and RAC ♦♦♦♦♦.

WEB: www.buttermilklodge.com

B&B from £20.00 to £30.00
€25.39 to €38.09

PATRICK & CATHRIONA O'TOOLE
Proprietors/Hosts

Mastercard

Visa

Closed 07 January - 01 February

Room rates are IR£ per room per night

CONNEMARA COUNTRY LODGE

WESTPORT ROAD, CLIFDEN,
CO. GALWAY
TEL: 095-22122   FAX: 095-21122
EMAIL: connemara@unison.ie

GUESTHOUSE P   MAP 6 F 10

Delightful Georgian home with spacious bedrooms, 2 mins walk from Clifden, on extensive grounds with large private car park. All bedrooms are en suite with TV, tea/coffee making facilities, telephones and hairdryers. Why not join Mary for an evening of traditional Irish music and song in her large lounge - a truly unique experience - as Mary is a well known performer. Her home and ballad singing have recently been recorded for broadcasting on American TV. French and German spoken.

B&B from £20.00 to £30.00
€25.39 to €38.09

MARY CORBETT
Proprietress

Mastercard

Visa

🔥♨🐾📞🔒⬜T C💧☀⛵🍴🎵P🛗
10 10

Open All Year

DUN RI GUESTHOUSE

HULK STREET, CLIFDEN,
CO. GALWAY
TEL: 095-21625   FAX: 095-21635
EMAIL: dunri@anu.ie

GUESTHOUSE ★★★   MAP 9 C 12

Centrally located in picturesque Clifden. Dun Ri is newly built and specially designed to offer a high standard of accommodation. The spacious and luxurious bedrooms are all en suite. Facilities include TV, phone, hairdryer and tea/coffee. Private parking is available. Ideal base to enjoy all Connemara has to offer - golf, fishing, walking, sandy beaches, cycling, horse riding, excellent restaurants and pubs.

WEB: www.connemara.net/dun-ri

B&B from £20.00 to £25.00
€25.39 to €31.74

MICHAEL KING
Proprietor

Mastercard

Visa

🔥♨🐾📞🔒⬜T C U P
10 10

Closed 03 November - 01 March

ERRISEASK HOUSE HOTEL & RESTAURANT

BALLYCONNEELY, CLIFDEN,
CO. GALWAY
TEL: 095-23553   FAX: 095-23639
EMAIL: erriseask@connemara-ireland.com

HOTEL ★★★   MAP 9 C 11

Set amidst breathtaking scenery right on the shore of Mannin Bay - with our beach just a short walk away over own fields. Starting from here, you can explore the coastline and walk along the numerous sandy beaches for hours. Enjoy the excellent cuisine in our own restaurant overlooking Erriseask Peninsula and Bay, (table d'hôte, à la carte, menu digustation). Local amenities include Connemara Golf Course, pony trekking, sea and lake fishing.

WEB: www.erriseask.connemara-ireland.com

B&B from £40.00 to £50.00
€50.79 to €63.49

CHRISTIAN & STEFAN MATZ
Proprietors

American Express

Diners

Mastercard

Visa

🔥♨🐾T P alc🍴🍷
12 12

Closed 25 September - 01 May

B&B rates are IR£ per person sharing per night incl. Breakfast

FOYLES HOTEL

CLIFDEN, CONNEMARA,
CO. GALWAY
TEL: 095-21801   FAX: 095-21458
EMAIL: foyles@anu.ie

HOTEL U   MAP 9 C 12

Foyles Hotel, formerly Clifden Bay Hotel, is situated on the square in Clifden. Connemara's longest established hotel, it has been owned and managed by the Foyle Family since 1917. Facilities include, direct dial phone, tea/coffee tray, multi-channel colour TV and hair dryers in all bedrooms. There is a pleasant patio garden to the rear of the hotel. Golf, horse riding, deep sea fishing and tennis are all available locally. Logis of Ireland, Central Reservations tel. 01-6689743.

WEB: www.foyleshotel.com

B&B from £35.00 to £50.00
€44.44 to €63.49

EDDIE FOYLE
Proprietor

American Express
Diners
Mastercard
Visa

Midweek specials from £90.00

28 28

alc

Closed 03 February - 15 March

JOYCES WATERLOO HOUSE

GALWAY ROAD, CLIFDEN,
CONNEMARA, CO. GALWAY
TEL: 095-21688   FAX: 095-22044
EMAIL: pkp@joyces-waterloo.com

GUESTHOUSE ★★★   MAP 9 C 12

Romantic lodge on edge of Clifden Town (10 mins walk). Relax with a genuine Irish coffee in front of a glowing fire after settling into your spacious 4 poster or king-size en suite room embellished with special touches. South facing superior rooms are furnished with sofas in bay windows to enjoy glorious countryside views. A refreshing relaxed home, tempered with our knowledge of local activities. Superb breakfast menu, and our evening meals are a must. Secure private parking. AA ◆◆◆◆.

WEB: www.joyces-waterloo.com

B&B from £20.00 to £30.00
€25.39 to €38.09

PATRICIA & P.K. JOYCE
Hosts

Mastercard
Visa

Weekend specials from £56.00

8 8

Open All Year

MAL DUA HOUSE

GALWAY ROAD, CLIFDEN,
CONNEMARA, CO. GALWAY
TEL: 095-21171   FAX: 095-21739
EMAIL: info@maldua.com

GUESTHOUSE ★★★★   MAP 9 C 12

Mal Dua House, winner of the RAC Little Gem Award for 2000, offers luxury in a relaxed atmosphere and provides personalised hospitality and excellent food with peace and quiet as the theme. This non-smoking house offers bedrooms with a high level of luxury and comfort. The Dining Room overlooking the landscaped gardens invites you to enjoy a light repast and select wines whilst the Mal Dua Afternoon Tea is a particular favourite served in the Drawing Room. AA ◆◆◆◆◆. RAC ◆◆◆◆◆. Member of Les Routiers. Courtesy minibus. Bicycles for hire.

WEB: www.maldua.com

B&B from £35.00 to £40.00
€44.44 to €50.79

THE BYRNE FAMILY

American Express
Diners
Mastercard
Visa

Midweek specials from £95.00

14 14

Inet

Open All Year

Room rates are IR£ per room per night

O'GRADY'S SUNNYBANK GUESTHOUSE

CHURCH HILL, CLIFDEN,
CO. GALWAY
TEL: 095-21437 FAX: 095-21976
EMAIL: info@sunnybank.com

GUESTHOUSE ★★★★ MAP 9 C 12

Restored 19th Century residence of 4★★★★ rating uniquely situated one hundred metres from town centre. The guesthouse is surrounded by landscaped gardens which contain many interesting features. It is owned and run by the O'Grady Family who have long experience in the restaurant and hospitality industry and are recipients of many awards of excellence. AA ◆◆◆◆ and Highly Acclaimed RAC. Galtee Breakfast Award. Amenities include swimming pool, sauna, tennis court.

WEB: www.sunnybankhouse.com

Member of Premier Guesthouses

B&B from £20.00 to £40.00
€25.39 to €50.79

SHANE O'GRADY
Proprietor

Mastercard

Visa

🏨🅿️🕿️🅃❄️🛎️♨️♨️🚶⛵🅿️🅂
8 8

Closed 06 November - 01 March

ROCK GLEN COUNTRY HOUSE HOTEL

CLIFDEN, CONNEMARA,
CO. GALWAY
TEL: 095-21035 FAX: 095-21737
EMAIL: rockglen@iol.ie

HOTEL ★★★★ MAP 9 C 12

A delightful country house hotel run by the Roche Family. The restaurant is well known for its excellent cuisine (2AA Rosettes). Lovely rooms, have the full range of facilities for your comfort. All weather tennis court, croquet, putting green and snooker room. A short drive is Connemara's 18-hole golflinks, horse riding, trekking and fishing arranged nearby. Guided walks to historical sites. Clifden has many art galleries and shops where you can buy local handcrafts, tweeds, linens. Visit Kylemore Abbey, Victorian Gardens and National Park.

WEB: www.connemara.net/rockglen-hotel

Member of Manor House Hotels

B&B from £57.00 to £70.00
€72.38 to €88.88

JOHN & EVANGELINE ROCHE
Proprietors

American Express

Diners

Mastercard

Visa

☺ Week partial board from
£575.00

🏨🅿️🕿️🅃🅲🅼❄️♨️🚶⛵🅿️🅿️
26 26
alc

Closed 30 November - 12 February

STATION HOUSE HOTEL

CLIFDEN, CONNEMARA,
CO. GALWAY
TEL: 095-21699 FAX: 095-21667
EMAIL: station@eircom.net

HOTEL U MAP 9 C 12

Modern hotel adjacent to the old station house which has been restored as a pub and restaurant. Rooms are spacious, warm and designed for the modern traveller. Leisure centre with indoor pool and conference facilities for 250. A heritage site complete with museum, old railway buildings, a village of crafts, antique and designer shops and 11 holiday homes complete what is the most exciting resort complex in Ireland. A warm, friendly and relaxed atmosphere awaits you at the Station House.

WEB: www.stationhousehotel.com

Member of Signature Hotels

B&B from £40.00 to £65.00
€50.79 to €82.53

CIAN LANDERS
General Manager

American Express

Diners

Mastercard

Visa

🏨🅿️🕿️🅃🅲❄️🅲🅲🅼🅲🅂♨️
78 78
🏠🚶⛵🅿️🅂🅰️alc Inet

Closed 25 December

B&B rates are IR£ per person sharing per night incl. Breakfast

PASS INN HOTEL

KYLEMORE, CONNEMARA,
CO. GALWAY
TEL: 095-41141 FAX: 095-41377
EMAIL: passinn@indigo.ie

HOTEL ★★ MAP 9 D 12

Family owned and managed where you are assured a warm welcome, comfortable & restful holiday. Beautifully situated on a 4 acre site overlooking mountains and Kylemore Lake. Ideal base for leisure activities including fishing, diving, pony trekking and hiking. In both restaurant & lounge bar each window affords a view of magnificent scenery, serves vegetarian menu & local caught fish a speciality, also when available organic produce. Restaurant (and 1st Floor Bedrooms) Non-Smoking.

WEB: http://passinn.irishbiz.com

B&B from £30.00 to £45.00
€38.09 to €57.14

ROSE RIMA
Owner

American Express
Diners
Mastercard
Visa

🙂 3 days B&B and Dinner from
£139.00

10 10

Open All Year

ST. CLERANS

CRAUGHWELL,
CO. GALWAY
TEL: 091-846555 FAX: 091-846600
EMAIL: stclerans@iol.ie

GUESTHOUSE ★★★★ MAP 6 G 10

The Georgian style house is situated 35km east of Galway City. It was considered by the late owner, film director John Huston, to be 'one of the most beautiful houses in Ireland'. American entertainer and present owner, Merv Griffin, has carefully restored St. Clerans to its original splendour and decorated the house with art treasures from around the world. St. Clerans provides a calm and serene location for true relaxation.

WEB: www.merv.com

Member of Ireland's Blue Book

B&B from £115.00 to £190.00
€146.02 to €241.25

SEAMUS DOOLEY
General Manager

American Express
Mastercard
Visa

12 12

Open All Year

CONNEMARA COAST HOTEL

FURBO,
CO. GALWAY
TEL: 091-592108 FAX: 091-592065
EMAIL: sinnott@iol.ie

HOTEL ★★★★ MAP 6 F 10

Perched on the shores of Galway Bay and just 10 mins from the west's most vibrant city. The Connemara Coast is an ideal base offering many options for your precious leisure time. Experience unspoilt sea and landscapes within sight of the Aran Islands and Connemara magic. Luxurious public areas, ample free secure car parking, an award winning bar and leisure centre provide a unique setting to relax and enjoy Galway at its best.

WEB: www.sinnotthotels.com

B&B from £40.00 to £90.00
€50.78 to €114.28

PAUL O'MEARA
General Manager

American Express
Diners
Mastercard
Visa

🙂 Weekend specials from £95.00

112 112

Open All Year

Room rates are IR£ per room per night

LADY GREGORY HOTEL

**ENNIS ROAD, GORT,
CO. GALWAY**
TEL: 091-632333 FAX: 091-632332
EMAIL: ladygregoryhotel@eircom.net

HOTEL ★★★ MAP 6 G 9

Situated in the west of Ireland near Coole Park, home of Lady Gregory in the town of Gort, with its many historic and local attractions. A warm friendly welcome awaits you as you enter the architectural splendour of the Lady Gregory Hotel. 48 beautifully appointed rooms, Copper Beech Restaurant, lively Jack B Yeats Bar and magnificent Gregory Suite. Relax in our Kiltatan Reading Room. Discounted green fees available from reception for Gort Golf Course located less than 1 hour from Shannon Airport.

WEB: www.ladygregoryhotel.com

B&B from £35.00 to £65.00
€44.44 to €82.53

LEONARD MURPHY
General Manager

American Express
Diners
Mastercard
Visa

Weekend specials from £89.00

48 48

P Inet FAX

Closed 24 - 27 December

SULLIVAN'S ROYAL HOTEL

**THE SQUARE, GORT,
CO. GALWAY**
TEL: 091-631257 FAX: 091-631916
EMAIL: jsullinsauc@eircom.net

HOTEL ★★ MAP 6 G 9

Sullivan's Hotel is family run and managed, fully licensed and open all year round. Situated on main west of Ireland road, in close proximity to Coole Park, home of Lady Gregory, Thoore Ballylee, Kilmacduagh and the Burren. TV and telephone in all bedrooms, en suite rooms, meals served all day - bar food, à la carte dinner at reasonable rates. Available locally: golf, pony trekking, fishing. Pub of the Year Award 2000.

B&B from £22.50 to £34.50
€28.57 to €43.80

JOHNNY & ANNIE SULLIVAN
Proprietors

American Express
Diners
Mastercard
Visa

12 12

Open All Year

DAY'S HOTEL

**INISHBOFIN ISLAND,
CO. GALWAY**
TEL: 095-45809 FAX: 095-45803
EMAIL: dayshotel@eircom.ie

HOTEL U MAP 9 C 12

Inishbofin, 6 miles from the mainland of Connemara, is one of the most westerly in Ireland. Day's Hotel, formerly the landlord's residence, commands exquisite views over the harbour. This long-established family-run hotel has well-appointed rooms and most are south facing. The family specialise in offering a warm welcome, friendly efficient service and excellent food, particularly seafood. In the evening social life in the hotel or the adjoining pub tends to be lively and musical.

WEB: www.inishbofin.com

B&B from £30.00 to £40.00
€38.09 to €50.79

BRENDAN & BRIDIE DAY
Proprietors

American Express
Mastercard
Visa

14 10

Closed 31 September - 01 April

B&B rates are IR£ per person sharing per night incl. Breakfast

CO. GALWAY
INISHBOFIN ISLAND / KINVARA / LEENANE

DOONMORE HOTEL

**INISHBOFIN ISLAND,
CO. GALWAY**
TEL: 095-45804   FAX: 095-45804
EMAIL: reservations@doonmorehotel.com

HOTEL ★★ MAP 9 C 12

Uniquely situated on a beautiful and historic island, commanding magnificent views of the surrounding sea and islands. Inishbofin, a haven for artists, fishermen, bird watchers, nature lovers or those who just wish to escape from the hectic pace of life. Fine sandy beaches. Sea trips and boat angling can be arranged. Facilities for divers. Excellent shore fishing. Doonmore Hotel is owned and managed by the Murray Family, unpretentious but friendly and comfortable.

WEB: www.doonmorehotel.com

B&B from £25.00 to £30.00
€31.74 to €38.09

AILEEN MURRAY
Manager

American Express
Mastercard
Visa

19 19

Closed 10 October - 11 April

MERRIMAN INN & RESTAURANT

**MAIN STREET, KINVARA,
CO. GALWAY**
TEL: 091-638222   FAX: 091-637686
EMAIL: merrimanhotel@eircom.net

HOTEL ★★★ MAP 6 G 10

Located in the picturesque fishing village of Kinvara, The Merriman opened in April '97. Named after the famous Irish Poet, Brian Merriman, this 32 bedroomed hotel has one of the largest thatched roofs in Ireland. Overlooking Galway Bay, the Burren, the hills of Connemara, Kinvara is an ideal touring base. Dunguaire Castle, a short stroll away, where an enjoyable medieval banquet can be experienced. Excellent restaurant & bar provide for friendly, comfortable & value for money hotel.

WEB: www.merrimanhotel.com

B&B from £32.50 to £42.50
€41.27 to €53.96

NIAMH O'DONNELL
Manager

American Express
Diners
Mastercard
Visa

32 32

IRISH HOTELS FEDERATION

Closed 22 December - 31 January

LEENANE HOTEL

**LEENANE, CONNEMARA,
CO. GALWAY**
TEL: 095-42249   FAX: 095-42376
EMAIL: leenanehotel@eircom.net

HOTEL N MAP 9 D 12

On the shores of spectacular Killary Harbour at the start of the Western Way lies one of Europe's oldest coaching inns playing host to kings and mortals for centuries. All lovers of fine fresh food will find much to appreciate in the restaurant. Enjoy golden tranquil beaches, mountain climbing, adventure centres, scuba diving and pony trekking all within ten minutes drive.

WEB: www.connemara.net/leenanehotel

B&B from £38.50 to £52.80
€48.88 to €67.04

CONOR FOYLE
Assistant Manager

Mastercard
Visa

☺ Weekend specials from £79.00

29 29

Closed 03 November - 11 April

Room rates are IR£ per room per night

WEST 371

PORTFINN LODGE

**LEENANE,
CO. GALWAY
TEL: 095-42265   FAX: 095-42315
EMAIL: rorydaly@anu.ie**

GUESTHOUSE ★★   MAP 9 D 12

Portfinn Lodge is a family run guest house offering 8 comfortable rooms en suite including double and triple bedrooms, a guest lounge and a restaurant which has an international reputation for its fresh seafood. Rory and Brid Daly will be delighted to make you feel welcome. An ideal centre from which beaches, walking, angling, clay shooting, watersports etc. are easily reachable. When in Connemara, stay at Portfinn.

WEB: www.anu.ie/portfinn

B&B from £25.00 to £35.00
€31.74 to €44.44

BRID & RORY DALY
Owners

Mastercard

Visa

8 8

Closed 01 November - 31 March

ROSLEAGUE MANOR HOTEL

**LETTERFRACK, CONNEMARA,
CO. GALWAY
TEL: 095-41101   FAX: 095-41168
EMAIL: rosleaguemanor@ireland.com**

HOTEL ★★★★   MAP 9 C 12

Rosleague is a Regency manor now run as a first class country house hotel by Mark Foyle and Eddie Foyle. It lies 7 miles north west of Clifden on the coast overlooking a sheltered bay and surrounded by the Connemara Mountains and beside the National Park. It is renowned for its superb cuisine personally supervised by the owners with all the amenities expected by todays discerning guest. Also a member of Ireland's Blue Book.

WEB: www.connemara.net/rosleaguemanor.ie

Member of I.C.H.R.A. (Blue Book)

B&B from £45.00 to £80.00
€57.14 to €101.58

MARK FOYLE/EDDIE FOYLE
Manager/Owner

American Express

Mastercard

Visa

15 15

Closed 01 November - 01 April

MEADOW COURT HOTEL

**CLOSTOKEN, LOUGHREA,
CO. GALWAY
TEL: 091-841051   FAX: 091-842406
EMAIL: meadowcourthotel@eircom.net**

HOTEL ★★★   MAP 6 H 10

Newly extended and refurbished the Meadow Court Hotel's en suite rooms have full facilities, multi channel TV, hair dryer and garment press. Superb dining is on offer in our award-winning restaurant renowned for its outstanding cuisine. Enjoy after dinner drinks in our Derby Bar. Situated on the main Galway Dublin Road 2 miles from Loughrea, 18 miles from Galway, convenient to all local 18-hole golf courses, angling, horseriding, water sports. Banqueting & conference facilities. Carpark.

B&B from £30.00 to £50.00
€38.09 to €63.48

TOM & DAVID CORBETT
Directors

American Express

Mastercard

Visa

20 20

Closed 25 December

B&B rates are IR£ per person sharing per night incl. Breakfast

CO. GALWAY
LOUGHREA / MAAM CROSS / MOYCULLEN

O'DEAS HOTEL

BRIDE STREET, LOUGHREA,
CO. GALWAY
TEL: 091-841611 FAX: 091-842635

HOTEL ★★★ MAP 6 H 10

O'Deas Hotel is a family hotel, a Georgian town house hotel, of character with open fires and within walking distance of Loughrea's game fishing lake. It is an ideal touring base situated on the N6 (exactly halfway between Clonmacnoise, 35 miles to the east and the Cliffs of Moher, 35 miles to the west). The start of the Burren country is just 12 miles away. Galway City 20 miles.

WEB: www.commerce.ie/odeashotel

Member of Logis of Ireland

B&B from £35.00 to £45.00
€44.44 to €57.14

MARY O'NEILL
Proprietor/Manager

American Express
Mastercard
Visa

25 25
alc

Open All Year

PEACOCKES HOTEL & COMPLEX

MAAM CROSS, CONNEMARA,
CO. GALWAY
TEL: 091-552306 FAX: 091-552216
EMAIL: peacockes@eircom.net

HOTEL N MAP 6 F 10

Newly built and situated at the Crossroads of Connemara, Peacockes is surrounded by breathtaking scenery. All rooms are en suite and a family room is included. Enjoy a drink beside the open turf fire in the Bog Dale Bar. Within the Complex also are The Quiet Man replica cottage and craft shop. Peacockes is an ideal base for Hill Walkers, Cyclists and Botanists while Golfing, Horse Riding, Fishing and Water Sports are also available locally.

WEB: www.peacockes.net

B&B from £25.00 to £55.00
€31.74 to €69.84

BASIL KEOGH
Managing Director

American Express
Diners
Mastercard
Visa

☺ Weekend Specials from £75.00

25 25
S alc

Closed 23 - 26 December

MORAN'S CLOONNABINNIA HOUSE HOTEL

MOYCULLEN, CONNEMARA,
CO. GALWAY
TEL: 091-555555 FAX: 091-555640
EMAIL: cbinnia@iol.ie

HOTEL ★★★ MAP 6 F 11

A hidden jewel, 16km from Galway City just off route N59. Overlooking Ross Lake and the rolling hills of Connemara. Quality food and magnificent views. It is the warmth and genuine hospitality of the Moran Family that make a visit to this delightful hotel a memorable experience. Angling centre on hotel grounds, own boats and gillies. 60,000 acres of internationally renowned lake and river systems. Atlantic Ocean 20 minutes. 5 golf courses and many walking routes nearby.

B&B from £35.00 to £45.00
€44.44 to €57.14

PETER & BERNADETTE MORAN
Proprietors

Mastercard
Visa

☺ Weekend specials from £72.00

20 20
alc

Open All Year

Room rates are IR£ per room per night

GALWAY BAY GOLF AND COUNTRY CLUB HOTEL

ORANMORE,
CO. GALWAY
TEL: 065-682 3000 FAX: 065-682 3759
EMAIL: reservations@lynchotels.com

HOTEL U MAP 6 G 10

Ideal for both leisure & corporate breaks, this hotel combines a PGA 18-hole golf course with outstanding views over Galway Bay. Set amongst acres of forest walks, Galway, just 10 mins drive & the Burren and Connemara a short distance. 92 en suite rooms await as does the finest local and international cuisine in the multi-award winning Grainne Uaile à la carte restaurant, plus the craic agus ceoil of the hotel's unique Didean Bar. Free ValuPass discount booklet to 25 local attractions. Conference facilities for 275. A leading wedding venue.

WEB: www.galwaybayhotel.com

Member of Lynch Hotels

B&B from £40.00 to £65.00
€50.79 to €82.53

MICHAEL B LYNCH Group MD
Hugh Coyle General Manager

American Express
Diners
Mastercard
Visa

😊 Weekend specials from £96.00

92 92

alc Inet FAX

Open All Year

ORANMORE LODGE HOTEL, CONFERENCE & LEISURE CENTRE

ORANMORE,
CO. GALWAY
TEL: 091-794400 FAX: 091-790227
EMAIL: orlodge@eircom.net

HOTEL ★★★ MAP 6 G 10

This manor house hotel 8km from Galway City in the picturesque village of Oranmore, overlooking Galway Bay and on the edge of oyster country. 3km from Galway Airport. Equestrian, golfing and walking pursuits all within 3km of the hotel. Full leisure facilities with a 17m swimming pool and computerised TechnoGym. Your host and his efficient staff radiate a welcome and warmth reminiscent of the old country houses of Ireland.

WEB: www.oranmorelodge.com

Member of Logis of Ireland

B&B from £40.00 to £90.00
€50.79 to €114.28

BRIAN J. O'HIGGINS
Proprietor

American Express
Diners
Mastercard
Visa

😊 Weekend specials from £89.00

56 56

S alc

Closed 23 - 27 December

QUALITY HOTEL AND LEISURE CENTRE GALWAY

ORANMORE,
CO. GALWAY
TEL: 091-792244 FAX: 091-792246
EMAIL: qualityhotelgalway@eircom.net

HOTEL ★★★ MAP 6 G 10

This luxury hotel is ideally located on the N6 approach to Galway, adjacent to the picturesque village of Oranmore & just 5 mins drive from Galway City. Facilities incl spacious rooms, Furey's Well traditional pub with regular entertainment & all day menu, Furey's Relish Restaurant, residents' lounge & a superb leisure centre with a 20m pool, jacuzzi, hi-tech gym, steamroom, sauna, therapy & solarium. Rooms to accommodate up to 2 adults & 2 children. Golf, karting, horseriding nearby.

WEB: www.qualityhotelgalway.com

Member of Choice Hotels Ireland

Room Rate from £49.00 to £109.00
€62.22 to €138.40

DERMOT COMERFORD
General Manager

American Express
Diners
Mastercard
Visa

😊 Weekend specials from £79.00

93 93

♫ P S alc

Closed 24 - 26 December

B&B rates are IR£ per person sharing per night incl. Breakfast

BOAT INN

THE SQUARE, OUGHTERARD,
CO. GALWAY
TEL: 091-552196   FAX: 091-552694
EMAIL: info@theboatinn.com

GUESTHOUSE ★★★   MAP 5 E 11

3*** guesthouse in the heart of Oughterard, just 25 minutes from Galway. 5 minutes to Lough Corrib and redesigned 18 hole golf course. Ideal base to explore Connemara. The Boat Bar and Restaurant offer an imaginative choice of food, drink and wine. Enjoy the continental feel of our terrace and rear gardens. Live music in the bar. All bedrooms en suite with TV, radio, phone and tea coffee making facilities.

WEB: www.theboatinn.com

B&B from £20.00 to £25.00
€25.39 to €31.74

MICHAEL MURPHY
Proprietor

American Express
Diners
Mastercard
Visa

Weekend specials from £53.00

10 10

Closed 25 - 26 December

CONNEMARA GATEWAY HOTEL

OUGHTERARD,
CO. GALWAY
TEL: 091-552328   FAX: 091-552332
EMAIL: gateway@iol.ie

HOTEL ★★★   MAP 5 E 11

This hotel, full of character and style, just 16 miles from Galway City at the gateway to Connemara. Set in attractive grounds, the emphasis is on warmth and hospitality. Turf fires, pine panelled lobby and bedrooms all en suite with tea/coffee making facilities, add to the overall comfort. The bar, restaurant and indoor heated swimming pool are equally attractive and nearby, there is golf and fishing in abundance. Outdoor tennis court, putting green and croquet lawn.

WEB: www.sinnotthotels.com

B&B from £40.00 to £70.00
€50.79 to €88.88

TONY BELLEW
Manager

American Express
Diners
Mastercard
Visa

Weekend specials from £85.00

62 62

IRISH
HOTELS
FEDERATION

Closed 01 December - 14 February

CORRIB HOUSE HOTEL

BRIDGE STREET, OUGHTERARD,
CO. GALWAY
TEL: 091-552329   FAX: 091-552522

HOTEL ★★   MAP 5 E 11

Character at the gateway to Connemara the Corrib House Hotel is 17 miles from Galway City and 1 mile from Connemara. 27 comfortable en suite rooms, turf fires and our renowned Owenriff Restaurant with superb food and wine list. 4 championship golf courses within 30 miles, the world famous fishing on Lough Corrib (1 mile) and magnificent walking and hiking - a few of the pastimes available while staying with us.

B&B from £26.00 to £37.00
€33.01 to €46.98

CONOR MCNAMARA
Manager

American Express
Mastercard
Visa

27 27

IRISH
HOTELS
FEDERATION

Closed 23 - 28 December

Room rates are IR£ per room per night

CORRIB WAVE GUEST HOUSE

PORTACARRON, OUGHTERARD,
CONNEMARA, CO. GALWAY
TEL: 091-552147   FAX: 091-552736
EMAIL: cwh@gofree.indigo.ie

GUESTHOUSE ★★★   MAP 5 E 11

Panoramic lakeside guest house - the home of Michael & Maria Healy. As our guests, you are assured of a warm welcome to a family home with every comfort and Irish hospitality, superb home cooking, excellent wines, beautiful en suite bedrooms (all with double and single beds), TVs, hairdryers. Spectacular views, turf fire, peace & tranquillity. Angling specialists, boats, engines. Boatmen for hire. Wild brown trout, salmon, pike, lakeside walks. 18 hole golf 1km. Colour brochure on request.

B&B from £22.50 to £25.00
€28.57 to €31.74

MARIA & MICHAEL HEALY
Proprietors

Mastercard
Visa

3 B&B, 3 dinners from
£110.00 to £117.50

9 9

Closed 20 December - 02 January

CURRAREVAGH HOUSE

OUGHTERARD, CONNEMARA,
CO. GALWAY
TEL: 091-552312   FAX: 091-552731
EMAIL: currarvagh@ireland.com

GUESTHOUSE ★★★★   MAP 5 E 11

A charming country mansion, built in 1842, situated beside Lough Corrib in 60 hect. of private woodland. The relaxing atmosphere & classically simple menus receive much international praise. Own fishing, boats, tennis court, with golf & riding locally. Recommendations: Egon Ronay, Guide Michelin, Footprint Guide, Lonely Planet, Karen Brown's Irish Country Inns, Good Food Guide, Good Hotel Guide & many other international hotel & food guides. You should stay at least 3 nights to absorb the atmosphere and gently explore Connemara.

Member of Ireland's Blue Book

B&B from £54.00 to £70.00
€68.57 to €88.88

HARRY & JUNE HODGSON
Proprietors

Mastercard
Visa

15 15

Closed 21 October - 31 March

LAKE HOTEL

OUGHTERARD,
CO. GALWAY
TEL: 091-552275   FAX: 091-552794

HOTEL ★★   MAP 5 E 11

Situated in the picturesque fishing and golfing village of Oughterard, within easy access to Connemara's rugged hills and hidden lakes and only 20 minutes drive to the City of Galway. Choice of 4 Championship Golf Courses and numerous Fishing Lakes. Family Run Hotel under the personal supervision of the McDonnell Family.

B&B from £25.00 to £40.00
€31.74 to €50.79

GERRY MCDONNELL & FAMILY
Proprietors

American Express
Diners
Mastercard
Visa

20 20

Open All Year

B&B rates are IR£ per person sharing per night incl. Breakfast

MOUNTAIN VIEW GUEST HOUSE

AUGHNANURE, OUGHTERARD,
CO. GALWAY
TEL: 091-550306 FAX: 091-550133

GUESTHOUSE ★★★ MAP 5 E 11

Situated just off the N59, 24km from Galway City and within 2.4km of Oughterard, with the Connemara Mountains in the distance and Lough Corrib nearby. Leisure activities include; golf at the renowned Oughterard Golf Club, established walks along scenic routes, boating or fishing on Lough Corrib. Guests can relax in the lounge with open turf fire and sample some of the cuisine before retiring to en suite bedrooms with TV, direct dial phone, tea/coffee making facilities and hairdryer.

B&B from £18.00 to £23.00
€22.86 to €29.20

PATRICIA & RICHARD O'CONNOR
Proprietors

Mastercard
Visa

☺ Weekend specials from £50.00

🛏🚗☎🅣🄲♥CM❄♨🅟🛎
10 10

HOTELS FEDERATION

Closed 24 - 26 December

RIVER RUN LODGE

GLANN ROAD, OUGHTERARD,
CO. GALWAY
TEL: 091-552697 FAX: 091-552669
EMAIL: rivrun@indigo.ie

GUESTHOUSE ★★★★ MAP 5 E 11

River Run Lodge sits on the Owenriff which flows into Lough Corrib. Just minutes walk from the heart of Oughterard you'll find landscaped gardens, patios and riverside walks. A lodge warmed by light wood and lit by natural hues. Comfortably traditional spacious bedrooms and cosy lounges. A riverside restaurant with menus to rival any city repertoire. Book your slice of peace and quiet in the ideal base for exploring Connemara.
AA ◆◆◆◆◆.

WEB: www.connemara.net/riverrunlodge

B&B from £27.50 to £39.50
€34.92 to €50.14

TOM & ANNE LITTLE
Proprietors

American Express
Mastercard
Visa

🛏🚗☎🅣❄♨🅟❀🅢🄰alc
6 6

HOTELS FEDERATION

Open All Year

ROSS LAKE HOUSE HOTEL

ROSSCAHILL, OUGHTERARD,
CO. GALWAY
TEL: 091-550109 FAX: 091-550184
EMAIL: rosslake@iol.ie

HOTEL ★★★ MAP 5 E 11

Ross Lake House is a wonderful Georgian house set in the magnificent wilderness of Connemara. Six acres of mature gardens surround the house creating an air of peace and tranquillity. Hosts Henry and Elaine Reid have beautifully restored this manor house to its former glory. A high quality Irish menu is prepared daily featuring a tempting variety of fresh produce from nearby Connemara hills, streams and lakes as well as fish straight from the Atlantic.

WEB: www.rosslakehotel.com

Member of Green Book of Ireland

B&B from £50.00 to £70.00
€63.49 to €88.88

ELAINE & HENRY REID
Proprietors

American Express
Diners
Mastercard
Visa

🛏🚗☎🅣❄♨🅟🅢🄰alc
13 13

HOTELS FEDERATION

Closed 31 October - 15 March

Room rates are IR£ per room per night

SHANNON OAKS HOTEL & COUNTRY CLUB

PORTUMNA,
CO. GALWAY
TEL: 0509-41777 FAX: 0509-41357
EMAIL: sales@shannonoaks.ie

HOTEL R MAP 6 I 9

Shannon Oaks Hotel & Country Club lies adjacent to the 17th century Portumna Castle and estate, by the shores of Lough Derg. All our rooms have satellite television, D.D. phone and an en suite bathroom. A distinguished menu of classic and fusion Irish dishes are available each evening. Our leisure centre, with its indoor heated swimming pool, sauna, steam room and gymnasium provides the stress free atmosphere in which to relax and unwind.

WEB: www.shannonoaks.ie

Member of Signature Hotels

B&B from £56.00 to £60.50
€71.11 to €76.82

BARRY MAHER
General Manager

American Express
Diners
Mastercard
Visa

63 63

Open All Year

LOUGH INAGH LODGE

RECESS, CONNEMARA,
CO. GALWAY
TEL: 095-34706 FAX: 095-34708
EMAIL: inagh@iol.ie

HOTEL ★★★ MAP 5 D 11

Lough Inagh Lodge was built in 1880. It offers all the comforts of an elegant modern hotel in an old world atmosphere, open log fires in the library and oak panelled bar symbolises the warmth of Inagh hospitality. The lodge is surrounded by famous beauty spots including the Twelve Bens Mountain Range and the Connemara National Park. Kylemore Abbey is also nearby.

WEB: www.commerce.ie/inagh/

Member of Manor House Hotels

B&B from £60.50 to £82.50
€76.82 to €104.75

MAIRE O'CONNOR
Proprietor

American Express
Diners
Mastercard
Visa

☺ Weekend specials from £119.90

12 12

Closed 13 December - 12 March

RENVYLE HOUSE HOTEL

RENVYLE, CONNEMARA,
CO. GALWAY
TEL: 095-43511 FAX: 095-43515
EMAIL: renvyle@iol.ie

HOTEL ★★★ MAP 9 C 12

Historic coastal hotel set amid the magical beauty of sea, lake and mountains, the keynotes are warmth and comfort with award winning fine fare. Turf fires and cosy lounges make you relax and feel at home. Golf, tennis, horse riding, swimming pool, snooker, boating, fishing are the facilities to name but a few. Wonderful walking and cycling routes throughout an area that hosts a vast National Park.

WEB: www.renvyle.com

B&B from £40.00 to £75.00
€50.78 to €95.23

VINCENT FLANNERY
General Manager

American Express
Diners
Mastercard
Visa

65 65

Closed 02 January - 29 February

B&B rates are IR£ per person sharing per night incl. Breakfast

ELDONS HOTEL

ROUNDSTONE, CONNEMARA,
CO. GALWAY
TEL: 095-35933   FAX: 095-35722
EMAIL: eldonshotel@eircom.net

HOTEL ★★   MAP 9 C 11

Situated in the village of Roundstone, has a view of the harbour and Twelve Ben's mountain range. We are a newly built, family run hotel, offering bedrooms all with private bathrooms, colour TV and D.D. phones. Locally; 18 hole golf course, sea angling and windsurfing school. Our Beola Restaurant has been operating successfully for many years and is renowned for its fine food, with lobster being its speciality. Credit cards taken. New Annex consisting of 6 superior rooms with a lift.

WEB: www.connemara.net

B&B from £30.00 to £45.00
€38.09 to €57.14

ANN & NOLEEN CONNEELY
Owner/Chef

American Express
Diners
Mastercard
Visa

Closed 11 November - 15 March

ROUNDSTONE HOUSE HOTEL

ROUNDSTONE, CONNEMARA,
CO. GALWAY
TEL: 095-35864   FAX: 095-35944
EMAIL: diar@eircom.net

HOTEL ★★   MAP 9 C 11

Roundstone House Hotel is a family hotel situated in the picturesque village of Roundstone. Roundstone is a fascinating place for a holiday offering a wide range of interests for the holiday makers. Many outdoor activities are available locally including sea angling, watersports, hillwalking, pony trekking and a championship 18 hole golf course nearby. Come to beautiful Roundstone for a holiday to remember.

Member of Village Inn Hotels

B&B from £31.50 to £39.00
€40.00 to €49.52

MAUREEN VAUGHAN
Proprietor

American Express
Mastercard
Visa

Closed 30 October - 02 April

AN CRUISCIN LAN HOTEL

SPIDDAL,
CO. GALWAY
TEL: 091-553148   FAX: 091-553712
EMAIL: info@cruiscinlanhotel.com

HOTEL P   MAP 5 E 10

Newly reconstructed family run hotel situated in the heart of Spiddal. All rooms en suite, colour TV, direct dial phone line. Ideal for canoeing, sea angling and touring Connemara and the Aran Islands. Enjoy a drink in the bar or a meal in our restaurant with panoramic views of Galway Bay.

WEB: www.cruiscinlanhotel.com

B&B from £39.00 to £89.00
€49.52 to €113.01

JOHN FOYE

Mastercard
Visa

Closed 23 - 28 December

Room rates are IR£ per room per night

BRIDGE HOUSE HOTEL

**SPIDDAL, CONNEMARA,
CO. GALWAY
TEL: 091-553118   FAX: 091-553435**

HOTEL ★★   MAP 5 E 10

Enjoy a friendly relaxed atmosphere at Bridge House, a small hotel set in the heart of Spiddal Village - the home of traditional Irish music. Ideally situated to tour the many beauty spots of Connemara. Minutes walk from the sea. Trips to the Aran Islands arranged. All rooms en suite, colour TV, direct dial telephone. Award winning restaurant - fresh seafood a speciality - privately owned - personal service. Discover the difference for yourself.

PARK LODGE HOTEL

**PARK, SPIDDAL,
CO. GALWAY
TEL: 091-553159   FAX: 091-553494
EMAIL: parklodgehotel@eircom.net**

HOTEL U   MAP 5 E 10

The Park Lodge Hotel is owned and run by the Foyle Family. It is situated on the coast road from Galway to Connemara, 16km west of Galway City and just east of Spiddal Village. Most of the 23 bedrooms have a view of Galway Bay. There are also seven detached cottages on the grounds, each self-catering and fully equipped for 5 persons. Cottages open all year.

WEB: www.failte-ireland.com/parklodgehotel

TIGH CHUALAIN

**KILROE EAST, SPIDDAL,
CO. GALWAY
TEL: 091-553609   FAX: 091-553049**

GUESTHOUSE ★★★   MAP 5 E 10

Tigh Chualain is a charming, family run 3*** guesthouse, 16km west of Galway City and 2km west of Spiddal Village, en route to the Aran Islands' Ferry. Overlooking Galway Bay, with a nearby Blue Flag beach it is in the heart of the Connemara Gaeltacht. An obvious starting point for exploring the rugged beauty of Connemara with its manifold attractions. All bedrooms are en suite with direct dial telephone and colour TV.

B&B from £30.00 to £55.00
€38.09 to €69.84

ESTHER FEENEY
Manager

American Express
Mastercard
Visa

☺ Weekend specials from £80.00

🏨🚗☎T✦⋃PS🅿alc
10 10

IRISH HOTELS FEDERATION

Closed 20 December - 01 March

B&B from £29.00 to £52.00
€36.82 to €66.03

JANE MARIE FOYLE
Manager

American Express
Diners
Mastercard
Visa

🏨🚗☎🛆✦C♥CM✿⋃PS
23 23

🅿♿

IRISH HOTELS FEDERATION

Closed 01 October - 31 May

B&B from £18.00 to £20.00
€22.86 to €25.39

NORA & COLM FOLAN
Proprietors

☺ Midweek specials from £50.00

🏨🚗☎C✿🅿P
9 9

Closed 31 October - 01 April

B&B rates are IR£ per person sharing per night incl. Breakfast

ACHILL CLIFF HOUSE & RESTAURANT

KEEL, ACHILL ISLAND,
CO. MAYO
TEL: 098-43400 FAX: 098-43007
EMAIL: achillcliff@anu.ie

GUESTHOUSE ★★★★ MAP 9 C 14

Family run guesthouse with a warm welcome. AA ◆◆◆◆. Spacious smoke free rooms, orthopaedic beds, sauna, fully licenced restaurant with a selection of fine wines. Fresh local produce with seafood a speciality. Dining room looks out on to magnificent scenery. Ideal base for walking, climbing, fishing, sightseeing, painting, photography, writing. Bus stops at door. NRB approved. Tempting choices for breakfast. Friendly host recommends a 3 day stay.

WEB: www.achillcliff.com

Member of Premier Guesthouses

B&B from £25.00 to £48.00
€31.74 to €60.95

TERESA & JJ MCNAMARA
Proprietors

American Express
Mastercard
Visa

Midweek 2 B&B and 1 Dinner from £69.00

10 10

Open All Year

GRAYS GUEST HOUSE

DUGORT, ACHILL ISLAND,
CO. MAYO
TEL: 098-43244

GUESTHOUSE ★★★ MAP 9 C 14

Vi McDowell welcomes you to Grays where you are assured of a restful holiday, with good food, comfort and personal attention. Turf fires and electric blankets. Late dinner is served at 7pm. There are three lounges, colour TV, table tennis room and croquet lawn and swings in an enclosed garden.

B&B from £25.00 to £30.00
€31.74 to €38.09

VI MCDOWELL
Owner/Manager

15 15

Closed 24 - 26 December

OSTAN OILEAN ACLA

ACHILL SOUND,
CO. MAYO.
TEL: 098-45138 FAX: 098-45198
EMAIL: reservations@achillislandhotel.com

HOTEL U MAP 9 C 14

Enjoy the panoramic views of Achill Island from our new luxury hotel situated at the gateway to Achill Island. In our elegant Seafood Restaurant choose from a wide range of local produce. Relax and enjoy a drink in our friendly traditional bar. Convenient to Blue Flag beaches, the highest cliffs in Europe, golf courses, pitch and putt course, outdoor activities. A warm friendly welcome awaits you at Ostan Oilean Acla.

WEB: www.achillislandhotel.com

B&B from £30.00 to £50.00
€38.09 to €63.49

MICHAEL MCLOUGHLIN

American Express
Mastercard
Visa

Weekend specials from £80.00

16 16

Open All Year

SLIEVEMORE HOTEL

**DUGORT, ACHILL,
CO. MAYO
TEL: 098-43224 FAX: 098-43236**

HOTEL ★ MAP 9 C 14

This historic building dates back to the 1830s and became Achill's first hotel in 1840. Standing on the slopes of Slievemore Mountain (Achill's highest point 2,204ft) it affords the energetic a start for walks and climbs with stunning beauty and views. Within a few minutes' walk you have one of Dugort's two blue flag beaches with views of north Mayo across Blacksod Bay. Beside this beach is a small harbour and nearby the famous seal caves.

B&B from £22.00 to £25.00
€27.93 to €31.74

TIM & AIDEEN STEVENSON
Owners

Mastercard

Visa

🛏️🅿️📞T▲⚡C CM❄️🎵📶🚲
16 9
🆂🏧alc🚬

Open All Year

BARTRA HOUSE HOTEL

**PEARSE STREET, BALLINA,
CO. MAYO
TEL: 096-22200 FAX: 096-22111**

HOTEL ★★ MAP 10 F 15

Bartra House Hotel, situated in Ballina, is a family business run by brothers Paul and Noel Regan. Located near the famous River Moy and with two golf courses within easy reach, it is the ideal base for such holidays. The hotel boasts 20 bedrooms all en suite, with colour television and telephone. Our restaurant is famous for its superb food and service and our function room can cater for up to 200 people for dinner.

B&B from £30.00 to £45.00
€38.09 to €57.14

PAUL AND NOEL REGAN
Directors

American Express

Diners

Mastercard

Visa

✓/🐦

😊 Weekend specials from £75.00

🛏️🅿️📞TC🍴CM🎵📶🆂🏧alc🚬
17 17

Closed 25 December

BELLEEK CASTLE

**BELEEK, BALLINA,
CO. MAYO
TEL: 096-22400 FAX: 096-71750
EMAIL: belleekcastlehotel@eircom.net**

HOTEL U MAP 10 F 15

Historic, romantic, set in 1000 acres of woodland on banks of River Moy - Wine/dine till midnight - Gourmet organic food enthusiasts welcomed - 'Perchance to Dream' in a four poster. For your added pleasure: tour of 16c castle armoury, giant fossil exhibits, Spanish Armada Bar, dramatic artifacts and timbers salvaged from Galleons wrecked off Irish west coast 1588. Sporting: international surfing, golf, fishing, tennis, riding, ten stables in castle.

WEB: www.belleekcastle.com

B&B from £42.35 to £78.65
€53.77 to €99.86

**MARSHALL & JACQUELINE
DORAN**

American Express

Mastercard

Visa

🛏️🅿️📞T❄️U🎵🅿️🏧alc Inet
16 16

Closed 24 - 27 December

B&B rates are IR£ per person sharing per night incl. Breakfast

DOWNHILL HOUSE HOTEL

**BALLINA,
CO. MAYO**
TEL: 096-21033 FAX: 096-21338
EMAIL: thedownhillhotel@eircom.net

HOTEL ★★★ MAP 10 F 15

A 3*** family run hotel beside Europe's best salmon fishing river, the Moy, 1km from Ballina, adjacent lake, course & deep sea fishing. Golfers paradise, 6 x 18-hole courses nearby. Set in tranquil gardens, friendly service, excellent cuisine and superb facilities. Eagles Health & Leisure Club, heated pool, children's pool, sauna/jacuzzi/sunbed. Floodlit tennis courts. Conference centre. Piano Bar with international entertainment June-Sept. Rest of year weekends (entertainment).

WEB: www.downhillhotel.ie

B&B from £50.00 to £61.00
€63.49 to €77.45

MICHAEL MCKEIGUE
General Manager

American Express
Diners
Mastercard
Visa

Weekend specials from £127.00

50 50

Closed 22 - 27 December

DOWNHILL INN

**SLIGO ROAD, BALLINA,
CO. MAYO**
TEL: 096-73444 FAX: 096-73411
EMAIL: thedownhillinn@eircom.net

HOTEL ★★★ MAP 10 F 15

A family-run 3*** hotel, located 1 mile outside Ballina town on the main Sligo Road (N59). Contemporary in its design with 45 well-appointed triple rooms. All rooms are en suite with multi-channel TV, hairdryer and direct dial phone. The region offers superb fishing on the River Moy, Lough Conn and Killala Bay. An excellent selection of golf courses: Enniscrone, Ballina, Carne, to mention but a few. Enjoy a drink at the bar or a meal in our Terrace Restaurant. Rest assured!

WEB: www.downhillinn.com

Member of Holiday Ireland Hotels

B&B from £28.00 to £36.00
€35.55 to €45.71

JOHN RAFTERY/NICOLA
MOYLETT Proprietors

American Express
Mastercard
Visa

Weekend specials from £62.00

45 45

Closed 24 - 30 December

RIDGEPOOL HOTEL, CONFERENCE AND LEISURE CENTRE

**BALLINA,
CO. MAYO**
TEL: 096-24600 FAX: 096-24602
EMAIL: ridgepoolhotel@eircom.net

HOTEL P MAP 10 F 15

Located in the heart of Ballina, the Ridgepool Hotel is graced by its view onto the world renowned Ridgepool fishing area of the River Moy. It boasts 70 luxury en suite bedrooms, 2 executive suites & 3 penthouse suites. Our Leisure Centre incorporates a gymnasium, steam room, sauna, jacuzzi, pool, solarium and changing facilities. The conference centre will furnish you with a comprehensive, competitively priced, thoroughly professional package no matter what the occasion.

WEB: www.ridgepoolhotel.com

B&B from £55.00 to £85.00
€69.84 to €107.93

CONOR O'CONNELL
General Manager

American Express
Diners
Mastercard
Visa

Weekend specials from £129.00

75 75

Open All Year

ROCKS

FOXFORD ROAD, BALLINA,
CO. MAYO
TEL: 096-22140
EMAIL: therocks@eircom.net

GUESTHOUSE ★★ MAP 10 F 15

Built and designed by the present owners. This beautiful residence offers good hospitality and atmosphere. All rooms en suite with hairdryers, TV and internal phone system. Guest tea & coffee room and guest lounge. Large landscaped gardens - front & rear - children's playground and barbeque. Ideal location for touring the scenic North West. All fishing arranged on River Moy - Lough Conn - estuary and sea with gillie and boats. Pony riding, golf, swimming and mountain climbing nearby.

B&B from £18.00 to £22.00
€22.86 to €27.93

MARGARET CUMISKEY

🛏🚭🕿T🅰C🔆♨UJP
6   6

Open All Year

BREAFFY HOUSE
BUSINESS & LEISURE HOTEL

CASTLEBAR,
CO. MAYO
TEL: 065-682 3000 FAX: 065-682 3759
EMAIL: reservations@lynchotels.com

HOTEL ★★★ MAP 9 E 14

Breaffy House Hotel is a 3* manor style country house hotel, situated on 82 acres of grounds and gardens, just 4km from Castlebar. All 60 rooms are en suite, with direct dial phone, TV/radio, hairdryer, trouserpress and tea/coffee making facilities. Enjoy the relaxed and comfortable Mulberry Bar and Lounge, with superb food in the Garden Restaurant. The hotel has a gymnasium and conference facilities for 250. The hotel is the ideal base to explore the beauties of Mayo and is 30 mins from Knock and Westport. A leading wedding venue.

WEB: www.breaffyhousehotel.com

Member of Lynch Hotels

B&B from £40.00 to £65.00
€50.78 to €82.53

MICHAEL B LYNCH Group MD
David Ryan General Manager

American Express
Diners
Mastercard
Visa

😊 Weekend specials from £96.00

🛏🚭🕿📺T🅰C🔆CM🔆📷UJP
60   60
S🅰alc☕

Closed 23 - 26 December

DALY'S HOTEL

THE MALL, CASTLEBAR,
CO. MAYO
TEL: 094-21961 FAX: 094-22783
EMAIL: stay@dalyshotel.com

HOTEL U MAP 9 E 14

The longest established hotel in Castlebar (1795) tastefully renovated and refurbished. Combines all of what is good from both old and new. Centre piece of the beautiful Mall - a mature, tree lined park in the heart of the town. Attractive bar, charming restaurant and spacious bedrooms ensure an enjoyable and pleasurable stay. Indoor pool and leisure complex closeby (.5km). Outdoor activities including angling can be arranged. Ideal base for touring the West, Blue Flag beaches nearby.

WEB:www.dalyshotel.com

B&B from £30.00 to £36.00
€38.09 to €45.71

RUAIRI HUGHES
General Manager

American Express
Diners
Mastercard
Visa

🛏🚭🕿T🅰C🔆CMUJ♫PS🅰
23   23
alc☕

Closed 24 - 25 December

B&B rates are IR£ per person sharing per night incl. Breakfast

HENEGHAN'S GUEST HOUSE

NEWTOWN STREET, CASTLEBAR,
CO. MAYO
TEL: 094-21883   FAX: 094-26476
EMAIL: heneghans@eircom.net

GUESTHOUSE ★★★   MAP 9 E 14

Charming town house, built by our grandparents in 1932, it has hosted generations of Irish and international guests. Restored and tastefully refurbished, we offer warmth, comfort and great food in the centre of Castlebar. All rooms en suite with TV, hairdryers, tea/coffee, direct dial phones. Relax in our courtyard garden & library or use as the ideal base for touring the West. Genealogical information supplied. Arrangements made for walking/golfing/fishing. Packed lunches available.

WEB: www.castlebar.ie/heneghans/

B&B from £20.00 to £24.00
€25.39 to €30.47

BRIDGET & ROISIN HORKAN
Proprietors

Mastercard

Visa

7 nights one night free

88

Closed 24 - 25 December

JENNINGS HOTEL & TRAVELLERS FRIEND

OLD WESTPORT ROAD, CASTLEBAR,
CO. MAYO
TEL: 094-23111   FAX: 094-23111
EMAIL: patj@anu.ie

HOTEL ★★★   MAP 9 E 14

Jennings Hotel & The Travellers Friend, Hotel & Theatre is a luxurious family 3*** facility. Contemporary style new rooms & suites with air-conditioning, data-ports, VCR, hairdryer, trouser press. Combine with a new 1920s style restaurant & new conference rooms to provide excellent facilities for meetings/banquets. Personalised service, excellent cuisine, theatre shows, afford total comfort without compromise. Dedicated Business Centre. Adjacent to Institute of Technology, Mayo General Hospital and Aldi Shopping Centre.

Member of MinOtel Ireland Hotel Group.

B&B from £40.00 to £55.00
€50.79 to €69.84

PAT AND MARY JENNINGS
Proprietors

American Express

Mastercard

Visa

27 27

Closed 24 - 25 December

KENNYS GUESTHOUSE

LUCAN STREET, CASTLEBAR,
CO. MAYO
TEL: 094-23091
EMAIL: kennysguesthouse@focus-ireland.com

GUESTHOUSE ★★★   MAP 9 E 14

Our family-managed guesthouse is tastefully decorated and furnished to a very high standard. All guests rooms are en suite with direct dial phone, TV and hairdryer. Relax in our residents' lounge with complimentary tea/coffee or avail of the numerous facilities nearby e.g. organised walks, fishing trips, bowling, swimming, golf, fine restaurants and entertainment. Ideal base to explore the unspoilt areas in the west. Private car parking. Reasonable prices for business or leisure.

WEB: www.focus-ireland.com/kennysguesthouse

B&B from £20.00 to £30.00
€25.39 to €38.09

SUSANNA & RAYMOND KENNY
Owners/Proprietors

Mastercard

Visa

88

Open All Year

Room rates are IR£ per room per night

WELCOME INN HOTEL

NEW ANTRIM STREET, CASTLEBAR, CO. MAYO
TEL: 094-22288 FAX: 094-21766
EMAIL: ifh@iol.ie

HOTEL ★★ MAP 9 E 14

The Welcome Inn Hotel is a professionally managed family hotel in the capital town of County Mayo. We provide first class service at reasonable rates. We have ultra modern facilities combined with a very friendly and welcoming attitude. Ours is an ideal base from which to tour and view some of the world's most breathtaking scenery. We look forward to welcoming you. A member of Irish Family Hotels Marketing Group Int.
Tel 353 - 458 67307.

Member of Irish Family Hotels

B&B from £33.00 to £45.00
€41.90 to €57.14

ANN MCHUGH
Director

American Express
Mastercard
Visa

☺ Weekend specials from £70.00

🛏🍴☎🖥❄T C ♥CMU♩♫🔲
39 39

🄰🄻🄲☕🍵

IRISH HOTELS FEDERATION

Closed 24 - 27 December

ASHFORD CASTLE

CONG, CO. MAYO
TEL: 092-46003 FAX: 092-46260
EMAIL: ashford@ashford.ie

HOTEL ★★★★★ MAP 9 E 12

5* Ashford Castle has long been considered one of Ireland's most outstanding properties - and has adapted the facilities to cater for the demands of today's discerning clientele. Now a total resort, guests can enjoy complimentary golf and the health club facilities which comprise a fully equipped gymnasium, sauna, steamroom and whirlpool. Other sports to be enjoyed are horseback riding outdoor & indoor, falconry, cruising and fishing on Lough Corrib. Nightly entertainment is provided.

WEB: www.ashford.ie

Member of Relais & Châteaux

Room Rate from £146.00 to £350.00
€185.38 to €444.41

BILL BUCKLEY
Manager

American Express
Diners
Mastercard
Visa

🛏🍴☎🖥❄T C ♥CM✱🔲🔍🔍
83 83

🆙♩♫🄿🄰🄻🄰🄻🄲

IRISH HOTELS FEDERATION

Open All Year

LYDONS LODGE

CONG, CO. MAYO
TEL: 092-46053 FAX: 092-46523
EMAIL: lydonslodge@eircom.net

HOTEL ★★ MAP 9 E 12

Lydons Lodge combines the most modern amenities with old world charm. Located in Cong, village of 'Quiet Man' film fame it offers salmon, pike and famous Lough Corrib wild brown trout fishing. Boats, engines and boatmen can be arranged. Choice of 3 local golf clubs, horse riding and tennis. Minutes' walk from Ashford Castle and gardens. Hill walks and mountain climbing with spectacular lake views, an archaeological and geological paradise. Traditional music and bar food.

WEB: www.lydonslodgefreeservers.com

B&B from £25.00 to £30.00
€31.74 to €38.09

FRANK & CARMEL LYDON
Owners

American Express
Diners
Mastercard
Visa

🛏🍴☎🔲TCMU♩♫🄰🄻🄲
11 11

IRISH HOTELS FEDERATION

Closed 05 November - 01 February

B&B rates are IR£ per person sharing per night incl. Breakfast

RYAN'S HOTEL

CONG,
CO. MAYO
TEL: 092-46243 FAX: 092-46634
EMAIL: michaelv@indigo.ie

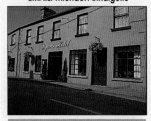

HOTEL ★★ MAP 9 E 12

The idyllic riverside setting of Ryan's Hotel is more than matched by the outstanding service and lovely surroundings inside. Just a few minutes' walk from the infamous free fishing Brown Trout lake Lough Corrib, the hotel is ideally situated for touring the west coast including the breathtaking views of Connemara. Because of its unique beauty, Cong was chosen by John Ford for his film The Quiet Man.

Member of MinOtel Ireland Hotel Group

B&B from £29.00 to £42.00
€36.82 to €53.33

MICHAEL & GERALDINE RYAN
Owners

Mastercard
Visa

12 12

alc

Closed 04 January - 08 February

TEACH IORRAIS

GEESALA, BALLINA,
CO. MAYO
TEL: 097-86888 FAX: 097-86855
EMAIL: teachior@iol.ie

HOTEL N MAP 10 F 15

Situated in an area of unrivalled beauty, Teach Iorrais is one of the most exclusive and luxurious hotels within Mayo. The hotel boasts 31 exquisite en-suite bedrooms which are decorated to the highest standard and offer awe-inspiring views of the surrounding Neiphinn Mountains and the Atlantic Ocean. An Neiphinn Restaurant offers the best of fine dining in a relaxing and intimate environment. Carne Links Golf Course located 15 minutes drive from hotel.

WEB: www.teachiorrais.com

B&B from £28.00 to £48.00
€35.55 to €60.95

CARMEL GALLAGHER
Manager

American Express
Diners
Mastercard
Visa

☺ Weekend specials from £79.00

31 31

S alc

IRISH HOTELS FEDERATION

Open All Year

CILL AODAIN HOTEL

MAIN STREET, KILTIMAGH,
CO. MAYO
TEL: 094-81761 FAX: 094-81838
EMAIL: cillaodain@eircom.net

HOTEL R MAP 10 F 14

This RAC 3*** hotel is set in the centre of historic Kiltimagh. Furnished with flair and imagination. Has pannelled lounges and open fires. The restaurant which has received many accolades is open for dinner each evening. The bedrooms, with all amenities, are individually furnished and decorated. Kiltimagh is one of Ireland's most famous small towns. 5km off Galway to Sligo Road. Member of Village Inns of Ireland.

Member of Village Inn Hotels

B&B from £28.00 to £42.00
€35.55 to €53.33

TONY MCDERMOTT
Innkeeper

American Express
Diners
Mastercard
Visa

☺ Weekend specials from £85.00

12 12

alc

IRISH HOTELS FEDERATION

Closed 24 - 26 December

Room rates are IR£ per room per night

BELMONT HOTEL

KNOCK,
CO. MAYO
TEL: 094-88122 FAX: 094-88532
EMAIL: belmonthotel@eircom.net

HOTEL ★★★ MAP 10 G 13

A haven of hospitality nestled at the rear entrance to Knock Shrine off N17. The hotel radiates Old Country Warmth from the moment you arrive. Recently RAC 3*** accreditation is added to Irish Tourist Board 3*** and AA 3*** status. Our An Bialann Restaurant is the recipient of 3 AA Rosette Awards. All day carvery is available and our specially developed Natural Health Therapy packages compliment our services. All rooms tastefully furnished with direct dial phone, TV, tea/coffee making facilities.

WEB: www.belmonthotel.ie

Member of Logis of Ireland

B&B from £30.00 to £48.00
€38.09 to €60.95

TERENCE EGAN
Manager

American Express
Diners
Mastercard
Visa

64 64

Open All Year

KNOCK HOUSE HOTEL

BALLYHAUNIS ROAD, KNOCK,
CO. MAYO
TEL: 094-88088   FAX: 094-88044
EMAIL: hotel@knock-shrine.ie

HOTEL ★★★ MAP 10 G 13

Knock House Hotel opened in May 1999 and is located in 100 acres of parkland, behind the famous Marian Shrine, just minutes from the Basilica. The foyer of local limestone and a glazed area give unparalleled views of the surrounding countryside. 6 guestrooms have been especially designed to cater for wheelchair users. The Four Seasons Restaurant is ideal for snacks and full meals, and is open all day.

WEB: www.knock-shrine.ie

B&B from £37.00 to £43.00
€46.98 to €54.60

BRIAN CROWLEY
Manager

Diners
Mastercard
Visa

68 68

Open All Year

KNOCK INTERNATIONAL HOTEL

MAIN STREET, KNOCK,
CO. MAYO
TEL: 094-88466 FAX: 094-88428

HOTEL ★★ MAP 10 G 13

Knock International Hotel was opened in 1986 by Mary and Edward Curry, who have been catering for pilgrims for years at Fairfield Restaurant. Set in own gardens only minutes from Knock Shrine. Also only 10 minutes from Knock Airport. The Currys are joined in the operations by their family and the hotel is especially suited for weddings and functions. Credit cards, Access, Visa.

B&B from £25.00 to £32.00
€31.74 to €40.63

MR & MRS EDWARD CURRY
Owners

Mastercard
Visa

10 10

Closed 13 October - 29 March

B&B rates are IR£ per person sharing per night incl. Breakfast

HEALY'S HOTEL ON THE LAKE

PONTOON, FOXFORD,
CO. MAYO
TEL: 094-56443 FAX: 094-56572
EMAIL: healyspontoon@eircom.net

HOTEL ★★ MAP 9 F 14

Get away from all the fuss of busy city life, Healys on the Lake is magic. It is located in the heart of Mayo. Ireland's best location for Golf and Fishing. Owner managed and friendly Co. Mayo staff. Healy's Restaurant *probably the best food in the West*. Scenically overlooking Lough Cullen, adjacent to Lough Conn, 10 minutes from the River Moy, one of Western Europe's best salmon rivers. Healys is 30 mins from Enniscrone and Carne Golf Links.

WEB: www.irelandmayohotel.com

B&B from £20.00 to £25.00
€25.39 to €31.74

JOHN DEVER
Proprietor

American Express
Diners
Mastercard
Visa

Open All Year

PONTOON BRIDGE HOTEL

PONTOON, FOXFORD,
CO. MAYO
TEL: 094-56120 FAX: 094-56688
EMAIL: relax@pontoonbridge.com

HOTEL ★★★ MAP 10 F 14

Family managed hotel on the shores of Lough Conn and Cullin in the centre of Mayo. Famous for trout and salmon fishing - River Moy, golf, horseriding, scenery, central for touring. Twin Lakes Restaurant. Live musical entertainment nightly during season. Tennis court, sandy beaches, conference facilities. Families welcome. School of flyfishing, landscape painting and cookery. Leisure Centre opening Spring 2001.

WEB: www.pontoonbridge.com

B&B from £55.00 to £65.00
€69.84 to €82.53

BREETA GEARY
General Manager

American Express
Mastercard
Visa

Open All Year

ARDMORE COUNTRY HOUSE HOTEL AND RESTAURANT

THE QUAY, WESTPORT,
CO. MAYO
TEL: 098-25994 FAX: 098-27795
EMAIL: ardmore@anv.ie

HOTEL ★★★★ MAP 9 E 13

Ardmore Country House and Restaurant is a small luxurious 4**** hotel, owned and managed by Pat & Noreen Hoban and family, offering warm hospitality. Ardmore House is idyllically situated overlooking Clew Bay with breathtaking sunsets, in the shadow of Croagh Patrick. The Restaurant offers the best of local produce, including fresh fish from Clew Bay, organic vegetables and herbs from local producers and a selection of Irish farmhouse cheeses. All bedrooms are non-smoking.

WEB: www.ardmorecountryhouse.com

B&B from £60.00 to £80.00
€76.18 to €101.58

NOREEN & PAT HOBAN

American Express
Mastercard
Visa

☺ Weekend specials from £135.00

Closed 01 February - 01 March

Room rates are IR£ per room per night

ATLANTIC COAST HOTEL

THE QUAY, WESTPORT,
CO. MAYO
TEL: 098-29000 FAX: 098-29111
EMAIL: achotel@iol.ie

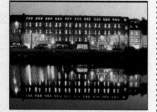

HOTEL N MAP 9 E 13

Recently established as one of Westport's finest and most popular hotels, situated on the waterfront at Westport Quay overlooking Clew Bay. Superb contemporary cuisine in our unique top floor restaurant -The Blue Wave. The Atlantic Club features pool, gym, sauna, steamroom & massage, including seaweed hydrotherapy bath treatments. Championship golf, angling, scenic walks, islands & blue flag beaches nearby. Your perfect base to explore beautiful Westport. Callsave 1850 229000

WEB: www.atlanticcoasthotel.com

B&B from £40.00 to £65.00
€50.79 to €82.53

JIM MULCAHY
Manager

American Express
Mastercard
Visa

☺ Weekend specials from £90.00

85 85

Closed 23 - 27 December

AUGUSTA LODGE

GOLF LINKS ROAD, WESTPORT,
CO. MAYO
TEL: 098-28900 FAX: 098-28995
EMAIL: info@augustalodge.ie

GUESTHOUSE ★★★ MAP 9 E 13

Augusta Lodge is a purpose-built 3*** guesthouse situated just 5 minutes walk from the town centre of Westport. A warm and friendly welcome awaits you in this family run guesthouse and Liz and Dave will ensure that your stay is a memorable one. A golfer's haven with tee times and reduced green fees arranged at Westport and adjacent courses. Putting green on site for guests use. Listed in all leading guides.

WEB: www.augustalodge.ie

B&B from £18.00 to £30.00
€22.86 to €38.09

LIZ O'REGAN

Mastercard
Visa

☺ Midweek specials from £54.00

10 10

Closed 23 - 27 December

CASTLECOURT HOTEL CONFERENCE AND LEISURE CENTRE

CASTLEBAR STREET, WESTPORT,
CO. MAYO
TEL: 098-25444 FAX: 098-28622
EMAIL: castlecourt@anu.ie

HOTEL ★★★ MAP 9 E 13

Perfectly located in the heart of Westport, the tourist haven of Mayo; a genuine welcome and warm atmosphere awaits you at this spectacular hotel, run by the Corcorans since 1971. The hotel has been refurbished and extended. Guests can enjoy 140 luxurious rooms, indoor heated swimming pool, children's pool, sauna, steamroom, sunbed, children's creche, health suites for aromatherapy & massage, hair salon, 200 car spaces, conservatory concorse and an award winning restaurant.

WEB: www.castlecourthotel.com

Member of Holiday Ireland Hotels

B&B from £40.00 to £72.00
€50.79 to €91.42

JOSEPH & ANNE CORCORAN
Managers

American Express
Diners
Mastercard
Visa

☺ Weekend specials from £95.00

140 140

Closed 24 - 26 December

B&B rates are IR£ per person sharing per night incl. Breakfast

CENTRAL HOTEL

THE OCTAGON, WESTPORT,
CO. MAYO
TEL: 098-25027 FAX: 098-26316
EMAIL: centralhotel@anu.ie

HOTEL U MAP 9 E 13

A warm friendly newly renovated hotel, perfectly located in the heart of Westport's beautiful town. All bedrooms are en suite with TV, direct dial phone, iron and iron board. Enjoy dining in our Wyatt Restaurant, our lively J. W's Bar. Bar food served all day. 4**** leisure facilities available for our guests 50 yards from hotel. Local activities: Golf, angling and scenic walks.

WEB: www.thecentralhotel.com

Member of Logis of Ireland

B&B from £35.00 to £45.00
€44.44 to €57.14

CIARA TEMPLE
General Manager

American Express
Mastercard
Visa

 Weekend specials from £89.00

35 35

Closed 24 - 25 December

CLEW BAY HOTEL

JAMES STREET, WESTPORT,
CO. MAYO
TEL: 098-28088 FAX: 098-25783
EMAIL: clewbay@anu.ie

HOTEL U MAP 9 E 13

Enjoy our warm friendly family run hotel situated in Westport Town centre. Our newly renovated hotel has 28 en suite rooms finished to the highest standard of comfort. Guests can enjoy the Old World charm of the Tubber Bar that features traditional music. The Riverside Restaurant overlooking the Carrowbeg River offers an imaginative menu, modestly priced. Local attractions include Westport Leisure Park, golfing, angling, pony trekking, scenic walks/drives, beaches.

WEB: www.clewbay.anu.ie

Member of Village Inn Hotels

B&B from £32.50 to £50.00
€41.26 to €63.49

DARREN MADDEN & MARIA
RUDDY Proprietors

Mastercard
Visa

 Weekend specials from £80.00

28 28

alc Inet

Closed 22 - 27 December

HOTEL WESTPORT

THE DEMESNE, NEWPORT ROAD,
WESTPORT, CO. MAYO
TEL: 098-25122 FAX: 098-26739
EMAIL: reservations@hotelwestport.ie

HOTEL *** MAP 9 E 13

This uniquely comfortable, friendly hotel is set in its own tranquil parklands, in the heart of Westport Town, offering a unique experience in relaxation and leisure. Our state of the art conference centre and ultra modern swimming pool/leisure centre offer an excellent range of accommodation with delightful food, wine, entertainment for your business or leisure break. Local attractions: golf, scenic walks/drives, cycling, angling, pony trekking, beaches. Callsave: 1850 53 63 73

WEB: www.hotelwestport.ie

B&B from £65.00 to £75.00
€82.53 to €95.23

GERRY WALSHE
General Manager

American Express
Diners
Mastercard
Visa

 Weekend specials from £99.00

129 129

Open All Year

Room rates are IR£ per room per night

KNOCKRANNY HOUSE HOTEL

WESTPORT,
CO. MAYO
TEL: 098-28600 FAX: 098-28611
EMAIL: info@khh.ie

HOTEL ★★★★ MAP 9 E 13

Situated on a hillside overlooking picturesque town of Westport, Knockranny House Hotel enjoys unrivalled views of Clew Bay & Croagh Patrick. The hotel is full of character with log fires creating a warm and relaxed atmosphere. The restaurant 'La Fougère' offers excellent cuisine with an emphasis on fresh seafood and the finest local ingredients. Westport is a charming town with a lot to offer. Local activities include golf, angling, horse riding, water sports and much more.

WEB: www.khh.ie

B&B from £65.00 to £85.00
€82.53 to €107.93

GERALDINE & ADRIAN NOONAN Proprietors
American Express
Mastercard
Visa

54 54

Closed 23 - 27 December

KNOCKRANNY LODGE

KNOCKRANNY, WESTPORT,
CO. MAYO
TEL: 098-28595 FAX: 098-28805
EMAIL: knockranny@anu.ie

GUESTHOUSE ★★★★ MAP 9 E 13

Knockranny Lodge is a beautifully appointed 4**** guesthouse. It has the peace and tranquillity of the country and yet is only 5 mins walk to town. Relax and enjoy a cup of tea or coffee in our welcoming lounge. All of our en suite bedrooms have direct dial phone, multi-channel TV, trouserpress and hairdryer. Private tennis court and car park. We have full use of swimming pool and leisure complex in nearby sister hotel.

WEB: www.anu.ie/knockrannylodge

B&B from £25.00 to £45.00
€31.74 to €57.14

MARY MCDERMOTT
American Express
Diners
Mastercard
Visa

Weekend specials from £79.00

12 12

Closed 01 December - 30 January

OLDE RAILWAY HOTEL

THE MALL, WESTPORT,
CO. MAYO
TEL: 098-25166 FAX: 098-25090
EMAIL: railway@anu.ie

HOTEL ★★★ MAP 9 E 13

Get away from it all and be pampered in this tastefully appointed 18th Century coaching inn. Standard and superior accommodation. Renowned for traditional country fare and fine wines. Genuine hospitality and warm welcome in relaxing intimate surroundings. Conservatory restaurant, residents' lounge and library, turf fires, original antique furniture adorn. Patio and garden area. Organic vegetable garden for restaurant. Recommended in all leading guides, Egon Ronay, AA Rosette winner.

WEB: www.anu.ie/railwayhotel

B&B from £35.00 to £70.00
€44.44 to €88.88

KARL ROSENKRANZ
Owner/Manager
American Express
Diners
Mastercard
Visa

15 15

Open All Year

B&B rates are IR£ per person sharing per night incl. Breakfast

WESTPORT WOODS HOTEL & LEISURE CENTRE

QUAY ROAD, WESTPORT,
CO. MAYO
TEL: 098-25811 FAX: 098-26212
EMAIL: info@westportwoodshotel.com

HOTEL ★★★ MAP 9 E 13

Friendly, cosy hotel with fabulous 'Beech Club' leisure centre, set in mature woodland, overlooking private lake. Enjoy unforgettable family holidays with our famous Kiddies Club or treat yourself to a terrific theme break, ranging from golf and murder mystery to bridge and short mat bowls. Glorious golden getaways are a speciality in this welcoming establishment. Situated on the road to the harbour, the hotel is ideally located for lots of fascinating day trips - Kylemore Abbey, Achill, Clare Island, Croagh Patrick plus lots more.

WEB: www.westportwoodshotel.com

B&B from £40.00 to £65.00
€50.79 to €82.53

MICHAEL LENNON &
JOANNE McENIFF

American Express
Mastercard
Visa

Open All Year

ABBEY HOTEL

GALWAY ROAD,
ROSCOMMON TOWN
TEL: 0903-26240 FAX: 0903-26021
EMAIL: cmv@indigo.ie

HOTEL ★★★ MAP 10 I 12

This eighteenth century manor has been carefully transformed into an exceedingly well appointed country house hotel beautifully set in four acres of private lawns, the Abbey offers excellent accommodation, the old wing rooms are a special feature, and a fine restaurant open to non residents. The hotel is three star rated by Bord Failte, AA and RAC. Recommended in most guide books. Roscommon Town is on these holiday routes, Dublin/Westport, Shannon/Donegal and Belfast/Galway.

Member of Coast and Country Hotels

B&B from £45.00 to £55.00
€57.14 to €69.84

TOMMY & ANYA GREALY
Manager/Manageress

American Express
Diners
Mastercard
Visa

Closed 24 - 26 December

GLEESONS TOWNHOUSE & RESTAURANT

MARKET SQUARE,
ROSCOMMON TOWN
TEL: 0903-26954 FAX: 0903-27425
EMAIL: gleerest@iol.ie

GUESTHOUSE ★★★ MAP 10 I 12

Magnificent Townhouse/Restaurant in a tastefully restored listed 19th Century Town House with an attractive finish of cut limestone and blue Bangor quarry slates. Located in the town centre next door to the Tourist Office/Museum. We offer superb accommodation with all 19 rooms built to a 4 star standard. Private car parking. Experience "The Manse" Restaurant where all the old values of guest satisfaction comfort and value for money prevail. Fully licensed for beers/spirits/wine. Anglers/Golf facility centre on-site. Conference facilities available.

WEB: www.gleesonstownhouse.com

Member of Premier Guesthouses of Ireland

B&B from £27.50 to £37.50
€34.92 to €47.62

MARY & EAMONN GLEESON
Proprietors

American Express
Diners
Mastercard
Visa

☺ Weekend specials from £69.00

Open All Year

Room rates are IR£ per room per night

O'GARA'S ROYAL HOTEL

**CASTLE STREET,
ROSCOMMON TOWN
TEL: 0903-26317 FAX: 0903-26225**

HOTEL ★★ MAP 10 I 12

O'Gara's Royal Hotel family run, situated on the Dublin to Castlebar/Westport route. 19 bedrooms en suite, radio, direct dial phone, TV, video, hair dryer. Comfortable modern dining room with good food and friendly service. Coffee dock/carvery. Spacious lounge bar with pleasant surroundings. Private car park. A warm welcome awaits you. Available 3 new conference rooms fully equipped with the latest facilities. Golfing holidays a speciality with a number of top golf courses locally.

B&B from £25.00 to £34.00
€31.74 to €43.17

AILEEN & LARRY O'GARA
Proprietors

American Express
· Mastercard
Visa

☺ Weekend specials from £70.00

19 19

HOTELS FEDERATION

Open All Year

REGANS

**MARKET SQUARE,
ROSCOMMON TOWN
TEL: 0903-25339 FAX: 0903-27833**

GUESTHOUSE ★★★ MAP 10 I 12

Regan's is a family run 3*** licenced guesthouse situated in Roscommon Town Centre. It provides a central base to explore the town and environs. Regans boasts a fine bar, restaurant and 14 en suite bedrooms, all with satellite TV and direct dial phone facilities. We have also added a new dimension by way of two bedroom self-catering apartments. Our restaurant offers good quality food at a reasonable price. Also available is a fully equipped conference room. A warm welcome awaits you.

B&B from £25.00 to £25.00
€31.74 to €31.74

EAMON & DOMINIC REGAN
Managers

American Express
Mastercard
Visa

14 14

Open All Year

FOREST PARK HOTEL

**DUBLIN ROAD, BOYLE,
CO. ROSCOMMON
TEL: 079-62229 FAX: 079-63113**

HOTEL ★★ MAP 10 I 14

Family run hotel, in own gardens on main Dublin Road. 1km from town centre. All rooms en suite with T.V. & Welcome Tea Tray, most with a garden view. Full Restaurant & Bar facilities with food bar open daily. Ideal touring centre close to Lough Key Forest Park, Boyle Abbey, Arigna Drive & newly restored King House. Available locally are 9 Hole Golf, Fishing, Walking, Cycling & Animal Farm. Close to Knock & Sligo Airports. We wish you a pleasant visit.

B&B from £35.00 to £45.00
€44.44 to €57.14

MICHAEL GILMARTIN
Manager

American Express
Diners
Mastercard
Visa

12 12

HOTELS FEDERATION

Closed 24 - 26 December

B&B rates are IR£ per person sharing per night incl. Breakfast

ROYAL HOTEL

BRIDGE STREET, BOYLE,
CO. ROSCOMMON
TEL: 079-62016   FAX: 079-64949

HOTEL ★★ MAP 10 I 14

Royal Hotel is over 250 years old.
Under the new ownership since
December 1999 of Nelson Chung &
Adrian Bouchier, General Manager, it
consists of 16 en suite bedrooms.
Coffee shop open daily serving hot
food from 8 a.m to 6 p.m. Chung's
famous Chinese restaurant is also
part of the hotel opening at 6 p.m.
nightly until late. AA***. Private car
park. Member of MinOtel Marketing
Group, Ballycanew, Co. Wexford.
Tel.353-55-27291. Fax:353-55-
27398

Member of MinOtel Ireland Hotel Group

B&B from £40.00 to £48.00
€50.79 to €60.95

ADRIAN BOUCHIER & NELSON
CHUNG

Mastercard

Visa

☺ Weekend Specials available

16 16

a/c Inet FAX

Open All Year

SHANNON KEY WEST HOTEL

THE RIVER EDGE, ROOSKEY,
CO. ROSCOMMON
TEL: 078-38800   FAX: 078-38811
EMAIL: shnkywst@iol.ie

HOTEL ★★★ MAP 11 J 13

Situated on N4 Dublin Sligo route,
2km from Dromod Train Station, this
beautiful 40 bedroom hotel with
Greek, Georgian and modern
architecture offers panoramic views
of Shannon River from both
bedrooms and roof gardens. All
rooms are well appointed with direct
dial phone - modem compatible.
Rooskey Inn and Kilglass
Restaurants offer excellent choice of
cuisine. Leisure club and tennis
court. Enjoy scenic trips on Shannon
Queen. While away your time in
elegant and peaceful surroundings.

WEB: keywest.firebird.net

Member of Best Western Hotels

B&B from £39.50 to £46.50
€50.15 to €59.04

DAVID O'CONNOR
General Manager

American Express

Mastercard

Visa

40 40

P S a/c

IRISH
HOTELS
FEDERATION

Closed 25 - 26 December

Room rates are IR£ per room per night

Les Routiers
25 Vanston Place
London SW6 1AZ
Great Britian

Phone: ++44 20 7385 6644
Fax: ++ 44 20 7385 7136
Email: info@routiers.co.uk
Website: www.routiers.co.uk

Your guarantee of great value, good food and a warm welcome.

Les Routiers offers an unrivalled selection of hotels and restaurants for leisure or business travellers throughout the whole of Ireland. Why not visit one of our award winning establishments and experience excellent accommodation, enjoy innovative cuisine, avail of our conference facilities and varied selection of leisure pursuits or simply relax with a round of golf on one of Ireland's many wonderful courses.

Les Routiers is your guarantee of quality.
If you are travelling to Ireland - go Les Routiers.

For details of our wonderful establishments, either look at our website, send us an email or send for brochures.

For details in Ireland, contact Noel Stewart on ++353 87 230 9814
or fax ++353 1 295 1356, email on: ireland@routiers.co.uk

Be Our Guest

2001

HOTEL AND GUESTHOUSE
RESERVATIONS
FREEPHONE

To book any of the premises in this Guide ring toll free on

* +800 36 98 74 12

Be Our Guest

or visit our web site at

www.irelandhotels.com

On-line Reservations from Spring 2001

+ denotes international access code in country where call is made
g. from UK   access code 00
     USA   access code 011

Powered by: 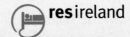 **res**ireland

WHERE TO STAY
WHEN YOU PLAY!

Accommodation	Courses	Be Our Guest Page Number	Golf On Site	All Inclusive Package	Tuition Available	Cart Available	Arrange Tee Off Times	Advance Reservations	Clubs For Hire	Transport	Preferential Green Fees	Caddy Available
ANTRIM Continued												
Causeway Coast Hotel & Conference Centre	Royal Portrush, Portstewart, Castlerock, Ballycastle, Bushfort, Gracehill	49		•	•	•	•	•	•		•	
Comfort Hotel Portrush	Royal Portrush, Portstewart, Castlerock, Ballycastle, Bushfoot, Gracehill	50		•	•	•	•	•	•	•	•	•
Hilton Templepatrick		51 ⛳18	•	•	•	•			•		•	
Magherabuoy House Hotel	Royal Portrush, Valley, Portstewart, Castlerock, Bushfoot, Ballycastle	50		•	•	•	•	•	•			
Tullyglass House Hotel	Galgorm Castle Golf and Country Club	47		•							•	
ARMAGH												
Silverwood Golf Hotel and Country Club	Lurgan, Portadown, Banbridge, Tandragee	52 ⛳18	•		•	•	•	•	•	•		
BELFAST												
Aldergrove Hotel	Allen Park Golf Centre, Massereene Golf Club	53					•	•		•		
Posthouse Premier Belfast	Malone Golf Course, Mount Obor Golf Club, Belvoir Park Golf Club	55						•	•			
DERRY												
Edgewater Hotel	Portstewart, Royal Portrush	58			•	•	•	•	•			
Brown Trout Golf & Country Inn	Royal Portrush, Portstewart, Castlerock	57 ⛳9	•	•	•	•	•	•	•	•	•	•
DOWN												
Burrendale Hotel and Country Club	Royal County Down, Kilkeel, Downpatrick, Ardglass	60			•	•	•	•	•		•	
Chestnut Inn	Royal County Down, Ardglass, Spa, Ballynahinch, Bright	59							•			
Royal Hotel	Bangor, Clandeboye, Blackwood	59	•									
FERMANAGH												
Mahons Hotel	Castle Hume, Enniskillen	64		•	•	•		•	•	•	•	•
EAST COAST												
DUBLIN												
Abberley Court Hotel	Citywest	67		•	•	•	•	•	•			
Aberdeen Lodge	St Margarets, Portmarnock, Woodbrook, Dun Laoghaire, Sea Point, Druids Glen	67		•	•	•	•	•				
Abigail House	Druids Glen, European Club, Woodbrook, Powerscourt, Charlesland, Old Conna	127			•	•	•	•	•			

⛳18 = Full 18 Hole   ⛳9 = 9 Hole   ⛳3 = Par 3

WHERE TO STAY WHEN YOU PLAY!

DUBLIN Continued

ACCOMMODATION	COURSES	BE OUR GUEST PAGE NUMBER	GOLF ON SITE	ALL INCLUSIVE PACKAGE	TUITION AVAILABLE	CART AVAILABLE	ARRANGE TEE OFF TIMES	ADVANCE RESERVATIONS	CLUBS FOR HIRE	TRANSPORT	PREFERENTIAL GREEN FEES	CADDY AVAILABLE
Adams Trinity Hotel	Royal Dublin, Portmarnock, Druids Glen, City West, Luttrellstown, Malahide	68						•		•		•
Alexander Hotel	Royal Dublin, Portmarnock, Druid's Glen, St Margarets, Luttrellstown	69						•	•	•		•
Arlington Hotel	St Margarets, Portmarnock, Island, Luttrellstown, Citywest, Royal Dublin	71						•	•	•		•
Ashview House	St. Margarets, Dublin Country Golf, Hollystown, Ashbourne and Corrstown	129	•	•	•	•	•	•	•	•	•	
Carriage House	St Margarets, Portmarnock, Skerries, Balbriggan, Hollywood, Luttrellstown	125	•	•	•	•	•	•	•	•	•	•
Charleville Lodge	St. Margarets, Luttrellstown, The Links, Portmarnock, The Island Golf Links	80	•	•	•	•	•	•	•	•	•	
City West Hotel, Conference, Leisure & Golf Resort		127 ▸18	•	•	•	•	•	•	•	•	•	
Clarion Hotel Dublin IFSC	Clontarf, Portmarnock, St. Anne's, Royal Dublin, St. Margaret's	82		•				•		•		•
Clarion Stephens Hall Hotel & Suites	St. Margaret's, Portmarnock Links, Citywest, Luttrellstown Castle	82		•				•	•	•		•
Clifton Court Hotel	St. Margaret's, Portmarnock, Citywest, Royal Dublin, Luttrellstown	83						•	•			
Clontarf Castle Hotel	Royal Dublin, Clontarf, St Annes, St Margarets, Portmarnock	83		•			•	•	•	•	•	•
Court Hotel	Druids Glen, European, Roundwood, Woodbrook, Charlesland, Powerscourt	123	•	•		•	•	•	•	•	•	•
Davenport Hotel	Druid's Glen, Royal Dublin, Portmarnock, St Margarets, Luttrellstown	84						•	•	•		•
Deer Park Hotel and Golf Courses		122 ▸18	•				•	•	•		•	
Drury Court Hotel	Edmondstown, Luttrellstown Castle, St. Margarets	86						•	•			
Dunes Hotel on the Beach	Donabate, Turvey, Beaverstown, Belcarrick, Island/Corballis	119	•	•	•	•	•	•	•	•	•	•
Fitzwilliam Hotel	Portmarnock	88						•				
Georgian Hotel	K Club, Druids Glen, St Margaret's, Portmarnock	89					•	•				
Gresham Hotel	St. Margaret's, Hollystown, Portmarnock, Grange, Royal Dublin, Howth	91						•	•	•	•	
Hedigan's	Clontarf, Royal Dublin, St. Annes, Howth, Portmarnock, Sutton	93						•	•	•	•	
Hilton Dublin	St Margarets, Druids Glen	94		•				•		•		•

▸18 = Full 18 Hole   ▸9 = 9 Hole   ▸3 = Pa...

WHERE TO STAY
WHEN YOU PLAY!

ACCOMMODATION	COURSES	BE OUR GUEST PAGE NUMBER	GOLF ON SITE	ALL INCLUSIVE PACKAGE	TUITION AVAILABLE	CART AVAILABLE	ARRANGE TEE OFF TIMES	ADVANCE RESERVATIONS	CLUBS FOR HIRE	TRANSPORT	PREFERENTIAL GREEN FEES	CADDY AVAILABLE
DUBLIN Continued												
Island View Hotel	Corballis, Malahide, Portmarnock, Howth, Donabate, Island	126	•	•	•	•	•	•	•	•	•	•
King Sitric Fish Restaurant and Accommodation	Deerpark, Howth, Royal Dublin, Portmarnock, St Margaret's, The Island	123				•	•		•		•	•
Kingston Hotel	Powerscourt, Charlesland, Old Conna, European, Druids Glen, Portmarnock	121	•		•	•	•	•	•	•	•	•
Marine Hotel	Royal Dublin, Portmarnock, St. Margarets, The Island, St Anne's, The Links	128	•		•	•	•	•	•	•	•	•
Mercer Hotel	Portmarnock, St Margarets, City West	102	•			•	•	•	•		•	•
Merrion Hall	Portmarnock, Royal Dublin, Elm Park, Castle, Milltown and Druids Glen.	102	•		•	•	•	•	•		•	•
Mont Clare Hotel	Royal Dublin, Portmarnock, Luttrellstown, St. Margarets, Druids Glen	104						•			•	•
Old Dubliner Guesthouse	Royal Dublin, Clontarf, St. Annes, St. Margarets, City West, Deer Park	106					•	•				
Plaza Hotel	Ballinascorney, Citywest, Newlands, K-Club, Powerscourt	109						•				•
Portmarnock Hotel & Golf Links	Portmarnock, St. Margaret's, Royal Dublin, Malahide, The Island	126 ▶18	•		•	•	•	•	•	•	•	•
Posthouse Dublin Airport	Hollystown, St Margaret's, Portmarnock, Malahide, Forest Little, The Island	120				•	•		•		•	•
Quality Charleville Hotel and Suites	St Margarets, Portmarnock, Royal Dublin, Citywest, K-Club, Luttrellstown	109	•		•	•	•	•	•	•	•	•
Redbank House Guesthouse & Restaurant	Skerries, Laytown, Bettystown, Baltray, Portmarnock, St Margaret's,	127	•			•	•		•		•	•
Redbank Lodge & Restaurant	Balbriggan, St Margaret's, Portmarnock, Baltray	128	•			•	•		•		•	•
Royal Marine Hotel	Dun Laoghaire, Woodbrook, Killiney, Greystones, Seapoint, Druids Glen	122				•	•	•	•		•	•
Shelbourne Dublin	St. Margaret's, Druids Glen	112	•			•	•	•	•		•	•
Spa Hotel	Hermitage, Citywest, Knockanally, Lucan, Luttrellstown	124	•			•	•	•	•		•	•
Stephen's Green Hotel	St. Margaret's, Druid's Glen, Portmarnock, Royal Dublin	114								•	•	•
Stillorgan Park Hotel	Druids Glen, Portmarnock, Woodbrook, Woodenbridge, Powerscourt, European	118	•			•	•	•	•		•	•
Temple Bar Hotel	St. Margarets, Luttrellstown, Portmarnock Hotel and Golf Links	115									•	•

 18 = Full 18 Hole   9 = 9 Hole ▶3 = Par 3

WHERE TO STAY WHEN YOU PLAY!

ACCOMMODATION / COURSES	BE OUR GUEST PAGE NUMBER	GOLF ON SITE	ALL INCLUSIVE PACKAGE	TUITION AVAILABLE	CART AVAILABLE	ARRANGE TEE OFF TIMES	ADVANCE RESERVATIONS	CLUBS FOR HIRE	TRANSPORT	PREFERENTIAL GREEN FEES	CADDY AVAILABLE
LOUTH											
Ballymascanlon House Hotel	131	18	•		•	•		•		•	
Boyne Valley Hotel & Country Club — Baltray, Seapoint, Laytown/Bettystown, Dundalk, Headfort (Kells), Ardee	130		•	•	•	•	•	•		•	
Fairways Hotel — Ballymascanlon, Dundalk, Killin Park, Greenore, Warrenpoint, Carnbeg	132		•			•	•	•	•	•	•
Hotel Imperial — Ballymascanlon, Dundalk, Greenore	133		•		•	•	•	•	•	•	•
McKevitt's Village Hotel — Greenore	130		•			•	•	•		•	•
Westcourt Hotel — Seapoint, Baltray, Balbriggan, Bettystown, Headfort, Dundalk	131		•			•	•	•	•	•	•
MEATH											
Conyngham Arms Hotel — Sea Point, Ardee, Headfort, Royal Tara	136		•			•	•	•		•	•
Neptune Beach — Laytown & Bettystown, Sea Point, County Louth/Baltray, Royal Tara	134		•	•	•	•	•	•		•	•
Old Darnley Lodge Hotel — Royal Tara, Delvin Castle, Headfort, Trim, The Glebe	134		•	•		•	•	•		•	•
WICKLOW											
Arklow Bay Hotel — European, Arklow, Woodenbridge, Blainroe	140		•	•	•	•	•	•		•	•
Blainroe Hotel — Blainroe, Wicklow, Woodenbridge, European	138		•	•		•	•	•		•	•
Chester Beatty Inn — Druids Glen, Woodenbridge, Blainroe, European, Powerscourt, Delgany	142		•			•	•	•		•	•
Cullenmore Hotel — Druids Glen, Charlesland, Wicklow, Blainroe, European Club, Delgany	142		•			•		•	•	•	•
Glenart Castle Hotel — Arklow, Woodenbridge, Druid's Glen, Coolattin, Blainroe, European	141		•	•	•	•	•	•	•	•	•
Glendalough Hotel — The European Club, Woodenbridge, Charlesland, Druid's Glen, Blainroe	147		•		•	•	•	•		•	•
Glenview Hotel — Charlesland, Druids Glen, Delgany, Powerscourt, Glen-O-The-Downs	146		•		•	•	•	•		•	•
Hunter's Hotel — Druid's Glen, European, Blainroe, Powerscourt, Woodenbridge, Delgany	148		•			•	•	•		•	•
Lawless's Hotel — Woodenbridge, Coolattin, European, Blainroe, Arklow, Druids Glen	143		•			•	•	•		•	•
Rathsallagh House, Golf and Country Club — Mount Juliet, Carlow, Baltinglass, K Club, Mount Wolseley, Druids Glen	145	18	•	•	•	•	•	•	•	•	•
Tinakilly Country House and Restaurant — European, Druid's Glen, Blainroe, Woodenbridge, Wicklow, Delgany	148		•	•	•	•	•	•		•	•

18 = Full 18 Hole   9 = 9 Hole   3 = P...

WHERE TO STAY WHEN YOU PLAY!

ACCOMMODATION	COURSES	BE OUR GUEST PAGE NUMBER	GOLF ON SITE	ALL INCLUSIVE PACKAGE	TUITION AVAILABLE	CART AVAILABLE	ARRANGE TEE OFF TIMES	ADVANCE RESERVATIONS	CLUBS FOR HIRE	TRANSPORT	PREFERENTIAL GREEN FEES	CADDY AVAILABLE
WICKLOW Continued												
Tulfarris Golf & Country House Hotel	Tulfarris, Ratsallagh, City West	144 (18)	•	•	•	•	•	•	•	•	•	•
Vale View Hotel	Woodenbridge, Arklow, Blainroe, Wicklow, European, Glenmalure	143			•		•	•	•		•	
Valley Hotel and Restaurant	Woodenbridge, European, Arklow, Courtown, Blainroe	149					•	•	•		•	
Woodenbridge Hotel	Woodenbridge, Blainroe, Arklow, European Club, Mill Brook, Glenmalure	149	•		•		•	•	•		•	
Woodland Court Hotel	Powerscourt, Woodbrook, Druids Glen, Charlesland, Old Conna, Kilternan	145			•		•	•	•		•	

MIDLANDS & LAKELANDS

ACCOMMODATION	COURSES	PAGE	GOLF ON SITE	ALL INCLUSIVE	TUITION	CART	TEE OFF	ADVANCE RES	CLUBS HIRE	TRANSPORT	PREF GREEN FEES	CADDY
CAVAN												
Cabra Castle Hotel		152 (9)	•	•	•	•	•	•	•	•	•	
Lacken Mill House and Gardens	Cavan, Slieve Russell, Belturbet, Delvin Castle, Longford, Virginia	151		•			•	•	•		•	
Park Hotel	Cavan Golf Club, Headfort Golf Club, Kells	153 (9)	•				•	•	•		•	
Slieve Russell Hotel, Golf & Country Club		152 (18)	•	•	•	•	•	•	•	•	•	
KILDARE												
Curragh Lodge Hotel	Cill Dara, K Club, Curragh, Rathsallagh, Naas, Killeens	153		•			•	•	•		•	
Glenroyal Hotel, Leisure Club & Conference Centre	Knockanally, K Club, Killeen, Castlewarden, Bodenstown, City West	156		•			•	•	•		•	
Hazel Hotel	Cill Dara, Portarlington, Curragh, Heath, Athy	157		•			•	•	•		•	•
Hillview House	K Club, Citywest, Curragh, Naas, Luttrellstown Castle, Knockanally	157		•			•	•	•		•	
K Club	Luttrellstown Castle, Druids Glen, Portmarnock Links, Rathsallagh, Hermitage	159 (18)	•		•		•	•	•		•	
Standhouse Hotel Leisure & Conference Centre	The Curragh, Athy, Rathsallagh, Cill Dara, K.Club, and Naas Golf Clubs	155		•			•	•	•		•	•
LAOIS												
Hibernian Hotel	Abbeyleix, Mountrath, The Heath, Rathdowney	159						•	•		•	
LONGFORD												
Longford Arms Hotel	Longford	161		•	•	•	•	•			•	
MONAGHAN												
Four Seasons Hotel & Leisure Club	Rossmore, Nuremore, Armagh, Castleblaney	162		•				•	•		•	

18 = Full 18 Hole   9 = 9 Hole   3 = Par 3

WHERE TO STAY WHEN YOU PLAY!

ACCOMMODATION	COURSES	BE OUR GUEST PAGE NUMBER	GOLF ON SITE	ALL INCLUSIVE PACKAGE	TUITION AVAILABLE	CART AVAILABLE	ARRANGE TEE OFF TIMES	ADVANCE RESERVATIONS	CLUBS FOR HIRE	TRANSPORT	PREFERENTIAL GREEN FEES	CADDY AVAILABLE
MONAGHAN Continued												
Glencarn Hotel and Leisure Centre	Castleblayney, Mannon Castle, Rossmore	163		•			•	•	•		•	
Nuremore Hotel & Country Club	Nuremore, Baltray, Headfort, Dundalk, Greenore, Royal County Down	162 ▶18	•	•	•	•	•	•	•	•	•	•
OFFALY												
Bridge House Hotel & Leisure Club	Esker Hills, Tullamore	165		•	•		•	•	•		•	•
Brosna Lodge Hotel	Birr, Esker Hills, Tullamore, Glasson, Portumna, Ballinasloe	163		•	•		•	•	•		•	•
County Arms Hotel	Birr, Tullamore, Nenagh, Roscrea, Mount Temple, Esker Hills	163		•	•		•	•	•		•	•
Doolys Hotel	Birr, Esker Hills, Roscrea	164		•	•		•	•	•		•	•
Kinnitty Castle Demesne	Birr, Glasson, Esker Hill, Roscrea, Tullamore and Castle Barna	164		•	•		•	•	•		•	•
Moorhill House Hotel	Esker Hills, Tullamore, Daingean, Mount Temple, Birr, Glasson	166		•	•		•	•	•		•	•
Sea Dew Guesthouse	Esker Hills, Castle Barna, Tullamore	166		•			•	•	•		•	
Tullamore Court Hotel	Tullamore, Esker Hills, Castle Barna, Mount Temple, Glasson, Birr	166		•	•		•	•	•		•	•
WESTMEATH												
Austin Friar Hotel	Mullingar	169		•	•		•	•	•		•	
Bloomfield House Hotel & Leisure Club	Mullingar, Glasson, Mount Temple, Esker Hills, Athlone, Tullamore	169		•	•		•	•	•		•	
Creggan Court Hotel	Glasson Golf & Country Club, Athlone, Moate, Mount Temple	167		•			•					
Greville Arms Hotel	Mullingar, Glasson, Mount Temple, Tullamore, Longford, Esker Hills	170		•	•		•	•	•		•	•
Hodson Bay Hotel	Athlone, Glasson, Mountemple, Ballinasloe, Roscommon, Esker Hills	169 ▶18	•	•	•		•	•	•		•	•
Lakeside Hotel & Marina	Glasson, Athlone, Mount Temple, Moate	167		•	•		•	•	•		•	
Prince of Wales Hotel	Glasson, Mount Temple, Athlone, Ballinasloe, Tullamore, Galway Bay, Moate	168		•	•		•	•	•		•	•
Royal Hoey Hotel	Mount Temple, Glasson, Hodson Bay	168		•	•		•	•	•		•	•
Shamrock Lodge Hotel and Conference Centre	Glasson, Athlone, Moate, Mount Temple	168		•			•					

406

▶18 = Full 18 Hole   ▶9 = 9 Hole   ▶3 =

WHERE TO STAY WHEN YOU PLAY!

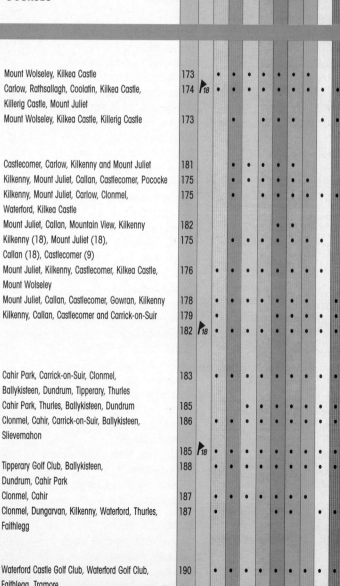

ACCOMMODATION	COURSES	BE OUR GUEST PAGE NUMBER	GOLF ON SITE	ALL INCLUSIVE PACKAGE	TUITION AVAILABLE	CART AVAILABLE	ARRANGE TEE OFF TIMES	ADVANCE RESERVATIONS	CLUBS FOR HIRE	TRANSPORT	PREFERENTIAL GREEN FEES	CADDY AVAILABLE
SOUTH EAST												
CARLOW												
Dolmen Hotel & River Court Lodges	Mount Wolseley, Kilkea Castle	173		•	•	•	•	•	•	•		
Mount Wolseley Hotel, Golf and Country Club	Carlow, Rathsallagh, Coolatin, Kilkea Castle, Killerig Castle, Mount Juliet	174 ⚑18	•	•	•	•	•	•	•	•	•	•
Seven Oaks Hotel	Mount Wolseley, Kilkea Castle, Killerig Castle	173									•	•
KILKENNY												
Avalon Inn	Castlecomer, Carlow, Kilkenny and Mount Juliet	181		•	•	•	•	•	•	•		
Brannigans Glendine Inn	Kilkenny, Mount Juliet, Callan, Castlecomer, Pococke	175		•	•	•	•	•	•	•		
Butler House	Kilkenny, Mount Juliet, Carlow, Clonmel, Waterford, Kilkea Castle	175		•			•	•			•	
Carrolls Hotel	Mount Juliet, Callan, Mountain View, Kilkenny	182					•	•		•		
Club House Hotel	Kilkenny (18), Mount Juliet (18), Callan (18), Castlecomer (9)	175		•	•	•	•	•	•		•	
Hibernian Hotel	Mount Juliet, Kilkenny, Castlecomer, Kilkea Castle, Mount Wolseley	176	•	•			•	•			•	
Kilkenny River Court Hotel	Mount Juliet, Callan, Castlecomer, Gowran, Kilkenny	178					•	•			•	•
Metropole Hotel	Kilkenny, Callan, Castlecomer and Carrick-on-Suir	179		•	•	•	•	•	•	•	•	•
Mount Juliet Estate		182 ⚑18	•	•	•	•	•	•	•	•	•	•
TIPPERARY SOUTH												
Cahir House Hotel	Cahir Park, Carrick-on-Suir, Clonmel, Ballykisteen, Dundrum, Tipperary, Thurles	183		•	•	•	•	•	•	•	•	•
Cashel Palace Hotel	Cahir Park, Thurles, Ballykisteen, Dundrum	185		•			•	•			•	•
Clonmel Arms Hotel	Clonmel, Cahir, Carrick-on-Suir, Ballykisteen, Slievemahon	186		•	•	•	•	•	•	•	•	•
Dundrum House Hotel		185 ⚑18	•	•	•	•	•	•	•	•	•	•
...en Hotel	Tipperary Golf Club, Ballykisteen, Dundrum, Cahir Park	188		•	•	•	•	•	•	•	•	•
...earns Hotel	Clonmel, Cahir	187		•	•		•	•			•	•
Hotel Minella & Leisure Centre	Clonmel, Dungarvan, Kilkenny, Waterford, Thurles, Faithlegg	187		•			•	•			•	
WATERFORD												
...lfry Hotel	Waterford Castle Golf Club, Waterford Golf Club, Faithlegg, Tramore	190		•	•	•	•	•	•	•	•	•

⚑18 = Full 18 Hole   ⚑9 = 9 Hole   ⚑3 = Par 3

WHERE TO STAY WHEN YOU PLAY!

Accommodation	Courses	Be Our Guest Page Number	Golf On Site	All Inclusive Package	Tuition Available	Cart Available	Arrange Tee Off Times	Advance Reservations	Clubs For Hire	Transport	Preferential Green Fees	Caddy Available
WATERFORD Continued												
Bridge Hotel	Waterford Castle, Faithlegg, Waterford, Tramore, New Ross	190		•	•	•	•	•	•		•	
Clonea Strand Hotel, Golf & Leisure	Gold Coast, West Waterford, Dungarvan, Lismore	198	18	•	•	•	•	•	•		•	
Dooley's Hotel	Waterford, Tramore, Faithlegg, Waterford Castle, New Ross	191		•	•	•	•	•	•	•	•	
Faithlegg House Hotel	Waterford Castle, Tramore, Waterford Golf Club	200	18	•	•	•	•	•	•	•	•	
Gold Coast Golf Hotel & Leisure Centre	Gold Coast Golf Course, Dungarvan Golf Course, West Waterford Golf Course	198	18	•	•	•	•	•	•	•	•	
Granville Hotel	Waterford, Faithlegg, Waterford Castle, Tramore, Dunmore East	192		•	•	•	•	•	•	•	•	
Hanoras Cottage	Clonmel, Carrick-on-Suir, Dungarvan, West Waterford, Gold Coast, Cahir Park	197		•	•	•	•	•	•	•	•	
Haven Hotel	Faithlegg, Tramore, Waterford, Waterford Castle, Dunmore East	199		•	•	•	•	•	•	•	•	
Ivory's Hotel	Dunmore East, Faithlegg, Waterford, Waterford Castle, Tramore, Williamstown	192		•	•	•	•	•	•	•	•	
Jurys Waterford Hotel	Waterford, Waterford Castle & Country Club, Faithlegg, Tramore	192		•	•	•	•	•	•	•	•	
Lawlors Hotel	Dungarvan, West Waterford, Gold Coast	198		•	•	•	•	•	•	•	•	
Majestic Hotel	Tramore, Waterford, Faithlegg, Waterford Castle, Mount Juliet, Dunmore East	201		•	•	•	•	•	•	•	•	
O'Shea's Hotel	Tramore, Faithlegg, Waterford Castle, Waterford, Dungarvan	201		•	•	•	•	•	•	•	•	
Ocean Hotel	Waterford, Waterford Castle, Faithlegg, Dunmore East, Tramore	200		•			•	•	•	•	•	
Rice Guesthouse Batterberry's Bar	Dunmore East, Faithlegg, Water Castle, Tramore	194				•	•	•	•	•	•	
Three Rivers Guest House	Faithlegg, Dunmore East, Tramore, Waterford Castle, Waterford, Mount Juliet	197		•	•	•	•	•	•	•	•	
Tower Hotel & Leisure Centre	Waterford Castle, Waterford, Faithlegg, Tramore	194		•		•	•	•	•	•	•	
Waterford Castle Hotel, Golf & Country Club	Tramore, Waterford	195	18	•			•	•	•	•	•	
Woodlands Hotel	Waterford Castle, Waterford, Faithlegg, Tramore, Dunmore East	195		•			•	•	•	•	•	
WEXFORD												
Bayview Hotel	Courtown Harbour, Ballymoney, Coolattin, Enniscorthy, Woodenbridge, Arklow	206				•	•	•	•	•	•	
Clarion Brandon House Hotel & Leisure Centre	New Ross, Mount Juliet, Faithlegg, Rosslare Strand, Waterford, Enniscorthy	210		•	•	•	•	•	•	•	•	

 18 = Full 18 Hole   9 = 9 Hole   3 =

WHERE TO STAY WHEN YOU PLAY!

Accommodation	Courses	Be Our Guest Page Number	Golf On Site	All Inclusive Package	Tuition Available	Cart Available	Arrange Tee Off Times	Advance Reservations	Clubs For Hire	Transport	Preferential Green Fees	Caddy Available
WEXFORD Continued												
Creacon Lodge Hotel	New Ross, St. Helens Bay, Faithlegg, Scarke, Mount Juliet	211	•	•	•	•	•	•			•	•
Horse and Hound Inn	New Ross, Wexford, Rosslare, Waterford, Mount Juliet	208	•					•				
Kelly's Resort Hotel	Rosslare Championship, Rosslare 12 Hole, St. Helens Bay, Wexford, Enniscorthy	213	•	•	•	•	•	•	•	•	•	•
Murphy - Floods Hotel	Enniscorthy	207	•			•	•	•			•	
Riverbank House Hotel	Wexford, St Helens, Rosslare	203	•			•	•	•			•	
Riverside Park Hotel	Enniscorthy, Rosslare, St Helens	208	•			•	•	•			•	
Talbot Hotel Conference and Leisure Centre	St Helens, Wexford, Rosslare, Enniscorthy and Courtown	204	•		•	•	•	•			•	
Treacys Hotel	Enniscorthy, Courtown, St Helen's Bay, Mount Wolsley, Mount Juliet, Waterford Castle	208	•		•	•	•	•			•	
Tuskar House Hotel	St. Helen's, Rosslare Strand, Wexford, Mount Juliet, Waterford, Enniscorthy	215	•	•	•	•	•	•			•	•
Whites Hotel	Wexford, Rosslare, St. Helen's Bay, Enniscorthy	204	•	•	•	•	•	•			•	•
Whitford House Hotel	St. Helen's Bay, Wexford, Rosslare, Rathaspeck (par 3 golf)	205	•		•	•	•	•			•	•
SOUTH WEST												
CORK												
Abbey Hotel	Killarney, Kenmare, Macroom, Lee Valley, Dooks	233	•				•				•	
Actons Hotel	Kinsale, Old Head of Kinsale, Fota Island, Bandon, Harbour Point	346	•			•	•	•			•	•
Aherne's Townhouse & Seafood Restaurant	Fota, Youghal, Faithlegg, Waterford Castle, Old Head Kinsale, Little Island	258	•	•	•	•	•	•	•		•	•
Ambassador Hotel	Cork, Fota, Douglas, Monkstown, Harbour Point, Water Rock	218	•		•	•	•	•	•		•	•
Ballylickey Manor House	Bantry, Glengarriff	233	•				•	•			•	
Baltimore Bay Guest House	Skibbereen	234	•				•	•			•	
Baltimore Harbour Hotel & Leisure Centre	Skibbereen, Bantry	234	•		•	•	•	•			•	
Blarney Park Hotel	Lee Valley, Harbour Point, Fota, Muskerry, Mallow	237	•		•	•	•	•	•		•	•
Blue Haven Hotel	Kinsale (Farrangalway, Ringenane), Old Head	247	•		•	•	•	•	•		•	•
Carrigaline Court Hotel	Old Head of Kinsale, Fernhill, Monkstown, Kinsale, Douglas	238	•		•	•	•	•	•		•	•
Casey's of Baltimore	Skibbereen	234	•				•	•			•	•
Castle Hotel & Leisure Centre	Macroom Golf Course, 18 hole Parklands Course	252	•			•	•				•	

WHERE TO STAY WHEN YOU PLAY!

ACCOMMODATION	COURSES	BE OUR GUEST PAGE NUMBER	GOLF ON SITE	ALL INCLUSIVE PACKAGE	TUITION AVAILABLE	CART AVAILABLE	ARRANGE TEE OFF TIMES	ADVANCE RESERVATIONS	CLUBS FOR HIRE	TRANSPORT	PREFERENTIAL GREEN FEES	CADDY AVAILABLE
CORK Continued												
Celtic Ross Hotel Conference & Leisure Centre	Skibbereen, Bandon, Lisselan, Old Head, Kinsale	255	•		•		•	•	•	•	•	•
Christy's Hotel	Muskerry, Lee Valley, Fota Island, Harbour Point, Mallow	237	•		•		•	•	•	•	•	•
Clarion Hotel - Morrisons Island	Fota Island, Frankfield (Cork City), Muskerry (Blarney), Lee Valley	220	•		•		•	•	•	•	•	•
Colla House Hotel	Coosheen, Bantry, Skibbereen	256	•				•	•		•	•	•
Colneth House	Kinsale- Farrangalway, Ringanane, Old Head	248	•				•	•	•	•	•	•
Commodore Hotel	East Cork, Midleton, Cobh	242	•									
Deerpark Hotel	Charleville	239					•	•	•	•	•	•
Devonshire Arms Hotel & Restaurant	Youghal, West Waterford, Fota Island, Harbour Point, Lismore	258	•				•	•	•	•	•	•
Dunmore House Hotel	Macroom, Bandon, Skibbereen, Monkstown, The Island	240	•				•	•	•	•	•	•
Eldon Hotel	Skibbereen, Bantry, Glengarriff, Schull, Clonakilty	257	•				•	•	•	•	•	•
Fernhill Golf & Country Club	Douglas, Monkstown, Harbour Point, Kinsale - Old Head, Cork, Fota	238 ▶18	•				•	•	•	•	•	•
Glenvera Hotel	Fota Island, Harbour Point, Cork, Water Rock, Douglas, Lee Valley	223	•				•	•	•	•	•	•
Hayfield Manor Hotel	Lee Valley, Fota Island, Cork, Harbour Point, Douglas, Old Head of Kinsale	224	•				•	•	•	•	•	•
Hibernian Hotel	Mallow, Lee Valley, Charleville, Doneraile, Fota Island	253	•					•	•	•	•	•
Imperial Hotel	Fota Island, Douglas, Cork Golf Course, Muskerry Golf Course	225	•				•	•	•	•	•	•
Innishannon House Hotel	Old Head Of Kinsale, Bandon, Kinsale, Lee Valley, Lisalawn, Farran Galway	246	•				•	•	•	•	•	•
Jurys Cork Hotel	Lee Valley, Harbour Point, Douglas, Cork, Muskerry	225	•				•	•	•	•	•	•
Jurys Inn Cork	Little Island, Harbour Point, Lee Valley, Monkstown, Cork	226	•				•		•			
Kierans Folkhouse Inn	Kinsale, Farrangalway, Fota, Lee Valley, Harbour Point, Old Head of Kinsale	248	•				•	•	•	•	•	•
Lodge & Spa at Inchydoney Island	Old Head of Kinsale, Bandon, Dunmore	241	•		•		•	•	•	•	•	•
Long Quay House	Kinsale Golf Club, Old Head Golf Links, Ringenane Kinsale	249	•				•	•	•	•	•	•
Lotamore House	Cork, Harbour Point, Fota Island, Water Rock, Lee Valley, Kinsale	227	•				•	•	•	•	•	•
Maryborough House Hotel	Douglas, Fota Island, Cork, Kinsale Old Head, Harbour Point, Monkstown	228	•				•	•	•	•	•	•
Metropole Ryan Hotel and Leisure Centre	Fota Island, Little Island, Harbour Point, Muskerry, Kinsale	228			•		•	•	•	•	•	•

410

▶18 = Full 18 Hole   ▶9 = 9 Hole   ▶3 =

WHERE TO STAY WHEN YOU PLAY!

ACCOMMODATION	COURSES	BE OUR GUEST PAGE NUMBER	GOLF ON SITE	ALL INCLUSIVE PACKAGE	TUITION AVAILABLE	CART AVAILABLE	ARRANGE TEE OFF TIMES	ADVANCE RESERVATIONS	CLUBS FOR HIRE	TRANSPORT	PREFERENTIAL GREEN FEES	CADDY AVAILABLE
CORK Continued												
Midleton Park Hotel	Fota Island, Cork - Little Island, Harbour Point, Water Rock, East Cork	255		•	•	•	•	•	•	•	•	•
Moorings	Kinsale, Old Head of Kinsale, Bandon, Fota, Cork, Harbour Point	249		•	•	•	•	•	•	•	•	•
Old Bank House	Old Head of Kinsale, Kinsale, Farringalway, Little Island, Fota, Lee Valley	250		•	•	•	•	•	•	•	•	•
Quality Hotel and Leisure Centre	Dunmore, Kinsale, Bandon, Skibbereen, Lisselan	242		•		•	•	•	•	•	•	•
Quality Shandon Court Hotel	Fota Island Golf Course, Cork Golf Course, Blarney Golf Course	228		•	•	•	•	•	•	•	•	•
Seven North Mall	Cork, Douglas, Fota Island, Harbour Point, Monkstown, Muskerry	230		•	•	•	•	•	•		•	•
Springfort Hall Hotel	Mallow, Charleville, Doneraile, Kanturk, Blarney, Adare	254		•			•	•	•		•	•
Trident Hotel	Kinsale Golf Club, Fota Island, Old Head Golf Links, Lee Valley	251		•	•	•	•	•	•	•	•	•
Victoria Hotel, Macroom	Lee Valley, Macroom	252		•	•	•	•	•	•		•	•
Victoria Hotel, Cork	Fota Island, Cork Golf Club, Monkstown Golf Club, Douglas, Lee Valley	231		•	•	•	•	•	•	•	•	•
Vienna Woods Hotel	Cork, Harbour Point, Fota, Old Head of Kinsale Water Rock, Silver Springs	231		•	•	•	•	•	•	•	•	•
WatersEdge Hotel	Fota Island, Harbour Point, Cobh, Water Rock, East Cork	243		•	•	•	•	•	•	•	•	•
West Cork Hotel	Skibbereen, West Carbery	257			•	•	•	•	•	•	•	•
Westlodge Hotel	Bantry, Bantry Bay	236		•			•	•	•		•	•
White Lady Hotel	Kinsale, Old Head of Kinsale, Farren Galway, Ringenane	251		•	•	•	•	•	•	•	•	•
KERRY												
Abbey Gate Hotel	Tralee, Ballybunion, Killarney, Dooks, Waterville, Kerries.	298		•	•	•	•	•	•	•	•	•
Aghadoe Heights Hotel	Waterville, Ballybunion, Kenmare, Killarney, Beaufort, Ring of Kerry	275					•	•	•		•	•
Arbutus Hotel	Killarney, Ballybunion, Waterville, Dooks, Tralee, Ring of Kerry	276		•			•	•	•		•	•
Ashville Guesthouse	Killarney, Ross, Dunloe, Beaufort, Waterville, Dooks, Ballybunion	276			•	•	•	•	•	•	•	•
Ballyseede Castle Hotel	Tralee, Ballybunion, Killarney, Kerries, Dooks, Dingle, Waterville	298		•	•	•	•	•	•	•	•	•

 18 = Full 18 Hole  9 = 9 Hole   3 = Par 3

WHERE TO STAY WHEN YOU PLAY!

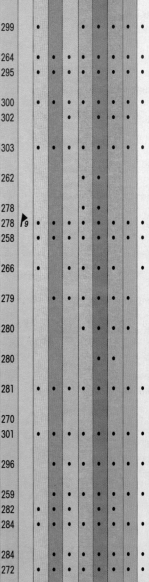

Accommodation	Courses	BE OUR GUEST PAGE NUMBER	GOLF ON SITE	ALL INCLUSIVE PACKAGE	TUITION AVAILABLE	CART AVAILABLE	ARRANGE TEE OFF TIMES	ADVANCE RESERVATIONS	CLUBS FOR HIRE	TRANSPORT	PREFERENTIAL GREEN FEES	CADDY AVAILABLE
KERRY Continued												
Barrow House	Tralee, Ballybunion, Killarney, Waterville, Dooks, Dingle	299	•				•	•	•	•	•	•
Benners Hotel	Ceann Sibeal (Dingle),	264	•	•	•	•	•	•	•	•	•	•
Bianconi	Killarney, Beaufort, Dunloe, Killorglin, Dooks, Waterville	295	•	•			•	•	•	•	•	•
Brandon Hotel	Tralee, Ballybunion, Waterville, Dooks, Killarney	300	•	•			•	•	•	•	•	•
Brookhaven Guesthouse	Waterville, Dooks, Parknasilla, Tralee, Kenmare, Ballybunion, Ring of Kerry	302	•	•			•	•	•	•	•	•
Butler Arms Hotel	Waterville, Dooks, Killarney, Tralee, Ballybunion, Ring of Kerry	303	•	•			•	•	•	•	•	•
Caragh Lodge	Dooks, Beaufort, Tralee, Killarney, Waterville, Ballybunion	262						•	•			
Castlelodge Guesthouse	Killarney Golf Course, Ross Golf Course	278						•	•			•
Castlerosse Hotel & Leisure Centre	Killarney (3 courses), Beaufort	278	•	•			•	•	•	•	•	•
Cliff House Hotel	Ballybunion Old Course and Cashen Course, Tralee, Killarney, Lahinch	258	•	•			•	•	•	•	•	•
Dingle Skellig Hotel	Ceann Sibeal Dingle, Castlegregory, Tralee Golf Club, Killarney, Dooks	266	•				•	•	•	•	•	•
Earls Court House	Killarney, Waterville, Ballybunion, Tralee, Beaufort, Dooks	279					•	•	•	•	•	•
Failte Hotel	Killarney Golf & Fishing Club, Beaufort, Ross, Dunloe, Castleross	280					•	•	•	•		
Foley's Townhouse	Killarney, Barrow, Beaufort, Dooks, Ballybunion, Waterville	280						•	•			
Fuchsia House	Killarney, Ballybunion, Waterville, Beaufort, Tralee, Dooks, Old Head	281	•				•	•	•	•	•	•
Glencar House Hotel	Killarney, Beaufort, Dooks, Waterville, Killorglin	270	•				•	•	•	•	•	•
Grand Hotel	Tralee, Ballybunion, Waterville, Dingle, Dooks, Killarney	301	•	•			•	•	•	•	•	•
Grove Lodge Guesthouse	Killarney, Killorglin, Dooks, Beaufort, Gap of Dunloe, Dingle	296					•	•	•	•	•	•
Harty Costello Town House	Ballybunion, Tralee, Listowel, Ballyheigue, Killarney	259					•	•	•	•	•	•
Holiday Inn Killarney	Killarney Golf & Fishing Club, Ross, Dunloe, Beaufort	282	•	•			•	•	•	•	•	•
International Best Western Hotel	Killarney, Beaufort, Killorglin, Dooks, Ballybunion, Tralee	284	•				•	•	•	•	•	•
Kathleen's Country House	Killarney, Beaufort, Dooks, Dunloe, Ross	284					•	•	•	•	•	•
Kenmare Bay Hotel	Ring of Kerry, Kenmare, Killarney, Tralee, Ballybunion, Waterville	272	•	•			•	•	•	•	•	•

▶18 = Full 18 Hole ▶9 = 9 Hole ▶3 =

WHERE TO STAY WHEN YOU PLAY!

Accommodation	Courses	Be Our Guest Page Number	Golf on Site	All Inclusive Package	Tuition Available	Cart Available	Arrange Tee Off Times	Advance Reservations	Clubs for Hire	Transport	Preferential Green Fees	Caddy Available
KERRY Continued												
Killarney Avenue Hotel	Killarney, Ballybunion, Tralee, Waterville, Beaufort	285	•		•	•	•	•	•	•	•	•
Killarney Court Hotel	Killarney, Beaufort, Dunloe, Ross	285	•		•	•	•	•	•	•	•	•
Killarney Heights Hotel	Killarney, Beaufort, Waterville, Dooks, Ballybunion, Tralee	286	•		•	•	•	•	•	•	•	•
Killarney Lodge	Killarney, Waterville, Ballybunion, Tralee, Dooks, Beaufort	286			•	•	•	•	•	•		
Killarney Park Hotel	Killarney, Ballybunion, Tralee, Waterville, Dooks, Beaufort	287			•	•	•	•	•	•	•	
Killarney Royal	Killarney, Tralee, Dooks, Waterville, Beaufort, Ross.	287			•	•	•	•	•	•	•	
Killarney Ryan Hotel & Leisure Centre	Killarney, Dooks, Tralee, Ballybunion, Waterville, Beaufort	287			•	•	•	•	•	•	•	
Killarney Towers Hotel & Leisure Centre	Killarney, Ballybunion, Tralee, Waterville, Beaufort	288	•		•	•	•	•	•	•	•	•
Killeen House Hotel	Killarney, Waterville, Tralee, Dooks, Ballybunion, Beaufort	288	•		•	•	•	•	•	•	•	•
Kingfisher Lodge Guesthouse	Beaufort, Dunloe, Castlerosse, Killarney, Ross	289			•	•	•	•	•		•	•
Lake Hotel	Killarney (3 courses), Beaufort, Dooks, Ballybunion, Waterville, Tralee	289	•		•	•	•	•	•	•	•	•
Lakelands Farm Guesthouse	Waterville Golf Course	303			•	•	•	•	•	•		•
Listowel Arms Hotel	Ballybunion, Listowel, Tralee, Killarney, Lahinch, Waterville	296			•	•	•	•	•	•	•	•
Marine Links Hotel	Ballybunion, Old Course & Cashen, Tralee, Killarney, Lahinch, Dooks	260			•	•	•	•	•	•	•	•
McSweeney Arms Hotel	Killarney, Ballybunion, Waterville, Dooks, Beaufort, Tralee	290			•	•	•	•	•	•	•	•
Muckross Park Hotel	Beaufort, O'Mahony's Point, Killeen, Fossa, Ross, Ring of Kerry, Tralee, Ballybunion, Waterville, Dooks	291						•	•	•	•	
Oakland House	Killarney, Ross, Beaufort, Waterville, Dunloe, Dooks	291			•	•	•	•	•	•		
Oakley House	Tralee, Killarney, Dooks, Ballybunion, Waterville	301			•	•	•	•	•	•	•	
Park Hotel Kenmare	Ring of Kerry	273 18			•	•	•	•	•	•	•	•
Parknasilla Great Southern Hotel		297 9			•				•	•	•	•
Pax House	Ceann Sibeal (Dingle)	269						•	•	•		•
Randls Court Clarion Hotel	Killarney, Tralee, Beaufort, Dooks	292	•			•	•	•	•	•		
Rivermere	Killarney (O'Mahony's Point and Killeen), Dooks, Ballybunion, Waterville	292			•	•	•	•	•	•		
Riversdale House Hotel	Kenmare, Killarney, Waterville, Parknasilla, Dooks, Ring of Kerry	273			•	•	•	•	•	•	•	•
Rosegarden Guesthouse	Kenmare, Ring of Kerry, Parknasilla	274				•	•					

 ▸18 = Full 18 Hole   ▸9 = 9 Hole   ▸3 = Par 3

WHERE TO STAY WHEN YOU PLAY!

ACCOMMODATION	COURSES	BE OUR GUEST PAGE NUMBER	GOLF ON SITE	ALL INCLUSIVE PACKAGE	TUITION AVAILABLE	CART AVAILABLE	ARRANGE TEE OFF TIMES	ADVANCE RESERVATIONS	CLUBS FOR HIRE	TRANSPORT	PREFERENTIAL GREEN FEES	CADDY AVAILABLE
KERRY Continued												
Ross Hotel	Killarney, Ballybunion, Tralee, Waterville, Dooks, Beaufort	293			•		•	•	•	•	•	•
Scarriff Inn	Waterville, Kenmare, Sneem, Killorglin, Tralee, Ballybunion	261			•	•	•	•	•	•	•	•
Sheen Falls Lodge	Kenmare, Ring of Kerry	274	•	•	•			•	•		•	•
Smerwick Harbour Hotel	Ceann Sibeal (Dingle)	269	•	•	•			•	•		•	•
Smugglers Inn	Waterville, Killarney, Dooks, Tralee, Ballybunion, Kenmare, Parknasilla	303	•	•	•			•	•		•	•
SHANNON												
CLARE												
Aberdeen Arms Hotel	Lahinch Championship, Lahinch Castle, Woodstock, Dromoland Castle	322			•	•	•	•	•	•	•	•
Aran View House Hotel & Restaurant	Lahinch, Doolin Pitch & Putt	309			•		•	•	•	•	•	
Atlantic Hotel	Lahinch Championship Course and Castle, Woodstock, Ennis, Spanish Point	322			•	•	•	•	•	•	•	•
Ballinalacken Castle Country House & Restaurant	Lahinch, Lahinch Castle, Woodstock, Galway Bay, Dromoland Castle, Ennis.	309					•	•	•	•	•	•
Bellbridge House Hotel	Spanish Point, Lahinch	325			•		•	•	•	•	•	
Bunratty Castle Hotel	Shannon, Dromoland, Lahinch, Limerick	307			•		•	•	•	•	•	•
Burkes Armada Hotel	Spanish Point, Lahinch, Kilkee	326			•		•	•	•	•	•	•
Central Guesthouse	Kilrush Golf course, Kilkee Golf course, Doonbeg Golf course	320			•	•		•	•		•	•
Carrygerry Country House	Dromoland, Woodstock, Shannon	327					•	•	•		•	•
Clare Inn Golf & Leisure Hotel	Ennis, Dromoland, Limerick, Adare	310					•	•	•	•	•	•
Clarehills Guesthouse	Woodstock Golf Course, Ennis Golf Course, Lahinch Golf Course, East Clare	312						•	•		•	
Dough Mor Lodge	Lahinch Golf Club (36 holes)	322	▸18					•	•		•	
Dromoland Castle	Lahinch, Ballybunion, Shannon	326	▸18					•	•		•	
Falls Hotel	Lahinch, Dromoland, Ennis, Kilkee, Shannon	316						•	•	•	•	•
Fitzpatrick Bunratty	Shannon, Dromoland, Woodstock, Ballykisteen, Limerick County	309			•			•	•	•	•	•
Fountain Court	Ennis, Woodstock, Dromoland, Lahinch, Shannon, East Clare	312						•	•		•	•
Greenbrier Inn Guesthouse	Lahinch Championship Course, Lahinch Castle Course	323			•	•						
Grovemount House	Lahinch	316			•	•	•	•	•	•	•	•

▸18 = Full 18 Hole   ▸9 = 9 Hole   ▸3 =

WHERE TO STAY
WHEN YOU PLAY!

ACCOMMODATION	COURSES	BE OUR GUEST PAGE NUMBER	GOLF ON SITE	ALL INCLUSIVE PACKAGE	TUITION AVAILABLE	CART AVAILABLE	ARRANGE TEE OFF TIMES	ADVANCE RESERVATIONS	CLUBS FOR HIRE	TRANSPORT	PREFERENTIAL GREEN FEES	CADDY AVAILABLE
CLARE Continued												
Halpin's Hotel & Vittles Restaurant	Ballybunion, Lahinch, Kilkee, Dromoland, Woodstock, Shannon	317		•		•	•	•	•			•
Kincora Hall Hotel	East Clare	319	•			•	•	•		•	•	
Magowna House Hotel	Woodstock, Ennis, Lahinch, Dromoland Castle, Shannon, Kilrush, Kilkee	313		•		•	•	•	•		•	•
Oak Wood Arms Hotel	Shannon, Dromoland	328		•		•	•	•	•		•	•
Ocean Cove Golf and Leisure Hotel	Kilkee Bay, Kilrush	317		•		•	•	•	•		•	•
Old Ground Hotel	Lahinch, Woodstock, Ennis, Dromoland, Shannon, East Clare	314		•		•	•	•	•		•	•
Sancta Maria Hotel	Lahinch, Lahinch Castle, Woodstock, Dromoland, Kilkee, Galway Bay	323		•		•	•	•	•		•	•
Shamrock Inn Hotel	Lahinch Championship Course, Spanish Point, Woodstock, Ennis	324		•		•	•	•	•		•	•
Temple Gate Hotel	Woodstock, Ennis, Lahinch, East Clare, Shannon, Dromoland	314		•		•	•	•	•		•	•
West County Conference & Leisure Hotel	Ennis, Kilrush, Kilkee, Dromoland	315		•			•	•	•		•	
Westbrook House	Woodstock, Ennis, Dromoland, Shannon, Lahinch and East Clare Golf Clubs	315		•		•	•	•	•		•	•
Woodstock Hotel		315 18	•	•		•	•	•	•		•	•
LIMERICK												
Adare Manor Hotel & Golf Resort		336 18	•	•	•	•	•	•	•	•	•	•
Carrabawn House	Adare Manor, Newcastlewest, Adare, Dromoland, Charleville, Limerick Golf & Country Club	336		•		•	•	•	•		•	•
Castletroy Park Hotel	Castletroy, Limerick County (Ballyneety), Dromoland, Adare	329					•	•	•		•	•
Castle Oaks House Hotel & Country Club	Limerick, Nenagh, Shannon, Castletroy, Limerick County	337 18	•			•	•	•	•		•	•
Clonmacken House Guest House	Dromoland, Shannon, Ballyclough, Castletroy, Ballykisteen, Adare Manor	330		•		•	•	•	•		•	•
Devon Inn Hotel	Newcastlewest, Killeline, Ballybunion, Killarney, Tralee	338		•		•	•	•	•		•	•
Dunraven Arms Hotel	Adare, Adare Manor, Limerick, Ballybunion, Lahinch	336		•		•	•	•	•		•	•
Fitzgeralds Woodlands House Hotel & Leisure Club	Adare Manor, New Adare, Newcastle West, Ardagh, Charleville, Ballyneety	337		•		•	•	•	•		•	•
Greenhills Hotel Conference/Leisure	Ballyneety, Shannon, Castletroy, Ballykisten, Dromoland, Limerick	331		•		•	•	•	•		•	•

18 = Full 18 Hole   9 = 9 Hole   3 = Par 3

WHERE TO STAY WHEN YOU PLAY!

ACCOMMODATION	COURSES	BE OUR GUEST PAGE NUMBER	GOLF ON SITE	ALL INCLUSIVE PACKAGE	TUITION AVAILABLE	CART AVAILABLE	ARRANGE TEE OFF TIMES	ADVANCE TEE RESERVATIONS	CLUBS FOR HIRE	TRANSPORT	PREFERENTIAL GREEN FEES	CADDY AVAILABLE
LIMERICK Continued												
Jurys Limerick Hotel	Castletroy, Limerick (Ballyclough), Co. Limerick (Ballyneety), Shannon	332		•		•		•		•		
Limerick Inn Hotel	Castletroy, Limerick (Ballyclough), Shannon, Adare, Limerick County	333		•		•		•		•	•	
Limerick Ryan Hotel	Limerick, Castletroy, Adare, Shannon, Ballykisteen, Limerick County	333		•		•		•		•	•	•
Rathkeale House Hotel	Adare, Adare Manor, Killeline, Newcastlewest, Charleville, Ballybunion	338		•		•		•		•	•	
Shannon Grove Guesthouse	Castletroy, Limerick, Ballyneety, Lahinch, Adare, Clonlara	334						•		•	•	•
South Court Business and Leisure Hotel	Limerick, Adare, Dromoland, Ballybunion	334		•		•		•		•	•	•
Two Mile Inn Hotel	Castletroy, Limerick, Shannon, Dromoland, Adare	335		•		•		•		•	•	
Woodfield House Hotel	Shannon, Dromoland, Ballykisteen, Limerick Country Club, Woodstock, Bodyke	335		•		•		•		•	•	
TIPPERARY NORTH												
Abbey Court Hotel	Birr, Nenagh, Roscrea, Portumna	339		•		•		•		•	•	
Anner Hotel & Leisure Centre	Thurles, Dundrum, Templemore	340		•		•		•		•	•	
Dromineer Bay Hotel	Nenagh, Roscrea	339		•		•		•		•	•	
Grant's Hotel	Roscrea, Birr, Nenagh, Mountrath, Esker Hills	339		•		•		•		•	•	
Tower	Roscrea, Birr, Nenagh, Mountrath	340		•		•		•		•	•	
WEST												
GALWAY												
Abbey House	Barna, Galway, Galway Bay, Athenry, Oughterard	342		•				•				
Abbeyglen Castle Hotel	Connemara	363		•	•	•	•	•	•	•	•	•
Acorn Guesthouse	Galway Bay, Salthill, Oughterard, Athenry, Gort, Loughrea	343		•	•	•	•	•	•	•	•	•
Adare Guest House	Galway Bay, Oughterard	343		•	•	•		•	•	•	•	•
Alcock and Brown Hotel	Connemara	364		•	•	•		•	•	•	•	•
Anno Santo Hotel	Glenlo, Athenry, Galway, Oughterard, Galway Bay	343		•	•			•	•	•	•	•
Ardagh Hotel & Restaurant	Connemara	364				•	•	•	•	•	•	•
Ardilaun House Hotel, Conference Centre & Leisure Club	Galway, Oughterard, Galway Bay Golf & Country, Athenry, Lahinch, Connemara, Barna Golf Club	344		•	•	•		•	•	•	•	•
Ballynahinch Castle Hotel	Connemara Championship Golf Course	361		•		•		•	•	•	•	•
Ben View House	Connemara	365				•		•	•	•	•	•

416

18 = Full 18 Hole   9 = 9 Hole   3 = F

WHERE TO STAY WHEN YOU PLAY!

ACCOMMODATION	COURSES	BE OUR GUEST PAGE NUMBER	GOLF ON SITE	ALL INCLUSIVE PACKAGE	TUITION AVAILABLE	CART AVAILABLE	ARRANGE TEE OFF TIMES	ADVANCE RESERVATIONS	CLUBS FOR HIRE	TRANSPORT	PREFERENTIAL GREEN FEES	CADDY AVAILABLE
GALWAY Continued												
Boat Inn	Oughterard, Barna, Ballyconneely, Galway Bay, Salthill, Glenlo	375		•	•	•	•	•	•	•	•	•
Connemara Coast Hotel	Barna, Oughterard, Galway Bay	369		•	•	•	•	•	•	•	•	
Connemara Gateway Hotel	Oughterard, Barna Golf and Country	375		•	•	•	•	•	•	•	•	•
Corrib House Hotel	Oughterard, Connemara Isles, Galway Bay, Bearna, Ballyconneely	375		•	•	•	•	•	•	•	•	•
Corrib Wave Guest House	Oughterard	376		•	•	•	•	•	•	•	•	
Dun Ri Guesthouse	Connemara	366		•	•	•	•	•	•	•	•	
Foyles Hotel	Connemara	367		•	•	•	•	•	•	•	•	
Galway Bay Golf and Country Club Hotel	Galway Bay (PGA)	374 ⚑18	•	•	•	•	•	•	•	•	•	•
Galway Bay Hotel, Conference & Leisure Centre	Galway, Galway Bay, Athenry, Bearna, Gort	348		•	•	•	•	•	•	•	•	
Galway Ryan Hotel & Leisure Centre	Galway Bay, Galway, Athenry, Oughterard, Roscam, Rosshill	349		•	•	•	•	•	•	•	•	
Hayden's Gateway Business & Leisure Hotel	Ballinasloe, Glasson	360		•	•	•	•	•	•	•	•	
Hotel Sacre Coeur	Bearna, Galway, Athenry, Tuam, Oughterard, Galway Bay	250		•	•	•	•	•	•	•	•	
Inishmore Guesthouse	Barna, Galway Bay, Oughterard, Athenry, Salthill	251		•	•	•	•	•	•	•	•	
Lady Gregory Hotel	Gort	270		•	•	•	•	•	•	•	•	
Lake Hotel	Oughterard Golf Club and other local championship courses	276		•	•	•	•	•	•	•	•	•
Lochlurgain Hotel	Bearna, Galway, Athenry, Gort, Oughterard and Galway Bay	253		•	•	•	•	•	•	•	•	•
Mal Dua House	Connemara Golf Club, Oughterard Golf Club	367		•	•	•	•	•	•	•	•	
Mountain View Guest House	Oughterard, Galway, Connemara, Westport	377		•	•	•	•	•	•	•	•	
O'Deas Hotel	Loughrea, Curragh, Gort, Galway Bay	373		•	•	•	•	•	•	•	•	
O'Grady's Sunnybank Guesthouse	Connemara, Ballyconneely, Westport, Oughterard	368		•	•	•	•	•	•	•	•	
Peacockes Hotel & Complex	Oughterard, Ballyconneely, Glenlo Abbey, Barna, Westport	373		•	•	•	•	•	•	•	•	•
Quality Hotel and Leisure Centre Galway	Athenry, Galway, Galway Bay, Loughrea, Glenlo Abbey, Gort	374		•	•	•	•	•	•	•	•	•
Renvyle House Hotel	Connemara, Westport, Oughterard, Pebble Beach	378 ⚑9	•	•	•	•	•	•	•	•	•	•
River Run Lodge	Oughterard	377		•	•	•	•	•	•	•	•	•
Shannon Oaks Hotel & Country Club	Portumna, Galway Bay, Birr, Glasson, Gort, Lahinch	378		•	•	•	•	•	•	•	•	•
Station House Hotel	Ballyconeely (Connemara), Oughterard, Westport	368		•	•	•	•	•	•	•	•	•
Westwood House Hotel	Barna, Oughterard, Ballyconneely	358		•	•	•	•	•	•	•	•	•
Zetland Country House Hotel	Connemara	363		•	•							

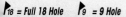 ⚑18 = Full 18 Hole ⚑9 = 9 Hole ⚑3 = Par 3

WHERE TO STAY WHEN YOU PLAY!

ACCOMMODATION	COURSES	BE OUR GUEST PAGE NUMBER	GOLF ON SITE	ALL INCLUSIVE PACKAGE	TUITION AVAILABLE	CART AVAILABLE	ARRANGE TEE OFF TIMES	ADVANCE RESERVATIONS	CLUBS FOR HIRE	TRANSPORT	PREFERENTIAL GREEN FEES	CADDY AVAILABLE
MAYO												
Atlantic Coast Hotel	Westport, Enniscrone, Carne, Ballyconneely, Castlebar, Ballinrobe	390		•	•	•	•	•	•	•	•	•
Augusta Lodge	Westport, Enniscrone, Belmullet (Carne), Mulranny, Clew Bay	390						•	•	•	•	•
Bartra House Hotel	Enniscrone, Ballina, Cairn, Rosses Point, Strandhill	382		•	•	•	•	•	•	•	•	•
Castlecourt Hotel Conference and Leisure Centre	Westport, Ballinrobe, Castlebar, Belmullet, Clew Bay, Enniscrone	390		•	•	•	•	•	•	•	•	•
Central Hotel	Westport Golf Club	391		•	•	•	•	•	•	•	•	•
Daly's Hotel	Belmullet, Castlebar, Westport, Balla, Enniscrone, Three Oaks	384		•	•	•	•	•	•	•	•	•
Downhill House Hotel	Ballina, Enniscrone, Carne (Belmullet), Rosses Point, Strandhill, Westport	383		•	•	•	•	•	•	•	•	•
Downhill Inn	Rosses Point, Enniscrone, Belmullet, Westport, Strand Hill, Ballina	383		•	•	•	•	•	•	•	•	•
Healy's Hotel On The Lake	Castlebar, Ballina, Westport, Enniscrone, Carne	389		•	•	•	•	•	•	•	•	•
Hotel Westport	Westport, Castlebar, Ballinrobe, Carne	391		•	•	•	•	•	•	•	•	•
Jennings Hotel & Travellers Friend	Castlebar, Westport, Three Oaks, Ballinrobe, Belmullet, Enniscrone	385		•	•	•	•	•	•	•	•	•
Knockranny House Hotel	Westport, Castlebar, Ballinrobe, Clew Bay, Achill, Mulranny	392		•	•	•	•	•	•	•	•	•
Knockranny Lodge	Westport	392		•	•	•	•	•	•	•	•	•
Ostan Oilean Acla	Keel, Mulranny, Westport, Carne, Castlebar.	381	•				•	•	•	•	•	•
Ridgepool Hotel, Conference and Leisure Centre	Ballina	383					•	•	•	•	•	•
Ryan's Hotel	Westport, Clifden (Ballyconneely), Galway, Ballinrobe	387		•	•	•	•	•	•	•	•	•
Teach Iorrais	Carne Links Golf Course	387		•	•	•	•	•	•	•	•	•
Westport Woods Hotel & Leisure Centre	Westport, Castlebar, Ballinrobe, Clew Bay, Carne (Belmullet)	393		•	•	•	•	•	•	•	•	•
ROSCOMMON												
Abbey Hotel	Roscommon, Glasson, Athlone	393		•	•	•	•	•	•	•	•	•
Gleesons Guesthouse & Restaurant	Roscommon	393		•	•	•	•	•	•	•	•	•
O'Gara's Royal Hotel	Roscommon, Glasson, Longford, Athlone	394	•					•	•		•	
Royal Hotel	Roscommon, County Sligo, Strandhill	395								•		•

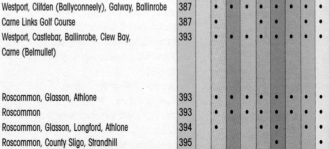

▶18 = Full 18 Hole   ▶9 = 9 Hole   ▶3 =

IRELAND FOR
Fishing
HOTELS & GUESTHOUSES

Ireland is accepted as being the outstanding
angling holiday resort in Europe.
Whether you are a competition angler,
a serious specimen hunter, or just fishing while on
holiday, you are sure to enjoy yourself here.
With over 14,000km of rivers feeding over 4,000
lakes and with no part of Ireland over 112km
from sea, Ireland can, in truth, be called
an angler's dream.

So come on and get hooked!

ANGLING FOR A PLACE TO STAY!

We invite you to sample the fishing, the countryside and the friendship of the Irish people and then to stay in some of Ireland's most charming accommodation. We have listed a range of hotels and guesthouses which are either situated with or near angling facilities. Your host will assist you in arranging your angling itinerary. A full description of the hotels and guesthouses can be had by looking up the appropriate page number. Premises are listed in alphabetical order in each county.

ACCOMMODATION	TYPES OF FISH	BE OUR GUEST PAGE NUMBER	COARSE FISHING	GAME FISHING	SEA FISHING	BAIT AND TACKLE	BOATS FOR HIRE	DRYING ROOM	PACKED LUNCHES	GILLIE	TACKLE ROOM	FREEZER	PERMITS REQUIRED
NORTH WEST													
DONEGAL													
Abbey Hotel	Pike, Roach, Perch, Bream, Eel, Salmon, Trout, Tope, Cod	26	•	•	•		•	•	•		•	•	•
Arnolds Hotel	Brown Trout, Salmon, Sea Trout	33		•				•	•			•	
Bay View Hotel & Leisure Centre	Salmon, Trout, Shark, Pollock, Cod, Conger, Turbot	34		•	•	•	•	•	•		•	•	
Great Northern Hotel	Pike, Perch, Salmon, Trout, Pollock, Cod, Ling, Plaice, Shark, Sole	31	•	•	•		•	•	•		•	•	
Lake of Shadows Hotel	Salmon, Sea Trout, Wild Brown Trout, Tope, Haddock, Cod, Whiting, Pollock, Coalfish, Gurnard, Plaice	30		•	•	•	•	•	•		•	•	
Ostan Na Rosann	Brown Trout, Sea Trout, Salmon, Cod, Mackerel, Shark, Turbot	33		•	•	•	•	•	•		•	•	
Ostan Na Tra (Beach Hotel)	Shark, Cod, Haddock, Ling, Conger, Gurnard, Pollock	32			•	•	•	•	•		•	•	
LEITRIM													
Bush Hotel	Bream, Roach, Rudd, Tench, Pike, Perch, Eel, Trout	39	•			•	•	•	•		•	•	
NORTH													
ANTRIM													
Bushmills Inn	Roach, Bream, Haddock, Salmon, Cod, Plaice, Whiting, Sea Trout	47	•	•	•		•	•	•		•	•	
ARMAGH													
Silverwood Golf Hotel and Country Club	Bream, Pike, Perch, Salmon, Trout	52	•	•			•		•			•	

ANGLING FOR A PLACE TO STAY!

ACCOMMODATION	TYPES OF FISH	BE OUR GUEST PAGE NUMBER	COARSE FISHING	GAME FISHING	SEA FISHING	BAIT AND TACKLE	BOATS FOR HIRE	DRYING ROOM	PACKED LUNCHES	GILLIE	TACKLE ROOM	FREEZER	PERMITS REQUIRED
BELFAST													
Aldergrove Hotel	Bream, Eel, Pike, Roach, Trout, Salmon	53	•	•		•	•		•				•
DERRY													
Brown Trout Golf & Country Inn	Salmon, Trout, Pike, Bream	57	•	•		•				•	•	•	•
DOWN													
Royal Hotel	Cod, Skate, Mackerel, Haddock, Whiting	59			•	•	•			•			
FERMANAGH													
Mahons Hotel	Roach, Bream, Pike, Perch, Trout, Salmon, Pollock, Cod, Conger, Mackerel	64	•	•	•	•	•	•		•	•		•
EAST COAST													
DUBLIN													
Old Dubliner Guesthouse	Bream, Roach, Perch, Salmon, Trout, Cod, Plaice, Whiting, Mackerel, Bass	106	•	•	•	•	•						
Redbank House Guesthouse & Restaurant	Mackerel, Cod, Pollock, Codling, Ling, Skate	127			•	•		•	•	•		•	
Redbank Lodge & Restaurant	Bass, Shark, Skate, Conger Eel	128			•	•			•	•		•	
Royal Marine Hotel	Cod, Plaice, Pollock, Ling, Dab	122			•	•			•	•			
Stillorgan Park Hotel	Bass, Sea Trout	118			•	•		•	•	•	•	•	
WICKLOW													
Valley Hotel and Restaurant	Brown Trout, Pike, Perch, Roach, Rainbow Trout	149	•	•		•		•		•	•		•
MIDLANDS & LAKELANDS													
CAVAN													
Hotel Kilmore	Pike, Perch, Bream, Roach, Trout	151	•	•		•	•	•	•	•		•	•
Keepers Arms	Pike, Bream, Hybrid, Roach, Tench	152	•			•	•	•	•	•			
Lacken Mill House and Gardens	Pike, Bream, Roach, Perch, Tench, Rudd, Trout	151	•	•		•	•		•	•	•	•	

421

ANGLING FOR A PLACE TO STAY!

ACCOMMODATION	TYPES OF FISH	BE OUR GUEST PAGE NUMBER	COARSE FISHING	GAME FISHING	SEA FISHING	BAIT AND TACKLE	BOATS FOR HIRE	DRYING ROOM	PACKED LUNCHES	GILLIE	TACKLE ROOM	FREEZER	PERMITS REQUIRED
CAVAN Continued													
Sharkeys Hotel	Pike, Perch, Bream, Rudd	153	•			•	•	•	•			•	
KILDARE													
Hazel Hotel	Pike, Rudd, Roach, Eel, Tench, Perch, Salmon, Trout	157	•	•			•		•			•	•
K Club	Salmon, Trout, Trout, Carp, Tench, Bream, Rudd	159	•	•					•			•	•
LAOIS													
Hibernian Hotel	Pike, Roach, Perch, Rudd, Tench, Salmon, Trout	159	•	•					•				
LONGFORD													
Longford Arms Hotel	Perch, Pike, Eel, Bream, Salmon, Trout	161	•	•					•			•	
MONAGHAN													
Glencarn Hotel and Leisure Centre	Perch, Bream, Pike, Trout	163	•						•				
OFFALY													
Brosna Lodge Hotel	Bream, Tench, Rudd, Roach, Perch, Brown Trout, Pike, Salmon	163	•	•		•	•	•	•	•	•		
Doolys Hotel	Trout, Salmon	164		•		•			•	•			
Kinnitty Castle Demesne	Rudd, Perch, Tench, Pike, Bream, Salmon, Brown Trout	164	•	•			•		•	•			
Moorhill House Hotel	Bream, Chub, Dab, Eel, Gurnard, Perch, Pike, Roach, Rudd, Brown & Rainbow Trout & Salmon	166	•	•		•	•	•	•	•	•		
WESTMEATH													
Austin Friar Hotel	Pike, Trout	169	•	•					•				
Creggan Court Hotel	Bream, Eel, Pike, Salmon, Trout, Pike, Tench, Rudd, Roach	167	•	•			•		•				
Greville Arms Hotel	Pike, Trout	170	•	•					•				
Hodson Bay Hotel	Bream, Perch, Pike, Brown Trout	167	•	•			•		•	•			
Lakeside Hotel & Marina	Trout, Pike, Bream	167	•				•		•	•	•		
Royal Hoey Hotel	Pike, Bream, Perch, Salmon, Trout, Cod, Mackerel	168	•	•	•		•	•	•				

422

ANGLING FOR A PLACE TO STAY!

ACCOMMODATION	TYPES OF FISH	BE OUR GUEST PAGE NUMBER	COARSE FISHING	GAME FISHING	SEA FISHING	BAIT AND TACKLE	BOATS FOR HIRE	DRYING ROOM	PACKED LUNCHES	GILLIE	TACKLE ROOM	FREEZER	PERMITS REQUIRED
SOUTH EAST													
CARLOW													
Seven Oaks Hotel	Breem, Perch, Roach, Pike, Eel, Salmon, Trout,	173	•	•		•			•	•	•		•
Dolmen Hotel & River Court Lodges	Pike, Salmon, Trout	173	•	•		•							•
KILKENNY													
Butler House	Brown Trout, Salmon	175		•		•			•	•	•		•
Kilkenny River Court Hotel	Trout, Salmon	178		•		•			•		•		•
Mount Juliet Estate	Salmon, Trout	182		•		•			•	•	•		•
TIPPERARY SOUTH													
Cashel Palace Hotel	Perch, Salmon, Brown Trout, Grilse	185	•	•		•			•	•	•		•
Dundrum House Hotel	Trout, Salmon	185		•		•			•	•	•		•
WATERFORD													
Belfry Hotel	Roach, Dace, Pike, Bream, Salmon, Trout, Flounder, Plaice, Ray	190	•	•	•	•			•		•		•
Bridge Hotel	Salmon, Trout, Sea Bass, Plaice, Cod	190	•	•	•	•			•		•		•
Clonanav Farm Guesthouse	Wild Brown Trout, Salmon	196		•		•			•	•			•
Lawlors Hotel	Roach, Dace, Salmon, Trout, Shark, Mackerel, Codling, Plaice, Brill, Bass, Turbot, Wray	198	•	•	•	•			•		•		•
Majestic Hotel	Pike, Salmon, Trout, Mackerel, Cod, Shark, Sea Bass, Plaice	201	•	•	•	•			•		•		•
WEXFORD													
Hotel Saltees	Cod, Bass, Mackerel, Pollock	209			•	•	•		•		•		
Quay House	Bass, Pollock, Coalfish, Codling, Tope, Spurdog, Ballan, Wrasse	210			•	•	•		•				
Riverside Park Hotel	Salmon, Trout, Bass, Mackerel, Shark, Plaice, Pollock	208		•	•	•			•		•		•
Talbot Hotel Conference and Leisure Centre	Salmon, Trout, Roach, Bass, Cod, Pollock, Ling	204	•		•	•	•		•				
Whites Hotel	Bream, Roach, Perch, Pike, Salmon, Trout, Cod, Mackerel	204	•	•	•	•			•				

ANGLING FOR A PLACE TO STAY!

ACCOMMODATION	TYPES OF FISH	BE OUR GUEST PAGE NUMBER	COARSE FISHING	GAME FISHING	SEA FISHING	BAIT AND TACKLE	BOATS FOR HIRE	DRYING ROOM	PACKED LUNCHES	GILLIE	TACKLE ROOM	FREEZER	PERMITS REQUIRED
SOUTH WEST													
CORK													
Aherne's Townhouse & Seafood Restaurant	Salmon, Trout, Shark, Cod, Ling, Conger	258			•	•			•	•		•	•
Ambassador Hotel	Pike, Bream, Salmon, Sea Trout, Cod, Pollock, Conger, Ling	218	•	•	•	•			•				•
Baltimore Harbour Hotel & Leisure Centre	Bream, Eel, Pike, Trout, Salmon, Pollock, Ling, Cod, Turbot, Skate, Shark	234	•	•	•		•		•				•
Carrigaline Court Hotel	Blue Shark (June-Sept), Ling, Pollock, Conger, Cod, Sea Trout	238		•	•		•		•				•
Casey's of Baltimore	Pike, Ling, Cod, Pollock, Mackerel, Turbot, Skate, Shark	234	•		•		•		•				•
Castlehyde Hotel	Bream, Eel, Salmon, Brown Trout, Rainbow Trout,	244	•	•	•				•	•		•	
Celtic Ross Hotel Conference & Leisure Centre	Bream, Roach, Tench, Trout, Salmon, Cod, Shark, Wrasse, Flat Fish	255	•	•	•		•		•				•
Colla House Hotel	Shark, Conger Eel, Cod, Mackerel, Ling, Flat Fish	256			•				•				•
Commodore Hotel	Ling, Cod, Pollock, Conger	242			•		•		•				
Coolcower House	Bream, Rudd, Tench, Eel, Pike, Perch, Salmon, Trout	252	•	•			•		•		•	•	
Creedon's Hotel	Bream, Pike, Perch	245	•				•			•			
Dunmore House Hotel	Bass, Cod, Mackerel, Skate, Whiting, Ling	240			•		•		•				•
Eldon Hotel	Pike, Bream, Tench, Trout, Salmon, Shark, Mackerel, Pollock	257	•	•	•		•		•	•		•	•
Hibernian Hotel	Bream, Pike, Perch, Trench, Trout, Salmon	253	•				•		•				•
Innishannon House Hotel	Salmon, Sea Trout, Brown Trout, Shark, Cod, Ling, Skate, etc.	246		•	•		•		•				•
Kierans Folkhouse Inn	Ling, Cod, Congor, Blue Shark, Sea Bass, Pollock	248			•		•		•				•
Longueville House & Presidents' Restaurant	Brown Trout, Salmon	253		•			•		•	•			•
Maryborough House Hotel	Bream, Perch, Pike, Trout, Rudd, Eel, Salmon, Shark, Ling, Conger, Pollock, Cod, Ray, Wrasse	228	•	•	•		•		•				•
Midleton Park Hotel	Rainbow Trout, Brown Trout, Salmon, Roach, Shark, Cod	255		•	•				•				•
Quality Shandon Court Hotel	Pike, Shark, Trout, Salmon, White Fish, Prawn, Conger, Ling, Pollock, Cod, Whiting, Mackerel	228	•	•	•	•	•		•	•		•	•
Springfort Hall Hotel	Trout, Salmon	254	•	•	•				•	•		•	•

424

ANGLING FOR A PLACE TO STAY!

ACCOMMODATION	TYPES OF FISH	BE OUR GUEST PAGE NUMBER	COARSE FISHING	GAME FISHING	SEA FISHING	BAIT AND TACKLE	BOATS FOR HIRE	DRYING ROOM	PACKED LUNCHES	GILLIE	TACKLE ROOM	FREEZER	PERMITS REQUIRED
CORK Continued													
Trident Hotel	Ling, Cod, Conger, Wrasse, Pollock, Mackerel, Blue Shark	251			•	•	•		•				
Victoria Hotel, Macroom	Bream, Pike, Perch	231	•					•			•	•	•
White Lady Hotel	Shark fishing our speciality, Cod, Pollock etc	251			•	•	•		•				
KERRY													
Aghadore Heights Hotel	Salmon, Sea Trout, Brown Trout, Mackerel, Pollock, Cod	275		•	•	•	•	•	•	•	•	•	•
Abbey Gate Hotel	Salmon, Sea Trout, Brown Trout, Mackerel, Pollock, Dog Fish etc.	298	•	•	•	•	•	•	•				•
Barrow House	Salmon, Shark, Bass, Wrasse	299		•	•	•							•
Benners Hotel	Pollock, Mackerel, Cod, Sea Trout, Salmon, Ray, Shark	264		•	•	•	•		•				•
Brandon Hotel	Cod, Sea Trout	300		•	•								•
Brookhaven Guesthouse	Bream, Pike, Chub, Rudd, Roach, Tench, Salmon, Trout, Pollock, Mackerel, Whiting, Plaice, Ling	302	•	•	•	•	•		•			•	•
Butler Arms Hotel	Salmon, Trout, Bass, Pollock, Cod, Shark, Mackerel, Whiting	303		•	•	•	•	•	•	•			•
Caragh Lodge	Brown Trout, Salmon	262		•			•	•		•			•
Castlelodge Guesthouse	Trout, Salmon	278	•	•			•	•					•
Castlerosse Hotel & Leisure Centre	Trout, Salmon	278	•	•			•						•
Cliff House Hotel	Salmon, Brown Trout, Shark, Monkfish, Bass, Cod, Ray, Pollock, Ling, Tope, Turbot	258		•	•	•	•		•				•
Derrynane Hotel	Mackerel, Pollock, Shark	261			•	•	•						•
Dingle Skellig Hotel	Pollock, Garfish, Blue Shark, Tope, Dogfish, Ling, Whiting, Ray	266		•	•	•	•		•				•
Earls Court House	Salmon, Trout	279		•			•			•		•	•
Glencar House Hotel	Salmon, Trout, Sea Trout, Tope, Pollock, Cod, Ling, Mackerel, Ray, Shark	270		•	•	•	•	•	•	•			•
Grand Hotel	Perch, Trout, Pike, Salmon, Dog Fish, Pollock, Ray, Monkfish	301	•	•	•	•	•		•			•	•
Inveraray Farm Guesthouse	Salmon, Brown Trout, Perch, Peel	284		•				•					•
Killarney Court Hotel	Pike, Trout, Salmon	285	•	•	•		•	•		•		•	•
Killarney Heights Hotel	Pike, Eel, Trout, Salmon	286	•	•			•			•		•	•

425

ANGLING FOR A PLACE TO STAY!

Accommodation	Types of Fish	Be Our Guest Page Number	Coarse Fishing	Game Fishing	Sea Fishing	Bait and Tackle	Boats for Hire	Drying Room	Packed Lunches	Gillie	Tackle Room	Freezer	Permits Required
KERRY Continued													
Killarney Park Hotel	Brown Trout, Salmon, Sea Trout	287		•		•		•	•		•	•	
Killarney Royal	Brown Trout, Salmon	287		•		•		•	•			•	
Killarney Ryan Hotel & Leisure Centre	Coarse Fish, Salmon, Trout	287	•	•		•		•	•		•		•
Kingfisher Lodge Guesthouse	Salmon, Trout, Sea Trout, Pollock, Ling, Coalfish, Mackerel, Wrasse, Shark	289	•	•	•	•	•	•	•	•	•	•	•
Lake Hotel	Salmon, Trout	289		•		•	•	•	•		•	•	
Lakelands Farm Guesthouse	Salmon, Sea Trout, Pollock, Bass, Shark, Ling, Mackerel	303		•	•	•		•	•		•	•	
Listowel Arms Hotel	Pike, Perch, Eel, Salmon, Trout, Ling, Ray, Bass, Pollock, Cod, Monkfish, Tope	296	•	•	•	•		•	•		•	•	•
Moorings	Salmon, Trout, Cod, Pollock, Mackerel, Shark, Turbot, Sea Trout, Salmon, Plaice	297		•	•	•	•	•	•		•	•	•
Muckross Park Hotel	Salmon, Brown Trout, Tench, Rainbow Trout	291	•	•	•	•		•	•	•	•	•	•
Riversdale House Hotel	Bream, Chub, Dab, Eel, Roach, Rudd, Tench, Brown Trout, Rainbow Trout, Salmon, Bass, Cod	273	•	•	•	•	•	•	•		•	•	•
Scarriff Inn	Mackerel, Pollock, Salmon, Mackerel, Pollock, Pike, Bass	261	•	•	•		•		•		•	•	•
Sheen Falls Lodge	Salmon, Trout, Shark, Mackerel, Pollock, Skate, Conger, Eel, Dogfish	274		•	•	•	•	•	•	•	•	•	•
Smerwick Harbour Hotel	Plaice, Turbot, Sole, Mackerel, Cod, Pollock, Conger, Shark	269		•	•	•	•	•	•		•	•	•
Smugglers Inn	Sea Trout, Salmon, Brown Trout, Bass, Cod, Mackerel, Shark, Plaice, Turbot, Sole, Monkfish	303		•	•	•	•	•	•		•	•	•

SHANNON

CLARE

Accommodation	Types of Fish	Page No.	Coarse	Game	Sea	Bait	Boats	Drying	Packed	Gillie	Tackle	Freezer	Permits
Aberdeen Arms Hotel	Bream, Chub, Tench, Perch, Eel, Dab, Roach, Salmon, Trout, Plaice, Monkfish, Shark, Mackerel, Cod, Ling, etc	322	•	•	•	•	•	•	•	•	•		•
Bunratty Castle Hotel	Salmon, Trout, Cod, Mackerel, Bass, Pike, Bream	307	•	•	•		•		•		•		
Atlantic Hotel	Bream, Perch, Pike, Tench, Bass, Blue Shark, Conger Eel, Ling, Salmon, Trout	322	•	•	•	•	•	•	•		•	•	•
Dromoland Castle	Pike, Trout, Bream	326	•	•	•	•	•		•	•			
Fountain Court	Pike, Bream, Tench, Salmon, Brown Trout, Mackerel, Skate, Pollock, Cod, Hake, Shark	312	•	•	•	•	•	•	•	•	•	•	•

ANGLING FOR A PLACE TO STAY!

ACCOMMODATION	TYPES OF FISH	BE OUR GUEST PAGE NUMBER	COARSE FISHING	GAME FISHING	SEA FISHING	BAIT AND TACKLE	BOATS FOR HIRE	DRYING ROOM	PACKED LUNCHES	GILLIE	TACKLE ROOM	FREEZER	PERMITS REQUIRED
CLARE Continued													
Grovemount House	Roach, Trout	316	•	•			•	•					
Kincora Hall Hotel	Tench, Bream, Roach, Perch, Pike, Eel, Trout, Salmon	319	•	•		•	•	•	•	•		•	•
Ocean Cove Golf and Leisure Hotel	Cod, Pollock	317			•	•	•	•	•	•	•	•	•
Woodstock Hotel	Pike, Bream, Tench, Perch, Salmon, Mullet, Brown & Sea Trout, Cod, Skate, Pollock, Shark	315	•	•	•	•	•	•	•	•	•		•
Carrygerry Country House	Bream, Pike, Perch, Rainbow & Brown Trout, Mackerel, Bass, Cod	327	•	•	•		•		•	•		•	•
LIMERICK													
Adare Manor Hotel & Golf Resort	Salmon, Trout	336	•				•	•		•		•	•
Castle Oaks House Hotel	Pike, Bream, Tench, Eel, Trout, Salmon	337	•	•		•	•	•	•	•		•	•
Fitzgeralds Woodlands House Hotel & Leisure Club	Pike, Trout, Salmon	337	•				•	•		•		•	•
Leens Hotel	Salmon, Trout, Ray, Bass, Pollock, Cod, Monkfish	335	•	•	•	•	•	•	•	•	•	•	•
Limerick Ryan Hotel	Pike, Perch, Roach, Trout, Salmon	333	•	•		•	•	•	•	•	•	•	•
Rathkeale House Hotel	Pike, Perch, Roach, Trout, Salmon	338	•	•			•	•		•	•	•	•
Two Mile Inn Hotel	Pike, Perch, Salmon, Trout	335	•	•			•			•		•	
TIPPERARY NORTH													
Abbey Court Hotel	Pike, Perch, Bream, Roach, Brown Trout, Salmon	339	•	•		•	•	•		•		•	•
Dromineer Bay Hotel	Pike, Bream, Roach, Rudd, Perch, Eel, Salmon, Trout	339	•	•		•	•	•		•	•	•	•
WEST													
GALWAY													
Ardilaun House Hotel, Conference & Leisure Club	Salmon, Brown Trout, Sea Trout, Rainbow Trout	344		•		•	•	•	•	•	•		•
Ballynahinch Castle Hotel	Salmon, Seatrout, Brown Trout	361		•		•	•	•	•	•	•	•	•
Ben View House	Salmon, Trout, Bass, Herring, Whiting, Pollock, Plaice	365		•	•	•	•	•	•	•	•	•	•

ANGLING FOR A PLACE TO STAY!

ACCOMMODATION	TYPES OF FISH	BE OUR GUEST PAGE NUMBER	COARSE FISHING	GAME FISHING	SEA FISHING	BAIT AND TACKLE	BOATS FOR HIRE	DRYING ROOM	PACKED LUNCHES	GILLIE	TACKLE ROOM	FREEZER	PERMITS REQUIRED
GALWAY Continued													
Boat Inn	Perch, Pike, Eel, Pike, Salmon, Brown Trout, Sea Trout, Shark, Cod	375	•	•	•	•	•	•	•		•	•	
Corrib House Hotel	Salmon, Trout, Perch, Pike, Shark, Cod	375	•	•	•	•					•	•	•
Corrib Wave Guest House	Pike, Perch, Brown Trout, Salmon	376	•	•	•	•	•	•	•	•	•	•	•
Eldons Hotel	Shark, Pollock, Cod, Mackerel	379			•							•	
Galway Bay Golf and Country Club Hotel	Bream, Eel, Pike, Roach, Trout, Salmon, Bass, Cod, Mackerel, Plaice	374	•	•	•	•	•		•	•	•	•	•
Galway Bay Hotel, Conference & Leisure Centre	Bream, Roach, Perch, Rudd, Salmon, Brown Trout, Blue Shark, Cod, Ling, Pollock, Ray, Surnard, Eel, Plaice	348	•	•	•	•					•	•	
Galway Ryan Hotel & Leisure Centre	Pike, Perch, Bream, Roach, Salmon, Brown Trout	349	•	•	•	•				•		•	•
Hayden's Gateway Business & Leisure Hotel	Pike, Trout, Salmon	360	•	•		•	•		•	•	•	•	•
Lake Hotel	Pike, Perch, Trout, Salmon, All species	376	•	•	•		•	•		•	•	•	
Lough Inagh Lodge	Salmon, Sea Trout, Brown Trout	378		•	•		•	•	•	•		•	
Menlo Park Hotel & Conference Centre	Perch, Pike, Trout, Salmon, Mackerel, Pollock, Ray, Tope, Bullhuss, Wrasse	353	•	•	•						•	•	
Moran's Cloonnabinnia House Hotel	Bream, Roach, Rudd, Pike, Wild Brown Trout, Salmon, Sea Trout, Shark, Bass, Pollock, Cod	373	•	•	•	•	•		•	•	•	•	•
Mountain View Guest House	Salmon, Trout, Pike, Perch, Bream	377	•	•	•	•	•		•	•	•	•	•
O'Deas Hotel	Trout, Pike, Perch	373	•	•		•					•	•	•
Peacockes Hotel & Complex	Salmon, Sea Trout, Shark, Cod, Pollock, Mackerel, Ray	373	•	•	•	•					•	•	•
Pier House Guesthouse	Blue Shark, Cod, Pollock, Ling, Ray, Mackerel	359			•	•	•			•	•	•	•
Renvyle House Hotel	Brown Trout, Salmon, Sea Trout, Cod, Shark, Eel, Mackerel, Pollock	378	•	•	•	•	•			•	•	•	•
River Run Lodge	Pike, Perch, Roach, Salmon, Trout	377	•	•	•				•	•	•	•	
Station House Hotel	Pike, Perch, Roach, Brown Trout, Salmon, Sea Trout, Plaice, Mackerel, Monkfish	368	•	•	•	•					•	•	•
Zetland Country House Hotel	Pike, Salmon, Trout, Bass, Blue Shark, Cod, Hake, Mackerel, Plaice, Pollock, Ray	363	•	•	•					•	•	•	•
MAYO													
Achill Cliff House & Restaurant	Flat fish, Cod, Ling, Conger, Shark	381			•	•	•		•	•		•	
Atlantic Coast Hotel	Eel, Pike, Perch, Salmon, Trout, Sea Trout, Brill, Mackerel, Ling, Pollock, Ray, Shark, Herring	390	•	•	•	•					•	•	•

ANGLING FOR A PLACE TO STAY!

ACCOMMODATION	TYPES OF FISH	BE OUR GUEST PAGE NUMBER	COARSE FISHING	GAME FISHING	SEA FISHING	BAIT AND TACKLE	BOATS FOR HIRE	DRYING ROOM	PACKED LUNCHES	GILLIE	TACKLE ROOM	FREEZER	PERMITS REQUIRED
MAYO Continued													
Bartra House Hotel	Perch, Pike, Eel, Bream, Salmon, Trout, Wrasse, Cod, Mackerel, Conger, Eel	382	•	•	•	•	•	•		•	•		•	•
Daly's Hotel	Pollock, Ray, Shark, Herring, Pike, Perch, Mackerel, Salmon, Sea Trout, Brown Trout, Cod, Whiting, Ling	384	•	•	•	•	•		•		•	•	•	•
Downhill House Hotel	Pike, Salmon, Trout, Sea Trout, Sole, Bream, Brill, Mackerel, Ling, Cod, Monkfish	383	•	•	•	•	•			•	•	•	•	•
Downhill Inn	Eel, Pike, Sea Trout, Salmon, Brown Trout, Mackerel, Cod, Monkfish	383	•	•	•	•	•			•	•	•	•	•
Healy's Hotel On The Lake	Pike, Perch, Salmon, Brown Trout, Sea Trout	389	•	•	•	•	•		•	•	•		•	•
Hotel Westport	Pike, Perch, Bream, Salmon, Trout, Pollock, Dog Fish, Cod, Whiting, Blue Shark, Ling, Tope, Skate	391	•	•	•	•	•			•	•		•	•
Knockranny House Hotel	Pike, Salmon, Trout, Cod, Sea Trout, Whiting	392	•	•	•	•				•			•	•
Ostan Oilean Acla	Cod, Ling, Conger, Shark, Mackerel, Trout, Brill, Whiting, Ray	381		•	•	•				•			•	
Ridgepool Hotel, Conference and Leisure Centre	Bream, Eel, Trout, Salmon, Bass, Mackerel	383	•	•	•	•	•		•	•	•	•	•	•
Ryan's Hotel	Brown Trout, Salmon - also Pike, Perch and Roach Hake, Mackerel, Plaice, Pollock, Ray	387	•	•					•		•		•	•
Teach Iorrais	Salmon, Trout, Cod, Mackerel			•	•	•	•		•	•			•	•
ROSCOMMON													
Royal Hotel	Salmon, Trout, Pike, Perch	395	•	•	•	•				•			•	•

IRELAND FOR

Conferences

HOTELS & GUESTHOUSES

Small meetings or large conferences are part
and parcel of life in Irish hotels and guesthouses.

What makes Ireland special as a venue
is the warmth of the welcome you will receive,
coupled with excellent facilities
which can be tailored to your needs.

If you have an agenda, we can supply
the venue.

SELECT A VENUE FOR YOUR AGENDA

We will be glad to see you and work with you to make your meeting or conference a successful one. Choose from the wide selection of special facilities throughout the country as shown here. A full description of the hotels and guesthouses can be had by looking up the appropriate page number. Premises are listed in alphabetical order in each county.

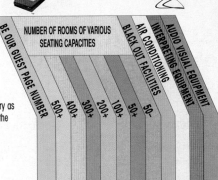

ACCOMMODATION	CONTACT PERSON	BE OUR GUEST PAGE NUMBER	500+	400+	300+	200+	100+	50+	50-	BLACK OUT FACILITIES	AIR CONDITIONING	INTERPRETING EQUIPMENT	AUDIO VISUAL EQUIPMENT
NORTH WEST													
DONEGAL													
Abbey Hotel	Jim White	26		1	1	1	1	1		•	•	O	O
Bay View Hotel & Leisure Centre	Noel O'Mahony	34		1				1		•	•		O
Central Hotel, Conference & Leisure Centre	Michael Naughton	26		1	1	1	1	1		•	•	H	O
Dorrians Imperial Hotel	Mary Dorrian	29			1		1	1		•	•		H
Great Northern Hotel	Philip McGlynn	31	1	1	1	1	1	1	1	•	•	H	O
Inishowen Gateway Hotel	Sean O'Kane	30		1			1	2	1	•	•		O
Ostan Na Rosann	Lewis Connon	33		1	1	1	1	1		•	•	H	H
Redcastle Hotel	Margaret Patterson	37		1				1		•		H	H
Sand House Hotel	Paul Diver - Manager	38						1	3	•		H	H
LEITRIM													
Bush Hotel	Joseph Dolan	39			1	1	3	2	3	•	•	H	H
Landmark Hotel	Mary Stillman	39			1	1	2	2		•	•	H	O
SLIGO													
Beach Hotel and Leisure Club	Audri McArdle	44					1	2				H	H
Sligo's Southern Hotel & Leisure Centre	Kevin McGlynn	42	1	1	1	1	1	2	4		H	H	O
Tower Hotel	Ian Hyland	42					1	1	2	•		H	H
NORTH													
ANTRIM													
Ballymac	Cathy Muldoon	51						1		•		1	O
Bushmills Inn	Stella Minogue	47						1	2	•	•	H	O
Causeway Coast Hotel & Conference Centre	Mary O'Neill	49			1	1	2	2	2	•	•	H	O
Comfort Hotel Portrush	Mary O'Neill	50						1	1	•	•	H	O
Hilton Templepatrick	Wilma Lindsay	51	1			2	5	7	3	•	•	H	O
Magherabuoy House Hotel	Miss Anna Conn	50		1		1	2	2	3	•		H	O

SELECT A VENUE FOR YOUR AGENDA

ACCOMMODATION	CONTACT PERSON	BE OUR GUEST PAGE NUMBER	500+	400+	300+	200+	100+	50+	50-	BLACK OUT FACILITIES	AIR CONDITIONING	INTERPRETING EQUIPMENT	AUDIO VISUAL EQUIPMENT
ANTRIM Continued													
Quality Hotel	Nina Kelly	48		1	1	1	2	3		•	•	H	O
ARMAGH													
Silverwood Golf Hotel and Country Club	Miriam Callan	52			1	1	1	2		•			O
BELFAST													
Aldergrove Hotel	Laura Maxwell	53				1	2	5		•	•	H	O
Dukes Hotel	Yvonne McNally	53				1	2	3		•	•	H	H
Dunadry Hotel and Country Club	Sheree Davis	54			1	1	2	4	5	•	•		O
McCausland Hotel	Adrianne Carr	55					1	2		•	•	H	H
Park Avenue Hotel	Angela Reid	55		1	1	2	3	6	7	•	•	H	O
Posthouse Premier Belfast	Rachael Clarke	55					1	9		•	•	H	O
Wellington Park Hotel		56		1	1	2	3	4	9	•	•	H	O
DOWN													
Royal Hotel	Hazel Smith	59						1		•			O
DERRY													
Brown Trout Golf & Country Inn	Bill O'Hara	57						2		•	•		
FERMANAGH													
Killyhevlin Hotel	David Morrison	63	1			2		2	3	•	•	H	H
Mahons Hotel	Joe Mahon	64		1		1		1		•		H	O

EAST COAST

ACCOMMODATION	CONTACT PERSON	BE OUR GUEST PAGE NUMBER	500+	400+	300+	200+	100+	50+	50-	BLACK OUT FACILITIES	AIR CONDITIONING	INTERPRETING EQUIPMENT	AUDIO VISUAL EQUIPMENT
DUBLIN													
Abberley Court Hotel	Karen Garry	67						2		•	•	H	O
Aberdeen Lodge	Pat Halpin	67						2		•	•	H	H
Academy Hotel	Glen Fanning	68						5		•	•	H	C

432

H = Can Arrange Hire   O = Available On Premise

SELECT A VENUE FOR YOUR AGENDA

ACCOMMODATION

DUBLIN Continued

Accommodation	Contact Person	Be Our Guest Page Number	500+	400+	300+	200+	100+	50+	50-	Black Out Facilities	Air Conditioning	Interpreting Equipment	Audio Visual Equipment
Airport View	Anne Marie Beggs	118							1	•			H
Alexander Hotel	Siobhan O'Hare	69		1	1	2	4	5	1	•	•	H	O
Arlington Hotel	Andrea Inglis	71							2	•		H	O
Ashling Hotel	Dermot Lambe & David Lane	72				1	1	1	5	•	•	H	H
Belvedere Hotel	Marion Heneghan	73					1			•			H
Berkeley Court	Michelle McDermot	74	1			2	1		3	•	•		H
Brooks Hotel	Anne McKiernan / Fionnuala McParland	76						1	3	•	•	H	O
Burlington	John Conmee	77	1	3			3	2	9	•	•	H	H
Buswells Hotel	Aileen Mangan	77						1	3	•	•	H	O
Camden Court Hotel	Elaine Silke	78							4	•	•	H	H
Cassidys Hotel	Carol	79						1	1	•	•		H
Central Hotel	Gwen McGauley	80						2	4	•		H	H
City West Hotel, Conference, Leisure & Golf Resort	Fiona Killilea	127	1		2			3	10	•	•		O
Clarion Hotel Dublin IFSC	Jane Curley	82						2	7	•	•		O
Clontarf Castle Hotel	Deirdre Kavanagh	83		1			3	2	1	•	•	H	H
Conrad International Dublin	Sandra Cummins	84			1				4	•	•	H	H
Court Hotel	Joe Conlon	123			1	2	2	5		•	•	O	O
Davenport Hotel	Siobhan O'Hare	84		1		2	2	2	4	•	•	H	O
Eglinton Manor	Rosaleen Cahill O'Brien	86							1	•	•		
Finnstown Country House Hotel	Oonagh Brien	124				1		2	4	•		H	O
Fitzpatrick Castle Dublin	Monica O'Byrne	123	1	2	2	2	2	7	5	•		H	O
Fitzwilliam Hotel	Lesley Mangan	88						2	1	•	•	H	H
Grand Hotel	Bernadette O'Connor	125	2			1	3	6	9	•	•	H	O
Great Southern Hotel Dublin Airport	Louise Maguire	119			1	1	3		8	•	•	H	H
Gresham Hotel	Ian Craig	91			1	2	3	8	22	•	•	H	H
Hilton Dublin	Triona Horgan	94			1			4	7	•	•	H	O
Holiday Inn	Ciara Hamilton	94						1	1	•	•	H	H
Hotel St. George	Reception	95							1				
Jurys Ballsbridge Hotel & Towers	Conor O'Kane	96	1				2	2	8	•	•	H	H
Jurys Inn Custom House	Stephen Johnston	97				1			3	•	•	H	H
Lansdowne Hotel	Margaret English	100				1	1	1		•	•	H	H
Marine Hotel	Sheila Baird	128						1	6	•	•	H	H
Mercer Hotel	Caroline Fahy	102				1	1		3	•	•	H	O
Merrion Hall	Pat Halpin	102							2	•	•	H	H
Merrion Hotel	Orla Duff	103							2	•	•		O

H = Can Arrange Hire   O = Available On Premises

SELECT A VENUE FOR YOUR AGENDA

Accommodation	Contact Person	Be Our Guest Page Number	500+	400+	300+	200+	100+	50+	50–	Air Conditioning	Black Out Facilities	Interpreting Equipment	Audio Visual Equipment
DUBLIN Continued													
Mespil Hotel	Emma Allen	104							2	•			O
Mont Clare Hotel	Siobhan O'Hare	104					1	3	6	•	•	H	O
Ormond Quay Hotel	Conor Byrne	106						1	3	•		H	H
Orwell Lodge Hotel	Reception	107						1	2				
Paramount Hotel	Gary Taylor	108							1	•	•	H	O
Plaza Hotel	Deirdre Neill	109			1		2	2	8	•	•	H	H
Portmarnock Hotel & Golf Links	Caitriona Loughrey	126				1	2	2	2	•	•	H	H
Posthouse Dublin Airport	Valerie Markey	120					1		6	•	•	H	H
Quality Charleville Hotel and Suites	Ann Byrne	109							3	•		H	H
Radisson SAS St. Helen's Hotel	John Coleman	118			1	1	3	6	5	•	•	H	O
Red Cow Moran Hotel	Karen Moran	111	1	1	1	2	5	5	16	•	•	H	O
Royal Dublin Hotel	Louisa Owens	111			1		2	3	4	•		H	H
Royal Marine Hotel	Tracey Johnson	122		1			1	2	4	•		H	H
Sachs Hotel	Ann Byrne	112					1	1	1			H	H
Shelbourne Dublin	Richard Margo	112		1			2	2	6	•		H	H
Sheldon Park Hotel & Leisure Centre	Maura Bissett	112	1	1	1	2	3	2	9	•	•	H	C
Spa Hotel	Betty Dolan	124	1	1	1	1	1	1	1	•		H	H
Stephen's Green Hotel	Sally Hughes	114							6	•	•	H	C
Stillorgan Park Hotel	Ailbhe Winston	118		1			1	5	9	•	•	H	H
Temple Bar Hotel	Justin Lowry	115						1	4	•		H	H
West County Hotel	Reception	117					1	1	2	•	•	H	
Westbury	Jane Howley	117				1	2	1	1	•	•	H	H
LOUTH													
Boyne Valley Hotel & Country Club	Noel Comer	130	1	1	1	2	1	2	3	•		H	C
Carrickdale Hotel & Leisure Complex	Breige Savage/Declan O'Neill/Fiona Clerkin	131	1			1	1	1	1	•	•	H	C
Derryhale Hotel	Liam Sexton	132					1		2	•		H	
Fairways Hotel	Brian Quinn	132			1	1	1		4	•	•	H	
Hotel Imperial	Peter Quinn	133					1	2	2				
McKevitt's Village Hotel	Terry and Kay McKevitt	130						1	1	•			
Westcourt Hotel	Barry Tierney	131			1	1	2	3	5	•	•		
MEATH													
Ardboyne Hotel	Bernie McHugh	135				1	2	3	4	•	•	H	
Broadmeadow Country House & Equestrian Centre	Sandra Duff	133							2			H	

H = Can Arrange Hire   O = Available On Premis

SELECT A VENUE FOR YOUR AGENDA

Accommodation	Contact Person	Be Our Guest Page Number	500+	400+	300+	200+	100+	50+	50-	Black Out Facilities	Air Conditioning	Interpreting Equipment	Audio Visual Equipment
MEATH Continued													
Conyngham Arms Hotel	Graham Canning	136					1	2	1	•	•	H	O
Headfort Arms Hotel	Vincent Duff, General Manager	134		1						•	•	O	O
Neptune Beach Hotel	Anita Byrne	134				1		2			•	H	O
Old Darnley Lodge Hotel	Mary Murphy	134			1			1		•	•		O
Station House Hotel	Chris Slattery	135				1				•	•	H	O
WICKLOW													
Arklow Bay Hotel	Monique Freeman	140	1	1	1	1	1	2	2	•	•	H	O
Blainroe Hotel	Annie Friel	138						1	2	•	•		O
BrookLodge	Evan Doyle	142		1		1		2	2	•	•	H	O
Cullenmore Hotel	Dirk Van Der Flier	142						1	2		•		H
Glendalough Hotel	Patrick Casey	147				1		2			•		O
Glenview Hotel	Annemarie Whelan	146				1	1	2	2	•	•	H	O
Hunter's Hotel	Nicola Coffey	148						3			•		O
La Touche		147											
Lawless's Hotel	Seoirse or Maeve O'Toole	143				1			1	•		H	O
Rathsallagh House, Golf and Country Club	Catherine Lawlor	145			1				1	•		H	O
Summerhill House Hotel	Michael Blake	146				1		1	5		•	H	H
Tinakilly Country House and Restaurant	Brenda Gilmore	148						1	3	•	•		O
Tulfarris Golf & Country House Hotel	Liz Hayes	144				1	4	3	7		•		O
Woodenbridge Hotel	Esther and Bill O'Brien	149		1				1			•		
Woodland Court Hotel	Eileen Murphy	145						1	4	•	•	H	O
MIDLANDS & LAKELANDS													
CAVAN													
Hotel Kilmore	Bernie McHugh	151	1			2	3	3	4	•	•	H	O
Park Hotel	Mary McMillan	153						1	2	•			O
Sharkeys Hotel	Goretti Sharkey	153		1				1	1	•	•		O
Slieve Russell Hotel, Golf & Country Club	Vari McGreevy	152	1	1	3	3	3	4	7	•	•	H	O
KILDARE													
Ambassador Hotel	Brian Johnston	155				1	2	2	3	•	•	H	O

H = Can Arrange Hire   O = Available On Premises   435

SELECT A VENUE FOR YOUR AGENDA

ACCOMMODATION	CONTACT PERSON	BE OUR GUEST PAGE NUMBER	500+	400+	300+	200+	100+	50+	50-	BLACK OUT FACILITIES	AIR CONDITIONING	INTERPRETING EQUIPMENT	AUDIO VISUAL EQUIPMENT
KILDARE Continued													
Curragh Lodge Hotel	Liam McLoughlin	153							2	•	•	H	H
Glenroyal Hotel, Leisure Club & Conference Centre	Helen Courtney	156		1	2	2	2	4	7	•	•	H	O
Hazel Hotel	Margaret Kelly	157			1	1	1	1	1	•	•		O
Keadeen Hotel	Michelle Kelly	158	1	1	1	1	3	4	7	•	•	H	O
K Club	Kerri Wells	159					1	1	3	•	•	H	O
Standhouse Hotel Leisure & Conference Centre	Shane D'Arcy	155	1	1	2	3	4	4	7	•	•	H	O
Straffan Lodge Hotel	Derek O'Farrell	156						1	1	•			O
LONGFORD													
Longford Arms Hotel	James Reynolds	161	1				2	3		•	•	H	H
MONAGHAN													
Four Seasons Hotel & Leisure Club	Orla McKenna	162	1	1	2	2	4	4	5	•	•	H	O
Glencarn Hotel and Leisure Centre	Patrick McFadden/Fiona Dooley/Kathleen Lavelle	163	1	1	1	3	3	3	5	•	•	H	O
Nuremore Hotel & Country Club	Helen Woods	162	1				2	3	4	•	•	H	O
OFFALY													
Bridge House Hotel & Leisure Club	Colm McCabe	165	1	1	2	2	3	4	9	•	•	H	C
County Arms Hotel	William Loughnane	163			1		1	2	2	•		H	H
Doolys Hotel	Jo Duignan	164				1			1	•			C
Kinnitty Castle Demesne	Elaine Kirwan	164				1	1	2	2	•		H	H
Tullamore Court Hotel	Ann Lynch	166	1	1	2	2	3	4	8	•	•	H	C
WESTMEATH													
Austin Friar Hotel	Patrina Mullen	169							1	•	•	H	
Bloomfield House Hotel & Leisure Club	Ita Purcell	169			1	2	3	5	7	•	•	H	
Creggan Court Hotel	Gerard Moylan	167							1	•	•	H	
Greville Arms Hotel	John Cochrane	170				1	2	1	2	•		H	
Hodson Bay Hotel	Catriona Connolly	167	1	1	1	2	3	4	4	•	•	H	
Lakeside Hotel & Marina	Maureen Flynn	167	1	1	1	1	1	1	1	•	•	H	
Prince of Wales Hotel	Gael C Allen	168			1				2	•	•	H	

H = Can Arrange Hire   O = Available On Premis

ACCOMMODATION	CONTACT PERSON	BE OUR GUEST PAGE NUMBER	500+	400+	300+	200+	100+	50+	50-	AIR CONDITIONING	BLACK OUT FACILITIES	INTERPRETING EQUIPMENT	AUDIO VISUAL EQUIPMENT
WESTMEATH Continued													
Royal Hoey Hotel	M. Hoey	168					1	2	3	•	•		O
Shamrock Lodge Hotel and Conference Centre	Pamela Wilson/Karen Smyth	168			1		1		1		•	H	O
SOUTH EAST													
CARLOW													
Dolmen Hotel & River Court Lodges	Nora Duggan	173	1	2	2	2	2	3	8	•	•	H	O
Mount Wolseley Hotel, Golf and Country Club	Cathy Walsh	174						1	3	•	•	H	H
Seven Oaks Hotel	Kathleen Dooley	173	1					1	2	•			H
KILKENNY													
Butler House	Gabrielle Hickey	175					1	2				H	O
Hibernian Hotel	Joe Kelly	176						1	2	•	•		O
Hotel Kilkenny	Brid Crawford	176		1	1	2	3	4	7	•	•	H	H
Kilkenny Ormonde Hotel	Sheena McCanny	177		1	1		1	1	8	•	•	H	O
Kilkenny River Court Hotel	Eleanor Begley	178				1			4	•	•	H	H
Mount Juliet Estate	Aine O'Hare	182					1	3	2	•	•	H	O
Newpark Hotel	Orla Gray	179		1	1	1	2	2	7	•	•	H	O
Springhill Court Hotel	Trish Murphy	180	1			1	1	2	3	•	•	H	O
TIPPERARY SOUTH													
Cashel Palace Hotel	Susan Murphy	185						1		•		H	H
Clonmel Arms Hotel	Neilus McDonnell	186		1		1	1		1	•	•	O	H
Dundrum House Hotel	Ms Deirdre Crowe	185		1					1	•	•	H	O
Glen Hotel	James Coughlan	188			1	1	1		1	•	•		H
Hotel Minella & Leisure Centre	Elizabeth Nallen	187	1			2	2	4	5	•	•	H	O
WATERFORD													
Belfry Hotel	Sharon Reid	190						1	1	•	•	H	H
Bridge Hotel	Catherina Byrne/Rosemary Ahern	190			1	1	2	3	4	•	•	H	O
Clonea Strand Hotel, Golf & Leisure	Mark Knowles or Ann McGrath	198			2	2	3	4	5	•	•	H	O
Dooley's Hotel	Margaret Darrer	191				1	2	1	4	•	•	H	O

H = Can Arrange Hire   O = Available On Premises

SELECT A VENUE FOR YOUR AGENDA

Accommodation	Contact Person	Be Our Guest Page Number	500+	400+	300+	200+	100+	50+	50-	Air Conditioning	Black Out Facilities	Audio Visual Equipment	Interpreting Equipment
WATERFORD Continued													
Faithlegg House Hotel		200				1		1	3	•		H	O
Gold Coast Golf Hotel & Leisure Centre	Ann McGrath or Maire McGrath	198					1	3	4	•	•	H	H
Granville Hotel	Richard Hurley	192					1	2	1	•		H	H
Jurys Waterford Hotel	Aine Aspel	192	1					1	2	•		H	H
Lawlors Hotel	William Buckley & Anne Marie Daffy	198		1		2	3	4	5	•	•	H	O
Majestic Hotel	Annette Devine	201					1	1	1	•	•	H	H
Tower Hotel & Leisure Centre	Padraig Penney	194	1	1	2	2		5	3	•			H
Woodlands Hotel	Marguerite Fitzgerald	195	1						3	•		H	H
WEXFORD													
Ashdown Park Hotel	Catherine Fulvio	209	1							•	•	H	O
Clarion Brandon House Hotel & Leisure Centre	Sean Reed	210				1			1	•	•	H	O
Ferrycarrig Hotel	Caroline Roche	202		1	1	1	1	1	2	•	•	H	H
Marlfield House Hotel	Margaret Bowe	209							1	•		H	O
Riverside Park Hotel	Jim Maher	208	1			2		4		•	•	H	O
Rosslare Great Southern Hotel	Pat Cussen	215					1		1	•		H	H
Talbot Hotel Conference and Leisure Centre	Niamh Lambert	204			1	1	2	3	4	•	•	H	O
Whites Hotel	Jaquie Nolan	204			1	1	2	3	7	•		H	O

SOUTH WEST

Accommodation	Contact Person	Be Our Guest Page Number	500+	400+	300+	200+	100+	50+	50-	Air Conditioning	Black Out Facilities	Audio Visual Equipment	Interpreting Equipment
CORK													
Actons Hotel	Angela Leany/Anne Marie Cross	246	1						2	•	•	H	
Ambassador Hotel	Mark Hornibrook	155						1	1	•		H	
Baltimore Harbour Hotel & Leisure Centre	Fiona O'Sullivan	234					1		1			H	
Blarney Park Hotel	Aidan Grimes	237				1	2	2	3	•	•	H	
Carrigaline Court Hotel	Bernadette C. Kirby	238		1				2		•		H	
Celtic Ross Hotel Conference & Leisure Centre	Nollaig Hurley	255					1	1	1	•		H	
Doughcloyne Hotel	David Harney	221					1	1	2	•	•	H	
Fernhill Golf & Country Club	Alan Bowes	238					1			•		H	
Fernhill House Hotel	Teresa O'Neill	240			1					•	•		
Glengarriff Eccles Hotel	Geraldine Owens	245					1	1		•		H	
Great Southern Hotel	Freda Darcy	224					1		5	•	•	H	

H = Can Arrange Hire   *O = Available On Premise*

SELECT A VENUE FOR YOUR AGENDA

Accommodation	Contact Person	Be Our Guest Page Number	500+	400+	300+	200+	100+	50+	50-	Air Conditioning	Black Out Facilities	Interpreting Equipment	Audio Visual Equipment
CORK Continued													
Hibernian Hotel	Catherine Gyves	253					1	2	4	•			O
Imperial Hotel	Aideen Murphy	225		1			1	1	4	•	•	•	H O
Innishannon House Hotel	General Manager	246						1	1		•	•	H O
Jurys Cork Hotel	Niamh Hynes	225	1				1	1	5	•	•	•	H H
Lodge & Spa at Inchydoney Island	Sales & Marketing Manager	241		1				1	2	•	•	•	H O
Longueville House & Presidents' Restaurant	Aisling O'Callaghan	253							2	•			H H
Maryborough House Hotel	Mary Motherway	228		1	1		2	2	2	•	•	•	H O
Metropole Ryan Hotel and Leisure Centre	Fiona Keohane	228	1	1	1	2	2	6	11	•	•	•	H H
Quality Hotel and Leisure Centre	David Henry	242				1	4	4	1	•	•	•	H H
Quality Shandon Court Hotel	Tracy Hoary	228					1	3	4	•	•	•	H H
Rochestown Park Hotel	Liam Lally/Claire Cullinane	229	1	1	2	2	3	5	9	•	•	•	H O
Silversprings Moran Hotel	Tracey Moran	230	2		4			2	6		•	•	H O
Springfort Hall Hotel	Paul Walsh	254				1	1	2	3	•			O
Trident Hotel	Hal McElroy/Una Wren	251					1		4	•	•		H O
Westlodge Hotel	Eileen M O'Shea	236					1			•	•		H H
KERRY													
Abbey Gate Hotel	Patrick Dillon	298			1	1	1	3	3	•	•		H O
Aghadoe Heights Hotel	Emma Phillips	275						1	2	•	•		H
Barrow House	Noelle Crosbie	299						1		•			H H
Brandon Hotel	Louise Langan / Mark Sullivan	300	1	2	2	3	4	4	4	•	•		H O
Castlerosse Hotel & Leisure Centre	Michael O'Sullivan	278					1		1	•	•		H H
Dingle Skellig Hotel	Colin Aherne	266					1		2	•	•		H O
Dromhall Hotel	Derek Carrol	279				1				•	•		H H
Gleneagle Hotel	Cara Fuller	282	2	2	3	3	4	4	4	•	•		O O
Grand Hotel	Dick Boyle	301	1					3	6	•	•		O O
Holiday Inn Killarney	David Hennessy	282						1		•	•		H O
Kenmare Bay Hotel	Terry O'Doherty	272		1			1			•	•		H O
Killarney Court Hotel	Robert Lyne	285					1			•	•		H O
Killarney Great Southern Hotel	Michele King	285	1				1	2	2	•	•		H H
Killarney Heights Hotel	Bernadette Cassells	286			1			2		•	•		H
Killarney Park Hotel	Niamh O'Shea	287					1	1	3	•	•		H O
Lake Hotel	Tony Huggard	289						1	2	•	•		H O
Listowel Arms Hotel	Kevin O'Callaghan	296				1	1	1	1	•	•		H H

H = Can Arrange Hire   O = Available On Premises

SELECT A VENUE FOR YOUR AGENDA

Accommodation	Contact Person	Be Our Guest Page Number	Number of Rooms of Various Seating Capacities							Black Out Facilities	Air Conditioning	Interpreting Equipment	Audio Visual Equipment
			500+	400+	300+	200+	100+	50+	50-				
KERRY Continued													
Muckross Park Hotel	Lisa Cronin	291			1			1	1		•	H	H
Parknasilla Great Southern Hotel	Jim Feeney	297						1	1		•	H	H
Riversdale House Hotel	Peter O'Sullivan	273	1							•	•	H	H
Sheen Falls Lodge	Ms Carmel Flynn	274					1	1	2	•	•	H	O
SHANNON													
CLARE													
Aberdeen Arms Hotel	Brian Hegarty	322			1					•	•		H
Bunratty Castle Hotel	Kathleen McLoughlin	307					1	1	2	•	•	H	H
Burkes Armada Hotel	John Burke Jnr.	326			1			1		•	•		H
Clare Inn Golf & Leisure Hotel	Anne O'Toole Group Sales Manager	310		1				1	1	•		O	O
Dromoland Castle	Stella Rochford	326		1	1	1	2	3	6	•	•	H	O
Falls Hotel	Joe Leonard	316			1				2			H	C
Fitzpatrick Bunratty	Maria O'Gorman Skelly	309	1		2	1	6		1	•	•	H	C
Halpin's Hotel & Vittles Restaurant	Pat Halpin	317						2		•	•	H	H
Kincora Hall Hotel	John O'Connor	319				1						H	C
Magowna House Hotel	Gay Murphy	313			1			1		•	•	H	C
Oak Wood Arms Hotel	Stephen Keogh	328			1			3	3	•	•		C
Ocean Cove Golf and Leisure Hotel	Anne O'Toole, Group Sales Manager	317					1	3		•		O	C
Old Ground Hotel	Phil Sherlock	314			1			1	1	•	•		H
Shannon Great Southern Hotel	Pat Dooley	334			1			3		•	•	H	C
Temple Gate Hotel	John Madden	314				1	1	2	1	•	•	H	C
West County Conference & Leisure Hotel	Anne O'Toole, Group Sales Manager	315	3		1				6		•	O	C
Woodstock Hotel	Marian Kelly	315			1			2	1	•	•		H
LIMERICK													
Adare Manor Hotel & Golf Resort	Yvette Kennedy	336			1	1	1			•		H	
Castletroy Park Hotel	Ursula Cullen, Sales Manager	329		1	2	4	4	5	9	•	•		H
Cruises House	Carole Kelly	330						1				H	
Devon Inn Hotel	William Sheehan	338		1	1	1	1	2	1		•	H	
Dunraven Arms Hotel	Louis Murphy	336		1	1	1	2	4	5	•	•	H	
Fitzgeralds Woodlands House Hotel & Leisure Club	David or Karen	337			1	1	2	3	3	•	•	H	

H = Can Arrange Hire O = Available On Premises

SELECT A VENUE FOR YOUR AGENDA

ACCOMMODATION	CONTACT PERSON	BE OUR GUEST PAGE NUMBER	500+	400+	300+	200+	100+	50+	50-	BLACK OUT FACILITIES	AIR CONDITIONING	INTERPRETING EQUIPMENT	AUDIO VISUAL EQUIPMENT
LIMERICK Continued													
Greenhills Hotel Conference/Leisure	Sarah Greene	331	1	1	1	1	2			•	•	H	O
Jurys Limerick Hotel	Linda Walsh	332						1	2	•	•	H	H
Kilmurry Lodge Hotel	Gerard Lane	337			1		2	1	2			H	H
Limerick Inn Hotel	Patricia Ryan	333	1	1	1	2	2	2	2	•	•	H	O
Limerick Ryan Hotel	Claire Kennedy	333					1	5	5	•		H	H
Rathkeale House Hotel	Gerry O'Connor	338			1		1		1	•	•	H	O
South Court Business and Leisure Hotel	Anne O'Toole, Group Sales Manager	334	1			2	8	2	2	•	•	O	O
Two Mile Inn Hotel	Ann Hackett	335			1		1			•		H	H
Woodfield House Hotel	Austin Gibbons/Mary Gleeson	335						2	1	•	•	H	O
TIPPERARY NORTH													
Abbey Court Hotel	Tom Walsh	339	1	1	1	2	3	3	6	•	•		O
Anner Hotel & Leisure Centre	Nollaig Howell	340		1	1	1	2	3		•		H	O
Dromineer Bay Hotel	Gerry Callanan	339			1								O
WEST													
GALWAY													
Abbeyglen Castle Hotel	Paul Hughes	363					1	1	1	•		H	O
Ardilaun House Hotel, Conference Centre & Leisure Club	Thomas MacCarthy O'Hea	344			1	1	1	2	3	•	•	H	H
Connemara Coast Hotel	Jason Foody	369		1	1	2	2	5	8	•		H	O
Corrib Great Southern Hotel	Micheal Cunningham	346	1			2		1	3	•	•	H	O
Corrib House Hotel	Conor McNamara	375					1						H
Galway Bay Golf and Country Club Hotel	Anne O'Toole, Group Sales Manager	374					2	2	3	•	•	O	O
Galway Bay Hotel, Conference & Leisure Centre	Virginia Connolly	348	1	2	2	2	2	5	5	•	•	H	O
Galway Great Southern Hotel	Robert Byrne	349					1	1	3	•	•	H	O
Galway Ryan Hotel & Leisure Centre	Duty Manager	349							2	•	•	H	H
Hayden's Gateway Business & Leisure Hotel	Anne O'Toole, Group Sales Manager	360			1		1			•		O	O
Lady Gregory Hotel	Mary Sheehan	370			1			2		•	•	H	O
Menlo Park Hotel & Conference Centre	David Keane	353			1	1	1	2		•	•	H	O

H = Can Arrange Hire   O = Available On Premises

SELECT A VENUE FOR YOUR AGENDA

H = Can Arrange Hire   O = Available On Premis[es]

ACCOMMODATION	CONTACT PERSON	BE OUR GUEST PAGE NUMBER	500+	400+	300+	200+	100+	50+	50-	BLACK OUT FACILITIES	AIR CONDITIONING	INTERPRETING	AUDIO VISUAL EQUIPMENT
GALWAY Continued													
Oranmore Lodge Hotel, Conference & Leisure Centre	Mary O'Higgins	374		1		1	1	1		•	•	H	H
Park Lodge Hotel	Jane Marie Foyle	380					1	1	1		•	H	H
Peacockes Hotel & Complex	Mary Carroll	373	1			1	1			•	•	H	H
Quality Hotel and Leisure Centre Galway	Rhona Kearney/Dermot Comerford	374						1	6	•			H
Radisson SAS Hotel	Ulla Virkkula	354	1						11	•	•	H	O
Renvyle House Hotel	Vincent Flannery	378					2	1	1	•	•	H	O
Salthill Court Hotel	Joseph Hallinan	356					1			•	•	H	H
Shannon Oaks Hotel & Country Club	Barry Maher	378	1				1	1	2	•	•	H	O
Station House Hotel	Cian Landers	368			1			2		•	•	H	H
Westwood House Hotel	Karina Dunne	358			1	1	1	3	4	•	•	H	O
MAYO													
Atlantic Coast Hotel	Catherine O'Grady-Powers	390					1		3	•	•	H	O
Breaffy House Hotel	Caitriona Gavin	384			1	1	1		5	•	•	H	O
Castlecourt Hotel Conference and Leisure Centre	Joe Corcoran	390	1	1	1	2	2	3	3	•	•	H	O
Downhill House Hotel	Kay Devine & Rachel Moylett	383	1		1	1	1	2	3	•	•	H	O
Hotel Westport	Gerry Walshe & Ruth Farrell & Rhona Chambers	391			1		1	3	1	•	•	H	O
Jennings Hotel & Travellers Friend	David McManus	385	1	1	2	2	3	3	4	•	•	H	O
Knock House Hotel	Brian Crowley	388					1	1	1				O
Knockranny House Hotel	Carol Noonan	392	1	1	1	1	2	3	3	•	•	H	O
Pontoon Bridge Hotel	Breeta Geary	389			1	1	2	2	2	•	•	H	H
Ridgepool Hotel, Conference & Leisure Centre	Conor O'Connell	383					1		4	•	•	H	O
Teach Iorrais	Carmel Gallagher	383				2				•	•	H	
Westport Woods Hotel & Leisure Centre	Michael Lennon	393				1	1	1	2	•	•	H	
ROSCOMMON													
O'Gara's Royal Hotel	Larry O'Gara	394					1	2	1	•	•		
Royal Hotel	Adrian Bouchier & Nelson Chung	395						1			•		O

AVOCA
HANDWEAVERS

Welcome to the colourful world of Avoca, where our seven magical shops are crammed with beautiful things, most of which are made exclusively by Avoca. Savour our restaurants where our delicious lunches are legendary. Visit any one of our shops and be sure of a warm welcome and an experience with a difference.

Tel: 01 286 7466
Fax: 01 286 2367

Open 7 Days

Kilmacanogue	Avoca Village	Powerscourt House Shop	Molls Gap	Bunratty	Letterfrack	Suffolk St.
Bray, Co. Wicklow	Avoca Co. Wicklow	Enniskerry Co. Wicklow	Killarney, Co. Kerry	Co. Clare	Co. Galway	Dublin 2.

Heritage Island

is a group of the most prestigious heritage attractions in all of Ireland...

The centres range from historic houses, castles, monuments, museums, galleries, national parks, interpretative centres, gardens and theme parks.

Visitors can avail of big savings by displaying the *Heritage Island Explorer* coupon at the following attractions, which will entitle them to reduced admission, many two for one's and special offers...

Armagh
- Armagh Planetarium

Cavan
- Belturbet Station
- Cavan County Museum
- Cavan Crystal Visitor Centre
- Maudabawn Cultural Centre

Clare
- Bunratty Castle and Folk Park
- Clare County Museum
- Craggaunowen

Cork
- Cork City Gaol
- Millstreet Country Park
- Mizen Vision
- Old Midleton Distillery

Donegal
- Donegal County Museum

Down
- Castle Ward
- Exploris Aquarium
- Mount Stewart House and Gardens
- Somme Heritage Centre
- St. Patrick Centre

Dublin
- Ceol - The Irish Traditional Music Centre
- Dublinia
- Guinness Storehouse
- Hot Press Irish Music Hall of Fame

Dublin (continued)
- ICON - Home of Baileys® in Ireland
- James Joyce Centre
- Old Jameson Distillery
- St. Patrick's Cathedral
- Trinity College Library and Dublin Experience

Fermanagh
- Belleek Pottery Visitor Centre
- Castle Coole

Galway
- Galway Irish Crystal Heritage Centre
- Kylemore Abbey and Gardens

Kerry
- Crag Cave
- Jeanie Johnston Visitor Shipyard
- Kerry the Kingdom

Kildare
- Irish National Stud, Japanese Gardens & St. Fiachra's Garden
- Steam Museum

Limerick
- Adare Heritage Centre
- Hunt Museum, Limerick
- King John's Castle
- Limerick County Museum

Louth
- County Museum, Dundalk
- Millmount Museum

Meath
- Kells Heritage Centre
- Trim Visitor Centre

Monaghan
- Monaghan County Museum

Offaly
- Birr Castle Demesne & Ireland's Historic Science Centre
- Tullamore Dew Heritage Centre

Roscommon
- Cruachán Aí Visitor Centre
- King House
- Lough Key Forest Park
- Strokestown Park

Sligo
- Drumcliffe Church and Visitor Centre
- Michael Coleman Heritage Centre

Tipperary
- Brú Ború

Waterford
- Waterford Crystal Visitor Centre
- Waterford Treasures at the Granary and Reginald's Tower

Westmeath
- Athlone Castle Visitor Centre
- Belvedere House, Gardens and Park

Wexford
- Irish National Heritage Park
- National 1798 Visitor Centre

Wicklow
- Avondale House
- National Sealife Centre
- Powerscourt House and Gardens
- Russborough
- Wicklow's Historic Gaol

Heritage Island members confirmed as at August 2000. Heritage Island can not accept responsibility for any errors or omissions.

For full details on centres, opening times, discounts and special offers see Heritage Island Touring Guide 2001 available at Tourist Information Centres, nationwide.

Heritage Island,
37 Main Street,
Donnybrook, Dublin 4.
Tel: + 353 1 260 0055
Fax: + 353 1 260 0058
E mail: heritage.island@indigo.ie
Web: www.heritageisland.com

CUT ALONG DOTTED LINE

HERITAGE ISLAND EXPLORER

Display this coupon at any Heritage Island Centre to qualify for redu admission. Touring Guide available at Tourist Information Offices throughout Ireland, or contact www.heritageisland.com

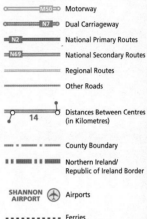

I R I S H
HOTELS
F E D E R A T I O N

KEY TO MAPS

13-14	15
9-10	11-12
5-6	7-8
1-2	3-4

Grid rows numbered 22 down to 1. Columns A B C D E F G H I J K L M N O P Q R.

Place names on map: COLERAINE, LETTERKENNY, DERRY, BALLYMENA, LARNE, COOKSTOWN, DONEGAL, BELFAST, SLIGO, ENNISKILLEN, ARMAGH, NEWRY, MONAGHAN, BALLINA, CAVAN, DUNDALK, CASTLEBAR, DROGHEDA, WESTPORT, ATHLONE, DUBLIN, GALWAY, TULLAMORE, PORTLAOISE, ENNIS, ARKLOW, CARLOW, LIMERICK, KILKENNY, TIPPERARY, WEXFORD, TRALEE, CLONMEL, WATERFORD, KILLARNEY, CORK, BANTRY

LEGEND

Symbol	Description
M50	Motorway
N7	Dual Carriageway
N2	National Primary Routes
N69	National Secondary Routes
	Regional Routes
	Other Roads
14	Distances Between Centres (in Kilometres)
	County Boundary
	Northern Ireland/ Republic of Ireland Border
SHANNON AIRPORT	Airports
Holyhead	Ferries
Hill of Tara ◇	Heritage Sites

N

MAGNETIC

Variation 10°45' (1990)

```
0    5    10   15   20   25km
0         5         10      15miles
```

SCALE 1 : 625 000

DISTANCE CHART
in Kilometres

Headers (diagonal): ARMAGH, ATHLONE, BELFAST, CARLOW, CLIFDEN, CORK, DERRY, DUBLIN, DUNDALK, ENNISKILLEN, GALWAY, KILKENNY, KILLARNEY, LARNE, LIMERICK, PORTLAOISE, ROSSLARE HARBOUR, SHANNON AIRPORT, SLIGO, TRALEE, WATERFORD, WEXFORD, WICKLOW

ARMAGH	ATHLONE	BELFAST	CARLOW	CLIFDEN	CORK	DERRY	DUBLIN	DUNDALK	ENNISKILLEN	GALWAY	KILKENNY	KILLARNEY	LARNE	LIMERICK	PORTLAOISE	ROSSLARE HARBOUR	SHANNON AIRPORT	SLIGO	TRALEE	WATERFORD	WEXFORD	WICKLOW
159																						
66	224																					
211	108	248																				
316	171	370	256																			
380	219	423	187	287																		
114	225	118	309	303	460																	
129	124	167	82	296	256	233																
45	142	82	166	314	340	158	84															
81	127	135	240	237	346	98	175	101														
238	92	303	177	79	206	216	233	192	169													
245	121	282	39	248	148	335	114	200	242	196												
388	229	430	235	89	480	303	348	356	214	196	470											
105	264	40	287	411	462	122	206	121	174	343	320	470										
279	119	320	138	184	101	369	192	238	245	105	114	109	356									
208	71	250	37	229	174	287	82	167	192	150	50	221	285	109								
282	201	320	93	348	206	385	151	237	324	269	100	272	356	204	130							
293	134	345	163	172	126	357	216	261	261	93	138	134	380	24	134	229						
148	116	203	224	167	336	134	213	171	68	142	237	345	240	235	187	319	224					
382	222	423	242	288	121	472	296	341	349	208	216	32	460	103	213	291	127	338				
285	167	324	74	296	126	383	156	240	290	217	48	192	359	124	97	81	148	283	211			
264	184	301	76	330	187	365	132	219	306	250	81	254	338	187	113	19	209	299	272	61		
185	138	222	61	311	256	293	56	140	221	232	100	303	259	193	82	118	216	238	296	135	100	

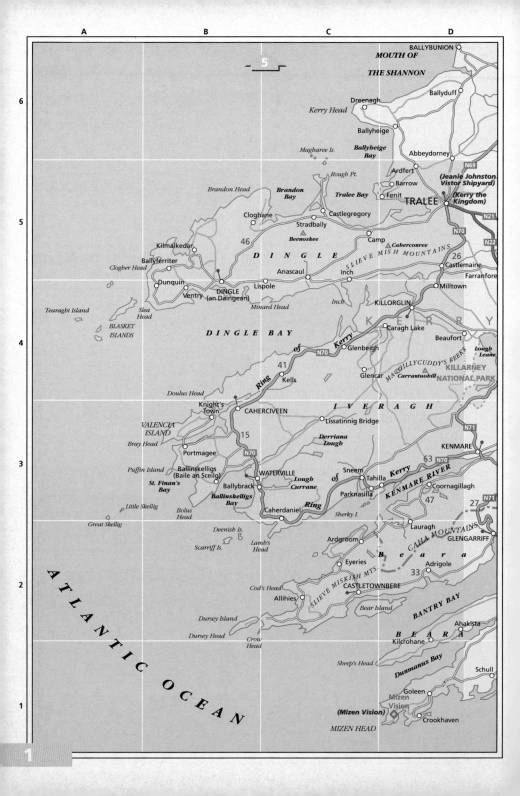

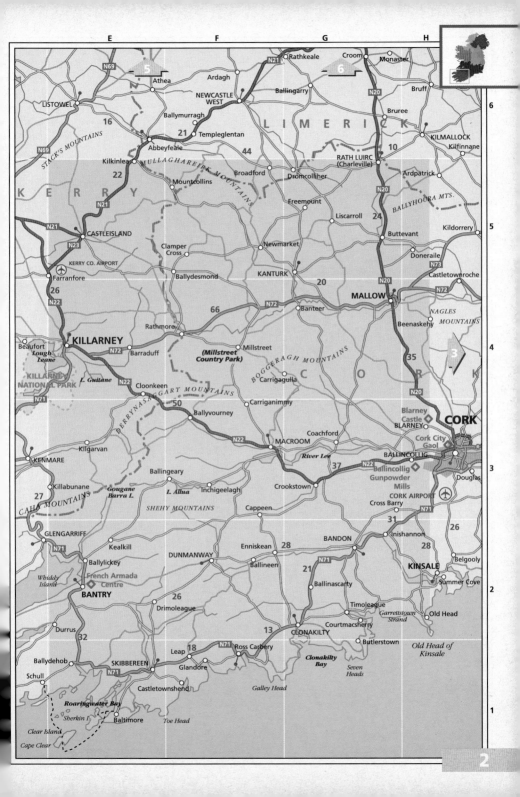

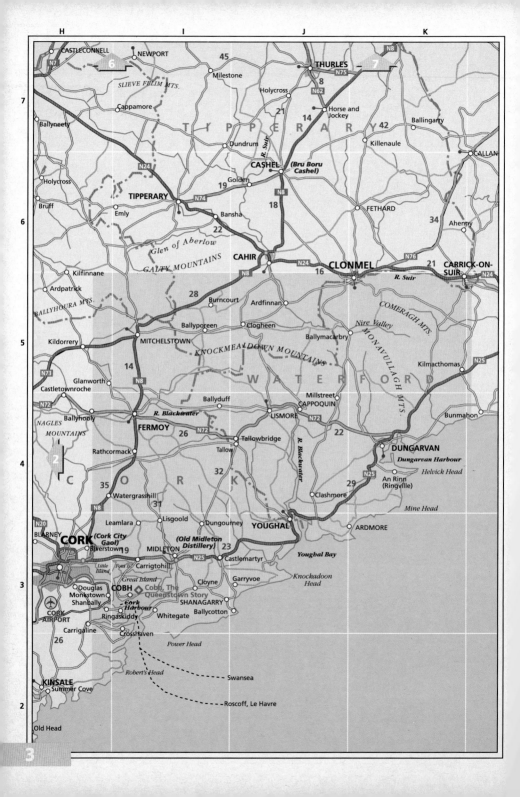

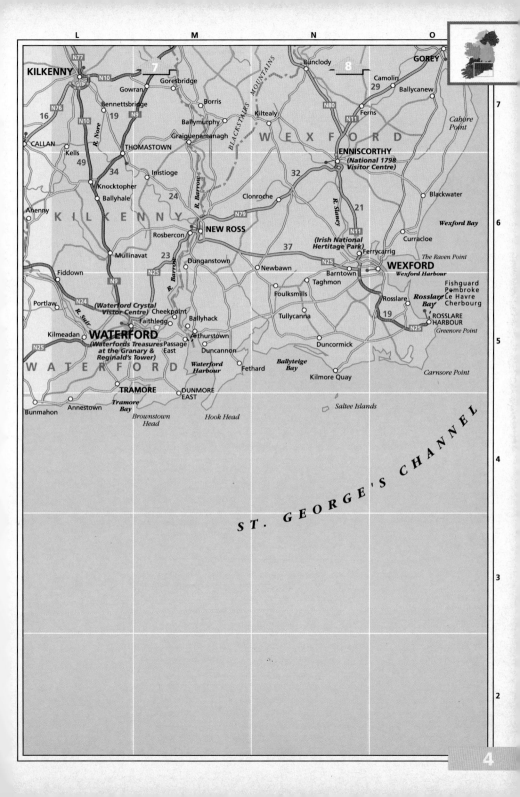

KILKENNY

7

Gowran

Goresbridge

Bunclody

Camolin
29

GOREY

Ballycanew

N76
16

N10

Bennettsbridge
19
N9

Borris

Kiltealy

Ferns
N11

8

N80

Cahore
Point

7

CALLAN

N10

Ballymurphy

Graiguenamanagh

W E X F O R D

Kells

R. Nore

THOMASTOWN

49
34

Inistioge

ENNISCORTHY
(National 1798 Visitor Centre)

32

Knocktopher

Ballyhale
24

Clonroche

R. Slaney

21

Blackwater

Ahenny

K I L K E N N Y

R. Barrow

N79

NEW ROSS

Wexford Bay

6

Rosbercon

37

Curracloe

(Irish National Heritage Park)

N11

The Raven Point

Mullinavat
23

Dunganstown

Newbawn

Ferrycarrig

WEXFORD

Wexford Harbour

Fiddown

N25

R. Barrow

N9

Taghmon

Barntown

Fishguard
Pembroke
Le Havre
Cherbourg

Portlaw

N24

Foulksmills

Rosslare

Rosslare Bay

(Waterford Crystal Vistor Centre)

Cheekpoint

Ballyhack

Tullycanna

19

ROSSLARE HARBOUR

R. Suir

Faithlegg

WATERFORD

Arthurstown

N25

Greenore Point

Kilmeadan

(Waterfords Treasures at the Granary & Reginald's Tower)

Passage East

Duncannon

Duncormick

5

N25

W A T E R F O R D

Duncannon

Waterford Harbour

Fethard

Ballyteige Bay

Kilmore Quay

Carnsore Point

TRAMORE

DUNMORE EAST

Bunmahon

Annestown

Tramore Bay

Brownstown Head

Hook Head

Saltee Islands

S T . G E O R G E ' S C H A N N E L

4

3

2

4

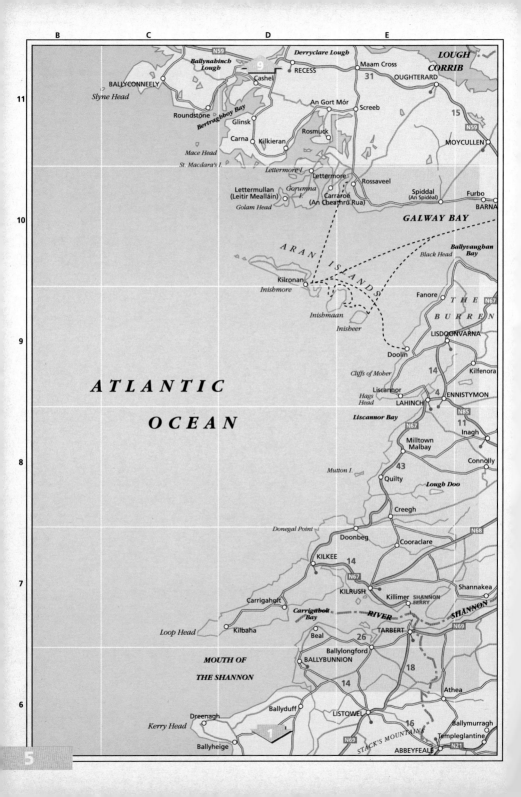

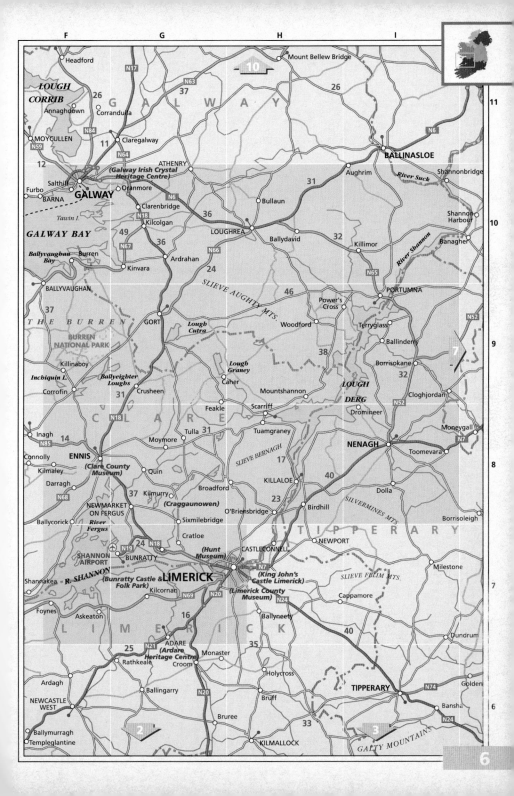

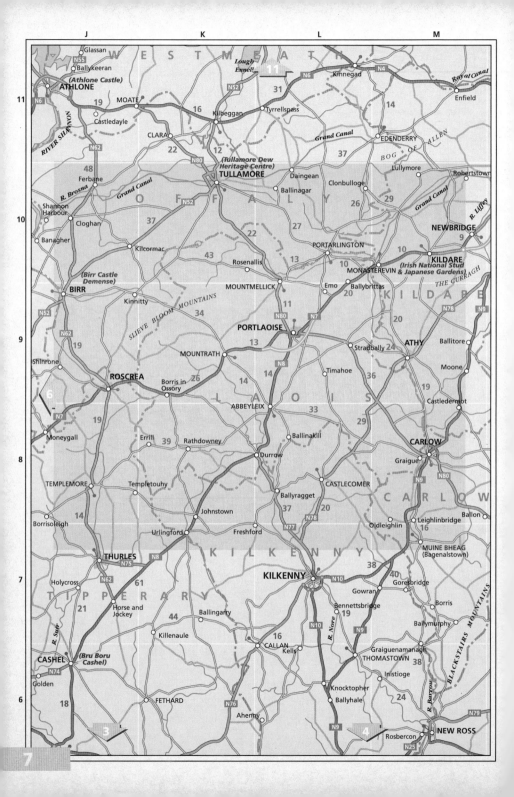

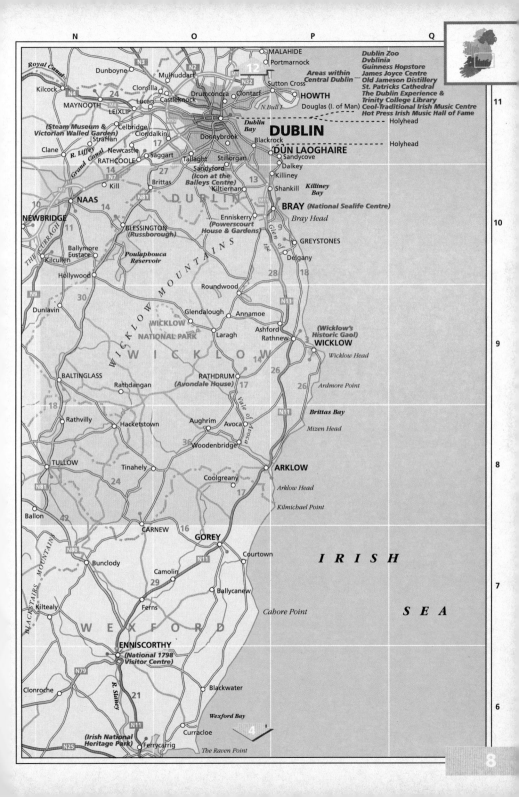

N   O   P   Q

Dublin Zoo
Dvblinia
Guinness Hopstore
James Joyce Centre
Old Jameson Distillery
St. Patricks Cathedral
The Dublin Experience &
Trinity College Library
Ceol-Traditional Irish Music Centre
Hot Press Irish Music Hall of Fame

MALAHIDE
Portmarnock
Sutton Cross
Areas within
Central Dublin
HOWTH
Douglas (I. of Man)
N. Bull I.
Holyhead
Holyhead

Royal Canal
Dunboyne
Mulhuddart
Kilcock
Clonsilla
Maynooth
Lucan
Castleknock
LEIXLIP
Drumcondra
Clontarf
Dublin Bay
DUBLIN
(Steam Museum &
Victorian Walled Garden)
Celbridge
Clondalkin
Staffan
Donnybrook
Blackrock
DÚN LAOGHAIRE
Clane
R. Liffey
Newcastle
Saggart
RATHCOOLE
Tallaght
Stillorgan
Sandycove
Dalkey
Kill
Brittas
Sandyford
(Icon at the
Balleys Centre)
Kiltiernan
Killiney
Killiney Bay
Shankill
NAAS
Brittas
BRAY (National Sealife Centre)
Bray Head
NEWBRIDGE
Enniskerry
(Powerscourt
House & Gardens)
Ballymore
Eustace
BLESSINGTON
(Russborough)
Glen of the
GREYSTONES
Kilcullen
Poulaphouca
Reservoir
Delgany
Hollywood
Roundwood
Dunlavin
Glendalough
Annamoe
Ashford
Rathnew
(Wicklow's
Historic Gaol)
WICKLOW
Laragh
Wicklow Head
WICKLOW
NATIONAL PARK
WICKLOW
BALTINGLASS
RATHDRUM
(Avondale House)
Ardmore Point
Rathdangan
Rathvilly
Hacketstown
Aughrim
Avoca
Vale of Avoca
Brittas Bay
Mizen Head
Woodenbridge
TULLOW
Tinahely
ARKLOW
Coolgreany
Arklow Head
Ballon
Kilmichael Point
CARNEW
GOREY
Bunclody
Camolin
Courtown
I R I S H
Kiltealy
Ferns
Ballycanew
Cahore Point
S E A
W E X F O R D
ENNISCORTHY
(National 1798
Visitor Centre)
Clonroche
R. Slaney
Blackwater
(Irish National
Heritage Park)
Wexford Bay
Curracloe
Ferrycarrig
The Raven Point

11

10

9

8

7

6

8

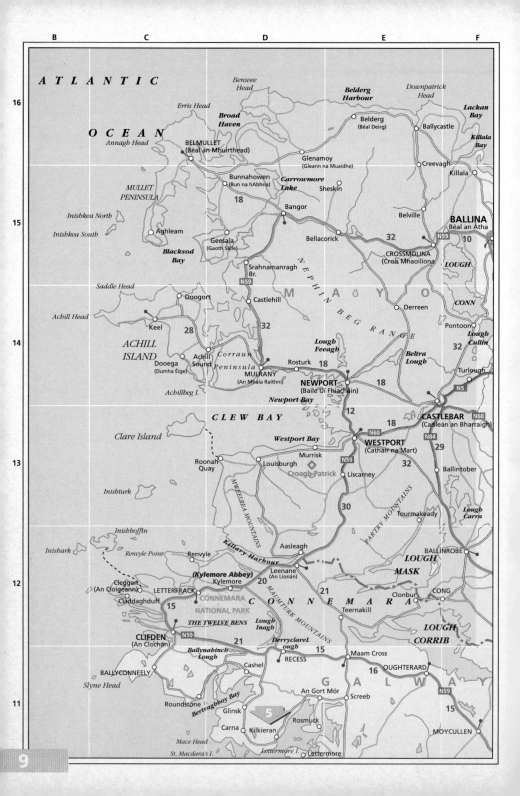

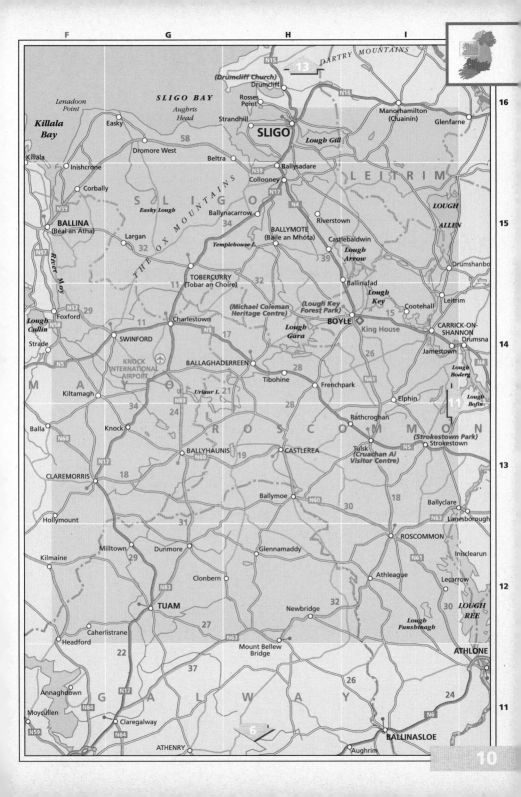

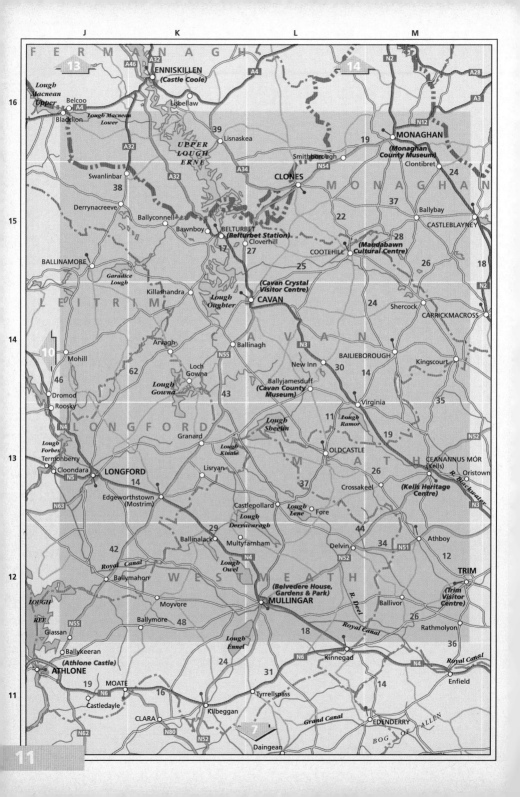

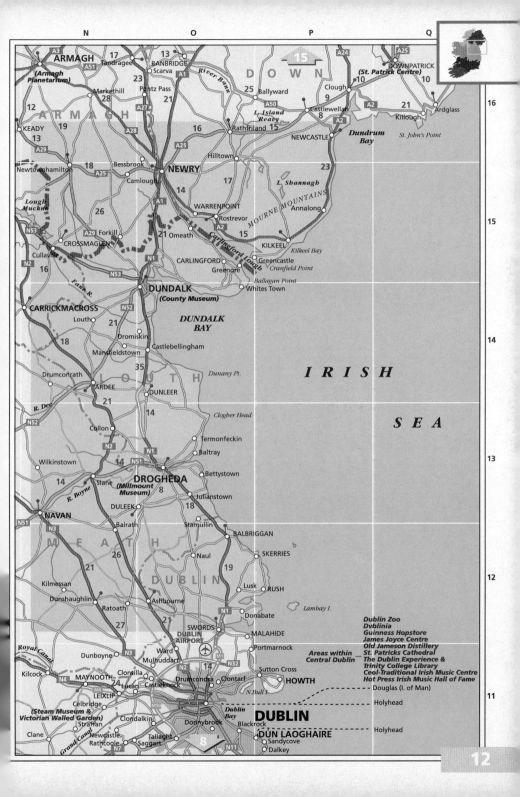

ARMAGH 17 Tandragee 13 BANBRIDGE
(Armagh Planetarium) Scarva
A3 A51 D O W N 15 A24 DOWNPATRICK
(St. Patrick Centre)
23 Poyntz Pass A50 Ballyward Clough 10
Markethill 28 25 Castlewellan 9
21 Ballyward 8 A2 21 Killough Ardglass
12 KEADY 19 A28 16 Rathfriland 15 NEWCASTLE Dundrum Bay St. John's Point
A R M A G H A29 A25 Hilltown
13 A29 18 Bessbrook NEWRY 23
Newtownhamilton A25 Camlough 17 L. Shannagh
Lough Muckno 26 A1 14 WARRENPOINT Annalong
N53 A29 Forkill Omeath Rostrevor M O U R N E M O U N T A I N S
CROSSMAGLEN 21 Carlingford Lough 15 KILKEEL Kilkeel Bay
Cullaville 16 N1 CARLINGFORD Greencastle Cranfield Point
Fane R. N53 Greenore Ballagan Point
DUNDALK Whites Town
(County Museum)
CARRICKMACROSS N52 DUNDALK BAY
Louth 21
18 Dromiskin I R I S H
Mansfieldstown Castlebellingham
35 Dunany Pt.
Drumconrath L O U T H
ARDEE DUNLEER S E A
R. Dee 21
14 Clogher Head
N52 Collon
Wilkinstown N2 Termonfeckin
14 N51 Baltray 13
14 Bettystown
Slane DROGHEDA
R. Boyne **(Millmount Museum)** 8 Julianstown
NAVAN DULEEK 18
N51 N3 Balrath Stamullin
M E A T H BALBRIGGAN 12
26 Naul
21 SKERRIES
Kilmessan D U B L I N 19
Dunshaughlin Lusk RUSH
Ratoath Ashbourne Lambay I.
27 N1 Donabate 11
SWORDS
DUBLIN AIRPORT MALAHIDE
Dunboyne N3 Ward Portmarnock
Kilcock Mulhuddart N32
MAYNOOTH 24 Lucan M1 Sutton Cross
N4 Clonsilla Drumcondra 14 Clontarf HOWTH
Celbridge Castleknock N. Bull I.
LEIXLIP M4
(Steam Museum & Victorian Walled Garden) Clondalkin M50 Dublin Bay
Straffan Donnybrook DUBLIN
Clane Newcastle Tallaght Blackrock
Rathcoole Saggart 8 DÚN LAOGHAIRE
N11 Sandycove
Dalkey

Areas within Central Dublin
Dublin Zoo
Dvblinia
Guinness Hopstore
James Joyce Centre
Old Jameson Distillery
St. Patricks Cathedral
The Dublin Experience &
Trinity College Library
Ceol-Traditional Irish Music Centre
Hot Press Irish Music Hall of Fame
- - - - Douglas (I. of Man)
Holyhead
- - - - - Holyhead

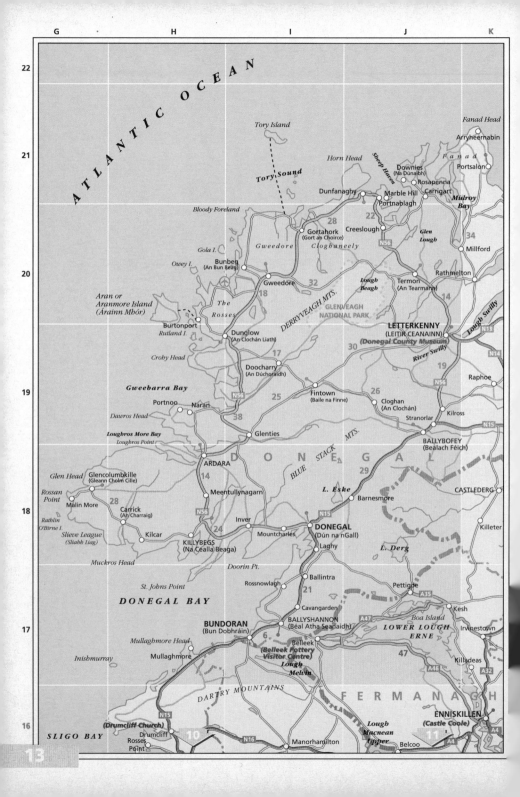

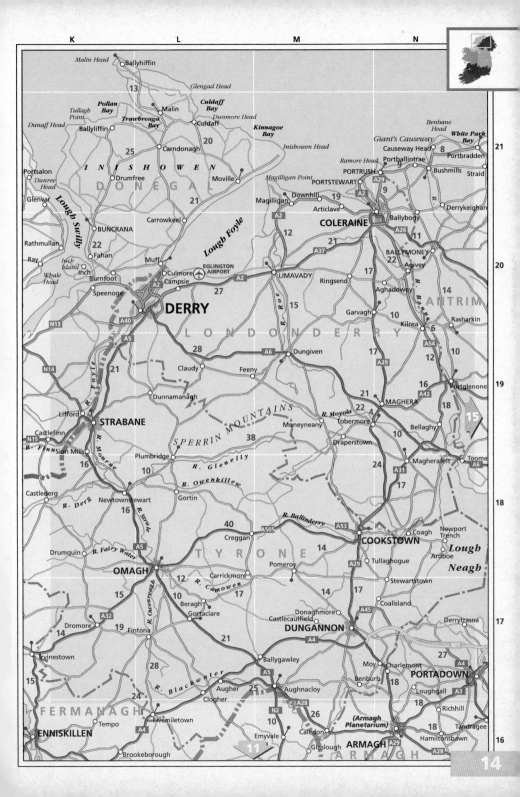

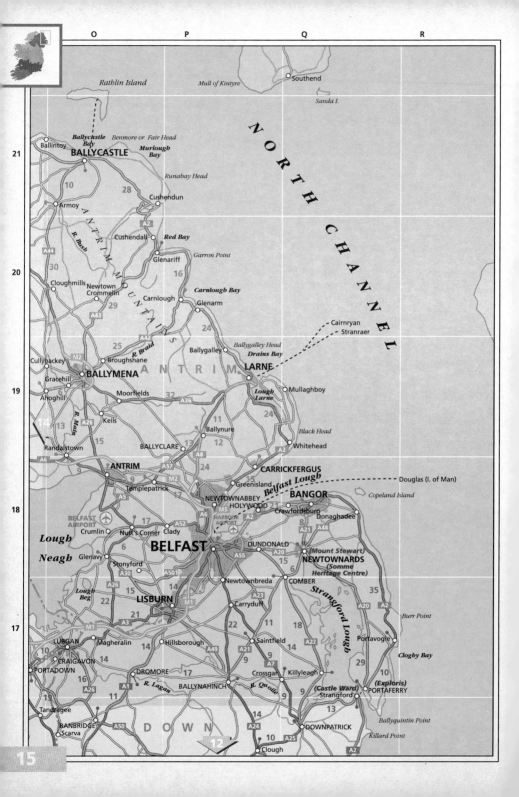

GUINNESS

Holiday Competition

Guinness invite you to Be Our Guest in any of the hotels or guesthouses featured in Ireland's favourite and most successful accommodation guide. (Value of prize £1,000).

[Excluding peak periods and subject to availability]

Simply complete the sentence below in 10 words or less:

I would like to win this wonderful prize because

_____

_____

Replies clearly marked Holiday Competition to:

Irish Hotels Federation, 13 Northbrook Road, Dublin 6, Ireland.

Closing Date for Entries 31st August 2001

(Photocopies not accepted)

Name: _____

Address: _____

_____

IRISH HOTELS FEDERATION

CALENDAR OF EVENTS

Throughout the year, Ireland has a great range of social, cultural and sporting events. The big cities and even the smallest villages have festivals, whether in honour of a goat, as at Puck Fair, or to celebrate the oysters in Galway.

Listed below is a small selection of well known events/festivals which take place. There are, of course, many others, whether music or sport. **Please contact your nearest Irish Tourist Board office for confirmation of dates and a full calendar of events. (TBC = Dates to be Confirmed)**

MARCH

07 - 11 March	Dublin Boat Show
16 - 19 March	St. Patrick's Festival 2001, Dublin
27 March - 01 April	The Irish Masters Snooker Tournament, Goffs, Kill, Co. Kildare
29 March - 08 April	Dublin Film Festival, Dublin

APRIL

27 March - 01 April	The Irish Masters Snooker Tournament, Goffs, Kill, Co. Kildare
29 March - 08 April	Dublin Film Festival, Dublin
07 - 11 April	World Irish Dancing Championships, South Court Hotel, Limerick
13 - 16 April	Circuit of Ireland Rally, Enniskillen, Co. Fermanagh & Bundoran, Co. Donegal
14 - 17 April	Kerry Arts Easter Weekend Festival, Tralee, Co. Kerry
17 - 22 April	Pan Celtic Festival 2001, Tralee, Co. Kerry

MAY

03 - 06 May	Cork International Choral Festival, Cork
10 - 13 May	Murphy's International Mussel Fair, Bantry, Co. Cork
19 - 20 May	A.I.M.S. Choral Festival, New Ross, Co. Wexford
24 - 28 May	Fleadh Nua, Ennis, Co. Clare
30 May - 03 June	Writers' Week, Listowel, Co. Kerry
31 May - 04 June	Murphy's Cat Laughs Comedy Festival, Kilkenny City

CALENDAR OF EVENTS

GUINNESS.

JUNE

30 May - 03 June	Writers' Week, Listowel, Co. Kerry
31 May - 04 June	Murphy's Cat Laughs Comedy Festival, Kilkenny City
09 - 17 June	Guinness Bloomsday Festival, Dublin
10 June	Tesco/Evening Herald Women's Mini Marathon, Dublin City
15 - 24 June	Eigse Carlow 2001 Arts Festival, St. Patrick's College, Carlow
28 June - 01 July	Murphy's Irish Open, Fota Island, Cork
29 June - 01 July	Budweiser Irish Derby Weekend, The Curragh Racecourse, Co. Kildare

JULY

28 June - 01 July	Murphy's Irish Open, Fota Island, Cork
29 June - 01 July	Budweiser Irish Derby Weekend, The Curragh Racecourse, Co. Kildare
01 - 07 July	Synge Summer School, Rathdrum, Co. Wicklow
07 - 14 July	Willie Clancy Summer School, Miltown Malbay, Co. Clare
08 - 13 July	Bard Summer School, Clare Island, Co. Mayo
10 - 15 July	Galway Film Fleadh, Galway City
17 - 29 July	Galway Arts Festival, Galway City
28 July - 11 August	Yeats International Summer School, Sligo
29 July - 07 August	Mary from Dungloe International Festival, Dungloe, Co. Donegal
29 July - 12 August	Wicklow Regatta Festival, Co. Wicklow
30 July - 05 August	Guinness Galway Race Meeting, Galway

CALENDAR OF EVENTS

GUINNESS

AUGUST

28 July - 11 August	Yeats International Summer School, Sligo
29 July - 07 August	Mary from Dungloe International Festival, Dungloe, Co. Donegal
29 July - 12 August	Wicklow Regatta Festival, Co. Wicklow
30 July - 05 August	Guinness Galway Race Meeting, Galway
08 - 12 August	Kerrygold Horse Show 2001, Royal Dublin Society, Dublin
10 - 12 August	Guinness Puck Fair, Killorglin, Co. Kerry
10 - 19 August	Kilkenny Arts Festival, Kilkenny City
16 August	Connemara Pony Show, Clifden, Co. Galway
24 -26 August	Fleadh Ceoil Na hEireann, Listowel, Co. Kerry
24 -29 August	Rose of Tralee International Festival, Tralee, Co. Kerry
31 August - 02 September	Cape Clear Island International Storytelling Festival, Cape Clear Island, West Cork

SEPTEMBER

31 August - 02 September	Cape Clear Island International Storytelling Festival, Cape Clear Island, West Cork
01 September - 07 October (TBC)	Matchmaking Festival, Lisdoonvarna, Co. Clare
(TBC)	Guinness All-Ireland Hurling Championship Final, Croke Park, Dublin
(TBC)	Guinness All-Ireland Football Championship Final, Croke Park, Dublin

live
life
to
the
power
of

CALENDAR OF EVENTS

(SEPTEMBER CONTINUED)

07 - 09 September	Clarenbridge Oyster Festival, Clarenbridge, Co. Galway
26 September - 07 October	Waterford International Festival of Light Opera, Waterford
27 - 30 September	Galway International Oyster Festival, Galway City
29 September - 07 October	Ballinasloe International Horse Fair and Festival, Ballinasloe, Co. Galway

OCTOBER

01 September - 07 October (TBC)	Matchmaking Festival, Lisdoonvarna, Co. Clare
26 September - 07 October	Waterford International Festival of Light Opera, Waterford
29 September - 07 October	Ballinasloe International Horse Fair and Festival, Ballinasloe, Co. Galway
(TBC)	Dublin Theatre Festival, Dublin
02 - 04 October	National Ploughing Championships, Ballacolla, Co. Laois
11 - 14 October	25th International Gourmet Festival, Kinsale, Co. Cork
14 - 21 October (TBC)	Cork Film Festival, Cork City
18 October - 04 November	Wexford Festival Opera, Wexford
26 - 29 October	Guinness Cork Jazz Festival, Cork City
29 October	Dublin City Marathon, Dublin City

Capture the Action
Go Greyhound Racing

ENJOY THIS GREAT EVENING SPORT

Enjoy superb facilities and experience thrill packed greyhound racing in a friendly atmosphere.
Race meetings normally commence at 8.00pm Mon.-Sat. inclusive (occasionaly Sunday meetings).
For details see local / national papers

IRISH GREYHOUND RACE NIGHTS

MONDAY: Harold's Cross (Dublin), Dundalk, Limerick, Enniscorthy, Newbridge, Derry, Ballyskeagh.

TUESDAY: Mullingar, Thurles, Tralee, Waterford, Galway, Youghal.

WEDNESDAY: Shelbourne Park (Dublin), Cork, Kilkenny, Dungannon.

THURSDAY: Shelbourne Park (Dublin), Cork, Enniscorthy, Limerick, Lifford.

FRIDAY: Harold's Cross (Dublin), Kilkenny, Longford, Galway, Youghal, Newbridge, Derry, Dungannon, Ballyskeagh.

SATURDAY: Shelbourne Park (Dublin), Dundalk, Limerick, Cork, Mullingar, Thurles, Waterford, Lifford, Ballyskeagh.

Irish Greyhound Board
Bord na gCon

INDEX OF HOTELS & GUESTHOUSES GUINNESS.

472

Magical Blarney

INDEX OF HOTELS & GUESTHOUSES GUINNESS.

INDEX OF HOTELS & GUESTHOUSES GUINNESS

INDEX OF HOTELS & GUESTHOUSES   GUINNESS

477

INDEX OF HOTELS & GUESTHOUSES GUINNESS

478

INDEX OF HOTELS & GUESTHOUSES   GUINNESS.

479

INDEX OF HOTELS & GUESTHOUSES   GUINNESS.